The L/L Research
Channeling Archives

Transcripts of the Meditation Sessions

Volume 15
January 3, 1999 to May 19, 2002

Don
Elkins

Jim
McCarty

Carla L.
Rueckert

Copyright © 2009 L/L Research

All rights reserved. No part of this book may be reproduced or used in any form or by any means—graphic, electronic or mechanical, including photocopying or information storage and retrieval systems—without written permission from the copyright holder.

ISBN: 978-0-945007-89-0

Published by L/L Research
Box 5195
Louisville, Kentucky 40255-0195

E-mail: contact@llresearch.org
www.llresearch.org

About the cover photo: *This photograph of Jim McCarty and Carla L. Rueckert was taken during an L/L Research channeling session on August 4, 2009, in the living room of their Louisville, Kentucky home. Jim always holds hands with Carla when she channels, following the Ra group's advice on how she can avoid any possibility of astral travel.*

Dedication

These archive volumes are dedicated to Hal and Jo Price, who faithfully and lovingly hosted this group's weekly meditation meetings from 1962 to 1975,

to Walt Rogers, whose work with the research group Man, Consciousness and Understanding of Detroit offered the information needed to begin this ongoing channeling experiment,

and to the Confederation of Angels and Planets in the Service of the Infinite Creator, for sharing their love and wisdom with us so generously through the years.

Table of Contents

Introduction 6
Year 1999 8
    January 3, 1999 9
    January 17, 1999 15
    February 7, 1999 19
    March 21, 1999 23
    April 18, 1999 29
    May 2, 1999 36
    May 23, 1999 43
    September 12, 1999 48
    September 26, 1999 53
    October 3, 1999 58
    October 17, 1999 63
    November 7, 1999 70
    November 21, 1999 75
    December 5, 1999 81
    December 19, 1999 88

Year 2000 92
    January 2, 2000 93
    January 16, 2000 97
    February 6, 2000 102
    February 20, 2000 110
    March 5, 2000 117
    March 19, 2000 123
    April 2, 2000 128
    April 16, 2000 134
    May 7, 2000 143
    May 21, 2000 149
    September 10, 2000 154
    September 23, 2000 160
    October 1, 2000 167
    October 15, 2000 172
    November 5, 2000 179
    November 19, 2000 185
    December 3, 2000 193
    December 17, 2000 198

Year 2001 202
    January 6, 2001 203
    January 14, 2001 208

January 21, 2001	216
February 4, 2001	222
February 11, 2001	229
March 4, 2001	236
March 18, 2001	243
March 25, 2001	248
March 29, 2001	253
April 1, 2001	257
May 6, 2001	262
May 20, 2001	268
August 29, 2001	272
September 2, 2001	277
September 16, 2001	281
September 23, 2001	288
October 7, 2001	295
October 21, 2001	301
November 4, 2001	306
November 18, 2001	312
December 9, 2001	317
December 23, 2001	321
Year 2002	**328**
January 6, 2002	329
January 20, 2002	332
February 4, 2002	339
February 10, 2002	343
February 24, 2002	350
March 7, 2002	356
March 17, 2002	361
April 7, 2002	366
April 21, 2002	371
May 5, 2002	377
May 16, 2002	385
May 19, 2002	391

Introduction

Welcome to this volume of the *L/L Research Channeling Archives*. This series of publications represents the collection of channeling sessions recorded by L/L Research during the period from the early seventies to the present day. The sessions are also available on the L/L Research website, www.llresearch.org.

Starting in the mid-1950s, Don Elkins, a professor of physics and engineering at Speed Scientific School, had begun researching the paranormal in general and UFOs in particular. Elkins was a pilot as well as a professor and he flew his small plane to meet with many of the UFO contactees of the period.

Hal Price had been a part of a UFO-contactee channeling circle in Detroit called "The Detroit Group." When Price was transferred from Detroit's Ford plant to its Louisville truck plant, mutual friends discovered that Price also was a UFO researcher and put the two men together. Hal introduced Elkins to material called *The Brown Notebook* which contained instructions on how to create a group and receive UFO contactee information. In January of 1962 they decided to put the instructions to use and began holding silent meditation meetings on Sunday nights just across the Ohio River in the southern Indiana home of Hal and his wife, Jo. This was the beginning of what was called the "Louisville Group."

I was an original member of that group, along with a dozen of Elkins' physics students. However, I did not learn to channel until 1974. Before that date, almost none of our weekly channeling sessions were recorded or transcribed. After I began improving as a channel, Elkins decided for the first time to record all the sessions and transcribe them.

During the first eighteen months or so of my studying channeling and producing material, we tended to reuse the tapes as soon as the transcriptions were finished. Since those were typewriter days, we had no record of the work that could be reopened and used again, as we do now with computers. And I used up the original and the carbon copy of my transcriptions putting together a manuscript, *Voices of the Gods*, which has not yet been published. It remains as almost the only record of Don Elkins' and my channeling of that period.

We learned from this experience to retain the original tapes of all of our sessions, and during the remainder of the seventies and through the eighties, our "Louisville Group" was prolific. The "Louisville Group" became "L/L Research" after Elkins and I published a book in 1976, *Secrets of the UFO*, using that publishing name. At first we met almost every night. In later years, we met gradually less often, and the number of sessions recorded by our group in a year accordingly went down. Eventually, the group began taking three months off from channeling during the summer. And after 2000, we began having channeling meditations only twice a month. The volume of sessions dropped to its present output of eighteen or so each year.

These sessions feature channeling from sources which call themselves members of the Confederation of Planets in the Service of the Infinite Creator. At first we enjoyed hearing from many different voices: Hatonn, Laitos, Oxal, L/Leema and Yadda being just a few of them. As I improved my tuning techniques, and became the sole senior channel in L/L Research, the number of contacts dwindled. When I began asking for "the highest and best contact which I can receive of Jesus the Christ's vibration of unconditional love in a conscious and stable manner," the entity offering its thoughts through our group was almost always Q'uo. This remains true as our group continues to channel on an ongoing basis.

The channelings are always about love and unity, enunciating "The Law of One" in one aspect or another. Seekers who are working with spiritual principles often find the material a good resource. We hope that you will as well. As time has gone on the questions have shifted somewhat, but in general the content of the channeling is metaphysical and focused on helping seekers find the love in the moment and the Creator in the love.

At first, I transcribed our channeling sessions. I got busier, as our little group became more widely known, and got hopelessly behind on transcribing. Two early transcribers who took that job off my hands were Kim

Howard and Judy Dunn, both of whom masterfully transcribed literally hundreds of sessions through the eighties and early nineties.

Then Ian Jaffray volunteered to create a web site for these transcriptions, and single-handedly unified the many different formats that the transcripts were in at that time and made them available online. This additional exposure prompted more volunteers to join the ranks of our transcribers, and now there are a dozen or so who help with this. Our thanks go out to all of these kind volunteers, early and late, who have made it possible for our webguy to make these archives available.

Around the turn of the millennium, I decided to commit to editing each session after it had been transcribed. So the later transcripts have fewer errata than the earlier ones, which are quite imperfect in places. One day, perhaps, those earlier sessions will be revisited and corrections will be made to the transcripts. It would be a large task, since there are well over 1500 channeling sessions as of this date, and counting. We apologize for the imperfections in those transcripts, and trust that you can ascertain the sense of them regardless of a mistake here and there.

Blessings, dear reader! Enjoy these "humble thoughts" from the Confederation of Planets. May they prove good companions to your spiritual seeking. ♣

For all of us at L/L Research,

Carla L. Rueckert

Louisville, Kentucky

July 16, 2009

Year 1999
January 3, 1999 to December 19, 1999

L/L Research

L/L Research is a subsidiary of Rock Creek Research & Development Laboratories, Inc.

P.O. Box 5195
Louisville, KY 40255-0195

www.llresearch.org

Rock Creek is a non-profit corporation dedicated to discovering and sharing information which may aid in the spiritual evolution of humankind.

ABOUT THE CONTENTS OF THIS TRANSCRIPT: This telepathic channeling has been taken from transcriptions of the weekly study and meditation meetings of the Rock Creek Research & Development Laboratories and L/L Research. It is offered in the hope that it may be useful to you. As the Confederation entities always make a point of saying, please use your discrimination and judgment in assessing this material. If something rings true to you, fine. If something does not resonate, please leave it behind, for neither we nor those of the Confederation would wish to be a stumbling block for any.

CAVEAT: This transcript is being published by L/L Research in a not yet final form. It has, however, been edited and any obvious errors have been corrected. When it is in a final form, this caveat will be removed.

© 2009 L/L Research

Sunday Meditation
January 3, 1999

Group question: We would like to ask Q'uo about guilt. When we feel guilt we are usually overtaken by the feeling and don't know where it comes from. Could you give us information about where guilt comes from and how to work with guilt in our spiritual evolution.

(Carla channeling)

We are those of the principle known to you as Q'uo. We greet you with joy in the love and the light of the one infinite Creator. It is a great blessing for us to be called to your group, and we bless and thank each who is a part of the circle of seeking this day.

Your question concerns guilt, and as we talk upon this interesting subject we share opinion rather than speaking as authorities over you. We would ask that each who hears use personal discrimination, for that which we have to say is opinion and may or may not be that which is of help to you personally. If it does not constitute a resource for you, if it does not fit in with that which resonates with you, then we ask that you simply leave it behind and move on.

As this instrument was tuning and challenging our contact earlier, the instrument, as is her habit, challenged us three times. In the first two challenges our impression was that this instrument was exercising her own discrimination in being certain of the vibration received. However, in the third challenge the instrument carefully described that facet of Jesus the Christ which identifies this entity to her. The nailing of the body upon the tree of wood to take upon the self the sins of humankind, to love others to the point of death, is to this instrument the great characteristic of Christhood that has riveted the instrument's mind for many years. And it is this characteristic which gives us a place to begin to speak about guilt.

The cultural religion, shall we say, differs from the pure religion in that the belief itself is eviscerated and removed, but the form remains. The non-Christian or secular expression of the Creator in Jesus the Christ, then, would be the golden rule in which one at least gives unto others as one would give to the self. But this cultural willingness to die for the sake of another as the highest good places a standard of service to others and giving without expectation of any return that is, in Earth terms, absolute. When one gives the life, one has given all and can not any longer give, for the incarnation has ended in that form. Naturally, gifts can continue to be given and, indeed, are far more easily given when discarnate. However, it is the incarnate aspect that creates the sacrifice of self for the good of another.

Each comes into incarnation with a personality already set up to be created. There is some play in the way in which the personality develops, but its conscious resources, an easily achieved asset, are set in place before incarnation. Consequently, some entities have a far keener sense of justice, fairness, sharing and giving than others coming into incarnation. Whatever this basic bias of given personality is, the cultural norm for parents is to attempt to increase the instinctively solipsistic infant in its supply of love for others and service to others. Small children are routinely taught to share their playthings, their sweets, and their good times. There is training concerning many behaviors starting with the word, "should." One should keep one's hands in one's lap at the table. One should be respectful to one's mother. One should avoid murdering anybody. At every level of a child's upbringing these enculturated biases are repeated and reiterated until they are inculcated into the basic emotional vocabulary of the logic of the deeper mind. Not that mind which moves beyond self, but that portion of the self within incarnation which lies below the limn of consciousness.

Consequently, when one has become enculturated with the bias towards service to others that the society offers, when one has digested this incoming data and responded to it according to its own biases, the biases of the personality shell, then each individual is left with a more or less threshold of guilt. To some the voice of authority remains dim throughout life and the basic nature of the personality shell has a deafness to the suffering of others. When there is no guilt displayed the medical person attempting to place this entity would call such an entity one who lacks any social behavior or psychopathic. For it is assumed by the healing professions by your peoples among your peoples that guilt is a natural function of the psyche. This instrument has called it "shoulding" all over yourself. And, indeed, when a sensitive entity takes the club of guilt and beats the self about the head and shoulders, metaphysically speaking, that damage is very real and the pain very great.

As you can see, depending upon the basic personality shell of the entity and the amount of enculturation that has stuck with the entity, there are varying degrees of guilt. Needless to say, those who are already oriented towards service to others and who are consciously working upon spiritual evolution tend far more towards a ready acceptance of guilt than those whose viewpoint is less broad. Thus, the very entities who are sensitive enough to be in pain because of guilt receive the more substantial amounts of guilt from their catalyst. It is as though the Creator were adding insult to injury by offering more guilt to those who are already sensitive to it, who are already responding to it by increases in their level of service to others.

The justice of this can only be seen from the standpoint of learning. The feeling of guilt, like many of the negative emotional systems of feeling, is designed to place one in a position in which it is possible to polarize. Now, service to self, in itself, does not necessarily bring great polarity. Many entities upon your sphere indeed live their entire lives in service to those about them without thinking unduly of it or considering it something that can be worked with or maximized. And for these entities the opportunities that awakened souls see are simply unnoticed and unused. However, we may encourage each of you, as those sensitive and consciously awake in the world of spirit, to see that the feelings of "should" are a catalyst to be praised and to be used. When one experiences this emotional set called guilt, one is experiencing a fear that one has not done enough, and, again, the term, "enough," is relative to the personality shell's capabilities and the amount of effort that the entity has put into actualizing the potential for service to others that is within the personality.

Thus, in a way, the more times one feels guilt, the more times one thinks, "Is that enough?" the more one is asking the self to polarize towards service to others without expectation of return. We would not necessarily encourage each to respond automatically to such feelings of "not enough." For sometimes that guilty feeling of not enough is simply an instinctive reaction, one that cannot be pinned down to specific lacks within the self or within the behavior of the self. We encourage, rather, the noticing of such an emotional system of weather, shall we say, having blown into the mental and emotional bodies with an eye to evaluating, as honestly and accurately as possible, the opportunity for increased service. When there is no opportunity for increase of service the guilt felt is as that phantom pain coming from the limb that has been amputated. There is, indeed, no actual physical limb there, simply a body so habitually used to experiencing that physical leg that the form-maker body continues to hold that idea in place, the body then feeling all of the pain of the amputated leg.

In some cases, and as entities become more inclined to spiritual work this becomes more true, the guilt is vestigial and unhelpful, for nothing can be done to ameliorate the situation about which the guilt is felt. A good example of this is the feelings of family in the event of suicide. Even those who are not related to the family member but were friends will consider to themselves immediately upon hearing of the demise of such an entity in suicide all of the things that could have been done had the person realized in what bad shape the entity was. Even though the entity has moved on and nothing can be done these phantom feelings are very real and must be dealt with as though they had something to do with consensus reality. When feelings arise of guilt and fear to which the entity cannot find any response, it is then that the entity does well to work upon the discipline of the personality and the discipline of the will. The discipline of the personality is involved in such a case in allowing the entity to sit with, to accompany, to be one with this feeling, to allow it to express and to give it respect and to be a witness to it. The use of the will, then, is that which asks the personality to let those feelings go, to let them be balanced by the awareness that all that has been done is all that can be done and that it is time to move on.

When an entity experiences guilt and finds it to be of this type, we would recommend this general way of working with the dynamics involved. When an entity finds itself feeling the fear of not having done enough and when further detailed examination confirms that there is indeed more that can be done, then it is that we encourage the seeker to view such feelings as good and productive catalyst. For it is not just the willingness to serve others that creates polarity but also the willingness to work upon the self to find ways of becoming more capable of giving, for that giving of self is a kind of muscle and it atrophies in those who do not use it. For those who use it, however, for those who exercise the vigilance to catch the process of guilt and choose a response to it rather than simply drowning in it, there is the possibility of deepening the faculties of will and faith and of using those to pray and to ask and to humbly entreat the one infinite Creator to give grace to become more able to give without thinking of the return.

Not all guilt, then, is good. Some guilt is a knee-jerk response to a catalyst that is truly not there in any sense of being able to work with that catalyst. But when there is something to work with it is work in consciousness that is extremely central to spiritual evolution, for it is to the [more highly] polarized entity that opportunities will come to give of the self gladly, to give not because of the cultural expectation or because of the nature of the personality but because the entity has come consciously to be aware of the way that polarity works, of the way that the schoolroom of Earth works, and such a student shall always excel over most other students. For if there is a motivation to work, the work goes quickly and more easily and with a sense of satisfaction when the test is over.

The illusion which this instrument calls Earth or the Earth plane is designed as a sea of confusion. It is designed in such a way as to greatly discourage entities from being able to cope from the standpoint of the intellect. It is designed to toss people out of their intellects on their ear, to bring them to their knees and place them in the sanctum of the heart, humbled, tired and ready to learn. Know this, just as love casts out fear, love casts out guilt. To remove guilt from oneself it is not enough to do all that one can. It helps to do all that one can, for that surely is enough, but, emotionally speaking, enough is never enough. There is always more that one might be able to do: one more cheek that can be turned; one more mile that can be walked in another's shoes; one more activity that can be helpful, or the refraining from one more activity that might be helpful. There is no logical end to guilt. It is not subject to logic. It is, instead, a tone in the music of the emotional body.

However, this tone can be worked with musically just as the instrument tuned itself for the contact: by prayer, silence, singing and praise. So the seeker can tune the purity of that emotion called guilt, combing from it the less beautiful pithiness of fear and self-condemnation and bringing more and more into focus by an increasing array of verniers that tune ever more finely until that feeling of guilt is as a beautiful tone, a beautiful and true emotion. For, indeed, that feeling that one cannot do enough is permanent within your illusion. It will recur for the reason that one cannot achieve the perfect behavior in one's own eyes. One cannot ever fully be satisfied that enough is enough. And so one is left with the awareness that one has this tone or chord of tones within one, but that it too has its place in the universal personality that is the self, that one is capable of comforting the self after all that has been done is done with the pain that remains. One can forgive oneself for being human. One can forgive oneself for not being able to sacrifice the self to the point of death. One can acknowledge, when faced with this catalyst, that the best one could do is not the best, but that is all right. That is as it should be. That is part of the perfection that is hidden within this sea of confusion.

When one has finished rocking and hugging and loving this imperfect being that wants so much to serve, then one can send that child within with a lighter heart by suggesting to the self within that uplifting of the self from the worry of the close view, that one can, by will, step back from the situation and from the emotions to a perspective that takes less into account [the foreground] of the present happenings and brings into sharper relief the basic principles involved.

We honor the one known as Jesus the Christ and, indeed, honor that vibration which is the Christ as being the highest vibration of love that is achievable so far within the infinite creation. We indeed bow to that and come in the name of that and hope to be able to serve to the point of that rude wood cross: the nailed hands, the pierced side. Yet we, in our present situation, do not have that physical sacrifice to make. We do not have the capacity for the kind of guilt that you feel within your illusion. We do not have the ability to be confused and in that confusion to call upon faith. Nor have we the ability to be angry with ourselves and then to forgive ourselves. For, as we are able to see into the roots of mind, we can see that in each system of illusions there are limitations which are set for a reason and that that reason is condign, helpful and enlightening. Upon the Earth plane you have the ability to be utterly dashed, completely confused, thrown to your knees by life, and you have the capacity to tune your responses to that catalyst which brings you down, which makes you feel into the dark side of your personality.

Do not be beaten about by your own feelings of guilt. But, rather, see them as opportunities to do work in consciousness, to forgive the self for being human, to analyze the situation to see whether or not the guilt is productive, to work upon releasing that guilt if it has not been productive, to work upon using that guilt in the highest and best way if there still is something that one can see to be done. Above all these considerations, above all manifestation and illusion the reality, as far as we know, is the perfect outworking of perfection: love reflected in love, moving through each instrument that is a soul of a person and out into the world. As you receive your catalyst, bless it and break yourself open to receive it with the most love of which you are capable in a stable manner. Do not move yourself beyond that which you can do without damage to yourself. Do not ask that which you are not ready for of yourself, but rather be sensitive to the opportunities that these negative feelings, so called, of guilt bring rise to.

And you, as is right within your schoolroom, shall follow in the steps of the cross. You shall have the chance to break yourself open and to pour out your energy, your time, and your attention. When you choose to do this, be aware that it is a sacrament, that you are on holy ground, and that you need to be fastidious in your orientation to the light, not condemning the self in any way for that which has not been done or that which has been done awry, but without heat and in perfect peace, moving back into the situation in mind, finding the balanced and appropriate response, choosing the most generous level of service of which you are capable. This is part and parcel of the teaching of third density. This is one way to move the entity from head to heart and for you to experience it is proper and desirable for those who wish to increase their rate of acceleration of spiritual evolution. In all things, find the love and find within the self the response to that love which most truly expresses yourself.

As in many things it is not so much what you do in the manifested world but how you do it, with what love you do it, with what gentleness and compassion for the self and for the other self and for the entire suffering Earth plane. In the awareness of the suffering of the world one can feel guilty for those who do not eat. Saints can feel guilty because they have not beaten themselves twice a day with chains but only once. You cannot remove this type of lesson from the life experience, so we ask that you see it as a course of study, and like many such a course, one which is helpful although the tests are frequently difficult. Above all, we encourage that you laugh, that you take these things to some extent lightly, that you are able to lift yourself from such considerations and move into awareness of the beauty of the present moment. For this is the center of things. This is the less confused place from which to cast one's eye upon the situation at hand. Laughter and merriment are most helpful spiritual disciplines and we encourage their use, especially for those who are serious students and who can become heavy with their concerns for doing things well.

We would at this time transfer this contact to the one known as Jim, leaving this instrument with thanks in love and in light. We are those of Q'uo.

(Jim channeling)

I am Q'uo, and greet each again in love and in light through this instrument. It is our privilege at this time to offer ourselves in the attempt to speak to further queries which those present might have for us. Is there another query at this time?

Carla: One question. I notice that when I say your name in channeling there seems to be an "a" before your name when I verbalize it. I wondered what I was picking up?

I am Q'uo, and am aware of your query, my sister. We are, as you are aware, a principle which has been created or constructed of two different mind/body/spirit complexes, each of which contains its own signature vibration or sound vibration which designates and identifies the entities involved. The beginning of the identification which you have noticed is that sound of, as we have discovered your peoples call it, the spheres, the great Aum which those of Ra partake of in a more balanced fashion. Thus, this sound of the "a" is a kind of bleed-through or a vibratory range that somewhat overlaps the blending of our two sound-vibration complexes, overlaps and underlies, for this sound of the spheres is that music that is available to any entity which has tuned itself to the one creation.

Is there a further query, my sister?

Carla: Yes. I noted that you spoke of the two social memory complexes involved, and for a while I felt that there was a third one involved, namely Hatonn, and that that entity had come on board with the principle in order to deal with some of the needs of some of the members of the circle at that time, and when that entity left perhaps Hatonn left also. Is this correct?

I am Q'uo, and am aware of your query, my sister. And though this supposition upon your part has its correctness it is not simply enough to say that that is correct, for there are many entities of the social memory complex nature which have been attracted to and have spoken to this group in its history, as you would say. When such a commitment and communication has been made it is never broken but remains as a link so that when this group gathers in its circle of seeking there are many who are drawn to it and do not participate directly in the spoken communication but which lend their vibratory presence to this circle of seeking, and any of this group of entities may be called upon by any in your circle of seeking for special communication, shall we say, that is, the calming effect that one group may have for a certain entity, the inspirational effect that one group may have for another entity. In general, there is much support that is available to this circle of seeking from those of the Confederation of Planets in the Service of the One Infinite Creator.

Is there a further query, my sister?

Carla: No, thank you for the information. It is fascinating and good to know.

I am Q'uo, and again we thank you, my sister. We would ask for a final query at this time if there is one.

R: The answer you have just given about the entities being present when the circle is together has touched upon a feeling that I had and I wanted to voice it. When I listen to Q'uo I really take Q'uo to represent a Brotherhood of Brothers and Sisters of Sorrow, as Ra has called it. I wanted to thank you for bringing it up because it has cleared up something for me because I felt there were more than just two entities involved and you have put it into a structure that my mind can deal with better. I appreciate that comment.

I am Q'uo, and we are responding to your response to us, my brother, and we thank you for the grasping of the nature of this contact in a more full sense, for as each in the circle is more able to appreciate that which is offered it makes the service which we have to offer take on a certain ease of momentum, shall we say. We are always gratified to be called specifically by this group, but we would reiterate that when any of the Confederation entities have been called that there is the joining of the particular entities called by others who are attracted by the seeking of the group. For as the group in which you sit gathers itself together and shares with the others of the group the concerns of the heart, the concerns of the mind, and the concerns of the day there is created a certain vibratory level which is likened to a calling for service in these areas from entities that are, shall we say, specialists and whose desire is to provide information and inspiration to those of the Earth population who would seek such solace.

As to the beginning of the New Year of your experience, we find that such demarcations of time, and especially this one, are helpful to each entity in that it provides a clean slate in the mind of the entity upon which can be written the new and more refined aspirations that the entity may desire to express within its own life pattern and [may] find it more easily able to do so when it feels that there is a new opportunity presented. Much as a level of a new incarnation offers the freedom of expression to an entity, so does this beginning of a new calendar year for your peoples.

We are those of Q'uo, and would at this time express our appreciation to each here for inviting our presence in your circle of seeking this day. It is a great honor to be able to do so and we would hope that each entity would use the discrimination native within each to take those words which ring of truth that we have spoken this day and use them as each will, leaving behind those that do not have that ring of truth at this time. At this time we shall take our leave of this instrument and this group, leaving each in the love and in the light of the one infinite Creator. We are known to you as those of Q'uo. Adonai, my friends. Adonai.

L/L Research

L/L Research is a subsidiary of Rock Creek Research & Development Laboratories, Inc.

P.O. Box 5195
Louisville, KY 40255-0195

www.llresearch.org

Rock Creek is a non-profit corporation dedicated to discovering and sharing information which may aid in the spiritual evolution of humankind.

ABOUT THE CONTENTS OF THIS TRANSCRIPT: This telepathic channeling has been taken from transcriptions of the weekly study and meditation meetings of the Rock Creek Research & Development Laboratories and L/L Research. It is offered in the hope that it may be useful to you. As the Confederation entities always make a point of saying, please use your discrimination and judgment in assessing this material. If something rings true to you, fine. If something does not resonate, please leave it behind, for neither we nor those of the Confederation would wish to be a stumbling block for any.

CAVEAT: This transcript is being published by L/L Research in a not yet final form. It has, however, been edited and any obvious errors have been corrected. When it is in a final form, this caveat will be removed.

© 2009 L/L Research

Sunday Meditation
January 17, 1999

Group question: We would like to ask a question about control over one's daily round of activities, or the lack of control, the feeling of having lost power to be able to affect the outcome of any situation. And this is balanced with the realization that every situation offers us the opportunity to gain from it whatever we need to gain from it and that there is no way that we can lose. It is all a matter of adopting the attitude that all is well and all is one and that the moment offers each of us just what we need to grow. So we would like Q'uo to comment on the concepts of the seeming loss of control, the being able to focus one's attention in the moment upon what is going on, and that the moment offers us the love that we need in that moment.

(Carla channeling)

We are those of the principle known to you as Q'uo, and we greet you in the infinite love and light of the one Creator, whom we serve. We thank each that has joined the circle this day. Our gratitude and our blessing go with you, for you enable us to offer our service. And thus you offer us learning and growth and the ability to serve as we had hoped to. May we say that although we are most happy to be able to share our opinions with you, we are not an authority. We are simply those who are upon a path which this instrument calls the King's Highway. We seek that love and that truth and that way that is so close to us that we cannot express it, yet we know that it is still a mystery and that that mystery recedes before us as we go forward. And so, as we share our opinions with you, we also ask that you use your powers of discrimination, for all that we say shall not be resources for you. And we would ask that you take those thoughts that are helpful and leave the rest behind. This we would greatly appreciate.

You ask us concerning power and control. The song which you have used to tune your circle this day talks of footsteps on the water that lead the singer back to who he is. This instrument immediately thinks of the one known as Jesus the Christ, who walked upon the water and who gave to her the identity in which she rests. The one known as Jesus did not find it remarkable to walk upon the water, nor did the one known as Peter, who sprang from the boat when he saw his teacher coming and walked upon the water also to him until he realized that he was a human and that humans sink. And so down he went until the one known as the Christ reached out a hand to him and lifted him up. Such is the nature of faith.

Faith is not something one can plan to acquire. Upon this King's Highway there is no hostel at which you can purchase faith nor any school at which you may learn faith. Rather, faith is expressed in the middle of utter confusion, in the midst of the grand chaos that is the nature of your third-density physical illusion.

Let us look at the creature that you are. You are a citizen of eternity. Your essence is infinite, and you have no limit. This is your nature, for are you not one with the original Thought, that Logos which may so weakly be called Love? And this Creator that is beyond, and yet contains all things, has that nature of intelligent infinity. And this birthright is yours, but you have chosen, at this time, to take this illimitable consciousness and to place it gently and lovingly and hopefully within a jar of clay, within that chemical electrical distillery which is your physical vehicle and with this physical vehicle, this hairless great ape which so gallantly carries you about for your entire incarnation, comes an intelligence that is not unlimited but is limited, that is not eternal but is time bound. And these two natures dwell within you, interacting in many, many ways. When the mind that comes with the physical vehicle is in command of consciousness there inevitable and instantly comes those feelings of limit, disappointment, worry and an endless series of reasoning designed to solve specific problems. For the mind that comes with the physical vehicle is carefully designed to solve problems and make choices.

To this mind all things can be measured and when one has measured a situation, got its inseam and its outseam, taken all of this down, then the mind makes a choice. And the body must follow. This is the state of what we might call spiritual sleep. The entity depending completely upon the rational, limited mind may well make brilliant choices and solve many hard problems, but there will not be that feeling of ease or space or love that is your birthright. This is as it should be, this relatively commonplace placement of the consciousness that is eternal under the threshold of conscious awareness, what this instrument would call consensus reality. And so to the unawakened spirit it is the subconscious mind, the deeper mind, which contains all of the nature and the characteristics of the citizen of eternity that has hoped, by taking incarnation, both to learn and to serve.

No matter how confused or chaotic the sea of confusion about you is, no matter how limited you may feel, there is a higher truth, a deeper truth, if you will, a broader truth, that lies waiting, hoping, its hand raised to rap upon the door of your consciousness at all times, for you to woo and court and open those doors of deeper consciousness. As a limited being, your feet are upon the earth, your roots go down into the earth itself. You are connected to all that is earthly, to those wonderful energies of earth, rock, fire, water, plants and animals. The physical body itself has the instinctual grace of animal and plant life, that turning towards the light, that moving to survive, to continue. But as a citizen of eternity you root yourself in what this instrument would call heaven. It is as though the roots of the tree were at the very top and the branches came down into the illusion. When you reach into the roots of the mind, then, you are reaching into heavenly things. All of this you have within you. It all lies waiting behind doors which are locked against the hasty, the unthinking, the careless seeker.

That sense of power that is, shall we say, not of the illusion is within these rooms of self, these structures of deep mind. The desire to control, a sense of power that comes with that desire, is a perfectly natural, instinctual part of the human animal. It is, of course, a desire that is fated to be thwarted, this being one of the great points of the incarnation and the illusion into which you step the moment of your first breath.

And so, as a citizen of Earth you are destined to spend your time paddling about in the archipelago of confusion which is third-density existence, finding a dry place here and a dry place there, making your way but constantly being buffeted by that which you cannot, in an earthly sense, control or have power over. And if you focus into that life view that feeling of peace that each seeks shall ever be illusive, for the whole purpose of physical incarnation is to so confuse and baffle the mind that it has to let go. This instrument is fond of saying that the spiritual journey is one from head to heart.

The techniques of using the intellect bring one to many brilliant conclusions, none of which move one into those depths of awareness and comfort and peace which knowing the truth in any moment can make you feel. Each has had these moments of infinite peace and joy. Each has felt the self open and something stretch and flex and enjoy existence, locked so long in those deep guarded rooms. And what are the keys to these rooms? One door is only opened by silence, and we heartily recommend that each of you spend time in silence whenever you can … thirty seconds, five minutes. A little silence will go a long way.

There is another door that can only be opened by the key of patience. Patience that is not pinned to any expectation. Let us look at this a moment. What are your expectations? Do you have many? What are your desires? Do you have a raft of them? Do you have just a few? If your expectations are more than modest, if they are ambitious, if there is a plan—this instrument's mind immediately remembers the Soviets' five year plans which never seem to work—then each plan that is made is destined to be left behind. And even when a plan comes out exactly right often it does not give one the expected feelings. No, rather, patience is that which releases expectation and simply waits, not knowing what is to come, not necessarily even guessing what is to come but, rather, moving in that openness of heart which is as a seat upon which to sit in that house, that room of patience.

Remember that expectations are dangerous things; desires are powerful things. Dangerous and powerful because they create an energy that will not be balanced until you achieve your expectations and your desires. And yet nothing is as it seems within your illusion. Consequently, each desire that is granted will bring with it great catalyst, for it will not be what you thought it would be.

And there is a door in the deep mind that can only be opened by the key of faith. When this instrument was in extremity, very close to death, she taped a message where she could read it from the bed upon which she lay. It read, "Faith, the final frontier," making the pun upon the Star Trek, "Space, the final frontier." It was meaningful to this instrument, and we pull it from her memory so that we may talk about the unknown land into which faith is an entry. Faith is not faith in anything. Faith is the knowing of things that are not seen, the sureness that one is in the right place. Faith is illogical and cannot be defended rationally, and yet the more time that you spend in this room within the deep mind the more you shall flower as an entity, able to do that work which each truly came to do. For, indeed, what do you wish to control? Over what do you wish to have power?

In things of the spirit, those who work within service-to-others polarity will find that there is only one area which needs work. It is not the world that needs work. It is not others that need to change. It is the self that is the province and the realm over which each entity has the right to work, to hope, to dream, and to walk that spiritual path.

The mind asks you, "Where are you going?" "How do you get there the best way?" This is logical. This sometimes works spiritually, but not often. What works spiritually, rather, is that faithful patience that, when in doubt, sees the doubt, sits with the doubt, accepts the doubt, forgives the doubt, and then chooses to rest in faith. We do not mean to suggest that action is not a good idea. You came here to be confused. You came here to act. You came here to make mistakes, to judge yourself, to do all of the things that you will learn are not particularly loving or wise.

You will notice that we have not talked about a room of wisdom, for it is our humble opinion that wisdom is not the lesson for which you are ready at this time. For you see, wisdom may only be studied, with good results, when an entity has learned the lesson of love and compassion. Wisdom is a dead thing unless it comes from that resoundingly open heart that is able to allow the infinite love of the one Creator to go into the self, to be blessed by the self, and to move on from the self into the Earth plane without significant distortion. This is what you came to do. And it is not a doing but a being that you came to offer as your gift. You came to sacrifice your very self. Your whole incarnation is a gift to Earth. Certainly you hoped to do personal work here. And certainly you hoped to serve by what you do and what you say, but how much more central is your responsibility to meet the moment with a loving and opened heart. And it is this which is the province and realm over which you have control. This is where your power lies, in the momentary decision to seek the love in that moment. As the one known as Ra has said, "Where is the love in this moment?" is a helpful question at any juncture, but especially when the spirit is weary or overwrought.

And there is one final door that can only be opened by the key of honest love. And this is the holy of holies. This is the mercy seat. If you can enter that door, all the rest shall open also. If you can dig in the soil of your nature, down into the roots of mind, past the confusion that is your topsoil, past the difficulties that are your fertilizer, if you can get through that to the rock, that rock is love. Take this moment just to feel how much the Creator loves you. Oh, how the Creator loves each one of us! Every hair. Every freckle. Every folly and mistake.

All these things are part of a wonderful tapestry, a tone poem of emotion and concern and caring that is your signature, and the Creator loves every bit of color and tone and energy and pattern that you have created with your life. How you are loved. Know this. Dwell upon this, for this is deep truth, and it may free you a little at a time from those human concerns that seem to create the atmosphere where you are not appreciated, where there is no balance to life, where those things that you attempt to do to aid others do not seem to find their mark.

And you also have within you tremendous stores of this energy that is love. Yet it is not that you have these things within you precisely. Rather, as this instrument said earlier, it is as though you only have them when you know that they are coming through you, not from you. For those things which are human are limited, and if you attempt to love the world from your conscious self you shall run out quickly. You shall feel burnt out, and weary, and certainly sapped of energy. Rather, we would suggest that model where you see yourself as a transmitter and receiver of vibrations of a certain kind. You both receive them and you send them. And if you allow it, you create a circuit [amid] infinite intelligence, which is that flowing, knowing, growing place that each of you has visited many times, that each of you yearns for when things become fuzzy and muddled.

We are not saying that entities such as yourselves do not often run into brick walls where it was hoped would be open road. We are saying, rather, that these brick walls are part of the illusion and are not particularly interesting compared to the wooing and the courting of that self within which is a citizen of eternity and which may choose at each juncture, in each instant, to focus, as the one known as Ra said earlier, upon the main thing. And that main thing is always, eternally, love. May you be guided again and again into situations where you may take those keys of patience, love, simple persistence, hope and faith and may find for yourself those places which rest you, which comfort you, which are merciful balms to your weary soul.

We would at this time transfer this contact to the one known as Jim. We would take our leave of this instrument in the love and in the light of the one infinite Creator. We are those of Q'uo.

(Jim channeling)

I am Q'uo, and greet each again in love and in light through this instrument. It is our privilege at this time to offer ourselves in the attempt to speak to any further queries which those present may have for us.

Carla: I have a question about working on my book. I have tried to divide things up by the energy centers and have found a difficulty doing that. Various issues hit upon more than one chakra. If you take sex, for instance, it certainly is a red-ray issue, and also a yellow-ray issue, and so forth. I wonder if you could comment on this? I am looking for a better direction for dividing the book and the material.

I am Q'uo, and am aware of your query, my sister. We wish to be of service without the, shall we say, doing of the homework, but can begin to open the door which you, yourself, opened at the end of your query by suggesting that there are topics such as the one mentioned, that is, the sexual energy exchange, and many others, that can be pursued to present the student of the spiritual journey with an overview of this journey using experiences with which it is most familiar. These combined then can become the vehicle to share that aspect of the devotional life which you wish to share with others.

Is there a further query, my sister?

Carla: No. I'll look over what you just said. Thank you.

I am Q'uo, and we thank you once again, my sister. Is there another query at this time?

(No further queries.)

I am Q'uo, and as it appears that the queries have found their end we would once again thank each entity present in this circle of seeking for inviting our presence this day. We are most honored and privileged to have been able to join you here. And we remind each that there are many such as ourselves that walk with each upon that journey of seeking and becoming and knowing the one infinite Creator. We are known to you as those of Q'uo. Adonai.

L/L Research

L/L Research is a subsidiary of Rock Creek Research & Development Laboratories, Inc.

P.O. Box 5195
Louisville, KY 40255-0195

www.llresearch.org

Rock Creek is a non-profit corporation dedicated to discovering and sharing information which may aid in the spiritual evolution of humankind.

ABOUT THE CONTENTS OF THIS TRANSCRIPT: This telepathic channeling has been taken from transcriptions of the weekly study and meditation meetings of the Rock Creek Research & Development Laboratories and L/L Research. It is offered in the hope that it may be useful to you. As the Confederation entities always make a point of saying, please use your discrimination and judgment in assessing this material. If something rings true to you, fine. If something does not resonate, please leave it behind, for neither we nor those of the Confederation would wish to be a stumbling block for any.

CAVEAT: This transcript is being published by L/L Research in a not yet final form. It has, however, been edited and any obvious errors have been corrected. When it is in a final form, this caveat will be removed.

© 2009 L/L Research

Sunday Meditation
February 7, 1999

Group question: The planetary awakening to unseen essences such as angels, guides and spirit guidance is part of our awakening to an even larger self-realization of direct co-creatorship with intelligent infinity. Could you speak of the process that is taking place, in which we are coming to actual awareness of our role as co-creators, with specific focus on how we are learning to become direct conductors of the eternal energies?

(Carla channeling)

We are those known to you as Q'uo. Greetings in the love and in the light of the one infinite Creator. We thank this group, as always, for calling us to share our views and to take part in your meditation. This experience is precious to us for each of your vibrations is beautiful and we greatly appreciate to be able to blend with that. Also, we thank you because this sharing of opinions gives us the opportunity for service to others in the way that we feel our gifts are best shared. As always, we would ask that from these thoughts each take only that which has personal meaning, leaving the rest behind. For each seeker has excellent powers of discrimination, and we encourage their use. There is no authority greater than the authority of the inner heart and that feeling of rightness.

You ask this day for us to share our opinions on how awakening entities are coming to experience a universe in which time and space have given way to infinity and eternity and the seeking of the metaphysical self has become more important than the approval of the world or any worldly gain which does not have its roots in love: the love of one doing the service, the love of one offering the self. Many entities are awakening now to their spiritual identity. This is the time for the blooming of those feelings and awareness that have long been hidden. This is the time of the blossoming of those entities upon your planet who have become aware of themselves as citizens of eternity.

It is our opinion that all things are one, that all there is dwells within each entity. It is our feeling that each entity contains the infinite creation. All things are thought, all thoughts, all emotions, all that is seen, all that is sensed in any way has manifestation to the outer eye but first has roots within that inner being that is connected, not with larger spaces, but with infinity itself. For each of you is that holographic image of all that there is. Each of you is one thing. The small self cannot grasp the unity that is the truth of all your peoples upon your sphere of Earth. It seems obvious to the outer eye that each entity is a person unto herself, and yet just as a child awakens for the first time in her mother's arms and becomes aware of a new world of sight and sound and sensation, just so does the spiritual self within the human being awaken to an alarm that only it can hear.

No two entities have the same clock setting. There is no one time for spirits within bodies to awaken. For each seeker that time of awakening is perfect and right although it may not seem right to others. It always shall come to the one who is ready to deal with the implications of the new inner birth that constitutes the awakening into realization of the self as a spirit independent of space and time but wholly dependent upon love and light. For each is love and light, yet each also transduces love and light as it streams from the infinite Creator into the Earth plane. And so each of you, no matter the age or any details about the person, each who is awakening is a receiver and a transmitter of vibration.

Your scientists tell you that all that there is is made up of particles of energy vibrating at various speeds and creating various energy fields. One such energy field is that in which is contained the spirit of each of you, and when that spirit awakens there is no going back to sleep. Once awake, the seeker must remain awake and alert. The question then becomes, "How can I help this process of awakening along? How can I accelerate the pace of my spiritual evolution?" We would suggest several ways in which this can be encouraged.

Firstly, we would suggest that each awakened soul choose for the self that rule of life which most nurtures the spiritual child within, that child that dwells in the heart and can become mature only as the outer self makes room and time for it. Time spent in silence, whether formal meditation is offered or whether it is simply sitting, greatly aids the spiritual self within. Further, it helps to align the seeker with her personal destiny, for each has come with gifts to share, lessons to learn, and service to offer. Each has planned for the self companions along the way and good work to do, and each has hoped that within the veiled conditions of the physical illusion that constitutes consensus reality upon your planet that the awakening would occur and the choices would begin to be made which would more and more allow the spiritual self within to mature.

Meditation is not the only technique or method whereby one may encourage one's own spiritual evolution. Certainly, the attempts to offer service to others always creates a more spacious environment for the spiritual self to grow in. Certainly, reading and listening to inspired and inspirational material is helpful. More helpful, however, than any of these practices is the persistent focus upon the mental and emotional awareness of the nature of the self within incarnation upon planet Earth. For as we said, each of you is as the radio: receiving and transmitting vibratory energy as good feelings, as good words, as good deeds. All of these are equal in the world of metaphysics, for thoughts are metaphysical things and have shape and substance and reality in the world of spirit. That is why the intentions, the desires, and the prayers of the seeker are so important.

The greatest single practice for bringing seekers into more and more direct awareness of their role here within the planetary rise in vibration is simply to be, to be the deepest and most profound and true self of which one is capable. In this being there is a releasing of the doing, for, metaphysically speaking, it is not these but rather being and essence which are the gifts that we have to give to each other. When a seeker becomes aware that it is a creature of will, discipline and faith then that person can simply allow those instreaming vibrations of love and of light to move through the physical, mental, emotional and spiritual channels of the body and out into the world that so desperately needs those vibrations of undistorted love and light.

Each seeker is here to become a direct co-creator by allowing that which is, the Logos, that one great original Thought, to be us and to move through us and out into the Earth plane. By blessing this energy and yet not holding it, by knowing there is enough, an infinite amount of this love and light, that it cannot be spent, the seeker is affirming that which is. We wish each entity those delights of travel, those mountaintop experiences, those great and profound realizations that come. Those times are precious, and yet each of you will find that when all is said and done it is the vibratory level of the beingness of each entity that sticks in the mind and in the heart like no other sense memory can. Each of us knows blessing when we experience it. All of us have known these entities who, by their very being, improve the vibrations of a place. Yet always know that it is not from you that these things come. It is through you. There is not a key that unlocks the doors of the heart that has anything to do with the human mind or the will in the worldly sense of that mind. Rather, it is the naked soul, the bare and unadorned spirit that is the object of perfection, that is love itself, and that is each of you.

May you find ever more creative ways to share the infinite love and light that will come through you by blessing that energy and by consciously sending it out into the world. We encourage each who hears these words to take the self very seriously in terms of developing a daily practice that feeds the metaphysical self, whether by meditation or prayer, contemplation or rumination, the gazing at inspiring objects, or the reading of inspired words. You will find these techniques of entraining the mind to be most helpful. There are many ways in which the person who sees the hunger and the thirst of the self that is emerging for metaphysical truth to offer that truth to the inner self. It is our opinion, however, that truth is a fluid and changing thing and very personal and subjective in its nature. For each entity there will be landmark truths that come and stay for a very long time. There will also be truths that are seen to transform and to migrate as lessons come to one and as the self develops.

We encourage each of you to trust in the self, to listen to those hunches and intuitions that are the only voice into the conscious mind of the deeper and larger self that exists below the threshold of consciousness. Each of you is as the fruit of the true vine. Each of you has roots in heaven. Within each of you dwells perfection, truth and infinite love. Spiritual maturity comes to those who seek to run the straight race regardless of what others may think. Move slowly and thoughtfully and wait for inspiration. Maturity will come faster to those who yield their ambitions and ask, "What is the Creator's will for me today? Where is the love in this moment?" The love in this moment is you. May you carry that truth and wear it as a crown and even when the crown sits heavy upon the head, may you serve, may you reach out to others, may you respond to requests for help with the best that is in you. May you encourage others in their paths, for you are the hands, voices, the caring of the infinite Creator within the Earth, you and none other. As the old chant goes, "May you love each other. May you care for each other. And may you bring each other home."

We would at this time transfer this contact to the one known as Jim. We would leave this instrument in love and in light. We are those of Q'uo.

(Jim channeling)

I am Q'uo, and greet each again in love and in light through this instrument. At this time it is our privilege to offer ourselves for further queries which those present may find value in the request. Is there another query at this time?

Carla: I would like to ask two questions for P. Firstly, what is the origin and purpose of the B'hai faith?

I am Q'uo, and am aware of your query, my sister. And we would greet the one known as P, who has for a great period of time has been seeking in the faith in which the query is rooted and is a friend of this group that is dear to each. The origins of this particular path of seeking the one Creator lie in the recent past, as you would measure time, that is, within the last 200 of your years, and lie with one who found a personal path that was able to allow this entity to experience the one infinite Creator and to realize the unity of all things through this experience of unity with the one Creator. Thus, this entity who had for a great portion of its life sought that which is called truth, that which is called the origin of all that is, was able, through a blending of various other paths in their rituals of observances, was able to create a meaning whereby not only was it able to experience the unity of all things but was able to offer this experience to others as well, as it was the life's purpose for the incarnation to put the self in such a position that it was able to make a contact with that which is called intelligent infinity and offer this contact as the eternal waters of life, to be then one who was able to provide this service to others in as egalitarian a means as possible, shall we say. Thus, the origin of many such mystic paths is that journey which begins and ends inside the human heart, for as all such paths to unity the way of the heart is that which moves most quickly there.

Is there a further query, my sister?

Carla: Yes. Her second question is just to comment on her experiences of the last year in any way in which you would care to share. She doesn't wish for you to infringe upon free will, just comments.

I am Q'uo, and am aware of your query, my sister. Looking now at that which has been the experience of this entity, in metaphysical terms, we see that there is the dedication of the heart to seek in truth that which are the proper steps for this entity to follow and that there has been a great degree of success in bending the will of the self to new dimensions that seem on the one hand to restrict and yet on the other hand to free. The balance of attitude with which this entity sees its journey and its relationship to others is to be recommended, for within the balanced attitude, seeing the experience of others as a valuable journey and the seeing of the journey of the self as being that which is to move in harmony with certain other selves which have formed a primary place within this entity's being. The difficulties that the entity experiences are the, shall we say, friction where the rougher portions of the personality meet the reality of dealing with other selves who also have the tendency towards humanity—that is, to err. The ability to accept, to forgive, and to renew the dedication of the self to the seeking of the One in all, is the quality that has sustained this entity and will continue to do so.

At this time we feel that we have given that which is appropriate for this entity and would ask if there would be any further queries?

Carla: I know P thanks you for that. I have a question of my own. I was pondering D's words in the process of putting them on the tape concerning guides from the inner planes or spiritualist type guides such as doctors, Indians, the Holy Spirit, people who have the awareness of the help of fairies or of angels and all of these discarnate and magical beings. They all seem to have the same kind of service to offer to us in third-density bodies on Earth. What I was wondering was is there an element of creatorship where those of us who expect fairies get fairies, and those who expect Indians get Indians, and those of us who expect UFO contact get that? Is there some way that we come into the mix that assigns guidance? Different people have different methods of guidance?

I am Q'uo and am aware of your query, my sister. It is truly said that these entities of an unseen nature move to inspire and to guide and to bring into contact those influences that are most helpful to the entities that call them. And it is also well said that it is oftentimes the expectations of those who call that determine the nature of the response in the form of one kind of guide or another. And it is a possibility of many that there are previous incarnational experiences that determine that kind of essence that is called for and seen and experienced. For there are throughout the one creation many, many different forms of guidance that are available to third-density entities and these forms of guidance may refine their formation to be more in alignment with that basic vibratory essence of the calling entity. Thus, each entity will experience that which it truly desires and which it has made room for in its metaphysical system of apprehending that which is.

Is there a further query, my sister?

Carla: No. That was it. Thank you very much.

I am Q'uo, and we thank you again, my sister. Is there another query at this time?

(No further queries.)

I am Q'uo, and we would at this time express our great gratitude to those which are present and to those who are in distant meditative circles adding their energy and essence to this one for inviting our presence and our participation in your seeking this day. It is, as always, a great honor and we walk with many who echo our gratitude. At this time we shall take our leave of this instrument and this group, leaving each, as always, in the love and in the light of the one infinite Creator. We are known to you as those of Q'uo. Adonai, my friends. Adonai. ✦

L/L Research

L/L Research is a subsidiary of Rock Creek Research & Development Laboratories, Inc.

P.O. Box 5195
Louisville, KY 40255-0195

www.llresearch.org

Rock Creek is a non-profit corporation dedicated to discovering and sharing information which may aid in the spiritual evolution of humankind.

ABOUT THE CONTENTS OF THIS TRANSCRIPT: This telepathic channeling has been taken from transcriptions of the weekly study and meditation meetings of the Rock Creek Research & Development Laboratories and L/L Research. It is offered in the hope that it may be useful to you. As the Confederation entities always make a point of saying, please use your discrimination and judgment in assessing this material. If something rings true to you, fine. If something does not resonate, please leave it behind, for neither we nor those of the Confederation would wish to be a stumbling block for any.

CAVEAT: This transcript is being published by L/L Research in a not yet final form. It has, however, been edited and any obvious errors have been corrected. When it is in a final form, this caveat will be removed.

© 2009 L/L Research

Sunday Meditation
March 21, 1999

Group question: How can we use our desires and expectations in a balanced way to grow spiritually?

(Carla channeling)

We are those of the principle known to you as Q'uo. Greetings in the love and in the light of the one infinite Creator. It is our privilege and our blessing to join you in your meditation, to experience the beauty of your vibratory patterns, and to be able to speak with you our opinions upon the subject that you have requested this afternoon. We are most happy to speak with you concerning desire and the balancing and use of desire. We ask only that each of you listens with a careful and discriminating ear, for truth is a personal thing. That which is true is true one person at a time, one creation at a time, for each of you is the center of your creation, which is no one else's. You and your creation are unique, and you will resonate to those truths that constitute an asset and a resource to you. When you feel that resonance, you may trust it. And when you do not, we ask that you leave our humble thoughts behind. For we are as you: pilgrims upon a spiritual journey. And though this instrument is fond of saying that she never metaphysician she didn't like, we continue to insist that we are as you, perhaps further along in the great circle from source to source. But we walk the same road, and we seek and desire the same things. Calls such as yours are most precious to us, and we thank you especially for allowing us to practice our form of service to the one infinite Creator, for we are within your inner planes at this time specifically for the answering of calls by groups and entities such as you.

Let us focus upon desire. What is the nature of desire? It is our limited understanding that the Creator Itself used the function of desire, which is also called free will, when It decided that It would know Itself. It's desire was knowledge of Itself, and so the Creator flung out all the densities of experience, all the infinities of galaxies and stars and planets and consciousness so that It might experience Itself. As the nature of the Creator is infinite love, so did It create all Its parts as infinite love, and each of you is as a sun or a planet in being created of infinite love, having the nature of infinite love. Each sentient and non-sentient being, each poppy, each breeze, each animal and tree and human being, is the result of that desire of the Creator to know Itself. The Creator has, from the beginning of Its creation, found Itself utterly in love with each iota, with each soul. The Creator is delighted, thrilled and fascinated, and so the Creator has an attitude of love and feeling of that love radiating to every sentient being. The Creator remains fascinated. What will happen next? wonders the infinite part of deity.

Since the nature of deity or Godhead resides completely within love and the desire to know the dimensions of that love, it is only suitable and appropriate that each soul that awakens to its spiritual identity becomes aware of itself as a creature of desire. As the one known as R said earlier in this discussion, "I thought that I was on a high spiritual plane only to discover that I still have many, many desires." May we say to each of you that you shall never find yourself lacking in desires. This is the nature of your being. It is the nature of space and time which creates dimensions in which you may follow your desires. So it is entirely appropriate that each of you has desires and that each of you works within the self in consciousness to know better the desires of the heart, to refine the desires of the heart, and to discipline the personality that would go forth into the world that it may have the armor of light, that it may have the resources which it needs in order to remain aware to an increasing extent of the patterns and ramifications of the desires of the heart.

As the one known as Jim said earlier, there are many, many entities upon your plane of existence who find themselves unable to fit into the myth and mythical system of the culture in which they may find themselves. These wanderers are those pilgrims which do not have a place to stay upon the road, who do not have a handy chapel that they may go into and find themselves at rest. For many, these culturally pervasive religious influences have not been able to offer the rest and the peace which constitute spiritual balance to the pilgrim that is perforce abroad upon the spiritual path. You see, once an entity has awakened to itself as a citizen of eternity and has become aware of that essence of self that is infinite and that shall not go down to the dust, that entity then hungers and thirsts for that of the spirit which may come into the consciousness and deflect the conscious mind during the everyday existence. It is significant to us that so many of your people feel that it is impossible to maintain a spiritual practice in everyday life. This is notable because [you are] the entity that you are, having the nature of love and of love's desire: to love and be loved, and then having that feeling that one cannot bring this into the everyday sphere.

There is, more and more, within the heart of the seeker a feeling of imbalance, a feeling of not being able to express the essence of self. When that lack of center, that lack of peace, exists within the heart of the seeker there shall inevitably be a feeling of imbalance and a feeling of restlessness, of itchy feet, a desire to get on with and through whatever is keeping the spirit from the love of the infinite Creator. Further, it is telling that within your society the solution of bringing the spiritual into the everyday is to take time out from the everyday to go to a weekend conference or a spiritual convention or some grouping where one may trust that there will be spiritual food and there will be the time-out from the everyday life taken for spiritual work. Mind you, we are not criticizing those who offer or those who take spiritual courses or weekends or conventions or workshops. These are wonderful means of sharing and caring and learning and service. However, the source that can be most deeply secure and reliable for each seeker is the innermost heart, for in the deep heart there is a tabernacle and within this tabernacle, in all of its infinity, lies the one Creator, patiently waiting for the seeker to open the door to their own heart. It is not in the reaching out that the most trustworthy grounding of desire may be had but, rather, in the smaller and smaller, quieter and quieter, energies of the self. For each of you is a hologram of the Creator. Each of you is already that which each seeks, but this treasure lies buried within the deeper self, not so much, shall we say, closeted away as behind a door which has a key, and that key is silence.

When an entity thinks of desire, the word itself has overtones of passion, sexual or sensual in nature, certainly vital. The connotations of desire are warm, hot, burning. And each experiences desires in a tremendous array of levels so that when one attempts to talk about desires with others, even those of like mind may become lost in the semantics of "desire for what?" Are some desires more balanced than others? Is it more appropriate to desire the higher things than it is to desire those shallow and materialistic things of the Earth world? The key here, we feel, is balance, as several of you have mentioned this afternoon. That word, balance, is most important. We would note that to our way of thinking that there is no particular necessity to begin with the higher desires. Indeed, we would recommend against it for those who have not done a good deal of work in consciousness, and the reason is that each is a creature of many parts, with various energies which the body and the mind and the spirit experience. All need to be balanced, and it is our feeling that it is far better actually to begin working with the so-called lower energy centers and chakras when one is doing so-called spiritual work.

The three lower energy centers that we have talked about before are those centers with the colors of red, orange and yellow: the base or first chakra being the red chakra and containing those issues of survival, sexuality, and vitality; the orange-ray, that belly chakra, wherein the issues of personal ethics, personal choices, and personal relationships are worked upon; and that yellow energy center which is sometimes called the solar plexus center, which treats with the energies having to do with society and societal groups, the ethics and the relationships and the responses which the seeker may choose to offer to those catalysts which may come about. These are the chakras which need to be open and in minimal balance in order that the full energy that the Creator offers may come from the base of the body up into the heart. To do work in consciousness in the higher energy centers when the heart is not receiving full energy is to risk what this instrument would call burnout, ill health, scattered personality, and other ailments—mental, spiritual, and physical—that are the result of attempting to do high intensity, high energy work in consciousness when the heart does not have enough power to keep all things in balance.

This instrument is fond of a writer and mystic called Evelyn Underhill. Within this saintly and delightfully humble woman's work there lies the suggestion that one may think of the spiritual self as a house with two floors. Upon the first floor there is the eating, the drinking, the sleeping, and all those things which the body and the mind must do to maintain the self, to provide for the self, and to make the household that may then offer rest and security to the seeker. The one known as Evelyn asks how the seeker might feel if it ignored the dirty dishes, the unmade bed, the wonderfully creative mess that entities can make of those possessions that they have. Walk up the stair and go into the upper room. To some, this would be very easy to do. And yet the one known as Evelyn suggests that this is putting cart before horse. This is moving too quickly for the whole being to follow. And so we would say to you that we agree with this sentiment, that we do feel it a holy and loving work to balance those feelings concerning existence, sexuality, person, personal relationships, family relationships, and societal relationships. All these are blessed and important concerns. They are not the small change to be tossed away so that one may go higher. They are the steps which you must be able to trust, going up that staircase to the upper room. And we ask each of you to be especially aware of the beauty and the divinity of simple things. For these things will feed you and will balance you and will open your heart.

Once you have entered the open heart, once you feel able to bear the silence of that inner voice which speaks, not to the ear but to the heart, you rest balanced and ready to look at the deeper desires of that heart. Again and again, you will find your heart closing. You will find your relationships coming out of balance. And we say to you, take no worry from such. This is the way of things. For all things go in spirals. That which you meet today you shall meet again in a week, a month, or a year, just to be sure that you have gotten that particular point. You will see the same lessons repeated and yet not repeated, for you have spiraled into a different person, and at the new level you need to be tested. Therefore, when you find yourself moving back out of the open heart, back out of balance with relationship or with the self or with the health, or with the depression, know that this is not stepping backwards but spiraling into a review, a test, if you will, of that which you have already learned. If you spend any time at all condemning yourself for once again experiencing catalyst of this particular kind that you see repeating we ask you to put it out of your heart and forgive yourself for being who you are.

You see, within desire there lie choices which are very subtle. When you reach that point in your spiral where you get the lesson again, it is very, very easy to move back into the lower energies, meanwhile berating yourself for being within the lower energies. Yet know that you will be working with these lower energies every day and every night of your incarnation. Many times you will not even be aware of the work that you are doing in these lower energies, for the more discipline that you bring to your way of living, your rule of life, as this instrument would call it, the more you do rest in faith and do not contract away from the catalyst that constitutes this review, this test of your awareness of your balance. It is not only the balance, often, that is tested. It is your awareness of the process. When you can win through in a confused situation to a remembrance, a memory of the way catalyst works, of the process in which you are taking part, the more you will be able to move smoothly, gracefully and cooperatively into doing the work at hand, without condemnation of self or of others, forgiving completely that which this density of experience confers upon each and every sentient citizen of eternity. For each of you is human; each of you, therefore, cannot help but make errors. That is the nature of third density, of the human experience, of the spiritual path at the point which you are now, that you will constantly be tossed into confusion, difficulty and aggravation. This is simply in order to set the stage for your journey from the intellect to the heart.

It is often seen as desirable to live the life in a carefully thought out manner, and certainly we would not say that thought given to a way of life is unwise or unspiritual. Rather, we would say that there is a kind of wisdom that appeals to the intellect but which is false, for your density is not the density of wisdom. The greatest wisdom that you shall ever learn in your density at this time is that you cannot know anything. In other words, that your incarnation is based completely upon faith. You have no backstop of destiny. You have no eternal parent that will tell you what to do. You are on a journey in uncharted waters and your intellect will not be able to be so wise as to steer your spiritual journey. Many mistakenly attempt to live a spiritual life coming from the intellect and from wisdom. However, this energy does not make use of the open heart, and it will not take you far. And those seas into which it pitches you will be as confusing as the seas you left behind to seek for wisdom. It is our understanding, rather, that your density is a starkly simple stage set for making one choice again and again, and that is the choice to love and to be loved. The one known as Ra has said in each moment ask yourself, "Where is the love in this moment?" This question contains the seed of the heart's opening and polarizing, and we are aware that that is what each of you wishes to do: to become more awake and aware of the true nature of the self, to be more and more able to express that essence in the daily life.

These are desires that all have in common. For each, the ship upon which each finds herself is without a lodestone or rudder. But, rather, there is a sail which may be moved about by the seeker to catch the winds of spirit. Once one has been able, even for a short time, to run before the wind of spirit and to feel the sails billow, one has become able to recognize what it feels like to be in the rhythm and in the rightness of things. For truly we say to you, to the best of our knowledge, each has a destiny. Each has a mission. Each has come into incarnation with gifts to share, with a mission to fulfill, a service to do, and with learning to accomplish. The learning is always about love. The serving is always about trusting in the rightness of the moment. Again and again we have heard the question, "What can I believe in? How can I have faith?" We say to you that when your desires come into balance, then it is that you are most liable to experience the harvest and the blooming of faith, for faith is not faith in anything. Faith is simply an attitude which is part of your spiritual being. Faith is that which knows that all is well and that all will be well. It cannot be gotten at by trust in any other person. It can only be experienced in midair after one has leapt from the precipice safely. In midair one finds oneself marvelously able to cultivate faith, and you will find, as you work with your desires, that there is a place or balance which you will come to recognize. There is a comfort in sensing that one is centered, that one is on the beam, that one is in rhythm and in cooperation with one's destiny.

We hope that we have been able to describe some of the processes that go into arriving at the inmost heart and becoming aware that within it lies the Creator and that you may go in and tabernacle with that Creator and allow that Creator to be actively indwelling so that when you come out of that inner room of prayer, meditation and silence you will feel the energy of spirit moving through you, and you will know that, thankfully, you are no longer depending upon a pitifully small amount of human love which comes from you, but you have been able to open up the instrument of self that infinite love and light may flow through you and out into a hungry, thirsty world. It is our feeling that this being in the self is the highest mission of all people, that living a devotional [life] in the midst of all the everyday confusion is each spiritual entity's first vocation. And I think we may say that once one attempts, on a regular basis, to live the life from this point of view, the rhythms shall grow more obvious, the music more clear, and the love more flowing as though each petal of each flower, each bird that sings, each iota of the Creator's universe are harmonizing with you, aware of you, and in love with you as you with all of them.

We thank you for allowing us to speak upon this subject, and would at this time transfer the contact to the one known as Jim. We are those of Q'uo, and thank this instrument for its service. We leave it in the love and light of the one Creator, whom we serve with all our love and might.

(Jim channeling)

I am Q'uo, and greet each again in love and in light through this instrument. At this time it is our privilege to offer ourselves to any further queries which may have come upon the minds of any present. Is there another query at this time?

T: Is it best to attempt to create your desires, or is it better, to use the basketball phrase, "let the game come to you," and do what comes the best you can and make your desire to do the will of God and not put too much of your own coloring on the interpretation?

I am Q'uo, and am aware of your query, my brother. To use your analogy of the game of basketball, it is well to find oneself within the flow of life as a result of observing those experiences which come to you and which come through you. You are, as a conscious being, as one who is moved by forces which are great and unseen in the life pattern, for each has chosen a kind of curriculum, you might say, in which the opportunities to learn that which remains as lessons for you will be presented to you and will be presented as often as is necessary for you to understand their impact and the effect that love has with the open heart. Thus, it is our suggestion to each seeker of truth that you move as lightly as possible through your daily round of experience, looking for those experiences which leave a mark upon your inner being, which remain with you and affect you as that which has been drawn to you.

Is there a further query, my brother.

T: No, thank you.

I am Q'uo, and we thank you, my brother. Is there another query at this time?

Carla: To follow up on T's question, if one does have a burning desire of some kind is there the way to go concerning focusing on that desire, or is it simply to step back and say, "Thy will be done"?

I am Q'uo, and am aware of your query, my sister. If in the observation of the experiences which are yours over a period of time it is discovered that there is a passion for this or for that avenue of expression, then it is well to follow such a passion and trust that such a passion is the will of the Creator for you at this time. For this feeling of passion is, indeed, one of the most effective ways for the subconscious mind, or the will of the Creator to move through the subconscious mind, and to move the conscious entity in such and such a fashion.

Is there a further query, my sister?

Carla: Not on that subject. I do have a question of my own and it's OK if you can't comment, because it is specific. I have noticed this week my own anger very strongly, and I wondered if there were any psychosomatic connection between cleansings that I have done with my body this week and the more easily felt negative emotion of anger?

I am Q'uo, and am aware of your query, my sister. As you have surmised, we must tread carefully that we do not infringe upon your free will. We may suggest that those experiences that have been yours this week in the way of cleansing have accentuated the continuing tendency for the transparency of the self, as we may put it. That is to say, the physical condition that you have experienced concerning pain for a great portion of your incarnation has had the effect, shall we say, of wearing the nerves thin so that there is a more easily recognized emotional response to the environment about you. The fragility of your own physical vehicle has as its analog within the mind a psychology [of] the feeling that one must take care and be careful, and when there is another within the life experience that seems to be careless in regards [to] relationships with you—for example, the entity pulling in front of your automobile in a careless fashion—then there is as a result within your physical and emotional being a tendency towards the defensive reaction: the fear, the anger, and so forth.

Is there any further query, my sister?

Carla: No, thank you.

I am Q'uo, and again we thank you, my sister. Is there another query at this time?

R: Can you tell me whether the books by Carlos Casteneda are of the path of that which is not?

I am Q'uo, and am aware of your query, my brother. But we find that there is a line beyond which we may not go in describing the nature of these or any volumes as being of the path of that which is not or the path of that which is, the path of negativity or the path of positively. These choices, my brother, are most important for each seeker of truth to make for himself or herself, and this choice we find that we must leave to you.

Is there another query, my brother?

R: No, not on this subject. Thank you anyway.

I am Q'uo, and we thank you for your query, my brother. Is there another query at this time?

(No further queries.)

I am Q'uo, and as it appears that we have exhausted the queries for the nonce we shall take this opportunity to thank each present for inviting our presence in your circle this day. It has been a great honor and privilege for us to walk these few steps with you. We are known to you as those of Q'uo, and would at this time take our leave of this instrument and this group, leaving each, as always, in the love and in the light of the one infinite Creator. Adonai, my friends. Adonai.

L/L Research

L/L Research is a subsidiary of Rock Creek Research & Development Laboratories, Inc.

P.O. Box 5195
Louisville, KY 40255-0195

www.llresearch.org

Rock Creek is a non-profit corporation dedicated to discovering and sharing information which may aid in the spiritual evolution of humankind.

ABOUT THE CONTENTS OF THIS TRANSCRIPT: This telepathic channeling has been taken from transcriptions of the weekly study and meditation meetings of the Rock Creek Research & Development Laboratories and L/L Research. It is offered in the hope that it may be useful to you. As the Confederation entities always make a point of saying, please use your discrimination and judgment in assessing this material. If something rings true to you, fine. If something does not resonate, please leave it behind, for neither we nor those of the Confederation would wish to be a stumbling block for any.

CAVEAT: This transcript is being published by L/L Research in a not yet final form. It has, however, been edited and any obvious errors have been corrected. When it is in a final form, this caveat will be removed.

© 2009 L/L Research

Sunday Meditation
April 18, 1999

Group question: Our question today has to do with the concept of finding the Creator in each aspect of our everyday lives. We can understand intellectually how the Creator has made all that there is and eventually we progress through all of the experiences and all is one again, but we are wondering if Q'uo can give us information today about how to find the Creator in each moment, whether we are washing dishes or driving a car, or fleeing attacks in Kosovo, or flying in an airplane, or whatever we might be doing. It's easier to see the Creator in the good moments but it's harder when we find things bad or boring or nonsensical or absurd, how do we find the Creator there?

(Carla channeling)

We are those of the principle known to you as Q'uo. We greet you in the love and in the infinite light of the one Creator in whose name we come. We thank you and bless each of you for calling us to your circle of seeking. It is both our privilege and our pleasure to share our opinions with you on the interesting subject of daily spirituality. We ask of you only that you listen to our words as to those of a brother or sister, for we are not perfect nor any kind of authority over you but, rather, we are those who are pilgrims on what this instrument calls the King's Highway. We are in service to the one infinite Creator, and as we seek we know you also seek this beauty, this truth, this mystery, this way, this life. It is good to have such companions, and as we said, a great blessing to us to be able to be of service in this way. And we thank each.

As we rest in the comfort and the beauty of your blended vibrations we find ourselves aware of much each of you already knows from experience, from suffering and undergoing great difficulty, from being held together and lifted up by the love and the light of the one infinite Creator. Each has beautiful stories to tell of those times when everything seemed clear and the creation truly did seem to be one beautiful, harmonious symphony of people and relationships and nature and things great and small, all moving together with rhythm and pulse and a lovely dance that was new every moment. It is not simply with the intellect that each of you has had these experiences, but with the whole self. Each has had these transcendent times when the world simplified itself and the love could be seen. We are grateful for the beauty of those memories and those awarenesses within you, for this gives us common ground. We do not have to convince or persuade any that spirituality is a very real and a very intimate thing, for each of you has had those feelings from deep within the self, and each more or less trusts those experiences. We would encourage you to continue to trust those memories, for whenever times of ineffable harmony come, however they come, through what suffering they come, or as what gift out of nowhere, they are the gems hidden within the ore of common life, so far. And what a blessing it is to stumble across a perfect diamond or ruby, to see the crystalline nature of truth which has been realized in some way.

And now each is filled with the appetite for living at this level of harmony and justice and that feeling of rightness. You crave and seek with all your heart to enlarge those experiences and to enhance the possibility of having those times come upon you, for surely we may say that there is no guaranteed entrance into a state of mind or heart within which, while the illusion of normal life is full and living, you may control your state of mind or your awareness, for we would not be telling the truth were we to say that we have the solution that can erase the illusion and leave you in sure possession of the truth that lies within the illusion. And may we say that were we able to guarantee to each within incarnation upon your planet at this time that each would be able to be completely free of the illusion, we would not wish to ruin the experience of suffering which each of you desired to undergo.

Let us look at this point, at this issue of the desirability of suffering. Why would a spirit in full and conscious knowledge of the love of the Creator voluntarily place herself within the veil of forgetting and then ask herself to undergo a certain level of suffering and learning and transformation? Why would [you] wish to plunge into the difficult and confused sea of illusion that your Earth plane represents? That which places you within this illusion is infinitely and intimately tied to the Creator Itself and to the free will that has begotten the universe and that calls each spark of the Creator onward to reach once again that source and ending of all. Why would any do this, except for the simple reason that it is the nature of each spark of the Creator to wish to learn and to serve. Now, we come to you hoping to be of service to you, and as we speak to you we find ourselves learning twice as much as each of you may perhaps learn from those things that we say. Such is the nature of any gift that is given, that it comes to bless the giver twice and three times and a hundredfold.

Before incarnation each of you saw clearly what it was to live by faith, what it was to affirm in each moment the holy nature of that moment and the blessed nature of the holiness of the self. Each saw this clearly, and we see this clearly, for we do not have that veil of illusion that has dropped upon you as you have taken on yourselves the flesh and blood and biochemical mechanisms which move you about within your lifetime that you experience. We see clearly, but because we see so clearly our choices are easy. There is no effort in choosing to radiate or, rather, to allow the radiation through us of the infinite love and light of the one great original Thought which is Love. It is not that this is easy. Rather, that this is inevitable given our view which is clear. Therefore, we cannot polarize towards loving more or serving more or learning more. We cannot become, this instrument would say, better people. We cannot improve our vibratory complex very easily at all within this state which we now enjoy. That which we do to increase our polarity is done with infinite time and patience compared to the rough and tumble and very quick energy exchanges and learnings that are available to those who do not know and cannot see the truth plainly.

Faith to us is simply a word, a word that means the knowledge that all is well and the knowledge that all shall be well. To us it is not amazing to look out of the window and see snow and call it snow. There it is. Yet this within your world is not at all clear. We are not speaking now of snow. We are speaking of the ability of each heart to see that it is love itself and to see that each atom, each iota, each mote of stuff visible or invisible is instinct with the love and the light of the one infinite Creator. From your viewpoint as third-density human beings dwelling within physical bodies, what you gaze at may not speak to you. As the one known as R said, "A floor is only a floor. Dust is only dust. The broom is only a broom." To us, with our clear vision, every manifested atom, dust, floor and broom is alike, a beautiful, living, transformative piece of the Creator's manifestation.

The ability to call upon that part of the self that is already aware of the truth and sanctity of daily living is to call upon a part of the self that this instrument would call the Holy Spirit. The self is a concept that is extremely rich. When one looks at oneself in the mirror or looks at another self, another being, it is easy to see that which is immediately visible to the physical self, and one gathers great quantities of information from gazing in the mirror or from looking at another: the color of the hair, the health of the complexion, age, weight, general characteristics of all kind can be easily noted and filed away. But within that mirror's image, within that other self that you see lies a limitless and infinite self, a self that is connected to all other selves and to all parts whatsoever of the creation of the Father. This connection is so powerful that to gather together in groups, even small groups, is to gather tremendous amounts of energy, and if each of you can sense into the flow of energy around the circle in which you sit you may indeed experience for yourself the great amount of light energy that coming together with one purpose and hope has given to you. Each connection that is made between spirits such as yourselves is a connection that is greatly sanctified and blessed and holy, and it is the reason that you feel that need to come into groups and to express your love of the Creator in some way as a group. The energy of each multiplies the energy of each, so that together you are far more than the sum of yourselves.

You have become an infinite power for love and light, and this is a resource that we are glad that you are taking part in, not only because we feel close to each of you as we meditate with you but also because we have heard the sorrow of the brothers and sisters of those upon your planet, and we know that the light energy that you gather in groups such as this will have a great healing effect upon the suffering of the world as a whole. For each light that connects with another becomes a stronger and stronger light and a lighthouse, shall we say, if there is a group that continues so that entities who have been within the circle know that there is a light source within a certain place. And so entities have come to depend greatly upon churches and synagogues and temples and places where entities may gather for spiritual healing and service. And this is the Sunday mentality that each of you grew up with and is familiar with and is what most of those whom you may know find acceptable as the extent to which they wish to express spirituality in their lives. This is the easy spirituality: the gathering together in groups and the raising of the group spirit. It is much more difficult within the illusion for an entity to come into remembrance of its own nature by himself.

The one known as N spoke earlier of the isolation that a painful condition might give to a patient who does not look sick but who indeed suffers great pain. There is a spiritual isolation that entities may easily feel as they go about their daily round of activities. This isolation is based upon the incoming data from the outside environment which is fed through a number of biases that filter information and prioritize its use. Were each of you to know this and pay attention to all of the incoming data that your senses receive each would become paralyzed with the flood of information. Consequently, each spirit within flesh begins very early to learn what can be taken in, what must be taken in first and acted upon, what is secondly important and what is only in the third place important, and so on. And we would suggest that each of you has adopted biases that cut into, and, in some cases, delete completely the large amounts of data received which are helpful to one which is attempting to break the bonds of Sunday spirituality and come into a closer relationship with the spirit that lies within.

Now, each within this circle has achieved a high measure of dependability and functionality within the society and the culture within which you live. Each has made the choices which have brought each to this point of awareness because those choices seemed necessary. What we are suggesting is that it is possible through observation to reprioritize some aspects of incoming data in order that either different filters are used or certain classes of material are reprioritized and noticed at a higher level than was previously done. One example of this is the creation of the Father. It brings to the eye most of all, certainly to the nose, to the ears, to the senses altogether, the feel and touch and taste of creation itself: the elements of earth and air, wind and fire, the incredible complexities of a life that seems infinitely fertile and wonderfully abundant. Each bush, each blade of grass, each leaf upon a tree, each cloud within the sky, carries a beauty that is ineffable and that hides from the notice of the everyday awareness because it cannot be used in the acquisition of comfort or safety or that money that is needed to assure the comfort and the food of the self and the family.

This, shall we say, is one fairly large category of data that tends to be prioritized quite low, and, therefore, tends not to be appreciated or reacted to at the level of the whole conscious self. Certainly, an entity may feel better in the sunshine than in the shade, may enjoy a sunny day more than a rainy day. But to appreciate each drop of rain or each ray of sunshine, to see each blade of grass as the miracle that it is, this is seldom done because it has no survival value. It is not that which the nuts and bolts needs of humankind would say is part of a necessary awareness of life. And yet it is this aspect of things, the beauty, the wholeness of each creation, that can bring home to the spirit the lessons of faith and hope and love that each does indeed yearn for in that spirit within the self that is a citizen of eternity and not simply a personality that develops and becomes ill and goes back into the dust from which it came.

We are suggesting that each of you is more complex than you may be aware, that you have more needs than can be satisfied with the data prioritization that you now employ. There is that need to go back into the deep programming of the self and to ask, and ask again, and ask again, that self within to pay attention, to take in and to notice the lessons that each blade of grass may teach. And what are those lessons, you may ask? Let us look at that blade of grass. You see the tip of the plant as it comes forth from the fertile soil. You see the hope of its greening in those cold days of the first part of Spring when the earth is still chilly and it is brave and courageous for the seed to start reaching towards that wintry sun that is a bit more to be seen in the sky but does not yet come with that summer warmth that is easy to grow under. Underneath the soil lie those roots which have made it through the deepest sleep of winter on faith alone. That grass has rested within its roots and its seed and accepted the dying of that self that was, is responding to a new life with all the power of its tiny form, and if some weeder such as this instrument should attempt to take that blade of grass from its home, which unfortunately [is] in some flower box that she wishes to weed, it will resist with every fiber of its being, for it loves life. It knows not how to do otherwise than to reach for the light and to bless all who may tread upon it. And this is one blade of grass, so ask to yourself what lessons lie within the floor and the broom and the dust.

Might you see, then, that the dust expresses a patience, a contentment of being what it is. Dust is, indeed, the most patient of friends. It will stay precisely where it is. It will not travel, for it knows its place and is happy with its place. And that place is upon that which was at one time the tree, and this tree has undergone great suffering. These planks of wood have been torn from the ground by huge saws. They have been rammed into sawmills and made to be peoples' floors and as peoples' floors they are yet willing to lend the beauty of their grain, the softness of their spring underfoot, and the ability to hold that lovely, patient dust. And these gifts they give to you and to all who no longer find them.

And so that incredible being that has the power of locomotion and the power to pick up things and place them otherwise than where they were, this being has manufactured a wonderful instrument for addressing the replacement of dust upon floors with cleanliness upon floors. And this being comes to sweep away that which is old and that which has done its work, to take it up and place it back within the province of the unimproved earth. And in this humble and surely boring little chore there lies the excellence of spiritual inquiry, that desire to uncover beauty, that desire to cleanse and bless one's environment, to take a magical sense of cleanliness and give it to the surroundings which it enjoys. The sweet earth is expressing a spiritual love when it expresses a desire for cleanliness.

The inspiration for cleanliness is indeed spiritual. And the ritual of making that which is dusty into that which shines with cleanliness is a spiritual ritual. The one known as Jim has often spoken of his Sunday morning house-cleaning as part of the family plan, for the one known as Carla goes to church and sings to the infinite Creator and goes through the ceremony of the holy communion. Meanwhile, the one known as Jim is taking all of those things which may have gone awry, that dirt which has fallen or spattered or come upon the things of daily use and with great love and great feeling of the ritual of cleanliness has blessed the entire house with loving and careful attention. And we will guarantee each of you that when you have cleaned your space, when you have cleansed your living place, those coming through the door and entering your magical aura may well never realize why they feel so welcome and so comfortable within your space, but you will know that it is because you have loved your space and have spiffed it up and shined it up until it is proud of itself and feels very ready to bless all who come within its purview. There is nothing that you see that is not holy. There is nothing that you do that cannot be holy. Nothing in your environment is dead. All is alive, made with love and manifested with light. All things are available to those who live by faith as ways to express faith and love and hope.

We cannot cause each of you to sense this. Were we to impose our will upon you in some way, to give you visions of the holiness of the everyday, we would choose not to, for we would simply be doing your learning for you and the realization would have no real power within you. Indeed, each of you must live by faith, completely by reason of your own free will. Each of you must learn the lessons of love and service for yourselves, chosen only by your own free will. When the free will of an entity turns towards faith there is the tendency and the temptation to reach out as if there is something out there that can be gotten into the light, into the mind, that will change things. Yet we say to you that in terms of the spirit the knowledge, the awareness, the transformation that you seek lies waiting within you, and it is to those who reach into the self that faith will come.

We spoke earlier of the Holy Spirit. It can be imagined as that which comes from without, as that which is exterior to the self. And certainly it is, shall we say, exterior to the conscious self. But the spirit of the one infinite Creator is far closer to you than your bones, or your muscle, or your flesh. It is far closer to you than your hearing, or your eyes, or your senses. You are made of faith and love. The Holy Spirit is with you in an intimate and inner way as a true portion of your being, as that portion of the self that knows and that can inspire. This instrument calls upon the name of Jesus and yet Jesus said, "I am the way." By whatever name you call love, you are calling *(inaudible)*.

Within those gifts that are yours by nature you are not calling upon something that you must go out and get, for the Creator is the "I" of you. When you say "I am," you are speaking also of the Creator. When you say "I am," you are speaking of love. You are speaking of holiness. You are speaking of faith. And this awareness is part of your web of perception that has been prioritized so low that it does not come up into the conscious mind.

We are being asked by this instrument to finish this portion of the meditation, and so we would conclude through this instrument by suggesting that the life lived in faith begins with the assumption that all is well and that all shall be well. We are suggesting that to live in faith you claim faith, that you live in a magical world. You claim the magic of your "I," your "I am." If you wish to bring the holy within your daily awareness, you claim the holiness of your self and reprioritize those things to which you pay attention, so that you may be better served by those things about which you think and by those ways in which you form biases and opinions. That which you seek lies within you. The ground whereon you are sitting is holy ground. Begin with the assumption of that which you seek, and you will begin to uncover the simple truth that that which you seek is right there, closer than your breathing, nearer to you than your hands or your feet.

We would at this time transfer the contact to the one known as Jim that we may answer any questions that you may have at this time. We leave this instrument in love and in light. We are those of Q'uo.

(Jim channeling)

I am Q'uo, and I greet each of you again in the love and the light of the infinite Creator. At this time it is our privilege to offer ourselves in the attempt to speak to any further queries which those present might have for us. Is there another query at this time?

Carla: I have been struggling with a tendency to be angry and go on the defensive, but I don't know how to get out of that feeling from the inside out. I find it almost impossible to claim myself as anything other than the anger that I feel at that time. Could you make any comments or suggestions?

I am Q'uo, and am aware of your query, my sister. We find that we may speak on some aspects of this problem, shall we say, but there is much yet which will need to be discovered through your own efforts. We may suggest that the long-term press of pain upon the physical vehicle wears both upon the physical vehicle and upon the mental support framework, shall we say, the nerves and the nervous system, as you would call them. For as one has the experience of the physical pain repeated in a nearly constant fashion at various locations within the physical vehicle there is the tendency [of] what we have heard called the transparency of the experience in which there is the response or knee-jerk action, as it has been called, that appears within the behavioral patterns of the entity so experiencing pain. Thus, it is a kind of wearing upon the machinery that has its effect upon you at this time. However, there is the potential of the reprogramming of the system of response so that there is less likelihood of losing one's center or balance in a mental and emotional sense when [one] feels the confusion or startled response as a result of interacting with other entities within one's environment. This is something which takes the conscious attention to reprogram these responses and is nearly as constant in its requirements for application as is the pain which it is seeking to ameliorate.

Is there a further query, my sister?

Carla: No. I'll have to read that over.

I am Q'uo, and we thank you once again, my sister. Is there another query at this time?

T: Keeping free will in mind, how do I recognize the reason for the fears that I experience. Why am I afraid? Why am I uneasy?

I am Q'uo, and am aware of your query, my brother. We would comment by suggesting that the fears of any moment might best be explored by entering that state of consciousness which is available when one is in the meditative state. That is, to retire upon a regular basis to that inner room where one may look at the environment in which the fear was experienced, the thoughts that accompanied such fear, the responses that arose within one, and so forth, so that one may examine, as well as one can in an intellectual sense, the nature of the experience and how it affects one's being.

This exploration may best be accomplished while one is in the meditative state, for while one is in this state there is the easier access, shall we say, to the subconscious level of the mind complex, and from this level of being it is possible to make connections between that which is experienced consciously and the source of such experience and the response of the self to this experience. Thus, this is a careful study which one may make of the self. This is an enhanced level of seeking or course [of] experience in that the fears that one may explore also represent some aspect of the primary lessons which one is working upon during the length of the incarnation. Thus, when one is exploring one's fears one is continuing the exploration that was set forth for the incarnation before it began.

Is there a further query, my brother?

T: No. Thank you very much.

I am Q'uo, and we thank you very much, my brother. Is there another query at this time?

R: As I sit in meditation my mind picks up on a situation or pattern and works with a thought and creates what I call a mind movie that goes on and on. I can consciously stop this and return to silence and then it begins again. I try to allow a place for that pattern, but I still wonder if there is something else that I can do with it, or just leave it?

I am Q'uo, and am aware of your query, my brother. The minds of most third-density entities such as yourselves are quite stimulated and active upon many levels as a result of the progress, shall we say, of the way of life which is experienced and created as an experience by your peoples. There is the tendency to apply the self liberally throughout the daily experience, to spread oneself thinly, shall we say, to engage the mind often as a means by which one navigates through the cultural experience. This experience has been enhanced by many tools and gadgets that take one quickly here and there and require from one a great deal of information, time, effort and thought. Thus, the mind is like a plant which has been given a great deal of water, of soil, of sun, of nutrients, and of attention and has grown in large degree as a result of this overemphasis on its functioning into a kind of machine which has a momentum of its own being, we shall say, for we find a difficulty in adequately describing how active the mind complex of your peoples is.

We find that the meditative state is, indeed, that place where one may approach the quieting of the mind yet find time and again examples of its rambunctiousness. That you are able to become aware of this chatter or momentum of the mind and have been able from time to time to be able to displace this chatter with the one-pointed focus upon the silence within is an achievement of note and is the path towards the eventual balancing of this mechanism so that there is the possibility of entering into a sacred place within the mind complex and be unhindered by the activity of the constant stream of thoughts that is the natural concomitant to the kind of style that most of your people find themselves living.

Thus, our suggestion to you is to continue that which you have done tirelessly and that is to notice when the mind is running and then to place that mental picture aside so that the main focus of the mind may return to that one-pointed focus upon stillness. This is an exercise which does engage the mind upon a simpler level than the normal daily routine. If there is a scent of incense or a sound as of your music or your chanting that you find relaxing, we would suggest that you engage these activities to enhance the process of relaxing the mind process.

There is no easy answer for any entity within this environment who wishes to find the peaceful place within, for each must deal with this mental activity and the tendency to take over the focus. We can only suggest your perseverance and the application of the light-hearted attitude in so doing. For it is the effort that you make, the regularity of your meditations, that is of importance in the real gain from this stage of the meditative practice. As you continue to invest your time and your effort there also [is] a momentum of this investiture that is made that will eventually take its hold upon the meditative endeavor.

Is there a further query, my brother?

R: No, not on this subject. I will have to sit with those suggestions.

I am Q'uo, and we thank you, my brother. Is there another query at this time?

Carla: How can R prepare himself for meeting a girlfriend to be a companion?

I am Q'uo, and am aware of your queries, my friends. When an entity finds that there is a portion of the self that resides in loneliness and wishes to be accompanied by another it is well to do those things which one would normally and naturally do to make oneself available for the finding of such a friend. We find that this is well-known by the one known as R in that this entity is active in placing itself in its environment in which there is the likelihood of finding the female of the proper persuasion.

However, we would also suggest that there is the possibility of placing oneself in the meditative state upon the regular basis, as is always our suggestion, for the meditative state is a means whereby the subconscious mind and other resources of the entity may be accessed so that the direction or plan may first be formed in this place, then fleshed out, shall we say, within the physical illusion in which each moves.

Within the meditative state it is well to look at the self and to see the self as it is, shall we say, to look at the heart of the self and see where there might be the company provided by the self for the self so that the self is enhanced in its view of itself. This is to say that an entity may find that there is a missing piece, a place, an avenue of interest that, when explored, feels like going home. That there is a completion upon this avenue, that a direction that may be found will allow a certain passion within to be released, from self to self, so that there is the possibility of the completion that occurs first within. Then it is followed within the physical illusion by the physical expression for the self, respect for the self, and excitement of the self for the life experience.

Again, we have not provided a course of study or reflection which is easily achieved, for there is within each entity a place whereby the self may expand in its view of itself, that is to say, a place where a new level of learning, a new level of resonance, may be discovered. When this place is found there is the possibility, then, of having this new level of experience be reflected within the daily round of activities.

Is there a further query, my friends?

R: No. You have given me a lot to think about, and thank you for the words of encouragement. Thanks to Carla as well.

I am Q'uo, and we are grateful that we are able to be of some small service. Is there a final query at this time?

(No further queries.)

I am Q'uo, and as it appears that we have exhausted the queries for the nonce we would take this opportunity to thank each for inviting our presence in your circle of seeking this day. We are most grateful to be able to walk with you for a few steps upon your journey. We would also remind each that each has many such friends that walk with you, and wait with you, and rejoice with you at each step and praise with you the unity of the one Creator. We are known to you as those of Q'uo, and would take our leave of this instrument and this group at this time, leaving each, as always, in the love and the light of the one infinite Creator. Adonai, my friends. Adonai. ☙

L/L Research

L/L Research is a subsidiary of Rock Creek Research & Development Laboratories, Inc.

P.O. Box 5195
Louisville, KY 40255-0195

www.llresearch.org

Rock Creek is a non-profit corporation dedicated to discovering and sharing information which may aid in the spiritual evolution of humankind.

ABOUT THE CONTENTS OF THIS TRANSCRIPT: This telepathic channeling has been taken from transcriptions of the weekly study and meditation meetings of the Rock Creek Research & Development Laboratories and L/L Research. It is offered in the hope that it may be useful to you. As the Confederation entities always make a point of saying, please use your discrimination and judgment in assessing this material. If something rings true to you, fine. If something does not resonate, please leave it behind, for neither we nor those of the Confederation would wish to be a stumbling block for any.

CAVEAT: This transcript is being published by L/L Research in a not yet final form. It has, however, been edited and any obvious errors have been corrected. When it is in a final form, this caveat will be removed.

© 2009 L/L Research

Sunday Meditation
May 2, 1999

Group question: Today we would like to get some information that would help us to clarify the work that we do in our daily lives that is of a metaphysical nature. Usually one, or many people, or lots of people, think that the spiritual journey consists of operating in the higher energy centers from the heart on up, through the throat and brow, and doing these things that seem obviously of a spiritual or metaphysical nature. But we are wondering how to focus one's life on the spiritual journey while living the everyday life that has various relationships that are going well or poorly but is where we really live. Could Q'uo give us some information to help us clarify how we focus on what really is our spiritual work each day?

(Carla channeling)

We are those known to you as Q'uo, and we greet you in the love and in the light of the one infinite Creator in whose service we are. We thank you for bringing this circle together, for seeking truly, and for calling us to share in this circle of seeking. We hope that we also may be counted as true pilgrims and we feel the blessing both of being able to share in your circle and for being able to perform the service which we dwell within your inner planes at this time in order to offer. It is a great opportunity that you offer us and we accept it eagerly, with the one stipulation that each take from what we say those things that seem to be helpful, leaving the rest behind.

You ask us this day concerning clarity, the clarity that would create for each of you the way in which to see the events and happenstances of your everyday life in the most useful, the most clear, the most lucid, the most spiritually helpful standpoint. We give to this instrument a view of a memory which she has, for we wish to go in somewhat a different direction than this instrument expects, and so we chose out of her store of memory that clear memory which is useful to our purposes at this time.

This instrument was experiencing at the time of this occurrence a nearly complete lack of life; that is, this instrument was very close to death at the time of this experience. It was aware that it was in extremity. The instrument was in the hospital. Her physical body was not functioning adequately. The concern of those surrounding the instrument was intense. In this environment the instrument lay in a state of prayer. Far from being lucid, the prayerful state of this instrument was described by her at the time as a fog, a mist on the waters. This was literally the vision which the instrument was aware of at the time. She was aware of herself as a spirit, not resting in or on the waters but being at the water and seeing through the fog two lights as stars would appear, beaming ever so dimly through the fog. Sometimes she could see them. Sometimes she could not. But more and more it became a vision that had its own reality.

There was a moment of sudden realization in which she grasped the fact that these lights were spirits, spirits whom she could identify, and she realized that these two entities, her relatives, were praying for her, dwelling with her in thought, accompanying [her] in the hour of extremity. As she became aware that this was, indeed, a specific vision and not a passing miasma or phantasm she saw the fog lift and the sky light up with literally millions of lights. And she again had that realization in which she realized that these were all of the entities which dwelt upon Earth who were, at that moment, in a state of prayer, doing work for those who suffered upon Earth. None, or almost none, of these entities knew of her or her extremity and yet they appeared in her universe as spirits because they were praying to lessen the suffering of humankind.

This vision has a clarity to it that is born of the depth of reality and the shallowness of personality. Although the instrument was aware of the first two who prayed, once the universe was realized as being a way to see prayer help, the way to see energy coming to help the instrument, the instrument immediately transcended personality and saw those who were vibrating in Christ-like love. We choose this memory because it strips away so many layers of perception and habit in the way in which entities tend to think about themselves, what they are doing, how they are doing, and how they can do better in attempting to be those who live like a spirit, those who are working from a metaphysical frame of reference. The pursuit of spiritual evolution is a pursuit in which almost every temptation to follow this or that avenue is a temptation toward folly, for the instincts that the physical and mental parts of the personality have are instincts which show no clarity or very little clarity when it comes to what is actually taking place spiritually, from moment to moment in the passage of everyday life.

Because this instrument was in an extremely precarious position, it was therefore more open to awareness that followed no obvious logic. What we ask you to do at this juncture is to take a moment and move into that space in which you are a light. We would pause at this time and allow each of you to move into that space where spirit is real in you.

(Pause)

As each of you struggles with this concept each begins to see how deceptive rational thought is when it comes to spiritual matters. In attempting to see the self as a light there is that feeling of self-judgment that comes immediately, that feeling that, "I am not a very bright light." The feeling that, perhaps, "I am not even lit all of the time." That feeling of all limits washing away, shores receding and disappearing and the self finding itself in the midst of a trackless ocean of experience in which there is more fog than light.

We have said many times through this instrument and through many other instruments that what you are is a vibration. That you are a metaphysical entity that is expressing in a complex of vibrations that is as clearly and uniquely yourself as your name. Indeed, that is clearer than any name because it is an encompassing, complete rendition of the self. There may be two or more John Smiths, or Jane Does, or even Jim McCartys, or R's, but there is only one vibratory complex that has configured itself in precisely the way that you have. No one thought up your vibratory complex. No one named you this vibratory signature. By direction and misdirection by things done and left undone, by the uncountable totality of everyday moments mounting one upon the other, without effort, without guides, without knowledge for the most part, of what is occurring, you simply are. You can poke. You can probe, but you cannot break down [the] metaphysical vibratory complex that is one precious, infinite and much loved being.

The Creator is vitally interested in each configured being. The Creator grasps the totality of this vibratory complex and echoes back to the being a validation without judgment, created utterly of love—creative and destructive, all-powerful love. It is this vibratory complex that is you as a light being. It is this light being that you are. You are not your body. You are not your personality. You are not your mind. You are not your emotions. You cannot exhaust the qualities of yourself regardless of how long you look, how deeply you search, or how prayerfully you mine the rich lode of the deep mind in attempting to affix to the self a deeper and more permanent personality. That is to say, that the building up of the magical personality, as this instrument has often called the work of disciplining the self, while it is a good and even an important adventure to be on, it has a limited use, a use within the illusion rather than a use that will alter the configuration of your vibration.

Indeed, we could gaze at the entire spectrum of conscious methods of working upon the discipline of the personality and point out that they are or constitute a materialistic view of spiritual evolution. This instrument immediately thought to herself, "How can there be spiritual materialism?" because the first dynamic, the first paradox, is the dynamic between the spiritual and material worlds, and this is so. This is spiritual work as seen by and as taught by entities within the spiritual illusion of Earth. This does not mean that the discipline of the personality is a bad idea. There is tremendous clarity to be gained by such a spiritual practice. There is tremendous advantage to be gained in working with many spiritual practices, and one of the things that spiritually awakened beings do is find and employ spiritual practices that feel useful and fertile and productive. But, you see, when you are thinking about becoming more spiritually productive, you are thinking about being spiritual in the same way that you would think about finishing your physical labor for a given period. It is the work ethic of your culture carried over into the spiritual life. Again we say, we are not in any way attempting to discredit those efforts which you make to become a better spiritual being. It is simply to point out that what you are spiritually will express itself the most clearly when there is no thought taken as to how one is doing spiritually.

The being that you are is only lightly connected to the body that you experience or even the incarnation that you experience. In truth, at the level of clarity which we are able to express through this instrument, that vibratory complex that expresses self when the infant cries its first cry is not difficult at all to pick out of a metaphysical lineup of those beings that are ending their incarnation. The change from the beginning of incarnation to the end of incarnation in vibratory complex is minimal. Although it is far more possible to make substantive changes in that vibration within your third density than it is in any other density that is higher, yet still that with which one began the incarnation is going to be pretty much that which one takes out of the incarnation.

This does not mean that spiritual work is useless. It simply means that the power to be is so all-encompassing that the distortions laid upon that basic vibration of infinite love are quite, quite small compared to the core reality of limitless light itself vibrating in undistorted love, or, shall we say, in minimally undistorted love. For all that is manifest as vibration has the distortion of free will and is, therefore, not a pure love vibration. Each of you is not here to work upon one's quality of life. This is not what we are suggesting. What we are suggesting is that the material part of spirituality concerns itself with patterns of interaction between beings. The densities are schools in which spiritual entities learn with increasing efficiency to interact with each other with minimal distortion. This is quite different from the self as a configuration of light.

What we would suggest to each of you when the way seems clouded and conflicted is that you separate reality from illusion, that you call to remembrance who you are and how you are, that you call to remembrance with full respect who other entities interacting with you are and how they are. That you be able to see the difference between the self and that other self as inevitable beings that are as they are and self and other self as those who have been offered the opportunity to work within an illusion in such a way as to discover as much as possible about loving interaction. It does not cure problems if you see that those having the problems are simply beautiful configurations of light. But it gives to the seeker something that does not need work, something that is already perfect, in the self and in the other self. It gives to the seeker that ability to move into distortion with an awareness that it is distortion even when the most exacting spiritual practices are being observed and the most discipline of personality is being accomplished.

It may seem unfair that so much of spiritual seeking is in the spiritually material sector when what the soul thirsts for is that sense of self, other self, and Creator as light. But it does set a baseline against which work within an incarnation can be seen for what it is. This instrument would call it homework, and, indeed, many are those upon your sphere who have shaped the spiritual life as a process of learning, a school of instruction. This is a pretty good metaphor, a useful tool in thinking about specific difficulties. We are aware that this question comes from each within the circle and those writing in from outside the circle having that feeling of wanting to know more about work on this or that energy center, this or that chakra, this or that relationship, this or that process. And each of you will find yourself leaping nimbly from precipice to midair to abyss and back again as the various moments of living and experiencing pass in this time and space illusion that you enjoy, indeed, that we also enjoy.

We assure you that there are realizations to be gained and lessons of love to be learned just as you have been going about learning them through your meditations, through your attempts to balance experience, through your concern for and work upon core interactions and core relationships. We may say to the one known as P that this desire for work, desire for understanding of experiences, is a good and a proper desire, and yet as with all desires there is no achieving of the objective that will satisfy the depth of that desire because of the fact that entities are configurations of light; that is to say, because they are vibrations. Any and every thought that an entity can have about identity, relationships, spiritual work, or any matter whatsoever are like that desire for food that is not satisfied by the eating of food. There is a thirst and a hunger in spiritual work that cannot be satisfied by spiritual work or by spiritual attainment. All spiritual attainment in the end is nonsense, one with the illusion that spawned it. And yet, it is the nonsense that each came here to prosecute with the highest degree of integrity, love and respect of which each is capable and will hope to become more capable.

The being that you are attempting to create, you see, is, and [yet] cannot be that light being, for that light being is pretty much as it is and will change only through unimaginable eons of time. The whole octave of experience shall have its way with that vibration and [you] will still be you. However, you actually think to create an entity that never was until you put yourself into the rhythms and the intentions of a way of living that will bring you closer and closer to a goal that you can only dimly sense, and that goal has to do with the way you interact with other selves. The entity you are attempting to build is the world soul or the social memory complex, as this instrument would say it. Light simply is. Yet time and space create the need for movement and it is in becoming aware of graceful movement in habit, in ways of thinking, in disciplines of the personality, in purification of the emotions, that you may reliably hope and trust that you will make progress, that you will at the end of an incarnation be measurably more able to see the self and the other self without significant distortion when first you grasped the fact that you were alone in this illusion and wailed your first wail upon being born.

We appreciate greatly the depth of this question. We are extremely thankful to have been able to make this attempt to share with you our limited understanding of the issues involved. In your beingness, we salute you. And in your patterns of doing, we salute you as well. Each level is acceptable and true. In terms of remembrance, we would suggest the key advantage of the memory that you are as you are and others are as they are and that you and they are both perfect. Indeed, we suggest that each think of self and other self as this instrument does the Christ. You are that ideal, that archetype, that loves so deeply and so generously. You are easily capable of Christhood as is everyone you meet. The desire to affect that outcome, that hunger and thirst for righteousness, will not prove false, simply somewhat limited.

We would at this time end with some reluctance. Let this be the totality of our initial discussion of this interesting subject. For this instrument is expressing to us in no uncertain terms that our time is up. We realize that there are other questions at this time and in hopes of being able to speak with you further upon those topics we would at this time transfer this contact to the one known as Jim, leaving this instrument in the love and in the light of the infinite One. We are those of Q'uo.

(Jim channeling)

I am Q'uo, and I greet each of you again in the love and the light of the one infinite Creator through this instrument. We would now ask if we might speak to any further queries which those present might have for us?

Carla: I would like to start off just by asking why I was moved to tears by something which never moved me to tears before when I was reliving that memory. I was feeling intense emotion. I couldn't say whether it was happy or sad. It was an almost unbearable intensity of emotion. Any comments you could make on why that happened might have some bearing on the message, I would think.

I am Q'uo, and am aware of your query, my sister. The image of the light and the love filled beings at the heart of the light is a revealing of a connection to love which opens the heart and releases the emotions in many. That it should do so within your own being is not surprising. To discover that one is loved to such an extent that the heart of another beats for another for you is overwhelming to many who have not felt such love before.

Is there a further query, my sister?

Carla: No. Not about that. Thank you. In thinking about P's questions I would just ask if you have a message for P, if there is something you would respond to in those many specific requests for information that would help the way she is working on herself right now?

I am Q'uo, and am aware of your query, my sister. We are aware that the one known as P has offered the service of many of those concerns which are upon her mind at this time, and we do not wish to seem to weigh them less importantly, shall we say, than does she, for each has its focus and opportunity for learning. But we wish to offer our service which does not infringe upon another entity's free will by providing for them the direction or heart of a concern which is of necessity theirs to discover. For to feel that there is experience and information of importance within a certain set of circumstances is the domain of the seeker of truth. But we would comment to this entity by suggesting to it that each flower grows where it is planted, and where this entity has found itself situated within this illusion at this time may not be the most comfortable of circumstances but is the situation in which its higher self felt it most helpful to be. For it provides the lessons that are not easy but are to the heart of its incarnation.

To learn to love and accept that which seems unlovable and unacceptable is, indeed, a worthy challenge, and we would encourage this entity to look about it and to discover that those entities within its circle of experience are those which have come together with it to dance the dance of this illusion's catalyst, shall we say. Each entity has that to offer that is important to the one known as P, and we would encourage perseverance. We would encourage the opening of the heart in a relentless fashion, and we would encourage the seeing of the one Creator in the smallest of moments and in the most difficult of circumstances.

Is there a further query, my sister?

Carla: Yes, but from my standpoint rather than P's. For many years I have heard people ask about specific questions and this kind of question was taken and discussed by inner guides or other entities and the person asking the question felt a great deal of valuable material was gained through such questions and answers. I have also felt that it is a distraction. Is this an unfair judgment on my part? What is the basic nature or value of asking metaphysical sources about specific circumstances or relationships?

I am Q'uo, and am aware of your query, my sister. We of the Confederation of Planets in the Service of the One Infinite Creator have found that it is most appropriate for us to speak upon those queries which are of a philosophical or generally applicable level of principle. For we are not native to this planetary sphere and are not able to see with a clear vision the means by which to avoid infringing upon free will without applying this general principle of replying only to general philosophically oriented queries. It is so very easy to feel one has helped another by giving the answer to specific queries such as the ones which this entity has offered and then witness the loss of the power to seek and discriminate on the part of such a seeker when a source such as are we is trusted more in this area more than is personal discrimination. Thus, we leave it to those of this planetary sphere—those who inhabit its outer planes and those who inhabit its inner planes—to deal with the issues of specificity: the determining of dreams, the meaning of a book, the coincidence of a friend, and so forth. That these events do have a meaning and a purpose in the incarnation is without dispute. The great value of their determination is that the seeker herself shall make this determination and thereby strengthen her ability to discriminate that which has value to it by the exercise of the intuition, the releasing of the power of the subconscious mind, the harmonizing of that which is the conscious mind with the subconscious mind so that like a muscle that is well exercised there is strength developed in the area of discrimination as well. We apologize for our inability to be of service in these areas but would feel that we are of a greater service by refraining from comment.

Is there a further query at this time?

Carla: No. Not now. Thank you very much for myself and for P.

I am Q'uo, and we thank you and the one known as P. Is there another query at this time?

R: So you are in a way doing the same thing that we are doing on our path, looking for catalyst that comes your way and then strengthening your muscles of discrimination and then finding the best way to use it so that you can move along on your own path?

I am Q'uo, and am aware of your query, my brother, and in the general sense you are quite correct, for always is it necessary to exercise the muscle of discrimination. There are many potential avenues of service provided all seekers of service at all levels of experience. It is to those who exercise most carefully, or shall we say lovingly, or shall we say wisely, the ability to choose the path, for there are always considerations of appropriateness, of infringing upon another entity's free will choices in his or her own journey. Each of us as a portion of the one Creator is most carefully and closely connected to every other entity. As we give our energies, attention and concern, love, and light, information and inspiration, we affect those to whom we speak and with whom we share these energies. It is well to affect others in a fashion which provides an opportunity for discovery from within that entity. This is difficult to do. However, the attempt is worthwhile, and we continue to make it, as do each of you. And as we travel this journey, wishing, indeed, to place one spiritual foot in front of the other, we do not wish to negate that which we are nor that which we have been, wishing to leave them for they fall short of some standard, but have learned to accept all that we are, all that we have been, and all that we shall become, as portions of the one Creator.

Is there a further query, my brother?

R: I was trying to do as you advised earlier in the session and move into a place of light, but I was having trouble doing that and wondered if it would help if I were to focus on an emotion and then follow that emotion to the place of light?

I am Q'uo, and am aware of your query, my brother. This is somewhat difficult to give a clear response to for the emotional aspect of most entities' complex of being is that weighing of the value of a thing by the emotion it causes to arise in response. The emotional aspect of most entities' complex points to those areas of concern and of immediate attention, shall we say.

However, the desire to seek in a spiritual sense the nature of one's journey and the nature of truth, of love, and so forth, is the, shall we say, directional arrow that points the way and which opens a door within the essence of one's being so that one may feel a connection with all things, including the quality of the one Creator called light. Thus, we would point one to this concept of desire and will, the concept of faith that might be more helpful in opening the avenues to the inner being rather than relying upon the qualities of emotion.

Is there a further query, my brother?

R: If we continue to talk about this question from today and fashion another query from it would you want to talk further about it?

I am Q'uo, and am aware of your query, my brother, and, indeed, we would be happy to speak upon this query again or one similar to it if you would care to consider and rephrase the query for another working.

Is there another query at this time?

Carla: I was struck by a statement from you that we were able to interact with others and create social memory complexes and get together more and more. My mentality said that, well, you don't want us to become exactly alike, and I feel this is so. Would the model, then, of such an interaction be one of infinite harmony rather than unison?

I am Q'uo, and am aware of your query, my sister. We would agree that this is a good representation of the nature of the blending of the various portions of the one infinite Creator, into a kind of choir that each entity contributes to by the uniqueness of its voice.

Carla: So the angels' songs are really harmonious emotions and harmonizing personalities. They don't just chant "Hallelujah! Hallelujah!" Their every fiber of every being is like a song to the Creator. Is that what you are saying?

I am Q'uo, and this is correct, my sister. Is there a final query?

Carla: No. I am done and I just want to thank you for a fascinating session. Well done.

I am Q'uo, and we would also thank each of those present for preparing a query full of nuance and rich with the heart-felt desires of each present and those not present as well.

At this time we would take our leave of this instrument and this group, leaving each in the love and in the light of the one infinite Creator. Adonai, my friends. Adonai. ✦

L/L Research

L/L Research is a subsidiary of Rock Creek Research & Development Laboratories, Inc.

P.O. Box 5195
Louisville, KY 40255-0195

www.llresearch.org

Rock Creek is a non-profit corporation dedicated to discovering and sharing information which may aid in the spiritual evolution of humankind.

ABOUT THE CONTENTS OF THIS TRANSCRIPT: This telepathic channeling has been taken from transcriptions of the weekly study and meditation meetings of the Rock Creek Research & Development Laboratories and L/L Research. It is offered in the hope that it may be useful to you. As the Confederation entities always make a point of saying, please use your discrimination and judgment in assessing this material. If something rings true to you, fine. If something does not resonate, please leave it behind, for neither we nor those of the Confederation would wish to be a stumbling block for any.

CAVEAT: This transcript is being published by L/L Research in a not yet final form. It has, however, been edited and any obvious errors have been corrected. When it is in a final form, this caveat will be removed.

© 2009 L/L Research

Sunday Meditation
May 23, 1999

Group question: The question this week has to do with three weeks ago when we began to ask about the devotional life and how to live the devotional life, and we would like to follow up that question by asking how we find more and more of that which we really are, that which is the heart of our being. We would like to hear whatever Q'uo has to say about ways to discover more of our true nature, how to observe our true nature, how to become aware of our true nature, our true being, that which we had planned before the incarnation to have as an opportunity, a way of expressing our soul essence.

(Carla channeling)

We are those of the principle known to you as Q'uo. We greet you in the love and in the light of the one infinite Creator. We are most happy and blessed to be included in your meditation this day, and we appreciate greatly your question for us. Truly, the mystery of deity is wrapped up in this question of how to be one's true self. For as the one known as Jim read from the *Law of One* material earlier this day, each is the Creator. And the challenge before all living in illusion is how to become more aware of that personhood as infinite Creator.

The workings of what this instrument would call God and men are as complex and as assorted and varied as the grains of sand upon the shore. It is difficult to comprehend the myriad numbers of sparks of the Creator that are, just as you or we, attempting to be their true selves. It is hard to fathom that, even upon your planet, one small entity amidst a million or a billion other planetary entities, there is such a long history of people such as you attempting to survive, to relate to each other, to accomplish physical and societal, mental and emotional goals. It is difficult to imagine the thousands of years during which the human experience has basically remained the same. This instrument thinks back over all of the reading that she has done through a long succession of classes and learning experiences, and no matter what the century or the millennium, the human heart has remained the same: seeking wisdom, seeking compassion, seeking the truth, concerned for basically the same things century after century, millennium upon millennium.

As each entity sits in this circle of seeking she brings to this moment the sum total of all that has been undergone, all that has lasted through the chances and changes of daily living. In one field of energy there lies for each that history of the life and, taken to a bigger scale, the history of that spirit whose personality shell is now occupying the chair. For each of you and each of us has a tremendously long and varied history of incarnations and experiences and gifts and graces and opportunities, and were we to speak upon any one of you, upon all that that one entity is, we could not exhaust the subject through any amount of time, for each of you is all that there is. Each of you is full and whole and infinite.

As always, [for] one attempting to come to a place of more awareness the tool of choice is silence. In meditation and in prayer much may be accomplished beneath the surface of that beingness that is each of you. Without words to limit, without thorns to inhibit, the silence speaks in the free and open manner of deity. The more of silence that one may eat as food, the more deep shall come that awareness of the Creator speaking within that system of energies that is the being that is each of you. We hear you speaking of the desire to serve, the desire to give of the self to others and to the planetary energy, and we applaud that hope and that energy, for each of you was indeed careful to include unique gifts in the personality that you chose for this incarnation. And it is wise to seek out one's gifts and to find ways to use them in the service of others.

Perhaps we may say that when the word "wise" or "wisdom" is heard, we have not yet gotten to the heart of meaning for this particular density. The lesson that is before you at this point is undoubtedly not about wisdom, not about being wise, but rather about discovering the spring of infinite love. The rational mind can do just so much when it comes to seeking out the wellspring of one's being. It can put you in a good place. It can arrange an environment for best effect. But once the stage is set, there seems to be nothing but a beating heart, a resting body, an alert and seeking mind that thirsts for the Creator, and time. And in this curl of body and silence and time there is that feeling of being alone, being still, and being at sea. And the rational mind asks how this curl of energy and hope and time can bring one to oneself.

Individuality is a very deceptive thing. We are not denying each of you your individuality at all, but it is a puzzling thing in that it predisposes one to thinking that the goal is to find more of one's individuality, that in becoming more of oneself one shall become more individualized. This, however, is not our understanding of the way one becomes more fully or wholly oneself. The rational mind wants to reach out and pull in all of those things that will be useful and helpful in the search for the heart itself. There is that feeling of accretion, of collecting resources that will be of help in this search. Yet it is our feeling that the becoming more of oneself is a process of things falling away, a process of subtraction.

The model that we give this instrument is the model of an entity who works upon two levels. On the outer level the seeker who wishes to become more itself deals with the environment about it, attempting to place itself more and more in an environment that it finds conducive to the giving of its gifts and the learning of its lessons and the keeping of its promises in relationships and ethical considerations, and in all those matters of personal honor and duty. There is a valid benefit gained by the seeker as it simplifies and regularizes its environment in such a way as to find fruitfulness of self in all of those ways that entities think of being fruitful in avocations and vocations. There is a legitimate outer work that is helpful to doing, and we would not say that one who wishes to move more into the heart of oneself should forgo working on the discipline of the personality, the purification of emotion, and the development of the magical personality. These are just and helpful uses of the mind, of the attention, and of time.

However, in terms of doing the inner work the challenge is to find ways to allow that which is not the heart of self to fall away. It is not that one decides to remove self identification from this or that pattern of living or distortion of mind, but the seeker who feels that it knows what is to be dropped in order to be more the heart of self is deluding itself at some level, for there is no way from within the self to see into the patterns of energy that are, in essence, distortions of the one infinite Creator. Consequently, there is no rational way to become more and more undistorted. Working to become less distorted is a distortion itself, and the seeker who attempts to guide itself in the ways of becoming the Creator is, instead, most likely developing patterns of thinking that are in and of themselves an additional distortion, so there is the addition of distortion rather than the subtraction of distortion.

What we are trying to say is how easy it is to work too hard at something that is not actually work at all but, rather, a growing willingness, and this is the heart of what we would like to say this day. This place of willingness that things may change in any way, seemingly inwardly or seemingly outwardly, it is this attitude of open possibility, of lack of fear when viewing the present or the future that is a kind of key. And if you can do nothing else from what we suggest this day but cultivate an attitude of willingness to be swayed by the tides of destiny, then we are more than happy.

You are something that is whole and unifying and simple. You are infinite love, infinite light, infinite energy, stepped down and stepped down until you can exist within this particular illusion with this particular kind of physical vehicle, this particular energy shell that we have called the personality. It is as though out of an infinite universe you came through density after density and experience after experience, looking and laughing and gazing and enjoying, and came to this particular planet and said, "Here, I shall plant myself. Here I shall learn to blossom. Here I shall enjoy the sun and feel the rain. Here I shall be born and die." And you descend through the inner planes, through each level at which you make choices, until you have chosen this body, and this time, and this set of circumstances, and suddenly you are born. And this is the present moment of all times, and this is the place out of all places, and this is the density, and this is the experience.

And somehow it seems a miracle that is out of time that has burst upon the Earth like a sun. This is you. This is here. And this is now.

Think of yourself in this way, as a sun or a blossom. Anything but a human. For to think of oneself as human is always to move to the outer, for your true self is no outer thing. You true self is without distortion, and infinite in love. We cannot teach you how to realize compassion. You cannot teach yourself how to realize the compassion that is locked within you. And even with the dint of the hardest and most intransigent work upon the self, you cannot add one whit of compassion to your personality. You can teach yourself to perform compassionate acts, but the key to that infinite compassion that is truly yours is not to be found within teaching and learning. It is locked within the present moment, and it is when you go into the present moment that you are vulnerable to a deeper realization of yourself.

And so what we encourage this day is a heightened awareness of the value of losing yourself in the present moment. When one talks about the devotional life, again one is pulled into thoughts of the outer world. The question that you ask when you ask to learn more of your true self is a question that has no answer but only a direction, a direction that says, "into the present moment, into life." Not living, not a process, but that state of being that lies beyond all process. It should be utterly simple to allow distortion to fall away, and yet it is as far from simple as the challenge of the sculptor who is looking at an ovoid rock which he wishes to carve into a likeness. The likeness dwells within that rock. It is a matter of chipping away at the rock until it has the requisite form to satisfy the maker.

Let us move back into the image of the self in the water. The self has a relationship to the water of being in that the self is a bubble upon the sea of being that wishes to dissolve into that sea, and yet it is the essence of being an individual that you cannot, for the term of this experience, this incarnation, dissolve. This is not your time to dissolve. This is your time to be a bubble. The bubble has a skin, the coherent shell that holds the self apart from the water. And within that bubble there is, one would say, nothing and yet it is within that bubble of individuality that your true self lies. So you may accept being that bubble on the water, but you are touching the water. You are carried along by the water, and we encourage in each of you a sense of that rhythmic and pulsing wave effect that this instrument would call destiny. You have little or no choice as to how the wave on which you are sitting will go. You may, perhaps, position yourself so that the waves do not toss you unduly, yet you are directionless, except for the water. Where the water takes you, you shall go.

And there is an endless art in the observation of this wave action and in those creative attempts to come more into congruency with the line of energy of this wave action. Your responsibility as a personality shell is to be present during this experience of individuality, to observe, and to respond. As you do this outer work, yet still realizing that you are the bubble on the ocean, you set up for yourself that two-layered plan of attack, the outer layer being largely the attempt to come into rhythmic harmony with that energy of destiny that shall give you the experiences that you hoped for, those limitations that will help teach, and those opportunities to share the gifts that you brought with you. Meanwhile, always reserving some of the self for the immediate experience of diving into the present moment. This instrument was earlier speaking of the bliss while working in the garden, talking to the plant life, and working with the devic energy, and she wondered, "Is it out of proportion to its actual import?" and we would say to this instrument, "No, it is not at all out of proportion." It is an instance where this instrument did dive into the present moment to find the heart of bliss that is within each present moment.

We encourage each, then, to find those situations within which it is the easiest to forget the self completely and simply to be. For this particular entity, that is, this particular instrument, being in the garden, interacting with second-density energies, is one excellent set of conditions that encourages this particular seeker to come completely out of herself and into the moment. We encourage each to find those situations that so encourage each. For some it is great music. For others it is art. For some a tramp in the woods. For others the contemplation of the structure of thought that is majestic. What all of them have in common is the result, that explosion of the limited self into the infinite present. Each of you is a blossom. Turn towards the light.

We ask each of you to remember the help that awaits the seeker. You are not alone as you seek to be. There is at many levels help, guidance, encouragement and comfort. As always, we encourage patience, persistence and a sense of humor. For those who seek outwardly there are many accomplishments that can be pointed to. For those who seek to be truly themselves there is only the joy of bursting the bubble and becoming the ocean. We encourage you to continue this seeking in all faith and all hope.

We would at this time conclude this contact through the instrument known as Jim. We leave this instrument in love and in light. We are those of Q'uo.

(Jim channeling)

I am Q'uo, and I greet each of you again in the love and the light of the infinite Creator through this instrument. At this time we would offer ourselves to the possibility that there are further queries that rest upon the minds of those present. If there are further queries, may we ask to hear the next query, please?

R: Why was this universe set up as it is? This octave set up with learning about interactions that collapses into another octave?

I am Q'uo, and am aware of your query, my brother, though we do not expect to be able to give a complete answer to a query which is as broad as the creation itself. But we may give some thoughts that we ourselves have considered concerning the nature of the creation as it is and as we have experienced it.

We are aware that there are those who move as completed beings, those which you have called the Logoi, who have the responsibility of taking the stuff, shall we say, of the infinite mind of the one Creator and refining it in such a way so that those entities such as ourselves and yourselves who are under the care of the Logoi are offered greater and greater opportunities to both know the self at its heart and to know the one Creator at Its heart, and to find that one is in the same place when one knows the self and the Creator.

The infinity of creation is dwarfed by the infinity of the Creator, and as each entity which each of us and you is discovers more of the one Creator and more of the self, each is exploring more intensely one energy center until it is explored in completeness so that the opportunity for a quantum leap to another energy center is offered to the self.

Thus, each entity in each density is offered increasing opportunities to know more of the creation, the Creator, and the self. By offering steady increments of the one Creator the very structure of the creation allows for a steady growth of each entity rather than an overstimulation which would cause the burning out of those receptors of stimuli which the senses of each entity in each density offers. Thus, each entity is offered a reliable means by which to journey through the creation so that it is a perfectly balanced and self-generating curiosity inspiring mechanism, shall we say. We feel that this is perhaps the best way in which we may describe the creation, for there are infinite ways in which it may be described, and each is in its own way correct, for each perceives that which it is ready to perceive and will move up the centers of energy within the physical, mental and spiritual complex vehicles.

Is there a further query, my brother?

R: Are the completed beings, the Logoi, within time and space or do they stand apart from it as shepherds who then drive the others until all becomes one again and goes into another creation?

I am Q'uo, and am aware of your query, my brother. Your latter assumption is more nearly correct, for the Logoi entities are without time and space; that is, they are as the shepherds you have described which care for those who are within their provenance. These Logoi entities are entities of completion who, themselves, have not partaken in the progress of evolution from first density to second and so forth but, from the beginning of the creation, are entities of completion, who look upon the previous octaves of beingness for the seeds that shall grow into the next octave of beingness.

Is there a further query, my brother?

R: So because of their completeness of being the Logoi have the ability to perceive other octaves of experience and I guess it is their choice that they stand apart rather than become part of the Creator?

I am Q'uo, and am aware of your query, my brother. Rather than saying that it is their choice it is more their nature as a given that they are one with the Creator yet are enough different that they have the ability to harvest that which has been learned in previous octaves of experience and expand upon these seeds, these lessons, these crystallizations of being, and to partake in further octaves of being.

Is there a further query, my brother?

R: It is always fascinating to hear you talk about the larger picture. Thank you. I don't have any more questions today.

I am Q'uo, and we thank you for those queries which you have offered us with a whole heart. Is there a further query at this time?

(No further queries.)

I am Q'uo, and again we thank each present for inviting our presence in your circle of seeking this day. It has been, as it always is, a pleasure to join each this day and we remind each that we walk with you at all times for we are one in love and in light and in our common bond of seeking the one Creator together. We invite each to call upon us to deepen your meditative state at any time. At this time we shall take our leave of this instrument and this group, leaving each in the love and in the light of the one infinite Creator. We are known to you as those of Q'uo. Adonai, my friends. Adonai. ✤

Sunday Meditation
September 12, 1999

Group question: What words of inspiration would Q'uo have for those people who have been on the path of seeking for a long time? They are very familiar with their catalyst. They have seen it come around again and again. Maybe they are beginning to wonder if they are ever going to get anywhere with their catalyst. So we would like to ask Q'uo what words of inspiration Q'uo would have for people who might be getting a bit burnt out on the spiritual trail?

(Carla channeling)

We are those of the principle known to you as Q'uo, and we greet you in the love and in the light of the one infinite Creator in whose service we come to you this day. May we say what a joy it is to rekindle the contact that we have enjoyed with your group of seekers for some of your time now. The opportunity that you offer us is greatly appreciated. The energy that you bring to us as you endeavor to aid in your own spiritual evolution is very inspiring to us, for we are aware of the darkness in which you labor and the thick illusion which conceals from you within your illusion the true shape of the form of that catalyst which comes to you.

This instrument has been a fan of the television series, *The X-Files*, and we find in her memory many instances where these two agents of the government had no light but their flashlights to peer into the darkness of their own seeking for their own truths, and so it is with each of you. You have the flashlight of hope, and faith, and will to see into the inky blackness of that spiritual night which both day and night upon your Earth world are.

We hear with sympathy the pain and the effort in the question for us today concerning seekers who have been upon their path for a long time, long enough to begin to see into the patterns of learning which are cyclical in nature. These patterns of learning are different for each seeker due to the arrangements that each seeker has made before the incarnation. Each entity will have an unique set of incarnational lessons. In some cases, this list of lessons is very short. Perhaps one or two themes were chosen to work on during this incarnation. In these cases perhaps the pattern is more easily seen more quickly. This does not mean that it is easily balanced. Others have more complex and interrelated incarnational lessons. And to the ear of logic such lessons are baffling because the connections between the various levels of the lessons are not logical. We cannot say that they are illogical. Perhaps the expression would be extralogical.

If the seeker recognizes himself in this description then perhaps we can simply say that for you the patterns may not seem regular for some time, during which there is much confusion. However, we always encourage that patience which waits to see more of the pattern, for those patterns which are not yet completely seen will look chaotic and will seem to have no order. Nevertheless, this is the creation of the Father, and in that creation there is infinite order.

You ask us for inspiration in words to those who are tired and burnt out on the spiritual path. In a way, anything that will be put into words will be inadequate to the task of lightening the feelings of being heavy laden that drown the senses of the seeker who is weary. What words can change darkness to light, or sadness to joy, when the ineluctable facts that have given rise to the weariness remain as they are? For each entity has vigorously and eagerly created incarnational lessons that are tremendously challenging. What words can make someone forgive the self for being so eager to learn, so eager to learn that the plate of life is overfilled with things to digest during the lifetime?

Before the incarnation began each seeker gazed upon the life to come as though it were a gem, a ruby, an opal, a diamond, with each facet fascinating and pure in its lucid power. Each of you held this gem of incarnation in your figurative hand and gazed upon it with joy and eagerness to begin. Before incarnation the pattern was there for you to see in all of its detail. In that state the look into the actual lifetime lived in space and time looked tiny, as the moon looks just so large as the thumbnail when it rises. Unfortunately for the temperament, the moon that was the size of the thumbnail is now seen [as] a planetoid with crevices and mountains and dust and earth. It is not small at all, and the pattern has nowhere to express itself. For that faculty of knowing and vision is closed somewhere around the moment of the birth into the Earth plane.

This instrument recently held a baby that was less than five hours old. The nails upon the hand of this infant were so tiny that they could barely be seen, and yet they were perfect in every detail. The tiny little mouth, [eyes] barely large enough to see, the tiny form, so new to breathing and crying and expressing the self within the illusion. It is probable that already this tiny infant had feelings of weariness and despair, wondering where all the quiet has gone, where all the wisdom and knowledge and closeness[of] the bond with the mother [has] gone. Why is it colder? Why do I have these coverings upon my body? What is this thing called life? The veil drops and does not rise again and is it any wonder that the seeker grows weary? And yet we say to you that you can at any moment turn a corner within your self and come upon a new world.

We would ask you to move with us in thought. Take the attention within. Move into the darkness of your own mind, breathing in and breathing out. Allow the tension to move deeper and deeper within the self, down through the roots of mind, through the archetypical mind, through the mind of Christ. Feel the tides of time and space flicker and vanish. Feel the stars themselves give way to that which is neither light nor dark but Deity Itself. Feel this energy of Deity that rests and yet contains all creations that are, all that were and all that shall be. And yet you are balanced, looking nowhere, sensing nowhere, bound in one mote of lucid energy. You have nowhere to go, for you are everywhere that is. You have no knowledge to give for you are everything that is. At this state there are no cycles to complete. There is nothing to do. There is nowhere to go. All is perfect now. Allow this awareness to move back into time and space, back into the stars, into the Earth plane, into your physical vehicle. This is the essence of you, resting within a vessel of clay. You are beyond description. You are beyond all worlds, all space and time. You are perfect. Remember this feeling. Come back again and again to this tabernacle of no time and no space where you are and you are perfect, and there is nowhere to go and nothing to do. For this is the truth about you; beyond all your endeavors and all your suffering this remains the truth of each.

Now let us turn and look upon the landscape that offers itself to you. There, just there, is, indeed, the catalyst that you know so well. There the pen to write. There the decision to make. There the life to live. There the grace to write. Are you rats in a maze? Do you see your higher self as the scientist that is running you mindlessly through a useless task? As the one known as St. Paul would say, "May it never be!" Far closer to the truth is that your higher self is a spiritual entity with a healthy appetite who signed you up for, perhaps, more courses than you wished that you had now that you are at least through at least half of your semester at school in the Earth school. There is one difference in this Earth school from all schools that you are familiar with, and that difference is that there is no requirement for you to make a grade. There is no teacher to set an arbitrary standard that you must achieve.

Rather, you are completely in charge of how much you wish to learn, how far you wish to take each portion of phase of each lesson. You may not feel that you have control, and this is frustrating. But we say to you that you do have full control over your incarnation. If you are too weary to move on, if that is the sense that you get at this point, then we say to you, lighten the load. Remove expectations from your own self and allow yourself to play, to be as the daisies that dance upon the wind, carefree and blameless. You do not have to learn today. You do not have to work today. You have to do only that which is in your heart to do.

When you become frustrated with the self, with the lessons, with the pattern, then it is that we encourage the lifting of the self from pain. And how is this done? For some personalities it is accomplished by moving into the silence, by going for the walks, the meditative reflective times. For other personalities it may be that the choice is to remove the self physically from that which is frustrating, turning the attention to others things. But whatever your personality, we suggest to you that the inspiration that lifts frustration is within you and within this moment if you can but allow the self to express its nature through your instrument. For you are not as you think you are, but, rather, you are a personality shell that distorts the love and the light of the one infinite Creator in just this and that way. You are an instrument. You are an instrument of a certain kind. You are a citizen of a world that you do not see. The great baffling thing about spiritual seeking is that you seem to be in one world, a world with sidewalks and chairs and furniture and cars and movie theaters. Yet in actuality, once you awaken spiritually, you are in a creation of energy fields and all of your work is upon your energy field, the vibration of that field and its dynamics when coming into contact [with] other fields of energy. Each person that you encounter has a field of energy, and you will interact with that energy in certain ways suggested by your distortion and the distortion of the other self. Ideas are fields of energy, and as you come into contact with them there are dynamics between the field of energy that is you and the field of energy that is an idea or an ideal quality that you may wish to pursue.

You are, as a spiritual seeker, in a universe of thought, of being, of essence. It will always be frustrating to live in two worlds, but it is just that dynamic that creates the fertile field for your acceleration of spiritual evolution. Know yourself to be ever on the path and yet ever at rest. Know yourself to be ever learning, yet always knowing. Know yourself to be ever striving, yet always having arrived at precisely the place for which the strife exists. Knowing the self, allow the self to be the self. Release and release and again release the self from the stricture of making sense, of coming up to snuff, passing the grade. Each release, each forgiveness, each new level of acceptance will bring its own inspiration and offer its own opportunities for transformation.

We would at this time transfer this contact to the one known as Jim that we may conclude this session through this instrument. We leave this instrument with thanks, love and light. We are those of Q'uo.

(Jim channeling)

I am Q'uo, and greet each again in love and in light through this instrument. We have taken a great deal of pleasure in presenting our offering to you this session of working, and we would ask if our speaking or any other impetus has brought any other queries to your minds. If so, we would be happy to speak to them now.

Carla: I would like for you to speak more about living in two worlds at once. It seems to me that the frustration, the pain of living, is in trying to deal with the light and see things in a spiritual way and yet there is just no way to escape the fact that we live in the Earth plane and life as it is.

I am Q'uo, and am aware of your query, my sister. This is a query which each seeker, from the depths of its soul, asks of any entity which will answer. For it is most difficult for the spiritual seeker who wishes with all its heart to hew to the upper level, to the higher road, to the spiritual journey, to have to dip again into the illusion of third density and to move within a realm that seems to be muddied, confusing and chaotic. This is the nature of your illusion. For if all were as the time/space realm, that is, clear to the eye, to the heart, to the mind, and to the experience of each moment, then there would be no challenge to the seeker to enlarge its scope of being, its realm of possibility, to gain more experience in the rather efficient way that the third density has of impressing upon the seeker the urgency of catalyst. There is within your illusion the benefit of the seeker who wishes to know and yet does not know, and the benefit that we find here is that the angst, the frustration that comes from wishing to know that which is beyond the illusion, beyond the grasp, is that it motivates the seeker to move forward even when the seeker does not recognize forward as forward. For each catalyst, each experience, each event within your illusion has the ability to temper the heart of the seeker, shall we say, the will of the seeker, the faith of the seeker.

There is within frustration an inevitable rededication of the self to seeking, for the temptation is to stop, to quit, to rest, to have done with it. Yet, though this may momentarily give solace to the mind of the seeker [there is] no quitting, no true stopping. Though one may rest there is always the journey that waits before one. And the heart of each seeker seeks the heart of the one Creator. There is no better way to put it. And when heart seeks heart, there is the motivation to move forward, to learn from that experience, that catalyst about one, enough to move yet a small bit forward, to feel the desire afresh. To feel motivated again. And so this wishing to know what seems beyond knowing is enough, for there is within each frustrated moment the tempering, the hardening, the building up of inner desire to know, to grow, to share, to experience again the great round and round of this illusion. For though frustration may grow greatly there is still in the heart the knowledge that this is as it should be, this is as it must be, this is as it was planned. There is a recognition of the rightness of frustration so that when its fury has worn off there is reborn the kernel of desire, the seed of knowing, the seed of knowledge.

Is there a further query, my sister?

Carla: And when there is bitterness, what can I say to such a person?

I am Q'uo, and am aware of your query, my sister. There may be nothing that will satisfy one that feels bitter to the point of quitting, wishing to quit, laying down the desire and withering upon the spot. And, yet, when one feels such desperation and anger to this point of bitterness, perhaps being heard is all that is necessary, and yet one wishes to give more, to share what is in one's heart the difficulties that you have experienced, the frustrations that you share in common …

(Side one of tape ends.)

I am Q'uo, and am again with this instrument. It is important to make the effort to share with one who has become embittered that which one feels about being bitter, the fruits of bitterness, that there is a lesson that can be learned from bitterness, that there is always an opportunity to begin again. There is always the opportunity every experience that one has had, to drop the illusion of activity, to retreat to a quiet, remote and isolated place within the mountaintops of meditation, to seek there the soothing hand of the one Creator upon the fevered brow, to open the heart finally and fully one last time, to throw down the weight of worry, the burden of frustration, and to ask with a full and bursting heart to be again a child of the Creator, to see again with new eyes, to move again with trembling legs, to ask again the eternal questions, to build the faith and the will to continue.

Is there another query, my sister?

Carla: On another subject I would like just a short answer. Is it all right if I ask some questions in the future about various facets of the book I am writing? I don't want to presume that your agency would help me in writing the book.

I am Q'uo. Yes. We hope that was short enough.

Carla: That was sufficiently short. Thank you very much.

I am Q'uo. We are always happy, my sister, to speak to any queries that you may have for us. We will always give those responses that we are hopeful that are helpful.

Is there another query at this time?

R: I don't have an actual question, but I wanted to speak and offer greetings to all the entities of the Confederation that join us here and to thank you for the words of encouragement. Thank you for your company.

I am Q'uo, and we appreciate your comments. We are always grateful to be able to speak to this group and to entertain those queries which we feel come from the heart, for we are also those of the heart and recognize the great desire which fuels the desire of each seeker which hears our words, both those present and those that are removed from this group but who shall hear these words nonetheless.

At this time we shall take our leave of this group and this instrument, leaving each, as always, in the love and in the light of the one infinite Creator. We are known to you as those of Q'uo. Adonai, my friends. Adonai. 🌸

Sunday Meditation
September 26, 1999

Group question: The question this week concerns our desire to know what we are doing when we attempt to serve another person. Could Q'uo talk to us about the equality of service, if such is so, between washing dishes, raising children, sending rockets to the moon, teaching, feeding thousands, whatever we may do? We would like some information about what we really are doing when we serve another person.

(Carla channeling)

We are those known to you as the principle of Q'uo. We greet you in the love and in the light of the one infinite Creator, and we thank you for calling us to your circle of seeking this day. We are most happy to share our thoughts and our opinions with you on the nature of service to others and what is involved in serving another. This is certainly a fascinating and central topic. We ask of you that you listen to what we have to say with a good deal of discrimination, taking that which seems to you to have use and leaving the rest behind. We encourage each always to use those inner powers of discrimination to sift and test data and thoughts that you receive from the world that is around you. For many are the thoughts that those around you think, and yet not all of these thoughts are helpful.

We come as those with a simple and single message: that all is one and that that one thing is the infinite Creator which is also Love. We see a universe which is unal, unified, of one piece, of one thing. We also, as you, see an infinite array of universes, all of which are unique, different one from the other as snowflakes are, as people are, as all living things are, both obviously of one kind and obviously of infinite variety. We see in our way of looking at the universe that there is a natural instinct implicit in the parts of this unity that is all that there is to fit together in such a way that all are fed and all needs are met. We see a universe in which there are orders of beings, and we see the order of being that is the level of your present incarnational experience as level three, the first two levels being inanimate or seemingly inanimate matter such as rocks, water, air and fire and animate objects, those plants and animals which can turn towards the sun and move about under their own power.

We see this level three as being one in which the instinct to serve remains within the heart while a veil is drawn over the deep memory of why this desire is so deeply ingrained. It is an instinct for beings of level three to wish to be of service, to wish to have a purpose, to wish to help or improve the situations in which they find themselves. The instinct is there. It depends greatly upon the culture in which entities of this density grow up as to how any individual might come to think about the question of how to be of service. In the culture which has produced those which sit in this group we see a heavy emphasis upon activity and accomplishment of a physical type. Thusly, it is normal for each of you, when thinking about service to others, to think in terms of actions that take place in the outer world.

However, when entities such as yourselves commit themselves to living a life of service and seek it, they are working as citizens of eternity rather than citizens of space and time. For the world of the seeker who has become consciously aware of the desire to seek further and who is consciously attempting to live such a life, the terrain shifts from the world of physical objects and activities to a world of thoughts, ideas and intentions. These two worlds merge within the seeker, for the seeker is living in two worlds at the same time. The seeker is living in a very physical consensus reality, in which consensus reality rules apply, and in that world it would seem obviously better to feed one thousand people than to feed one, to heal one thousand people than to heal one, to console one thousand people than to console one. Further, it would seem obvious that the seeker who is putting in a considerable amount of her energy and her time upon seeking within the self, meditating, spending time in contemplation, that this kind of activity was not serving others. It would seem obvious that this kind of activity is selfish and service to self. The confusion that the seeker often feels is because these two worlds are offering conflicting pictures and giving conflicting information. For within the world of spirit it is not at all obvious that it is better to heal a thousand than to heal one. It is not at all obvious that spending time upon one's development as a person is selfish. In fact, to the contrary, in the world of metaphysical existence time spent upon developing the gifts and skills of the spirit can be clearly seen to be service to others' work of the highest order. Let us look at this concept.

When this instrument thinks of one who has excelled beyond any other in service to others, this instrument immediately thinks of Jesus the Christ. Here was an entity who did not behave according to the normal standards of the culture in which he lived. Because this entity's father was a carpenter this entity would be considered to be a carpenter, for that was the way of the culture into which this entity was born. This entity did not satisfy the requests of consensus reality that were thrust upon him by the world in which he lived. Rather, this entity was moved by inner direction, first to seek out the wisdom within its own culture, then to seek out the wisdom of other cultures in lands which neighbored his own. This entity did not ever hold a job or earn money. This entity, thusly, did not contribute to society in the accepted ways of his culture, nor did this entity marry, have children and become husband, father, advisor and wise old man. Rather, this entity wandered from place to place, owning very little, seeking within his own heart, moving according to those inner dictates that called to him from planes beyond the one in which he dwelled.

Fasting, praying, talking to those who wished to talk about the spiritual journey, this entity eventually gathered about himself students, and gradually the entity began to have abilities that were remarkable. And, yet, the healings and the manifestations which the one known as Jesus eventually became able to offer to those about him were not a product of any [part] of the outer or consensus world, but, rather, were the fruit of a long and arduous process of self-discovery and purification of self which this very gifted individual felt called to pursue. When this entity then was able to open a channel within which miracles could take place, the entity was able to do this not through anything that he did but through that which he was. This was an entity who had worked long and hard to open up the deeper levels of his own mind, consciousness and heart.

When this instrument challenges us in the name of Jesus the Christ we are able to answer her not so much because this entity died on a cross, hoping to save the world by its sacrifice, but rather because this entity had a quality of being that was maximal in terms of the purity and profundity of his intention. Or to put it another way, because of the utterness of his love.

Each of you has a heart full of love. And, yet, because it is a human heart with a human love, the human supply will run out quickly when it is placed under stress. The hope that each seeker has of becoming a person that may hold a higher quality of love is the hope of moving more and more into the world of eternity and away from the world of space and time, cause and effect, quantity and quality and differentiation. The one known as St. Paul the Apostle wrote[1] most beautifully that one may do all

---

[1] *Holy Bible*, Corinthians 13:1-3: "If I speak the languages of men and of angels, but do not have love, I am a sounding gong

manner of wonderful things, but if one has not love, one is nothing but a noisy gong or a clanging cymbal1. And perhaps this seed thought may open to you the nature of service to others. For it is not what service you do, it is the love with which you do this service that makes all services equal. It is not the healing or the feeding or the changing or the washing that you [do]. It is the quality of love with which you do it.

How can you develop your being to be capable of ever more fullness of love, but by moving within and paying attention to the self and the processes of the self. And many times this process feels selfish, self-absorbed and narcissistic. You think to yourself, "I am taking these walks and having these thoughts and basically screwing around, not being useful." And we put ourselves down for the very thing that will go furthest towards deepening our quality of selfhood. We say, "we," because it is not only in third density that this is an issue. We still very deeply hope and pray to learn more about how to serve.

One thing we have come to know for ourselves with great certainty is that it is in the opening of the self to the processes of spiritual evolution and the seating of these openings with daily and with repetitive exercises that realizations have the best atmosphere into which to come. You are as a human being at the third level, just at the beginning of the road that is infinite, just making the acquaintance of the self, just finding out precisely who and what you are. And as you work with the self and pay persistent attention to the thoughts of the self you are working to open and deepen the shuttle or linkage from the world of space and time to the world of eternity. You are a place in which two worlds meet. And as spiritual entities you are attempting to be, and in that being, to yield to and embrace love itself.

This instrument has thought much of late upon the many false steps that she considers that she has made as she has persisted in attempting to create what she calls the *Wanderer's Handbook*. We say to you for each person, for each intention to serve, this is the pattern to expect. That pattern of many false starts which seem upon the surface to be useless and yet

which are very rich in learning. Many times of seeming paralysis in which there does not seem to be any way to move forward, and many times of seeming success where there seems to be progress, there seems to be success. The further that one gets from one particular process the easier it is to use hindsight, to look back and say, "There, just there was when I really found pay dirt. There was the time of service. There was the time when I did it right." And yet this, too, is an illusion, for at the level of essential being there is no sense of failure at the false starts. There is no sense of failure at the times of paralysis. And there is no sense of success when the world says that you have success. But rather, there is the one infinite Creator. There is the self utterly with the one infinite Creator and hoping through faith and will to become more and more like the infinite Creator. And less and less like a dream within a dream within a dream.

Where is reality to a spiritual entity but in the present moment and within the love within that moment? Why are all ways of service equal? Because they all address the same thing. They all come from the same being. Each entity came into incarnation with gifts, with endowments of nature, and when one considers what to do with the self it is well to consider with the eye of reason the self and the gifts of the self. What are the natural proclivities, natural affections of the self? For truly these preferences are there for a very good reason, not to distract or disturb or move someone off the path, but rather to help point out the path that is to be taken. Seen with the eye of reason it is perfectly logical to look for the service that one may do in terms of one's gifts, in terms of what one person can do. Can this one person do physical things? Can this person heal? Can this person teach? These are questions the self can ask of the self when looking at the question of service. And yet seen with the eye of faith the question is not, "What are my gifts?" But rather, "What is Your will for me, infinite One? What good works have You prepared for me to walk in? Help me to see better. And when I see them, help me to meet them."

We are, in your world, as smoke or haze. We are a melody upon the wind. We are a thought within the mind. We are an energy and a level of awareness into which this entity which is our channel has tapped. We very deliberately are not flesh and bone, those who come into your skies, those who land upon

---

or a clanging cymbal. If I have the gift of prophecy, and understand all mysteries and all knowledge, and if I have all faith, so that I can move mountains, but do not have love, I am nothing. And if I donate all my goods to feed the poor, and if I give my body to be burned, but do not have love, I gain nothing."

your earth. We do not see our service as including the outer manifestation that proves us to be real. We wish simply to be a quiet and available voice upon the wind, for this is where we perceive our service to lie. In terms of the world, our service is obscure and, in many ways, meaningless. But we continue to be satisfied with the blessings that this kind of contact has offered to us, for we believe that it is not our words but, rather, the vibration that accompanies our words that is essentially our service. You know our hearts, for we have opened them to you, and you feel comfort from our beingness. And in this we are satisfied that we have offered the highest service that we know how to offer.

Again, we know we give comfort and reassurance. We know that we give food for thought. But we would say that our perception of how we are serving is that we offer a quality of beingness that underlies these messages that speaks not of us but of the one infinite Creator. We do not want you to look at us. We want to join you in looking at the one infinite Creator. We see that in you. You see that in each other and in us, and that quality of comfort and reassurance and belonging moves from the Creator to us to you and out into the world. And we can see the energy moving that we allow through us and that you then allow through yourself, and we are humbly and profoundly satisfied. And we would encourage each of you to see yourself as one who has within that being of self those seeds which flow out of the self to comfort and reassure those about you. See yourselves as those through whom undistorted and infinite love and light may move.

You have prepared good works for yourself to walk in. You do not know what scale they might be on or what direction in which they might lie until you find your feet moving instinctively and naturally and your direction finds itself and there is a moment of realization and a pattern, for a moment, is clear and you say, "Oh, now I understand." These moments are rare. But they are a blessing when they come. Wait for these moments in perfect faith. They will come. And know that your highest and best service will be opened to you one moment at a time.

The one known as R speaks of entering this or that avenue for additional service, and we would say move with that which moves your heart, but know that if such and such a choice were not made, if the entity did not go forth into another environment but stayed within the one which offers comfort and pleasure at the present time, yet still the same quality of service would be offered, would come about. Indeed, one cannot escape one's opportunities for growth and for service. They are so much a part of the warp and woof of the incarnational experience that there is no escaping them. Your purposes will find you where you are if you listen. And so we simply ask you to rest, insofar as you are able, in the sure knowledge that you are not alone, nor are you lost. All that you hoped for and seek will come to you in ways that surprise you often but in ways that are still recognizable in terms of your hopes and your dreams. Hew always to those dreams. Encourage the faith that lies within you. And relax into the moment with its joys and its sorrows and its dailyness. And know that in the most simple and everyday atmosphere stunning and powerful forces are at work and will reveal self to self and service to the seeker.

We would close this communication through the one known as Jim. We leave this instrument in love and in light. We are those of Q'uo.

(Jim channeling)

I am Q'uo, and greet each of you again in love and in light through this instrument.

At this time it is our privilege to offer ourselves in the attempt to speak to any further queries which those present may have for us. Is there another query at this time?

Carla: Yes, I sensed that there was a lot of material that I did not get to, and I wondered if you could just continue the train of thought and open to some of what I was not able to open to through the one known as Jim.

I am Q'uo, and you are correct, my sister, in your supposition that there is a great deal of information that is available upon this topic. We are aware, however, of the time restrictions that this group has set for itself, and we are attempting to observe those restrictions so that we do not overtire those present. Thus, we have found a place that is, as you would say, good for the stopping and would focus now upon any short queries before ending this session.

Carla: I would just say that it is frustrating sometimes to have the bridge to the subconscious open and to see the immensity of the structure of thought that is behind the little bit that I am able to say, and I wish that I could move into those immense structures of thought and explore.

I am Q'uo, and we would agree with you, my sister, that there is a great deal of organized information that is available upon not only this topic but upon most topics that are the subject of our speaking to this group. This is so because, of course, as you all are aware, there is a very close connection between all thoughts of each entity. For the one Creator is alive and well and thinking mightily upon all things. And yet does not all of this fine and intricate structure dissolve into the one unifying concept of Love that has created all of us, the thoughts that we think and the means by which we think and observe our thinking. There is as much to be said about such topics as there is time to say it, and of course, within the third density most especially, there are time parameters into which various portions of experience are placed. Then, as we communicate with you we also seek to observe the patterns of your life, the ways in which information is sought, and we look at that which we have to offer of our own opinion and seek to form it into a shape which will fit your needs. If there were only five of your minutes, for example, to give information upon this topic we would attempt to hit more of the high points, shall we say, than attempt to interweave a more intricate connection of these points as was our desire during this session of working.

Is there another query at this time?

Carla: Yes, I have one on a completely different topic. I got an e-mail from a fellow who had an experience where in a dream or somewhere he saw a skull which shot out a green light from its eyes into his eyes. When that happened he could feel that he was changed and he saw his shadow walk up to him and join him, and from that time he has cleansed his body. He is now a vegetarian and seeks in meditative and contemplative ways and he has asked about the shadow. Is it something added to him or some part of him rejoining him, or what was happening here?

I am Q'uo, and am aware of your query, my sister. Indeed, within the dreaming state there is the opportunity for each entity to feel a revitalization, a rejuvenation, a rededication and an inspiration which will move one beyond one's previous self. In experiences as the one described today where there is a connection made with the self that is profound and powerful, one may look to the addition of those latent powers, those essences of the subconscious mind that become available to the conscious seeking self. Thus, in this particular experience the shadow may well represent those hidden attributes that this entity has programmed previous to the incarnation as additions that would be sought at some point within the incarnation and made available as doors to the subconscious mind, that dark and hidden place of power, are opened to the conscious mind. Thus does the subconscious mind join with the conscious mind in the conscious seeking during the incarnation.

Is there a further query, my sister?

Carla: No. I thank you for that answer.

I am Q'uo, and we thank you, my sister. Is there another query at this time?

R: No. Not from me. Thank you for all that you have said.

I am Q'uo, and we thank each present for inviting us to speak our simple thoughts and opinions this day. We would again ask each to use discrimination in choosing that which to place within the life pattern and that which to leave behind. We are those of Q'uo, and would take our leave of this instrument and this group. We leave each in the love and in the light of the one infinite Creator. Adonai, my friends. Adonai. ✡

Sunday Meditation
October 3, 1999

Group question: Our question this week has to do with desire. We would like to know what it is to balance desire. A lot of times we think we know what we want. We think we understand that if we had a certain ability or a certain thing we would be able to function more efficiently. We would be more whole. We would be more balanced. And then when we do achieve that it turns out to be other than what we thought. We would like Q'uo to give us information about working with our desires. How do we determine what we really want rather than what we think that we want?

(Carla channeling)

We are those known to you as the principle Q'uo. We greet you in the love and in the light of the one infinite Creator. We cannot say how blessed we feel to be called to your circle of seeking on this day of your fall as the creation about you has begun to release its summer heat and to prepare itself for the sleep of winter. The desire of each tree and bush and flower for growing and turning to the light must gaze at this time of autumn knowing its time of sleeping and regeneration is soon to arrive. And while the ground and the second-density trees and creatures of the shrub and forest have no trouble adjusting their desires to fit the harmony of temperature and inner direction, the third-density humans upon your sphere do, indeed, have no winter of sleep and regeneration but rather an endless, or seemingly endless, succession of hopes, ideals, wishes and desires of all kind that seem to know no season and sometimes seem to give one no rest.

We are most happy to speak to you upon the subject of desire. We ask only one thing and that is that you listen to what we have to say with a jaundiced and careful ear and heart, for we would not wish to place a stumbling block before any who seeks. Rather, we wish to offer thoughts that have been useful in our own development. It is our service to you to do this. We are delighted to do this, but we do not wish to pretend to be authorities. For we are not authorities, but those who walk with you upon a spiritual path that, as far as we know, is endless. The rising and falling of desire can well be said to be the hallmark of the experience of being self-conscious. Not only your third-density human experience but also the experience of higher densities. There is ever the finer tuning of desire, the finer delineation of the shape of energy of desire.

Indeed, it may be said that in a very powerful way desire is necessary to the third-density experience, or to the fourth, fifth, sixth-density experience. So let us move back to take a longer view of this that is called desire. This instrument has received from those who have had unusual experiences, and we find in her memory a recent letter that gives us a good place to start speaking of desire. This entity was able to move out of his body in a daydream-like state, not in a sleeping state, but in a very relaxed and self-confident state. He was able to leave the area in which his body was placed and eventually to leave the planet. At first, he could not move beyond a certain distance but then, he wrote to this instrument that in the metaphysical or time/space continuum the mode of motivation or movement was love. Love, therefore, took him by his will on a tour right up to the point at which he felt that he could not and would not go further. We offer this experience in order to be able to talk about the relationship about the great original Thought or Logos, which is love or desire.

Desire feels, when one is in an incarnation and experiencing the momentary arising of it, very straightforwardly a desire for acquisition. It feels like it has an object, in other words. And for the most part, those things which entities among your peoples desire have what this instrument would call a simple location. One desires a meal or a girlfriend or to go someplace or to read a certain book. These are things in the outer world that can be achieved and brought into the dwelling place and possessed. And as the one known as R noted, it seems that these desires have a very short shelf life after the acquisition of the object. Once the object is acquired it is no longer desired. As long as desire remains at this level and is seen as that which is desire of an object we have to approach the subject in a certain way and that would be to speak of certain ways of estimating the value of various desires.

However, there is another level of desire with which those present all have considerable experience and that is the desire for purity, for truth, for beauty, for light, for true love, for true love between people, for true relationships between people. And this level of desire has a life that is denied to desires for things which can be acquired in the physical world. This level of desire places a seeker in a different world where she is able to see objects, both metaphysical and physical, not with the eye of the physical world but with the eye of the heart, what the one known as Ken Wilbur has called the eye of contemplation. These desires for a higher way are wise, wise desires and we would encourage each of you to stoke these fires of hope and faith and will and ask for your highest desires with abandon and greed. For these desires for a higher way of being, a higher method of seeing, will cool the fire in the oven of desire so that you as an instrument of the divine are tempered and strengthened.

You shall not, to the best of our knowledge, probably ever be able to experience a lack of desire. For you dwell within a physical vehicle which must eat, which must have a place, which must put onto the body protective clothing against the elements. As long as you carry this structure of flesh, the chemical, the biological reactions which move the physical vehicle from infanthood to growth to decay to death will continue unabated, that being the nature of that physical vehicle and the nature of the physical world into which this vehicle has been born. The poet which this instrument knows as Tennyson called the nature red in tooth and claw. Everything must eat, and so the universe of the body is full of that which is eaten and that which eats. It is full of the tiniest organization of molecules which make up the simplest life form, having unending desire and with each iota of consciousness there come new and greater levels of physical desire.

There is no harm, error or sin in desire. It is simply logical to satisfy appetites. Each organism has instinctual appetites and the fulfilling of them is appropriate and, shall we say, planned for by the infinite Creator. Indeed, desires are to be protected in that it is well for all that draws breath, shall we say, within your physical world to have that which is needed to sustain life.

The kind of desire that tends to provide excellent catalyst for growth and good food for thought is what we might term mental/emotional desire. The one known as R spoke of that desire to get those things which he might need at a later time. The one known as S spoke of the desire to come into a more integrated or full understanding that would illuminate the experience that he was having that would make things more make sense. As the one known as R noted, [when] these particular desires were dropped others would take their place. And in this context we would use something else out of this instrument's memory: a story that is given as what this instrument calls a koan, a parable, shall we say, that helps seekers to gain realization.

This story, in brief, is that there was a holy man, an anchorite, one who had been given a room where he might put his bones and a daily bowl of meager soup and bread that kept body and soul together. And in this room this entity sat in meditation all his waking hours, waiting on the truth, resting in the divine, at peace, and feeling no rising desire. Years went by and then one day the door to his humble room burst open and into the room came a woman he had never seen before. She placed a baby in his arms. She had told her parents that this holy man was the father of her child, and she was giving the child to him. After contemplating this gift for a time this holy man set out for the sea coast very near the street on which he lived and obtained work of the most humble kind, carrying heavy things on and off the ships that traded at that port. With the money that he made, he purchased food and fed and clothed and tended the child that had been given to him. Several years went forward in this way, and then one day his door burst open again and this woman entered again, having decided that she wished for her child after all. He gave her the child who was by now passed the toddler stage, arranged his limbs for meditation and rejoined the light that he had left behind when the gift of the child was his.

To the one who has no arising desire the universe is free. It is a gift. And every blade of grass, every ray of sunlight, every kind word, every gentle glance, is a beauty and a truth. When you have no arising desires you may feel the grass and the elements, the dance of the wind, the dance of fire, the dance of water, and the dance of earth. And the universe lies before you infinitely complex, infinitely unified, at one with itself, at one with you, part of you, as you are a part of it. May we say that we do not expect many moving through third density who experience this state of no desire for longer than, say, a moment, an hour, or an afternoon. Times of feeling this peace indeed are gifts that come now and again, and while you were experiencing this peace you wondered why you ever desired anything. But that setting of full and open heart of faith, that ultimate balancing will that would allow such a state, are genuinely not helpful for the purposes of evolution in spiritual terms. The design of your physical vehicle as human beings is not an error or a whim but, rather, it is the result of experimentation on the part of what this instrument would call the Deity. Creations before this one that you now experience have tried various kinds of ways in which entities could accelerate the pace of their spiritual development, and, so far, what has been found is that placing a veil over the truth and the beauty and the ultimate goodness of all that exists is very helpful for the developing spirit.

If you are as the trees and the flowers then you know without having to reach that all is well, that all is one, and that all is a dance. But humans with this knowledge will not move themselves forward spiritually but rather tend to remain in the state in which they were born. It is actually the arising of desire creating discomfort that motivates entities on so many levels and this motivation of people who wish to simplify or clarify or solve the perplexing questions of what to desire and how to desire it are what open people to new thoughts, new ideas, new practices, and new ways of looking at things. There is, of course, much of skill but more of art in learning your own self, of using the mind carefully in a limited fashion to analyze just what level this desire is on, how true to myself, the seeker, is this desire, how honest and pure is this desire.

There are many ways to use the emotions in working with the desires of the heart, the emotions, and the mind. We would like to take another half hour to speak of the desire to know, but we shall content ourselves here with saying that the intellectual and the emotional parts of the self often so combine as to create a very intense desire to know, and this desire has power both for good and for ill in terms of the evolution of the spirit. Here we would perhaps offer a warning that we have offered many times and that is the warning of the nature of the mind as compared to the nature of consciousness. It is easy to confuse the mind with consciousness, but they are separate things. You are, in terms of your physical vehicle, an almost hairless great ape. You have an excellent mind capable of abstract thought, self-reflection and many, many other things. It is basically a choice-making tool.

When faced with something the physical mind wants to solve the problem. It is not comfortable. It is not used to thinking about or analyzing or sitting with what is perceived as a desire that needs to be fulfilled. For your everyday existence, for meeting society's demands, and for keeping body and soul together, this is an excellent tool. It is not to be confused with the consciousness that you are. That which you are is not a citizen of time or place. You are not of this Earth. You are not of this era. Before time began, you existed. In all possible creations you exist. You are one with the infinite Creator. Being able to separate these two strands of being is sometimes extremely helpful when you are working with desires. For that which you are as a citizen of eternity is, in itself, what this instrument would call a safe place to rest from this seemingly ceaseless process of arising desire and the satisfaction or the disappearance of desire.

Be sure that when you use the mind you use it as you would any tool or resource. Be sure that you do not allow the mind to use you. For, as we said, the mind of the physical vehicle has a life of its own, and it can and it will drive your consciousness to distraction if you allow the mind to race away with you. It is a good tool. It is a poor, poor master. Rather, we would suggest that you come to the working with desire from the heart because the heart is that point within the energy system of the body wherein the one infinite Creator dwells and awaits the reaching of the hopeful heart. It is as though that which you most keenly desire with your spirit and your soul is already within you, more yours than your breathing or your heartbeat, closer to you than your own bones and flesh, so that the judgment and analysis and understanding that you have within you and can apply to questions that you have about desire are in place, waiting for you to achieve the quietness and confidence of self, to turn to them and to allow them their full sway.

Whether a seeker decides to get this car or that computer or that larger tent in a very important way makes almost no difference in the spiritual life of the seeker that makes these choices. But when you move into the area of desires for qualities, for truth, for higher spiritual capacity, then you are beginning to work with desires that are very helpful in terms of acceleration of your spiritual self, the moving forward of that process of the evolution of the spirit for which you took flesh in the first place. When next you have these desires for things or for qualities gaze at them from a secure and restful place from within your own heart, knowing that you have all that you need if you are one with the infinite Creator, yet knowing that you dance the dance of life. And while you are moving through the steps of this beautiful and intricate dance, desires shall arise and may well be satisfied. Know that this is a not only accepted but protected activity, that you have not cast yourself into the outer reaches of foolishness simply because of desire. For it is your nature and your glory to desire, but what shall you desire? There is always the choice.

We would at this time make an offer and also leave this instrument. Our offer, as always, is if there is a desire for help as you are seeking, say, to deepen a meditation or a contemplation, we are happy if you will call on us to be with you, not to speak with you but simply to add our meditation to your own. For in many cases this actually helps in stabilizing or deepening a meditative state and is part of that which we are allowed to do without infringing upon free will. Call us mentally to you by our name, and we are glad to be with you at any time.

We would at this time leave this instrument and transfer this contact to the one known as Jim. We thank this instrument. We are those known to you as those of Q'uo.

(Jim channeling)

I am Q'uo, and greet each again in love and in light through this instrument. It is our privilege at this time to offer ourselves to speak to any further queries which those present may have for us. Is there another query at this time?

S: I have been participating with a group which purports to be Zetas and I have doubts about the service orientations of those of that group. Could you give me your perspective?

I am Q'uo, and am aware of your query, my brother. It is our great desire to be of service through speaking to groups such as this one, for in so speaking we have the opportunity to walk with each a certain distance, shall we say, upon the journey of seeking. And if we may speak in a manner which offers catalyst and inspiriting we feel blessed. We at all times seek to avoid infringing upon the free will of any entity to whom we speak. There are many ways in which free will may be abridged, and we are aware that if we give a blessing or a warning to an entity such as yourself who is working with other groups then, perhaps, our speaking will carry too much weight in that regard. Therefore, in matters such as this we leave the process of discrimination to you, my brother, for we are aware that you are able to assess the nature of any information which comes within your provenance. Thus, we must apologize for not being able to give you that which you seek in this case, for we would not take from you the opportunity to exercise your own powers of discrimination.

(Side one of tape ends.)

I am Q'uo, and am again with this instrument. Is there any other query, my brother, to which we might attempt to respond?

S: Yes. There has been a gentleman named C, a young man who through the internet has been asking me for advice, spiritual and otherwise, and I am not quite sure how he fell into it, and I am concerned that I am giving him good advice. I ask for your thoughts on that.

I am Q'uo, and am aware of your query, my brother. We would suggest to you that as you have come in contact with this entity that there is no mistake or happenstance about the crossing of your paths. This entity has been drawn to you, for there is within this entity's subconscious feelings the impulse to seek information from those sources which it values. Thus, as you speak with this entity and share with him that which is your best and highest information and inspiration you give to him that which he seeks. You must also realize that this entity is, as yourself, one who is able to discriminate between that information that he receives that is helpful to him and that information that is not helpful to him. Thus, we would encourage you in your sharing information with this entity that you …

(Transcript ends.)

L/L Research

L/L Research is a subsidiary of Rock Creek Research & Development Laboratories, Inc.

P.O. Box 5195
Louisville, KY 40255-0195

www.llresearch.org

Rock Creek is a non-profit corporation dedicated to discovering and sharing information which may aid in the spiritual evolution of humankind.

ABOUT THE CONTENTS OF THIS TRANSCRIPT: This telepathic channeling has been taken from transcriptions of the weekly study and meditation meetings of the Rock Creek Research & Development Laboratories and L/L Research. It is offered in the hope that it may be useful to you. As the Confederation entities always make a point of saying, please use your discrimination and judgment in assessing this material. If something rings true to you, fine. If something does not resonate, please leave it behind, for neither we nor those of the Confederation would wish to be a stumbling block for any.

CAVEAT: This transcript is being published by L/L Research in a not yet final form. It has, however, been edited and any obvious errors have been corrected. When it is in a final form, this caveat will be removed.

© 2009 L/L Research

Sunday Meditation
October 17, 1999

Group question: The question this week has to do with whether or not it is possible in this day and age and in the place in which we live for us to use meditation and personal works to become the seeker we hope to be, to achieve that state of being that will allow us to radiate the love and the light of the Creator and to continue to expand as learning and growing beings. Or is it still necessary to retire to a cave in the Himalayan Mountains and meditate for twenty years with some small chance for success, of some hope of achieving a realization of who we really are?

(Carla channeling)

We are those of the principle known to you as Q'uo. Greetings and blessings in the love and in the light of the one infinite Creator. We thank each of you for all that you have sacrificed, all that you have sought, that has brought you to this circle of seeking at this time. We thank you that you have called us to your session of working. We wish you to understand what a blessing it is to us to be able to share our thoughts with you, to be able to fulfill that which is our chosen service at this time. Please know that you serve us far more than we could ever serve you with our humble words by providing us with the opportunity to experience what it is to be called, to be asked to share. We will, indeed, share all that we can share through this and other instruments this day. We ask but one thing of each of you, and that is that you listen to our thoughts and our opinions with a careful and discriminating ear and heart, for that which we have to say may or may not be that which is needed by you at this time. And for us to be considered by you as an authority to which you must listen is obnoxious to us, for that would mean that we were, instead of helping, being a stumbling block before you. Therefore, we ask that you take those thoughts that ring true to you and leave all the rest behind. We trust your powers of discrimination and we ask that you also trust your own inner knowing, for each has a personal truth to which each needs to hew.

You ask this day concerning the unfolding of spiritual evolution and the ways in which you can encourage that within yourself. You ask if the practices of meditation and personal work are enough, are sufficient to open the process of evolution for you and so encourage and promote that evolution, that you will be able to see and realize that you are where you should be, doing what you should be doing as an authentic being.

We find that the question is such that we cannot say yes and no, but, rather, we must discuss these concepts. And so we shall begin. Let us look at the nature of each of you, for what are you? What is your nature? Each of you, through personal work, has begun to realize the most basic truth, which is that each of you is the Creator, and within incarnation each of you is the co-Creator of experience for yourself. But what, then, is the Creator? The word, "logos," in Greek means "word." But more it may be seen to be a word denoting all-inclusive thought or being. What is the nature, then, of this original Thought or Being that is the Creator? It is our understanding that the nature of the Creator, the nature of the creation that has been formed in the image of the Creator, is love. This is your basic identity. Each of you has within you a spark that vibrates precisely at the original vibration which is the Logos. The Creator is not out there, but, rather, the Creator is within each of you already, the heart of your identity and your being. There is nothing you can do, think, say or believe that can separate you from this basic selfhood. You cannot give it away. You cannot lose it. You can, however, and easily, become distracted from it and move into other areas of thought that are not so directly of the one infinite Creator. No matter how far you go, however, in your straying from love and from your own identity as love, it shall not leave you, and you shall always have this inner source of all that you seek closer to you than your very thoughts and heartbeat.

And what, then, is the nature of this spark? This instrument would say that it is a vibration. And that is close enough for us. The original vibration, then, is the reality within every illusion which you experience. This anchoring vibration can be overlaid by any number of vibratory complexes, for each receives an unending supply of the pure vibration of love that is the moving energy of the cosmos. Each takes this vibration into the various bodies from the gross to the finer and distorts that vibration in various ways as it moves through that vessel which is your mind, body and spirit. And, thusly, to those who have the ability to see through the veil each entity speaks itself in vibration with a distinctive and utterly unique identification.

Since the very nature of your being is vibration it will not surprise you that we would ask you to evaluate those ways in which you characteristically distort the original vibration of love. Now, there are various ways to distort or block or over-activate the vibratory energy that feeds and fuels your being. Those of you who experience incarnation in third density at this time are experienced souls. This is due to the fact that through what this instrument would call the time of harvest there is a tremendous opportunity for relatively rapid soul growth, and this has meant that there are far more entities wishing to take incarnation upon your Earth plane than there are opportunities for these souls to come into physical vehicles. And so those who have incarnated into your plane of existence at this particular time for this particular planet are those with a seniority by vibration. This means that each of you is already capable of doing relatively, shall we say, "advanced," for want of a better word, work in consciousness.

Each of you has many assets and resources in place. Among these resources are meditation, and each of you has personal practices: the reading, the contemplation, the solitary walking, the discussion with companions, the work in healing, the work with various structures of thought which provide ways of thinking about the issues that matter to you. All of these are valuable. Meditation especially, as each who has heard us before is aware, is that which we most encourage and recommend as a daily practice. So let us look at the concept of having a daily practice, for beyond any particular avenue of personal or spiritual growth there is the keenness of desire that seeks with a heart full of hope for that feeling of authenticity of self which allows the self to release the strictures that have provided spiritual and emotional discomfort.

We cannot say what any one seeker shall find useful for herself. We do feel that entering the silence is universally helpful, but there is a range that is fairly extensive from soul to soul in terms of what techniques or modes of spiritual seeking shall be more efficacious at any given time. However, in each case the dailyness of the practice is that which is very helpful, that which will, indeed, suffice to bring the seeker more and more to herself, to an awareness of the self as a whole and radiant being. Remember that beyond all illusion, each of you is vibration. If you think, for instance, of an engine in a car that develops a certain speed of turning because of the fuel fed to it you can see that various kinds of practices will move that vehicle which is yourself at various rates of speed, with various rates of efficiency, for each of you is an unique being and you will not react or respond to various elements of practice in the same way that any other entity would. And so there is a continual seeking and searching through the aisles of the supermarket of philosophy, metaphysics, spirituality and religion that each seeker does go through seeking those resources that for that seeker do that job that the seeker feels needs to be done. Consequently, much is left to you, at least in terms of what we would encourage each of you to do. We cannot encourage for each a specific practice that is the same for each, but, rather, we can simply encourage the dailyness of such practices.

It is as though the self were a bit scattered in the normal dailyness of living. There are the calls upon energy for those with whom you are in relationship. There are the calls upon your energies for those things you need to do in order not to be a burden to others: the gaining of the money for the necessities, and the enjoyments of a physical life. There are many, many things, ways of thinking, modes of thinking, that move one to various levels of the mind, the shallow or surface mind, the levels of mind just below the limn of consciousness, and those levels that are in the deep mind that this instrument would call archetypal or archetypical. Some entities will wish to work on the surface questioning the form of their practice, moving into rituals that feel right, using the moments to generate within the self-realizations of beauty and delight. Indeed, there is that practice that is legitimate of focusing completely upon the surface and delighting completely in the very chores and minutiae of the day. This is a legitimate practice, a dharma that is blessed and that works for some entities.

There are those who find their delight in logic and intellectual inquiry whose approach to the spiritual is of a—we look in this instrument's mind for a word and do not find one—aesthetic approach to the deeper self. And to that person the delight of perfect ideas moves that person into the authenticity of its own being. There are those such as this instrument who dwell in what we would call an emotional approach in which the responses to incoming data are monitored for the purity of the emotions evoked, and there are practices which encourage this accuracy of notation. This instrument would call this level the life in faith, and it is a kind of way of centering the self which lends itself to those who are of a mystical nature. There are those who thirst so for true spiritual food that they are not satisfied with anything less than the archetypical foundations of consciousness, and these entities are like explorers of the deep who bring treasures from mines deep within the Earth and open them to the light within themselves. This also is a legitimate way of approaching the job of cooperating with one's own spiritual evolution.

Most entities work on more than one of these levels, and some entities work on all of these levels. Consequently, it is additionally helpful to many entities to practice the facility with which they slip from level to level within themselves. For the way the self works is a structure but one unlike any other entity's structure. And so there is a good deal of inner exploration which is very productive in terms of identifying for the self those modes of inquiry that will be the most helpful assets in working with one's destiny.

We would venture to say that within third density what most often disturbs the spiritual seeker is the veil itself, that veil of forgetting that drops over the infant soul as it enters into the Earth plane. Gone is that knowledge of identification with the Father. Gone is the awareness of other selves as the self and all selves as the Creator. Come, instead, is a world in which people observe forms but not essences, doing but not being. And, yet, this is a school carefully designed for maximum learning. How can one learn when one is so bemused, confused and flustered by this unknowing?

Look at that. Look at the conundrum, the enigma of the veil. Before you came here you knew who you were. Why did you work hard and rejoice when you succeeded in getting a place within this Earth plane which you now enjoy? Why the confusion? Why the necessity to backtrack, as it may seem to each, and learn again who your real self is, what the real self is, what the quality of realness is? But you see, the point of your density is singular. There is a choice that needs to be made. It is a choice which this instrument would call one of polarity. Do you seek to serve others, or do you seek to serve yourself? Each path, in our understanding, is equally valid. Each path has its adherents. Both paths come together a bit further along the evolution of the spirit for each of you.

One path, in our opinion, that of service to others, is favored by the infinite Creator. It is the path upon which we have chosen to move, and we are aware that each within your circle has chosen that path of service to others. And this awareness brings to what practice that each of you has the additional practice of constantly looking at one's intentions to see where the desire for service truly lies. And it is always fruitful to look back over the situations through which you have gone with an eye to pinpointing for the self the self's own actual orientation as evidenced by that which one has gone through.

And so we would say a resounding yes, a heartfelt affirmative to the question. In the city or in the country, in any place where you are, if you have a daily practice is it enough? Yes. Whatever is heartfelt to do that daily brings you to yourself is sufficient for you. You are not expected to figure it all out. That is not what this density that you are experiencing is for. It may be a wonderful luxury that certainly has occurred to this instrument, and undoubtedly to each, in the past and hopefully in the future, that there is that moment when all is one. All can be seen to be perfect, and there is nowhere that pulls, no place that one wishes to go, for all is perfect as it is. These moments of bliss and joy, indeed, perhaps days or weeks of bliss and joy, come not due to work but because it is time. For you cannot learn on a schedule the lessons of spirit. The spirit moves as the wind and comes when it will and teaches with breath-taking honesty when it will. And when it will not it sends its messengers everywhere to give you hints and little bits of encouragement that keep you seeking. But there is no scheduling those moments of utter authenticity, nor is it a realistic expectation of the self that the self shall one day come to a mode of living in which the utter authenticity of the self runs on a continuous basis.

This instrument would perhaps choose the one known to her as Jesus to be an exemplar of undistorted love, and yet we say to her and to each of you that this entity, as devoted a servant to the Creator as he was, had many moments and many days and many weeks and many months in which confusion reigned and the puzzle was not solved. And the hunger and the thirst for truth and beauty was unfulfilled. These seasons of weal and woe are extremely helpful and very deeply to be appreciated, for in addition to bringing to one that catalyst that one needs in order to learn, these seasons of dryness and aridity of spirit deepen and purify the vessel within. For each truly is a channel, an instrument.

Think of the musical instrument that is played by the wind of the instrumentalist. The air moves through the instrument and under the clever movement of the fingers various tones come forth expressing, when they are played as written, flights of music that lift the heart and encourage the spirit.

And each of you has this hollowness that is filled with the love and the light of the infinite Creator. What this instrument and perhaps others within this room hope for is that the self will become transparent so that the wind of spirit that is blown through will come out as it went in, totally undistorted by the self. For if the self can allow infinite love and light to move through the self, then that self has the capacity to bless that love and light that flows through it and offer that that has been brought through to the Earth plane. Indeed, it is our feeling that this is the basic work of all spiritually awakened people, this essential beingness of self that does not distort the love that flows through the instrument of selfhood. Beyond all the beautiful tunes that your instrument might play with the various distortion of the various energy centers there is the wonderful ability to do that essential work that is the work of being that allows love and light to flow into the Earth plane undistorted.

We have talked to you often of being versus doing. Of essence versus action. It is our humble opinion that each, indeed, needs to address the beingness of the self, and we ask each to think on this for the self, to look at the question of whether there is releasing and surrender that might create a more pure way of being. Very often that which most constricts the spirit from its evolution is that which hampers beingness and no amount of good works, good actions, or good thoughts, no amount of practice of any kind can address this rather deep and subtle question: what shall you surrender in order to more fully be yourself? As each faces the chances and changes of daily living we encourage each to look for those things that can be surrendered and look for those things which can be taken up and embraced, for there shall be an ever-evolving panoply of choices for each of you to make. We encourage you to move forward in a faith that all that you need will come to you, and all that you must crave and learn will be before you in its own time.

We are sorry that we have spoken longer than we should. We heard the recording device come to its end and realized that we should have been at ours. However, we would like at this time to transfer this contact to the one known as Jim in order that we may answer any questions that may be upon your minds at this time. We leave this instrument in love and in light and transfer now. We are those of Q'uo.

(Jim channeling)

I am Q'uo, and greet each again in love and in light through this instrument. It is our privilege at this time to offer ourselves in the attempt to speak to any further queries which those present may have for us. Is there another query at this time?

S: I recently purchased an audio cassette device that was to help clear geopathic lines around my home and work with nature spirits. I am curious as to what results, if any, I have been able to accomplish?

I am Q'uo, and am aware of your query, my brother. As we observe the device and the activity which you have employed in order to work with those more elemental spirits within your home environment we find that your desire to communicate with these entities is that which has been most successful rather than the gadget, shall we say, that you have employed though there is an efficacy attached to this gadget that is powered by your desire and your intentions. For these intentions are from your heart, and it is upon this level that communication may be established with such entities.

Is there another query, my brother?

S: With your communications here, what are some of the things that you have learned?

I am Q'uo, and am aware of your query, my brother. And we are gratified to say that our learning that has been associated with this group and with this kind of service with other groups has been focused in the area in learning to accept limitations, though they be great, and to persevere beyond the seeming boundaries that are created by one's own mind. For each of us in this creation—and we speak of all entities of which we are aware—desires to know the one Creator, and yet each of us has put before ourselves various hurdles, shall we say, various levels of lessons that seem to bind us, to keep us from moving in the desired direction. These, however, have the ability to reveal to us the necessary steps to take to move beyond them if we become able to accept that which we are, that is, the one infinite Creator. This ability to accept our nature as the Creator, for each entity, is that which is somewhat beyond the reach and thus propels us onward in our great journey of seeking.

We have also learned that which you call humor, that which we would call the sense of proportion, where it is discovered to be helpful to see the self in a lighter manner. Though the seeking be the sole desire of the entity and the knowledge of truth, love, wisdom and so forth is that which is sought with every fiber of the being, yet there is the enhancement to the process that humor brings. For if one can lighten the point of view, can lighten the intensity of emotion in even that situation that seems the gravest, then there is the freedom to move more as in a dance, more as with the flow of the universe.

We have learned much of the nobility of the human spirit, the desire to be of service to others beyond all cost to the self. Constantly we see entities who are willing to do whatever is necessary in order to serve their brothers and sisters who suffer within the illusion of this third density. We are most honored to witness this nobility and this humility, for it shows to us the very heart of the one Creator that wishes to love and serve all as the self.

Is there a further query, my brother?

S: Concerning past inventions in this world. One was the eternal candle, how that was constructed and made, and the second one was the Bessler Wheel constructed in the 1700's. How were these constructed?

I am Q'uo, and am aware of your query, my brother. It is our purpose as members of the Confederation of Planets in the Service of the Infinite Creator to speak upon those topics of a philosophical nature which entities who are desirous of moving their evolutionary process along may be able to utilize in so doing. We are marginally able to speak upon areas which lie outside of the philosophy of being, shall we say. The topics that you have mentioned are somewhat removed from our main desire or purpose, and in utilizing an instrument such as the one we now utilize, that is, in the conscious meditative state, we are unable to access the necessary terms to give technical descriptions such as the ones which would be necessary this case. Therefore, we must apologize for our lack of breadth and our lack of words upon this particular topic.

Is there another query, my brother?

S: There seems to be a life-long strife between my wife and her mother. It seems hurtful to my wife, with the strange and bizarre behavior from her mother. She was asking me what she should do, and I would like to help. How can I help her?

I am Q'uo, and am aware of your query, my brother. As is oftentimes the case, entities who are of what you call a bloodline relationship are of such a relationship for in such relationships lessons of a most intensive nature may be undertaken that would not be possible with other entities that would not be in one's proximity for the length of time and the intensity of experience that one would have, in this case, [in] the mother and daughter relationship.

We would recommend, as we would in many such instances, that the loving acceptance of the process is the first foundation stone to lay in the attempt to serve another entity. For if one is able to see that the difficulties shared in such a relationship are also offering opportunities for the opening of the heart, each to the other, then the proper valuing of the experience may be appreciated. When one sees that such a relationship is sacred in its nature and fertile in the possibility of producing the open heart, then it is possible to see the interrelationship of the entities as that which will eventually produce the desired opening of the heart. As one supports each in the process one may retire periodically to the meditative state to look more deeply at that which occurs in the daily round of activities, for those experiences which, shall we say, push the various buttons, each of the other, and result in the heated words, the hurt feelings, and the overall confusion as regards the entire situation, one may begin to see a pattern in the relationship where there is the possibility of progress as each is able to accept what previously seemed unacceptable, each is able to love what previously [was] seen as unloveable. The process of being able to see and accept more and more of the other self as whole and perfect allows the self to do the same with the self. For in each instance it is a process of learning that occurs within each individual entity and then is offered in love and service to the other.

Tolerance, the light touch, the sense of humor, the acceptance of the process, all of these are ways in which you may serve an entity in such a relationship.

Is there another query, my brother?

S: No. Thank you.

I am Q'uo, and we thank you once again. Is there another query at this time?

D: Is it useful or wise for me to use the analogy of sun, earth, moon and universe to define the nature of the self as a constructed being?

I am Q'uo, and am aware of your query, my brother. And we would suggest that this is indeed efficacious for it is a system of construction which not only draws its usefulness from the nature of the qualities you have invoked, but also draws its efficacy from your very effort at constructing this analogy. For each seeker of truth constructs a personal mythology or means by which the universe is viewed as well as the entity's journey through it. Thus, you are as the magician who is able to gather the tools for its working and by arranging them in such and such a fashion is able to build a useful channel for information and inspiration to move through.

Is there a further question, my brother?

D: Is there truly a distinction between the allness of God, the embodying of the Creator, and the enlightening of the Father?

I am Q'uo, and am aware of your query, my brother. Again, we would suggest that those distinctions which have value to you with these terms and phrases are those which will allow you to experience a greater revelation and be able to experience this as one who can share it with others. Thus, that which you do in the use of these terms is that which makes plain to you [the] goal of your understanding.

Is there another query, my brother?

D: Does one ever lose the incredible sense of loneliness?

I am Q'uo, and am aware of your query, my brother. And we are aware of this loneliness of which you speak, for there are many such as yourself who have removed themselves from other realms of clearer experience and understanding and have chosen to enter this illusion of separateness, of seeming separateness, each from the other, in order [that] those who are seen as brothers and sisters of sorrow may be served with all one's being. In this service there is the distant memory of those realms from which one comes, of those friends which one has agreed to work with, and of the purpose of the incarnation which is seen to be the pearl of great price, the service of others, no matter the cost to the self. And the cost to many such selves is that feeling of alienation, of isolation, of loneliness, of being cut off from that which is of the most worth to the self, of being away from home, of not being able to return home. This is a feeling which each entity shall live with for the entire incarnation, for it was seen previous to the incarnation as that which was necessary to endure, yet that which was possible to endure, and that which, indeed, may even aid in the achieving of the service to others. For it is a way of propelling the self, shall we say, upon the subtler, more spiritual realms so that the desire of the heart to serve others and to know the one Creator might be realized.

There are many, my brother, who walk with you in an unseen fashion so that in truth one is never truly alone. There is a goodly company of such angelic presences that is with each such entity within this third-density illusion. There is much of hope and sustenance that can be gained from attempting to speak to these entities within one's daily meditations, to become more aware of their walk with one in the daily round of activities. For truly, the efforts of each within this third-density to serve those brothers and sisters of sorrow are recognized and great praise and thanksgiving is given for each such effort. There is, indeed, my brother, a heavenly choir that accompanies you upon this great journey of seeking and service.

Is there another query at this time?

D: Is the path that we walk simply God's individuation of Itself seeking to know Itself, unify Itself, and simply create ideals of Itself that incorporate or encompass infinite opportunities, possibilities, gestalts, and so on, and is there tension that is created within this vast array of experiences that we have in which simply those who serve others and those who serve themselves are a catalyst for this process to unfold individually, relationally, socially, planetarially and so on?

I am Q'uo, and am aware of your query, my brother. And we would respond by saying that we could not have said it better. For, indeed, all of the experience of the one Creator in all densities of illusion is the Creator knowing Itself through infinite means, infinite entities, and the polarity of the light and the dark, that which you have called service to others and service to self. Thus, the creation itself is held in place by this dynamic tension. And thus the Creator is able to play in those fields of flowers that It has created for Itself.

Is there another query, my brother?

D: Is the opportunity available for us, and is the role that we play in serving others simply assisting in everyone knowing themselves, establishing rules and ideas so that from self knowledge collective ascension transpires within the context of a social group of people through time?

I am Q'uo, and am aware of your query, my brother. And we would respond by saying once again that you have eloquently stated your perception and an accurate perception of that which is. There are many, many entities that move upon this great journey of seeking, that move as in a dance, in a harmony that is unseen by those who do not look, and yet they dance to the tune, to the beat of the heart of the one infinite Creator. Yes, all dance and move in rhythmic patterns. The balance in all of the creation is one and is perfect. That which each does as his or her own contribution to this great dance and journey of seeking is that which has been planned aforetimes, shall we say. There is a pattern to movement, a pattern to thought, a pattern to seeking, a pattern to suffering, a pattern to all that is.

Is there another query, my brother?

D: I am done. Thank you.

I am Q'uo, and we thank you, my brother. Is there another query at this time?

(No further queries.)

I am Q'uo, and as we observe the last inchoate queries fading from the minds we have once again come to an ending to a session of working with this group, and we are most grateful to each for inviting us to your circle of seeking this day. We are always honored to be able to share our thoughts and humble opinions with those who call to us. And we would suggest to each gathered today that we have been especially honored to join each this day and would greet those who are new to this circle, yet not new to this group, and remind each present that we are available upon your mental request to join you in your personal meditations in order that we might help to deepen those meditations without any spoken words or thoughts. Just our vibrations moving in harmony with yours. We are known to you as those of Q'uo. At this time we shall take our leave of this instrument and this group, leaving each, as always, in the love and in the light of the infinite Creator. Adonai, my friends. Adonai. ✣

Sunday Meditation
November 7, 1999

Group question: Our question this week has to do with being able to live in the moment. How can we live in the moment more consistently? Can we ask for assistance from our higher selves to help us to live in the moment? What are the advantages of living in the moment?

(Carla channeling)

(A recording problem rendered portions of this recording inaudible.)

We are *(inaudible)*. We ask that as we offer these thoughts and opinions that each that hears them submits them to the inner knowing and discernment that each has in abundance. For not everything that we have to offer may aid everyone equally and we would not wish to constitute a stumbling block. So we feel free to speak *(inaudible)*.

That mindfulness and remembrance is so effortless to muscle and bone, to bloom and bud and to all second-density but which so escapes third density mentality.

If you will cast your mind upon the world of nature you may quickly see how single-mindedly the flower, the tree, the bush *(inaudible)*. Breathing in and out of each other's lives, the textures and colors and pigment as the leaf turns towards the sun and the hunger and appetite of the animal kingdom brings them to interact with each other in absolute mindfulness. The animal and the plant are held gently, safely and completely in the hand of the Creator. The ways of each species provide a seamless garment in which each movement of each part of nature is interwoven to create the tapestry that the eye of the third-density human falls upon and does not see, for who can see into the magnificence of such perfect orchestration of all beings moving in rhythm and harmony?

And yet second-density is not the density that is the highest. Rather, the third density, with its seeming lapses into unmindfulness and unawareness, is actually that giant step forward that those who are chauvinistic about the human race have been proclaiming for years. And, indeed, the human race is a noble and strong race of entities. Third density has its marvels and miracles and we would not want you to feel that you have lost something by moving from second density to third, for you have not lost that ability to be a perfect part of a perfect creation. It has simply gone underground in your mind. But every cell of your body knows what it is, where it is, and who it is. Every iota of your being at the cellular level is mindful and knows its source.

And so, perhaps, we would begin this consideration by recommending to each the continuing dedication to reentering the body, seeing that body as one of perfect health and perfect rhythm, feeling within the self, within the muscle and bone the rightness of this precise manifestation at this precise time. For each of you has a niche in the harmonics of the Earth plane. Each of you is essential to that overall balance of energies which the planet itself vibrates in. You may trust your bodies in their rhythms, in their cycles, and it is very, very good to remind the self, when you catch yourself being disrespectful to your own body and the wisdom of your own body, that it actually knows a great deal more than the mind of the human, that the heart and every cell of that body, which may seem at times nothing but a mechanical physical vehicle, to revisualize and to understand that body as a perfect and graceful body, one that is beautiful in its own way, one that has great wisdom in and of its own. This constitutes a tremendous resource for the mindful person. For in exercising that physical vehicle, in walking among things of nature and working within the realm of nature, these activities tune and harmonize your body with all of the bodies of plant and animal with which it comes in contact. For a walk is not simply putting one foot in front of the other. A walk is also a recapturing of the perfection of the being that you are.

Indeed, it is well to think of yourself as a dancer through life, for each of you dances or walks, is graceful or isn't, and these infinitesimal changes in the way you think about yourself and the way you think about the body can, indeed, bring you to more mindfulness as you revisualize yourself in perfection, in harmony, and in unity.

When the life force of a human is new the animalness of the human is ascendant and the infant is always in the present moment. For it is largely unawakened to the Earth plane, and, for the most part, as it moves into the Earth plane it is the physical vehicle that is a perfect and energetic body. As the young child begins to gain the concept of itself as a being apart from the rest of the universe that spontaneous position of the self in the moment becomes more and more tenuous until often by the time a child has entered school the self-consciousness of the human has become entirely ascendant, and the young soul is already concerning itself with the past and the future, plans that have gone wrong and plans that have not yet come to fruition. And the march to ever less mindfulness has begun.

It is typical of the training that the culture offers to the individual that the spontaneous and rhythmic harmonization of the self with all will be systematically and thoroughly interrupted, for it is not useful for society to have a tribe of completely mindful and aware beings. Rather, what is the easiest block of entities to govern turns out actually to be those who have turned their concept of themselves over to the orthodox ways of thinking and then have begun to measure themselves by those yardsticks that the culture and the society puts forth. As each becomes a so-called adult, each more or less finds itself necessarily moving into those areas of work and employment and the chores of living that constitute keeping body and soul together for those within third density.

In the culture in which you now enjoy living the hope is not that the entities will be mindful, but, rather, that they will be mind-persuaded in the ways in which the culture wishes its citizens to think, behave and move. As far as an unawakened spirit can tell, what is required of it is that it get a job, pay for the privilege of having space in which to live and food to eat. This economic concern, namely, that each citizen will take care of itself and its dependents, ranks far above any consideration in terms of public policy of the spiritual evolution of its citizens. Naturally, this not being the obvious concern of governmental or cultural entities this has never, for the most part, been questioned. No one expects the government or the culture to require mindfulness of its citizens.

However, we would say more than this. In order to become a citizen of eternity it seems necessary to become one that is athwart society. You may think of it in terms of being radical or in terms of being other than the mind control of the culture. This may seem an extreme statement but there is a seduction of principles and values that goes on within the daily intellectual life that the culture offers through its newspapers and various other information sources which offers to its citizens much information *(inaudible)*.

(Inaudible) just as it should be, the past, present and the future nicely falling into the patterns of intellectual consideration while unbeknownst to this tidy arrangement the portion of the self having to do with eternity is completely other than this stream of time that so dominates thinking in what this instrument would call consensus reality. You must decide *(inaudible)*. You must decide to abandon society within your inner selves and hew instead to the ideal. This will take you out of time. This will

give you the present moment. You cannot hold this present moment. You cannot cherish it or shape it or put it safely away some place. Now it kisses you on the lips and then it is gone. *(Inaudible)*.

The present moment comes to you and stays with you. It is catching the magic, of letting go of the past and the future that is the trick. How to catch the self on the hinge of the present moment? How to recapture the self from consensus reality? This instrument has often felt it useful to use the sounds within its experiences on a daily basis to encourage mindfulness: the striking of the clock, the ringing of the phone. If one is in a school situation, the bell between classes. These sounds are helpful reminders, or they can be made so. And so one thing the seeker may do to encourage mindfulness within the self is to analyze the sights and the sounds and the hues of various colors that are in *(inaudible)*. Identifying those sounds that are repeated each day and then training the self to use those questions, those hints, and not to use them in a way that stays in the mind but rather to move into the awareness of them as bells that ring within the heart, that have reverberation within the vastness of the deep mind, so that the deep mind itself is awakened by this sound; the phone, the doorbell, any repeating sound can be a tocsin that tolls, "Remember, remember, remember."

There are many ways to slip out of consensus reality and into the kingdom of the Father, as this instrument would call it, to join the dance of the flowers and the trees and the stars and the wind and the rain. Some have found music to bring their hearts back to the present moment. Some find the present moment in the exhaustion of dance. Some find it within the repetition of outer observances. Indeed, there are those among your peoples who for thousands of your years have had access to the repetition through each day of a long life of what this instrument would call services. Some having more separate services per day in which the Creator was the center of the focus of worship. Some more. Some moving the student into days and weeks and months of constant meditation. All of these practices that you are aware of through your travels through the supermarket of spiritual resources have much to offer to the person who is seeking to turn the mind from not simply the things of society but from time itself.

Try each of these avenues of remembering and see which of them work for you. But above all realize that there is a switch, shall we call it, in the deep mind, a toggle switch that is on and off. And when it is on, you are in consensus reality and working within the strictures of society. Move that switch in thought, not in action, but in thought, and you are a subversive element, as far as time is concerned. For you now stand upon the eternal and time means nothing. And, ah, the bliss, the relief, the release of experiencing the plenum that is all that there is in the present moment. Let your hearts be open. And know that within you there is the bliss of this present moment. To get to it, often it is not a matter of adding things but of subtracting things and not things that are out there but the things of the mind, the things of the intellect, the things that you may never have questioned seriously having to do with time and responsibility.

We invite you to a land which is one turn past tomorrow and just a few doors down from yesterday. We invite you to open and empty yourself and to ask. To open, to be empty, and to ask. Each time that you feel that you would wish to enter the present moment, be open, become empty, and see what happens. We would encourage each to use meditation with regularity in order to seat and regularize this process. And we are always glad to be with you in that meditation.

At this time we would transfer this contact to the one known as Jim. We thank this instrument, and leave it in love and in light, for we are those of Q'uo.

(Jim channeling)

I am Q'uo, and greet each again in love and in light through this instrument. At this time it is our privilege to offer ourselves in the attempt to speak to any further queries which those present may have for us. Is there another query at this time?

R: Can a deeper portion of ourselves be used in the third density by the conscious mind to achieve mindfulness?

I am Q'uo, and am aware of your query, my brother. And we are glad that we did not speak too soon and exclude you from this opportunity to ask a query this day, for we are always happy to speak to this group and it is an unusual day when there is only one query.

The deeper self, or higher self, however one wishes to describe it, is a resource which is always available to each third-density entity; that is, from the higher self's point of view it is available. Yet there is seldom the clear and open communication between the conscious waking personality and the higher self from which it springs and which serves as a guide to each third-density representation. The higher self is a resource which is most usually contacted in the deeper states of meditation or within the state of sleep and dreaming, for this resource is one which is most subtle and one which observes the need to maintain free will most scrupulously. The higher self and the conscious waking personality that inhabit third density have, previously to the incarnation's beginning, planned together the lessons for that incarnation and have made ready an access means that the conscious self may utilize during the incarnation to receive information from the higher self. There is the necessity for the conscious self to be seeking in a clear and one-pointed fashion in order for the higher self to respond to the conscious self. For, as we mentioned previously, the subtleties of the nature of the higher self are such that the conscious self is frequently unaware that it is being aided when it is being aided. For the higher self is often the agency through which certain connections are made by the conscious mind, the intuitive mind, and the deeper portions of that same mind. The synchronicities which bring together various resources such as books, movies, experiences and other selves into the life pattern of the conscious self are those which are the handiwork, shall we say, oftentimes of the higher self. If one were to access or request access to this portion of this portion of one's own being for the purpose of remaining in a centered state of being, within the mindfulness of the moment, the very act of requesting assistance would be all that would be necessary for the achieving of this state of mindfulness for a certain period of your time. For the desire that would fuel the need to request assistance is the same desire that could be brought to bear upon focusing one's being upon the fullness of the moment that is always present. Thus, the higher self could be invoked in such an instance with success, yet it is the responsibility of each incarnated third-density entity to take that which is given, whether it be from the higher self or some other guide or teacher, and use it as he or she will. It is not the responsibility of the higher self or any other source to keep the third-density entity in any particular state of being, for the hallmark of third density and all of creation is the exercise of free will. Thus, the higher self is that source that is always available and which is always offering its assistance as requested.

Is there another query, my brother?

R: Is there any feedback that goes back when the conscious entity uses the information and says, "Thank you." Do you say thank you by paying attention? Does the flow go both ways?

I am Q'uo, and am aware of your query, my brother. This is correct, for the higher self is always aware of the experience of the third-density self, for each is so intricately a part of the other that it is not possible to experience an emotion within third density that the higher self is unaware of. Thus, when called upon by the third-density expression of its own being, the higher self listens with a careful ear and an open heart and is aware of each response.

Is there another query, my brother?

R: Is this concept also true when another entity such as one from the Confederation of Planets or a inner plane teacher like Aaron speaks and offers guidance and inspiration, then whoever comes across the material and finds inspiration and help within it?

I am Q'uo, and am aware of your query, my brother. This is also correct but is correct more to the specific case of each request, the lines of communication not being as intimate, shall we say, as are those between the higher self and the third density entity. Guides or teachers that are asked for assistance give it as freely in most instances but are not as congruently related to the third-density entity as is the higher self.

Is there another query, my brother?

R: I wonder, when a third-density entity requests help from one of the Confederation such as yourself, as the answer is given is it a community effort between the entity giving the answer and the higher self to shape the answer in the way that is most appropriate for the question?

I am Q'uo, and am aware of your query, my brother. And although this may be the case in some instances, for there is much freedom of possibility within such relationships, it is more nearly the case that the higher self and the third-density expression of itself will work together in the formation of the query that one such as we may then respond to, and in our response and in establishing a line of communication with an entity such as yourself, then there is the awareness upon our part of the impact of our response upon your nature or your being. However, our awareness of your gratitude or response to our query is more specific to the time during which we speak with you and you with us than the higher self's constant relationship with you.

Is there another query, my brother?

R: No. Thank you so much for speaking on this esoteric subject. And say hello to the other entities from your group that we get to hear from time to time.

I am Q'uo, and we are most grateful for your queries, my brother. And we have relayed your regards and they are also returned as well. Is there another query at this time?

Carla: I'd like to ask about this concept of self in the present moment being a rebel or subversive agent in regards to time. I was surprised at the energy that was in those concepts as I was channeling, almost as if there was an anger for the seduction of time. Could you speak to that a little bit? I had never thought of moving into the present moment as an act of rebellion or subversion.

I am Q'uo, and am aware of your query, my sister. The nature of your third-density illusion is one which is constructed in such a manner as to present one with a near constant experience of being out of the moment of remembrance, for it is when one is without such a centered state of being that one encounters the catalyst that one has incarnated to encounter. This is the purpose of this illusion: to give one those experiences that will throw one off one's center to the point that one is then put to the test, shall we say. The spontaneous response of each entity in such instances is the mark, the measure, the register for the entity and its ability and success in learning what it has come to learn. If one is able to achieve the centered state of being in which one is in, shall we say, the flow of the moment, in the center of things, then one is resting more securely in the bosom of the Creator, shall we say. That is a safe refuge from those slings and arrows of your outrageous fortune, for the entity that is able to retire in meditation, in contemplation, or perhaps in prayer to this safe tabernacle within is the entity that is not dealing as straightforwardly with the difficulties of the moment of the incarnation, and one which has returned in some sense to the unity of all things. It is from this unity with all things that entities move when they incarnate within this third-density illusion. Thus, to move and have one's being there, to expose oneself in a vulnerable fashion to the difficulties of this illusion of forgetting, is to partake in the manner that is desired, that is expected, that is set before all. Thus, to take oneself from the schooling at hand is to, shall we say, play hooky in a certain way.

Is there another query, my sister?

Carla: No. Thank you.

I am Q'uo, and we thank you again, my sister. Is there another query at this time?

(No further queries.)

I am Q'uo, and as it appears that we have exhausted the queries for this session of working we shall once again express our gratitude to each present for inviting us to join your circle of seeking this day. It has, as it always is, been a great pleasure for us to be with you and to speak with you, to listen to the beating of each heart, and the movement of the mind, as each seeks in this circle of meditation. We would take our leave at this time of this instrument and this group, leaving each in the love and in the light of the one infinite Creator. We are known to you as those of Q'uo. Adonai, my friends. Adonai. ✤

L/L Research

L/L Research is a subsidiary of Rock Creek Research & Development Laboratories, Inc.

P.O. Box 5195
Louisville, KY 40255-0195

www.llresearch.org

Rock Creek is a non-profit corporation dedicated to discovering and sharing information which may aid in the spiritual evolution of humankind.

ABOUT THE CONTENTS OF THIS TRANSCRIPT: This telepathic channeling has been taken from transcriptions of the weekly study and meditation meetings of the Rock Creek Research & Development Laboratories and L/L Research. It is offered in the hope that it may be useful to you. As the Confederation entities always make a point of saying, please use your discrimination and judgment in assessing this material. If something rings true to you, fine. If something does not resonate, please leave it behind, for neither we nor those of the Confederation would wish to be a stumbling block for any.

CAVEAT: This transcript is being published by L/L Research in a not yet final form. It has, however, been edited and any obvious errors have been corrected. When it is in a final form, this caveat will be removed.

© 2009 L/L Research

Sunday Meditation
November 21, 1999

Group question: We are wondering if Q'uo can give us some information about how the mirroring effect works and how we can utilize it in our own life. It is very hard to get an objective point of view about ourselves. We have a much easier time helping other people with their problems and catalyst and seeing things in an objective way. How can we use the mirroring effect in our daily lives to enhance our own understanding about ourselves?

(Carla channeling)

We are those of the principle known to you as Q'uo. Greetings in the love and in the light of the one infinite Creator. It is in the Creator's service that we come to this group this evening. May we thank each of you for desiring to know the truth and for calling us to your session of working. It is a great blessing for us to be able to speak to you in this manner, for it is through instruments such as this one that we are able to offer our ideas and opinions without trespassing on the free will of those whom we would wish to serve. Therefore, you serve us greatly by allowing us to serve you, for this is our path of service at this time, and to be able to exercise that which we came to offer is a great blessing. As always, we ask that each of you listen with a discerning and discriminating ear and heart to our thoughts and to the thoughts of any who would offer opinion and teaching. For truth is not a solid and unchanging thing. There are as many personal truths as there are persons or spirits, for each has an unique viewpoint. Therefore, those thoughts that we offer to you, take them or leave them as you wish and keep only those that you find helpful.

You ask us this day concerning how to make use of the catalyst that is offered to you in the form of those things about those with whom you are in relationship that catch the attention in irritation or aggravation or annoyance. You have said that you understand that these other entities all serve as reflections of yourself. And perhaps we can work upon this point a bit to bring it into a more lucid focus. Each of you and each of us are the one infinite Creator in each iota or atom or cell of our makeup. No matter who the entity is it is a portion of all that there is and all that there is exists in that portion in the way of holographic images. Thusly, when you see another entity and react to that entity, you are the Creator seeing the Creator. This is a truth about you, regardless of the situation in which one entity gazes upon another.

Throughout your recorded history it has been so that in the apparent world there were great differences between people. Some had great possessions and wealth while others had nothing or very little. Some have great influence and power while others are helpless and at the mercy of those who are powerful. The apparent inequities of the ages remain inequities because the Creator in each of you is at the core of each of you. It is the work of many, many incarnations to begin to bring the truth at the core of the being up into the light of conscious and consciously lived life. But no matter how deep the seeming vision, no matter how bottomless the abyss that seems to yawn between two people, no matter what the apparent inequity between two people, at the core each is joined to each forever in a unity that is endless and complete. Density may pass into density and octave into octave forever, and you shall still be one with every entity that has ever disturbed or bothered you, as well as one with every entity that has ever earned your respect, admiration, compassion or love. You have no room to pick and choose amongst the great variety that is apparent upon your Earth plane in terms of the truth of your being and the truth of the being of those with whom you come into contact.

Needless to say, it is not the function of the illusion in which you find yourself to bring the core truths to light. Rather, it is the function of the illusion in which you find yourself to toss you into a sea of confusion again and again and again, as often as this can possibly happen without completely deluging and foundering the spirit within. Now, each of you, as an eternal and infinite being, at one point before you decided upon incarnation within the Earth plane, sat down with your higher self and with the aid of the spiritual guides and considered carefully the life which you were about to embark upon. You considered the relationships that would give you the catalyst that you needed in order for growth to occur of a spiritual type. You considered these relationships well. From the standpoint of an entity which is not within the heavy chemical illusion of third density you gazed upon the richness of the learning experience awaiting you, and you gleefully rubbed your hands, thinking to yourself that this would be a wonderful adventure, an experience to remember, a great opportunity for increasing your polarity. This last is central, for each of you chose a catalyst that would work directly upon your polarity; that is, the intensity with which you desire either to serve others or to serve yourself.

It seemed so obvious to you, before incarnation, that these relationships that were being set up and the dynamics that would develop would be helpful. It simply did not occur to you that, perhaps, you might lose your way, that, perhaps, you might become completely overwhelmed by the sea of confusion, that you might temporarily and again and again drown in this confusion and become completely without hope. It was not obvious to you from the standpoint of infinity and eternity that minutes and hours could be endlessly long, that the dynamic of a difficult relationship could be excruciating emotionally, that the pain of living through relationships that were somewhat difficult over a period of time would be cumulative and distressing in the extreme. These things did not occur to the eager and ardent soul that you are in eternity and infinity. Simply put, it did not occur to you that the veil of forgetting would have such a powerful influence upon your awareness of the truth. However, it is just this deadening, numbing forgetting that places you in the optimal position for work in polarizing and sharpening and honing the desire to serve ever more truly, ever more deeply, ever more purely.

Nevertheless, here each of you is sitting in this circle with a heart still ardent and intentions still earnest, ideals still high. Yet each of you is bemused and concerned because of those things which you see as failures upon your part, failures to keep the cheerfulness, to feel the light and the love of the infinite Creator surrounding each and every situation. And we can only say to you in your darkness, in your searching, in your confusion, be at peace. Know that all is well. It is utterly and completely acceptable and a very helpful learning experience to feel irritation, aggravation and annoyance. It may be distressing. It may seem very confusing. And it may feel like an error that is dirty and sinful. Nevertheless, each time that you, as a consciously living entity, become aware that you are not treating another entity as the Creator you are in a very enviable position from the standpoint of one who has set before the self the race to run. For in this situation there is no human forgiveness possible. You see, each of you is deliberately cut off from your perfection. You embraced the humanity, which is error prone, because it was error prone, because you became blind and deaf and dumb to the full awareness of the one infinite Creator.

You may ask, "Am I supposed to flounder in this sea of confusion for my entire incarnation? Is there no way that I can improve at moving from the surface of a situation in which I experience catalyst to a deeper appreciation of the opportunities that this catalyst offers?" And we say to you, you may well attempt to become ever more quickly aware of the true situation and move from confusion to faith, but do not ever begrudge these irritations and annoyances in relationships that bring you to yourself.

Now, you have asked how you can work with the awareness that entities are a reflection of yourself, and we say to you work with them by releasing yourself and them from the strictures of humanity. It is not efficient or often possible to work with situations upon the level that the situation has occurred. In your humanity you have very limited resources when it comes to expressing love. Your supply runs out, and you are not expected, in and of yourself, to have infinite love. This is not within the capacity or the blueprint for human entities. It is necessary for the learning experience for an incarnation that you repeatedly come to the end of your human resources and then are forced to look at choices between despair and hope, between doubt and confidence, between giving up and keeping the faith. Thusly, we would suggest to each of you that when you begin to experience these irritations in a relationship between friends and relatives and loved ones move immediately to a position of forgiveness of self. For your real work in consciousness is not with another entity but with the self.

Now, in the example that this instrument gave in the conversation prior to this contact the entity involved was an entity which required that which this instrument was unable to offer with a full and open heart. This entity was immediately caught up in that situation with the mechanics of refraining of offering catalyst to the other entity. The one known as R, however, was precisely accurate in pointing out that there is an alternative to bearing difficulty in silence.

There are several alternatives to this. One is that choice of anger which, in a blaze of truth, blasts both self and other self in a fire of destruction, offering further catalyst to both entities. This is an acceptable way to work with the catalyst of irritation

There is the choice of attempting to express the feelings of the self to the other self. This choice is somewhat more skillful, taking into account as it does that the other entity in the equation of dynamics is also an infinite and eternal being which may wish to work carefully and thoughtfully upon its own inner processes. In such open communication there is much hope, and the faith that it takes to expose the poverty of the self to another is that effort put forth that does increase the polarity of the self. For there is that open-hearted communication in faith.

There is the choice that this instrument has repeatedly made in such a situation of maintaining a silence concerning the inner processes of irritation and anger and so forth. This can be a somewhat skillful choice if it is combined with a very light touch. The instinct of most entities in this situation is towards a heavier and heavier and ever more earnest and deeply felt concern. Whereas the more skillful approach to suffering in silence is to suffer in silence while amusing the self, finding inner laughter, and achieving a point of view that puts the entire foolish quarrel of humans and other humans into perspective as the blind leading the blind, both falling into the ditch.

Perhaps from this exposition you may see that we are not, as teachers, particularly concerned with which option you choose, for in each process lessons will be offered and learning will be possible. There are two elements at work when you are working upon polarity. One is faith, one is desire. Look to your desire that it may be of the highest and the best that you know. Look to the true and the good and the beautiful and hew as best you can to the high road, keeping in mind always that it is intention, not manifestation, that is important in the metaphysical universe of time/space. Keep in mind that it is faith that you are attempting to express in your life and in your being. Faith does not make sense. Faith gives one no avenue to pride. Faith seems to be the slenderest of all reeds to cling to, and yet the soul who lives by faith, the spirit who clings to faith, the one who refuses to let it go, is that spirit which shall achieve advances and polarity, and this is an achievement that redounds not to the incarnational self alone but to the eternal and infinite self.

Thusly, we ask that whether you burst into angry speech, keep silence, find communication, or simply work with the self to lighten the mood, do these things with an eye to keeping the faith. What is it to live by faith but to look at a situation that seems hopeless and say, "I believe that all is well." May we say that in our opinion this affirmation is one of the most powerful, enabling and ennobling of all learnings, of all expression, of all spiritual manifestation. The other is forgiveness. When you are looking at that part of your universal self that you do not wish to see—that is, when you are having difficulty with another entity—it may not seem possible for you to forgive that entity, and, by reflection, it may not seem possible for you to forgive yourself. And may we say further it is not possible to either forgive self or other self without a release of that self and an acceptance of help, for there is help at the core of your being waiting to be accessed, waiting to be asked. For the infinite Creator in infinite love and infinite patience sits in a humble chair in a little corner of your heart waiting to be called upon, waiting to be brought into the center of the heart, waiting to be noticed, waiting to be asked. In the beginning was the word, and the word was with deity and that Logos was deity, and that deity is Love, and that Love is you. At the heart of your being lie all the resources that you will ever, ever need. At the heart of your being lies infinite truth, infinite power, infinite strength.

When you can lay the burden of selfhood down and allow that core of self to speak as the little self, then you shall be overshadowed by infinite energy. And there are times when each of you has experienced this grace, times when you have prayed and received blessing, when it has become possible for you to love and forgive another and the self. Know that these things are possible. Know that it does not matter whether you have not succeeded or whether you feel that you have. For you are doing well simply to arise in the morning and breathe the air and respond as best you can to the busyness and the pleasure of the day.

All is well. This may be your mantra. All will be well. This will be your hope. Allow yourself to fail. Allow yourself to be upset. There is no disaster here, but only the opportunity for learning and growth. And know that help is always nearer than your breathing, closer than your own features or the breath in your body. Entities of great love and wisdom surround you, love you, want to support you. Lean into that invisible help and know always that all is well.

We would at this time transfer this contact to the one known as Jim. We leave this instrument, with thanks, in the love and in the light of the infinite One. We are those of Q'uo.

(Jim channeling)

I am Q'uo, and with this instrument again. We greet each again in the love and in the light of the one infinite Creator through this instrument. At this time we would offer ourselves in the attempt to speak to any further queries which those present may have for us. Is there another query at this time?

S: What do you do, how is your time spent, when you are not speaking with groups such as ours?

I am Q'uo, and am aware of your query, my brother. A large portion of our experience is that which reaches into realms which are not available to those of third density and which would not make much sense, shall we say, to those of your experience. What we attempt to do in relation to your planetary sphere is to monitor the progress of your peoples in discovering the concept of infinity, for it is this concept of infinite which is the key to unlocking the doors of unknowing, shall we say. The experience of the intellectual mind which is so much prevalent among the populations of your planet is an experience which is largely reserved for those of third density. For it is that which allows you to gain the greatest amount of individuality possible and to begin the process of opening the heart. For as each entity begun its experience in the first density of simple awareness, and having moved through this timeless experience into the second density of gaining the seeking and movement towards the light, this process of individuation, of moving seemingly away from the complete unity with all things, then gains its zenith within third density where the great intellectual ability is sacrificed, shall we say, by those who would open their hearts to the one Creator and Its creation. Thus, as we have been called by many such as yourselves, then we look to those who call and present ourselves in whatever form or fashion is most helpful to them, whether it be in a small number of cases such as the calling of this group to hear our words and opinions or to those who need an inspirational dream, shall we say, and, thus, a visitation within the sleep and dreaming portion of your experience, or whether it might be more helpful to provide a coincidental meeting of entities within the third-density illusion, that they might share with each other that they might share the seeking that grows within both hearts. Thus, we aim most of our efforts toward this planet and its harvest, which is ongoing at this time.

Is there another query, my brother?

S: How is your consciousness picked by those who you speak through or to? How is it determined who is paired with whom?

I am Q'uo, and am aware of your query, my brother. In the small percentage of entities with whom we deal where there is the opportunity for mind-to-mind contact and the expressing of the verbal representation of our thoughts, the group calling will determine whether the nature of the information sought is of an introductory or other nature. Far more entities request the introductory information which concerns the concept of the one great original Thought of the infinite Creator from which all of the creation has been made and the need for each entity to establish regular meditation times and practices so that more and more of this thought may be apprehended and utilized in the daily round of activities. When a group has persisted for a long enough period of time and has meditated faithfully, giving over a regular portion of the diurnal period to retiring to that sacred inner room to be in the presence of the one Creator, then there is the need for more intermediate information which Confederation entities are then able to give according to their own talents, shall we say. There are numerous entities within the Confederation of Planets in the Service of the One Creator who are able to serve in both the introductory and intermediate phases to groups such as this one. In those few groups in which there is the additional need for what you would call advanced information, there are also groups which are able to answer this call as well. The matching of groups which call with those who answer is upon the level of a natural affinity for that which is called and that which is shared, much as the simple analogy of the magnet which attracts the iron filings.

Is there another query, my brother?

S: I have recently purchased some quartz crystals and could you tell me how the energy through crystals manifests itself and the additional uses that I may make of them?

I am Q'uo, and am aware of your query, my brother. The study of those artifacts known as crystals is a large study which has been investigated in great detail by many of your peoples who have utilized such crystals for a great portion of time. For specific information, we would recommend that various texts upon this subject be studied. The general principle of the use of the crystal is that there is a geometrical and arithmetic relationship of various angles and sides and nature of the crystal itself which lends itself to certain kinds of uses depending upon the ability of the entity which utilizes the crystal to regularize and harmonize its own being, its own personality, with the crystal being used. Thus, the charging of any crystal is done by the focus of the intention within the heart and mind while in the meditative state upon the crystal which is held in various positions ranging from the lower to the higher chakras. This done over a period of time then creates a harmonic resonance, shall we say, between the entity and the crystal so that the crystal acts as that which magnifies the intentions of the entity using it. As we mentioned previously, the specific use to which the crystal is put is determined by the nature of the crystal, its size and its purity. The nature of the entity utilizing the crystal is as important if not more so than the nature and purity of the crystal used.

Is there a further query, my brother?

S: I have recently been reading and making my best attempts at DNA recoding and activation and I will ask you whether you can give me any comment on my progress in that direction?

I am Q'uo, and am enough aware of the query which you ask that we would request a good deal more information in relation to this subject area, for if we were to attempt to speak to this query at this time it would require us to infringe upon your free will by moving into those areas which are yet undiscovered.

Is there a further query, my brother?

S: I was wondering if during the dreaming stage that I could possibly meet with you and share your surroundings?

I am Q'uo, and am aware of your query, my brother. Such a meeting would, indeed, be possible if you are able to successfully navigate in a conscious fashion within your dreaming state. This is a skill which is achieved after a good deal of work, shall we say, over a period of time. Those who are able to move in a conscious fashion within their dreams are few upon your planetary surface. If you are able to accomplish this we shall be most happy to meet you there.

Is there another query, my brother?

S: No more from me. Thank you very much.

I am Q'uo, and we thank you again, my brother. Is there another query at this time?

Carla: I wondered, number one, as I get to working on various topics on my book there may be subjects which the archive material hasn't given us anything on. On those areas would it be acceptable for you to give me information to share with others through the book?

I am Q'uo, and we would be most happy to speak upon any subject within your outline, my sister.

Carla: My other short one had to do with some really strange things that have been happening while I have been working on the book on the computer. There have been so many gremlins lately and I have been taking this as a good sign. It means a good energy is building up on the project and has attracted attention. Would you agree?

I am Q'uo, and am aware of your query, my sister. The experience of the malfunctioning of the computer and its software is in most cases the normal working out of the interrelationship between the hardware and the software and the brain. However, there is some small degree of, as you would say, interference from the loyal opposition. However, we find that the project is being undertaken in the most appropriate attitude of praise and thanksgiving and the openhearted giving of love and light which is your great protection.

Is there a further query, my sister?

Carla: Yes. One more. I got a letter from a lady today who was in that hypnogogic state between sleep and waking and she was suddenly aware of a violent energy that was making a lot of noise and was entering at the heart, coming out the back, going into the back and coming out the front over and over. This went on for a while and at the end of this time everything shut down but she had a pain in her back and chest and was very uncomfortable. I suggested that she had either become aware of a psychic greeting within her finer bodies or that there was a process going on in the finer bodies that she became aware of in this state and was benign, and that moving back into her body and waking up she had gotten back in crooked at that energy center she had gotten stuck. I suggested that she make daily affirmations that her finer bodies were perfectly in alignment with her physical vehicle. Could you suggest anything further that might be helpful to her?

I am Q'uo, and am aware of your query, my sister. The refining of the affirmation to that which suggests to the deep mind that within the sleep state the body will readjust itself into the proper alignment with the energy centers would be that which may be helpful in finalizing the realignment that has been, as you have surmised, caused by the incorrect re-entry of the astral body into the third-density, chemical vehicle.

Is there a further query, my sister?

Carla: No. I will quote your response to her verbatim and let her work with it.

I am Q'uo, and we thank you once again, my sister. Is there another query at this time?

R: No question. Just want to say thanks for everything that you have shared with us.

I am Q'uo, and we are grateful for your words as well, my brother. For as we said in the beginning of this session it is your calling to us that is a great service to us. Without such a calling we would have no beingness within your illusion. At this time within this third-density planetary influence there is a great deal of calling for assistance from any source which may provide the green-ray opening of love and compassion. That is our great desire: to partake in the awakening of the heart energy center of all those who seek our assistance, for there is no greater calling than that which calls for love, that which calls to love, and it is that calling which we answer, and those from the far reaches of the one creation rejoice at the experience which each has upon this planetary influence in the opening of the heart.

At this time we shall take our leave of this instrument and this group, leaving each, as always, in the love and in the light of the one infinite Creator. We are known to you as those of Q'uo. Adonai, my friends. Adonai.

L/L Research

L/L Research is a subsidiary of Rock Creek Research & Development Laboratories, Inc.

P.O. Box 5195
Louisville, KY 40255-0195

www.llresearch.org

Rock Creek is a non-profit corporation dedicated to discovering and sharing information which may aid in the spiritual evolution of humankind.

ABOUT THE CONTENTS OF THIS TRANSCRIPT: This telepathic channeling has been taken from transcriptions of the weekly study and meditation meetings of the Rock Creek Research & Development Laboratories and L/L Research. It is offered in the hope that it may be useful to you. As the Confederation entities always make a point of saying, please use your discrimination and judgment in assessing this material. If something rings true to you, fine. If something does not resonate, please leave it behind, for neither we nor those of the Confederation would wish to be a stumbling block for any.

CAVEAT: This transcript is being published by L/L Research in a not yet final form. It has, however, been edited and any obvious errors have been corrected. When it is in a final form, this caveat will be removed.

© 2009 L/L Research

Sunday Meditation
December 5, 1999

Group question: What are the components of clear communication? How can miscommunication happen? What is said is not always heard or interpreted as it was intended. And would there be any non-verbal ways of communicating that would enhance our communication?

(Carla channeling)

We are those of the principle known to you as Q'uo. Greetings in the love and in the light of the one infinite Creator, in whose service we are. It is our distinct pleasure and blessing to be able to share your meditation this day and to be called to your circle that we may offer our poor thoughts and opinions concerning clear communication. This is a subject as interesting to us as to you since our form of service to others at this time is this speaking with words through channels such as this one.

The substantial and sometimes grave difficulties using your words certainly heightens the difficulties inherent in any communication, for words are as slippery as eels, and yet that is the medium of communication. And limited though it is, it must suffice for those in third density. May we say that we sympathize with each of you which attempts to express clearly thoughts and clusters of concepts within having to do with emotion and feeling and facts. It is in no wise an easy thing to be perfectly clear.

Let us look at the roots of communication, for it is from the root that the plant grows and much can be understood by gazing at this energy in its beginning state. Each of you is a complex of vibrations. The Creator Itself is a complex of vibrations. The universe, as far as we know, is a complex of vibrations, or more specifically of fields of energy with vibrational characteristics which interact with each other. Therefore, each of you, as a being, communicates by your very vibration, your identity. Those not within the veil of forgetting, that is, those not incarnate within third density, find this information of vibration helpful and much is communicated from person to person as the two entities feel their vibratory complexes beginning to harmonize and intermingle.

Also, beyond the limits of the veil of forgetting the communication most usually would not take place by using words but by offering concept complexes or balls of thought, we might call them, which are offered from one to another in a whole fashion so that the other may, herself, draw out the threads of communication that are offered there and see the entirely three-dimensional nature of even a single seed thought. So, the first thing that you communicate as an entity is your vibration, and from it people will take much. They will form an attitude towards you dependent upon how that vibration that is they and that vibration that is you are harmonizing. Neither you nor they may be aware that this subtle bodywork is going on, but bodies themselves are aware of these vibrational characteristics, and perhaps you have had the experience of cottoning to someone and not particularly liking someone else from the very instant of meeting. Often the communication of vibration has done its work before a word is spoken.

And, certainly, once an entity who wishes to communicate clearly grasps this vibrational nature of identity in a metaphysical sense the entity has become wise enough to work on or tune that vibrational nature of self that it may become more like the vibration of the Creator. For each of you has as the basic vibration the vibration of the Creator, and each of you has found ways to distort those perfectly harmonized vibrations in such and such a way, making the individual being of yourself a one of a kind. No one distorts that original Thought the same way as you. By taking thought, however, a seeker may, indeed, lessen the distortion of the vibration from the original Thought. And this is work well worth doing.

As we said, in your density it is necessary, for the most part, to use words to express opinion and fact. Your peoples have great numbers of words, many languages from which to choose. And each entity comes into her existence bombarded from the beginning with words, words, words. The process of maturation of the young ones of your species is a process of learning the words, learning the phrases, learning the behaviors, and then endlessly combining those learnings in ways that are taught as appropriate. And so each flower of self grows to bloom, grows to maturity, coming through the schooling process that teaches more and more words, more and more ways to use words and also that process teaches ways to think about the self, ways to think about others, so that by the time a young child has grown to adulthood she has an enormous quantity of information, some of which is words and the definitions of words and ways to use words, but a great deal of which is judgment or fear-based. For the culture in which you live teaches you to estimate the worth of an entity with whom you are going to communicate thought and from the results of that judgment to slant your communication in such a way as will, you feel, maximize the clarity.

For the most part, this process of learning produces fairly clear communication. When difficulties arise you may look for difficulties to arise when an entity is seen or assumed to be some nature on the surface that, in fact, the entity is not; for them, the carefully pointed communication is misaimed. When we speak to you through these instruments we play an endless and fascinating game wherein we assess the harmonics of each of those within the circle. We listen to the, shall we say, the sound of the hunger or the desire or perhaps we might say the color of that desire, and then we orient and slant our message, which is always the same message, in order to best serve the harmonics and the substantial nature of the group which we feel kinship with and are meditating with. Each time even the same people meet as a circle there are subtle differences in the inner harmonics of the group, and each time we assess anew before we begin to speak, for we would not wish to waste this opportunity to share our thoughts with you clearly.

Earlier conversation before this channeled communication talked about the way people do not listen to each other but rather each have things they wish to say to the other, and this is, of course, a very prominent way in which clear communication is sabotaged. If you become aware of a situation in which your words are not being heard, then it is that you may ask yourself whether you wish to be heard or whether you wish to allow the other self to express that which that self wishes to express and assume a role of simply listening. In many instances the appropriate response we would say, metaphysically speaking, is simply to abandon the desire to be heard and become a sounding board that can hear what an other self is attempting to say. This yielding up of the inner agenda and the thing to say is a mark of spiritual maturity. It is an action very difficult to complete, for there is within each self a deep well of desire to be heard, to be heard by the self, and to be heard by those other selves which have meaning for the self. And yet many times the straightest and shortest distance to clear communication is to become silent, to release the desire to be heard and to accept, temporarily, a role of purely listening.

May we say that when this decision is made it is a decision which places the self in a separated stance with regard to the other self. Consequently, when relationships are close in families or in communities it is not a wise choice to become the pure listener, for the harmonics within a family or within a spiritual community especially depend upon all of those involved being able not only to speak but also to listen. Thusly, if some give up that desire to speak that seems selfish and become pure listeners they have robbed the collective harmonized group of those things which they alone could conceive of, think through, and express. Thusly, we encourage each to see that it is a mark of respect for the other self to continue to attempt not only to listen but also to be heard.

Perhaps the next most usual or common way in which communications go awry is that situation in which the self does not want to speak what is actually true. This can be as innocent a situation as one's mother saying, "How do I look in this hat?" If Mother looks perfectly terrible in that hat, if that hat is an outrage and an eyesore, yet still a husband or a son is likely to say, "Oh, Mother you look wonderful in that hat." This is not clear communication. This is, however, loving communication. And we do not say that this is wrong, for there are many kinds of truth. And the truth that is being expressed by the compliment, while untrue about the hat, is certainly true about the regard that the family members feel about another family member. The desire in this circumstance is not, then, to express truth but to express love. And we feel that that has its own kind of truth to it.

However, there are many times when that which should be expressed, if truth were told, is that which the other does not want to hear. The word, "no," when permission is asked to do something. The words, "I don't know," when someone wishes you to have all the answers. These things are difficult to say. These things are even difficult to say to the self, and yet it does remarkably improve communication if the self does not edit to remove negative responses. Rather, we would suggest that when a situation arises that the self becomes aware that negative seeming truth must be told that there is a calm and quiet peace within. Perhaps even a small prayer may be uttered within, tuning the self toward the light, hoping that within that additional light there will be found ways to tell the truth that will be softer and yet still clearer than the abrupt, "I don't know," or, "The answer is no."

When the person facing this situation can realize the degree of fear that is distorting the challenge at hand, then it is that that entity becomes more and more skillful at looking straight at the fear involved and taking that fear within the heart and forgiving the self for being fearful. This work upon the self, over a period of time, begins to build up for the self a concept of the self as being flexible, able to learn new ways, unafraid to speak regardless of the consequences. It is as if you take a comb and comb through the difficulties and brambles that seem to be surrounding communication with this other self, combing away the tightness of spirit, combing the fear of ridicule, combing away the fear of making a mistake, combing away all the fear-based limitations that hedge you about as a communicator, until all that is left in your blue-ray energy field is an honest and open desire to give and receive information and love. Remember that communication itself is vibration. It has its own energy center, that blue-ray chakra in the throat.

Now, communication may come from any of the centers within your physical and finer bodies. When you experience substantial difficulties in communication, know immediately that you are not in blue ray. And take the time in your mind to contemplate the conversation that was not clear, looking for the signature of the energy center that is blocked, over-stimulated, or in some way distorted. Often you will find an orange-ray blockage when the conversation is between two people and about something that is between those two people. In this situation you are literally looking in a mirror and that which you think that the other has said is a reflection of that which you have said.

This instrument is perusing a book at this time about the living memory process and throughout the book the author keeps bringing up the qualities of interaction between two things, this author calling these two things tuning fork A and tuning fork B, or Albert and Betty. But let us say that you are Albert and the other is Betty. That which you say to the other self has a certain kind of energy. That energy moves to Betty, to tuning fork B, and is taken in by tuning fork B in a way that you could not predict but that is purely the choice of tuning for B. Then tuning fork Betty B responds to you and energy and information comes back to you altered by the other, and as you and Betty converse you are creating an entire energy system that is strictly between the two of you, that has energy and life and love.

In any conversation you are creating energy, light and memory, and you are watching something that is vivid develop. Consequently, one way to powerfully aid this process is to do some version of that which the one known as Ken Keyes has suggested in several of his books, and that is to use the phrase, "I am creating," when you are speaking to another and there seems to be a major difficulty in understanding each other. If someone says, "You hate me," to you, that is a clear communication of what that person thinks, but it is not particularly easy to respond to. If someone says, "I feel I am creating that you hate me," then it is that the other can say, "I am creating that I do not feel that I hate you, but I do hear that you feel that I hate you, so we must now find out why it is that you feel this." Any method that allows each person to take responsibility for that which he is hearing will improve communication in difficult situations.

The deepest aid to communication is character. If an entity has the humility and the patience to work with another entity to achieve clear communication nothing will keep that entity from achieving clear communication. But it is to the humble only that this becomes true. Your yellow-ray world, this world of Earth and the human experience is absolutely dependent upon communication. It is attempting to learn the lessons of love for individuals and for groups. So much about communication at the level at which you are now enjoying experience has the agenda of drawing groups together as well as drawing individuals together. There is an evolutionary drive towards harmonization of vibrations, and if you examine the kind of language that nations use with other nations you will see that despite many fears, despite many reservations, despite many warring hostile vibrations, groups of people can come to agreements in clear communication. And each of you knows from personal experience that clear communication from person to person is possible. Therefore, let your heart never be faint when you discover that you are unable to communicate. Then is the time to listen patiently, to ask humbly those questions that you have upon your mind and, therefore, to gather the information that you may need in order to grasp what someone is attempting to tell you. And when you are the one speaking and you find that your words are falling upon deaf ears then it is that you may call upon your humanity, call upon your patience and release, for the moment, in order that you may provide the service of understanding that which the other has to say to you. Once this has been done you may then reassess the possibility of communicating that which you needed to.

We show this instrument a beautiful flowing river, a river of golden rolling waters, bubbling and springing and singing. We show this instrument that with those who would communicate [they] must be as fish within that water, must feel that life-giving unifying water between the self and all other selves. See the self and all other selves as united within that golden stream that is flowing and bubbling at a very brisk rate at a very decided direction. It does no good to attempt to stop the water. It does not help to remove the self from the flow of the everyday. Rather, the good of it is always in realizing the praise and the thanksgiving for belonging in that water of life, for being in the flow of incarnation, and for having the opportunity to share this environment with others also breathing the water and living in the flow.

Perhaps the most helpful thing to remember about communication is that you are all one. You are all going through the same experience. You are intimate, intimate friends. This is the truth beyond the surface, behind the masks of personality and individuality. Above all things, keep that faith that each other self is as you are, no better and no worse. See that equality of self to self always, disregarding status and the details of wealth and position. Be heart to heart insofar as you can with each other self. And that attitude of love will greatly help the process of clear communication. Know that each of you has gifts. Some of you have blue-ray gifts of communication. Some of you have gifts elsewhere. It helps to know the self, to have confidence in the self. And so we encourage that within each.

More and more as you take responsibility for yourself, as you bring your energy centers to a real balance, you will become more and more skilled at feeling the point at which the communication has bogged down. Where is the energy that is tangled? Is it in the orange-ray of personal communication, or is it in yellow-ray of communicators working with institutions like marriage, work, and groups of all kinds? But above all, know yourself to be a child of the one infinite Creator. Rest in that identity. Rest in that love. And let that love feed your heart, your faith, and your will so that you may once again give a gladsome smile and try again to say things clearly and with love.

We would transfer this contact to the one known as Jim. We thank this instrument and leave it in love and in light. We are those of Q'uo.

(Jim channeling)

I am Q'uo, and greet each again in love and in light through this instrument. At this time it is our privilege to offer ourselves to additional queries which those present may have for us. May we ask if there is another query at this time?

S: I have been reading material that talks of the Guardian Races and the Ra Confederacy, and the question that I had on that is is there any other material available to us on the Law of One?

I am Q'uo, and am aware of your query, my brother. We find that there are many authors who, throughout the written history of this planet, have spoken of this law. Many poets, many musicians speak of the unity of all things. We are aware that you are intending to inquire of entities who are consciously writing of this Law or who have been able to make contact with entities such as ourselves who may speak of this Law, and, again, there are many, beginning with the text that is known among your peoples as the Holy Bible, for there are some instances within this work in which the concepts of the Law of One, and some of the distortions of the Law of One, are spoken of. There are entities who, from the ancient times, [have] spoken of this law in an oral tradition. The so-called Brotherhood of the Seven Rays is one such group that spoke concerning this law. Within your own time frame there has been much information channeled through the one known as Edgar Cayce in which the Law of One was revealed in some detail. Other entities, such as the one known as Brother Philip, have also shared information regarding this law.

Is there a further query, my brother?

S: A week ago I had some problems with my contacts and my eyes and have been unable to wear my contacts. I have been thinking all week what possible issue may be coming up as a result. Is there something that I am not seeing? Maybe you could shed some light on that area.

I am Q'uo, and am aware of your query, my brother. Without moving too far toward the precipice of infringement upon free will we may suggest that you may fruitfully look into the area of the Christmas season and some of the concerns, shall we say, that have been a part of your history that revolve about this season, so that the sight is less than clear and is somewhat irritated when the, shall we say, sore subjects are broached.

Is there another query, my brother?

S: The last time that we spoke I was asking about the DNA activation recoding and you mentioned that it would be an infringement on my free will to give me information about that, and I don't understand how it could be an infringement. Could you elaborate?

I am Q'uo, and am aware of your query, my brother. This particular area of inquiry is one which may offer a fruitful avenue of exploration to you. We are not desirous of influencing your choices to the degree that we would answer in great detail or even much detail at all in this area for we would prefer that you be able to make these choices for yourself. If you have a more specific query in this area to offer to us that is the result of your own consideration we would be more than happy to speak to that specific query rather than being asked by you to look into this general area and to elicit from it for you that which is of importance.

Is there another query, my brother?

S: OK. I guess maybe to take it a little further in, in these readings there was a mention of how the Earth at this time was increasing its activation that will come up over the next 17 years, the next 12 to 17 years, that will be available to all. I had a dream recently that I was at 4.4 and one of the things mentioned was that the ascension of most people would have to be 4.5, and I am trying to get a better understanding of what that means.

I am Q'uo, and we believe that we grasp your query. Please query further if we are incorrect. There are various points of harmony, shall we say, betwixt the energy centers of individuals such as yourself and the planetary entity that is the sphere upon which you now dwell. As the planetary entity moves through its process of evolution it, as do each of those entities such as yourself which live upon it, opens various doors, certain tones or themes are made available so that those entities such as yourself which are in the planet's care are able to take advantage of these doors, these tones, these reaches of possibility that allow each entity upon the planet to harmonize its own seeking with the planetary evolution. Thus, the interrelationship of this planetary entity and those upon it is that which can be utilized to enhance one's process of becoming aware of the nature of the self, of the creation, and the opening of the heart of the self through the acceptance of all that is.

Is there another query, my brother?

S: Do you have any suggestions or exercises or anything of that nature that would be of benefit?

I am Q'uo, and am aware of your query, my brother. And to this query we would respond by suggesting that it is well to take a portion of each and to reserve it for the meditation so that the events of the day may be reviewed in a brief manner in which time there is the feeling again of those efforts to communicate, to open the heart, to understand, to be more aware of the effect one's being has upon those about one. In short, this is an exercise in the increasing sensitivity of an entity to its own evolutionary process. The time spent in meditation reviewing the events that have left their mark upon the mind and upon the heart is a time during which that which has been learned can be seated more firmly within the self and that which awaits the learning can begin to be revealed to the conscious mind.

Is there another query, my brother?

S: That's all that I have for now. Thank you.

I am Q'uo, and we thank you, my brother. Is there another query at this time?

Carla: I would like to ask—I've noticed my eagerness this whole year to work on the handbook for wanderers. I know it must be somewhat out of balance. I was wondering if you could comment on this almost compulsion that I have to keep working as fast as I can in working on the book. Is there anything that I could do to bring more into balance? I don't want my great desire or eagerness to do the book to hurt its purity.

I am Q'uo, and am aware of your query, my sister. The project of the writing of this book may be likened to the preparation for the running of the race. The runner has trained well, has trained long, and now awaits the starter's gun. The pulse increases. The adrenaline is released and the mind is focused in a single fashion upon the running of the race. That there should be some increase in the level of anxiety before such a race or the writing of such a book is understandable, for there is the desire to accomplish each well. There is also the need to give over the project to those hands which are greater than your own, to the heart which is larger than your own. And though the one known as R has a large heart and great hands, we speak of the one Creator which is able to move through channels such as your own in a more balanced fashion when the dedication to a certain outcome is released enough that one can move with the possibilities, the difficulties, the frustrations, and the, shall we say, gremlins, as we have heard them called, in as easy a fashion as one can move with the work moving smoothly. Thus, one sees the one Creator moving in a rhythmic sense so that which seems to be a difficulty in the short run may seem either insignificant or an unseen ally in the longer run. For the quality of understanding is not a portion of this third-density experience, and much which occurs in your daily round of activities, even to the smallest of details, has a beneficial purpose which will not be understood in the moment of its occurrence, if ever. However, there is a purpose to even the smallest of experiences and the one Creator may utilize each experience for the accomplishment of a larger purpose or plan.

Is there a further query, my sister?

Carla: Yes. I have noticed that I am dropping off to sleep morning, noon and night, when I don't intend to, since I have started working on the book. Is this tendency benign?

I am Q'uo, and am aware of your query, my sister. The wear and tear of such a project has its toll. The sleeping is appropriate when one is weary.

Carla: Thanks. This lady that wrote in is named F and she lives in Brooklyn, New York, and she has a metaphysical TV show that goes out to about a million people in the New York City area. She and I have been writing for some time. Recently she sent me a transcript of an exchange between her and an entity that she calls A that she met through her ouija board. She has been talking to A for about 15 years and seems to relate to her in the same way a personal guide would. I see nothing but a benign relationship. She asks if you would comment on the relationship between her and A.

I am Q'uo, and am aware of your query, my sister. We look at this entity, the one known as F and the one known as A who is working with the entity known as F in order that there might be some guidance made available from sources that are, as you have surmised, benign and helpful for the one known as F. This relationship is one which has been established as a kind of rotating honor and duty, so that as one entity is within the incarnation the other remains exterior to it and serves as a guide to the one moving through the veil of forgetting. This relationship is old in terms of this cycle of experience, having begun early within the cycle, at a time when both were incarnate and shared a relationship which was that of what you would call the husband and the wife. The offspring of this mating were not just the physical children that is the usual produce of such relationships but were also concepts of the unity of all things and the creative power of love which each wished to share with others upon this planetary sphere and which each continues to share with those of this population.

Is there a further query, my sister?

Carla: No. Thank you, and I know F thanks you, too.

I am Q'uo, and we are most grateful to you as well, my sister. Is there another query at this time?

R: To follow up on the concept of one entity in the incarnation and one out of the incarnation, how does a concept of such a guide compare to the guidance provided to a person from his or her own higher self?

I am Q'uo, and am aware of your query, my brother. In most instances the type of relationship would be nearly identical. However, those guides are related to the higher self in the role of the male, the female, and the androgynous guide. The more personal guide may be more immanent or, shall we say, accessible so that there might be a more practical, shall we say, line of communication so that words and concepts, feelings and tones, may be transmitted upon a regular basis. Thus, the personal guide—which is an entity much like the one being guided, however having remained between incarnations in what you would call the time/space portion of this planetary vibration—then is able to make a reliable contact in some fashion with the entity entering the incarnation, for the purpose of enhancing a personal evolution in the day-to-day activities.

Is there a further query, my brother?

R: What you are saying is that with this case of two entities, one in and one out of incarnation, there is a more reliable chance of establishing a type of communication which will touch upon the conscious mind of the entity in incarnation, thereby enabling some flow of information between them, as opposed to the higher self which always communicates through the deeper mind and, therefore, is more in the form of concepts which do not relate to the logic of the conscious mind as well?

I am Q'uo, and we are grateful for your elucidation of our attempt to speak to your query. We feel that you have done a better job than we, and we thank you. Is there another query at this time?

R: No. Not a question. But a comment. It sounds like music to my ears when you inject some humor into the topics which we discuss here that feel serious and deep. Perhaps they are, but if you have more of it, just keep it coming.

I am Q'uo, and we also appreciate humor, for the sense of proportion is that which provides the better view to the restricted mind, and we appreciate your comments as well, my friend.

Is there a final query at this time?

(No further queries.)

I am Q'uo, and since we have exhausted the queries for this session of working we would again take the opportunity to thank each present for inviting us to join your circle of seeking this day. We are always filled with joy at this invitation and appreciate greatly the ability to speak with each. We remind each that we are not great authorities and do not wish any to take all of what we say as being the truth. Use your own powers of discrimination to chose that which has meaning and value for you, leaving all else behind.

We are known to you as those of Q'uo, and we would take our leave of this instrument and this group at this time, leaving each, as always, in the love and in the light of the one infinite Creator. Adonai, my friends. Adonai. ✤

L/L Research

L/L Research is a subsidiary of Rock Creek Research & Development Laboratories, Inc.

P.O. Box 5195
Louisville, KY 40255-0195

www.llresearch.org

Rock Creek is a non-profit corporation dedicated to discovering and sharing information which may aid in the spiritual evolution of humankind.

ABOUT THE CONTENTS OF THIS TRANSCRIPT: This telepathic channeling has been taken from transcriptions of the weekly study and meditation meetings of the Rock Creek Research & Development Laboratories and L/L Research. It is offered in the hope that it may be useful to you. As the Confederation entities always make a point of saying, please use your discrimination and judgment in assessing this material. If something rings true to you, fine. If something does not resonate, please leave it behind, for neither we nor those of the Confederation would wish to be a stumbling block for any.

CAVEAT: This transcript is being published by L/L Research in a not yet final form. It has, however, been edited and any obvious errors have been corrected. When it is in a final form, this caveat will be removed.

© 2009 L/L Research

Sunday Meditation
December 19, 1999

Group question: The question today has to do with the situation of when we find ourselves being of service, whether it is the work we do for our living or it is just a favor that we do for friends, and we do it over and over, how do we deal with the anger and the frustration and the negative emotions that come into our minds when we feel like we are being pushed beyond our limits, that there are so many people pulling us in so many different directions that we don't feel that we are really able to serve without feeling anger, frustration, doubt and being stopped in one way or another?

(Carla channeling)

We are those known to you as the principle, Q'uo. We greet you in the love and in the light of the one infinite Creator, in whose service we are. May we thank each of you in this circle of seeking for the sacrifices and processes which each went through in order to arrive at this working. It is a great blessing to us to be able to be called to groups such as this one for those who are seeking what this instrument would call the truth, for that is the service which we offer at this time. And the opportunity to speak through instruments such as this one is precious to us. We are glad to share our thoughts and opinions with you with the understanding that we are not authorities but, rather, fellow pilgrims upon the path of seeking the one infinite Creator whose mystery expands and recedes before us as we go. May we say that you are good company. We would like to also state at this time, since there is a concern, that this instrument challenges in the name of Jesus the Christ, and we were not able to meet this challenge we could not speak through this instrument. This is most satisfactory for us as we are the, shall we say, station to which this instrument seems best tuned and vice versa.

As we begin to look over this interesting subject of energy exchange and blockage we note that it is what this instrument would call the season of Advent, that time in your solar year when darkness claims your Earth plane the maximum amount of time during your days, the time when the light seems farthest. In this darkness the light is born, and into this darkness the light does come, and each of you is a repository of that light, and each of you wears the crown upon your head. And it is heavy. And this is as it should be. As the one known as Jim spoke earlier, from the standpoint of each of you before incarnation, each and every difficulty that you are having, from the depletion of your energy from unwise exchange, with disappointment in yourself for energy blockage, was gazed at with delight, with eager anticipation of running the straight race, serving with gladness and joy, being a light within the darkness of the Earth plane. From that vantage point the perfection of the pattern was seen, accepted and acted upon. It is, indeed, an innocence of soul and spirit that is bound to be lost, that idealistic, optimistic concept that the self has of the self's coming incarnation.

We would like to take each of you back to that position when you and your higher self and your guidance considered well what you wished to offer, what you wished to learn, and what you wished to share. And with a sense of adventure and creativity you chose those entities with whom you would collaborate, for in each unwise energy exchange and in each instance of blocked energy, not only are you involved and confused but also is the other self in the equation confused, puzzled, at a loss, feeling that there is imbalance and, in many cases, having not even the vocabulary with which to think about what is occurring. When each of you finished the play, set it in place, and entered incarnation, each of you went through what we have called the veil of forgetting. This veil is something that cannot be imagined from the standpoint of the higher self, from the standpoint of the inner planes, or any density but the third.

Let us look at the cause of this veil of forgetting, for there is good reason for it. That which entities learn with the book open may make sense for a little while, may enter the mind for the nonce, and an open book test may produce an excellent score. There have been many creations in which the veil of forgetting was not dropped over the third density, and it is from the failure of these entities to accelerate the pace of their own spiritual evolution that later creations decided to use a veil so that entities entering the density of choice would have no memory of the way things actually are upon which they could count to the exclusion of other information. In other words, this darkness of mind, this disconnection between the roots of mind and the conscious mind, was an adjustment made carefully and with measure in order to achieve an atmosphere in which work in consciousness could be done by faith alone and not, in any case, by authority or proof or empirical processes. For that which you most deeply are, that about which your self revolves, is an infinite, eternal, unique spark of the Creator. All that you wish to learn lies now perfected within you. All that you sense as imperfect lies in perfection within you. And, yet, through incarnations such as those as you are now enjoying you have placed yourself in a position to chose, by faith alone. How to proceed with your own spiritual studies? How to assess yourself? How to relate to other selves?

By enjoying this veiled experience each seeker was at once cast into a sea of confusion and safe at home. And it is this dual reality that each experiences: the seeing of the self as an imperfect, stumbling seeker and at the same time having the faint but unmistakable ring of an inner perfection and truth that cannot be denied. Once cast into this sea of confusion it is well for each to cultivate certain angels, shall we say, for we find among your peoples at this time much awareness, seemingly an increased awareness of inner plane entities such as angels and guides. There are habits of mind that are also angels. It is to be expected that as you come up against the various relationships which you set up for yourself before incarnation you will again and again be cast into the confusion of a precise kind. That is the very best teaching tool for you and the other self, that you will need to consult some angels and guides. We would suggest one of these angels might well be the angel of humility. If you are in a sea of confusion and if you feel that there are demands made upon your energy which are excessive, then it is no wonder that there will be disquiet within.

And, indeed, in terms of the stability and solidity of your waking personality there is no harm in drawing limits, in creating boundaries for relationships that allow you and the other self a measure of comfort and freedom. When you ask yourself, "How much can I give?" let the angel of humility take that question and shake off the dust of pride so that to the best of your conscious ability you define for yourself in each situation that seemingly imperfect but necessary boundary line that represents for you that which can be given with a full heart and an open hand.

We might suggest that you bid come the angel of gladness. For there is much inner noise which almost drowns out a yearning for clarity and balance. It is not in noise or contention but in quietness that each may find the peace to accept the limits of self and the limits of other self.

We could suggest that you bid come the angel of patience, for each process of your developing spirit must do its work through time until time is no longer. And there is no rushing the processes of spiritual evolution. There are times that will seem very wrong to a seeker when a complex outworking of inner processes is taking place. In some instances this becomes a certain kind of experience which this instrument would call initiation, and this dark Night of the Soul is also a process which is especially needful of the angel of patience. Again and again such a process will bring you to a feeling of urgency, and yet there is nothing to do. This is a frictive process which is, shall we say, a kind of tempering, a burning away of that which is stiff and unwieldy so that the instrument that you are becomes both stronger and more flexible.

We would urge you to bid come the angel of joy. Whatever you do, do not forget to take the moment to rediscover your joy. In each day and in each hour find the moment to remember with utter and whole joy who you are, where you are going, whence you came, and upon what errand you now are. You are loved. You came to reflect and share and transmute love in giving and receiving. That which your senses see and hear and feel and taste and touch is a panoply, a weaving and interweaving of a tapestry of unimaginable joy, of every color and emotion and sensation and inner process—the dark, the colorful, the pale. All of the various strands of your experience and your being are woven in light, in love, in joy, and to connect through the beauty of the grass, through the star in the sky, through the frost upon the pane, through the look in someone's eye, in every and any way to connect with joy is to come into the self most profoundly.

We would suggest that you bid come the angel of laughter. Dear ones, we, as well as you, can be serious to a fault. It seems sometimes that only earnestness and seriousness serve one in good stead in the spiritual search, but we share with you our conviction that the light touch is absolutely necessary in spiritual matters. For all that you think, all that you feel, all that you experience is a dream within a dream within a dream. The levels of illusion are many. We, ourselves, have not combed through the illusions to find that which is real. For us, as well as you, the mystery continues to draw us onward.

We can talk to you of resources for your seeking and for your study. What we cannot do, what only each of you can do, is express that which is you in an ever more whole and pure, and true way. The Creator loves you, each of you, and praises every distortion of the one infinite creative Thought of Love which has gone into making you just the precise vibratory complex that is you. Every quirk and cranny, every imperfection and quiggle that is in your nature is loved by the Creator. In terms of your relationship to deity, you are completely loved. You are not judged except by yourself.

Now, let us look at that. Of course, in terms of where the next incarnation will be, each walks steps of light after completing an incarnation to discover what density of light is most comfortable for that entity at that time, and in those terms there is, shall we say, an objective judging. It is not a judging except that it is a home-finding device, and where that light is most comfortable for you might be in third density, or fourth density. This is unknown until that particular process is gone through. However, within incarnation, within the life that you now experience, your judge is yourself, and you have a very stern judge. May we say that the experiences that each of you is having in which there is unwise energy expenditure or blockage there is the mirroring effect which provides each of you with a look at imbalances within the self, carefully reflected by an other self for your learning and understanding. We encourage you to listen to yourself when you think or when you speak concerning these relationships, for as you speak of other selves you are speaking wisdom that can be heard by you regarding that portion of your universal self which has aspects of the dynamic that you are experiencing as coming from an other self to you. When you look in the mirror you see a face you know of as yours. But when you are speaking with an other self you are still looking in the mirror.

This instrument is informing us that we need to move to the second portion of this meeting, and so we will conclude our thoughts through this instrument by encouraging each of you to love, accept and forgive as you can, when you can, and if you can, and to take note of those frustrations which you feel are overwhelming. Over time you will find repeated patterns, and we encourage you to spend some time gazing into those patterns, for they will yield to you information that you can use. We encourage you to encourage each other, to comfort each other, to serve as the listening ear and the supporting arm within the sea of confusion that you share with those that you love. Most of all, we encourage you to move as often as you can into what the one known as T was speaking of: those times of quietness and meditation that bring one to oneself, that bring one to one's heart, for within that heart which is the center of each of you is a tabernacle and in the holy of holies dwells the Most High, radiant, omnipotent, omniscient, more yourself than you. May you yield yourself up to that inner fire as often and as whole-heartedly as possible, for there is your anchorage, there your spiritual home.

We would at this time transfer this contact to the one known as Jim. We thank this instrument for its service, and we leave it in love and in light. We are those of Q'uo.

(Jim channeling)

I am Q'uo, and greet each again in love and light through this instrument. At this time it is our privilege to ask if there may be any further queries that those present might have for us. Is there another query at this time?

R: The last fifteen years of my life I have changed dramatically in ever accelerating paces in ways that I cannot comprehend. I look at myself now and fifteen years ago and I see a dramatic difference. I am attempting to comprehend to the best of my ability these changes.

I am Q'uo, and we are aware of the comments concerning the change in the life pattern in the one known as R, and we believe that this entity has well stated the changes that have occurred in his own structure of personality, shall we say. And this is the kind of transformation which each seeker has desired for the self, for as each incarnation is begun with a plan for the opening of the heart, the discovery of the self, and the sharing of the fruits of an open heart with others, so then each entity begins the great incarnational journey with goals that are similar to those shared by fellow travelers but with the means for achieving such goals that are unique to each entity. For as each entity enters the incarnation, so it is with the one known as R that there is the goal and the means, the opportunity, which is presented in a fashion which shall allow the blooming of the incarnation. There are those experiences which have been programmed to serve much as the water, the soil, the sun, and the fertilizer to the growing flower of self within. Many of these experiences have been what you would call difficult and have tested the inner resolve to move forward in spite of difficulty. Many experiences have been puzzling and have left a sense of questioning which has been pointed in an inward fashion so that the appropriate questions would be asked at the right time. Many experiences have been obviously preparatory, in that knowledge has been gained and practiced over time giving one an excellence of operation, shall we say, the operation of the incarnation. Some experiences have been for the purpose of bringing one to a synchronistic juncture, if we may call it that, so that there is …

We find that we must pause briefly so that the instrument be allowed to work the recording devices.

(Transcript ends.)

Year 2000
January 2, 2000 to December 17, 2000

Sunday Meditation
January 2, 2000

Group question: We have just started a new year and we are wondering, as we look back over the past year, we are wondering what we can learn from intellectually? What can we observe and benefit from? And how much does our intellect play into the growth that we do accomplish? We would also like to know what role gratitude plays in our evolution?

(Carla channeling)

We are those of the principle known to you as Q'uo. Greetings, in the love and in the ineffable light of the one infinite Creator, in whose service we come. We want to thank each of you for calling us to your circle of seeking this day. It is our privilege and pleasure to respond to your call for our thoughts and opinions. As always, we are most happy to be with you and to share with you anything that we feel or know, with the understanding, as always, that each of you will take from those things which we say only those thoughts that seem useful and good to you, leaving the rest behind. We are not an authority but, rather, we are your companions on the way.

The topic you have asked us to speak on this day is the place of the intellect in learning and assessing one's spiritual state and the place of gratitude in that same process of seeking ever more deeply and fully that truth that lies at the heart of things. As is often the case, we would begin by moving backwards from the question to a more fundamental place, that place which sees all of the incarnational experience of each entity on the Earth plane as a very small part of a lifetime that is eternal and a citizenship that is infinite, for each of you is a thought that has sprung from the Creator. From the Logos through many densities and experiences has come this present incarnational self with its burden of gifts and challenges. Each of you existed before time and space. Each of you will exist when time and space have no more meaning, and, yet, within each incarnation there is the hope of transformation. There are the lessons put before the self by the self. There are the gifts of the incarnations that you share. There are the sufferings of the incarnation to work with, to accept, to forgive, to heal.

Each who enters the Earth plane has these things in common, and truly each sub-sub Logos, each spark of the infinite Creator, each person, has within this small incarnation tremendous forces poised, waiting for the proper stimulation or invitation in order to exist, to guide, to help with healing processes. And if each has felt this hope that there are those forces, energies and essences that can help with difficult incarnational challenges, then we say that this hope is infinitely justified. For each of you is as the magician with the wand, in potential. Each of you has power and force, will, and faith. These things are stored in infinite supply in great storehouses that lie within each of you, awaiting only that awareness that calls in quiet confidence for the assistance that is already there.

Since each of you is as a thought we may see the tremendous and infinite complexity of that concept, for you are not a thought in the sense of being only one thing; that is, in the sense in which words are used. Certainly, each of you is one thing and the same thing, that being love. And yet each of you has colored that infinite love that is the core of being with those distortions which take the clear white light of limitless truth and shade it in rainbows of personality and character so that each of you is as a tapestry in which dark and light and colorful threads are woven together through your experiences, your sufferings, your joys, and your sorrows. And all of these threads—the light, the dark, and the color—are beautiful and the way that you put them together can be beautiful, even when the material seems very difficult and the experiences very dense and hard to bear.

Upon the human plane, then, on that level of conscious living from which each of you is asking this question, the prospect of gaining a great deal from the use of the conscious mind may be seen to be, at best, limited. Certainly, the use of the mind is recommended, and, certainly, there are more and less skillful ways to use the mind in that attempt to create for the self clearer understandings of the self and of the challenges and issues that are before not just the conscious personality but the metaphysical entity that each is.

May we say that the intellectual mind has implicit limitations, those limitations being the natural limitations of reason. Ratiocination is an exercise which is posited upon the faith and logic and reason. To a certain extent this faith is justified. However, that which is rational and reasonable is only a small part of this essence of self and, therefore, the use of the conscious mind has natural limitations. Reason cannot move down into the roots of being, for those roots are not reasonable or rational but are, rather, of that energy which this instrument is used to calling archetypal or archetypical. The essences of each of your beings have far more to do with intense purified emotion than with reason. This is a topic in itself that bears much inquiry.

And when we have finished with all of the avenues of thought that reason and logic and imagination can form and create there is much material of self remaining which has not been touched by the process of analysis and thought. When the one known as T brought up the question concerning gratitude the appropriateness of this direction of thought was extremely logical and reasonable in a profound sense, that sense being that the deeper reaches of thought and mind and consciousness and being are directly worked upon with far greater efficiency and effect by those energies which are usually called emotions or emotion-laden concepts such as gratitude, hope, faith and will. It is beyond all reason to expect within a little life to transform that infinite eternal being that you are, and yet within every incarnation this is possible and in many incarnations this is realized.

There is no incarnation that is just a punishment or just a vacation. All incarnational experiences are clear so that there are lessons to learn and gifts to share. And the channels in which each entity is moved to travel are those pathways of thought and habit that feel right to that entity and this is as it should be. For your essence, your deepest energy, is more feeling that thought, more energy than concept, and that which works best upon the deep self is essence, that essence of feeling as opposed to sense.

This instrument has often said it is not what happens to one, it is one's response to what happens to one which is the natural arena within which entities may wield their power and offer their truths. It is the attitude with which one meets the moment that sets and prepares the self to receive that moment's burden of joy or sorrow. If the attitude is gratitude, if the moment is met in thanksgiving, whatever comes at that moment is bid welcome, is embraced, and this is a very positive and excellent metaphysical stance with which to greet that which is occurring in the moment. This business of attitude is extremely central to the metaphysical learning experience and much wisdom is expressed by the entity who is working with the attitude with which she greets the moment. This is not a process much open to reason. Oftentimes, in any reasonable sense, there is little to give thanks for in a given moment, and there are what seem to be weighty reasons to meet the moment with fear and trembling. And yet in these moments, as in all moments, great skill lies in keeping the heart completely open and allowing love to flow through the self with that attitude of thankfulness and praise that looks for the very best that could be within the present moment.

There are many circumstances within your experience, and, certainly, within all third-density experience in which the self is very uncomfortable, in which there are many negative feelings of alienation, isolation, anguish, grief, anger and disappointment. And, yet, it is especially [important] in these times to cling to the same attitude of praise and thanksgiving with which the high points, the good days, of an incarnation are naturally greeted. It is when it makes the least sense to be thankful, to offer praise, and to have an open and flowing heart, that there is the most skill in choosing this response to life itself. For if each of you is a thought, and if that thought is love, then shall you not be at your most skillful in attempting to keep open a channel for that love that you are? It is as though the situations of life try to silence and make dumb that clarion love within. And, yet, they cannot silence you if you will not be silenced, for it is always your choice to cling to hope, to believe and have faith when there is no evidence to support such thoughts, such attitudes. It is when all seems darkest that you may, with the most direct apprehension, know and feel and sense that truth within, that unconditional and absolute love that created you and sustains you.

In the dark of the night that lies across the hearts of those who mourn and weep there is a humble dwelling, and in that dwelling that lives within your heart there is a principle, an essence, an absolute being that is Love. To this instrument that Love came down into the human condition as Jesus the Christ. To many to whom this is not meaningful the essence can remain unnamed and simply be Love, Love eternal, Love divine, Love creative and destroying, infinite Love. However you wish to frame it, this Love is with you in the darkness. This energy is faithful to the light with complete disregard to outer circumstance, for to love there are no outer circumstances but only infinite light and infinite love.

So, we certainly suggest that you make use of those faculties of intelligence and reason that help you to analyze what is happening to you, help you to keep yourself in a self-understood order, but, more than this, we would encourage the cultivation of purified emotions. Those emotions being faith and hope and charity. Encourage yourself to be faithful in meeting each moment with hope and gratitude, praise and thanksgiving. And, insofar as it is possible, we encourage each to find ways of strengthening these habits of mind so that, little by little, it becomes habitual to greet the moment with hope, to greet the situation with faith, to greet the relationship with gratitude, humility, patience and love. Where the intellect loses energy and is no more these deeper emotions become more and more and then oceans of energy offering infinite power and infinite grace to those who persist in seeking them. May we suggest to each of you the great benefits of disciplining your personality so that the first thought when engaged in a new situation is that thought of praise and thanksgiving. For when you stand upon that thought all that your outer circumstances can give to you will be grist for the mill, fodder to be chewed, experiences to be analyzed, to be loved, to be accepted, and to be forgiven.

We would at this time transfer this contact to the one known as Jim that we may continue this working through that instrument. We leave this instrument with thanks, in love and in light, for we are those of Q'uo.

(Jim channeling)

I am Q'uo, and I greet each again in love and in light through this instrument. At this time it is our privilege to offer ourselves to the further responding to any queries which may yet remain upon the minds of those present. Is there another query to which we may respond?

Carla: About a recent experience that I had, I had attempted to meet a relative's questions over many years on the subject of channeling with patience and tolerance and although this has seemed to be the right way to handle things in actuality, during this last Christmas I became unable to be tolerant and patient and expressed strong emotions such as anger and pain at this objecting that my relative was doing to me. It seemed to create a much more rapid and healing response from him than all my patience and tolerance had and this surprised me very much. I wondered if you could comment on this process?

I am Q'uo, and am aware of your query, my sister. As each of you move through the various levels and kinds of relationships with those who are close to you, you will find that there is a certain efficiency to speaking from the heart as contrasted to speaking from the mind or the intellect. For though the mind is quite useful in its ability to analyze experience and to chart a potential course of action, there is no efficiency greater than the spontaneous response of the heart that wells up from inside of one, for this tuning into one's emotions in an honest manner, without desire or manipulation, is that which speaks to another heart most clearly. For though each of you is able to, shall we say, put a good face on a situation by using one's intellect, this is only a stop-gap measure, for there is within each entity the sure knowledge of clear communication that is from one's heart and this kind of communication speaks more clearly than any other. For it tears away that facade or barrier which keeps one heart from another. All hearts know pain. All hearts seek solace. When one becomes aware of another's heart that is in pain then there is the greater likelihood that one will respond honestly with one's own emotions, the doors having been opened by the first to do so.

Is there another query, my sister?

Carla: No. Thank you. That was very clear.

I am Q'uo, and we thank you once again, my sister. Is there another query at this time?

Carla: Yes, I would just ask since this is the season of Jesus' nativity if there is anything that you would choose to say about this entity and this particular season of the year.

I am Q'uo, and am aware of your query, my sister. This season, that which gives the focus of attention for a moment to the life and love of the one known as Jesus the Christ is, for us, one of our favorite for observation among your peoples for it is at this time, especially within this particular culture, that many difficult relationships are made more smooth and loving as a result of the focus upon the Christ child coming into the world of illusion. It is at this time that many of your peoples find time to drop their usual cares and concerns and to make a pilgrimage to their own hearts, and, in so doing, also move in a compassionate vibration into the hearts of those about them. Though the practice of revering the life of the one known as Jesus is usually short lived, we find that the focus, even for a brief time, upon this entity's center or central message of love is most helpful to the entire planet, for as love becomes the focus for more and more of your peoples so does this vibration of love move in an harmonic manner around and throughout the planet itself. Thus, we rejoice with you at the birth of this entity in each heart that makes room for him, and we remind each that this pilgrimage to the heart is a journey that each can take at any moment. We thank each for making this journey. It is our privilege to walk with you upon it, for we also make the same journey.

Is there another query at this time?

Carla: No. Thank you.

I am Q'uo. As we have apparently exhausted the queries for this session of working, we would take this opportunity to thank each gathered here today for making those sacrifices necessary in order to form this circle of seeking. We are aware that each works with much catalyst in the daily round of activities and it is often not easy to remove oneself from that momentum. At this time we would take our leave of this instrument and this group, leaving each, as always, in the love and in the ineffable light of the one infinite Creator. We are known to you as those of Q'uo. Adonai, my friends. Adonai. ✼

L/L Research

L/L Research is a subsidiary of Rock Creek Research & Development Laboratories, Inc.

P.O. Box 5195
Louisville, KY 40255-0195

www.llresearch.org

Rock Creek is a non-profit corporation dedicated to discovering and sharing information which may aid in the spiritual evolution of humankind.

ABOUT THE CONTENTS OF THIS TRANSCRIPT: This telepathic channeling has been taken from transcriptions of the weekly study and meditation meetings of the Rock Creek Research & Development Laboratories and L/L Research. It is offered in the hope that it may be useful to you. As the Confederation entities always make a point of saying, please use your discrimination and judgment in assessing this material. If something rings true to you, fine. If something does not resonate, please leave it behind, for neither we nor those of the Confederation would wish to be a stumbling block for any.

CAVEAT: This transcript is being published by L/L Research in a not yet final form. It has, however, been edited and any obvious errors have been corrected. When it is in a final form, this caveat will be removed.

© 2009 L/L Research

Sunday Meditation
January 16, 2000

Group question: The question this week has to do with the concept of the rapture. Could Q'uo give us information about the process of rapture? Some say that people will go in the rapture without going through the process of death, and we are wondering what Q'uo would have to say about that and what value Q'uo might find in this for our own spiritual journeys.

(Carla channeling)

We are those of the principle known to you as Q'uo. We greet you in the love and in the light of the one infinite Creator in whose service we are. May we thank each of you who has come to be a part of this circle of seeking at this time. We are aware that in each case there was that hunger and desire to seek the truth, and we find this a great blessing to us, for being called to speak with you is what we consider our service at this time. So, meetings such as this one enable us to serve, and we are most grateful for the opportunity. As always, we would ask that each consider those things which we have to say, keeping those which ring true and dropping all information which does not ring true for you. For we would not wish to be a stumbling block to any.

Your group question concerns that which this instrument has called the rapture and others have called the ascension, and, as is often the case, we find that we need to back up from that question to a more fundamental or basic stance. We would ask each of you, "What have you thought this day? What has occupied the mind? What has charged you with hope or with fear? What has your concern been this day?" For each of you is a creation of unique characteristics, yet at the same time each of you is the Creator. And at the very core of each of your beings there is that pure and undistorted love, that great original Thought from which all things were created and which moves through all created things to the extent that the distortions within those created things allows for the uninterrupted flow of that love.

Each of you, then, is a part of the Creator. Each of you inheres in the Creator and at the same time each of you has chosen at this time to manifest in a personality shell and a physical body within the illusion that you now enjoy. The nature of this manifestation is such that there will be distortion. It is impossible not to have distortion, for distortion is the very nature of space and time. The yearning for absolute purity, absolute truth, and absolute love is a yearning that was within you when you chose to move forth from what this instrument would call the Creator's house. That love has been with you as you have moved through many densities and many experiences, through many worlds, through many lifetimes, and it is that undistorted love that draws you ever onwards towards the source and ending of all that is.

So you may consider yourself as a distorted version of the Creator, each of you distorted in unique and fascinating ways, each of you having chosen the gifts that you would bring into manifestation with your personality shell, the limitations that you would set for yourself so that you may learn, the relationships that you chose specifically for their friction, for their catalyst, that you might experience that process of distillation wherein all of those things that move before the eye of mind bloom, stutter and fail. There are many tools that each of you has available in this journey that you take together and, yet, always alone.

One of those tools could be called imagination, and we would ask you to look at the material that the one known as P has brought to the attention of this group. We consider that source and many others to be valid and interesting resources from which to draw inspiration and structures of thinking. For you see, when you seek the truth, when you seek the nature of reality, you move quickly into uncharted seas within the deep mind. The deep mind does not think like the conscious mind, for to the conscious mind, to the intellectual mind, the tool of logic is considered useful and helpful. And, yet, as the one known as R said earlier, in matters of spiritual concern logic and reasoning often not only do not make the picture clearer but also may obfuscate those resources that are there.

The function of myth, then, is as a resource which aids the mind in its attempts to think about spiritual matters. When we say myth or mythical system we refer to the entire gamut of religions, philosophies and cosmologies, whether they be what this instrument would call orthodox or within the culture and society, or unorthodox and eccentric. It does not matter what the rest of the world thinks about any given system of mythical, religious or philosophical thought. Rather, it matters to each individual what structures of thought attract and awaken desire within that individual. When a mythical system or a portion of a mythical system rivets the attention then the seeker may know that this is fertile ground for investigation or contemplation, for deep thought over a period of time.

As long as this particular vision or structure or thought attracts the mind and the heart, then for that person this is precisely what that person needs to be looking at and thinking about, for each seeker will be drawn to those structures of thought that help that individual think about deity, devotion and service. Such is the nature of the human heart and the deep mind that it is often a process that cannot be predicted in any way. It is a process that is full of surprises. The thought that takes the mind and heart today places it then over a period of time into a gradually changing—we are having trouble finding a word in your language. We show this instrument a nautilus. The shell of the nautilus grows each year as the animal within the shell grows, making a beautiful curling and ever-widening horn. Such is the process of thinking about spiritual matters, having those feelings and experiences seated within the personality shell and moving around in a spiral fashion so that you are hitting the same material repeatedly and each time finding new avenues of thought to be created where before there was none.

So you see, working with mythical systems is something we feel is extremely helpful and valid. Those systems are there because inspired entities throughout your history have attempted in their own ways to share their visions of processes which they saw in a unique and interesting way. Such a piece of mythical architecture is the rapture or the ascension. We shall say through this instrument that which this instrument said herself earlier, that being that it is our humble opinion that the processes of spiritual evolution at work upon your planetary sphere at this time are metaphysical rather than physical. We do not in any way suggest that planet itself is not laboring difficultly at this time. Indeed, your sphere itself is undergoing a graduation and a birthing into a density more filled with the light of the one infinite Creator.

The suggestion has been made many times that the planetary sphere itself would, through the necessity of altering its magnetic polarity to some extent, shake off all life as a dog would shake off fleas. And indeed, one reason that wanderers first came to this particular planetary sphere was to transmute the infinite love and light of the one Creator through their physical and metaphysical instrument and out into the Earth plane, creating a net of light that would alleviate and ameliorate the tectonic distress which the Earth is now experiencing. It is our opinion that this plan, though working imperfectly, has reached a critical mass sufficient to enable your planet to suffer many smaller catastrophes that allow the majority of those upon your planet to continue to enjoy the illusion.

However, there is also another kind of graduation which is taking place among your peoples at this time. It is our opinion that this ascension or rapture is a way of describing what we have thought of before as steps of light. It is our feeling that when, as the one known as Jim said, the doors of death open for an individual that individual goes through as much healing as it needs to go through to recover from the stress of physical death, to gather the feet under the self within the new configuration, the new body, the new environment. There is the review of the incarnation which takes place when healing work has been accomplished so that the soul itself may, together with the higher self, review the incarnation and consider how that learning process went and what may need to be focused upon next in the never-ending process of spiritual learning.

At the point that this has been accomplished and the soul knows itself and is oriented to its surroundings it then comes to a kind of staircase, if you will, where there is a gradually increasing density of light. In this process the spirit simply moves forward into fuller light until it is receiving a maximum amount of light that it can enjoy in a stable manner. At this point the spirit stops. That point may be in third density. That point may be in fourth density, or even higher. Whatever amount of light is comfortable to that spirit is the appropriate density location for that entity in its next incarnation. Rather than there being a judge meting out judgment it is simply a matter of each spirit finding itself in the best place possible for new learning and growth.

We would turn now to the question of what the rapture, then, may be discussing. For it is an inspiring and riveting writing that has fascinated many, many seekers over thousands of years. It is our opinion that this writing moves into a very creative and useful way to look at death, to look at the death of the physical or mortal body. In a world of appearances the death of the physical body is the end of everything, the alpha and omega of dust and ashes. And, yet, the spirit within rebels at the limit of death, at the abruptness and dislocation of death, and it says, "There must be more. Surely I could not be stopped by this arbitrary exhaustion of flesh."

We have found in working with your peoples that it is almost impossible to be complete and satisfactory in our coverage of almost any subject, for wherever there are minds that think there will be the desire for complexity. Yet, our message is ever towards simplification. It is our feeling that at the very heart of each of you lies all that you will ever need to know, kept safe, secure and snug within your skeleton and musculature and all of those physical embellishments that create the fair physical body. To us, you are a vibration that we can see and feel and touch. To us, you are love, and as we gaze at you we see the reflection and it is love.

To us, each entity has already ascended. For to us the energy which is you is already perfect. We encourage each of you to seek in whatever way is helpful to you. As always, we encourage meditation. Simply lighting the candle and sitting with the candle is a life-changing habit if it be prosecuted through time. And we encourage all the other avenues of seeking as well. Most of all, we encourage you to believe in your own rightness, for that which inspires you may not inspire others. But that does not matter. That does not signify anything for you. Whatever moves you to think upon who you are, why you are here, where you are going, of these things we greatly approve. And because each entity is very much, and of necessity, alone in the seeking within, become more and more aware of the great aid you may be to each other by offering support and understanding wherever you can, by sharing honest emotion and opinion whenever you are asked, and by simply being there to give a smile to a stranger, or to simply interact as you go about your chores. Each of you with your many, many chores are all a' bustle, and we do enjoy tuning into groups such as this one and seeing all of the colors of your desires and hopes, your ambitions and your fears. Know that you are loved for who you are. We consider each of you our friends.

We would at this time transfer this contact to the one known as Jim. We leave this instrument in thanks, love and light. We are those of Q'uo.

(Jim channeling)

I am Q'uo, and greet each again in love and in light through this instrument. It is our privilege at this time to offer ourselves for any further queries which those present might have for us. Is there another query at this time?

P: Yes. I have a couple. I have some about addictions which are part of my path. Some people say if you don't do things their way that you can't make it to where you are going. There are all kinds of addictions: food, money, shopping, working, sex, etc. These are all lessons for us, for us to overcome. I can't help anyone else until I have overcome them to find the path out. I believe in the rapture. I want to go on the rapture and come back to help others when the time is right. That is the first part of the question.

I am Q'uo, and we have listened carefully to that which you have offered to us and we have not found a clear query at the present time. Could you requestion, please?

P: I am saying that there are many paths and everybody has to walk their own path. Some people don't understand that and will place judgment on you for not walking their path. Those people distress me because I like some of them and open my heart to them and share my soul with them. Then they find out certain things about me and it hurts and I am disheartened but I feel those addictions are still part of my path. The second question was, I have placed on this Bible here three amulets: a ring and two stones for E and M and I was wondering if they could be charged so that they could help open the hearts of those who own them?

I am Q'uo, and we appreciate that which you have offered to us. We are most happy to lend our healing vibrations to those amulets which you have offered for such. We bless each and bestow upon these objects of the third-density illusion those feelings of love and acceptance which you have spoken of as being somewhat lacking from those whose judgment is heavy upon yourself. We would agree that each entity has a path which is unique; whether this path has the accoutrements which you have called addictions or does not have such is of no consequence, for each entity will fashion that journey which has meaning for him or for her. And all portions of the journey through the third-density illusion are shrouded in mystery, for from mystery and into mystery each of you shall leave. For the one infinite Creator is beyond all understanding, and the one Creator exists in full in each, though there may be a disguise that is worn for a certain purpose and a certain time. This disguise shall, at a certain time, be dropped and each entity shall return again in full realization and experience of the one Creator. For each is made of nothing else. We are aware that each entity has those qualities which may be accepted or rejected by others or by the self, and the great lesson of this illusion is to love with an open heart, to accept without condition …

(Tape change.)

I am Q'uo, and am once again with this instrument. We apologize for the delay and for the pause that was necessary in order for those present to rejoin the circle of seeking. We would ask if there might be another query at this time?

Carla: I have noticed a lot of computer weirdness, the latest being that this week, again, even though the data base was found I couldn't open it, and I have not been able, by looking at myself and my experience, to find any psychic greeting component at all. It just seems like the typical glitches one runs across when one is working, but I do want to ask for any insight that you might have because I do want to enter working on this book with the best that I have to offer.

I am Q'uo, and am aware of your query, my sister. In this regard we may suggest that the genesis of the difficulty is simply that, as they are called, bugs in the software, and we observe that your patience in this regard is to be commended. For an undertaking of that which you speak is that which requires a certain gentleness balanced with a perseverance that will see you through the difficulties of any nature.

Is there a further query, my sister?

Carla: As a follow up, two things are happening: I am extremely content with less, and, number two, is the joy and the bliss that I feel comes from the less—being here, doing chores, weeding the garden, cooking in the kitchen, and just doing the normal things that we do. The small things seem to contain all of the truth and the beauty and the learning that I was looking for out in the world. Is this a typical progress, from your experience, from working with people in third density, that their bliss comes not from farther and farther out but from closer and closer in?

I am Q'uo, and am aware of your query, my sister. And, indeed, we find this is true not only for those of your third-density illusion but for all succeeding illusions as well. For the true richness of each experience is contained within the heart of the one who experiences. The one Creator, whole and perfect, is contained in each moment, each iota of experience for those whose hearts are open to love and to the one Creator. Then does this fullness of love and unity pour into the moment until the moment itself is whole and perfect, and the true richness of being is appreciated.

Is there another query, my sister?

Carla: No. Thank you very much.

I am Q'uo, and again we thank you, my sister. Is there another query at this time?

P: I wanted to know about the Mandelbrot Set, discovered back in 1981. I've seen films and pictures of it and it blows me away. It's an infinite mathematical formula that creates a stream of pictures. Scientists don't seem to know what to make of it. I feel it is the unified field that everyone is looking for. It is the way the creation is made, the blueprint. What are your insights on the matter, what it all means to us?

I am Q'uo, and am aware of your query, my brother. To give a full explanation of this Mandelbrot Set would not be possible within this illusion, for there is much that is beyond understanding, shall we say. But in the general gist of your understanding of this phenomenon we would agree that this is but another example of the perfection of the one Creation becoming apparent to those who peer for the first time beyond the boundaries of the illusion. The ability of the one Creator to reproduce Itself in an infinite action is that which is barely begun in this type of mathematical expression. Far more wonders exist, not only for the mind that can comprehend, but also for the heart that can open in full understanding and acceptance of the One in all.

Is there another query, my brother.

P: So, is the rapture going to happen?

I am Q'uo, and we would not infringe upon anyone's free will by revealing a yes or a no to such a query. Is there another query at this time?

P: No. I am done. Thank you very much.

I am Q'uo, and again we thank you, my brother. Is there a final query at this time?

Carla: Just on a whim I would ask if the Latwii portion of your principle is looking at any particular colors within our inner planes these days?

I am Q'uo, and am aware of your query, my sister. Those of the social memory complex known to this group as Latwii have been busying themselves with the qualities of communication which are located within the blue range of your spectrum of colors, as you call them. For this group has the need for the definition of this particular color as does the entire population of your planetary sphere at this time, for there is much within clear communication that can allow catalyst to be consumed, shall we say. There is much that needs to be said from heart to heart. Thus does the opening of this heart center of energy become that which is aided by the opening and balancing of all energy centers.

At this time we would thank each present for inviting us to join your circle of seeking this day. It is always the greatest of honors for us to be able to do so. We would remind each that we are happy to join each entity in his or her private meditations in order, not to speak in any words, but to deepen the meditation in order that there be more stillness of the mind and openness of the heart there, at the throne of the one Creator. We are known to you as those of Q'uo.

At this time we would take our leave of this instrument and this group, leaving each, as always, in the love and in the ineffable light of the one infinite Creator. Adonai, my friends. Adonai. ✤

L/L Research is a subsidiary of Rock Creek Research & Development Laboratories, Inc.

P.O. Box 5195
Louisville, KY 40255-0195

www.llresearch.org

Rock Creek is a non-profit corporation dedicated to discovering and sharing information which may aid in the spiritual evolution of humankind.

ABOUT THE CONTENTS OF THIS TRANSCRIPT: This telepathic channeling has been taken from transcriptions of the weekly study and meditation meetings of the Rock Creek Research & Development Laboratories and L/L Research. It is offered in the hope that it may be useful to you. As the Confederation entities always make a point of saying, please use your discrimination and judgment in assessing this material. If something rings true to you, fine. If something does not resonate, please leave it behind, for neither we nor those of the Confederation would wish to be a stumbling block for any.

CAVEAT: This transcript is being published by L/L Research in a not yet final form. It has, however, been edited and any obvious errors have been corrected. When it is in a final form, this caveat will be removed.

© 2009 L/L RESEARCH

Sunday Meditation
February 6, 2000

Group question: The question today has to do with the various frustrations and angers, all the various difficulties that come around in our lives periodically and seem to be part of our catalyst. What can Q'uo tell us about what it is possible to do intellectually, logically and consciously in learning from the catalyst, and when it is necessary to do something different, to give it up, to accept the situation, to have faith that everything is as it should be? What can Q'uo tell us about the different approaches, the intellectual, the acceptance, doing something different, giving ourselves a break? How can we know what is best for us to do at any certain time in our life experience?

(Carla channeling)

We are those of the principle known to you as Q'uo. We greet you in the love and in the light of the one infinite Creator, in whose service we are. It is a great blessing and a privilege for us to be called to your group this afternoon. We greatly appreciate each person which sits in this circle of seeking. We appreciate the desire that brought you to this circle and that brought us to you. It is a signal blessing to us to be able to speak through this instrument and other instruments to people such as you. For in this way we feel that we can share information and opinion without infringing upon the free will of any, for we wish our information to be taken lightly, in that we ask that you not think us to be an authority.

For we are not an authority over you, but, rather, are companions along the way that we both walk. We know that the way is dusty and we appreciate your company as much as you appreciate ours.

When this instrument was speaking to the one known as R earlier this afternoon the one known as R asked the instrument to ask a question of us within this session. That question was, do we remember the difficulties of third density? Is it possible for us to put ourselves into the experiences of third density? May we say that, yes, indeed, we do. Our third density was, in some ways, a simpler experience than the one which faces you at this time because of there being more of a consensus within the entire population concerning the choice of polarity. However, when the veil drops at the beginning of a third-density incarnation there is no possibility that any can proceed through the incarnative experience in a state of calm and peace.

So the first thing that we would like to focus upon is the situation, for it is the situation of third density that is at once its glory and its horror. It is seen as a glory for those outside the incarnation looking at the incarnative possibilities in learning and in service for those who undergo the veil of forgetting. It can be a horror when experienced within incarnation, especially when the tempo of confusion becomes so hectic that there is no longer any island of safety for the emotional and spiritual self but, rather, all seems completely involved in a desperate confusion.

Thusly, it is well to look at the basics of the situation, to begin to see into why you as a soul would have chosen to put yourself into the way of such suffering as you now experience. May we say that the stories that we spin are our suppositions and not fact, but we suppose that the Creator said to Itself, "I desire to know Myself." We suppose that it is this desire that birthed creation. This Creator, wishing to know Itself, spun out of Itself an infinite creation with an infinite number of unique souls, each of which contained the Creator within it. This creation was cast into the creation of light. Thusly, you, as a creation of love, were given a creation built of light in order that you might experience the illusion of time and space and cause and effect so that in this illusory dream each unique portion of the one infinite Creator could become an experiencer, a reasoner, a source of information for the infinite Creator about Itself.

Many things have been projected by entities within your third density and in many other densities concerning the nature of the one infinite Creator. And many are the commands of various religions concerning behavior towards the one infinite Creator. But, in truth, it was not that the Creator wished to be loved but, rather, that It wished to know Itself. Curiosity, then, the desire to know more, is built into the one infinite Creator's nature. It is only reasonable, therefore, that the infinite Creator would choose, at some point, to give Its souls free will.

The way that the densities of light were set up was that there was an octave of steadily increasing density of light and that there would be creatures native to each density that would be able to experience, express and communicate the nature of their experience to the one infinite Creator. These densities begin, in our system of describing them, with the first density, which is elemental, the density of rock, of earth, wind, fire, and water, of sky and sea. Those things which seem quite inanimate, yet they are fully vibrating with the love and the light of the one infinite Creator.

The second density is that density of reaching towards the light. And the natives of that density are your plant and animal kingdoms. They are not aware of self, yet they are aware of the light, and they move towards it.

The third density is the one of which you are now a part. It has often been called the density of choice. The reason for this descriptive name is that this is the density wherein consciousness itself, that is, the soul that you are, takes a second-density physical vehicle and attaches itself within that fleshly temple to experience the limitations of time and space, to experience the first awareness of self by self. In this third density, and only in third density, does the veil of forgetting drop as each soul incarnates into a physical vehicle. This density is full of confusion and is designed that way. And we will come back to this point.

The remaining densities are the fourth density, which many have called the density of understanding but which we would call the density of love; fifth density, in which souls take on themselves lessons of wisdom; sixth density, which is the density of unity, where love and wisdom find the way to meld and become one. This density is the first density wherein the positive and the negative paths are reconciled and all paradoxes solved. The seventh density has been called the density of foreverness, for in this final density before the octave souls spend their last days looking backwards and finally, full of spiritual gravity, are pulled back into the heart of the one infinite Creator to become quiescent and held completely in potential, only to be flung out again at the beginning of the next creation to experience more, to express more, and to inform the one infinite Creator of Its own nature.

In third density you are at the beginning of a three density walk, either on the positive path or the negative path, the path of service to others or the path of service to self. The choice of which path to follow is an extremely central part of what you as a soul hoped that you would successfully grapple with in this incarnation. Looking at this incarnative experience from before or after it the issues are clearly seen. Every human condition contains a lesson in love that can be taken either positively or negatively. Indeed, it is sometimes difficult but always possible to look at the present moment and find the love that is within that moment. This is often very subtle work and, meanwhile, very unsubtle confusion tends to reign.

Let us look at this confusion, for within each heart within this circle we see a puzzlement, a sincere wishing that there would not be so much confusion, and yet it is the specific purpose of third density to create massive and persistent confusion. You see, each of you came into incarnation with a clear set of lessons to learn and service to offer. You laid down relationships and situations that would produce the most catalyst and would offer you the most efficient possible opportunities to increase your polarity and to share your gifts. You also provided yourself with what this instrument would call a personality shell. And within that personality shell you offered to yourself the amount of intelligence that you thought would be helpful in order for you to do those things which you came to do. Consequently, the human situation is a soul who does not remember its lessons, does not know what service it came to offer, [and] is placed in what will continue to be, until the incarnation is through, a constant cyclical sea of confusion.

The personality shell, you see, has one aspect that can be very difficult to control. That aspect is the mind. The emotions of self, whether instinctual and second-density in origin, or whether of third-density origin, have a truth to them that does not depend upon the veil of forgetting. The feelings that each seeker has are trustable to a far greater extent than that which the mind puts out in the way of thoughts. Let us explain.

The intellectual mind is a portion of the personality shell and is designed to solve problems. The mind is an either/or instrument. It is designed to look at a situation and make a choice. On the surface of life, on the matter of whether to go straight or turn right, whether to keep an appointment or to change it, this choice-making equipment works very well. When the intellectual mind is dealing with the physical creation and the creations of humankind, the society and relationships, and so forth, this mind works well. However, this density is the density of the soul's awakening to an awareness of itself. So there comes that moment within the incarnational experience when the seeker realizes that something has changed, that there is a comfortable nest in which she seems to be sleeping so well, and, suddenly, she woke up. And she got up and she stretched and looked longingly at that nest and could no longer see it. This is the experience of awakening to the metaphysical nature of the self. It is a dislocating experience because it means that you are now the inhabitant of a completely different creation than the creation that you enjoyed up until the moment of awakening.

The creation into which the seeker awakes is the metaphysical universe. In the physical universe the goals tend to be achievements, things that can be done. In the metaphysical universe the issues have to do with essence and being. In this universe it is thoughts that are the deeds. It is intention and desire that are the actions.

Consequently, when the intellectual mind tends to analyze a situation that is metaphysical in nature it can only be effectual with the careful overseeing of the deeper self, that is, the more true nature of you. In other words, as a metaphysical entity, a citizen of eternity and infinity, you then turn and look back at the human situation, not with an idea to solve the situation, but with the idea to hone your intentions, your desires, and your vibration. Priorities for a metaphysical seeker are completely switched from the priorities of the physical person. And this is very confusing. Naturally, the soul tends to move back and forth between the two worlds and attempts to harmonize physical agendas and metaphysical agendas—and may we say that both physical and metaphysical agendas are valuable and are valuable equally. For you did not come into this density of choice to be aloof, wise and in control. You came into this experience so that you might surprise yourself and the infinite Creator. You came to experience new things and give yourself new catalyst to chew over and make into deep experience.

Let us look at a "for instance." This instrument was speaking about the irritation and aggravation that she felt at discovering that she was going to have a very sore hand at the same moment that she needed her hands to do a service that she truly wished to do. As a physical entity, this can only be bad news. As a metaphysical entity, there was almost immediately seen to be good news involved in the situation, for it asked both of the instrument and the instrument's mate that they put aside those things that they had previously planned to do and those methods of doing them that they had previously contemplated. And they were given the opportunity to work together or to find catalyst with each other of a negative nature to the point where they decided that they could not work together. In this instance, each of these seekers chose a high road, and, consequently, the experience of increased limitation has almost seemed to be rather an experience of increased freedom, the freedom to grow closer, to accomplish things as one being, to find the heart of cooperation and sympathy.

May we say that in many, many cases the lessons of love do not involve the great boon of companionship. In many cases the catalyst comes to one who must deal with it by oneself, or seemingly by oneself. And there is a tremendous loneliness and isolation that is felt by those who are adrift in the sea of confusion for one reason or another. Yet, we say to you that when you are at your lowest point, when hope seems to be the dimmest, then is the creative moment, the moment of unlimited possibility. For it is into the darkness that light must shine. Just as the trees in the winter stretch the roots down into the darkness and reach the naked limbs of winter to the sky, each of you has times of rooting darkness, times when it seems truly the Dark Night of the Soul.

And it is in just situations that the intellectual mind is finally brought to a standstill, is finally defeated, and knows that it cannot solve spiritual problems. And when that occurs the way of working moves from the head to the heart. Do not feel that you are less than an excellent seeker if you spend much time within your intellectual mind. You gave yourself a powerful intellectual mind in order to help with the confusion. But note the dark time when finally you listen to your heart and write it down as a red letter day, for when you come into your heart, and when you let your heart do your thinking, the intuitions that can arise can truly seem to simplify and harmonize the experience of being in the dark and being confused.

It is not that the heart is a place of explanation, for it is not. What is in the heart is your deeper self. What is in the heart ultimately is the one infinite Creator, and this is a Creator who has learned one thing for sure so far in Its infinite creations and that is that It loves each and every creation that It has made with a love that is so deep and so pure that the tiniest iota of skin or hair or thought or idea that occurs is important to the one infinite Creator. You cannot bore the one infinite Creator. It is endlessly fascinated by and interested in each of Its souls.

Thusly, when all human habitation fails to comfort or to simplify there is that tabernacle within the heart to which you may go in meditation, in contemplation, in prayer. In a moment of remembrance you may suddenly be in the light, bursting with joy and peace, and aware that things will rise, things will occur, and things will pass away. And that the one infinite Creator and you will be just fine in weal or woe, in life or death, moving through all of the interesting confusions and conundrums of everyday life. When you live in the heart you shall still be confused, but you shall not begrudge that confusion so deeply. Nor shall you find yourself in the state of irritation for as long a time, for the heart, in its intuitive way, has a kindness, a gentleness when the mind would cut with its sharp edges.

This is a great and central learning, and there is more to say concerning it, but we feel that we have made a good beginning. And we feel that it is a good point at which we shall pause and transfer this contact to the one known as Jim, for we are aware that there are still questions that you wish to bring up at this time, and this instrument is asking us to keep our speeches to a certain time limit. We understand this need and, truly, we know we have too many words. So, consequently, at this time we would transfer this contact to the one known as Jim. We would thank this instrument for its service and leave it in love and in light. We are those of Q'uo.

(Jim channeling)

I am Q'uo, and greet each again in love and in light through this instrument. At this time it is our privilege to offer ourselves in the further attempt to respond to those queries which those present may have for us. Is there another query at this time?

M: I have a question. With this six month automobile thing I'm doing, because it is a karmic relationship with another person, I don't know how to proceed at this point because I don't seem to be getting anywhere. I have tied up almost half a year's income, so it may sound silly, but something I've been pondering for quite a while.

I am Q'uo, and am aware of your query, my sister. When one finds that there is the confusion as to the next steps to take upon the journey of seeking it is well to consider the situation in which you find yourself and to utilize the facilities of the conscious mind to their fullest extent so that that which can be known is known to you. Then take the time from your daily round of activities each day, to retire in [to] meditation that those questions that have been asked consciously may sink further into the deeper portions of your mind and that connections [may] be made with those pre-incarnative choices which have been guiding you in a more or less clear fashion. And simply await the speaking of your own heart, of the Creator which moves inside of you. When you have stilled yourself to a point deep enough and regularly enough—and no one can say when this point is—but when it comes you will know it, then the direction will be made clear to you that you might move in the confidence of the one infinite Creator.

Is there a further query, my sister?

M: No. Thank you.

I am Q'uo, and we thank you, my sister.

Carla: Could I follow that up?

I am Q'uo, and we would be happy for you to do that, my sister.

Carla: When there is a money problem when it looks like you are going to lose everything, what do you suppose could be the lesson involved?

M: Not to put all your eggs in one basket?

I am Q'uo, and am aware of your query, my sister. When one seeks the highest path possible for the incarnation, one is then saying …

(Tape change.)

… When one has chosen the highest path for the incarnation, then one is saying to the self that all else must be subservient to that choice of love, whatever it may be. One must be willing to risk the loss of those things which may seem, for the moment, to be more important than following the path which is closest to the heart's desire. This is where the symbol of the Fool within your system of the tarot is seen to be walking from the cliff to be suspended in midair, ready to fall. However, the faith of the Fool sustains the next step, and the next, and the next.

Is there a further query, my sister?

M: No. Thank you. That was very comforting.

I am Q'uo, and again we thank you, my sister. Is there another question at this time?

Carla: I would like to read four questions from R, if that is all right. First, "I am vulnerable to being used by people who are more self-serving because I am lonely and want to be of service. I feel manipulated. What can I do?"

I am Q'uo, and am aware of your query, my sister. Again, we find that for each seeker of truth it is most salient and centrally necessary to take that time from the daily round of activities and to retire within the meditative state so that one may see the direction in which the feet are moving, may reassess, if necessary, the direction, the desire, the motivation. And, then, if there is the need for the movement in another direction that would balance that which was first chosen, then to place the feet there and to move in confidence there. We cannot choose for any, for this is the honor and duty of each: to make those choices that carry the metaphysical weight, shall we say, in the life pattern. We say to each that each within the heart knows the next step, the next, and the next. The daily round of activities within your current illusion is such that the frantic pace of existence often causes a blurring of the vision to the heart. Many do not seek the wisdom of the heart because of the commitment to the daily round of activities. We would ask each to look therein on a regular basis that one may develop a clear communication, with the heart, the intuition, the portion of the self that still moves in unity with all.

Is there a further query, my sister?

Carla: Yes, Q'uo. R asks, "It takes time for me to assimilate whole new concepts such as I have found in your group and to stay centered while I am doing that."

I am Q'uo, and am aware of your query, my sister. Each seeker will approach the learning of that which is set before him or her in an unique fashion. Allow the self to move in the way and at the speed which is comfortable for the self. Do not place too many demands upon the efficiency or the speediness of the learning process.

Is there a further query, my sister?

Carla: I hear that, Q'uo. R says that he is sensing to, "Do this, or don't do that," in his meditations. "Is this my imagination? How can I tell good suggestions from bad suggestions?"

I am Q'uo, and am aware of your query, my sister. As one develops the pattern of the daily meditation and becomes comfortable with the sitting within the silence and the seeking with the heart, there is the first inspiration that moves one in this or that direction. We would suggest that each entity move as the heart instructs, with the understanding that this is not a precise science, that there may be the times when one is uncertain, that the outcome of an action does not seem to be what was hoped for. Yet, we encourage each to reinforce the faith that the heart does know that which is needed. And as the seeking of the conscious self is more and more consciously and subconsciously sought in the daily round of activities and in the meditations that that which is the product of the seeking in the meditation may be followed with confidence and one may find that the feet are placed upon the firm ground though one may not consciously recognize the territory into which one has moved.

Is there another query, my sister?

Carla: Just to follow up with that: What you are saying is that with the faith you have to walk into the midair before the faith can kick in?

I am Q'uo, and am aware of your query, my sister. Indeed, each seeker must call upon the quality of faith again and again within the life pattern. This calling upon faith is that type of seeking which builds upon itself a kind of metaphysical momentum, shall we say. As one moves at first, the movement tends to be hesitant, not quite sure, timid, yet desirous of building the faith necessary to continue to move. And so the movement in faith does just this. The metaphysical muscles are built as are the physical muscles, with exercise.

Is there another query, my sister?

Carla: There is, but I would like to follow up on this question first. How do you balance moving in faith and discriminating?

I am Q'uo, and am aware of your query, my sister? We must pause briefly that this instrument be allowed to re-focus.

(Pause)

I am Q'uo, and am again with this instrument. The discrimination of which you speak is that which each entity is in the process of learning. The following of intuition, the movement according to inspiration, the ability to discriminate with some certainty of success, are all skills which are learned through the exercise of same. There are those times when the intellectual mind will enter the doubt or the fear and the process will become confused. This is the common practice when an entity is first becoming aware of the need to move the self by the heart rather than only by the head, shall we say.

Is there a further query, my sister?

Carla: Yes. Do they have difficulty understanding Earth problems and situations … but you already answered that, so you don't have to answer further. R also wants to say that he knows that you are trying to help him and he wants to thank you with all his heart.

I am Q'uo, and we also would thank the one known as R for offering these heartfelt queries to us and to this group. Is there another query at this time?

S: A couple of sessions back I was unable to attend and a couple of questions which were asked for me were lost and unrecorded. The first one was [about] my wife. She seems to be at a crossroads in her life. Work no longer gives her the same joy and satisfaction. She seems to think that her life should go in a different direction and she does not know where. She has physical ailments with her back and her feet that are not getting better. There is a lot of frustration and I don't know how to help. What can I do? How can I help? What suggestions or opinions do you have to help her?

I am Q'uo, and am aware of your query, my brother. We would again suggest that the meditative state is that place within each entity's experience where the self may face the self and seek the heart of self most lucidly. We would recommend for any such entity seeking the answer for the deepest questions of the incarnation that the meditative state is that place where such may be sought with security and with a certainty that can be found in no other experience. The entity of which you speak suffers the pains to those portions of the body used carrying heavy weights. The entity is aware of the weight upon the shoulders. The entity seeks the new direction but is unable to find the new path to travel until it is able to make the choice to leave the old path behind. This again requires the kind of faith that the Arcanum Number 22, the Fool, expresses as it moves in midair. Thus, we would recommend that this entity seek in the quiet times the depth of its heart's desire. Here the entity will find the direction pointed for the new movement. And yet the entire direction awaits the choice by the entity to no longer carry the weight that it now carries.

Is there a further query, my brother?

S: Yes, my youngest daughter at times seems to be fascinated with my mother, who died 11 years to the very day that she was born. What are the dynamics of her interest?

I am Q'uo, and am aware of your query, my brother. We wish to serve without infringing upon free will, and in this instance we find that we must choose our words carefully. The experience of the young entity's fascination with the one which came before it is the one which is supposed or surmised by those closest to it. More than this we cannot say at this time.

Is there another query at this time?

S: You many times say that you do not want to interfere with free will. It reminds me of the Hindu story of two men in a boat and one falls into the water. The man in the boat does not help him and says that it is his karma to drown. It might have been the other person's karma to save him. How do you know when you may infringe on free will?

I am Q'uo, and am aware of your query, my brother. We look at the choices which have been made by the entity in question. If the entity has begun to utilize the catalyst which has been placed before it in a direction which needs only confirmation in some degree, then we feel free to speak. If the entity has not yet used enough of the catalyst placed before it to be able to make this beginning choice, then we feel it is an infringement for us to make it for the entity.

Is there a further query, my brother?

S: Since they are using two tapes now, what caused both tapes to fail at the same time a couple of sessions ago?

I am Q'uo, and am aware of your query, my brother. We find that one tape failed due to a mechanical malfunction. We find that the primary tape failed due to the interference of one within the circle of seeking.

Is there a further query, my brother?

S: I have had problems with my eyes [from] just before Christmas and, since I don't "do sick," it really caught my attention. I was afraid that I might have missed the point of something that was presented to me. I might be thick in the head and just missed something. Could you comment on that, please?

I am Q'uo, and am aware of your query, my brother. In this instance we find that you were responding to a responsibility which had been placed on your shoulders which you wished was not so and in this instance refused to see a way of accomplishing this responsibility in a timely manner.

Is there another query, my brother?

S: A week ago my 20-year-old niece was in a very serious car accident and at a time in which our family was going to get together and heal wounds that had been out there for a long time. Her serious injuries have been a shock to all the family and could you tell me what were the dynamics to be learned and what are the effects for the family and my niece, particularly?

I am Q'uo, and am aware of your query, my brother. We find that the experience of the car accident involving your niece is one which may yet enable the harmonizing of difficulties within the larger family as it has become a focus point for the various entities of the family to gather about. For the one which has suffered the limitation of the physical vehicle due to the accident we would suggest that there are possible choices that this entity is now able to make, of necessity, that were receding, shall we say, from its conscious grasp as the direction it was moving its life pattern into was somewhat astray from that hoped before the incarnation began.

One may look to various other entities to see how such limitations may aid the overall incarnative process of seeking. The one known as Carla, for example, suffered the limitation of the physical vehicle due to the onset of juvenile rheumatoid [arthritis] at an early age within its incarnation, which had the effect of forcing its awareness into the self, that the meditative state, the contemplative, and the prayerful states be those which took precedence in the incarnation of the entity and allowed it to move into those areas which it has explored as its service ever since. The one known as Franklin Delano Roosevelt, as those who have read *The Ra Material* have understood, chose the paralysis of the lower portions of its physical vehicle as a balancing to the lack of compassion which it had shown to others in its rise to a powerful position. Thus, the limitation of the physical vehicle reignited a compassion within this entity for those about it.

When the physical vehicle is so limited in its ability to carry out its normal functions that it can no longer do so without the aid of others then one may see the necessity of the others' aid as being a significant portion of the incarnational pattern of the injured entity. The ability to give and to receive the vibrations of love may be learned in such a situation. The non-movement of the physical vehicle may also cause the entity to reinforce the looking within that we spoke of when referring to the one known as Carla. The initial response of the entity to this possibility may or may not be the recognition of its value but may, instead, be the complete denial of this need. Each seeker will need to work with the catalyst which is placed before it in the fashion which is most comfortable to it even though this working with catalyst may seem quite chaotic and destructive in its beginning stages.

Is there another query, my brother?

S: I am reminded of my father who had problems with his knees. Hilarion channeled that problems with one's knees is like an individual being cut off or not seeing his higher self. Could this be a somewhat similar situation?

I am Q'uo, and am aware of your query, my brother. And, indeed, this was the point to which we referred to when we spoke of this entity's need of the reevaluation of the incarnation and the partaking in the accident as being the catalyst which would bring this need to the fore.

Is there another query, my brother?

S: I recently finished Book Five of *The Law of One*, and I was wondering if you could tell us what Don Elkins is doing these days?

I am Q'uo, and am aware of your query, my brother, though we are not able to answer this query due to our desire to refrain [from infringing] upon the free will of some of those present.

Is there a further query, my brother?

S: I notice with physical exercise I don't seem to be very flexible and I was wondering if my physical inflexibility might indicate a mental inflexibility. Could you comment on that?

I am Q'uo, and am aware of your query, my brother. In this instance we would suggest that the physical inflexibility is more a product of a lack of use than the reflection of any mental inflexibility that may have an effect on the physical body.

Is there a further query, my brother?

S: Recently I fell and jammed two of my fingers and they were sore for many days and I could not think what I had done to cause it to feel such pain. What was going on there?

I am Q'uo, and … we correct this entity. The energy grows low. We are those of Q'uo, and are aware of your query, my brother. The awareness of the increased pain of your physical vehicle is a symptom of the overloading of that area of the physical vehicle in such a manner that the pain is accentuated according to the weariness of that portion of your vehicle.

Is there a further query, my brother?

S: Yes. There was some music that I had purchased called, "The Wing Makers." There were ten selections and I was told there were thirteen other selections available. Could you tell me where I could get those selections?

I am Q'uo, and though we are aware of your query, my brother, we find that we are unable to find a "search.com."

Is there any further query?

S: Yeah. When are you going to get an e-mail address?

We are those of Q'uo, and we are most grateful to each entity for calling our presence this day to this circle of seeking and would wish to speak at greater length to this group but find that the energy of this particular instrument grows low and, thus, we must take our leave of this instrument and this group. We leave each in the love and in the light of the one infinite Creator. We are know to you as those of Q'uo. Adonai, my friends. Adonai. ❧

Sunday Meditation
February 20, 2000

Group question: The question this week has to do with the concept of guides. We are wondering what is the best way for anyone who wants to get in touch with his or her guide to do that? And we are also wondering, if we are trying to get in touch with our guides and looking at our guides as something outside of ourselves, does that influence or affect our ability to get in touch with our guides? And if we are able to get in touch with our guides, does that add a responsibility to our life pattern?

(Carla channeling)

We are those of the principle known to you as Q'uo. Greetings in the love and in the light of the one infinite Creator. It is a blessing and a privilege to be called to you this afternoon. We wish to thank each of you for joining this circle of seeking and for calling us to your group. It is a great blessing for us to be able to share our opinions and thoughts and you greatly serve us by enabling us to offer our service, for this is the way that we are attempting to be of service at this time. As always, we would ask that you consider each of our thoughts to see if they resonate with your own needs, for we are not those in authority but, rather, your brothers and sisters who walk the same dusty path and make many mistakes. Thusly, take what is useful to you from what we say and leave the rest. We suggest that you do this with all sources of information. For truly, your inner discrimination will be that which resonates to what is right for you, which brings us to your requested topic, that of connecting with your guidance. For guidance is always available and there are many ways in which one may frame the search for becoming more and more skillful at the using of it.

To put this question in context we would like to talk about the worldly versus the metaphysical universe. The dilemma of those who wish to live their lives from a metaphysical point of view is that this metaphysical universe is not the universe in which consensus reality, or the physical reality you experience day by day, takes place. The concerns of the outer world can absorb all of one's time and attention. And, indeed, many there are upon your sphere who manage to move from birth to the end of an entire incarnation without even once suspecting that there is another universe which interpenetrates the physical universe whose laws are of a higher order than those of the physical universe. However, for most people there are at least one or two times during an incarnation when it is brought clearly to one's attention that there is a higher order of reality and that it sometimes affects physical reality.

For those who are gathered today there is a complete awareness of and a desire and yearning for that second universe of higher truth. Further, the body which carries you about contains what this instrument has called a biocomputer, the earthly brain, the choice-maker brain, that is built specifically to deal with the either/or questions of survival, protection of home and family, and the other concerns of the earthly life. The guidance system for the earthly brain is difficult to describe in earthly terms, but the word, intuition, surely covers it. However, for those who wish to become serious students, who have begun their path of wandering, their seeking for a true home, this either/or mentality does not satisfy for the simple reason that it cannot satisfy the needs of the metaphysical universe. However, each of you is also, and predominantly, a consciousness, an unique entity made wholly of love and light which goes through many physical vehicles in many densities and through many experiences within each density. This consciousness which is you can dip into the earthly universe, the physical world, by virtue of being wedded through the incarnational birthing process to a second-density physical vehicle; that is, your body. This consciousness, being a citizen of eternity, being infinite in nature, is completely adapted to doing work in the metaphysical universe. And each of you has, lying in potential within you, or should we say, within your consciousness, all of the guidance and information that you need. The challenge, of course, is how to gain access to that guidance, for however framed in conceptual structure, that guidance is a denizen of the deep mind, the roots of consciousness. And the door from the deep unconscious self to the conscious self must needs be opened or set ajar in some way in order for guidance to move into the conscious realm and become available in order that you may have access to it.

It is well to remember that guidance is definitely and always there, even when you are at the most seemingly far reach from it, even when you feel most blind, deaf and dumb. The guidance is there. The guidance is awaiting for your awareness. It is a matter of unblocking the channels of communication rather than searching for something that may or may not be there. We say this because in order to access guidance it is extremely helpful to be practicing a life in faith. We do not wish to imply a certain structure to a life in faith but rather wish to look at this quality of love that is faith. Faith is a paradox, for one cannot gain faith. One simply must leap into behaving as if one had faith in order to begin a life in faith. Thusly, the first act of faith is the leap into nothingness. Faith, after all, would not be faith if there were a way to rationalize it or prove that it existed by any reasonable inquiry. This makes faith a real challenge, for if you have not faith, then how do you achieve it?

That leap looks very foolish and feels very dangerous. And, yet, we say to you that if you can hold the essence of faith which is that all is well and that all will be well, if you can hold to this attitude, that faith will grow and flourish and bloom in amazing ways. And if you become overwhelmed with a lack of faith you have but to start over to take that leap again and the journey accelerates once more. There is never a failure that faith will not be recovered from. There is never a desert that is too wide for faith to cross. In faith, then, when you wish to seek guidance, you may approach this search in various ways.

This instrument, for instance, allows guidance to come to her by praying to the Holy Spirit. This guide, which she thinks of as an aspect of her higher self and which she objectifies as a portion of the Creator, is a projection of that essence within the deep mind that can be called guidance. Therefore, to this entity does not come a conversation but, rather, a feeling, an intuition, a sense of rightness. For this instrument this degree of clarity is completely sufficient and satisfactory. For many others there is a need to objectify guidance in persons and, thusly, many entities seek their guidance in the form of guides. Again, all that there is, is one, and in many ways and on the deeper levels all that is outside of the physical being is a projected portion of that physical being. If all things are one, then all that an entity sees is part of that entity and, in one sense, a projection of that entity. Each of you, you see, lives in a complete and unique universe, a creation of your own. It is slightly different but definitely different from that universe of each and every other spark of the infinite Creator that has been sent forth. As this instrument was saying earlier, there are non religious ways to set about discovering more about the guides that bless the entity with love and the desire to be of help in a spiritual or metaphysical sense.

These projections of the self that are guides are also entities with their own identities, their own histories, and, to some degree, their own agendas. Some entities feel that they have one major guide and it is to this one entity that the self goes. Indeed, some have objectified this guide to a great extent. Each of you has seen examples of channeling from inner guides that various sources offer and each is familiar with the concept of getting in touch with the guide. The project, shall we say, of reaching to discover information is best approached within a framework of a daily rule of life that includes a period of meditation during each day. The mind in the earthly sense has that tendency to continue working whether or not there is prominent stimulation from the outer world and, thusly, the inner world can be the world of one listening to a chatterbox.

Many are the conversations entities such as this instrument have with themselves, all in the imagination. And this energy generally moves according to the laws of inertia. It simply keeps going because that is what the mental biocomputer does. It runs. It operates. It is noisy. The idea, then, is to empty out the mental pockets and allow the earthly biocomputer to have a rest so that the consciousness may float free of the either/or demands of the earthly mind. Without the regular, habitual and persistent use of meditation it is very difficult to learn to stop the mind from running. And when the mind is running the deeper guidance is very difficult to contact.

Thusly, in order to prepare the ground for connecting with guidance it is a very skillful idea to place the self in the act of meditation. This is a tremendous commitment and it is a life-changer. This entity, for instance, is fond of saying that she does not meditate well. What she means is that she cannot completely shut off her earthly brain. Bits of conversations and music continue to filter through all efforts to shut down the noise of the mind. However [true], this objective concept of the self as not being good at meditating [is], this instrument would be the first to express the powerful work that meditation on a daily basis has wrought in her life experience. And indeed, any entity who has meditated for any length of time is aware that even a little of this silence of mind is a powerful accelerant of the process of spiritual transformation.

We would strongly recommend, therefore, that any who wish to connect with their guides do this in the context of daily meditational periods. Remember that although each of you came into incarnation fully aware of all of this that we are saying, during the birthing process the veil of forgetting dropped neatly and usually completely over the consciousness so that within the incarnation the path back to the metaphysical universe must be retraced step by step, and, in addition to the general confusion of the Earth plane, much must be unlearned from the standpoint of the metaphysical universe that is included in the cultural training of young entities. Many are those who have said that adulthood is that period wherein one attempts to undo the damage sustained during childhood. Much needs to be unlearned as the view shifts from the earthly and physical to the non-earthly and metaphysical. In one universe there are things, tables, people, planets, stars. In the other universe there are energies, thoughts, ideals, and as a metaphysical entity you are one who *is*, as opposed to the physical entity which [is one who] *does*.

Guidance is that connection between the metaphysical and physical universes which translates complex information concerning destiny and desire into earthly terms which steps down the energy of the cosmos so that the self within incarnation can accept energy and intuition and essence and open the mind to the translation that guidance will make of these things in offering them to the conscious mind.

The one known as R wondered if it would matter as to how one framed the request for this guidance and we may say that, indeed, this is so. If one frames the search for advice and wisdom as a search for guides, then it is very likely that entities, as opposed to energies, will be contacted. We may say that it is very difficult to express the nature of these essences and energies that are guides and guidance. Take, for instance, [that] of angels. Angels are another way of describing inner plane guides. When entities over a long period of time think along the same patterns and constructions of thought there is created by such thought the reality that such thought embodies. Thoughts become things and guidance becomes angelic. And it becomes true that for each entity there are several angels.

If we were to go through each culture and its religious beliefs we would find the channels and pathways by which that body of entities that believed in that wise perceived their guidance to be housed or contained within. And, thus, you have fairies and genies and inner planes masters and so forth. [There are] as many different ways to contact guides and guidance as there have been groups of people, or entities by themselves, who were seeking in a certain way with certain needs. What you may depend upon is that you fashioned for yourself, before incarnation, triggers [whose nature] would depend [upon] your appreciation and your awareness of the guidance that you need. As you seek for your guidance you need to follow that intuition that you have within you and those feelings that come from the heart. For it is the wisdom of the heart which often expresses through emotion only, that is the kind of beast, as this instrument would say, that guidance truly is. It is not an intellectual source. Guidance is not heavy on logic. Guidance can be paradoxical and, in many ways, can offer varying views on the same subject. What guidance is, as we said, is connections made within the self that enable the content of the deep mind to be moved close enough to the conscious mind that a translation of concepts into words and thoughts may take place. So what you are doing is asking the self to release the physical universe from consciousness and to move down into the roots of mind. Meditation is the specific way that we would suggest that this movement down into the roots of mind be approached.

Each entity will have a different experience when attempting to create the habit of daily meditation. For some entities it is a procedure that is very easy. Some entities offer to themselves within incarnation the gift of a quiet mind and economical thoughts, and for such entities meditation seems almost a natural way of life. For others, it seems most unnatural and is correspondingly difficult to create as a habit and, yet, we say to you that regardless of the subjective experience while gaining that habit of silence within each day, the progress is being made. It may feel as though one is coming up against a solid brick wall and going nowhere. We assure each that this is not so, that if the time is put in and the desire is true, the meditation periods will do their work and situations will begin to appear in a more lucid clarity. As the one known as Tom said earlier, it is not that the situation changes. It is that the response to the situation begins to change, which alters the situation, not for any other necessarily, but only for the self. Yet, since all metaphysical work is work on the self, this is a completely satisfactory situation.

We would suggest that it is well to develop one's personal way of approaching guidance, to put some time and concern in on clarifying to the self what is truly desired, what is truly sought, where the passion and the intensity of one's life is. For this process of seeking guidance and of listening to that guidance is an important part of accelerating the pace of your spiritual evolution. You will evolve spiritually regardless of what you do. The Creator's universe is somewhat efficient. Catalyst happens. Experience is gained. You do change. However, each of you is hungry for a faster pace of transformation, a more secure feeling that one is on one's way, that one is on the path. And certainly the whole process of meditation and of listening within that silence is central. We wish each of you the joy of finding your desires, of honing and sharpening those desires, and of seeking guidance in the pursuit of that thirst for truth, for love, for the Creator.

Remember that you may be part of others' guidance systems and you may not know it. Remember that when services small or large are done with love they will provide guidance regardless of who else is aware of your actions. When energy is put out it is not ignored, so that even if you do not know that you are guiding and the entity does not know that he is being guided by you, yet still this energy transfer will take place. So, at all times be aware of the ethical considerations involving relationships with others, for you do not know what service you might provide by simply being yourself.

We are with you in the silence. We sit with you in the darkness of the mind. There is love in that darkness. Know that it is there. Have the faith that your search is a good one, and allow. That is the word that opens the door once the silence is achieved. That word, allow. Allow the intuition to arise. Allow the still, small voice to speak. You will not hear, for it is silent. You can only act upon faith with that feeling of rightness.

We would at this time transfer this contact to the one known as Jim, thanking this instrument and leaving it in the love and in the light of the one infinite Creator. We are those of Q'uo.

(Jim channeling)

I am Q'uo, and greet each again in the love and in the light of the one Creator. It is our privilege at this time to offer ourselves in an attempt to speak to any further queries which those present may have for us. Is there any other query at this time to which we may speak?

T: I have had, for the last three or four weeks, several very strong dreams by spirit guides or guidance, and they are nudging me in a couple of directions. Away from a couple of things and towards a couple of things. I wondered what you could tell me about these dreams.

(Tape change.)

I am Q'uo, and am aware of your query, my brother. The experiences of which you speak are the natural function of the subconscious mind as it is working in tandem with the conscious experience due to the intense desire upon your part to know the appropriate steps to take in matters that are of importance to you in relationship with others. When the conscious mind has long sought a direction in which to move and has with an open heart found a kind of vulnerability, shall we say, then the subconscious mind moves through this desire and vulnerability and offers to the conscious mind the images and clues of the dream state. In this state there is the ability to impress upon the conscious mind a tendency, a direction, in which one may appropriately move one's being. We recommend that this dialogue with your subconscious mind be attended to so that the conversation might be attended to.

Is there another query, my brother?

T: No. Thank you very much.

I am Q'uo, and we thank you, my brother. Is there another query at this time?

Carla: I often get requests for questions to be asked by people who are not here. Is that a satisfactory thing to do? Or should people have to be here in order to ask questions?

I am Q'uo, and am aware of your query, my sister. We find that it is quite acceptable for queries to be asked of us for those who are not able to attend these sessions of working, and we are quite happy to give the best response that is possible without infringing upon free will.

Is there a further query, my sister?

Carla: Is there anything that I can do to prepare the mind of the person who is not present and is having a question asked for him that would help you in the answering?

I am Q'uo, and am aware of your query, my sister. The simple informing of such an entity that we desire to be of true service and that is a service which does not infringe upon free will is all that is necessary in this instance.

Carla: Thank you so much, Q'uo.

I am Q'uo, and we thank you, my sister. Is there another query at this time?

S: On previous sessions you mentioned that you have talked with this group and with others. Can you discuss some of the other groups that you talk with?

I am Q'uo, and am aware of your query, my brother. There are few groups such as this one that we actually speak with in the words of your culture. Many such groups are there around this sphere who in their meetings and meditations are inspired in images and what you would call intuition and hunches by those of our group and by those of others within the Confederation of Planets in the Service of the One Creator. The channeling process is one which is, though widely used in this culture at this time, one which we are able to pursue in only a few instances, for there is the need for anyone serving as an instrument to proceed in that service in a certain fashion which requires dedication and perseverance.

Is there a further query, my brother?

S: Is there any means that we can help you by as you help others? A kind word or encouragement or similar means that we in third density are more able to do that might be of help to your service?

I am Q'uo, and am aware of your query, my brother. We salute the desire to serve others in whatever way is possible for in any entity such as yourself and all those gathered in this circle there is a possibility of sharing information and inspiration with those that one meets in the daily round of activities. Indeed, each entity has the opportunity and the potential to serve as a beacon of light, as one who inspires faith and love in other entities. It is said often within your culture, and we find it true, that there is no end of good that a smile can do, for as each entity moves more frenetically in the pace of the culture oftentimes the simplest of courtesies are neglected and when remembered bring a great deal of encouragement to those entities with whom a smile is shared. To speak to another who has experienced a loss of significance, a difficulty in growth, a pain of the physical vehicle, and so forth, is a very helpful thing to do. Wherever there is the seed of love planted then there is a greater possibility of the open heart growing to fruition.

Is there another query at this time?

S: I have read about the planet Niberu which has a 3,600 year orbit in this solar system. Can you tell us how the catalyst from this planet will affect this world?

I am Q'uo, and though we understand that query which you ask, we are unable to speak to this query in any direct sense.

Is there another query at this time?

M: I would like to ask about kundalini energy and how we can grow from that energy and that type of meditation in yoga. Also what that energy can bring about in our growth.

I am Q'uo, and am aware of your query, my sister. The experience of the rising of the kundalini energy is one which is most powerful in its onset and requires that the entity which is undergoing this increase in awareness be most balanced, especially in the lower energy centers, that is, the red, the orange, and the yellow. For it is these centers of energy that form the foundation for the movement upward through the rest of the centers of energy. If this experience is undertaken without a proper balance in these centers there is the possibility of the loss of balance in the overall sense for the entity experiencing this growing awareness.

We would recommend that for any entity that is hopeful of igniting that [that] there be a careful examination of its own lower energy centers so that its ability to handle the increase of energy will be stable and remain so as the energy progresses through each ascending center. This may be undertaken in a daily pattern, shall we say, where the entity retires in meditation at the end of the day, looking at the experiences which have left their mark on the mind for that day and balancing each imbalance with its opposite so that the foundation is securely laid. This may take some of your time, for it is not a quick or easy process but one which takes dedication and repetition.

Is there a further query, my sister?

M: No. Thank you so much.

I am Q'uo, and we thank you my sister. Is there another query at this time?

S: Recently I had a period of twenty-four hours where my gums were swollen and infected and I had to seek medical attention for it. I am still mystified for what the catalyst was for that, and is there a better, more direct way to get my attention?

I am Q'uo, and it is in such a case as this one that we find ourselves unable to move very far with our response, for the experience of which you speak is one which, as you have said, is one which has left you mystified. It is such a mystery that provides you with the opportunity to begin the process of untangling, shall we say, the origin of such pain and suffering. When there is no beginning within the seeker's mind of the cause of such an experience we find, then, that we must remain mostly silent in order not to infringe upon free will by putting in the mind that which was not already there. However, we might suggest in this instance that you look at the energy center which is located at the point of your pain and begin there with a consideration of words spoken and the value of such.

Is there a further query, my brother?

S: No. Thank you.

I am Q'uo, and, again, we thank you, my brother. Is there another query at this time?

R: No question. Just wanted to thank Q'uo for looking after our free will and for the diligence in attempting to answer our questions, as repetitive as they seem to be.

I am Q'uo, and we are grateful for your words of support, my brother. For we are, indeed, hopeful of being of service with our humble words to this group and are also aware of the difficulties that each experiences in the daily round of activities. It is often a paradox that we observe entities which move with a great desire to be of service and in their desire to serve they stumble across this or that which seems to block the service, then, experiencing the blockage of service, ask all who may hear the cause of the blockage. When one wishes to serve such an entity it is apparently easier to give the answer rather than to withhold it and allow the entity to discover for itself in a manner which will carry true weight within the entity's total being than to simply experience what is given by another. Thus, the table we set for you is often not completely given with all courses available.

For this we apologize, for we are aware that many would rather have a simple and clear response, but in our estimation such is not always a helpful response, for entities learn most powerfully when the learning is from the self, with perhaps a clue or two from another.

Is there another query at this time?

S: To perhaps turn this around, can we answer any questions for you?

I am Q'uo, and this instrument's mind began to run wild with that one. We shall attempt to rein him in, for he was wanting to know who was going to win the Kentucky Derby. I am Q'uo, and we are without significant query.

Is there a final query for us at this time?

(No further queries.)

I am Q'uo, and we again would thank each present for inviting our presence and for putting up with our poor humor. We are always grateful to be able to walk for a moment in the world of your words. We assure you that we always accompany you in an unseen fashion and observe those gallant forays into the murky ways of the catalyst of this illusion that each of you makes each of your days, and we cannot thank you enough for your attempts to share your love and light with those who walk with you. For in this illusion at this time there are many who are in need of such inspiration and such light. None of you knows how great an effect that you have with the sharing of an open heart, a smile, an open hand, a suggestion and the simplest gestures of courtesy within your illusion.

We are those of Q'uo, and would at this time take our leave of this instrument and this group, leaving each in the love and in the light of the one infinite Creator. Adonai, my friends. Adonai. ✤

Sunday Meditation
March 5, 2000

Group question: The question this week has to do with what would be the best way to deal with criticism from another person that really hurts us, that makes us feel real bad, especially when we feel that the criticism is unjustified. As a more specific focus for that general query, we would like information on how to deal with people that are specifically trying to take our power, that we feel drained of energy by after we leave their presence?

(Carla channeling)

We are those known to you as the principle of Q'uo. Greetings in the love and the light of the one infinite Creator. We welcome each of you on this beautiful spring afternoon. Through your eyes we experience the beauty of your plant life as it blooms in the early spring chill. How beautiful your dwelling place is. We greatly appreciate being able to share your setting and meditation with you. As always, we ask that you hear everything that we say with a discerning and discriminating ear, listening for those thoughts that resonate within your own mind and heart. Keep those that do so resonate and leave the rest behind, please.

You ask this day about how to deal with situations in which an entity has said hurtful things or has treated you in such a way that you feel drained of energy or saddened or discouraged by the exchange. As we often do, we would like to take a few steps back from this specific query in order that we may talk about the background of this question. Each of you is a complex of vibrations. Your scientists can tell you this. This is not purely metaphysical truth. You are, in one way of looking at yourself, a system of energy fields. Each energy field has its life and essence and its way of interlocking with and interacting with other aspects of your energy, other fields of energy within your overall energy complex. You have spiritual energies, physical energies, emotional energies, mental energies, and these energies are a complex kind of signature that speaks your identity as clearly as your name, perhaps more clearly than the name you may share with someone else upon the planet which you now enjoy. You share the vibratory complex that you offer up at this moment with no one in the infinite creation. You are unique.

Each, seen from the viewpoint of a perfectionist, is somewhat out of balance with the self. Yet it is these eccentric balances that add to your charm and your uniqueness and enable you to offer the Creator a new and ever-changing picture of who and what It really is. Thusly, your Creator is delighted with you whether you are in happy times or in woe, whether you struggle or flow and swim easily with the current of your destiny. But to you, gazing within at your energies, there is not seen the charm and delight of your uniqueness. Rather, because as several have said this day in your discussion preceding this meditation, each has good days and bad days and there are sometimes less skillful ways in which we share our energies.

The energy system that you work with in receiving catalyst and processing it into experience is your physical body, together with the finer bodies that interpenetrate that physical body you can see, feel and touch. Often we suggest to you that it is not wise to use the logical mind, but in this particular case we encourage you when you are looking at how you are feeling with regard to another person that you do take stock, using the intellectual mind as well as the intuition, of the basic balances of the body at each center or chakra of energy. For it is at those chakras or energy centers that energy is exchanged between entities or people.

We would quickly review the basic seven energy centers we would suggest as a model for you to work with. The seven centers are the seven colors of the rainbow: red, orange, yellow, green, blue, indigo and violet. Each center has its domain and together they are as the path which the infinite energy of the one infinite Creator may travel, beginning with the red or base chakra. The first energy center that the incoming infinite light and love of the Creator touches is the red-ray energy center or chakra. To this energy center flow those issues that are the most basic: survival, the natural functions that are necessary for survival such as sexual reproduction, the achievement of a food supply, and so forth. Those who are blocked in the red-ray energy center have a straightened or narrow or low supply of energy moving throughout the rest of the energy system. Therefore, it is well, if you see some red-ray blockage within yourself, to lay all other concerns aside while you work upon this all important energy center.

The orange-ray chakra is up the spine from the red-ray chakra, in the area of the lower belly. And to this energy center come the issues of one person to another person. To this center come concerns of being controlled, or controlling others, the love of control, or the fear of control, the love of being controlled, or the fear of being controlled.

Within the solar plexus is the yellow-ray chakra or energy center and to this energy center come the issues of the self with regard to groups. You will find many family difficulties depending from this center as opposed to the orange-ray center because within the mind the family members are given a different kind of concern, attention and energy sharing than one gives acquaintances or strangers.

These three lower energy centers are very often the centers which you will find being blocked or being overstimulated when there are what this instrument would call personal problems between people. When there is a straightening or narrowing of the path of energy flow in these three centers the supply of energy reaching the heart chakra is diminished. Consequently, there is far less energy with which to respond to felt insult, offense or hurt feelings.

The higher energy centers are not those usually considered when thinking of how to deal with a difficult relationship or an unwise exchange of energy. However, it needs to be said that in the green-ray center there is great healing. In the blue-ray center of open communication even a little energy into this center can produce clear communication that is very helpful in situations sometimes. And certainly the indigo-ray center, which is that center which does work in consciousness, is one which the seeker is always attempting to use to some degree as the hope is held in the heart that the self is truly a seeker seeking for that which truly is there, as opposed to the self seen as a dreamer seeking for something that is not there, something that is only a dream. We can assure you that none of these energies or essences are at all dream related. Indeed, they are aspects of your nature that, to us, are far more real than your day-to-day experiences, for these are, as we said, the vibratory essences which are your signature in the metaphysical world. The saying that this instrument has is that you are what you eat. We would replace this adage with you are what you think.

What you ponder, what you hope, what your dream: these are more real than the day-to-day experiences on the deep level of work done in consciousness. Thusly, when you receive catalyst that seems to take your power away from you, to drain you, or seems to hurt the feelings, the first process, then, has nothing to do with any other person but, rather, has to do with working with the self to reestablish the feeling of wholeness of self that, in a metaphysical sense, implies safety. Sometimes there is fear connected with such a difficult relationship exchange. Sometimes there is anger, but, whatever the emotions are, the experience of being out of control and left to twist in the wind, shall we say, without any power, is that which needs to be looked at carefully. Think about the exchange that has taken place and, in the privacy of your own time, ask for the forgiveness that lies within you to come to aid you. You are a powerful being. Within you lie conduits that move deeper and deeper in mind until you eventually merge with the one infinite Creator. Nothing outside of you can destroy this wholeness. However, depending upon the circumstances, a difficult experience with another entity can make you feel like you are no longer whole, entire, intact or safe.

Thusly, the first work of the seeker is to reestablish the wholeness and integrity of the self. This instrument earlier suggested to one who was expressing the feeling of being drained that the physical motion of the scissors cutting be made over the energy center from which this sensation of being drained was being felt. We find this a perfectly sound suggestion because the work actually being done is being done in the metaphysical universe as opposed to the physical. You are not making motions in the air in the physical to any use. Rather, you are expressing an intention or desire in the metaphysical world, and in this universe thoughts are things and a thought pair of scissors will cut the thoughts of another who wishes to exchange energy in the sense of attempting to control or take the power of you. Thusly, once you have reestablished the integrity of your finer bodies you can begin to heal from this unwise exchange of energy.

The energy of forgiveness is one which is infinitely strong and yet very subtle. Sometimes it is difficult to pin down precisely whom you wish to forgive first. Are you upset with this other entity who has caused you seeming discomfort? Or are you more upset with yourself for being vulnerable to such unwise energy exchanges? If necessary, sit with this question in meditation and simply await a sense or a feeling of whom to forgive first. For both yourself and the other are involved in this exchange. Both are individuals, holy in their own right. The deeper truth of both beings is love. Once you are able to establish whom you need to forgive first then it is left for you to accomplish this by intention.

May we say that it is often not possible to forgive completely at the time that you would wish that all be forgiven. There are times when the disharmony within an energy center is such that such energy gets jammed and will not, shall we say, go through, much as a telephone call will not go through if the line is busy. Again, this may take time for you to work with. It is easier for you to forgive the other very often, than it is to forgive the self. It seems always that the seeker is disappointed with the self for having any problem whatsoever. It is easy to forget that the reason for incarnation, the reason for entering into a body, and entering the veil of forgetting as you do, is so that you will be confused and puzzled and have many uncomfortable experiences and undergo much suffering. This is difficult to remember when one is uncomfortable. And yet it remains true.

Once this process of forgiveness has been carried through to what you may feel satisfied with as an outcome, then it is time to begin to look to your systems of energies to see if they are, indeed, in balance. For the preparation for meeting the moment with an open heart does involve coming to a position within your energies wherein you feel relatively unblocked and able to allow the infinite energy of the one Creator to easily move through the system of energy centers traveling upwards into and then through all of the energy centers and then back out into the creation.

We took the time to go through these energy centers and to look at some of the, shall we say, high points of each center because this is a system which you can work with in many different ways. It helps to know how you are made. Any mechanism which is having difficulties remains broken until someone who knows how it is supposed to work can take it and work on it. Your metaphysical beings are such creatures. They do have a rhyme and a reason. They can, indeed, be drained of energy, and there are things that you can do to mend those broken places, but until you grasp how your energy works it is not so easy to sit down and begin to do the repairs. When you have gone through the processes of balancing and forgiveness then you are once again at peace and at rest, feeling relatively safe in your own skin. However, you remain vulnerable and this vulnerability is very, very important. It is central to the Earth experience.

We would like to frame this vulnerability in a more positive way, for each of you before incarnation was extremely eager to come into the Earth plane and to offer the life experience as a service and gift to the one infinite Creator. From a position before the dropping of the veil of forgetting you could see that you had an opportunity in the darkness of the Earth plane to live by faith. You knew that a life in faith outside of incarnation was very easy to achieve because you, like all other entities not in incarnation, were totally aware of the plan of the one infinite Creator, of the beauty of that plan, of the goodness of the adventure of attempting in a world where it was not at all obvious that love abides, that it would help your polarity tremendously to come into this darkness and to express a life lived in faith. It looked easier, by far, before incarnation than it does now. We are sure that this is an understatement for each of you. It does not look easy at all from within incarnation to deal with difficult people and situations, challenges that seem to rob you of energy.

However, all of these difficulties, all of these ways of moving beyond your ability to cope, are moments of great opportunity. For when you are beyond your ability to cope you still have one choice to make: despair or hope, giving up or digging in. Saying, "I'm finished," or saying, "I have just begun." You are entities of great power. Again and again your outer experience will seem to rob you of that power. Again and again there will be the level upon which this is accurate. There will be the level at which you have lost power and underlying this level of apparent experience is a faculty called faith. It lies like a floor that you must believe is there before you can feel it under foot. It is in times when you are helpless and hopeless and at the end of your human strength that faith will help you soar and fly far above all restraints and limitations. Faith is something that picked up weighs nothing but planted yields everything. It is in the air about you. It is in the heart within you. It is in the remembering of the mind that is disciplined to reject hopelessness, so you have good work to do when catalyst overcomes you.

Feel those feelings of helplessness, anger, grief, pain and puzzlement. Allow all of those strong emotions to wash through you, for they are cleansing to you. Moan and cry if you need to in the privacy of your own chambers. Do what you need to do to validate this experience that you are having. Don't say that it doesn't matter, because it does. These energies that you are experiencing as being drained are very real. But also move onto the next process. Invoke faith, forgiveness, and faith again. Surround and permeate yourself with faith.

The one known as Jesus the Christ wished with all its heart, all its soul, all of its strength, and all of its mind to take upon itself as it died the death of every other being in the creation. The difficulty with your doing the same thing is very simple. Is this your time to go to Jerusalem? Is this the time for you to be completely sacrificial of yourself? Do you feel that you will be of more help by being vanquished by this unwise exchange of energy, or do you feel that it would be of more service to the infinite Creator and the world in which you live for you to mend yourself, to re-establish your health, speaking metaphysically, and then to move on to further learning within this incarnation? This instrument, may we say, has at times been the martyr, offering the self in unwise energy exchange and not realizing that this was unwise. Each of you has had the temptation to be the martyr, to give of the self beyond all possible healing, until there is nothing left. You may be Christ-like. We do not say this is a poor choice. We only say consider well if you wish to remain bankrupt or if you wish to restore your own integrity.

We would suggest that, most of the time, skill lies in protecting and defending the self, metaphysically speaking, [so it] can repair its energy loss and again stand upon its own two feet, metaphysically speaking, ready once again to offer all, to love all, to serve and hold to high ideals as best as it can. New catalyst will come and new challenges, in each and every day. But you are a powerful entity. You can and you will learn more and more skill and take more and more courage, for each time that you go through the balancing, the forgiving, and the re-determining to live a life in faith, you open to yourself more of the power that lies in potential within you. You do not need to remain a victim. You may have relationship into which these periods of unwise energy exchange will come again and again. These are the relationships in the school of Earth that you prepared for yourself. You felt that you had plenty of ability to deal with these challenging personalities. You felt that you wanted to look in the mirror at these qualities within yourself projected onto others. When you are at your lowest, remember who you are. Remember the confidence you felt in yourself and then move into the ways of faith.

At this time we would transfer this contact to the one known as Jim. We thank this instrument and leave it in the love and in the light of the one infinite Creator. We are those known to you as Q'uo.

(Jim channeling)

I am Q'uo, and greet each again in love and in light through this instrument. At this time it is our privilege to offer ourselves to speak to any further queries which those present may have for us.

T: I understand the need for polarity. To experience one, you have to have the other. Most of my days are very positive but now and then I have one where I feel very negative about everything. As one becomes more positive does the need for the negative experience lessen, and when you have a number of positive experiences does that mean you need more negative to remind you where you are?

I am Q'uo, and we believe that we grasp your query, my brother. We would not suggest that there is a general rule for all entities, for the balancing process in which you are now partaking is one which you have been experiencing for some time now, where the outlook for the day, the attitude of the mind, is one which has moved in a, as you would call it, positive direction in which the joy and light of the Creator is more apparent to you because of work you have done upon yourself. On those days in which you experience the negative, the attitude [of mind] sees much of darkness about you and is the remnant of the prior perceptive abilities. Thus, you will find in your own abilities …

(Tape change.)

I am Q'uo, and am again with this instrument. To continue. There is a momentum that is possible to obtain either with the positive or the negative outlook, for as one feeds the beast, shall we say, so shall it grow. The momentum of the positive outlook for you now has begun to hold sway in a greater extent than in the past and this may be expected to continue.

Is there another question at this time?

T: No. Not at this time. Thank you.

I am Q'uo, and we thank you, my brother. Does another have a query at this time?

S: Our oldest daughter has very consciously avoided any contact with us. Phone calls go unanswered. My wife is quite concerned that our daughter needs our help or is in need of attention. My meditations tell me that she has done something and is afraid of our disapproval and wants to avoid us. Should we back off? Does she need our help in any way?

I am Q'uo, and am aware of your query, my brother. As the daughter has been aided in her leaving of the home environment and has now found a place in the physical world of her own it has the normal response that is to be somewhat divided, shall we say, in appreciation for its new position and in some trepidation for its security. Thus, one may expect that if aid is needed, it shall be requested. However, there is also the possibility that the entity known as the daughter is hoping to create the feelings of fear within the parental entities so that they will rush to an unasked aid or, perhaps, simply worry that their expectations were too high. The young entity must needs exercise its own muscles in order to grow strong. This, we find, is a portion of the philosophy which has put each in the position which each now occupies, and we would recommend that the course be stayed.

Is there a further query, my brother?

S: I have been in business for fifteen years and my wife has been in it with me for ten years, and we are contemplating the possible [closing] of the business and perhaps pursuing other ventures. It's not so much a spiritual question but a friend to friend question of having an opinion as to what we should do. Can you give me one?

I am Q'uo, and though we are aware of your query, my brother, we must respectfully decline to offer a friendly opinion for it would infringe upon your future in a manner which we would not wish to accomplish.

Is there any further query, my brother?

S: I guess I have to ask at least one question a week where you give me that response. Let me think of another one which I can put you on the spot with. It seems that I have had an infected hair on the back of my neck for years. It will sometimes scab up and go away and sometimes it occurs. Can you tell me what is the cause of that?

I am Q'uo. Buy pork bellies. We find that this response also causes this instrument to wonder, but we cannot offer any opinion other than this. Please forgive our shortness of words. We are sure that you understand.

Does any other entity within the circle have a query for us at this time?

R: No question. I just want to thank you and the other entities of the Confederation for joining our circle today.

M: I want to express my sincere appreciation as well.

T: I, too, want to thank you for speaking to us.

I am Q'uo, and we thank each of you for your gratitude. It is an attitude which is most helpful in this circle of seeking. May we ask if there is another query at this time?

Carla: If you had one thought that you would like to leave us with, what would it be—in regard to all that we have been talking about today?

I am Q'uo, and we are grateful for your query as well, my sister. We are not usually those who are quick to give a thought for the day, but we are aware of the concerns shared within this circle of seeking on this particular day. There has been much opening of the heart in true concern for the way in which the life pattern has unfolded for each in the recent of your past. We find that each is concerned that the correct approach, attitude and steps have been taken, that the best that each has to offer has, indeed, been offered. And we would recommend to each our thought for this day that the worries of each be released, that the concern which each feels for one another, for the self, for loved ones, for any situation in which each moves, that the proper attention has been given, for each is a sincere seeker of truth and offers that which is in one at each moment and at each turn in the daily round of activities. That there is any question here we understand for each of you within the illusion, for you move within the darkness of not knowing the complete connection of all things within the one creation. However, from our point of view we can assure each of you that each is moving in the appropriate direction, accepting that which must be accepted, and moving on as best you can. And the burden of your experience seems heavy upon your shoulders. The worries that propel you to take one step or another are yet another heavy weight that each could well do without, for there is no mistake that love cannot make whole. There is no missed step that cannot be corrected with compassion. Understanding will heal many wounds, my friends, especially those that are self-inflicted.

We would encourage each to move forward in joy, in love, in light, and in appreciation and exuberance for the life which each now shares upon your whirling ball of Earth. The one Creator is strong in each and is most pleased with that which you have accomplished. You cannot displease the one Creator, for all experiences, both those which you call negative and those which you call positive, are the food of life for the one Creator that wished to know the length, the breadth, the limits of love, if there are limits to love. What can love heal? How far can love move? How powerful is the love that made the one creation? Each of you tests these questions and many more within the daily round of activities and thus far no one has exceeded the bounds of what love can heal. Rest, then, in peace and in love and in light, my friends, for each of you is doing most well in the difficult journey of seeking the truth within the third-density illusion.

At this time we would take our leave of this instrument and this group, leaving each, as always, in the love and in the light of the one Creator. We are known to you as those of Q'uo. Adonai, my friends. Adonai.

L/L Research

L/L Research is a subsidiary of Rock Creek Research & Development Laboratories, Inc.

P.O. Box 5195
Louisville, KY 40255-0195

www.llresearch.org

Rock Creek is a non-profit corporation dedicated to discovering and sharing information which may aid in the spiritual evolution of humankind.

ABOUT THE CONTENTS OF THIS TRANSCRIPT: This telepathic channeling has been taken from transcriptions of the weekly study and meditation meetings of the Rock Creek Research & Development Laboratories and L/L Research. It is offered in the hope that it may be useful to you. As the Confederation entities always make a point of saying, please use your discrimination and judgment in assessing this material. If something rings true to you, fine. If something does not resonate, please leave it behind, for neither we nor those of the Confederation would wish to be a stumbling block for any.

CAVEAT: This transcript is being published by L/L Research in a not yet final form. It has, however, been edited and any obvious errors have been corrected. When it is in a final form, this caveat will be removed.

© 2009 L/L Research

Sunday Meditation
March 19, 2000

Group question: The question this week has to do with the discipline of the personality. We wonder what that might mean and how we can utilize it in our daily lives. Does it have more to do with how we respond to the things we do in our daily lives? Does it also include what we do in our daily lives? If, for example, we had six times during the day that we did meditation and prayer would it be a discipline of the personality in the positive sense for us to do these six meditations with a welcoming, relaxed, happy, open attitude, or would we still be exercising disciplines of the personality if we did it grudgingly or if we occasionally forgot? What exactly is the discipline of the personality, and how can we use it in our spiritual life?

(Carla channeling)

We are those known to you as the principle of Q'uo, and we greet you in the love and in the light of the one infinite Creator. It is our privilege for us to join your circle of meditation. We thank you for the beauty of your vibrations and the keenness of your desire to seek and know the truth. As always, we ask that those things that we say be tested by your own discrimination so that you keep only those things which seem helpful to you and release the rest from your memory.

You ask this day concerning the discipline of the personality. We are most glad to speak to you on this subject but, as is often the case, we would like to place this question in the context in which we see it, for this question is a question concerning what this instrument would call work in consciousness. This work in consciousness is a function of the indigo-ray or pineal energy center and there are strictures upon the appropriate occasion for doing such work which we would like to look at.

As this instrument is at this time working in the project of creating a handbook for wanderers it has had a good deal of occasion to reflect upon the basic arrangement or pattern of the metaphysical universe. Each of you as a physical entity and part of the physical universe is a human being with goals and interests, habits and preferences. The world seems to do unto you rather than you unto it. In the metaphysical universe this same situation takes on an entirely different cast. Rather than things in the world having weight, it is the thoughts and the intentions, the desires and intensifying effects and the blockages of energy and relaxing or limiting effects of catalyst that bear weight.

The person who is newly awakened to the way the metaphysical universe works will need to make a dramatic and often life-changing shift in thought in terms of what is valued or prioritized in the attention from moment to moment as the seeker is going through her day. The things of the world call upon the very persuasive levels of the senses and the errands and chores and busyness of the day intrudes greatly upon this basic frame of mind with which the person of the world goes about interacting with his environment. In terms of the metaphysical universe the everyday experience becomes the hallowed and greatly valued grist for the mill, as the one known as Ram Dass put it. And when one considers the same chores and concerns one is looking not simply for the completion of a list of things to do but also a way of going about the doing of these things that is informed and energized by the manner of being which underlies and undergirds the everyday experience.

It is in this regard that the discipline of the personality can come into play. However, it is important to note that the energy system of the mind, body and spirit of the complex of energies cannot be manipulated beyond certain limits. That is, if there is a blockage in the lower three energy centers, which have to do with survival, the way the self regards the self [or] relates to other entities one at a time, and the way the self relates to the groups of third density, such as the work environment and the family, then the power of the one infinite Creator that enters the body in infinite supply cannot come into the heart center with full energy. There are many ways to distort or block or confuse these lower energies.

The most likely culprit in the root-ray or red energy center is the self's basic opinion of the self as being either a deserving portion or an undeserving portion of the creation. Those who are harboring depressed thoughts and thoughts of suicide, for instance, will block almost all energy coming into the body system. Those with intense sexual cravings or with other ways in which the self has distorted the energies of sexuality and survival can also substantially block and hinder the life-force from moving into the body energy system and rising to the heart. Each of you knows already too well the difficulties of the orange and the yellow-ray energy centers, as the conversation before this meditation expressed eloquently. Each is working with the concept of self, with the concept of self in relationship, and with the concept of self in groups, in ways that distort and filter that energy. And each, being unique, is doing that distorting and partial blocking in her own way. And, therefore, each has what this instrument calls a knot to untangle that is unlike anyone else's knot, has the confusion to unravel that is not precisely not like anyone else's confusion.

And while these processes are going on it is not wise to attempt to work in the higher energy centers. This means that there are many times in each day where remedial and centering work in balancing the lower energy centers and clearing them is called for. There is not the work that is done once and then left but, rather, the metaphysical housework of clearing and re-clearing and re-clearing, cleansing and cleaning the energy centers, encouraging them by various means to be crystallized, balanced and energized so that more and more energy can be taken in and processed and transmuted as the energy moves up the energy system of the body. Each then must determine, daily, hourly, if it is an appropriate time to do work in consciousness. If it is an appropriate time to be looking at the discipline of the personality. Now that we have expressed our cautionary hope that each will refrain from doing such higher energy work until full energy is pouring into the heart we can take into consideration the discipline of the personality.

As a background to work in consciousness in general it may be noted that that energy which is called the rising of the kundalini is an energy placement that is heavily dependent upon the intensity and purity of desire and the type of desire that you as a soul or spirit are naturally and inherently feeling the need to express. In other words, there is energy entering the bottom of the energy system, coming up from the feet and into the root chakra and moving from there upwards. But there is also the inner light of the one infinite Creator that is called into the energy system through the gateway of intelligent infinity through the violet ray and into the green, blue and indigo energy centers. Work in the discipline of the personality is indigo-ray work. And it is facilitated greatly by persistent daily work on one's desire. For the more intense that desire the more powerful will be that energy moving through the gateway to intelligent infinity from above. And the more powerful will be the pull that pulls that energy up from the root chakra and to the meeting with that inner light that is called by the metaphysical worker in consciousness.

What one hopes for from the energy system in this regard is to have an intensification of the full power that is coming into the heart meeting in the indigo-ray center, and this is a goal which cannot be followed as a goal but, rather, lived as a process. For, again, this will not be work that is done once and never again. This is in no wise a work that after one has done it one may rest upon one's laurels. Rather, this is a continuing effort throughout the incarnation.

Now, let us look at the concept of the personality, for this is what one is attempting to discipline. It is our feeling that the personality shell is an artifact of the incarnation in which you are now enjoying existence. This personality shell was chosen carefully by you, picking from the gifts that you had worked upon in previous incarnations, choosing areas of weakness that would give dynamic to the catalyst that was desired for learning the specific lessons that you chose in this particular incarnation. It is not to be considered a real being but, rather, the outer shell of a being that is infinite. It is a face to meet the faces that one meets in the physical illusion, a voice to meet the voices, a way of thinking to meet the ways of thinking that one meets. Those of the Eastern religions tend to look at this as a fundamentally unreal entity and see the self as unreal. We note that this is, to us, a somewhat simplistic diminution of the actual situation.

However, we would agree that the ego is a good term for this personality shell and may be seen to be subject to the suspicions, shall we say, the justified suspicions of the spiritual seeker. For this personality shell is a collection of gifts, challenges, limitations and biases of all kinds which then is taken out of one's control, for the most part, while one is young in years and given a thorough enculturation from parents, teachers and others in authority during the young years of the incarnation. By the time the entity awakens spiritually and resolves to take responsibility for the self this personality shell has become huge. It seems very real. It seems to be indestructible and almost impossible to change in many ways. This is a semi-permeable illusion.

There is complete free will to alter the distortions of the self. It is simply that there is tremendous resistance to change from this personality shell. The value of the shell is that it is as the user interface between the self and the catalyst, those faces that meet you face, those thoughts that meet your thoughts, and so forth. It gives you a place to start. It gives you preferences and biases to begin with. It gives you, shall we say, the abode that is as the haven where the precious self within rests in potential, waiting for the opportunity to come forth.

Now, each of you has undoubtedly noted throughout your experience that bits and pieces of this personality shell will fall away, sometimes for clear reasons, sometimes for no apparent reason, at a certain point within the incarnational experience. This instrument has called this the subtraction process, and many have thought of it as the refining fire that tempers the self. One could see the action of catalyst and experience on this personality shell as that of the sculptor who skillfully or awkwardly is attempting to create a new shape out of the block of stone that is the personality shell. There is a far more vital and authentic being resting within this relatively non-vital shell. Consequently, the spiritual being within the worldly incarnation is as the mine of precious stones which has been overlaid with dirt. It is a wise and protective measure, given the circumstances of incarnation. This mining, then, can be seen as the discipline of the personality. The careful, slow, almost scientific excavation of the authentic self from the jagged edges and roughness of the personality shell is the goal of the worker in consciousness who is attempting the discipline of the personality.

Each personality will have significant areas where the self can see that there is metaphysical work to be done. This instrument, for instance, cyclically moves into an attitude of self condemnation because of its tendencies as a personality towards clothing itself in many, many varieties of outer skin; one layer of clothing after another is seen to be acceptable and then not acceptable. There is felt to be the energy given, for instance, as this entity has recently done, to the achievement of an Easter dress and hat because of this instrument's tendencies to think along the terms of appearance and wishing to have the clothing that it would prefer.

However, simply cutting off the self from the purchase of the clothing can be seen only to be working on the surface of the personality. In disciplining the personality it is far more telling if the worker in consciousness can see into the fear and the unworthiness, these being indigo-ray energies that are distorting the entity towards achieving further changes of clothing in order to defend the self and create that feeling that the self is in some measure of control. Each entity will have deeply personal areas where the energy is drawn and leeched away from metaphysical pursuits and it is to these rough places of the personality that the worker in consciousness will go in thought, not to condemn the self, not to attempt with the knife to excise surgically parts of the self, but, rather, to see these places as places where the earth is covering the jewels in such a deep way that the focus of service and learning is shifted to trivial concerns.

In no wise do we recommend that entities simply cut out those activities which the self considers beneath metaphysical notice. Rather, we would encourage each to come into a vision or an attitude concerning the self that—we offer this instrument the phrase, "My funny valentine." We find the words to this song very pointed in this regard. "My funny valentine, you look so laughable, unphotographical. You're my favorite work of art." This is how you may see yourself as a spiritual entity. As a funny, but very, very sweet work of art. Each entity in incarnation, especially in third density, is a puzzle, a mystery, and an enigma with funny quirks and uncommon lapses that don't seem to add up to a totally sensible human being, and, yet, with all of the preferences and biases and funny places yet still each of you is a beautiful and perfect sublime complex of vibrations that is unique and most beloved by the infinite Creator.

When you can have this attitude towards yourself, rather than a condemnatory or a judging attitude towards the self, this in turn frees the self to be the self without apology or guilt. And at the same time it frees the self to begin to consider where lies love in the personality and where lies fear. For fear is part of that dirt that covers the gems of the true and authentic self. What you are doing is panning for gold in a way. You don't want to take great chunks of your self and toss them to one side. You might miss a gem. You want to take a sieve and sieve each part of that earth, gazing at all that is you to see where the glimmer of treasure truly is. And as you sieve and discard the earth, you do not judge the earth but, rather, thank it for protecting that authentic self and offering it a haven within incarnation which is relatively safe, no matter what the outer circumstances, difficulties or tragedies in a worldly sense that the self may be going through.

We feel that this is sufficient material to begin this consideration and would at this time transfer this contact to the one known as Jim for further questions to refine this subject or anything that remains to be discussed at this working. We leave this instrument in thanks, love, and light and would now transfer to the one known as Jim. We are known to you as those of Q'uo.

(Jim channeling)

I am Q'uo, and greet each of you in the love and the light of the infinite Creator through this instrument. At this time it is our privilege to offer ourselves to speak to any further queries which those present might have for us. Is there another query at this time?

Carla: I would like to give the instrument a chance to ask any further queries on this topic since he is the one who brought it up. He can just ask it mentally and you can respond.

I am Q'uo, and we are aware that the one known as Jim will need to read that which we have given before further questions are offered. Is there any other query at this time?

Carla: Well, just to follow through the example of me with my clothes, would the discipline of my personality in this regard, then, be looking at this habit and this preference and seeing the energy that is caught there in a metaphysical sense rather than making a move to change my behavior? Would that be a discipline of the personality?

I am Q'uo, and am aware of your query, my sister, and we find that you are, indeed, correct in that when one is assessing the metaphysical treasure, the metaphysical value of an activity, an action, or a thought then one is beginning to build the foundation of that which shall, in total, for the entity become the discipline of its own personality. The personality in each instance, then, is offered an expression of itself in a fashion which allows for the understanding of the metaphysical nature of the action to be expressed. This is to say that all thoughts, and actions, words, and deeds may be assessed for the metaphysical quality that they offer to the individual. Thus, the entity in each instance is attempting to concern itself with those things which have value or growth. The metaphysical nature of each expenditure of energy is assessed and further expenditures of energy are arranged according to those qualities which the entity feels will help in personal growth.

Is there a further query, my sister?

Carla: So what I am hoping for when I am working on an area of my personality is that as I see into that area that I will have less and less to tie myself to that expenditure of energy. But is it also a discipline of the personality to go ahead and cut off the clothes-buying, in this particular instance, or is the metaphysical work best done by doing the thinking about it and then allowing spontaneous subtraction to take place?

I am Q'uo, and we are aware of your query, my sister. The expression of the discipline of the personality would be in that area where you felt there was the greatest potential for personal growth in the metaphysical sense, springing from your decision concerning purchasing or not purchasing further clothing. One may, for example, feel that there was growth potential in further purchases for they would add to the sense of worth for the self. Or one may feel that the metaphysical value would lie in the area of reducing the purchases or further purchases in this area would be felt to be of no value in the metaphysical sense. That is, there would be no increase in the sense of the worth of the self in so doing. This would depend upon the personality that was involved in such a purchase and how this entity viewed the self, the clothing, and the interaction of the two.

Carla: So you are saying that it isn't that one way is the right way, but that this is an area of play where we can make holy play out of improving ourselves or becoming more true to ourselves?

I am Q'uo, and we find that this is, indeed, correct, my sister, for it is the intention with which the activity is undertaken that determines its value in the metaphysical sense and the discipline of the personality would be that activity which the entity determined to be of metaphysical value.

Is there a further query, my sister?

Carla: One more. So if, for instance, we decided to be more disciplined about how much time we spent in formal meditation or offerings of some kind, what would make it a discipline of the personality would be the reason that we undertook such expenditure of energy. Is this correct?

I am Q'uo, and this is correct, my sister. Is there a further query, my sister?

Carla: No. Thank you.

I am Q'uo, and again we thank you, my sister. Is there another query at this time?

T: Yes. I mentioned earlier that I had an insight into my own possible motives, justification, or whatever, for certain service to certain people in my house, and it seems that part of this is ego or control factor on my part as much as wanting to help. I would like your comments on this type of thing when one undertakes a service and there are ulterior motives or things possibly of the personality that causes you to undertake this, that might not be the purest of motives.

I am Q'uo, and we believe that we grasp your query, my brother. In the situation of which you speak the underlying quality that is of significance is the intention upon your part is to be of service in an overall sense. This is to say, that the actions and attitudes employed with the desired end in mind …

(Tape change.)

I am Q'uo, and am again with this instrument. We shall continue. That situation of which you speak is one [in] which each entity involved is deemed to have a stake in the outcome of the endeavor. That is to say, that each entity will benefit from the action which has been undertaken, with the hope that the overall effect, then, will be for the growth of each entity. There may indeed be, as you have stated, certain hidden desires or portions to the agenda that one will be happy to see occur, yet we suggest that the overall desire for the benefit of all is the overriding consideration in this situation.

Is there a further query, my brother?

T: No. Thank you.

I am Q'uo, and we thank you, my brother. Is there another query at this time?

(No further queries.)

I am Q'uo, and we are also most grateful to each who has gathered here on this day and we would remind each that we are with you in your own meditations to aid in the deepening of your meditations. If you would ask us to join you there we would be most happy to do so. At this time we shall take our leave of this instrument and this group, leaving each, as always, in the love and in the light of the one infinite Creator. Adonai, my friends. Adonai. ✤

Sunday Meditation
April 2, 2000

Group question: The question this week has to do with protection. And we are thinking about two types of protection. First, the type that you would invoke from outside of yourself if you felt that there was a need for angelic protection, protection by Jesus, in asking a saint for protection or a guide or any other inner energy you felt was helpful. We would like Q'uo to speak to that type of protection and also relate it to the type of protection that comes from one's way of living, from focusing on the being, upon service to others. Ra said producing fruit was a protected activity. Would this have anything to do with refusing to be afraid of that from which you might need protection? Does it help to have an attitude of gratitude?

(Carla channeling)

We are those known to you as the principle of Q'uo. We greet each of you in the love and in the light of the one infinite Creator in whose service we are. We cannot express our delight to you and our pleasure at being able to join this meeting this afternoon. It is always a signal event when we are able to meet with this group. We would like to thank each for calling us to you by your desire for the truth. In that regard we would like to share with you that it is our perception that we are not authorities over you in any way, nor do we have what is, for you, necessarily the truth. We have opinions and thoughts which have come out of our experience, and we are happy to share this with you, for this is the nature of our service to the Creator at this time, to be in communication with those who seek information of this kind in this way.

However, we ask that each thing that we say be brought before each entity's discrimination, for you and only you will be able to feel the resonance of your truth when you hear it and when it comes into your heart. If there is not this solid feeling of resonance in our thoughts then we ask that you leave them behind, for what we are doing is not so much informing but, rather, sharing. For we are as you: students of the way. That way that calls all of us towards the mystery and the fullness of the one infinite Creator.

You ask this day concerning protection and because of the music which you played to begin to tune the session we would choose to begin with a discussion of the protection that can come from what the questioner called outer sources. The practice of calling for aid from a strong helper is as ancient as the belief that there are strong helpers. You must see your density as one in which you will inevitably, again and again, throughout your life be in the position of wishing to call for help from others. For the entire purpose of third density is socialization, the learning to give and to receive love and to give and receive lovingly that encouragement and support that is needed.

This instrument, for instance, in her tuning process habitually calls upon the archangels and all of the discarnate and angelic spirits that are within the inner planes of your planet. This instrument asks them to come and be a part of the session of working, helping to protect the instrument, the source of the contact, the contact itself, each person in the circle of seeking, the circle as an entity, and the physical space in which the meeting is taking place, the room, the house, and the surroundings. Each time that this instrument tunes itself for contact it goes through these preparatory protections. Further, it works with the energy centers of its body and wraps itself first in the protection of the body by the body and then the protection of the infinite white light of the one Creator.

May we say in this regard, then, that it is efficacious to call upon those entities, energies and essences to which an entity relates as ideas or ideals that are esteemed and admired. Calling for help sets up a dynamic within the inner planes as does any prayer. Indeed, we may include in this category specific worries which come repeatedly to the mind and begin to take over the mind. If these worries can be reformed into a more prayerful rendition so that help is asked this is an efficacious thing to do. However, you may note here that in this way of asking for protection danger is seen as "out there" and the protection against the danger is also seen as "out there"; that is, beyond the confines of the physical body and its thoughts and feelings and spiritual nature.

Consequently, there is a natural limit to this kind of request for help. The efficaciousness of these prayers and request for protection depend, in part, upon the attitude of the one praying towards the entities who are asked for help. If an entity is not actually one who believes or has faith that such calls for help will have an effect, then it weakens the prayer greatly. The faculty of faith, then, is signally important in asking for help from outer sources as well as in general.

To look at the attitude of the spiritually awakened entity who refuses outside help we would like to look at some of the actions of the teacher known to you as Jesus. This entity was extraordinarily aware of the issues involved in asking for protection. This is a time within what this instrument would call the church year when the one known as Jesus spent over a month in the desert. The story goes that this entity was fasting and being tempted. One of the temptations that this entity, Jesus, faced was the temptation to ask for outer help from angels. "Go ahead," suggested a negatively-oriented entity, "Throw yourself off of a high rock. Show me that the angels will catch you and not allow you to harm as much as your foot." Jesus remained on the rock. "You are hungry," came the voice. Make some bread out of that stone." Jesus ate locusts and starved. This entity grasped that he had no need of protection because he had nothing to fear. As the one known as T so accurately pointed out in an earlier discussion, an entity which has come to be fearless has come into a kind of balance that is beyond the forces of life and death. This may make such an entity seem weak-minded or [to be] missing the point. Someone new to the story of Jesus the Christ would at this point wonder what the point was of refusing any help when clearly there was no food, no shelter, and no comfort.

And, yet, to the one known as Jesus all that was necessary was the knowledge that he and the Father were one. He and the Father could be one in a desert with nothing to eat. He and the Father could be one in death when that illusion would vanish and he would once again, in spirit and in truth, be one with the Father. He could be one with the Father in any human situation whatsoever. And this was the value that this entity held above all others, seeing the primal nature of this utter belief in the unity of all things under the one infinite Creator.

There is a great key in this understanding. As long as an entity may tabernacle with the Most High, with El Shaddai, with the light, the Creator, the one original thought or Logos that is the Creator, all else has a habit of falling into place. This falling into place may include limitation, difficulty, illness and death. We do not say that fearlessness or faith will protect one from the natural processes of catalyst, declining health, or the natural end to an incarnation. However, let us continue to look at the attitude of the one known to you as Jesus the Christ. For if there was ever an entity which declined protection, this was the entity.

In its final days, knowing that this was its final few days upon the Earth, one night after dinner this teacher lovingly asked for its students to accompany him to a place where they could pray, for the one known as Jesus was fully aware that the time was almost gone and, oh, how this entity dreaded what was to come, as would any human in the bloom of life, young, and strong, and vigorous. It did not wish to lay itself down upon an altar as had Abraham done his son. He had no wish to immolate himself on some sacrificial fire. He wished to teach and to share and to love those who had been given to him. But the will of the Creator was pressing upon this entity's awareness, and he could not ignore the call that he felt was true. One last time he said in prayer, "O Father, please, if it is at all possible, let this not happen. Let me not have to do this." The answer was "no." Three different times he looked around to see if anyone was still praying with him and three times he found that all of his students were asleep and that he must meet this moment alone, vulnerable, completely undefended and unprotected.

When that moment came, when their little retreat was filled with soldiers suddenly, his students sprang to defend him. But he shook his head, "No," he said. "Put away your swords. My kingdom is not of this world. No fighting, please." He gave himself up to the authorities immediately and he walked willingly and sacrificially into his destiny. There must have been a thousand times in the next twenty-four hours before his death when he was tempted to say something in his own defense, to call upon powerful friends, or his heavenly Father, or some kind of angelic fix, but he never prayed, "Get me out of here." He was too busy watching for one more opportunity to love. When he was upon the cross at last, in the worst of his misery he kept finding little ways to show love. He saw his mother and suggested that one of his disciples take care of her and that she take care of him. He prayed for those who were murdering him, asking that his Father forgive them. No excuses. No anger. Just one more way to extend love, and when one of the two who were crucified with him mocked him and the other rebuked the first thief and said to Jesus, "Sorry about that. As for myself, do you suppose if you make it you could bring me along?" Jesus said "This day you will be with me in paradise." Anyone who hears this story knows two things for sure. Jesus the Christ loved and that thief was in paradise that day.

Now, how to bring such intense and pure love into your life, how to ask of that love to remove all fear we do not know, for with each entity the gifts of your incarnation, the circumstances of your incarnation, and the lessons that you came to learn will greatly shape the rhythm of your life. And those lessons that cycle through, again and again, for you may not seem at all the same as the lesson that is cycling for the next person, for your mate, or for your sister, or for your good friend. And, indeed, each of us, no matter what our density, if we are in incarnation, does have an agenda that we design for ourselves before we entered incarnation. This agenda involves relationships which need to be balanced and issues about which we have not yet learned enough to make skillful choices.

Now, both of these relationships and these issues will revolve around some aspect of the giving and the receiving of love to each other. As we said, your third density is a social density. You are here to learn to love, to give it and to receive it. You would be surprised how often it is that the giving of love is not difficult. It is the receiving of love. It is the surrender to love that is so hard, so very, very hard. And we know this because we have been through much more experience, but we still have that slight skin of separation between us and the goal that we see before us. We do not yet see that all things are one and that all expressions are one and, then, even the most fearsome and negative expression is a distortion of love. And, yet, we find that if we can move into that awareness that sees all entities and souls and all behavior as distortions of love, no matter how we feel about the actions involved we can continue to open our hearts and allow the love of the infinite Creator to flow through us and out into loving that distorted entity that is attempting to act negatively towards us. No matter how opaque the negative action may seem from the human standpoint, the rising to a level where all are seen as souls places the mind in a position which gives it the capacity to grasp that all is truly one, that all is truly well, and that all will truly be well.

Is this wellness congruent or synonymous with "well" in the worldly sense? By all means, no. That which is well in the spiritual sense may involve limitation, difficulty, disease or death. For these are processes that are part of life just as much as being born, being young, and learning new things, and so forth. The energies of living and of dying are companions within the density and its blood and bone aspect. This is a physical density. It is not an eternal one. That portion of yourself that is within incarnation and that will not continue after incarnation has every right to be afraid of death.

Again, it is a matter of a leap of faith with no proof whatsoever to come to the understanding or the acceptance of what this instrument would call faith. And there is in that faith a surrender or a leap involved and in this leap of faith there is the leaping into what is specifically and absolutely unknown. There is no cheating here. No one can know while jumping into midair that the parachute is going to open, and that is what faith is like. Because faith is that which looks at a situation in which protection is desperately needed apparently, judges the situation and sees no human avenue for help, and simply says, "All is well, and all will be well."

Where does this faith come from? We assure you it is a powerful protection. It is the most powerful protection that you can invoke. It involves you as a human and spiritual entity digging in your feet, metaphysically speaking, and saying, "Here I am. Listen to me. I am real. I am not what I was born, and I am not going to go away when I die to this reality. I am a citizen of eternity. I follow a higher law. I follow a higher way, a higher truth, a higher life." It is this identification with an idea or an ideal for which you would die and for which you are living that brings you to the courage to jump into midair and say, "I am doing this by faith, blind faith, and I will live by faith, blind faith, not words, not deeds, not reasoning, not wisdom, not logic, not what seems to be efficient or suggested. I will live by faith."

This entity, this instrument speaking, once was at the crossroads of life and death. And because the ailments involved were physical was fully aware of the tenuousness of her hold on physical life. In that situation this instrument's reaction was to put up two quotes. One was from her beloved St. Paul. It was a long passage about being bloody but unbowed, in difficulty yet lifted up, and it spoke to those pains and agonies which the instrument was going through. The other one was simply the re-writing of part of the opening monologue of the original version of the television program *Star Trek*. This entity laboriously wrote out, "Faith, the final frontier," and placed it where she could see it every minute of every day. For she knew that it was faith and only faith that would keep her alive. Faith that all was well and that all would be well. And as this instrument went through one emergency situation after another and then one difficult rehabilitation after another, she kept this motto with her as the watchword. Faith, the final frontier. And, truly, this motto was able to open every door, to quell every fear, to quiet every anxiety, but only because the instrument moved into a state of mind in which nothing actually mattered except remembering that watchword.

For a time it is very possible that this instrument was difficult to live with, for it was so keenly focused on the best protection it knew. And it is possible that when you sense a crux of destiny and do what you need to do within your own mind and heart and soul in order to hew to faith you may lose a friend or find that a family member does not understand you. Or that other entities feel that you are not exercising proper caution or care. And, yet, this attitude of faith is, to our knowledge, the key to the highest protection of life, of work, and of fruit that we know is effective within or without incarnation. This is a value and an asset that is powerful within third density particularly because it cannot be proven. There is no way that you can sit down with someone and justify faith. There is no way you can prove faith. You cannot argue someone into having faith. There is no reason or rhyme to faith. And, yet, it is our understanding that this is how the creation works. To those who have faith and move forward in that faith, the universe opens and the entity moves with increasingly unfettered foot through all the densities of love, of light, and of unity.

Now, how can you attempt to build your own faith? We would suggest three things to you. Firstly, we would suggest focusing upon love. This instrument is fond of saying "There is love in this moment. Where is it?" This instrument is incorrectly quoting those of Ra, but the idea is important. In all relationships there is a more loving path, and we encourage each to spend the time and the thought aforetimes, if possible, to see the way clear to cooperating with this path of love. This is not necessarily an easy choice, for the entities that one deals with are not designed to be pleasant or helpful necessarily in the usual sense, but, rather, may well have been chosen specifically because of their irritating and aggravating value, for it is in the friction and the heat of tempering and refining fire that the personality which you wish to improve will have the opportunity to improve. For that tempering and that friction begins to smooth away some of those aspects of personality that may not be so helpful in a spiritual sense. And they will not leave simply because you would rather that they not be there. They will leave when they fall away because they are no longer called upon. And the habit of not calling upon them will come because there will come a time of testing, and you will have learned enough to make a more skillful choice and to cooperate with the love in the moment rather than in the defense of the self.

The second aid to increasing the ability to choose faith is meditation. You will note that we do not ever lose an opportunity to encourage seekers to prayer, meditation, praise and thanksgiving. These powerful techniques of tuning the mind and the heart have a cumulative effect. The first time you choose to go into the silence or to have a conversation with the infinite Creator that is honest and deep and probing it may not seem to have amounted to much. But if you persist, then, moving into that silence again and again, that silence will expand and lighten and become the holy of holies in which you are sitting with the Creator. Indeed, the Creator sits already within your heart of hearts and waits for you to come and join Him.

The third aspect that will increase faith is the right use for the will. Indeed, faith and will go hand in hand and we encourage each of you to gain an ever increasing respect for your will. For it is your will that decides what you will desire, how you will desire it, and how strongly you will pursue it. We encourage each of you to hone and purify your desire. Always asking yourself, "Who am I? And what is my desire? What is my deepest self and what is my deepest desire?" For the more you know about yourself the more you will be able to come into acceptance and forgiveness of yourself. And the less that those of negative orientation can do to unbalance and topple you from this balanced view in which you are attempting …

(Tape change.)

The will can run away with the self and lead the self into most unwise areas of thought and interests. And that is why we emphasize the right use of will. Before you apply your will, before you decide to will that which you desire, we encourage each to look carefully at your desire to see if that desire is consonant with the laws of love that demand that all entities have free will and that the self never infringe upon that free will. Be very sure that you are following love and that your desire truly is a loving desire before you set your will behind it. For that which you will to desire you will receive. And each desire, when fulfilled, will have side effects which contain the possibility of adhering karma. Consequently, be very clear when you set your will, and gaze carefully at what occurs thereafter with an eye to maintaining a loving and giving and cooperative attitude concerning the outworkings of that fulfilled desire.

This is a good beginning, we think, upon the topic of protection, so this instrument is encouraging us to wrap it up for this day. We are glad, then, at this time to transfer this contact to the one known as Jim that if there are any further questions we may respond to them before the end of this session. We thank this instrument and leave it in love and in light. We are those known to you as those of Q'uo.

(Jim channeling)

I am Q'uo, and am again with this instrument. We greet you once again in love and light of the one Creator through this instrument. It is our privilege to ask if there might be any further queries to which we may respond?

S: This last week I have been quite depressed because our eldest daughter has chosen not to communicate with us and we don't know if she is OK, if she needs our help, or what. Could you give any information that I could give her mother as to how she is doing?

I am Q'uo, and am aware of your query, my brother. The young entity of which you speak is one who feels the need to express its own individuality in a manner which not only carries the nature of its own unique identity but also an emotional charge as well, for as this entity was encouraged to partake in the pursuance of its own individuality it was, shall we say, set upon this journey in a manner in which it was in some disagreement with and now seeks to express its own anger and sense of self in the refusal to communicate with you and the one known as C. We cannot speak in a specific sense for we are not privy to the details, shall we say, of this entity's experience but can give the report that it is well and is pursuing its own journey in its own way.

Is there another query at this time?

S: I've been reading recently on interesting magnetic devices and one thing interests me. They mention their source as the universal mind and can you expand on the reference to a universal mind?

I am Q'uo, and am aware of your query, my brother. Each entity which has individuality and, seemingly, its own separate mind, if it moved deeper into the roots of its own mind it would pass through those greater and greater accumulations of mind such as the racial mind, the planetary mind, the archetypical mind of the Logos, and eventually into that area of the intelligent infinity which you may call the universal or cosmic mind of the one Creator. Thus, each entity, if it is able to move in a conscious fashion past the veil of forgetting which separates your conscious and subconscious mind, it would eventually come to this source of all minds.

Is there a further query, my brother?

S: I have conversed with them a couple of times and my recent e-mail messages have not been responded to. Should I be patient in that respect?

I am Q'uo, and we suggest patience is always a virtue. Is there another query at this time?

S: No. Thank you.

I am Q'uo, and we thank you, my brother. Is there another query at this time?

Carla: Would it be helpful if I showed S the material on the gateway to intelligent infinity which has to do with opening to the deeper aspects of the mind?

I am Q'uo, and we find that this is completely at your discretion, my sister. Is there another query at this time?

(No further queries.)

I am Q'uo, and we are most grateful to each for inviting our presence this day. It is always a joy for us to walk with you in your meditative sessions and we look forward to each such event. At this time we shall take our leave of this instrument and this group, leaving each in the love and in the light of the one infinite Creator. We are those of Q'uo. Adonai, my friends. Adonai.

L/L Research

L/L Research is a subsidiary of Rock Creek Research & Development Laboratories, Inc.

P.O. Box 5195
Louisville, KY 40255-0195

www.llresearch.org

Rock Creek is a non-profit corporation dedicated to discovering and sharing information which may aid in the spiritual evolution of humankind.

ABOUT THE CONTENTS OF THIS TRANSCRIPT: This telepathic channeling has been taken from transcriptions of the weekly study and meditation meetings of the Rock Creek Research & Development Laboratories and L/L Research. It is offered in the hope that it may be useful to you. As the Confederation entities always make a point of saying, please use your discrimination and judgment in assessing this material. If something rings true to you, fine. If something does not resonate, please leave it behind, for neither we nor those of the Confederation would wish to be a stumbling block for any.

CAVEAT: This transcript is being published by L/L Research in a not yet final form. It has, however, been edited and any obvious errors have been corrected. When it is in a final form, this caveat will be removed.

© 2009 L/L Research

Sunday Meditation
April 16, 2000

Group question: The question this week has three parts. The first has do with information on what the experience each of us will face as we go through the experience of death will be like. We've heard a lot of things said about it, such as there will be guides and friends and teachers there to help orient us to our new environment. We would like Q'uo's perspective on what this death into life transition will be like. We also would like for you to relate that to the concept of what our entire evolutionary process is like from the third density on. Some writers here in the third density have mentioned the possibility of skipping the fourth density and going directly to the fifth, and we are wondering what Q'uo's take on that might be? The third part is information on how we can discriminate between positively and negatively oriented entities if a discarnate entity is in our daily lives and the information which we come across there.

(Carla channeling)

We are the principle known to you as Q'uo, and we greet you in the love and in the light of the one infinite Creator in whose service we are. We thank each of you for making the effort to join in this circle of seeking on this day, for, truly, it is a blessing and a privilege to be called to this group by the energy of your desire to seek and to know the truth. It is a blessing to us to be able to share our thoughts and also because this sharing of our thoughts with those who would seek to know them is our chosen area of service to others. And so we depend upon groups such as yours for our opportunities to be of service to your people. Consequently, you loom large in our life at this time. We are most grateful to you, and we know what it costs each of you to be here this day, the will and determination that it took to lay aside those other things that are of concern to you that you might seek in this manner. We greatly appreciate your dedication.

As we share our thoughts with you we wish you to know that we are those with opinions and information that we have come to feel is valuable in spiritual seeking, things that have stood the test of time for us. However, we also know that in speaking to a group we cannot be all things to all people. And, consequently, those things that we have to share may or may not resonate with your own personal truth, and we would suggest that each of you does have an extremely efficient and very sensitive apparatus of discrimination which is, for the most part, a portion of your intuition rather than a portion of your logical mind. When you hear our information do not simply ask yourself if it sounds logical, because we generally do sound logical. However, our truth may not suit your seeking at this point. For there is a movement and an aliveness to truth. It evolves for each seeker, and we would not wish you to hold on to something that might turn out to be a stumbling block. So use what seems helpful to you and, if you would, it would be very helpful to us if you would simply disregard and leave behind all other thoughts. Neither we nor any is an authority for you. You are an authority for yourself. We encourage you to trust in this energy of discrimination which you have within you, and when you sense a thought that resonates with your own, seize it and work with it. And when you do not, release those thoughts that do not ring true.

We are aware that we would speak to you this day about the processes involved in what you call the death of the physical body and would only preface our discussion of this interesting subject by noting that the living of the life is at least as interesting as the end of it so that we encourage each of you not only to think of the goal or ending of that great adventure in the middle of which you are now walking, but to think of the death of the physical body as a portion of an ongoing experience of living that is not ended by birth or death or any ending whatsoever. But, rather, that each of you is a citizen of eternity, that you were in your spiritual integrity a creation before the world was created, before the universe as you know it was created, indeed, before this octave of creation was present. For you have been a spark of the one infinite Creator, a child of the one great original Thought, for eternity. And there is no end to you, or to me, or to any part of the one infinite Creator.

Having said this we feel more comfortable with focusing upon this portion of the experience of incarnation which is the physical death and that which occurs directly after the physical death. Perhaps in order to create a more coherent explanation it would be helpful for us to look at the basic plan of what this instrument would call the octave of creation which represents the creation in which you are now involved. As the one known as D was saying earlier, this consists of the seven notes, shall we say, of existence in the octave that you now experience and we would ask you to think of this term, octave, as specifically musical or, alternately, that which is colored. One may either think of the musical scale of the first note through the seventh note ending in the octave of the first note, which is also the eighth note, the same note one octave higher. Or you may think of the rainbow with its red, orange, yellow, green, blue, indigo, violet, ending once again in that octave of color which is, shall we say, white or the octave density which moves without noticeable change into the first note or density of the next octave.

The first density is that density of elements where the lesson is simply being. The second density is that density which you enjoy when you step outside. It is the density of the animals and plants that turn towards the light. It is the density of awareness, not self-awareness but that awareness which is wishing to turn to the light, to seek the light for growth or food and so forth. Those which are animals within second density do not always seek the light for food directly but seek those plants and animals which have sought the light in terms of food. Consequently, this very large density is a density which is one with the infinite Creator. It is not self-aware, but it is aware of the truth. There was never a discontented flower, for instance, nor a rebellious wild creature. These entities know who they are and do not have questions concerning their nature.

It is in the third density which you now enjoy as what this instrument would call a human being that you experience that self-awareness that asks, "Who am I? Where am I going? What are my goals within this experience?" The higher densities after third density pivot upon third density because third density is the density wherein self-aware beings take stock of their situation and determine the nature of their further seeking. Seeking is all about loving. And the question becomes, "How do I express love?" Usually, this is conceived in terms of service and the question of how to love becomes the question of how to serve. There are two basic options for service to those who have come to this point in their spiritual evolution.

One option is to serve the Creator by serving others as though others were the same as the self. The other option is to serve others by encouraging them to serve the self. The rationale there is that the self is the Creator and, consequently, when others are serving you they are serving the Creator. This is called the service-to-self path as opposed to the service-to-others path. And in many ways it is difficult for those within third density, especially wanderers, to recognize the difference between service to self and service to others. For those who wish to help others in terms of service to self are often extremely dynamic and charismatic entities, who wish to control and manage the affairs of others for their own good, as the one known as M said earlier. This can be extremely fatiguing and difficult to deal with for those who are focused on service to others. And it is, indeed, a challenge when a service-to-others entity is faced with those who wish to control or manipulate. We can only encourage those who seek to advance themselves through service to others to continue in that path in faith that regardless of the seeming disadvantages of this attitude or point of view, the energies involved in responding always in terms of service to others over a period of time begin to have their own momentum, thereby moving the self into a point of view which is enough changed that the efforts of service-to-self manipulation are seen as less fear provoking and more provoking the desire to pray for, care for, and love those entities which seemingly would wish to manipulate you.

This kind of choice begins a process which we have called polarizing and for the rest of your third density experience, once you have begun to deal with this basic choice, you will be repeatedly, and on various levels as you proceed through the incarnation, be involved in times of observing, evaluating and responding to situations in which you have the repeated choice of service to self, by control, manipulation, fear and offense, or service to others with no control, no manipulation, and only blind faith and a hope of meeting others in their needs in such a way that you may be of service to them. This process of learning to love goes on through the next two densities. The next density of your experience after this one is the so-called density of love and understanding, the fourth density. The density after the density of love has been called the density of wisdom. You will note that the density of wisdom is not called the density of understanding, for understanding is that which is of the heart rather than the mind or the wisdom. In the sixth density, love and wisdom, which have been studied separately insofar as that is possible, are now considered in terms of their balance, one with the other, within the seeker. And so the sixth density is called the density of unification. Somewhere in the middle of this density those upon the path of service to others, or the negative path as this instrument has called it, face a choice once again. For they discover beyond a shadow of a doubt that they cannot move forward in their own spiritual evolution until they have accepted at last that the heart holds truth, and that other selves are the self. This is a crushing and an absolutely life-changing discovery to those of service to self and the phenomenon of reversal of polarity occurs at this point individually for each service-to-self entity. Each entity must make this choice again for the self: whether to stay with all that has been learned along the path of service to self, or whether to switch polarities and move further on, having accepted the unification of positive and negative paths as a positive path.

We have called these two paths the path of that which is, that is, the path of service to others, and the path of that which is not, service to self. And the reason that we call them in this particular way is that in service to self the heart is denied and ignored. Consequently, the main source of power for service-to-others entities, and the strongest source of power for all, is left out of the scheme of things. This is the great limitation and it is a denial. Consequently, we call service to self the path of that which is not.

After the unification occurs, the end of sixth density and the seventh density are those in which the selves gradually stop turning backwards to look at what has been and begin being drawn, as if by gravity, into the heart of the source of all that there is: the one infinite Creator. At the end of seventh density there is a movement into timelessness, and in this time of unknowing the heart of the Creator beats and another creation begins. This is the panoply of cosmology within which you are now experiencing the third of seven experiences or types of experience. And each of these densities represents a considerable length of your time.

However, your third density is the shortest of all densities, being only 75,000 years long. During third density the pattern of incarnation is, at first, quite automatic. Entities are graduating from second density because of the growing realization of love itself. As they become harvestable, for whatever reason, they are able to incarnate as individuated consciousnesses and they become what this instrument would call human. At first, incarnations are largely automatic. Little is known. Much is in chaos. And there is a little learning each time and then a relaxing from incarnation through death into the body of light that is yours between incarnations within the inner planes of this particular planetary sphere. During this time between incarnations there is first any healing that needs to take place from the incarnation, any traumas that need adjusting and comforting, and so forth. Then there is the opportunity for another physical vehicle, the descent into the world of heavy chemical bodies that your physical plane represents, the gathering of more catalyst, more information, more experiences, until the incarnational self is completely full and has done all that it has hoped to do within this particular incarnation, at which time it moves through the physical death again, the healing of the incarnation after death, and, gradually, as the incarnations mount up and the entity within begins to crystallize beyond the simple personality shell this between incarnations process becomes lengthened because there is more to heal, and because more and more, as entities become senior in their vibratory patterns they earn the right, more and more, to have a say in their own incarnational plan. At this point within third density upon your sphere, this being the end of that 75,000 year period, each entity that incarnates upon your planet is capable of graduation from third density to fourth. Each entity has chosen the incarnational lessons of the present lifetime and the relationships that it will use for learning and for service.

In this particular lifetime for each of you there is the potential of graduation at the end of this physical death experience. Now, let us say that the physical death is one thing to the body and another to the consciousness that the body is carrying about at this time. For each of you is not one being, but two. You are a second-density animal, a hairless or nearly hairless great ape, with certain instinctual patterns of behavior and a choice-making brain that is extremely good at choosing what to eat and how to survive and how to protect the family. And you are also this eternal being whose present life is merely a parenthesis in eternity. When the physical body is exhausted or is traumatized and can no longer sustain the breath of life the spirit itself does not miss a beat. There is no alteration in consciousness. It is as though you were continuing to observe but the nature of your observation changes. For, instead of observing the heart beating, the mind thinking about dinner, the feelings of the physical body as they move into your consciousness, suddenly you are experiencing what seems to be a physical body, what seems to be physical feelings, what seem to be physical incoming data. But the body itself has altered.

This instrument has had the experience of moving through the gate of death and so we are able to say through this instrument that this entity's first-hand experience was a valid one. And this entity's experience was simply that, the kidneys having failed in this instrument's body, it experienced a great deal of pain and then when death occurred, there was the cessation of the pain. There had been disfigurement of the body because of the lack of the kidneys working. Suddenly the body was fair and perfect. The clues mounted quickly, however, that the entire situation had changed. For when this entity spoke to a rose upon a fence an entire section of rose bush wound itself around this entity's arm, without thorns but with endless love. This entity could hear music and see it in the air. And the colors that this entity saw were more substantial and had a life of their own. They pulsed and glowed with a three-dimensional seeming energy that is lacking in the colors upon your planet

The experience expanded through the death process rather than being cut off and then changing or stopping altogether. This is the actual experience at the time of death. Indeed, it is so persuasive that many there are who die suddenly who take quite some time to realize that they have indeed passed through the gates of physical death and no longer have a body or an incarnation upon the planetary sphere.

Now we would address that which occurs at the time of graduation, and this, in part, moves into the second question which you have asked of us this day. Picture, if you will, a walk that is long and beautiful and seems to be completely a walkway filled with light. On either side of this walkway are presences that are extremely loving and nurturing and that guard each and every spirit that walks this path of light. Picture then, if you will, a light whose very nature changes, becoming more dense, more bright, and, in ways hard to describe, more challenging. It is as though elements have been added to this light as you move along this walk. The reason for this is that the nature of light changes by quanta. A photon within your density is not as complex as a photon within fourth density, which is not as complex as the photon in fifth density, and so forth. When you are walking steps of light you are walking to find your most comfortable and attractive place to be. You are looking for your new home.

This situation is somewhat complicated by the fact that many there are among your peoples now, including many within this room, who do not originally come from the Earth and its density system but, rather, have moved through third, fourth, perhaps fifth and sixth, to some extent, on other planetary spheres or on other planetary influences. Then you, perhaps, [have] come back to third density here. Why? For two basic reasons. Firstly, you wanted to undo a balance between love and wisdom that you felt could be improved upon and intensified. And so you came back to third density to remake the original choice and to reinvestigate the power of love, especially unlimited or unconditional love. Your second reason as a wanderer for coming here was to lend all of your being to what this instrument has called the ministry of essence upon planet Earth. It is a simple plan and it is the basic plan of wanderers upon planet Earth. The plan is basically to come into incarnation here and become subject to the laws of third density, to forget everything that you knew so well, and to exist within this density living a life of faith with no proof, no way to be sure that you are right, but only your heart telling you, "This is the way for me."

In this way you hoped to make the choice even more purely, even more surely, even more firmly than you did before. And so you are hoping to offer to the planet, as you make this choice, your being as you breathe in and as you breathe out. As you love and as you accept the love of others. This allowing of the infinite Creator's love and light to flow through each of you and out into the Earth plane accelerates the lightening energies of the planet and, consequently, makes it much more possible for the planet itself to move through what is being a somewhat difficult graduation. For the planet itself is also graduating into fourth density, moving into a new area of space and time and experiencing that addition to the photon that fourth density is bringing to the very physical creation in which you enjoy this continuing adventure.

The reason that this applies to the graduation context is that in that question that was brought by the one known as J the entities involved felt that, as wanderers from the fifth density, upon graduating from Earth's third density they would automatically move back into their home vibration. This is emphatically not true, and we felt that this is a very germane point, for all wanderers become Earth natives when they incarnate. The taking of a physical body is the taking of the blood, and bone, and the sinew of the entire human experience. There is no such thing as a tourist in the body on planet Earth.

All of you have become natives, whatever your planet or origin or your densities of previous experience.

This means that there is a very simple dynamic involved and it involves service to others, for the graduational criterion for positive polarity is that the seeker think more about serving others than about serving the self. The minimum grade for graduation from planet Earth is 51 percent service to others. Now, for those who are attempting to polarize service to self, the maximum grade is 5 percent service to others. To say that another way, the service-to-self entity must fight a graduation requirement in its purity of intention to serve the self. We may say that it is about as difficult to make the grade of 51 percent service to others or of 95 percent service to self. We are extremely pleased that each of you have chosen service to others, for that is the polarity that we also have chosen, and we would truly be out of our depth in attempting to be of service to those who were attempting to polarize along the other option.

For service-to-others entities, appreciate each moment and see what you can do to find the love in that moment. There is love in the moment. There is love in every moment. There is love in every thought. The question is: how distorted is that love? And one helpful discipline for the seeker is to look at that which comes before the attention with an eye to using both the intellectual mind and the intuition to ask the self questions about what one is perceiving. And, indeed, about how one wishes to respond to what one is receiving.

When an entity is able to walk the steps of light of graduation into fourth density and feel comfortable there, one is able to move into fourth density for the next experience. And this is true in a continuing way. If an entity is able to enjoy and use the light of fifth density or sixth density, the entity may, indeed, move back into that home vibration. However, it is first necessary to rediscover that deep self within this incarnation which you now experience to the extent that you are able to recapitulate that choice and the decisions that lead to being able to tolerate the light that is offered to those whose thoughts are more than 51 percent for other entities and how to serve them.

There is a tremendous amount of persistence and dedication involved in the processes of learning how to accelerate the pace of your spiritual evolution. And we would encourage each of you to take it slow, to attempt to seat experiences in silence, and to keep always before the self that light touch that is devoted to principles but not to the extent that the self and the principles become larger than the principles. Take the principles seriously. Take the self lightly, for you will be misunderstood. You will not always have anyone who is able to support or encourage you. There are aspects to the spiritual walk that are difficult. And, indeed, most of what this instrument would call the "good stuff," most of the pith and marrow of learning is received during times of intense suffering, limitation and change. Consequently, it is never obvious that this is a good thing. It is never clear that you are on the right track.

Occasionally all things may come together, and it is, indeed, a moment of clarity and delight. But again and again you as a seeker will be in the Dark Night of the Soul, looking for dawn but not at all sure that it will come. And all of this is a refiner of souls. You are engaged in distilling a truth and a duty that is so much larger and fuller and [more whole] than anything that you can imagine that we cannot express it to you. You are already a perfection that is the one infinite Creator, and yet you have this opportunity not to know and yet to seek. It is, in our experience, an absolute delight, and we feel that each of you here have had those moments of clarity and delight. We ask that you believe them, that you remember them and trust the memory. For these are little gems of your truth that have popped out into consciousness from that place where joy and purity and truth live within you. This instrument would say that they reside within the heart, and in a very real sense this is true. For it is through the heart center that these awarenesses are able to springboard from the unconscious or subconscious self into consciousness. In another way, we would say that these are energies of the deeper mind, this mind that attaches you to others, to the planet in which you now enjoy life, to all of life, and to the one infinite Creator.

This instrument is informing us that the time is nearly up for us to speak through this instrument. We do not wish to move beyond forty-five minutes. We have, in a sense, touched upon the discrimination between service-to-self and service-to-others sources within your reading and your hearing. And we simply encourage you to trust yourself. And at the same time to get to know that self that you are trusting ever more deeply, to consult your discrimination, and at the same time to strengthen your power of discrimination by trusting it, by using it, by seeing at first hand how it works. It is a faculty within you that is a gift from the one infinite Creator and from your higher self. And to this gift of discrimination is linked your guidance. We would encourage you to move into that place within the heart where you are able to ask within the safety of your own energy field, "Is this true for me?" If it is, move on it. Use it. Live it. Eat it. If it is not, walk on.

You will find those things that you need to be considering more and more coming to you in the words of a song, or the coincidences of a roadside sign, the flight of a butterfly or a bird, those things that pop into your reality seemingly from nowhere. All of these things are messages. And all of these things have something to say to you. Once you catch on to the synchronicity of spiritual events you will find more and more of your experience speaking directly to you in a spiritual sense.

May we say what a delight it has been to talk about these subjects through this instrument, and we would like to continue this meeting through the one known as Jim. We would leave this instrument in love and light. We are those of Q'uo.

(Jim channeling)

I am Q'uo, and greet each again in love and in light through this instrument. At this time it is our privilege to offer ourselves to speak to any query that those present might have for us of a shorter nature. Is there another query at this time?

D: My question centers on thinking why Ra built the pyramids for that land. Isn't part of the reason that the King's and Queen's chambers would open up the heart so that the Egyptian culture would be able to share love amongst the members of the culture? And the complement to opening up the heart was activating the brain so that true intelligence could be used in conjunction with opening the heart in the context of love and light or mind and spirit, in the context of personal development and social development of the culture as a whole?

I am Q'uo, and we are aware of your query, my brother. This query is large in its scope but one which hopefully will lend itself to an abbreviated response, for we are often known as those who speak for too long.

At the time of the construction of the Great Pyramid, that monument of antiquity located in the holy land that you call Egypt, the peoples of this culture were engaged in an appreciation of the one Creator which you may liken to that philosophy which you might call animism or paganism, in which the Creator was seen in all things and was everywhere present. Wonders were a part of this culture. The miraculous was seen as that which was as it should be: a portion of the everyday experience. However, the individual entities of this culture were of a nature that lent itself to being taught, shall we say, by those who were other than the self. Thus, the kind of spiritual awareness that was available to these entities was that which was handed down from one entity to another, from teacher to student. Thus, within the structure called the pyramid there were located those centers of energy that you have called the King's chamber, the Queen's chamber, and the resonating chamber below the surface of the earth. Within these central locations of swirling energy students and teacher could meet and be infused with the intelligent energy of the one Creator for the purpose of healing, the purpose of teaching, and the purpose of facing the self for the potential experience of being reborn, of finding a new life, a new direction. Thus, these centers of energy within the pyramid symbolized to the population of that culture the means by which teaching and enlightenment could be achieved. Thus, individuals were able to gain a certain amount of advancement, shall we say, within these structures and then were able to move within the culture and to share this teaching with a greater population. These structures, for the most part, were successful in being able to share with the population of that culture the advancement that was sought. However, there was, after a period of time, the reserving of these experiences within the pyramidal structure for only those who were of an advanced status according to the measure of wealth, power and position. Thus, as the information available within the structures became less and less available to the general population the purposes of the pyramidal structures were perverted. And those entities who had aided in the construction of the pyramids found it necessary to take stock of themselves, shall we say, and to find other avenues of service through which they might begin to correct the imbalances that were promulgated by the reserving of the use of the pyramids to those of power and wealth.

Is there a further query, my brother?

D: I recently submitted a manuscript to a series of publishers, and I was wondering if anything was going to come out of what I submitted, or if I still needed to do work, or do I need to take another approach, or what's up?

I am Q'uo, and am aware of your query, my brother. And, unfortunately, we are aware that to answer this query we move into an area in which we would be infringing upon your free will, for we are aware that you have made a great effort in personal sacrifice and achievement in order to have available these manuscripts and to submit them for further publication, shall we say. We recommend that one remember that there are no mistakes within this illusion, and the effort that you have put forth will produce its appropriate [result] and that there is the necessity for maintaining the faith in the perfection of all things in this instance.

Is there a further query, my brother?

D: Yes, I am curious. Could you share with me information about Jehovah, Yahweh, Id, the Council of Layette, and an entity known as Kingnah. I was wondering if you could share the types of entities that they are?

I am Q'uo, and am aware of your query, my brother. We find that there is only a certain distance that we may move in responding to this query, for there are elements of this query which also fall within the area of the infringement upon free will. We can suggest that there are entities such as Yahweh and Jehovah that are familiar to all who have appreciated the holy writings contained within your Bible and that these entities in their original and untarnished state were what you would call social memory complexes or groups of entities known by one name for the ease of identification by the populations that they chose to serve. These entities moved in service to those of not only this planetary sphere but also others as well, most notably those of the red planet that you call Mars who were in need of finding a new home upon which to continue their evolutionary process, having caused their original planetary sphere of home vibration to become inhospitable to life through bellicose action. Thus, these entities of the

Confederation of Planets in the Service of the One Creator set before the Council of Saturn a proposal for transferring and somewhat altering the genetic nature of the entities of the Mars experience that they might continue their progress towards the One on this planetary sphere. However, their efforts were not to go without meeting difficulties.

The enhancing of one group over another for the purpose of aiding that group's ability to apprehend the nature of infinity and of unity also creates an opening for negatively-oriented entities to communicate with the same Terran population and to give them the idea that perhaps they were special, they were elite, and that they were given this special nature in order that they might govern others and bring others into their influence of power. Thus, the experience of the ones known as Yahweh, the ones known as Jehovah, were difficult in that their efforts were lost to the groups of entities from the Orion constellation that moved also in service, yet moved in service of a negatively oriented nature and were able to make inroads for the first time upon this planetary sphere using the efforts first offered by others within the Confederation of Planets.

There is much that has been attributed to these entities that is not of their making. However, they were the first to offer the efforts that created inroads for a mixed contact, shall we say, and results which also were mixed in aiding the entities they desired to serve. Thus, upon reflection each of these social memory complexes have also sought to find other avenues of service to this planetary population that would balance the imbalances that they felt responsible for these many years ago.

Is there another query at this time?

D: One more. Do you have any suggestions that you could give that would assist me on personal healing in the areas of doing conscious out-of-body experiences and in opening the heart so that the love of God can simply be shared in a humble and consistent manner?

I am Q'uo, and am aware of your query, my brother. We would recommend that in addition to the offering of yourself in the early portion of your day to the one Creator, as you now do, that there be given over at this time a special meditation in which you visualize the heart being able to open to the extent that it can encompass greater and greater need from others for the love that can flow through it. That you see in your mind's eye the green-ray energy center vibrating with a greater and greater brilliance of an apple green. That you see this center becoming bright, vivid and crystallized. That for a few minutes of your time you offer yourself without condition, with the open heart, for the service of the one Creator in the face of each entity that you see in your daily round of activities.

Is there a further query, my brother?

D: No. Thank you very much.

I am Q'uo, and we thank you, my brother. Is there another query at this time?

C: I have a query and thank you for the opportunity. I recently learned of the term the neutral implant release, referring to the concept of voiding one's karma status in the third density. Could you help me understand and clarify some issues still unclear with this, such as what does this really mean in terms of voiding one's karma and does it have anything to do with releasing the death hormone, which voids remaining illness?

I am Q'uo, and am aware of the nature of your query, though we do not fully grasp the opportunity that could be offered to void the karma of the incarnation, for to our way of looking upon the opportunities provided by each incarnation, though each entity within the incarnation may see the karma that it has accumulated as a kind of weight or burden, we are not of the opinion that this is the most efficient way of looking at karma. For to be within your third-density illusion is a great privilege and honor. We see the ability of each entity within the third density to move ahead upon the evolutionary journey as being far, far greater than ever will be presented to an entity again in further densities. Thus, though your density may be one in which you move within a seeming darkness, lit only by the smallest of lights of your consciousness, yet this small light of your consciousness can accomplish a great deal within this illusion in a much shorter time than will ever be possible again. For those who move beyond your illusion find that the work that is able to be done there moves in a great extent because of the work that is done here, within the third-density illusion. Thus, we are unable to appreciate the desire to negate or remove one's karma. Perhaps we have misunderstood the query. Could you elucidate for us?

C: I think you've answered it adequately. It was a concept that was unclear to me, and I just wanted to find out your opinion.

I am Q'uo, and we hope that we have been helpful in this area. Is there another query at this time?

Carla: Could I follow up and ask if it would be possible that the good kind of elimination of karma would be forgiveness?

I am Q'uo, and am aware of your query, my sister. The ability to forgive, to have compassion for that for which there was previously no compassion, is the healing of the incarnation, as we have heard it said. Indeed, the efforts that each entity makes in every area of the incarnation may be aided by the ability to forgive, whether the forgiveness is of another or, more especially, of the self. For we find that forgiveness of another and of the self are intertwined in a manner that is irrefragable; that is, they are one. As you see another entity and feel one emotion or another for this entity, it is for yourself that this emotion is truly felt. For each entity is a mirror unto you that shows you yourself and the face of the Creator at the same time. When you are unable to perceive that this is what is being shown to you, then there arise a myriad of emotions, both those that are what you call positive and those that are what you call negative, that you attribute to this entity. When, through your own personal work and perseverance, you have been able to see that the world about you reflects your attitude back to you, then you are able to open the door to forgiveness, to compassion, to mercy, to understanding, and to those qualities that truly stop the wheel of karma and allow you that progress that you desire: the opening of the heart so that compassion is felt, not just for those about you, but for yourself, for the Creator, and for all of the creation about you.

Is there a further query, my sister?

Carla: One other question. The instrument now channeling you is going to write a letter this week correcting some errors concerning those of Ra being part of the Stargate Conspiracy. Would you like to express any opinion that would help the one known as Jim as he writes this letter?

I am Q'uo, and am aware of your query, my sister. And we would simply remind this entity, as we would remind each, that all entities are a portion of the same Creator. And that to salute that Creator in each is a firm foundation on which to begin.

Is there a further query at this time?

(No further queries.)

We are those of Q'uo. May we speak to any further queries at this time?

M: When you are dealing with times of hardship and you try to get through it the best you can, is it wise to take periods of rest before you jump back into the lion's den again?

I am Q'uo, and your query makes enough sense to us that we would say that you have answered your own query. Is there another query at this time?

(No further queries.)

I am Q'uo, and as it appears that we have exhausted the queries for the nonce we shall refrain from speaking overly long, for we do not wish to overtire those who have so generously offered their time and themselves for this circle of seeking. We thank each for bringing your queries and your heartfelt concerns, for it is to those of like mind that the journey is made easier by the companions that share it. We are known to you as those of Q'uo. We shall take our leave of this instrument and this group, leaving each in the love and in the light of the one infinite Creator. Adonai, my friends. Adonai. ✵

L/L Research

L/L Research is a subsidiary of Rock Creek Research & Development Laboratories, Inc.

P.O. Box 5195
Louisville, KY 40255-0195

www.llresearch.org

Rock Creek is a non-profit corporation dedicated to discovering and sharing information which may aid in the spiritual evolution of humankind.

ABOUT THE CONTENTS OF THIS TRANSCRIPT: This telepathic channeling has been taken from transcriptions of the weekly study and meditation meetings of the Rock Creek Research & Development Laboratories and L/L Research. It is offered in the hope that it may be useful to you. As the Confederation entities always make a point of saying, please use your discrimination and judgment in assessing this material. If something rings true to you, fine. If something does not resonate, please leave it behind, for neither we nor those of the Confederation would wish to be a stumbling block for any.

CAVEAT: This transcript is being published by L/L Research in a not yet final form. It has, however, been edited and any obvious errors have been corrected. When it is in a final form, this caveat will be removed.

© 2009 L/L Research

Sunday Meditation
May 7, 2000

Group question: Our question today concerns the concept of the emotions. A couple of months ago Q'uo described emotions as the thinking of the deep mind and said something about how we might be able to utilize our emotions in our spiritual evolution, and we would like for Q'uo to elaborate a little bit more on that today.

(Carla channeling)

We are those known to you as the principle Q'uo. Greetings in the love and in the light of the one infinite Creator. We thank you for calling us to your session of working this day. It is a great blessing to us to be able to speak with you on the subject of the emotions and their role in working to accelerate the rate of your spiritual and mental evolution. It is our privilege to be able to address this subject, but, as always, we ask that you refrain from following our suggestions without careful thought. For that we have to offer are opinion and consideration which we are glad to share with you as long as you understand that we are not authorities. We would not wish to be taken as authorities, for we are your brothers and sisters who walk the same dusty path that you do.

There is an irresistible pull to evolution. There is implicit in the structure of each density every potential outworking of every energy within that density. In a universe of builded light the subtleties are endless and, at the same time, progress through the gradually ascending densities is inevitable and irresistible. The only question that each entity faces is, "How quickly do I wish to progress?" There is no question that you will progress. It is as necessary to our nature to progress as it is for the iron to be drawn to the magnet. It is understandable that you might doubt this, for you see instances of your own lack of perceived progress, and you see apparent lapses in progression on the part of those with whom you come in contact. When these lapses are perceived it is easy to become discouraged, but we would encourage each of you to meet these judgmental feelings about the self and others with the courage of your conviction that all is proceeding according to an unseen plan.

You are, little by little, and step by step, gaining in experience and awareness, and each of you is on a path of strong progression. We encourage each of you to come into a fuller understanding, as time goes on, of the meaning of imperfection. It was not intended that third density be an illusion in which any conscious seeker after truth could honestly perceive the self as perfect. It was, in fact, designed into third-density experience that from beginning to end each person's personal experience will include perceptions of the self as being subtly or grossly imperfect, not once, not twice, not three times, but seven times and seven times seven. In other words, cyclically without an end throughout the incarnational experience.

This would seem to be a recipe for discouragement, heavy heartedness, and feelings of hopelessness. And yet the actual intent is the opposite. You see, as the spirit awakens this process of spiritual and mental evolution begins to accelerate. Whereas before awakening you were content to skate upon the surface of life as though it were a pond, once you have awakened you are aware of and drawn to the depths of each present moment. The profundities, implications, resonances and overtones of each present moment are infinite. The learning in each present moment is potentially infinite. The gateway to intelligent infinity lies within each present moment. As the spirit awakens it becomes gradually more able to hear the far more complex symphony of messages that are coming in within each present moment.

The resulting weight of experience can be crushing, and, typically, the spiritual seeker will scramble for a way to control this process which seems too chaotic to be useful. The first defense of an entity which wishes to control experience is the analytical, logical, reasoning mind. There is the desire to get hold of the experience, to rationalize it, and to understand the workings of it by analysis and logic. Great religious systems have been built which encourage and structure such intellectual and logical analysis of experience. We offer, for instance, the Buddhist, the yogic, and the Taoist systems of study, learning and worship as those systems which are primarily designed to utilize the intellect and the faculties of reason and logic in becoming able to distance the self from those things which are occurring to the self and which the self is feeling. We call this basic approach the way of wisdom. It has many advantages for the seeker, and for those who are unable to move directly to working with the emotions we encourage the pursuit of such study. For it does accelerate, to some extent, the evolution of spirit and mind. However, the way of wisdom as a general discipline—and here we do over-generalize for effect—is a way of remaining comfortable while learning, thus obviating the main thrust of the third-density experience.

There is another way to look at this process of learning from experience, and that is, shall we say, the way of the open heart, or the way of love. The religion which is known to this group as Christianity is a system of study, and learning, and worship which moves along this path of love or the path of the open heart. And it encourages the utilization of emotion. Now, let us look at why this might be. What are emotions exactly?

If you can gaze at the panoply and scope of your life experience, you can see a definite progression and coherent trail of emotions that are difficult and emotions that are wonderful. Both kinds of emotions have cropped up within the life experience in response to the difficulties and challenges of the incarnation and in response to the gifts and joys that are spontaneously given to the heart, whether it be the song of a bird, the smile of a child, a thought that is read in a favorite book or any other thing which has enlarged joy and encouraged faith within you as a spiritual seeker. For the most part it well may seem that the difficult emotions—anger, guilt, remorse, fear, grief, jealously, pride, alienation—are very much in the majority, and that the joyful emotions are given out with the miser's hand. And, indeed, this seems unfair. What is the justification for the surfeit of suffering that each awakening spiritual seeker seems to face?

Life is energy. Progress within life is a shift in energies. Everything that you do and everything that you think creates a certain vibrational energy, and the summation of all of these processes of energy changes and exchanges within your life represent an energy system or field that has a certain strength. To an awakened seeker who is pursuing the way of wisdom these energies move in a spontaneous manner and the seeker's goal is, more or less, to allow them to proceed. This allows the seeker to remain relatively peaceful and comfortable. However, this also creates a stiffness and resistance within the process of transformation, and this is where we get into what emotions are.

If the way of wisdom contains a linear structure so that one can follow one's processes and talk logically about them, it also holds the energy within the higher chakras or energy centers. Working with wisdom is not working with heart or with the lower energies but, rather, largely, the indigo-ray, and to some extent, the blue-ray energy centers. While it is good to do work in consciousness in this manner it is also somewhat imbalanced because there is no encouragement of the flow of energy through the system but, rather, the holding of energy in the higher chakras. Conversely, when one is working in the way of the open heart one is constantly faced with the entire spectrum of self, from the lowest and most primitive emotion, the desire for survival, the desire for sexual reproduction, the desire for food and safety, upwards throughout the system, touching all of the energy centers, rising as high as indigo ray, but again and again springboarding from the heart. So that instead of the seeker moving into and maintaining as a steady state reliance on the higher chakras, the seeker in the way of love has released the preference for work in the higher energy centers and has accepted the self as a full energy system and reconfigured the goal from staying in the higher energies to accelerating the flow of energy throughout the entire system. Instead of a safe but somewhat turgid and slow moving path of energy refinement the brother and sister of the open heart are attempting to take the whole self as it is and through blind faith alone and the processes of self-acceptance and self-forgiveness blessing, forgiving, redeeming, transforming and offering each and every emotion and sensation to the one infinite Creator.

This invigorates, energizes and enlivens the entire system. It is as if the owner of an automobile began running the engine through its paces in such a way that it began to burn off the carbon from the valves. The way of wisdom collects detritus, shall we say, the carbon on the valves that is not easily dealt with from the way of wisdom. The way of love is a rough and tumble way in comparison, but it also is the fast and cleaner way to use the energy system of the body, mind and spirit. For the emotions that are the responses to catalyst are the shadows, symbols, or increasingly as one progresses, the essence of deep and purified rivers of energy that abide within what your psychologist would call the unconscious mind. At the roots of consciousness lie rivers of purified emotion that are as gems, perfectly and regularly refracting from the white light of unlimited energy the colorations of energy which are called emotion which express essences which the Creator has previously learned about Itself. These essences are as great truths into which the seeker taps, however imperfectly and however distortedly, as it moves through catalyst and encounters difficulties and meets challenges.

Each has felt those moments when a tiny thing triggered a massive flood of emotion. And when this occurs it is an excellent signal from the self to the self that here is a gift that is imperfectly seen, perhaps, but that is real. That moves into the experience as a done thing, as something that is felt, not created. Emotions are messages from the unconscious or deeper self to the conscious self. Now, there are various levels of messages and various layers to emotions. It is not a simple practice to enter into one's emotions and to attempt to come into a deeper understanding of the heart of those emotions, not simply what triggered the emotion, but what kind of emotion it essentially is and what challenge it represents. In this wise it is often helpful to think of the centers of energy within the physical body, for difficult emotions often can be placed within certain energy centers and can be seen as messages expressing to the heart the need for working with those aspects of those emotions which are disturbing in such a way as to be able to balance and clarify those feelings. For there is a deeper truth within each emotion. The key to working on emotions is to realize the seat of emotion, shall we say, as being the green-ray energy center or heart chakra.

If one attempts to work with blocked and negative emotions from the energy in which they originate without moving into the heart chakra there is little chance or opportunity for self-forgiveness. Therefore, while it is very important to assess and evaluate such negative emotions as probably stemming from certain energy centers it is well to model the working with these essential and energetic nexi which are emotions with the model of keeping the energy in flow, moving again and again into the heart chakra and resting in that primary emotion which is called faith.

There is a deep well of emotion whose basic goal is to move all entities into unconditional love. It is towards unconditional love that the path of your spiritual evolution is irresistibly moving. This unconditional love is the most universal and powerful emotion and, indeed, is all that there is. In other words, the Logos Itself, the one great original Thought, is a purified emotion. It is not a thought precisely. A thought is linear. An emotion is global, universal, round, three-dimensional. It does not climb. It rolls. It does not fall. It continues to roll. Nothing can knock out the force of emotion. Indeed, it is that to which each must come in order to be able to graduate into the density of love which is your next experience.

Consequently, it is simply more efficient to choose the way of the heart, in our opinion, and to see the goal of working with difficulty, not in achieving happiness, peace, or content, but rather, simply in continuing to accelerate the pace of spiritual and mental evolution. The energy of the open heart is open ended. It does not attach an outcome. It simply seeks greater openness of self and a greater ability to allow these rising emotions to do the work of the refiner's fire. The seeker who has faith in the way of love has faith that no matter what comes she will be able to survive it. That no matter how much various difficulties cause suffering and pain she will be able to use those difficulties to refine those rivers of emotion that are rising to consciousness.

It is a bumpier and rougher ride to seek the way of the open heart than to seek the way of wisdom. It is a way which invokes faith without proof, reason or logic. There is no attempt to justify hardship, but neither is there the attempt to disempower hardship by rising above it. Rather, the way of the open heart is the way of vulnerability, of remaining open and weak in the face of strong and sometimes painful feelings. And, yet, because it sees the whole of imperfect selfhood as a beautiful and perfect thing in all its paradox it is the wiser path for your density. There is time enough to learn wisdom once you have learned to love fearlessly, to meet each moment with an open and unguarded heart.

This entity has experienced two pure emotions that it consciously knows of: grief and love. Neither experience shall ever be forgotten. When the seeker touches the heart of an emotion and it resonates purely, it is a life-changing event. Never again will grief lay waste to this instrument as it did before it experienced pure grief. And we might say that this is so for each shade of emotion, each tributary of each river of purified essence.

When each of you staggers under the load of difficult emotion we can only ask you to think on what you basically believe to be true about your incarnational experience. If you believe that your life makes sense, and this we truly believe is so, then you are able to see that each difficult emotion is a gift from the self to the self of the truth of what that self is processing at the moment and of its relationship to the deeper truths within. If the seeker can believe that the life makes sense, then there is that faith which can be called upon, that faith that says, "My life does make sense. These difficulties have a reason for being there. They are my way of learning past this moment." Then the seeker has a reason to work with these challenging and difficult feelings, to allow and even to encourage their movement through the energy system.

It may help, as it does this instrument, to think of the heart as a seat which contains deity so that there is, in emotions brought to the heart, a place where they can be laid and given away to the one infinite Creator, for many times emotions are overpowering and there is literally no way to do anything with them except to offer them up. But if they are offered up in faith, this too is working with emotions in the heart center and is part of work well done.

This instrument is informing us that we need to end our initial message, and we do so in hopes that we have given you some food for thought that may give you some comfort as well as some resources. We would at this time transfer this contact to the one known as Jim. We are known as those of Q'uo and leave this instrument with thanks in love and in light.

(Jim channeling)

I am Q'uo, and greet each again in love and in light through this instrument. It is our privilege at this time to offer ourselves in the attempt to answer any further queries which may yet remain upon the minds of those present. Is there another query at this time?

R: I have two. In your talk you said the gateway to intelligent infinity is present in every moment. Would you state that in other words to help me find entry into it?

I am Q'uo, and am aware of your query, my brother. By that statement we mean to say that each moment contains not only love but perfection. If one were to investigate all of the energies that have added themselves into that time period which you call the present moment, if you were able to investigate your own experience leading up to that moment, any such moment would offer you the opportunity of making contact with the one Creator, of experiencing the full presence of the one Creator. Thus, the use of catalyst is the variable which offers to each entity more or less of this opportunity to realize the perfection and the love contained in each moment. Thus, if one is able to fully utilize the catalyst that is presented to one, at any time that one is able to do this the doors to infinity open for you.

Is there another query, my brother?

R: Yes. I will have to think about that. The other question concerns another term that you have used and that is the purified emotion, and I would like to ask you to restate that in other terms.

I am Q'uo, and am aware of your query, my brother. The purified emotion is closely related to that which we spoke of in your first query, and this is the untangling process which each of you goes through as you utilize the catalyst which is given to you in your daily round of activities. As you are able to see where catalyst originates, to see its effect upon you, to see your response to it, to see those responses which you have made previously—this ability to see the nature of your experience is also the process of untangling those emotions which are fused together, perhaps in a confusing fashion, so that you are able to separate anger from jealousy, from disappointment, from doubt, from hilarity, from rage, from all the various sources which may be a portion of your experience, so that when you have discovered the sources of your feelings you will have found the various threads that together form the fabric or tapestry of your lives. You will see what part each emotion plays. A purified emotion is an emotion that stands alone, that is itself pure, that has one source and one effect in your being. It is not blended with any other emotion. It is not confused with any other emotion. It is itself a thing in itself.

Is there another query, my brother?

R: Is this purified emotion a reflection of the love and the light that is the universe?

I am Q'uo, and am aware of your query, my brother. We may further confuse you by suggesting that [in coming to experience] the love and the light that each so values as fundamental portions of this experience that each shares, the purified emotion occurs as that kind of feeling that is so basic within one that one is able to see the ramifications of this feeling, its source, its object, its effect, its continued presences within one. And there is a kind of satisfaction that comes from so seeing an emotion that will, indeed, reflect to you increased amounts of love and light. However, the purified emotion is, shall we say, a joy in that there is no confusion any longer as to its nature.

Is there a further query, my brother?

R: No. Thank you. I don't mind being confused, and I appreciate your attempt to make sense with words. That is very difficult.

I am Q'uo, and we thank you also for your ability to perceive the difficulty that each of us has with the word description of experience.

Is there another query at this time?

Carla: I have two questions from P that I would like to read. "Somehow, the year 2000 tripped a switch in me and I have been on quite an emotional rollercoaster, and I don't know where these deep feelings of anxiety come from, but I would say that they are blocking love from my heart. The anti-anxiety drug seems to have kicked in for the meantime, giving me much needed relief."

I am Q'uo, and we believe that we grasp the nature of this query. The feelings that one has about an event, or a person, or an experience such as the year that you have numbered 2000 may be investigated by the entity that so values it in order to see what value one has given to it. Look, then, within you to see each aspect of this event, this year, that has meaning for you. Dissect it, if you can, with pen and paper. Look to the essay, the driving out of the meaning within that you may not consciously be aware of. Make a list of those qualities that you feel are unique to this year 2000. Beside each quality give your emotional response, that which you feel about this quality. Take this list as that which you then remove yourself into meditation to consider. Look deeply at each quality, each emotional response and to their summation as well. Then you, yourself, shall find the triggers that have opened in your mental and emotional and, perhaps, spiritual energy systems, the torrent of emotions that now move through you. As you are able to untangle these various sources and qualities of emotion and experience then you will be able to see more clearly the power that you have given to this event and its effect upon you.

Is there another query, my sister?

Carla: Yes. His second question: "I would also like to ask what might be the effect of the May 5th planetary alignment and whether that might affect one's emotions?"

I am Q'uo, and am aware of your query, my brother. Again, we would recommend the same process be used for this event as well, for each of us creates the fabric of our experience by the expectations that we hold for certain kinds of events, of experiences, and of people. There are within each of us preconceived notions, shall we say, that we attach to certain events. Those of the astronomical and astrological and metaphysical moving together blend many powerful energies that only we can describe for ourselves. Thus, we recommend that this entity utilize the same procedure for discovering the value of this event which has now passed.

Is there a further query, my sister?

Carla: I would like to follow up on something that is common to P's question and the conversation I had with M before the channeling meditation, and it has to do with what you said earlier about blessing, forgiving, redeeming, accepting and transforming these difficult emotions. I was saying to M earlier that, "You are going to have to take care of yourself because no one else is interested in your having a happy heart. You are going to have to support your own work and your own security emotionally." I was just wondering if you could look into that. How do we support ourselves? How do we bring ourselves healing and comfort when we are dealing with these difficult emotions like anxiety?

I am Q'uo, and am aware of your query, my sister. Within your meditative state—and this is again our recommendation for the investigation of emotion, to use meditation—look, then, to those feelings which you have, for they are valuable in themselves. They are the temperature, shall we say, of your current experience. Each may be seen as a portion of a trail, a thread, that will lead one to more fruitful finding of the value of experience. The emotions that one feels at any particular moment give one a place to begin to assess that which is occurring in the life pattern, to see the honest and spontaneous response of self to self. Then, as one is able to utilize these emotions in the balancing process one shall find their opposite occurring. Thus, if you are able to relive a situation in which a strong emotion occurs and within the meditative state to see this occurring, giving it free reign, to become as large as you can imagine, then there is the opportunity for the polar opposite emotion to arise within the meditative state so that you begin to feel another way about a certain situation, person or event. Then allow this polar opposite emotion to get as large and as powerful as it can. When this has completed its growth and presentation to you, then accept yourself for having both of these means by which the Creator may know Itself in you, in your experience. Thus, you have taught to the Creator that which you have learned within the situation and you have seen a fuller expression of natural emotion within your being as a means by which you know the Creator in you. Thus, you, working with every emotion that leaves its imprint upon you, are able to see the full range of your beingness, the appropriateness of each facet of emotion, the direction that each emotion points towards the heart of being, so that eventually there is but one emotion for [every] event, that being compassion, love, forgiveness, mercy, understanding—all of those qualities of unconditional love.

Is there a further query, my sister?

Carla: Just to finish up, then all emotions, all these purified rivers of the Creator, empty into love or stem from love, or are a derivative of love, or are distortions of love?

I am Q'uo, and am aware of your query and also aware of the accuracy of each observation that you have made in asking it. For all does come from love. All exists in love. All is pointed towards love. The examined life is that life which is able to get a glimpse of this truth from time to time in the process of examining, balancing and accepting each emotion as it moves through your being and points towards each heart.

Is there a further query, my sister?

Carla: No. Thanks. That is a beautiful message.

I am Q'uo, and we thank you once again. Is there a final query at this time?

(No further queries.)

I am Q'uo, and as it appears that we have exhausted the queries for this session of working we shall thank each once again for inviting us to join you for your meditative session. We are filled with joy at each opportunity to do so. At this time we shall take our leave of this instrument and this group, leaving each in the love and the light of the one infinite Creator. We are known to you as those of Q'uo. Adonai, my friends. Adonai. ✻

L/L Research

L/L Research is a subsidiary of Rock Creek Research & Development Laboratories, Inc.

P.O. Box 5195
Louisville, KY 40255-0195

www.llresearch.org

Rock Creek is a non-profit corporation dedicated to discovering and sharing information which may aid in the spiritual evolution of humankind.

ABOUT THE CONTENTS OF THIS TRANSCRIPT: This telepathic channeling has been taken from transcriptions of the weekly study and meditation meetings of the Rock Creek Research & Development Laboratories and L/L Research. It is offered in the hope that it may be useful to you. As the Confederation entities always make a point of saying, please use your discrimination and judgment in assessing this material. If something rings true to you, fine. If something does not resonate, please leave it behind, for neither we nor those of the Confederation would wish to be a stumbling block for any.

CAVEAT: This transcript is being published by L/L Research in a not yet final form. It has, however, been edited and any obvious errors have been corrected. When it is in a final form, this caveat will be removed.

© 2009 L/L Research

Sunday Meditation
May 21, 2000

Group question: Our question today has to do with being of service to others and we would like some guidelines as to when we are actually being of service to others and when we have gone too far and infringed upon an entity's free will.

(Carla channeling)

We are those of the principle known to you as Q'uo, and we greet you in the love and in the light of the one infinite Creator in whose service we are. We thank you for calling us to your circle of seeking and for asking us the interesting question about the boundaries of service to others and free will. As we speak we would request that, as always, that each use his or her discernment to determine those thoughts of ours which may have resonance and which thoughts need to be left behind. We trust each seeker's discrimination and it would be a service to us if each could, indeed, leave behind those thoughts which do not ring true. For in their own way, such thoughts are a subtle infringement and we would not wish that. Authority itself has the ring of infringement and we would like to take away any taint of authority from our words, for we do not feel that we have any over you or that we are wiser than you but, rather, simply that we have more experience. We are glad to share that experience and our thoughts with you, but we greatly appreciate it if you would do us this favor.

The boundary between helping someone else and infringing on their free will was noted in the discussion which preceded this meditation as being somewhat moveable, or seeming to be moveable, and we would heartily agree. Indeed, for many within your density there is almost no action that can be taken of any kind that is not considered an infringement on free will. The character and temperament of each seeker or, shall we say more generally, each person upon your planet whether or not she is consciously seeking, is a completely individual one. Some entities are set up by the gifts that they brought into this incarnation and the experiences that have helped shape their opinion to feel that all helpfully meant suggestions are completely across the line and are not helpful at all but rather are seen as interference.

There are others of your density that are happiest when all of their decision are either made for them or are made very much with them in mind but not necessarily with their intense contribution. To such entities almost no act seen as helpful by the other is seen as infringement upon the part of the self. This is due to the entity's feeling that his opinions do not have worth. Therefore, there is clearly no arbitrary and theoretical line across which to step will be an infringement and before which no step will be an infringement. With each entity with whom you deal the boundaries and possibilities of the relationship will be unique.

We give this instrument the picture of the ship out on the ocean that the introductory song was singing about. In the spiritual sense each of us, we as well as you, is a wayfarer on a medium that seems far more watery than earthen in that there are no graven roads. There is no path in the pathless wilderness of the ocean except that which is laid down by the sextant and the other instruments of navigation. On a cloudy night such navigational aids may not be effective and so often each seeker is as the ship without a useful rudder. There is the yearning for the end of the journey, the desire for the home, but there is not the conscious awareness at the particular time of how to get there, what direction to take, or how to prepare for the weather upon the ocean. As that song said, each is in this sense a stranger, a single entity following the yearnings of the heart and attempting to make the journey that is before it. In this basic environment information is worth its weight in gold, and, in a way, when the entity who wishes to polarize service to others attempts to be of service to another entity that person is offering to a friendly ship information on the road, the weather, the state of the stars, the direction of home. The help may be very physical. It may be food to eat on the journey or warm covers for a chilly day or an ocean night, may be supply of some kind or gifts of goods. And in this way parents have for countless centuries of recorded and unrecorded history helped their children in a continuing round of a movement of the energy of goods and supply. And, for the most part, this is seen by both parties as a genuine gift of service that is appreciated and not considered to be an infringement.

The gifts of information as from a friend to a friend or from a teacher to a pupil can certainly be seen by most on that trackless main as a genuinely helpful gift. And in that category we would put such information as the weather and the stars and so forth. Each of you often has good opinions [for] the others that are sailing in the sea alongside you. Certainly, one key question when it comes to the dividing line between service to others that is well given and service that extends into infringement is the consideration of whether that stranger on the boat near yours has actually asked for such information. When needs are physical it is somewhat easier to see a need and to supply that need. There is a fairly clear, well drawn knowledge that each has of what it takes to keep the body and soul together during an incarnation.

The giving that is beyond the family, that which is called by this instrument charitable giving, is also of this kind in which it may be seen that there is no infringement and attempting to provide necessities for those who do not have them. When the gifts that one wishes to give are opinions and information then it becomes much less clear as to what is fairly given and what is excessive. So if there is within you a feeling of uncertainty about the gift of an opinion or a thought, ask the question to yourself, "Has this person requested this of me?" If the entity has, indeed, requested such information you are on very safe ground. You are free to give what information you have and what thoughts you may contain in the knowledge that they have been asked for.

When the information and the ideas are not asked for then it is well to ask the self, "If my thoughts were a handful of seeds, which seed would I want to sow first?" For you may consider the field of another person's consciousness as a field of earth which is able to receive ideas and to generate or create new life from those ideas if they are given the kind of interest and nutrition by that person that enables an idea to grow. The dropping of a seed is almost always that which is within the reach of fairness and justice. Attempting to plant the whole field with ideas and opinions that were not asked for is, in most cases, going to be seen as somewhat of an infringement.

And when there is a question about whether a relationship has been infringed upon we would strongly advise clear and honest communication. This instrument was saying earlier that clear communication is a gift, not one that is often easy to give and not one which is often easy to receive when the communication involves uncomfortable material. However, when two entities can communicate clearly they can together determine for themselves the actual situation as regards infringement. For it is entirely a contract that is unique to two individuals as to where the line is drawn between service and infringement.

Perhaps the greatest gift that each may offer is the self. There is a tremendous hunger in spiritually awakened entities for a companion or companions of like mind. There is comfort, even at sea in an open boat, at having a small fleet of small boats about one which are all headed for the same general destination and, therefore, may sail together helping each other with supply, information and essence. It is the essence of self that is the greatest gift. Certainly, when the seeker finds a companion that is of a like mind and that offers a helpful presence each to the other, there is great cause for rejoicing because there is beyond any gift of thing or idea an utter beauty in the gift of self to self that has a purity that cannot be matched by outer gifts of any kind.

Blessed is the seeker who stumbles [across] the great good fortune of meeting such a companion. For some this becomes the mated relationship of husband and wife. For some there is tremendous metaphysical attraction but there is not the kind of companionship that suggests a shared life, but rather a shared friendship that is a looser and more loosely fitting relationship but which has a tremendous amount to offer of that essence of self that is like the most haunting of perfumes, impossible to replicate anywhere else. How appreciated is that unique scent of self that is the essence of old friends. And how fortunate does the person feel who meets the new friend. How gifted and how cherished does a friend make you feel.

We encourage each to look for ways to share the self beyond any concept of sharing the ideas or the supply. Look for ways to share the beingness. On a fundamental level it is as though the entire creation of nature were already sharing its beingness at a very intense level, holding nothing back, doubting and fearing nothing whatsoever but giving all of the self all of the time, all of the color, all of the bloom, all of the glory. That it will last for only a brief period of bloom matters not to the flower or to the blossom on the tree but only that it is there today to vibrate in the air, to drink in the wind and the sun, and to share its scent with all those around it. This is also your heritage and your manifest gift to offer, your odor, your special scent, that which you have created of thought, feeling and experience that is a vibration unlike anyone else's and which makes your friends smile. How loved each of you is by the Creator who appreciates each essence and by those who appreciate each of you. Do what you can to become appreciators of all those around you. Perhaps you indicate only by your expression or your smile that you are entering fully into a moment with another, but that other senses the profundity of your gift.

One thing unique to the offering of the essence of the self is that it cannot infringe. The self has no words, no requirements, and no demands. Presence is the perfect present.

We would at this time transfer this contact to the one known as Jim. We greatly thank this instrument and this group for calling us, and we would like to further answer any questions that you have at this time. And so we leave this instrument in the love and in the light of the one infinite Creator and transfer to the one known as Jim. We are those known as Q'uo.

(Jim channeling)

I am Q'uo, and greet each again in love and in light through this instrument. It is our privilege at this time to offer ourselves in the attempt to speak to any further queries which those present might have for us. Is there another query at this time?

S: I have asked about our daughter in the past. Thank you for your past words. They were helpful. Another friend who is a walk-in mentioned that I should open up and share more or I may develop cancer. I have had phantom pains in my groin and I have been tripping about them. Could you tell me about those pains and what I need to be doing and be concerned about?

I am Q'uo, and am aware of your query, my brother. We are indeed heartened that you have rejoined this circle of seeking, for we are most honored to speak to each who comes with queries and with the open heart. We bless and welcome you once again.

As to the nature of those pains and questions that you have concerning the health and well-being of your physical vehicle, we would suggest that you are, indeed, very healthy, for the physical vehicle that you utilize to move about within this illusion is one which has a natural health to it. However, one can alter this health by offering to the deeper mind the questions that are in the form of doubts. One can erode one's own health by such doubts and fears, not usually in a significant sense, but in the sense that the physical vehicle will respond to the manipulations of the mind. For, indeed, the physical vehicle is a creature of the mind. It is well, therefore, not just to affirm one's health but to claim it, to live it, to exercise it, to go forth filled with it. We would recommend that you rest in the knowledge that your physical vehicle supports you as well as you support it. The pains that you have felt are not of consequence. They are, rather, fulfillments of expectations, more specifically, of fears that have no substance to them at the present time. Therefore, our recommendation [is] of the positive affirmations that remove doubt.

Is there a further query, my brother?

S: Yes. On a world event stage level, the drama of the Elian Gonzalez child seems to be a catalyst for millions of people. There seems to be more going on behind the scenes than is being reported. Could you share your perspective as to what is being played out?

I am Q'uo, and am aware of your query, my brother. The drama that surrounds this young entity is that which each feels it to be. Again, the minds of those observing this event will see what they wish to see, will see what they are told to see, and will see more than there is to see. For, indeed, the mind is a powerful source of seeing, of information. There is as much to this event as any says there is, for as soon as it is said, there it is. We look upon this young entity and many entities who have been placed in the public eye and see that the mass consciousness of many entities needed this young entity to focus upon in order to discuss and describe the nature of the lifestyle found in this young entity's two worlds. And the nature of the family itself, for this basic unit of support, nurture, teaching and guidance is one which has suffered, shall we say, significant loss of influence for many people within your planetary population. Many would have governmental powers, political powers, economic powers, and social institutions take from the family that which is its responsibility. An entity such as the one known as Elian can serve as a point of focus for people who need to bring into their own minds the topics of concern. Such entities are as the lightning rod which attracts the attention of a great deal of public energy, and by allowing this energy to be expressed then provide to many people an avenue not only for expression of emotions and thoughts and opinions but of the possibilities for their own life patterns to be altered by such discussions, depending upon the passion with which the discussion is carried out. Thus, the world stage is one which always offers to each individual entity whatever the entity desires. For if you look at the range of opinions and responses to every situation you will find that there is, indeed, a wide range, and one may pick and choose those areas of importance to one's own areas.

And those areas, therefore, will be important to each entity because each entity will make it so. This is the value of public explanations, displays and so forth. Each entity may take from it that which has value to it.

Is there a further query, my brother?

S: We were talking earlier of the opinion of Laura Jadzick/Knight having an opinion of *The Ra Material* and the events surrounding it. It seems to be another case where people can interpret and take from it what they will. Some of the comments were curious. I would like to know your response to it.

I am Q'uo, and am aware of your query, my brother. We look upon all such expressions of opinion as that. There are as many opinions as one can imagine and perhaps there are more. Indeed, as those of Ra mentioned within the material that has been published as *The Law of One*, there are many who feel that that work is of the devil. Many feel it is angelic. Many feel that it is of importance. Many feel that it has no significance. Again, this is all opinion. Each will take from what they see, what they see. Each person's journey is valuable in itself, and however they fashion that journey, and from whatever opinions they weave it, this is their journey. This is what is appropriate to them. It matters not whether the importance is shared by any other.

Is there another query at this time?

S: None at this time. Thank you very much.

I am Q'uo, and we thank you, my brother. Is there another query at this time?

Carla: I'd like to ask about my low energy level. I understand if you can't answer, but I am trying to take care of myself, but I haven't done very well. I have felt worse this last week than before. I deeply believe in what I am doing and usually look forward to working on the book project. But I seem to be doing too much. Do you have any pointers for me as to how to balance and re-energize myself?

I am Q'uo, and am aware of your query, my sister. We look upon this topic which you have expressed in terms of feeling that you have depleted your own energy and because of this observation suggest that it would be well if you were to rest for a period of days, giving yourself nothing of importance to do, luxuriating in whatever brings you rest, and letting your energies of your mind, your body especially, and your spirit recharge so that there might once again be a reserve upon which to call. We are aware that there are those duties which are of a regular nature which your perform each day and we would recommend that these be taken care of in a short manner by either neglect or a short [reply] to each entity, writing to inform them of your need for rest.

Is there a further query, my sister?

Carla: Could you tell me if three days of this would be enough? Five days?

I am Q'uo, and this will be your determination, my sister. As you are able to rest, it is then your estimation that will be important as to how you are rejuvenating.

Is there another query at this time?

Carla: No. That's it. Thank you very much.

I am Q'uo, and we thank you once again. Is there another query at this time?

S: The Derby and Preakness have been run. Did your horse come in?

I am Q'uo, and we are aware that this instrument was finally able to pick a winner after twenty-seven tries. We rejoice with him for his success as we rejoice with each of you in your successes.

S: So, who is your pick on the Belmont Stakes?

I am Q'uo, and we are happy when the underdog wins, but we see that there are no dogs in this race. Therefore, we shall be content with whatever outcome occurs.

Is there a final query at this time?

(No further queries.)

I am Q'uo, and we rejoice with each of you and take a great deal of pleasure in the mirth that this group has found in its seeking together. We are always privileged to join this circle of seeking and are aware that this shall be the final session of working that includes the channeling aspect for a portion of your time, and we would hope that each will remember that we walk with you in your seeking, immanent or not. All you need do is mentally request our presence and we will be glad to join you in your meditations. We are known to you as those of Q'uo, and we would now take our leave of this instrument and this group. We leave each of you in the love and in the light of the one infinite Creator. Adonai, my friends. Adonai. ☙

L/L Research

L/L Research is a subsidiary of Rock Creek Research & Development Laboratories, Inc.

P.O. Box 5195
Louisville, KY 40255-0195

www.llresearch.org

Rock Creek is a non-profit corporation dedicated to discovering and sharing information which may aid in the spiritual evolution of humankind.

ABOUT THE CONTENTS OF THIS TRANSCRIPT: This telepathic channeling has been taken from transcriptions of the weekly study and meditation meetings of the Rock Creek Research & Development Laboratories and L/L Research. It is offered in the hope that it may be useful to you. As the Confederation entities always make a point of saying, please use your discrimination and judgment in assessing this material. If something rings true to you, fine. If something does not resonate, please leave it behind, for neither we nor those of the Confederation would wish to be a stumbling block for any.

CAVEAT: This transcript is being published by L/L Research in a not yet final form. It has, however, been edited and any obvious errors have been corrected. When it is in a final form, this caveat will be removed.

© 2009 L/L Research

Sunday Meditation
September 10, 2000

Group question: Our question today concerns the seasons of awakening. Each person seems to have a time and a way of realizing more of the heart of the nature of the life experience and consciously becomes desirous of learning more of accelerating it, of growing, and really taking things in hand. We would like for Q'uo to speak to us of these seasons of awakening: how we might cooperate with them, foster them, and work with them, not only in ourselves but in other people as well.

(Carla channeling)

We are those of the principle known to you as Q'uo, and we greet you in the love and in the light of the one infinite creator in whose service we are. It is a great blessing to be called to your meeting, and we thank you for seeking this circle of seeking as part of your spiritual practice. We know that each of you sacrifices something in order to spend time in this search for truth, and we thank you, for it truly enables us to be able to share our service with you as we have hoped to do. For we are here as a service to those who are seeking and who wish another voice to consider.

We would ask that each be careful to realize that we are not authority figures but really brothers and sisters who travel the same spiritual road, who are looking for answers to the same mysteries. We are happy to share our thoughts but, as always, we ask that you leave behind those thoughts that may present a stumbling block. Take only those that are useful to you and move on. And we would encourage you to practice this discrimination with all sources that you may hear or read, for, truly, authority resides in the resonance between your own nature and that which you need. When you meet your own personal truth it has a resonance to it that is unmistakable, and we ask you to trust that and not some outer authority, no matter how persuasive or powerful.

You ask this afternoon concerning awakening and change. And since there are several levels of discussion in this subject we would choose the more general one with which to begin. We would discuss the basic concept of incarnational lessons. The mechanisms of change are somewhat cyclical and, spiritually speaking, descend from the level of preincarnative placement of the self and of the lessons of the incarnation that were set up by the self and by the higher self and other guidance, before incarnation. Before incarnation, each spirit that is now incarnate in a physical body on planet Earth had a great deal of say in choosing what lessons of love it wished to concentrate on during the upcoming lifetime and what outer services it might be able to specialize in sharing.

When the lifetime begins, memory of this process of choosing the basic themes of the incarnation or the basic lessons of the incarnation is removed. The veil descends, and in complete forgetfulness and innocence the physical child is born with a destiny that is, in some way, complete. This, however, does not abrogate free will. For it is the choices that this entity makes as it faces the relationships that it has chosen to offer itself and the catalyst that it has chosen to offer itself that will create the actual distortions that will be followed throughout the pattern of a lifetime. Consequently, the same relationships and the same situations may occur three different times but if the person is in three different states of mind the outcome of the same catalyst can be three different outcomes, and this is basically the structure of change throughout an incarnation. There will be a repeating theme, or perhaps two or even three themes, of incarnational lesson which bring up material having to do with one or another lesson of love that becomes familiar to the spirit in incarnation to some extent. Each time that it repeats it becomes a little clearer. At least that is the process that is hoped before incarnation.

In actuality many times a person in the midst of a difficult situation may choose to feel that it is the relationship or the situation that is at fault, rather than the self needing to pay attention to relationship or situation. Consequently, the solution chosen by the careless thinker may be to leave the relationship or leave the situation, thinking that another person or another situation will change that which is wrong. It is only when the pattern is repeated with another person or when another situation develops that brings in the same themes that the person may begin to feel that there may be a theme and that it may be worth attending to in hopes of learning the lesson, achieving the learning desired, and being able to move on to more interesting lessons. This is a general scheme of spiritual evolution that is at the unconscious level that is designed to work while the person is asleep, spiritually speaking, and designed to be very vulnerable to being accelerated by the person who has awakened.

Now let us speak concerning this situation where some are asleep and some are awake as spirits. The hope of each entity who enters the Earth plane at this time is graduation from this density. Each entity who has achieved incarnation at this time is capable of expressing full enough awareness of love and service to others to graduate this density in this lifetime with just a little more effort. In each case the spirit that each is before incarnation has real hopes of making some strides towards cementing that graduating ability, that ability to receive and transmit the light of the infinite Creator.

However, as we said, it is part of the plan of a school of life and love that depends on faith alone and not knowledge that all knowledge that can be proven of the reality of the spirit be removed from the conscious mind so that during incarnation the spirit that each of you is is faced with a journey that is strictly a journey of faith. There is really no way to prove spiritual principles, except by subjective experience and subjective conclusions drawn from subjective thinking. In other words, there is no objective spiritual proof possible. This is a protected illusion in which faith alone can bring the seeker through. The mechanism of destiny set by each before incarnation will periodically bring great confusion and trouble into the patterns of energy of each seeker, and it will attempt in a mechanical and rather blunt instrument sort of way to move the thinking of that person from head to heart, from intellect to openhearted love, and it will or will not have an effect depending on something that cannot be taught or bought or predicted or encouraged or manipulated, and that is the condign pre-set alarm clock of each individual within the Earth plane.

Each entity dwelling in an incarnative body has her alarm clock set for a certain triggered time. Now, many hit that triggered time and rather than waking up, hit the snooze button and go back to sleep. To some extent this tendency can be manipulated, but we would recommend that it be left completely to each seeker as to when that seeker will actually awake. For it truly is an awakening process. It is as if entities of Earth are born into a certain kind of dream which they can dream nicely all the way from cradle to grave. However, there is a likelihood that there will be an awakening from this level of dream into a higher and more overarching level of dreaming which involves more light and more so-called reality. And in this awakened state it can be seen that this incarnation is not simply the days and the nights of someone working until it falls into its grave but is the adventures in flesh of citizens of eternity that are not bound by time or space.

This is a huge change in consciousness: to become self-aware that one is a citizen of eternity. This is a real awakening, and when this occurs, there is a shift. It is as if before you were plodding upon the land,

and suddenly now you are on the ocean and moving quickly. And you cannot walk out of the boat and onto the water and onto safe shores. Indeed, you are on a path that cannot be predicted beforetime and that has many elements that are not linear. Consequently, there is a tremendous amount of experience that comes very quickly when the awakening occurs. To our way of thinking, it is a time for rejoicing when the spirit that you are has this sense of awakening to a deeper level of reality, to a fuller sense of life, to a wider appreciation of the possibilities of the present moment. It is not that learning can be accumulated like bricks until a wall can be built to house the knowledge of the mysteries involved in being who we are, but rather, that the fuller the light that we are standing in and working with the more of that light that we can send through our selves and into the creation to lighten those energy patterns about us.

When an entity wakes up it is as if a light has been switched on. It is not a light that can ever truly be put out again, for there is an awareness there. A change has been made, and it cannot be undone.

When the awakened entity views those who are still asleep it can seem desirable to shake them up and wake them up. And as the one known as S mentioned, it is perfectly all right when talking about things that interests us to mention such things and drop a seed here and there. There is no infringement on free will in doing so. However, to move further than the first mention of an interesting topic or thought without a substantially positive response is to begin to encroach upon that person's privacy and free will. We would encourage, rather, the attitude of trust and faith that each person's incarnational schedule is set as it should be, that if they are still asleep they should still be asleep, that something is going on that in the pattern of that person's life will work out perfectly for that person.

The person each needs to focus on in terms of spiritual work is the self. For, truly, the self is the universe. The self is the Creator. The self is all that there is. For all is one. The unity of all that there is is beyond understanding and an attempt to explain its nature devolves into paradox. This is as it should be, we feel, and we are, as we have said before, content to allow the mystery to escape us. We continue to pursue the mystery of deity, the mystery of essence, and although we have come to feel that we know many, many things we still find our reliance in the values upon which you are now focused: love itself. And that precious feeling, instinct, to help.

That desire is as a passion that shall burn through many lifetimes and many densities, and each of you will be that which brings beauty and healing, not because of the outer gifts that you share, but because of your being, because of the nature of your self as you meet the present moment. Regardless of the rate of change, indeed, regardless of the rate and pace of the busy days that each of you experiences, we encourage each of you to find time to be. For in the midst of whatever change you are, in the midst of whatever transformation, beyond all levels of alteration, you are who you are. And you have a basic nature and vibration that has been your signature of love for eons. All that you do within this incarnation shall burnish it up a little, shine it a bit, perhaps correct some distortion that you, as a spirit, see in the overall pattern as you gaze between lifetimes in leisure and patience.

But for now, have faith in yourself, and know that you need to spend that time just being, whether it is in meditation, taking a walk, sitting and holding hands and looking at the sunset, whatever chance that you have to share the silence and let the mind come to a halt and just be, take that moment and let your heart open and flower and blossom, and let your nature roll out in sympathy and harmony with all of the other natures of creation whatever. Let yourself sing like the stars, and the trees, and the wind and the fire at the heart of the planet, for you, as much as any of these elements of nature, are elemental, are yourself, are authentic and are a part of the good and the healing of your planet and your people.

May each of you take the time to become aware of yourself as these wonderful energy systems that allow the energy of the great original Thought of love to come rolling through and out into the Earth plane. Only entities and incarnations such as you can give that gift to the Earth. Many of you are wanderers who came here specifically to act as transducers for light upon Earth, to lighten the planet, to lighten the vibration, to help Earth at this time. All awakened entities, whether mature Earth natives ready for graduation or wanderers hopefully ready for the same graduation, now have this opportunity to lend their love and their light in service to those upon the Earth. We hope that you encourage and support each other as each of you attempts to become more truly yourself amidst all of the changes and transformations that you experience.

We would at this time transfer this contact to the one known as Jim. We leave this instrument in love and light, and with thanks. We are those of Q'uo.

(Jim channeling)

I am Q'uo, and greet each again in love and light through this instrument. At this time it is our privilege to offer ourselves in the attempt to answer any further queries from those in this circle. May we ask if there is another query at this time?

S: It's good to hear from you again. There is a girl whom we work with and her daughter is having health problems at 13 and they seem unusual at that age. Is there anything that we can do to help or advise? Any suggestions that you might have would be most helpful.

I am Q'uo, and am aware of your query, my brother. We appreciate the opening of the heart energy center upon your part in the consideration of that which would be helpful to the young entity of whom you speak. We are not those who give what you would call life readings or assessments of entities in order that one remedy or another be applied for any malady that may be found, for there are those who have this skill and use it well. We, on the other hand, are more philosophically oriented among those who seek to serve Earth at this time. And, thus, it would be our suggestion that any assistance given to this entity be that which is a natural outgrowth of the interaction between the group that is your family and the group that is this entity's family so that there be the normal progression of conversation which expresses the concern for the welfare of the young entity and the desire to be of service. When this seed is thusly planted and interest is noticed, then one may continue to water the seed with the attention that you may offer through one avenue or another. The choice of avenues is that which we would recommend by utilizing the intuition, the feeling within your deeper self that there is a path that can be taken and action that can be offered and, moreover, a concern, a love that can be shown by the entire process of interaction. Thus, the attention given to this situation may be nourished in love, contemplated with the mind, and directed with the intuition.

Is there another query, my brother?

S: Yeah, there is a tree in our backyard that's not been real healthy but provides wonderful shade and is a beautiful tree and it's something that we enjoy when we are outside. We wonder if there is anything that we can help with the health of this beautiful maple tree?

I am Q'uo, and am aware of your query, my brother. You will not be surprised to discover that our suggestion for this entity is similar to our suggestion to the previous entity. However, the means of communication between you and this entity may be somewhat different in that the second-density entities known to you as trees are those which also respond to that quality of love which comes from the open heart. Again, in this instance we would recommend that in the shading and protective arms of this entity you retire yourself into meditation seeking not only a direction for yourself but the establishment of a feeling-tone, shall we say, between yourself and this tree entity. Find the silence within and when that silence has been achieved, move in harmony and sympathy into a communication with the tree. Ask what it needs. Await a response which may or may not be in the form of your words. If you are able to perceive an image or a feeling that comes after the asking of the question, pay attention to that image and to that feeling. Follow either as a trail of communication is laid. Trust that this tree knows its needs and appreciates your love. Perhaps it will be necessary to achieve this meditation for a number of your days before there is a clear response. Perhaps the response will come immediately. However long or short the response time may be, then move in action according to that which you perceive, and trust your ability to perceive the response from the tree.

Is there another query, my brother?

S: I had many questions before coming here, yet they seem to escape me at this point, so I will turn the questioning over to anyone else who has one.

Carla: It's the first time I have had a chance to talk to you since I finished the handbook. I don't know if you have the capability to perceive what has been written, but if you do I would just wonder if you are satisfied with what is in it, or if you have other things that you would like to see in it?

I am Q'uo, and am aware of your query, my sister. We are most honored to have been mentioned in this work in a number of references. We are aware that this work has been one which is both fatiguing and enlivening, for the effort is great, yet the feeling of achievement that we feel within your energy system is substantial for the accomplishment of this work. We, of course, are not in the role of the critic, though if we were would have little purpose to fulfill, for we are aware that you have been most diligent in covering those areas which are of concern to entities such as yourself and many others like you who seek that which may be called the truth and seek it within a very difficult environment in which there is much of metaphysical or spiritual twilight, the lighting of the path for the next step of the path being dim in some cases, bright in others, various at all times, and we are aware that there are those concerns within this volume that are spoken to in a clear and enlightening manner so that those who are able to read this book may feel the same inspiration and information that has been felt by the few who have read it to date.

Is there a further query, my sister?

Carla: I had a gal write in to me that had a sore arm which she had abused physically and wore it out, with tennis elbow and golf arm and everything else wrong with it. She was afflicted by a new age healer who wrote her and upset her terribly and said she had all kinds of things wrong with her emotionally which were causing her to have this sore arm, and I wondered if you could comment with anything that I could say to this woman to express that it is not her fault that she has a sore arm. I really hate new age guilt and I really dislike doctors and healers who make their patients feel guilty for feeling bad. I know there is something between the psyche and the soma, but I would really appreciate any comments that you may have that I could send to this woman.

I am Q'uo, and am aware of your query, my sister. When we consider requests such as this we look again to the preamble that we offer before each contact is made with this and any other group that we are privileged to contact and that each entity present be encouraged to exercise the personal discrimination so that any information that comes before its notice be subjected to that inner knowing that each entity possesses that can direct it surely and safely along this journey of seeking the truth. For each entity's truth will be somewhat different though it partakes of the same great truth of the unity of all things created by love. Each entity must be aware that there is a unique journey that it is traveling and will travel. When information is made available that may or may not aid this journey then it is that the mind first looks at the information and assesses it upon an intellectual level and determines one thing or another about the information. Then the mind gives over the assessment of any information to what may be called the intuition, to the heart, to the deeper self, to that deeper knowing that each entity possesses. It is here that a feeling is generated in response to any thoughts about information offered. And it is this feeling from within that one must trust. We would suggest that this entity and any other entity in a similar situation take the information that has been given it into the meditative state after having considered it intellectually, and within the meditative state allow the feeling tones to arise from within that are the heart's response to that which has been given from without, and then to follow this feeling to its conclusion, whether it be to accept all, some or none of the information offered, and to do this with a feeling of love and gratitude for the Creator of us all and to the individualized portion of that one Creator which offers information to the one to be healed.

Is there any further query, my sister?

Carla: No, but I will be very happy to send that on to her. Thanks.

T: I have a question, if you still are up to it. I come here and always enjoy the silent meditation and I sit here and start meditating and sometimes, like today, I didn't hear anything that was said. I am just stoned and as high as I can be on the meditation, but could you comment on this incredible energy that I feel, and this whole process?

I am Q'uo, and am aware of your query, my brother. We are most pleased that you have been able to experience the basic vibrational frequency of our contact.

(Tape change.)

I am Q'uo, and am again with this instrument. The vibrational frequency that is the result of our vibrations and your own, blended in an harmonious fashion, is the heart of what we have to offer. It moves beyond words. It moves beyond feelings. It, hopefully, gives an inspiration to those who are able to perceive it. This inspiration is that which is as a, what you may call, blank check. One may take this inspirational energy and fill in the blank as to how it shall be used, what shall be considered, or if there shall be the thoughts related to it at all. In our speaking to you we not only infuse thoughts upon this basic carrier wave, but we fashion words that are in response to queries asked so that we take this basic vibrational frequency and shape a portion of it in such and such a fashion that it might communicate to both the mind and to the heart and, hopefully, to the spirit as well. If the words spoken during our sessions with you do not register then one may consider the possibility that these words were not for you this day and move on without a second thought. However, if one is also able to feel the inspiration of the basic carrier wave then the fundamental portion of our service to you has been accomplished and we are grateful to each for any opportunity to serve that was made available to us.

Is there another query at this time?

T: Yeah, if you're not too tired. I had a conversation with a crazy friend of mine who has never had anyone to talk to about things important to us. His wife has developed Alzheimer's and he is now back on the bottle. We talked and he wanted to know what faith was. He didn't know if he had any. I said that his feelings were like his faith and he should have faith in what comes out. Could you give a quick comment on faith?

I am Q'uo, and am aware of your query, my brother. The trust of which you speak in relation to faith is not only in one's feelings but the feeling that despite that which one sees and experiences that one knows that all is well, that one knows that all will be well, that what is occurring at any moment is appropriate and may be learned from in an effective manner which enhances the evolutionary journey. Each entity along this journey will have those times of doubt, of trial, of confusion, of feeling lost, of feeling alone. All of these and many more experiences are those which test one's character, which offer one kind of lesson or another. There are as many kinds of learning as there are entities to learn. However, in each experience and for each entity, if one can uncover that feeling of faith within and let it be the north star, the Polaris of the self, then one may move without fear and accept whatever is the daily round of activities as they come to one. For an entity that is filled with faith, there is no challenge too great. For any entity without faith, all challenges feel too great. Faith is that which one develops by wishing to develop faith. If one feels faith is lacking in the life pattern, begin to investigate the qualities of faith, the nature of faith, and begin to act as though you have faith, and faith will come to you. Moreover, faith will come through you, for faith is like love. It is a basic quality of this and all creations. If one can begin to exercise the quality of faith it is much like your physical muscle. It will grow in strength and ability.

Is there another query, my brother?

T: No. Thank you very much. That is wonderful. Thank you.

I am Q'uo, and, again, we thank you, my brother. Is there a final query at this time?

(No further queries.)

I am Q'uo, and we again thank each present for offering us the opportunity of joining your circle of seeking this day. It, as always, has been a great privilege to speak to each present, to offer our thoughts and words, humble as they are, to those concerns of heart and mind and soul. Know that you do not walk alone ever upon this journey. Not only do you have friends within your illusion, but there are those guides and presences that have been with you from the beginning of this illusion and who will not leave you until this illusion for you has ended as well. Each seeks a way to inspire, to guide, and to offer the hand when needed. In your meditations seek there the guidance from all those who wish you well upon the inner planes. We are known to you as those of Q'uo, and at this time we shall take our leave of this instrument and this group, leaving each, as always, in the ineffable light and love of the infinite Creator. Adonai, my friends. Adonai. ✜

Homecoming Session
September 23, 2000

Group question: The question this evening has to do with the fact that there seem to be changes in the world happening very quickly around us. As seekers, we are wondering if Q'uo could give us some idea as to how we can maintain our balance on our path while changes are happening so quickly around and within us?

(Carla channeling)

We are those of the principle known to you as Q'uo. We greet each of you in the love and in the light of the one infinite Creator in whose service we are. We wish to express our deep gratitude at your calling us to your circle of seeking this evening. We thank each of you for the sacrifices that you have made to be part of this circle. For each of you it has been a challenge, and the resulting desire to know the truth has been sharpened and honed and the energy that has been created is most beautiful. Your desire is as a beacon, and we thank you for the questions that you have asked and the hopes and the dreams that bring you to the restlessness of spirit that has caused this instrument and many among you to call yourselves wanderers.

Your desire to hear such information as we can offer through this instrument is also a great boon to us because this is our chosen path of service as a group at this particular juncture, so without being able to speak with groups such as you we would not be able to offer our service or to progress in our own learning. And so we thank and bless you for several things, not least of all the joy of sharing time with each of you.

We would ask of you that you take our word lightly, for we are not authorities. We are as you: pilgrims upon a dusty road. As the one known as V has said, each of us varies in our experiences, in the quantity of them, in the quality of them. And each of us knows the stones in the shoe, the dust upon the road, the light of hope in the sky amidst the clouds. We share a landscape, and we share in what may be called the journey. And as each of you has found many times already, the journey has many faces, challenges and surprises. And we are glad to look at these masks with you, for you have asked concerning keeping to one's path in the course of rapid change. And we would, indeed be delighted to share with you with the understanding that if any words that we say do not ring true to you, you will put them aside without a second thought and move on. For as the one known as A has said, that which is yours has a resonance, and you know it, and you feel it. And when it is not for you it is a dead thing and can easily be left behind. To hold to authority is to create a stumbling block. Hold only to your thirst, to your hunger, to your desire, to that passion that often seems so unfashionable within the mirrored walls of the world. For you need not look at those mirrors until you are ready to see that all things are the reflection of the self.

We would begin speaking concerning paths and change by speaking on the level at which there is no variation or shadow. For we would root that which we have to say in the truth of unity, in the circle view that sees the octave of experience, in the view that knows that each is the Creator. In a very real sense it is useful to think of all times and spaces as the final moment before oblivion, for, indeed, that is the precise link of a creation. That which seems eons is but a heartbeat of the one infinite Thought which is love. All that you will and have and are—experience, experienced, experiencing—is taking place precisely now. You are in a circle dance. Your movements contain eons of awkwardness, missed steps, and seeming mistakes of every possible kind and character. And yet, seen from the level of the circle dance, every mistake was part of a perfect pattern. Every foolish choice was that freedom that you could not otherwise have had. Every lifetime in which you spent years questioning this and that is seen within the level of the circle dance as the eccentric but perfect balancing dynamic that it was, that it is, and that it shall be.

Each of you, each of us within this group, each of those infinite sparks of the Logos, rest in unfathomable perfection drenched in a unity so profound that there is none to behold the light, but only the light. And this is your star being. This is your nature. Each of you has at the heart that fire of suns, that spark of creatorness that contains all that there is. And so, in a very important way, each of you is, beyond all changes, yourself. The you that was created before time and space, the only you that was ever you, the only you that will ever be you, you are unique. And truly are you precious and beloved to the Creator who values every distortion and seeming imperfection that has dented and banged you in the fire of learning and made you who you are. For you vibrate with a certain chord that cannot be duplicated, that is essentially you, that is most beautiful.

We realize that each of you would like to vibrate as the Logos. Each of you would like to have that perfect vibration of love, and yet we say to each of you how perfect you are as you are, as you turn, as you change, as you come to this moment. How well you hold within yourself the unity of all that there is. How gently do you cradle that being within that shall be and has always been a child of the one infinite Father. This instrument objects to the use of the word, Father. We object to the Father calling a Father, Mother. Consequently, shall we say, "celestial parent."

At any rate, beyond that level lies a life in which you are involved. Each of you has chosen to come into a heavy chemical illusion, and you have chosen to come into an illusion that is quite athwart your nature, for each of you remembers better ways to do things, better ways to live, better ways to think. And it is frustrating, indeed, for K to hold his laughter back, for those who attempt to work for the people they find in a way that enlarges the love within the world. We realize that there are very real challenges to expressing that level of self that is the soul of the spirit in the everyday life. And yet that is the level at which the self feels most authentic. That level at which the entire self can be shared.

There are so many calls upon the pilgrim self. It is extremely easy to move upon the surface of life as though one were skating upon the surface of a pond, or walking along the midways of a carnival, distracted by the rides and the amusements, busy with one thing and then another, and beguiled by the surface of things. Meanwhile, just beneath the level of the surface that self that has awakened to the spiritual path chews through catalyst with a voracious appetite. And the self is placed in one pickle after another, a puzzle followed by an enigma, followed by another challenge. As quickly as one can focus upon one thing there will come another. Whether the events are large or small often does not matter. It is the accumulation of changes that creates the sense of having lost one's sea legs or of even of having lost the lodestone by which one sets one's course. Certainly, it is easy to feel lost along the path, and there are, indeed, times when it is best to remove oneself from the path, one way or another, to go find a cave or a rock or a beautiful valley dotted with sheep and rest a while, and wait, and cultivate as a crop, patience.

For there are some things which continue to puzzle one for a significant period of your time. There are some riddles that do not have a ready solution. There are other times when the thing to do comes as if upon a wave and deposits itself at your feet, and when those gifts of the sea resonate with you, then we encourage you to move quickly. More than anything we encourage each of you to follow your discrimination. It is easy to doubt one's own judgment, and we have heard the one known as V speak concerning her lacks of awareness, and we have heard the one known as C say somewhat the same thing. But may we say that within our view these judgments of self are unfair and inadequate, and, in general, we would encourage all never to judge the self. This instrument calls it taking the spiritual temperature. May we say that it is an extremely rare seeker who is capable of seeing herself. Each of you was placed in this illusion precisely so that you would lose sight of your self. You were not put here to be intelligent and to make wise decisions. You were put here to make mistakes and to suffer. You see, each of you came here to get lost and to make what may be considered mistakes. Each of you hoped that when you plunged into this place of unknowing you would awaken to that instinct within you for faith, and you would choose to live by faith. You had hoped that you would take the opportunity of not knowing anything to choose, freely, the good, the true, the beautiful, the just, for no reason except that it is a beautiful thing to behold a fair and truthful principle.

And each time as a small new being, or as an adult being, you have heard stories of true heroism, love for others, and a nobility of the ordinary human being. Each of you has thrilled and known what it is to be a person of faith in a world that is dark. Each of you has seen what light a being can shine just by being who he is. You did not come into this world with high ambitions within the world. You may well create them within the world, and that is something to be encouraged if that is what you desire. But each of you came into this world in hopes that you would have the opportunity to choose to express love. You came to breathe the air, to love each other, to accept the love of each other, and to be yourselves. These are the ambitions with which you came into this world as a spirit: to be of service, to choose the good, to give and receive love. Every learning and every service has its roots in these simple hopes.

Of course, in the press of circumstance each spirit will often feel lost, abandoned, alone and without resources. This is part of the refining action of the illusion known as Earth. Consistently, again and again, you will find yourself in positions where you feel you are pressed against your own limitations, and it is at these times that the opportunities for faith are the greatest. And what is faith? We can say it in three words: all is well.

To keep one's feet, to keep one's balance, those three words are often as far as one needs to go if one is able to say them in quietness and in confidence. For truly, to the best of our knowledge, all is well. You are here. You are doing what you should be doing. You are experiencing. You are feeling. You are loving and you are being loved. You are extremely successful at being third-density human beings.

Do you come close now to that point where the light becomes fuller and your next incarnation works with different lessons in a different environment? Yes. For each of you, this is so. Whatever books you have read, whatever you think your level of awareness is, each of you is poised at graduation into fourth density. Each of you is eager for more light. And so you are in a wonderful position to gather experience, to make mistakes, to suffer from them, and to learn in the suffering even better who you are, why you are here, what you truly want to do, and who you truly want to become. And that which yesterday you dreamt, today you experience. That which today you dream, tomorrow you shall experience, until all that you have possibly imagined to desire has been experienced. So gauge carefully that which you desire, for you shall receive it.

Although we say in many different ways that you cannot lose your way amidst whatever change, we would say, as always, that a great aid in keeping one's balance in the midst of great transformation is the daily habit of silence. Whether it be contemplation, meditation, a silent walk, whatever it be that is your own prayer of the heart, open that heart to the silence daily and allow the experience that is coming through you to seat itself there. For time spent in silence is time spent with the Creator. And what a blessing for the Creator to spend time in silence with you. For there is no asking and there is no telling, but just the meaning. And the Creator craves your company and your communion and loves you so dearly, and waits for you so patiently to remember who you are, and whose.

May each of you be about your business. May each of you, as this instrument says, bring each other home. For you see, in that mirror world, each of you is, to the other, the picture of the self, the picture of the Creator. What shall you mirror by your thoughts this day? What Creator shall you be to those about you? And what being shall you be to yourself? May each of you enter your own heart in a mood to forgive completely, to fall completely in love with yourself just as you are. This is an important step in the evolution of the spirit, this ability to accept the self as it is, with every distortion, every folly, everything that the illusion seems to be telling you about yourself. For, you see, you are looking so hard at a personality shell that is not really there. Instead, depend upon that self that is beneath the surface, that will well up in the silence and tell you who you are when you need to know it, will give you new information when you need it, and may tell you to wait when you least want to hear it. Fall in love with that self that is you. Forgive and love that self, and you will find it easy to love the rest of the selves about you. Or at least as easy to love as it was to love the self.

We would at this time transfer this contact to the one known as Jim. We leave this instrument in love and light. We are known to you as those of Q'uo.

(Jim channeling)

I am Q'uo, and greet each of you again in the love and the light through this instrument. It is our privilege at this time to offer ourselves in the attempt to speak to any further queries which those present may have for us.

Is there another query at this time?

E: The sun and moon have a great deal of influence on us and is it by accident or design that they are the same size in the sky? That is, the moon perfectly superimposes the sun.

I am Q'uo, and am aware of your query, my brother. As it is the nature of the one Creator to allow for the expression of free will throughout the one creation, the formation of this creation in such and such a fashion is that which falls under the provenance of those entities which you would call the Logoi, which you have discussed this day to some extent. Thus, each entity of completeness that you see in your sky, known to you as the star, is an entity which takes the infinite mind of the one Creator and refines it in a fashion which this entity hopes will offer avenues of expression to the one Creator that are efficient in what you would call the evolutionary process. This extends to those bodies in your sky of which you have spoken that are arranged in a fashion which seems at first to be of chaos, and yet when investigated more closely reveals an order all about. The fact that the moon body of your local planetary sphere is of the identical size of the sun body at most opportunities of observation is of a nature of choice which is beyond our ken of understanding. Yet we do perceive that this choice was made consciously for a purpose that we are unable to plum, and this is not so unusual for us or for any who looks carefully at the one creation about one. For all about there are clues. There is a trail to the one Creator. There is a mystery that has a solution that reveals itself by slow degrees, and so we see that which is and ponder its meaning and take what we can from that which we observe. In short, we cannot give you the reason why but can say that this is so and was chosen so.

Is there a further query, my brother?

K: Will you speak to us of your knowledge of those who are known as the Children of the Law of One?

I am Q'uo, and am aware of your query, my brother. There have been various times in this planetary sphere's evolutionary process that some of the population of this entity has partaken in a more pure degree, shall we say, of the knowledge of the unity of all things. Many there have been upon this planetary surface who have felt in some way this harmonious unity and have, by their desire to know more, drawn to themselves information from those who are of the Law of One and members of what we have called the Confederation of Planets in the Service of the One Creator. And as these entities have been called to service by the population of this planetary sphere this service has taken various forms, not only the telepathic kind of communication that we engage in at this time but also the movement into the incarnative patterns of the planet as that which you have called the wanderer, moving in groups or clans, shall we say, that have had more or less influence at different portions of your planet's history. The most well known being that of the entities who incarnated within the eighteenth dynasty in the area of your holy land or that which is now called Egypt. There were those at this time who moved, shall we say, heaven and earth that the Law of One should become the means by which the One Creator was worshipped and the life upon the planetary sphere was lived. At other times, such as the movement of the Brotherhood of the Seven Rays into the area which you call Peru, in which time there was also the sharing of the information concerning the unity of all things. In each instance it was the intention of these entities that you have called the sons and daughters of the Law of One, or the Children of the Law of One, that it was given to the planetary population to understand that this was that which they were seeking by the nature of their beliefs. At this time there was also the movement of these entities and those of a similar nature to again share this law of singleness with those who seek such.

Is there another query, my brother?

(Tape change.)

Is there another query at this time?

S: In the last few months I have received a lot of help in my spiritual growth and I was wondering if you could tell me what help I have received. Who? What? Where? I was wondering if you could give me a little more detail on this.

I am Q'uo, and am aware of your query, my brother, and find that there is information of this nature which we may share but that there is some concern that we do not abridge free will. When an entity such as yourself seeks with a strong desire in the area of the spiritual evolution there are many unseen hands which move in concert to answer this call. Each entity such as yourself has those presences about him which are from birth given the honor and the duty to watch over and guide the progress of those within their care. In your case there are those who have been called, not only from birth, but according to the interests and areas of investigation which you have undertaken in this time period of which you speak. Thus, added to the angelic presences that are seen most commonly by your peoples as guides—those of the male and those of the female and those of the androgynous nature—there are also those inner planes teachers which have responded to the particular interests which you have given your attention to. Thus, not only do you find their influence in the books which make themselves available to you and the meetings of other entities in your daily round of activities that seem synchronistic but also in the moving into certain activities such as the joining of this weekend gathering of seekers that may seem in some to have been coincidental. Yet each step was carefully planned, not only by such invisible assistance but by those portions of yourself which you may see as your higher self, which is that great resource which may be called upon in the silence of the open heart. As one moves along the path of seeking the intensity of the desire is that which is seen as foremost in importance in responding to a seeker's call for assistance. Thus, you attract to you those whose desire to serve is as strong as your desire to seek. In this way there is the opportunity to give information in many forms that will assist in opening to the heart and to the mind those layers of self that are most in need of being explored.

Is there a further query, brother?

S: I would like to express my appreciation to those who have given me such assistance and I would appreciate it if it could continue. It has been enlightening and, at times, humorous.

I am Q'uo, and you may rest assured, my brother, that your gratitude is felt most purely by those who send their gratitude as well for the opportunity to be of service.

Is there another query at this time?

S: Yes, I think of you and who you are and what you are, and you mentioned you are service to others, blah, blah, blah. The information and the way you project things … did you go to channeling school, and take channeling classes, and have channeling parties with your channeling friends, and get a degree in channelology? I am curious on more details as to how you answer our calls.

I am Q'uo, and am aware of your query, my brother. We are members of those who are called the Brothers and Sisters of Sorrow. It is the sorrow upon the planetary surface and within the peoples of this planetary sphere that calls us here. This sorrow is expressed in many ways. That which you may call an intense desire to seek the truth is a shining light amidst the sorrow and that which gives great joy to all who beholds such light. And, yet, it is the sorrow that calls us here. The lack of knowledge of the one Creator. The lack of light. The lack of love. The heart that is closed. The mind that is beaten upon by the culture in which it cannot find expression. There are as many ways to feel and express sorrow in this third-density illusion as there are entities within it. And each seeks in some fashion that which may be called the truth. As we see those who express the kind of seeking and sorrow that we are able to respond to we are desirous in the extreme in moving to these entities in whatever way is possible. It is rare that we are able to speak as we do now, through instruments such as this one and others in a mind-to-mind contact that allows the expression of words. It is far more usual in our experience of serving entities such as yourselves that we would move in an unseen fashion, perhaps working in dreams, creating an opportunity in meditation to transmit a hunch, an intuition, a feeling, a direction, a thought, an image, a tone. In such a way are we most able to reach the greater majority, shall we say, of those who seek that which we have to offer.

Is there another query at this time?

V: May I know the nature, positive or negative, of the entity Turquoise?

I am Q'uo, and though we are aware of your query, my sister, we find that we are bated by the Law of Confusion from giving any information concerning this entity. We apologize for our lack of information.

Is there another query at this time?

S: I would like to ask for my bashful wife about the troubles of her feet, and I was hoping that you could tell me how we could alleviate the condition that troubles her?

I am Q'uo, and am aware of your query, my brother. Again, in order not to move beyond that line of infringement, we would suggest that it is well to look at the nature of the ailment, the arena, shall we say, in which this aliment has arisen. The nature of the experience that brings about the pain and the philosophical approach to this aspect of the life pattern that has brought this situation to the notice. If one is able to move along the trail of clues that the physical body gives one when the mind has not completely processed catalyst it is possible to find that area of movement that has yet to be investigated that will, when investigated, cause the cessation of the difficulty.

Is there a further query, my brother?

R: You speak with us of the entities that are gathered with this particular group, the Brothers and Sisters of Sorrow, and you have mentioned that you can be present with us in our personal meditations. Can you speak about that topic a bit?

I am Q'uo, and am aware of your query, my brother. Those of the Confederation of Planets in the Service of the One Creator who have been members, shall we say, of this group's circle of seeking are always, in some degree, aiding in the conducting of these sessions of seeking. Those of Hatonn, who were the first contact with this group many of your years ago, are more of what you would call the elder statesmen, lending their vibrations without dividing them into words. Those of Laitos, who have worked with many of the new instruments who have moved through this group, also have lent their vibration at this time and at any time that this group meets. There are those of Oxal, who have rarely in recent times been part of this group's activities in the sense of the telepathic channeling, yet who also lend their blessings and their vibrations to the seeking and the service within this group. There are others within the Confederation of Planets who have offered themselves over the years of this group's history in a manner which may be seen as sending the basic vibration of love that aids in each heart's opening in some degree to the messages offered by other members of the Confederation. Some there are who have not chosen what you call the naming, who are unseen and unnamed, who have had their influence and continue to do so within this group's circle of seeking. Each entity is available upon the mental request of any in this circle of seeking to join that seeker in the private meditation, not to speak or to communicate in words, but simply to lend the conditioning vibration which aids in the deepening of the meditation of those who call. This is our privilege and our honor, to aid each entity who calls in the meditative state. It is a steadying influence which brings a more focused approach for the seeker to the listening to the silence, to the one Creator, to the heart of the self.

Is there another query at this time?

K: Does the entity known as Edgar Cayce who passed from this life in January of 1945 live again?

I am Q'uo, and am aware of your query, my brother, and we would answer in the affirmative. Is there a final query at this time?

(No further queries.)

I am Q'uo, and as it appears that we have exhausted the queries for the nonce we shall once again express our great gratitude to each present for the great sacrifice that each has made to become a part of this community of seekers at this time and in this place. We would encourage each to see the self as a member of an even larger family of goodly souls who seek the One and who serve the One in all. Remember, each one of you, that you do not walk alone, that there are those who rejoice at every step taken with you, for this is a difficult illusion in which you find yourselves moving at this time. Your friends would seem to be confusion, doubt, fear, defeat, and being humbled daily by the difficulties of existing in such a heavy, chemical illusion. And yet, you do move with such encumbrances and yet the courage that each shows in continuing upon the journey, moving as the Fool from the cliff with no sure footing or idea of the next step, is that kind of action which inspires entities such as ourselves greatly as we observe the valor, the courage, the faith, the will, and the determination of so many seekers such as yourselves upon this planet at this time. The seeking is most intense. The service is ever more lovingly offered. The light shines ever more brilliantly through all of the difficulties and distress that are so much more apparent upon the surface of things in this illusion. We add our love and service to your own, as do many others, so that that which you accomplish can be seen to be as the fulcrum that allows a greater leverage in the overall evolution of this planetary entity.

We are known to you as those of Q'uo and at this time we would take our leave of this instrument and this group, leaving each in the love and in the light of the one infinite Creator. Adonai, my friends. Adonai.

Sunday Meditation
October 1, 2000

Group question: The question today concerns how we can get information from our bodies without having to get a cold, injure ourselves, or in some way bring ourselves bodily grief that is meant to get our attention on a problem we have ignored. We then learn moderation and care for ourselves, but we would like to know how to work with our catalyst without having to learn so much the hard way.

(Carla channeling)

We are those of the principle known to you as Q'uo. We greet you in the love and in the light of the one infinite Creator, in whose service we are. We thank you for calling us to your group this afternoon. We thank each of you for making those arrangements necessary in order to join the group. The desire and the hope for truth that you bring to the circle is beautiful to see. We enjoyed listening to your song for tuning and find many of the thoughts helpful for this particular subject of working with the various elements of your mind, body and your spirit in order to continue the revolving solution of issues that constitutes a major force in the movement of learning and the transformation of catalyst into experience.

As we speak we ask only one thing and that is that each of you distinguishes for yourself the resonance and the helpfulness of those thoughts which we offer, for truth is a personal thing and we do not expect or hope to hit the mark every time for everyone. Consequently, we just ask that those thoughts of ours which do not help are quickly left behind.

The song[2] asked the question, "What if God was one of us? Just a slob, like one of us? Just a stranger on the bus, trying to make his way home?" My friends, this is your situation. Each of you, in the core of your energetic body, is the Creator. Each of you is completely and wholly at the heart the Creator. You are one with all that there is. At the level of the heart of your being there is no difference between you and the Creator and all that there is. There is only an infinite amount of difference in each part of the Creator's view or perception of the scenery. There are infinite illusions. There are infinite impressions to be gathered within each creation. Consequently, the entire journey of awareness, from the first expression of light through all densities of an octave until light itself becomes absorbed once again in spiritual gravity, it is a journey home, and each of you is an energy system centered upon the Creator but full of your personality shell, your experiences, and the incoming catalyst that has your attention, and [each] is attempting, in her own way, to make her way home. It is a journey that will transcend this particular period of time that you experience now,

---

[2] Joan Osborne, "One Of Us," from the album *Relish* (1995).

the entire lifetime in which each of you now enjoys the dance of life, and all lifetimes and experiences between lifetimes that add up to the circle dance of becoming, being and being absorbed once again into absolute unity.

The particular place that you now occupy is a physical, electro-chemically based illusion which has much more heft and mass than the densities that are ahead of you but yet shares with the densities that are ahead of you the open book of self-awareness and all that that brings. The third density, then, is a hinge density where the evolution of mind and body becomes the evolution of mind, body and spirit. There is still much that is and can only be learned physically, in the muscles, the bone, and the blood. The illusion was set up so that there would be unavoidable physical experiences that would distort and shape the learning and the service of the incarnations. Some of the more obvious of these examples are the sexual urge and the urge for companionship. The body, the mind, and the spirit find themselves sometimes uneasy allies in the third-density illusion, attempting to integrate sources of information and kinds of information that are coming into the body, mind and emotional systems.

And many times, as the members of the circle have discussed, there are missed signals that, when missed result in becoming overstressed and developing injuries, or becoming overtired and developing a cold. We would start by suggesting that it is not considered a mistake by those who are looking at the third density from inner planes or from higher planes for entities within incarnation within the illusion to miss the signals before they move into the body. It is considered to be a normal behavior for third density. What each of you is beginning to sense into and beginning to wish for the self is the kind of facility and skill in reading the energy system that would be available without the veil. So the question becomes how to penetrate the veil of forgetting that lies between the conscious awareness of the intellect and the mind that is the daylight mind and the vast reaches of the mind that lies below the threshold of consciousness and that eventually takes in all that there is and the Creator.

The song, "What if God was one of us?" goes on to muse upon the situation that the deity faces. There's "nobody callin' on the phone, 'cept for the pope, maybe, in Rome." And this is certainly true within the illusion. This is the blindness of the situation that each of you is experiencing that is often so very maddening to the daylight mind, that the signal function of the conscious body is not working as it would very naturally in higher densities or between incarnations. The body must exceed natural boundaries in order for these subconscious sources of information more fully to be able to come into the conscious mind. Phone lines must be installed, in other words. And these are not the telephone lines of a linear space/time configuration that one could rig in any physical way or mechanically place within the body or within the mental system of the mind in order to get that signal system to work. That signal system was not intended to work in space/time.

However, each of you has a portion of self in time/space. The metaphysical identity of the self beyond the personality shell exists in time/space. When each of you achieves pure being, when you are expressing your essence, you are in time/space. That is where the effortlessness comes from when you are moving into the metaphysical universe. It is simply a shift in creations. Instead of the space/time universe where certain truths are held to be so, now you have entered a metaphysical universe where thoughts have become things and you have become a thought. Space has gone away. Time as you know it has gone away. But identity, energy focus and power have most certainly not disappeared but have, indeed, become clarified and illuminated by the underlying glow of creation in which all essence is held.

The singer went on to suggest that, "God is great. God is good. Yeah. Yeah." And this is one way to move into the metaphysical universe. Focus upon devotion is a metaphysical or time/space focus, and when the choice of the seeker is first to move into devotion and devotional principles such as thanksgiving and praise there begins to be established a point of view or an attitude which automatically links the seeker with its own subconscious or metaphysical mind. And in this attitude or construct of metaphysical being the connections become stronger and information moves into the conscious mind ever more quickly with iteration and experience until you are responding to better information and are finding a less troubled outer existence where instead of being surprised by your limitations you are responding to them in loving awareness of them.

We find in this channel's own experience that this particular entity has come through a week of having a chest cold and that it blames itself for not remembering that it needed more rest during times when a lot of group energy was being expressed in its environment. There were, of course, reasons for this instrument's forgetting that it knew that lesson. There was a perfectly valid reason that this entity subconsciously chose to have the experiences that would also cause it to go beyond its limitation and get the cold. And we concur that, not only for this instrument, but in each case where a limit has been overstepped and seeming disaster occurs, this is not a mistake. This is how is should be, for catalyst is gained, as the one known as S said, during the excessive activity that could not have been gained by acting in a balanced manner. In order words, it is not the business of those who come into incarnation upon a third-density planet to be right, to be balanced, or to be perfect.

Actually, each of you is here to go through the suffering, the pain, and the difficulties because of the refining, and purifying, and even chiseling aspects of the transformative process whence catalyst becomes experience. The basic tool for each application of practice that will yield better connections within the energy body is silence. We have said this in so many ways through the years through this instrument that we are aware that each of you is fully knowledgeable that we will talk about meditation or some other way of entering into and absorbing the information of silence. For silence is full of information, as the one known as J said. The very stars each have their song. All things in creation have their tune, and all blends in a marvelous harmony of the spheres that is endless and endlessly beautiful. But this beauty exists for the metaphysical entity that is attempting to begin the process of spiritual evolution in the bare bones of silence.

Whether it be the meditation of one who exercises or walks in nature, or whether it be the more formal practices of meditation, of contemplation, or of visualization, or whether even it is a practice that uses the everyday things of a normal life and workday to repeatedly center the self in moments of remembrance, the basic tool is silence, the moving into the consciousness of listening within.

You see, the information that is within the metaphysical portion of the body has its reflection in the feel and color of the energy of each chakra, and there are increasingly subtle levels of prescription about the energy system of the chakras and the connections between the chakras that will give fairly specific information about energy levels and where stress is and so forth. However, it is not the work of a short time to awaken the ability to read one's own psychic signature. There is a process of learning to visualize the system in some way that gives to the self fairly accurate information that can only be developed through a long period of time and experimentation with ways of visualizing and ways of interpreting what you have seen when you do the visualization process.

But whether you get the information from devotion, or from the silence of meditation, or from work with balancing the energy system of the body and asking it questions, or from hearing familiar sounds like the electronic beeps of the computer or telephone and using that beep to bring the self back to the remembrance of who it is, the basic key is to move into the silence and allow it to give its information and to do its transformative work. When one can work with the metaphysical structures that support life in third-density incarnation, then one can work better with the direct experience of the incarnation as well.

What if God were one of us? Just a slob like one of us? That is the situation. You are on a journey. You are very young gods. The journey has just begun. And there are many experiences through which you shall travel before you arrive home. But we may say this. Each of you and each of us is held in loving arms, and every step that each of us takes is accompanied by those spirits who love us and wish only to help us. We encourage each to lean into the support that lies within, and we encourage each to realize, more and more, the divinity of the imperfect self and the utter acceptableness of the imperfect self.

It is possible, if it is desired by a seeker, to enter into what this instrument would call body work and with a practitioner it is possible for a seeker to locate the places within the body's system of muscular and skeletal connections and skin and all else, those places of disharmony and conflict within the body. For the body carries memory in each of its cells, and each time that there is pain and sorrow, each time that there is anger and resentment, each time that there is any emotion that we could name to you, it is generally not so clearly expressed or not so completely acknowledged that it simply moves through the energy system and out. Usually a portion of the suffering of a moment will, indeed, move into the cellular structure of the body. For many entities it will settle in parts of the body that will talk to the body about what is occurring. If there is a sore back, it is sore from bearing the burden. If there are sore arms, they are sore from carrying too much. If there is the sore jaw that this instrument experiences, perhaps it is biting down on those things that it would say if it decided to allow itself to express itself in an unpleasant manner.

In each case where there are discomforts or pains within the body it is not simply that they are telling you what limitation you have gone beyond. They are also expressing the nature of a limitation and what kind of catalyst has brought the imbalance that is now being experienced. In extreme cases the body signals can include dysfunction that causes a change in the entire life. And again, this is often set into motion by those forces within the body, mind and spirit which are connected with choices made before incarnation concerning the lessons and the service which have been hoped to be encompassed in one incarnation.

It was an interesting question to ask, and we have greatly enjoyed playing with it, but as you may well realize we have only scratched the surface. So, if you wish to question further, that is certainly acceptable to us. At this time we would transfer the contact to the one known as Jim so that further questions may be asked if there is a desire. We thank this instrument and would leave it in love and in light. We are those of Q'uo.

(Jim channeling)

I am Q'uo, and greet each again in love and in light through this instrument. At this time it is our privilege to offer ourselves in the attempt to speak to any further queries which those present may have for us. Is there another query at this time?

S: I am curious to see if you have done any homework concerning a question concerning the relationship between the moon and the sun. Since you did not have an answer to that question last time, do you have it this time?

I am Q'uo, and am aware of your query, my brother. There are some mysteries that last longer than a week, and, indeed, this is the case with us.

Is there another query at this time?

S: I would be interested in having you search for the answer. You have the various resources of many densities in order to find the answer to that question. I would like to know not so much to have the answer but in order to find out how you go about finding the answer. I'll leave that for now and I'll query you next time.

The other question concerns the many equipment failures that happened during and just after the Homecoming weekend. What was going on last week to cause these problems to occur?

I am Q'uo, and am aware of your query, my brother. Though there was much of the excitement and energy moving through this group in that time period it would be normal to expect that these energies would affect a great many people and we feel that this was so for most of the entities who gathered here for the sharing of self with self. It is oftentimes during such gatherings that the mysterious occurs, and though we would like to add to the feel of mystery, for it is a pleasant experience to feel that one's energies have had an effect in the environment about one, we see that the failures of various electrical devices was simply coincidence.

Is there a further query, my brother?

S: When I read and hear people talk about their past lives, why don't they ever remember what they did in between past lives?

I am Q'uo, and am aware of your query, my brother. The experience that is had by those who have moved through an incarnation and who are in the time/space equivalent of the space/time illusion in which the incarnation was experienced go through a process which is most informative to a mind/body/spirit complex totality. However, many of these experiences taking place on the, shall we say, other side of the veil are of a nature which is difficult to access during an incarnation. However, there are some few who are able to do this. The number, however, is quite small, smaller even than those who feel that they are aware of previous incarnations. And we would suggest that the number of entities who are aware, in an accurate sense, of previous incarnations is much smaller than is believed. For the experience of remembering a previous incarnational experience is one which has a certain attractive glow to it, shall we say. It is in fashion to remember previous to the incarnation. We would suggest, however, that very few do remember a previous incarnation in an accurate way, so that the ability to remember an incarnation previous to this one, or the experience between incarnations previous to this one, is quite, quite rare. For each entity wishes that the veil of forgetting will, indeed, do what it does, and that is to make a complete block of all experience previous to the present incarnation in order that the present incarnation might be the sole focus of attention at this time. It is in such a situation that lessons are more purely and efficiently learned. If incarnations were able to be mixed so that memories of various incarnations blend through into the current incarnation the lessons and catalyst of the current incarnation would be diluted in such a fashion such as to reduce the efficiency of learning.

Is there a further query?

S: That's interesting. No further queries at this time. Thank you.

I am Q'uo, and we thank you, my brother. Is there another query at this time?

Carla: Are there reasons that free will is involved in not answering the question about the relative size of the sun and moon?

I am Q'uo, and am aware of your query, my sister. In this case this is not so. There are many, many physical, mental, emotional and spiritual coincidences that do, indeed, have meaning and may be pursued in various layers of uncovering the nature of the truth beneath them. In other instances we find that there is simply coincidence and that the coincidence is merely mechanical and unimportant. Into this category this falls for us.

Is there another query, my sister?

Carla: Yes. I went through regressive hypnosis and remembered a life in sparkling detail of another life lived on another planet, and a whole lifestyle. A friend of mine says that she remembers being an Egyptian god called Sekmet. I don't feel that I could bank on either one of our memories as accurate, and I wondered what these false images are that we think are incarnations from another time? Are they false echoes? Are they shadows that tell us something about ourselves that pierces the veil? Are there any uses to these memories at all?

I am Q'uo, and am aware of your query, my sister. In the specifics of this particular query we cannot answer in a definitive nature, for we are desirous of not infringing upon free will. However, in the general run of the query we may suggest that that importance which is placed upon the memory, however accurate or false it might be, is that quality of essence. The importance which a person places upon the supposed memory of a previous incarnation gives a person an idea of something of value resting there, taking a form as it will, being revealed as it is, being understood or misunderstood as it is. These are the facets of the gem of the incarnation. Seeing that which is of importance to the mind, to the emotions, to the spirit, to the body, this gives the self information from the self and it is unimportant as to whether or not this is an accurate memory. It is only important because the person feels that it is so.

Is there another query, my sister?

Carla: I really like that answer, by the way. I finished writing *A Wanderer's Handbook* some time ago and it is about 1280 pages. My editor thinks it should be published as it is with a good introduction explaining why it is so long, or, number two, that it needs to be edited down to about half its length and a lot of quotes from channeled entities such as yourself be replaced with a simpler and less convoluted language of me writing on those points. I would welcome any comments that you would have, as we are at this point now.

I am Q'uo, and am aware of your query, my sister, and again we must apologize for invoking the Way of Confusion, for we do not wish to influence you upon this matter for it is built upon the foundation of free will. We are happy to serve however we may. Is there another query?

Carla: No. Thank you very much.

I am Q'uo, and we thank you again, my sister. Is there another query at this time?

(No further queries.)

I am Q'uo, and as it appears that we have exhausted the queries for the nonce we would take this opportunity to thank each present once again for inviting us to join your circle this day. We are known to you as those of Q'uo. We leave each in the love and in the light of the one infinite Creator. Adonai, my friends. Adonai. ☥

L/L Research

L/L Research is a subsidiary of Rock Creek Research & Development Laboratories, Inc.

P.O. Box 5195
Louisville, KY 40255-0195

www.llresearch.org

Rock Creek is a non-profit corporation dedicated to discovering and sharing information which may aid in the spiritual evolution of humankind.

ABOUT THE CONTENTS OF THIS TRANSCRIPT: This telepathic channeling has been taken from transcriptions of the weekly study and meditation meetings of the Rock Creek Research & Development Laboratories and L/L Research. It is offered in the hope that it may be useful to you. As the Confederation entities always make a point of saying, please use your discrimination and judgment in assessing this material. If something rings true to you, fine. If something does not resonate, please leave it behind, for neither we nor those of the Confederation would wish to be a stumbling block for any.

CAVEAT: This transcript is being published by L/L Research in a not yet final form. It has, however, been edited and any obvious errors have been corrected. When it is in a final form, this caveat will be removed.

© 2009 L/L Research

Sunday Meditation
October 15, 2000

Group question: The question today has to do with the level of anxiety, and tension, and stress, and rush, and hurry, and angst, that we see all around us in the world today. We see it not only in others, but we see it in ourselves as we go through our daily round of activities. And we wonder if Q'uo could give us some information as to how we can deal with this angst as we deal with other people and as we see it in ourselves. Is there any message that is being delivered when a life is lived in this fashion? Is there anything that we should take from it besides what we see on the surface? We would appreciate anything that Q'uo might have to say.

(Carla channeling)

We are those of the principle known to you as Q'uo. Greetings in the love and in the light of the one infinite Creator, in whose service we are. As always, it is a great privilege to be called to this session of working, and we thank each in the group for asking for information of a metaphysical nature, for seeking for the truth, and for looking in unexpected places such as this group. We greatly appreciate the opportunity to share our opinion and our thought, with the understanding that these are opinions and not authoritative statements. We ask that each listen carefully to what we say with an eye to keeping that which resonates and releasing everything that does not, for we make no claims to be anything but your brothers and sisters in the metaphysical journey, in the school of learning that creation is, and in the opportunity to serve which creation constitutes also. May we learn and serve together and help each other. This is our hope and we assure you that you are aiding us, for to be able to respond to your call enables us to work on our chosen method of service to others at this time. This is a great blessing to us.

We enjoyed listening to your conversation concerning the various self-perceived imperfections of each person's efforts and living. From our point of view, since we are able to see the shining hopes and good intentions of the heart, each entity looks a great deal more successful, shall we say, than the opinion that each self has about itself. And we encourage each to realize that much of the self-perceived imperfection of the personality shell as seen by the awakening seeker is an artifact of culture and manifestation in general and can in no wise be translated to a linear manner to represent the actual placement of the vibratory pattern of the mind, the body, and the spirit. In actuality, the essence of each of you resonates far below the level of surface consciousness so that while the irritations and anxieties of the day may well destroy and cut up the conscious peace of the seeker as far as the self-perceived experience of the seeker, in actuality the service of the seeker, as far as offering its essence in a relatively positive way to this planet and to its people, continues to go on without a great deal of disturbance. This seems almost impossible to comprehend from the standpoint of the conscious mind because to the conscious mind there is no essence. To the conscious mind there is a system of thoughts about the self which constitute the virtual self.

Other selves are seen with much more balance by the self than the self because of the fact that they are not perceived as the self. Consequently, if you find yourself gazing at other people, concerned with their imperfections and sympathizing with them, we may encourage you to do the same with yourself. For that instinctual reaction that you have to the struggles of a person perceived by you as a well-intentioned person which perceives itself as imperfect, has more balance to it. And you may trust that the instinct that saw the love in another's heart is the shadow of that heart itself that is within you, that is in actuality transducing the love and the light of the infinite Creator in relatively unimpeded form despite surface angst and anxiety. There are many layers to the question of where an antsy feeling may come from.

The one known as R, in framing the question originally, asked if the experience of underlying antsy-ness was personal or cultural in nature. The basic question originally had to do with that underlying tone that lies behind actions rather than the actions or their irritability factors themselves; that is to say, that the one known as R was saying that there was this concern and that concern, this purchase and that change. But after those matters were disposed of, yet still there remained an underlying feeling of restlessness and anxiety, an itchiness that could not be explained by any particular physical or consciously known problem.

We may answer that, in general, there is both a cultural and personal component to such angst. Let us look at the cultural component first, or, shall we say, the global or transitional component, for there is within your inner planes a tremendous amount of change and transformation going on which has to do with not only the movements of the people upon this planet through metaphysical transformational times but also the planet itself, which is moving in its physical body and its finer bodies through just as substantial and primary a change. The pressure of growing electromagnetic alteration in the planetary web is creating energies which are perceived by sensitive people, especially those who have awakened spiritually, as creating new layers of vulnerability and fragility within the personality shell and the conscious mind. And this pressure comes not from the conscious mind but from the considerable depths of the subconscious mind, that portion of the mind being unable to speak but being far more nearly aware of the changing situation as regards the inner planes of the planet and as regards the energy system of each awakened seeker.

For those who have not yet awakened the same pressures are coming to bear, but the reactions widely vary. Some experience the so-called new age or transformational energies as activators of repressed negative emotion. It is as though instead of awakening the instinct for peace, unity, and harmony these energies are so sharply other than those energies which are useful to the personality shell and the energy setup of that unawakened being that there is a snap-back or bounce-back effect where these energies are distorted in a phase shift that is deleterious and that continues being deleterious until the unawakened seeker either chooses to awaken in the positive sense or chooses to become more negative. In other words, there is in the global energy web being received by the population of your planet an enhancer or exaggerator of choice. When there has been no choice made, the energies create a great deal of confusion.

Consequently, for this component of the angst affecting the peoples of your planet the most effectual way of dealing with it is to retain and maintain an awareness of choice, of the dimensions of personal choice, so that when energies begin to be more and more disturbed and when this itchiness, anxiety or angst moves into the weather of the mind, the body, and the spirit the more effectual views of the intellect and the analytical and reasoning abilities that are at the disposal of the seeker revolve around framing the situation in terms which offer to the self an ethical choice, a way to determine what is a service to others and at the same time what is a balanced action in terms of placing and maintaining the boundaries necessary for a peaceful self that has its own safety within itself.

The one known as S was talking about the need for balance to see both sides of a situation and yet to come to some decision that finds that which this instrument has often called the golden mean, the middle road that expresses both charity and wisdom and encapsulates the best of both. Oftentimes, this framework fails as this instrument was speaking earlier of with regards to her self. And we say, yes, often whether the reason for angst is cultural or personal, self-perceived failure will occur, and it is one more situation which is spiritual in nature which has a rhythm, and beauty, and a plan. The difficulty always is in retaining enough balance, faith and common sense to remember the truths and the principles that inform not just the conscious mind but the life and the essence of the being.

The instrument has a phrase that she often invokes when a situation seems hopeless. She will say, "Take it to a higher level." And we find this to be, in a global sense, in a transformational sense, sound advice. When it is perceived that there is a discomfort to the self this perception is simply the truth. It is a fact. The self is uncomfortable. It does not necessarily lead one to a specific response. Therefore, if it is possible in framing such a response, we recommend taking the opportunity to find the true and deep feelings of the heart on the subject which seems to be causing the anxiety. And moving with those feelings if at all possible. However, as we said, when self-perceived failure occurs we encourage each not to further berate the self for the failure, for it is only an apparent failure. In actuality, these actions, just like the action of elements with each other in chemistry or in alchemy, are going through certain transformations and changes and certain products are being created. The thing about chemistry, in general, is that if you do not like the results of an experiment you can start over and do it differently. And often in your receiving of catalyst you get the opportunity to repeat again and again and once again those things which you are rehearsing and practicing, so that you have any number of opportunities to look for that special grace which opens the heart.

Now, in addition to the planetary energy transformations that are now taking place upon your planet and are causing underlying anxieties and feelings of tension on a global basis there is also a self-perpetuation, self-regulating system of catalyst and experience that informs the gradual spiritual evolution of each awakened spirit. Each of you and each of us has a body system that is not a simple thing. Each of the seven sub-densities of your density has proper to it a physical or metaphysical vehicle or a combination of the two. Each of these vehicles has chakras. Each of these seven chakras in these seven finer bodies is related in some way and connected in some way to the chakra system of the physical body. Further, these bodies interpenetrate and there can come to be fairly interesting and unusual systems of connection where there have been repeated lessons distorted in a certain way and connections have been made between chakras or between chakras and the finer bodies and the chakras in the physical body. All of which can cause, shall we say, glitches in the system, places where energy is held, places where energy is leaking out through holes in the aura, places where there is overactivation so that there is a constant feeling of tension simply because a chakra has gone into a subjective perception that it is needed in an emergency activation, and so it is firing at full capability at all times. This is undesirable and unbalanced.

Indeed, it is far more desirable to have a relatively weak chakra system that has been balanced so that energy is coming through the entire system at however limited a rate and however slow a speed. Far better to have the system open and energy moving completely through it and out into the Earth plane than to have a tremendous amount of energy being pulled through the body because of an overactive chakra or chakra system while the energy system is not capable of transducing the energy as it moves through. The transduction of energy from the infinite energy that comes from the Creator is not a simple process in itself, and so this would be another area of inquiry to look into. However, we feel that there is too much detail in this for an introductory talk on anxiety and antsy-ness.

When the energy system of the body needs balancing there are many ways to work on the balancing of the system. It is always our first recommendation to use the key of silence, for silence, in one way or another, whether by silent prayer, by visualizations, by meditation, by contemplation, by simply walking in nature, silence has the space in it to hold divine thought. Divine thought is a natural balancer of energy systems. When your prayer goes up, when your call goes forth for inspiration and for peace, it is heard and immediately responses are being made. They are being made in silence. Consequently, if there is constant clamor in the mind and from the heart and from the spirit the responses will not be able to come through into the energy system. Therefore, using the silence after the prayer or the plea is a very helpful move to make, and we encourage it. We cannot say how long it may take in terms of your time for that feeling of response and healing and reassurance to move into the heart and to take root there, but we can say that it will shorten the time of healing, or, rather, it will shorten the time before the conscious mind will become aware of the healing, to move into the silence and to spend time simply resting in the knowledge that you have been heard.

The tuning song this day was, "Let It Be," and this is wonderful advice. When, as the one known as S said, you have done all that you can, what can you do but let it be? When you have given your all, when you have solved every problem you can find, what unrest and disquiet you are left with is an artifact of your energy system and the way that it amuses you at this time to think. Consequently, you can drive yourself crazy trying to think about how you think which is usually a bootless[3] inquiry. Or you can shake off the dull fatigue of trying to figure out that which cannot be figured out and determine that which is the next thing that feels right for you to do. For beyond all of the thoughts about living a life in truth, each moment there is a situation where there is an awareness that is caught in the flesh and we also are caught into a certain type of flesh and are embodied and have personalities. We are the limitless caught into limit. We are living paradoxes. We are not linear beings. We will often not make sense, and the angst and anxieties that come to those who are beginning to seek spiritually will always be vastly more deeply felt and more uncomfortable than those difficulties experienced by those not attempting to accelerate the pace of their evolution but are simply attempting to live through the day.

We are not those who would recommend the attempt to live through the day on its own merits. For we realize that seeing the self as a creature of work and food and rest creates a feeling of bestiality or animal nature that is simply not accurate in describing the nature of an awakened spirit. The awakened spirit will be more fragile, more tender, more easily bruised, and more in need of setting more firm boundaries, for there needs to be that place where it is safe to be yourself. We hope that each of you is able even in the darkest moments of anxiety and sorrow to support and encourage the heart of self to believe in yourself and to know that you are worthwhile and that those things that you hold dear, those principles that make your heart lift and your spirits soar, are, indeed, worth living for and worth dying for.

In personal anxieties as well as cultural and planetary ones it is also well to take it higher, remembering that as people in incarnation with relationships there will be times when there is found no higher ground. Nevertheless, my friends, that higher ground is there existing, if nowhere else, in your essential self, within your heart. Third density has to do with choice. This is the key to this question.

At this time we gratefully thank this instrument and transfer the contact to the one known as Jim. We are those known to you as the Q'uo. We transfer at this time.

(Jim channeling)

I am Q'uo, and greet each again in love and light through this instrument. It is our privilege at this time to offer ourselves in the attempt to speak to any further queries which those present may have for us. Is there another query at this time?

S: I've been dying these last two weeks just wondering what homework you have done and what answer you have for me. If you would be so kind, wow me.

I am Q'uo, and though we are not aware of a query, we are sure that there is one that you have for us. Would you please vibrate it at this time?

S: Certainly. It goes back to the question from last time and the time before which was the question of the size of the moon and the sun being the same size. The first time you did not know the answer. The second time you hadn't thought any more. And I was asking you if with your various resources you could find that answer and how you went about finding it.

I am Q'uo, and we are aware of your query, my brother. When we attempt to seek for that which we do not know, we look to the heart of our being for that which is important in our seeking. And when it is of great enough importance, then it is that we attempt to become that which we do not know. In this instance we do not seek for the answer for this information, for we feel that it is unimportant and is not central either to our service or our own learning. Rather, we would suggest that instead of being concerned with the external artifacts of the

---

[3] bootless: unavailing, useless, without advantage, unprofitable.

astronomical illusion that you look instead to the sun and the moon of your own inner being.

Is there another query at this time?

S: I guess our good friend R, whom we all think so highly of … to put it delicately, do you know any nice ladies that we could introduce him to, to kind of steer towards his way?

I am Q'uo, and though we are aware of your question, we are unaware of such an entity. Is there another query?

S: So, no match-making services. I guess I'll turn it over to others at this point. I've exhausted my tweaking of you today. Thank you so kindly.

I am Q'uo, and we are thankful to you also, my brother, though we have offered so little that is satisfying. Is there another query at this time?

Carla: I'd sort of like to follow up on what you said to S. The sun and the moon kind of moved me back to not only astrology but to alchemy. The Tree of Life figure, the glyph, is seen by some systems as having one side that is lunar and one side that is solar. There is a resonance in me as to what you suggested as the sunny self and the nighttime self, or the dark side, that are both us and hopefully well integrated, but sometimes it is very upsetting to see our dark side, or the moon, in us. Is that the direction of thought that you were suggesting?

I am Q'uo, and am aware of your query, my sister. Your interpretation of the sun and the moon of the inner self approaches that which was intended. There is much of the radiance and much of the magnetism, much of the male, much of the female, which each entity embodies within the incarnational life pattern. The information that was given through this group concerning the archetypical mind began to deal with some of this information, and we are glad that you have looked deeper than the surface of the, shall we say, original query.

Is there a further query, my sister?

Carla: I just want to share with you Don's joke about the moon and the sun. Don always felt that the moon was more important than the sun because it gave you light at night when you needed it.

I am Q'uo, and we, indeed, enjoy the humor of the sun and moon, and would add that we have also heard through a philosopher of yours that the old moon can be cut up into many small pieces to make more stars for the night sky.

Is there a further query at this time?

(Tape change. A portion was not recorded during the tape change.)

I am Q'uo, and am again with this instrument … that we carefully assess the line beyond which free will is infringed is known well by each in this group. When we attempt to determine what is of value for our own seeking we look at those qualities which are what you might call eternal, those qualities which are so now and ever, that we may apply them to our life pattern. Thus, there is much that comes before our notice that is of little import in our own seeking, for there is much that moves about one that is, shall we say, of a background kind of influence. That which is of central importance in our seeking, those qualities and principles which are true throughout all times and places, are those qualities upon which we would attempt to build our understanding, shall we say. And in our realm of experience understanding is possible, whereas in your third-density illusion understanding is not possible.

The intellectual mind offers so little that may assist one in the seeking that to pander to it and to fill it with useless facts is that which we see as being of not as service and continuing to lead an entity in the direction in which the illusion does such a good job already. For there is so much which one must know, or attempt to know, in order to cope within your daily round of activities. Thus, when we attempt to share with those within this illusion we look not only at that which is of service because it does not infringe upon free will but that which will move one more firmly towards the heart of the seeking, and that is, my friends, to move towards one's own heart in the interior sense, in the sense of opening the compassion for self and other self, in engaging the mercy, the willingness to forgive and be forgiven, the making of amends with those with whom you have a difficulty and disturbance.

Thus, what we see as helpful is oftentimes seen as not helpful to those who seek our assistance. And this is the way that we see the third-density illusion: so many entities moving in directions which do not directly aid in their own evolution. And, yet, in the long run of events there is no other journey that is taken. Thus, there is only the evolution of each entity at each instance in the life pattern. However, when we attempt to be of service to entities such as yourselves we feel that it is important that we maintain the focus upon those qualities that are not transient, that do not change from day to day and from illusion to illusion, and that we attempt to inspire that which is beyond the intellect. For there is so much that already requires the use of the intellect that many feel it is too reliable a partner in this seeking and serving. Thus, it is a delicate balance that we walk when we attempt to serve, yet we do so joyfully. And we do so without hesitation where we can, for it is a great honor for us to be able to move with you in your seeking and your service.

Is there another query, my brother?

S: No. I think that answers that. I will have to read the transcript and think about it. Thank you.

I am Q'uo, and, again, we thank you, my brother. Is there another query at this time?

R: I have a query about how you seek answers to that which you do not know. You said you first look into the heart of your being to see if there is value to that answer and if there is you will attempt to become that which is unknown. Is that a technique that can be used in the third density?

I am Q'uo, and am aware of your query, my brother. This technique has but limited use within the third-density illusion, for this illusion is one in which the veil of forgetting, as we have heard it called in this group, plays such an important role. This veil of forgetting allows each entity to focus upon the present life experience in a very focused manner. This same ability to focus in such a finely tuned fashion is that which mitigates against the ability to become that which is sought, for to do that one must be able to move through this veil and beyond the veil. The attempt to empathize with those about with whom there is miscommunication or difficulty of any kind has a limited possibility of success, for each entity is aware of its own emotions, thoughts, experiences, dreams and desires and can, therefore, begin to feel for another entity these same expressions of energy. Thus, there is some use in becoming or attempting to become another entity in order to understand that entity's relationship to the self. However, for other areas of investigation we feel that this is not a technique that would be helpful in your particular illusion.

Is there another query, my brother?

R: No. Thank you.

I am Q'uo, and we thank you, my brother. Is there another query at this time?

Carla: To follow up on S's question about dumbing down information to third density, because I am aware in the channeling process of having to translate concepts into words all the time, and I feel that I am getting bits of it and am doing the best that I can with it, but there is so much there I can't possibly express it all. Could you make any more comments about that? I can see the operation of the intellect here. It's not so much as there is a certain value placed on what we think about.

I am Q'uo, and am aware of your query, my sister. In your illusion there is the seeking for the heart of self. All queries of substance may be related to this seeking. We may share with each that desire to fully open the heart, each to the other, and may relate those queries of substance to this seeking. Thus, there is no necessity to, as you say, dumb down the answer for a query but to seek its simplest level of expression which each heart may understand.

Is there a further query, my sister?

Carla: No. Thank you.

I am Q'uo, and, again, we thank you, my sister. Is there another query at this time?

M: Am I using the medication that I am on as a crutch, or is it really helping me?

I am Q'uo, and am aware of your query, my sister. A direct answer is not possible for us here, for it is an infringement on free will for us to advise to the point of specificity. However, we would suggest that in your meditative state, as you ponder this query for yourself, you will be able to make a clear determination as to whether or not to continue this course of ingestion of prescribed medication. We encourage you to seek there your own answer and to trust in yourself in this seeking. For it is well said that each entity knows the answers within the heart to the queries which have importance to the heart.

Is there a further query, my sister?

M: No. Thank you.

I am Q'uo, and we thank you, my sister. Is there a final query at this time?

(No further queries.)

I am Q'uo, and we are also filled with gratitude for the opportunity to join this circle of seeking. We thank each individually for inviting our presence and for being able to accept little in the way of helpful responses in many cases, for we find the way of confusion often limits that which we may share. We hope that each will continue to seek with the strong desire that has brought each to this circle. We applaud the steps that each moves upon the inner journey of opening the heart and sharing the love that is found there with all that come across the path in the daily round of activities. We are known to you as those of Q'uo, and we would take our leave of this instrument and this group at this time, leaving each, as always, in the love and in the ineffable light of the one infinite Creator. Adonai, my friends. Adonai. ❧

L/L Research

L/L Research is a subsidiary of Rock Creek Research & Development Laboratories, Inc.

P.O. Box 5195
Louisville, KY 40255-0195

www.llresearch.org

Rock Creek is a non-profit corporation dedicated to discovering and sharing information which may aid in the spiritual evolution of humankind.

ABOUT THE CONTENTS OF THIS TRANSCRIPT: This telepathic channeling has been taken from transcriptions of the weekly study and meditation meetings of the Rock Creek Research & Development Laboratories and L/L Research. It is offered in the hope that it may be useful to you. As the Confederation entities always make a point of saying, please use your discrimination and judgment in assessing this material. If something rings true to you, fine. If something does not resonate, please leave it behind, for neither we nor those of the Confederation would wish to be a stumbling block for any.

CAVEAT: This transcript is being published by L/L Research in a not yet final form. It has, however, been edited and any obvious errors have been corrected. When it is in a final form, this caveat will be removed.

© 2009 L/L Research

Sunday Meditation
November 5, 2000

Group question: The question today has to do with change. Now, in the context of the perfection of the moment where all things are well, we realize that there is change that occurs at all times. And we are wondering as to how this change happens. How much is conscious and how much is subconscious? Is there a balance between change and keeping things the same that is well to maintain? Is there a certain amount of stability that is well in a seeker's life? How much of the change that is going on can we affect? How much is going to happen whether we have any input or not?

(Carla channeling)

We are those of the principle known to you as Q'uo, and we greet you in the love and in the light of the one infinite Creator, whose servants we are. We thank you for calling us to your group this evening, for the privilege of sharing our thought with you on the subject of change, and for the opportunity of sharing your meditation and your company and the beauty of your being. All of these things are a great privilege to us and a great blessing. We would ask of you one thing, and that is, as always, that you listen to us with discrimination, being fully aware that we are like yourselves, those who make errors and who are learning and changing. Therefore, nothing that we say should or needs to be taken as gospel. If any of our thoughts resonate in your own mind, then we offer them to you humbly. If not, then we ask you to pass them by.

Change is a fixture of all of the illusions of which we are aware. At the heart of creation is a constancy of metamorphosis that is, as far as we know, circular; that is, the creation as a whole can be said to have its source as its ending and its ending as its source, and all of that which stems from source and comes to an end is one unified entity, which is in a constant state of transformation.

All begins in the utter unpotentiated love, or Logos, that is the Creator unknown to Itself. The first distortion of this Logos is free will. And free will is the agent of change. In the Creator, and therefore in Its creation, through free will the Creator chooses that which you know as light and which we would call the manifesting principle. The child of free will and love, light in its first manifestation, may be seen as the sudden being of all that there is. Your scientists have envisioned this as inevitably explosive and have called the birth of creation the Big Bang. However, this is creation seen through the distortion of the lens of your third density in which time and space structure perception. In other illusions where time and space have different structures it may be seen that there is not the explosion but, rather, the transformative process which rolls from light to light to light, and by this we mean that there are levels of what this instrument would call rotation of light that create vast numbers of structures which are seen as systems of vibration and vibrational fields having their relative existence in various sizes or orders of your time and space so that from the smallest to the largest structure of vibration, from the lowest to the highest density of vibration, there are put in motion by the Logos systems which are destined to roll their metamorphoses from the position of what from your density would be the beginning of the creation to the ending of creation when all of these energies have reacted with all of the other energies which are appropriate for them to react with. All energy has been spent. All desire has been balanced and the exhausted and used energy and experience has been harvested or eaten by the one infinite Creator and absorbed at the end of creation. This describes the basic background against which self-aware entities such as yourselves and we experience and add our harvest to that knowledge the Creator has of Itself. This is the first and deepest level to change, and it is a design which accomplishes what in your bodies would be a heartbeat. For the creation is the body of the Creator, and an entire creation with all of the densities of an octave express one heartbeat of that creature, which is the Creator. This is in no way a literal rendering of a Creator which has a beginning and an ending. As far as we know, the Creator is infinite and is eternal.

However, there are quanta, or heartbeats, in which the Creator's knowledge of Itself is rendered open to alteration by the self-aware entities which are principles of the Creator, choosing by their free will to gather information and to process it in such and such a manner. And this the Creator can never know ahead of time and does not wish to know ahead of time. It is an important principle to the Creator: that Its portions that have been offered this background of densities and illusions have complete free will in looking at the creation around It, and responding to it, and in making those responses into a process of change, metamorphosis, and transformation of a certain kind. For each choice that each self-aware entity makes creates new possibilities, new patterns, and new potential choices that may add to the Creator's experience of Itself.

This basic structure of the long and winding road, as the song which this group listened to before the meditation referred to, is entirely as it is. There is no entry into altering the structure of the densities, of the illusions within the densities, or their progress. These are set and are as the house within which the self-aware sub-Creators, which are yourselves, we and all self-aware entities, have the opportunity to experience the light of life and the choices of a freely lived life.

The next level of change which we would address is that level which involves the self-aware entity which each of you is facing an incarnation upon your third-density world, choosing to come into incarnation and deciding upon the basic structure of that incarnation. For this, indeed, you do. And much that will affect the incarnation you and your higher self have decided upon beforehand. Now, this level of change is semi-permeable. It is not fully set; that is, before incarnation there is a review of the previous incarnation and a review of the basic stream of your soul. In the context of life between incarnations, time does not hold sway. And rather than a linear movement of incarnation after incarnation after incarnation, what your higher self is looking at is a circle of incarnations—past, present, and future—which are affecting what this instrument has been calling the soul stream, so that influences from various incarnations, lessons learned from various incarnations, lessons misaligned from various incarnations, information good and bad, is being filtered and refined and being placed into that repository of self that is far deeper than any personality shell which you experience as yourself within any one incarnation.

You and your higher self gaze at this, shall we say, pool of self and of lessons still to be learned from the relative standpoint of coming into this particular incarnation. And there is a careful choosing of the relationships which you hope you will be able to work on within this particular incarnation. There is a careful choice of the lessons which you feel are at the incarnational level and which you wish to address, no matter how many times you must repeat this lesson within the incarnation. Then there are secondary lessons which you place for yourself within the incarnation which are less set and are more a matter of contingency. If such and such a lesson is learned, then another and subordinate lesson may have the luxury of coming into the incarnational experience and being offered for experience. There is, further, the choice of what gifts you choose to bring into the incarnation in the hopes that you will be able to use them in terms of your learning and also in terms of what service you have hoped to offer.

Again, these things are set to an extent, but they are not fully set. And we have used the analogy before of these items being as the roadmap where it is decided that you as a person must go from Louisville, say, to the town of Chicago. That basic direction, that achieving of a different location, is as the choice that is set before you. In terms of actual catalyst that occurs to you, what happens is that you are offered again and again choices of ways to turn your vehicle. It is possible to get on an interstate highway and go directly to Chicago in a matter of hours. It is also possible to get on an airplane and go to New York, and then to Europe, and then to Asia, and then across the North Pole and back to California and hence to Chicago. In both cases, if you can arrive in Chicago, you have achieved your destination and you have learned your lesson. The question is: how much trouble do you want to make for yourself in getting to Chicago? And this is the kind of thing you seem to face in an incarnation.

With a person, for instance, if you are working on a relationship which spans several lifetimes you may well experience the desire to get to Chicago by way of New York, Europe and Asia. However, you will find that as you hit each new city—New York, London, Paris, Geneva—you will meet that entity that you left in Louisville. This entity, or one just like it, in terms of your incarnational lesson, will come before your face, not in order to bring you woe but, rather, in order for you to look upon an issue and begin to sit with that issue and to see into the nature, the shadows, the implications, of this issue, that which this relationship brings up. If there is an incarnational lesson involving service to others—and this is so often the case—it will come up again and again. It may come up in the matter of employment. It may come up in the matter of being responsible when others around you are not responsible. But again and again, if your business, your issue, within the incarnation is learning responsibility for the self and responsibility for fulfilling commitments then this seemingly arduous situation where someone else is not being responsible but you must be will come up again and again. If an issue repeats it is not in order to bedevil you or to trouble you or to bring you to despair but, rather, to open to you the depths and the riches of this suffering.

Always, when facing something that you have finally begun to recognize as an incarnational lesson our advice is first to give thanks that you finally have achieved the realization that this is an incarnational lesson. And then we encourage you simply to sit with this issue. It is not necessarily your issue to solve. It may be there is tremendous patience involved in this issue. It may be, indeed, that you cannot solve this issue within this incarnation. It may be that you have simply set up for yourself the continuing lesson of giving without expectation of return. And this could be done through the giving of money, through the giving of self to another in patient listening although that entity never listens to you. There are a thousand and one different ways that you can set up an incarnational lesson involved in learning a purifying and refining of the instincts of love and compassion.

So there is this level of semi-permeable setting of an incarnation where these are the constants of the incarnation. These are the things that you cannot get rid of, that you do not want to get rid of, that you will begin to appreciate as the spirit within you matures throughout the incarnation. At first these incarnational lessons seem to be insurmountable and impossible. And as they repeat and repeat and the learning curve gets a little shorter each time, the spiritually awakened person begins to see, not that she can succeed in conquering this catalyst, but that she can see the pattern of it and appreciate the sense of the plan. Once the level of comprehension has been achieved where the plan is seen to be benign then much of the heart is freed to open to the hope of the efficacy of the third level of change. And this is the exciting and fully alive portion of the structures of change which feed into the process of your self-aware progress through this lifetime, this, your third density, and all of the densities which are to come.

Become aware of yourself now as you sit in your chair. You know that you are a body. You can feel your weight. Perhaps you can feel your pulse in one part of your body or some slight electrical movement upon your head or upon the hairs upon your body because of the influence of this contact and the energy that is moving clockwise about the circle as you gather light into the circle by your desire to know the truth that you offer. And yet you are not your body. You are not that which has been born and will die. You are not bone and blood. You are part of the original Logos and in you is that which is prior to all else but the Logos. As the Logos chose free will, so you who have free will as part and parcel of yourself before manifestation. You cannot become a mindless creature. You are not without will and power. You have Creatorship. You are a person of infinite power. Of infinite love and infinite ability to manifest.

All of this, of course, is placed deeply within the heart that you bring into incarnation and bury within the deeper part of self which never comes into direct consciousness in the conscious daylight mind. Therefore, you are as a person in disguise, a Creator stepped down and stepped down and stepped down in vibration until you are able to enter the physical vehicle of a third-density great ape, that gallant physical vehicle that carries your consciousness about for the incarnation, that bears the stresses and strains of your learning, that does the will of your brain, your intellect, and eventually your consciousness, and that serves you with a body and a mind that has instincts that greatly influence the choices of the immature spiritual individual.

Consequently, the very first arena of change for the spiritual seeker is the alarm that awakens the spirit. We do not know any way to influence the timing of when that alarm clock goes off for each individual spirit. And so we would ask that this particular concern for the self or for any other self be removed from the arena of choice and change. Trust the self to know when it is time to awaken and trust that self again and again when it triggers an urgency for change. For there are, as we have said, these posts or stanchions that are part of the structure of each incarnation, that have been carefully set in place to cause a turn here and a swing there and a turn and a roll here and there. Sometimes these changes in direction seem to be coming from the blue, and yet they have been carefully placed and are doing what they should do in order to keep you pointed, to follow our original analogy, [not] to Chicago but to the issues of your incarnation and to the services which you wished to offer. So examine those things you cannot change for the potentials for learning and for service.

Now, as you approach each point of decision you are almost inevitably dealing with change, with the perception of change in your life, and here is where there is real excitement because there are two forces which are tremendously powerful and one overriding force, which we will speak of to conclude, that to our way of thinking are the greatest areas of potential within the incarnation. The first is faith. The one known as T spoke of faith, and we would agree that faith has a powerful effect upon how change occurs within the incarnation.

Now each, as we have said, has a fairly set personality shell, and each has a fairly set system of relationships, issues, learning and service. However, these factors only produce a fairly random series of crises, times when the spirit that is you must choose one way or another to act, to think, to be. Faith is a faculty which reaches into the heart and pulls from that place a faculty which believes not that which is seen but that which is hoped. It takes that which is hoped and places it in the position of being known and being believed. The choice of this attitude of faith that all is well and that the plan is good is that which will reliably illuminate that issue or that relationship with which you are sitting. It does not obviate the need for patience, tolerance, kindness or the innocent and heartfelt desire to communicate. But it creates a vibration of light that is far closer to the truth that is the Creator, to the vibration that is the one great original Thought. And it is as the element that enters a confused pattern and, by being placed in that pattern, stitches up the ravels of that pattern and creates a moment of clarity where the pattern emerges from the tangle and the structure is seen in one moment of crystallized learning.

And in those blessed moments of faith it is seen that all truly is well and that all will be well, and the bare memory of that moment is enough to illuminate and ease the entire process of transformation that would otherwise would seem a plodding and ungainly practice.

The second faculty that is most exciting to us and is very efficacious in creating positive as opposed to seemingly negative changes within the life experience is the faculty of will. Will may be seen as desire with a vector. Every entity has appetites. The physical body creates appetite as its first offering to the personality shell. The mental aspect of the physical body, with its predilection for choice making and for either/or, offers its refinements to the faculty of will. There become desires for this, desires for that. The consciousness itself has deeply seated desires that do not come from the body or from within the mind but from within the spirit. And these are deep desires of the soul that are often unspoken throughout the entire incarnation and, yet, even the shadows and echoes of these deep hungers of the heart affect the incarnation deeply.

The art and skill of developing the faculty of will is beginning to become aware of your desires, and as you become more and more aware of your desires becoming able to prioritize those desires, and sitting with them, beginning to see into them, and to choose those desires of the heart which you truly and deeply wish to follow. Once you have begun to identify those deep desires then it is that the faculty of will may begin to be pointed and the appetite and thirst may become a driving desire which may be expressed in prayer, in affirmation, in faith, in hope, in speech, in action, and in intention. The pointing and the continuation of desire is a faculty which will transform and accelerate the process of your spiritual evolution. This is perhaps the greatest of helpers in coming into a relative degree of mastery of the forces which are moving throughout your incarnation. The skill of pointing a desire is, paradoxically enough, that moment when it is seen that desire of the self and desire of the infinite One are one and the same thing. And there is a surrender of the small self to the Creator self so that these lower orders of body and mind and personality shell begin not to fall away but to have less sway over the incarnational process, over the thinking that feeds into the choices that you make.

That which lies beneath will and faith, like a blanket, is the Logos. And that Logos may be seen as the Creator. We say that this Logos is as the blanket because we feel that it is an apt simile of the spiritual walk, that long and winding road, to say that it is a walk in a cold climate. It is lonely, and the bed is the earth at the edge of the path. The ceiling is the stars above. And it seems a stark landscape often. For metaphysically, each truly walks alone as far as the making of choices and the creation of a tapestry of incarnational colors and textures. Each entity and each entity's choices are individual, to an absolute extent. Certainly, each walks with helpers. Each walks with spirit and the messengers of spirit, messengers of love, of understanding, of support and encouragement, and an awareness of this level of love from the Creator is helpful in softening that hard bed of earth and in bringing those cold stars closer.

But love is the blanket in which the seeker may roll up and rest at the end of the day, when will and faith are exhausted. That love lies within the heart and is accessible at all times. There is simply the choice made to crawl into that blanket and to roll oneself up in it. We greatly encourage this turning to love itself, turning to the heart within. For at the end of working with change there is great weariness and there is the need to rest. And this the Creator has provided for with a full and loving hand.

We are aware that the one known as J spoke of the difficulty that she had in comprehending this seemingly cruelty of one animal species preying upon another and perhaps we may speak of this at another time, but this instrument is telling us that we now have exceeded our time for speaking upon this subject. So, regretfully, we shall now release this subject for another asking or perhaps for the one known as Jim. We leave this instrument with thanks, in the love and in the light of the infinite One and transfer this contact to the one known as Jim. We are those known as Q'uo.

(Jim channeling)

I am Q'uo, and greet each again in the love and in the light of the one infinite Creator through this instrument. At this time it is our privilege to speak to any further queries which those present may have for us. Is there another query at this time?

Carla: Would you wish to take on that question that J raised before the session about animals killing each other and it being so difficult to deal with?

I am Q'uo, and am aware of your query, my sister. We shall offer a brief response with the invitation to ask further if there is more information desired. In this creation of the one Creator we spoke earlier of the nature of free will which makes change inevitable. For as the Creator has sought to know Itself through the operation of the creation, which each is somewhat aware of, each portion of the creation which is the Creator seeks to become more fully aware of the one Creator as the source of the self. Thus, there is inbuilt in all creation the desire to move, to know, to experience, to live, and to engage in each process of the living of the life, the experience of the world of the creation. So each portion of the one Creator partakes in some of that which is and some of that which is not. That is to say, each is a portion of the Creator, yet each acts as though it was alone in many instances. There is the process of individualization, of the intense focusing of consciousness so that it reflects an individual point of view, offering to the one Creator yet another avenue of knowing Itself.

As each portion of the creation begins to interact with each other portion within its realm of experience there is undertaken the qualities and responsibilities of individualized consciousness, the seeking for the self that guarantees survival, the interaction of the self with other selves that increases complexity and enriches experience, the movement of groups of selves that move as one and interact with other groups and individuals, with the environment, and so forth. As this interaction occurs there is what you may see as the living upon life, the Creator within each moving as an individualized portion or perspective of consciousness. Life lives with itself and upon itself so that in the reflection that is seen as perhaps the ending of an incarnation for one portion of one perspective, another portion of another perspective, which is still the one Creator, is enhanced while, perhaps, yet another is diminished. It is well to know and to remember that all of the creation is not only the one Creator but is an illusion of separateness.

No portion of the creation is lost, no matter what the change in consciousness or level of apprehension of consciousness is achieved. As you move about in your daily round of activities many millions are the miniscule life forms that give themselves and no longer exist in that form as your place your foot upon the ground, as your automobiles move in their realm of influence, as you breath the air and breath in many other minute forms of life that have but a tiny amount of what you call time in which to experience that which is theirs to experience. And yet the galaxies and the suns and the stars move in their realms as well, changing and transforming into that which is greater, that which is lesser, seen from a lesser point of view, and yet all is still the one Creator knowing Itself. For those who have opened their hearts in compassion to that creation which is theirs to experience within this third-density illusion it is difficult to see various forms of suffering and misery within your life experience. For the heart that is open to all feels the pain of privation, of disease, of isolation, of being unable to comprehend, of feeling the end of one experience as yet another begins. This is well, my friends, for it is, of necessity, a portion of the creation's evolutionary process that this heart opening and the feeling of the agony as well as the ecstasy of the creation about one is such. Yet we assure each that nothing, no portion of the Creator, no form of life or consciousness, is ever lost but is only transformed to yet another avenue or perspective for the Creator to know Itself.

Is there a further query?

Carla: To follow up. I've thought about this before and it is are we not also food but because we are self-aware that we become food of another kind. My thinking on this is that all of these thoughts, awareness, changes, conclusions, everything that we evolve through, in a way, that emotion and suffering and feelings, are they not food for the Creator, so that we are part of the food chain too?

I am Q'uo, and we are in agreement with the thoughts that you have spoken, my sister, and would comment by suggesting that each entity within any illusion or density is a portion of the Creator that gives entirely of itself, of its experiences, of its thoughts, of its past, its present, and its future to the one Creator, for each is the one Creator and the purpose of the entire creation is that the Creator may know Itself through Its infinite portions within creation.

Is there another query, my sister?

Carla: No. Thank you. That is fascinating.

I am Q'uo, and we would agree, my sister, that the entire creation is that which fascinates us in an absolute sense, for there is nothing but the one Creator knowing Itself in infinite variety. Is there another query at this time?

(No further queries.)

I am Q'uo, and we are well aware that we have spoken far longer than is our normal want, and we apologize for the wordiness and we would at this time thank each at this time for inviting our presence to your group this day. It is a great honor and privilege for us to join you in your circle of seeking. We are always aware that there is much more beneath the surface of your queries than first appears and we appreciate the sincerity and depth of seeking that this group brings to each gathering. We are known to you as those of Q'uo, and we would take our leave of this instrument and this group, leaving each in the love and in the light of the one infinite Creator. Adonai, my friends. Adonai. ✤

L/L Research

L/L Research is a subsidiary of Rock Creek Research & Development Laboratories, Inc.

P.O. Box 5195
Louisville, KY 40255-0195

www.llresearch.org

Rock Creek is a non-profit corporation dedicated to discovering and sharing information which may aid in the spiritual evolution of humankind.

ABOUT THE CONTENTS OF THIS TRANSCRIPT: This telepathic channeling has been taken from transcriptions of the weekly study and meditation meetings of the Rock Creek Research & Development Laboratories and L/L Research. It is offered in the hope that it may be useful to you. As the Confederation entities always make a point of saying, please use your discrimination and judgment in assessing this material. If something rings true to you, fine. If something does not resonate, please leave it behind, for neither we nor those of the Confederation would wish to be a stumbling block for any.

CAVEAT: This transcript is being published by L/L Research in a not yet final form. It has, however, been edited and any obvious errors have been corrected. When it is in a final form, this caveat will be removed.

© 2009 L/L Research

Sunday Meditation
November 19, 2000

Group question: The question today has to do with what happens to us when we pass through the doors of death from this illusion to the next, what happens then? Are we able to go on to another location and accomplish other work? If so, what would that be? Do we still have contact with our loved ones and can they become aware of this?

(Carla channeling)

We are those of the principle known to you as the Q'uo. We greet you in the love and in the light of the one infinite Creator, in whose service we are. And we thank you for bringing us to your group this day. It is a precious thing for us to be called to a circle of seeking such as your own. As we gaze and open our hearts to those who take part in this circle we experience great gratitude and a feeling of tremendous blessing for the beauty of each of you, your vibration, your hopes and your dreams are stunning to us. And your desire to know the truth is so inspiring to us, and it furnishes us with that which we hope for more than anything, and that is an opportunity to serve in the way that we have hoped to serve by sharing our thoughts with those who might wish to consider some alternative possibilities, thoughts and opinions that we may have to offer from our experience and our standpoint. We certainly do not claim to be authorities of any kind, and we would only ask each of you to listen to what we have to say with a feeling for what resonates to you. Take those thoughts which seem to be to you a resource and an asset and leave the rest behind. If you are able to use your discrimination then we feel we can speak to you without any infringement on free will. For truly we do not wish to place a stumbling block before any, and we honor free will and the discrimination of each. For each of you knows what is true for you, and you will recognize that truth when it comes to you. It will ring a bell deep in your heart. Do not accept authority or facts that do not resonate, for although they may be interesting they simply are not part of your personal and subjective path of seeking.

This day your question is about what happens when you as a flesh, blood, bone and sinew being perish and go back into the earth from which the elements of your body have come. Certainly, it is a fair question, for you exist in what seems to be a flesh, blood, bone and sinew world. To the outward eye, there is little that suggests that there is anything beyond the heat and the energy of physical existence. From the outward appearances of things it would appear that life comes up from the, what this instrument would call primeval ooze, flourishes for its season as does the grass and the flowers, and then sinks back into the earth. And many are those entities who have lived and died with no other feelings than that this was the situation.

It is our opinion that this is not at all the situation. From our standpoint we would say that this apparently real physical illusion in which you experience the dance of light is, in fact, a most thoroughgoing illusion, an illusion from the bottom up. We may make an inroad into this by saying that your own scientists are aware that the body which contains your consciousness and the chair upon which that body sits and the floor underneath that chair and the earth underneath that floor are all created by that which appears to be space, empty space. Matter itself has never been seen by your scientists although they have seen the path of the energy made by those seeming particles which seemingly create the energy fields and by this we refer to your photons or your electrons.

Beyond this model, which looks a great deal like the physical model of outer space with its far flung stars, there is, indeed, no physicalness to the physical illusion but, rather, a series of interpenetrating and hierarchical energy fields. The energy animating those fields is that which has the transcendent reality. The basis for this energy and the birthplace or spring of all that is, is that in which we greeted you: the love of the one infinite Creator. For this love is as the Logos that was referred to in that holy work which is called your Holy Bible by the one known as John when this entity said, "In the beginning was the Logos. In the beginning was the Word." This entity goes on to define this word as deity. But deity or God has developed connotations of great emotion, and instead we would refer to that energy that created all that is as love. For the Logos is the one great original Thought that is love.

Each star, each planet, each center of consciousness, and each atom has as its heart the Logos. All things are love. All things are the one infinite Creator in energy fields stepped down, and stepped down in order that experience might be gained by that which we would call the sub-Logos, for each of you and each of us is a sub-Logos, a part and portion of the Creator indistinguishable from the stuff of the Creator. This is that of which each of you was created, and this is that which makes each of you a citizen, not of time and space, not of beginnings and endings, but of eternity and infinity. This is your basic and continuing nature. The ones known as B and D have spoken of the concept of these sub-Logoi that each being is having been created before time, space, or the beginning of the creation as your scientists know it. And with this opinion we would agree. We believe this is the way the creation is designed.

The one known as L was speaking of the beating of the creation's heart, the explosion of experience from the Big Bang and the eventual spiritual gravity that pulls together into one locus that is beyond time and space all of the infinite reaches of creation. For the Creator has a heart that beats and each of its beats is a full and complete creation. And in each creation you, as sub-Creators, set out as explorers and voyagers on another incredible adventure of incarnation after incarnation, beginning as elements, moving through experiences as animals and trees and plants of all kinds until each comes to the experience of self-awareness.

This is the crux at which each of you is now, that which we have called third-density self-awareness. Up until this point the evolution which you have experienced has been of body, of mind, and of emotion. And you are ready now, as you begin to contemplate graduation from third density to fourth density experience, to contemplate the further evolution of your mind and your spirit.

When each physical entity comes into incarnation it is as though the consciousness that is your essence chooses to make an intimate affiliation with what this instrument would call a great ape. For each of you has the body of a fairly hairless great ape. Each of you has the instincts, the mind, the inclinations and the needs of this second-density entity that is the animal that has agreed to carry you about and to help you make the decisions of your life. One challenge, when you as a human being in third density come to consider the afterlife, is that challenge of separating in thought that being which is the great ape with its basic instincts, preferences and needs from that infinite and eternal consciousness which has entered into the body and which has worked and cooperated with the body and its mind in order to gain experience, to learn lessons, and to discover ways of being of service within this incarnation.

What dies when you as a person die? That is perhaps the first large question. And we would say to you it is the portion of yourself that you would call the body and the personality, for you see, when you came into incarnation you could not bring the depth and richness of your spirit into a personality shell.

For within the heart of your being you are the Creator and you are, therefore, all that there is. Furthermore, as a citizen of eternity you are not bound by time, so all of the subtleties and nuances of self that you have developed through the entire octave of densities of this creation have their shadow within your third-density experience. You know things that are out of time. They rest in the depths of your subconscious roots of mind, and only the tiniest portion of this knowledge is able to come through that threshold of consciousness which we have called the veil of forgetting which keeps the conscious mind relatively unaware of the depths of the ocean of consciousness beneath the limn of awareness. In dreams and in visions occasionally a glimpse of eternity will come, and the one known as L was speaking of those times when the plan, the purpose, is very clear and is seen to be adequate, elegant and simple.

For the most part, however, those positive assets and what seem to be negative limitations of personality are carefully chosen from the great circle of your true being so that you come into incarnation with a very decided set of preferences, limitations, talents and abilities that you have chosen, perhaps, because they would help you to learn those things which you felt you should learn. Perhaps, to help you pursue relationships which you felt would help you grow. And always to help you to manifest the gifts that you wished to share as a service within this incarnation.

When it is time to release the flesh, the blood, the time, and the space the question is "What survives?" And because this particular instrument has had an experience where it died and then came back to life after thirty seconds of death this instrument can say from sheer experience consciousness survives. By this we mean that at or close to the physical death the consciousness becomes aware that the physical body is becoming unviable. It has been linked throughout life to the physical body, through what this instrument has called the silver cord. Consider this simply as that which tethers the soul or the spirit to a particular body. Now, at or close to physical death this silver cord simply lets go. It may not immediately leave the body, especially if it is interested to see what may happen. Many are the spirits that choose to remain very close to the physical body until such time as all of those within that family, shall we say, have had the opportunity to express their grief and have some sort of farewell service. Often the honored guest at a funeral is the deceased, for it simply cannot leave until it sees what everyone is wearing, how everyone is feeling, if everyone is all right, from the most frivolous concern there is that entire constellation or universe of feelings for these people that have been so dear and so loving for so long and have had so much shared history.

But there comes the time, either at death or soon thereafter, when the consciousness becomes aware that it is time to move ahead. If it is an incarnational pause between two incarnations in third density the next step is what this instrument would call the review of the incarnation. In other words, there will be someone who comes to greet, welcome and guide that consciousness which has just moved into that metaphysical time/space which is the environment for the light body which spirits have between incarnations. That guide may be a loved one close in the birth family; it may be a close friend; it may be a beloved entity such as Jesus, the Holy Spirit, or a favorite saint. It will be that entity which the spirit most feels comfortable with. And with that help, the consciousness is taken to a comfortable place where she may watch what you could think of as a movie or a book with many pictures. For, truly, freed of the confines of time and space it is possible to riffle through the pages of an incarnations fairly quickly, assessing the damage, assessing the need for healing before further work is undertaken, and then assessing what might be the goals of the next incarnation.

Coming into this consideration are the relationships that have been experienced in the last incarnation and how they fell out as to balancing energies between two people. Other issues include what lessons might have been planned for the past incarnation and how those lessons were learned and what service was planned for that incarnation and how that went. There is no judgment involved in this review. There is no blame assigned if those things that were hoped to be accomplished were not. It is simply an evaluation process.

After this initial process, if there has been healing that has been needed, then that will take place. In the inner planes of this planet which each experiences between incarnations in third density the environment is pretty much up to the consciousness that dwells within the inner planes and has experiences to undergo. For some spirits healing will take place in what they conceive of as a hospital. Others will create for themselves a third-density life with a job and so forth, and will have their healing done in a familiar environment of this kind. This healing process is very much under the free choice of the spirit that is undergoing the healing. For you see, each of you between incarnations has no veil of forgetting and is totally aware that he is part of the Creator. He is loved by the Creator, and he is loved. Consequently, there is a gentleness and a charity in the way that the self talks to the self in between incarnations that you do not experience in the sometimes harsh criticisms that each levels at herself within incarnation.

Ultimately, when the consciousness feels that it is healed and that it is ready to take up further learning and further service within third density it moves into that portion of the inner planes where souls are being readied for incarnation. And again, with the aid of the higher self and any guides which the consciousness deems helpful, a plan for incarnation is created. The main lessons to be learned are set into place. The main relationships which the consciousness hopes to pursue are discussed with those other souls and spirits and agreements are made. And choices are made as to what shall be placed into the personality shell in terms of talents and gifts to share within incarnation. And the process begins again.

Because of the fact that there are those in this circle that are not going to have any more third-density incarnations we would mention, briefly, the graduation process from this density that each will go through at some point. We are aware that each has heard of ascensions, and catastrophes, and Armageddon, and people having a global catastrophe in which the world as we know it ends. It is our opinion that this is not the way the creation will work, not among your people. It is our feeling that each of you will be ready for harvest, either after this incarnation or very shortly. Each of you now in this circle has the capacity to be graduated from third density. In fact, each of those dwelling upon your planet at this time has the ability to polarize either in service to self or in service to others to an extent that is harvestable to fourth density. What this means is that each of you earned this incarnation by your basic state of awareness coming into incarnation. Each of you is able, if you wish, to achieve graduation from third density upon the physical death.

Now, the way this occurs begins very similarly to moving into the inner planes in which third-density entities spend time in between incarnations. There is the continuation of consciousness, and there is the being met by the guides, the Holy Spirit, Jesus, those entities in which the consciousness has reposed trust. However, if the consciousness is enough aware of the possibility of harvest it may, as soon as the review of the incarnation begins, ask to cut short all that lies between it and the steps of light. For there is a great hunger in many who are in incarnation on planet Earth at this time to go home. Now, some would frame this going home as going to a higher density. Others would frame going home as simply being with the Creator. However, the mechanism for moving from third density to densities which are more fully packed with light is what this instrument has called the steps of light. This is not quite an accurate description, but it is as close as this instrument can come to expressing what we offer her. What we offer her is a vision of a walkway, a broad and beautiful path of light.

The light along this path is most fastidiously guarded by entities which are extremely close to the one great original Thought, yet which still have some individuality. These are what we would call seventh-density entities. They make absolutely sure that the boundaries between the densities of third and fourth of light are precisely accurate and that higher densities as well along this path are fastidiously accurately observed. The consciousness, then, without seeing any boundaries or partitions in this light, is asked to walk along the path of light. When the entity gets to the place where the light is too much to bear, then that entity stops. The fullest amount of light that that entity can enjoy and work with defines the next density of that entity's experience. If it is third density, that entity will continue in third density. If it is fourth density, that entity will move into the inner planes of a fourth-density planet and prepare to start a cycle of fourth-density experience there. If the entity stops in fifth or sixth density, then that has become the native density of that entity, for that is the place that that entity can enjoy the experience of incarnation the most and can get the most out of it.

Beneath, above, and surrounding all of these details of continued existence is the love and the light of the one infinite Creator. Whether the next experience for each of you is in this density or in a higher density the purpose of incarnation remains the same. Each of you is asked to be yourself. For you are love. The great challenge is uncovering that love, freeing up that love, taking the pain and the suffering and the limitations away from the love that is in your heart. Each of you has, not just a temporary identity within this lifetime. Within this lifetime each of you is a citizen of eternity, and all that shall come to you is within your heart at this time. So we ask each of you to rest, both in the love and the light of the one infinite Creator and within the circumstances of your flesh and bone and blood and sinew. For all of these circumstances shall pass, and yet that consciousness which is you shall be, as it always has been, loving and loved, embracing and embraced by the one infinite Creator which is your source and ending.

We bow before the courage of you in third density, for you truly do dwell in a thick and heavy chemical illusion. And it is only by faith that you may hope and feel and know that all is well and that all will be well. We would at this time transfer this contact to the one known as Jim, thanking this instrument and leaving it in love and in light. We are those of Q'uo.

(Jim channeling)

I am Q'uo, and greet each, once again, in the love and the light of the one infinite Creator through this instrument. At this time it is our privilege to offer ourselves in the attempt to speak to any further queries which those present may have for us. Is there another query at this time?

S: There are many today from different densities that are here helping with the ascension process of this planet, and you have kindly joined us with your thoughts and ideas, so how come you haven't decided to take a dive in the gene pool and try your hand at third-density at this time?

I am Q'uo, and am aware of your query, my brother. As a grouping of entities we have done that which you now do and have moved through those times of choosing the manner in which we would pursue our further evolution beyond third density. Thus, we remember that which you now experience and it is the axis upon which our creation turns, for we are those who have chosen to serve the Creator in all, for by so doing we also advance ourselves as the Creator learns from and teaches to the Creator. There are also those of our grouping who take incarnation again in third density as those who serve as wanderers, answering the call of those upon planets such as your own.

(Tape change.)

I am Q'uo, and am again with this instrument. We appreciate your patience. Is there another query at this time?

S: You said there were some of those of your group that are acting as wanderers at this time. How are they doing and what are they doing?

I am Q'uo, and am aware of your query, my brother. As one might expect, the range of success is large and small, for there are many who move into the third-density illusion with the hope of serving not only by their presence in the lightening of the vibrations of this planetary sphere upon which they dwell, but there is also the hope that each will remember that which it came to do, the manner in which it came to serve, and in many cases this is so. And there is great rejoicing at such service well rendered. Others there are who have the same difficulties as do those natives to the third-density illusion in that they become somewhat, shall we say, lost within the great, heavy, chemical illusion that is your world. They seek in circuitous manner again and again to penetrate the veil of forgetting and yet are weighted down by the concerns and worries of this world. And some become caught within the illusion and must move again through the great cycle of being in order that in a future incarnation they might recapture that which was lost. And for some this might seem to be a situation in which there was sorrow at what seemed to be a failure in the service. And yet we say that there is no failure, for all service has it effect. The Creator learns from each entity that which is offered through the life experience, and there is an infinity of what you call time in which services may be offered. Thus, if one time does not produce the fruit, another season and another time shall surely do so.

Is there another query, my brother?

S: No. Thank you.

I am Q'uo, and we thank you, my brother. Is there another query at this time?

B: I would have a query. The feeling in the physical universe is that there is a great amount of chaos and, obviously, the burning of the stars. In the apparently parallel spiritual universe it seems that it is trying to become very smooth and a continuum of smoothness. How do those two work?

I am Q'uo, and am aware of your query, my brother. That which to the eyes of third density seems to be chaotic is, at another level of experience, that which has rhythm, motion, pattern. However, there are those mysteries for all created entities that go beyond the ability of mind, body and spirit to penetrate. For though we are all of the one Creator we never forget that the heart of the Creator is a mysterious love that has the power to create and to destroy that which we call universes, the very creation itself. So there is this movement of consciousness that is, itself, an infinite stream of being that may from time to time have ripples in it and eddies and that kind of experience which seems to be chaotic. Yet, when those consciousnesses which perceive it are able to become one with it through their understanding of it, then that which appeared to be chaotic then appears to be smooth and unified, harmonious, and able to be perceived in a fashion that is coherent.

Is there another query, my brother?

J: Is it possible according to the laws of incarnation that we at some point existed and met the loved ones that we know in this existence in previous lives and is it possible that we will meet them again in future incarnations?

I am Q'uo, and am aware of your query, my brother. This is indeed so. There are groupings or clans, if you will, of entities who move as a group through incarnational experience after incarnational experience. The relationships vary from one experience to another, oftentimes with some members of the grouping remaining in the inner planes of the planetary sphere offering their assistance in an unseen manner as guides and angelic presences, only to take incarnation once again in yet another experience so that as you move through this Earthly experience you may look about you to those who are your loved ones, those of your family, your friends, those of like mind and heart with whom you move in unison and see those who have been with you for many, many incarnations and experiences on not only this planetary sphere but others as well. For the third-density illusion which is now coming to an end on this planetary sphere is but a brief moment in that which you call time. And there is no time or limitation for the clans or groupings of consciousnesses that choose to move together for one reason or another in the seeking of the one Creator.

Is there another query, my brother?

D: I have a question about the number of people who are gaining understanding about the nature of the creation. Are we getting more understanding of how things really are in our world?

I am Q'uo, and am aware of your query, my brother. We would agree in principle with that statement which you have made, though we would not use the word "understanding," for, as we mentioned previously, especially for those within this third-density illusion, there is little that is understood, yet there is much that is desired to be understood. And it is that heart which desires to know the one Creator, that heart which sees the Creator in the friend, the family, the stranger, and in the mirror that is open to the graduation, the harvest that now beckons into fourth density. It is not what one knows or thinks one knows that will achieve the harvest, but it is the desire to know. The desire to serve and the desire to be the one Creator.

Is there another query, my brother?

B: In the various religious books of the various established religions they seem each to point to a future where there is sort of a nirvana, but none seem to be the same kind of nirvana. Could these exist parallel to each other at the same [time], one without the knowledge of the other?

I am Q'uo, and am aware of your query, my brother. The various terms that have been used in the many religions and spiritual practices upon your planetary sphere refer to various levels of experience in which union with the Creator is sought and for a brief time, as it is measured, is achieved. However, we would suggest that it is more the case that various cultures and religions have formed their own descriptive terms and phraseologies to reflect these levels of experience that each shares with the other, so that it is like various languages having a word for this or that experience in which the experience is the same, yet the word or phrase is different. It is a matter of perspective and experience within a culture that determines how the various steps of realization may be called or named.

Is there another query, my brother?

D: I have a query. As mentioned in the harvesting of the third-density entities moving into the fourth, is there any way to explain the experiences that might be had in the fourth density or what various purposes might be entertained in that density?

I am Q'uo, and am aware of your query, my brother. Though words fail to give a clear description of that which is beyond words we shall attempt to speak to this subject. Within the fourth-density experience the veil of forgetting that is so important within third density is removed, for no longer is there the need to make the choice of how to pursue learning and service further, the choice having been made in third density. Without the veil of forgetting the experience of each entity is much broadened and intensified for if you can imagine the ability to know the mind of another and to share that mind and the abilities in that mind and multiply that ability by the number of entities within the culture, within the race, and within the planet then one may begin to approximate the kind of consciousness that one may call a planetary consciousness that one may share with all others, for at this level of experience in the density of understanding and love there is no desire to hide any portion of the self from another. There is the desire, in fact, to join with others and point the needle of the compass, if you will, in one direction: in the direction of seeking and serving and becoming the one Creator. Thus, entities within the fourth-density illusion undertake the intensive learning of what it is to have complete compassion, understanding, mercy, forgiveness, and that which you call love. For at this level of experience the individual identity willingly blends with those of like mind and heart in the seeking and serving of the one Creator. Thus, the experience within the fourth-density illusion is far more harmonious than that within the third-density illusion where the choice of polarity is made in the fires of experience. As the soul is tempered in these fires then it is able to join with others of similar temper who also seek the One in a similar fashion.

The need for words, therefore, of a spoken nature is not necessary unless chosen. The communication is more of what you would call the telepathic nature but more than that which we do now, which is a word-by-word or concept kind of communication. The communication in fourth density is more of what you would call the gestalt, where an entire experience or picture with many thousands or millions of components may be transmitted instantaneously and true understanding achieved. There is no miscommunication at this level of experience. Thus, the harmony is most notable. However, since the harmony is notable and it is undeniable that the one Creator is at the heart of all, evolutionary experience is somewhat slowed in comparison to that which is possible within your third-density illusion. Thus it is that many of the fourth density seek to be of service to others by joining again the third-density illusion as those who are called wanderers and who seek with the great heart of compassion to share the love they know and have found within all creation with those who call for this kind of experience.

Is there another query, my brother?

D: In changing the subject, is there a description of time and how it is understood by various entities?

I am Q'uo, and am aware of your query, my brother. Again, we seek with words to do more than words can do, yet we will attempt to give you this description, which will be likened unto a river where time is seen as that which moves in a unified fashion, and yet moves within no boundaries of experience, which moves with a smaller influence, shall we say, being seen as more of an addition to experience rather than the nature of experience playing out from point A to B. Entities outside of the realm of time may look at time as being somewhat of a relic. However, there is the experience in appreciation of true simultaneity where entities may move into an experience of a certain kind of time for a certain intensity of experience until the experience is gained. Entities may, in fact, partake in various levels of time so that they may experience what you would see as the past before experiencing that which you see as the future. We realize that this term, time, and our description of it is somewhat confusing. We hope that our humble words have been able to elucidate in some small degree the nature of your query.

D: Thank you for that description.

We are most grateful to you as well, my brother, and would ask at this time if there is a final query.

B: Is it possible that planet Earth is being visited and has been visited by creatures from other parts of the galaxy or universe?

I am Q'uo, and am aware of your query, my brother. This is, indeed, so and has been for the entire lifetime of this planetary sphere, which includes that time before life as you know it began its cycle of experience here. There are those from all portions of the one creation who have been able to discipline their personalities to such a degree that they are able to move with unfettered tread throughout the one creation in what you would call zero time, for the creation is one being. And for those who have been able to master the disciplines, it is possible to move in thought from any portion of the one creation to any other portion of the one creation.

At this time we would like to thank each entity in this circle of seeking for inviting our presence here. It is a great honor and privilege for us to be able to join you in your circle when we are called, and we joyfully do so, again reminding each to take only those words and thoughts which we have offered which have meaning to you, leaving behind all others without a second thought. We are known to you as those of Q'uo, and we would take our leave of this instrument and this group at this time, leaving each, as always, in the love and in the ineffable light of the one infinite Creator. Adonai, my friends. Adonai.

Sunday Meditation
December 3, 2000

Group question: When we are trying to make a decision that is important to our spiritual lives, we often have to wait patiently, to take the matter to the heart, and we wonder how we can do this more effectively to gain the direction that we need to follow for our greatest growth? How do we discover what our direction is?

(Carla channeling)

We are those known to you as the principle of Q'uo, and we greet you in the love and in the light of the one infinite Creator, whose servants we are. It is our privilege and our blessing to be called to your group this afternoon, and, as always, we thank you for the desire for the truth and the thirst for deity that brings each of you to this circle of seeking. It is a great service to us to be able to share our thoughts with you, for this is the service we hope to offer at this time: to share our thoughts with those on your planet which might find some use in them.

As always, we ask that each use her powers of discrimination carefully, for we are not authority but, rather, fellow seekers and although we feel that we have experiences and thoughts that are worthy of sharing, we do not necessarily feel that our opinions are those which will resonate for other spiritual seekers in their particular patterns and processes, so we ask you to discriminate for yourselves and leave behind those thoughts that are not helpful.

The concept of discrimination is sometimes a difficult one for people who have been accustomed at times to feel that they, perhaps, are not entirely competent to judge any particular area or even in general. Many are the factors within your culture which tend to disenfranchise spiritual seekers from trusting in their own opinion and relying upon their own powers of discrimination. The bludgeoning of that blunt instrument known to you as school creates a respect for authority which is perhaps overstated. For in the realm of spiritual seeking truth is not a matter of authority. Truth is not subject to proof. Truth is, in fact, in any linear terms, entirely subjective. To get to a spiritual truth it first must be realized that this spiritual truth will be true only for you. It will not be true for another living human being.

Truly, each spiritual seeker is looking at one unique pattern and picture in looking at the self. It is almost impossible to extrapolate from something that is happening to someone else to something that is happening to you. You are an unique creature. Your incarnational lessons are carefully put in place. Each within this circle has accomplished a good many years of processing information and achieving realization after realization which has, each in its own way, encouraged, supported and helped to move forward that process of spiritual evolution of mind, emotions and spirit that each of you has thirsted for for many years. And, yet, the process does not end while life is extant within the flesh and bones of the incarnation. The learning process ripples merrily onward.

Let us look for a moment at this process. One thing we would note about this process is that it has themes that recur. For each entity there will be those incarnational lessons which cannot be identified quickly. The first time a crisis situation along certain lines comes up it is overwhelming. There is so much confusion that there is no seeming place where a person might find a place to stand, a ground of being, a trustable foundation from which to look at the situation and the environment of the situation. The second time this same incarnational lesson recurs it may be almost as completely baffling as the first time.

We will give an example that is part of this instrument's process about which it already knows, thereby avoiding infringement upon free will. This instrument has an incarnational lesson in which it gives without expectation of return. It is so accustomed now to this theme that when this situation occurs where the entity is giving and is not receiving anything back or is even receiving difficulty and resistance back from the loving offering of the self, this instrument simply becomes aware that the incarnational lesson is recurring again and this instrument assumes, then, that it is recurring at a slightly different level because there are nuances at this level that have not been covered before. And the pressures of spiritual evolution suggest further learning of these nuances. Therefore, this instrument is almost too willing to dash forward into the breach and serve that person who has no ability to offer a loving return that this instrument can recognize. Very well, in the case of this particular incarnational lesson this instrument is unlikely to be confused for very long when the cycle repeats and the lesson comes up again and that wind chime of the emotions begins to sound its motif and make that certain sound that brings forth the emotions associated with this lesson. So you see, over the passage of time learning occurs and the level of confusion ameliorates so that even though there is discomfort in the challenge of the situation there is not an overwhelming level of discomfort or confusion. The ground of being remains and this instrument is then able to call upon its faculties of will and faith.

Now, we take the liberty of moving to the situation, which faces the instrument, which prompted this particular line of questioning this afternoon. In this situation this instrument is dealing with an incarnational lesson concerning what best could be called limitations. It is very easy when there is more than one incarnational lesson involved in an incarnational plan to become puzzled or even confused as to which lesson is actually being recycled. Therefore, in this particular case, one suggestion that we would give to this instrument is to spend time resting in contemplation of the incarnational lesson of limitation, which this instrument has experienced cyclically throughout its incarnation. Much work has been done through the years in working upon this incarnational lesson. Work still needs to be done. There are nuances that need to be considered. This is absolutely normal for the progress of a spiritual seeker. It may not, perhaps, be completely standard that someone would choose more than one incarnational lesson. It is, indeed, a crowded agenda.

However, each personality shell that is chosen for an incarnation comes with certain characteristics. For some personality shells the characteristics include such a desire for working upon one shining goal that the hallmark of the incarnation is simplicity and one theme that recurs to the exclusion of all others. For other personality shells there has been what we might call spiritual ambition: the desire to learn more, the desire to progress at a more efficient and that which is seen subjectively as a more helpful rate. You will notice people with this type of personality shell over-committing themselves in good deeds, taking too many classes for their own comfort in schooling, and otherwise tending to overfill the time allotted for each day with what this instrument would call good things to do. In neither personality type is there more excellence than the other. It is a simple matter of choice. Each way of approaching an incarnation has its advantages. Each has its drawbacks.

For the entity with what may be called spiritual ambition, as well as for the entity who burns with one single flame or thirst, the dangers involved include coming to take this quest so seriously that the perspective of that ground of being is lost, and the seeker becomes overwhelmed with the details of whatever present situation has occupied the interest in mind, the emotions, and the time of the seeker.

Now let us step back and gaze at the actual situation. The actual situation is that there is no time or process or pressure to accomplish anything. Each dwells in eternity and all that has happened, is happening, and will happen is happening now, all at the same time, in perfect harmony, in utter perfection, and with an elegance and simplicity of pattern that is stunning, or would be if the pattern could be seen in its entirety.

There is no such thing as sequence. Space is an illusion. The bones, the flesh, and the mass of this particular incarnation are of an illusory nature that is very deep. Nothing that seems to be occurring upon the physical level has that kind of deep meaning that engenders fear, guilt, anger, remorse and all the other emotions that this incarnation creates as an illusion for the learning of the student. In other words, each seeker has put itself in a school of illusion in which things happen that are very strenuous, difficult and uncomfortable in many ways. And, yet, in the execution of these processes of suffering there is no animus, judgment or anger upon the part of the one infinite Creator.

The actual situation is that the one infinite Creator is issuing a vibration that is the creation. That creation is made up of the one great original Thought which is the Logos or love. The Creator is that love in utter unpotentiated fullness. The creation is that love in its potentiated form and light in its manifested form, and each of you as a creature of love and of light, of manifestation and of Logos, of Creator and illusion. And each of you dances the dance of Creator, moving to the dream of the illusion of sequence and meaning and living and learning. And, yet, each of you is already everything that each seeks to learn. So the actual process of spiritual evolution is one of subtraction, of allowing things to drop away in order to get to the heart of each perceived crisis or crux which occurs when an incarnational lesson, or a derivative of an incarnational lesson, recurs in the cyclical rhythms of the process of incarnation.

Now, each entity looking at the possibility of an incarnation upon planet Earth and an immersion into the illusion of third density was excited in the extreme about the extravagant possibilities for learning and for service that such an incarnation represents. Each in great anticipation set up what seemed to it to be very fruitful potential relationships, very helpful incarnational lessons which would sharpen the polarity of service to others, advance the evolution of mind, purify and discipline the emotions, and further the spiritual evolution of that soul which the personality shell brought into incarnation is only the shadow of. Each of you felt fairly optimistic about being able to penetrate the veil of forgetting. For the truth was so obvious before incarnation, so penetrating, so perfect. How could we truly forget? And, yet, the spirit comes into the flesh. The flesh comes into the world. The voices of the world come into the consciousness of the incarnated being, and confusion begins apace.

And so each in the childhood moves through a determined assault on the spirit. By the time that spirit has become mature enough to be able to work through those layers of enculturation the enculturation has become thick, dense and difficult to penetrate. That surety before incarnation has become utter unknowing. This is the plan. This is the way it is supposed to be. Each within incarnation is supposed to become a true Earth native and the awakening from that sleep of Earth is the hoped-for result of that thirst with which each incarnated in the heart of self, that thirst to know, that thirst to seek, that thirst to worship and simply to be one's deepest self.

We speak now to thirsty people, and we say to you, while we cannot hand-feed you water to quench your thirst, we can talk about the plan; the plan we see for each of you. For we feel that beyond all illusion, beyond all sequence, beyond all linear proof, beyond all illusion of any kind, it may be trusted by each of you that there is a plan, a carefully created, thoughtfully worked out plan that was created by yourself and by Spirit for this incarnation. Everything that is occurring is part of the outworking of this plan. It is an organic process, taking in great scoops, from anywhere within the illusion that comes into contact with the particular world of one seeker, that material which it needs in order to offer the various incarnational lessons in their various nuances needed as the cycles spiral and the learning and the process evolve. Therefore, what greatly aids the work of an entity in the midst of a perceived crux of incarnational lesson is not linear thought or analysis but, rather, a relaxation of all non-emotional processes, a refraining from intellectual thought, and a program of repetition of affirmations having to do with awakening, supporting and encouraging the faculties of faith and will.

Let us look first at faith. What is faith? Many would like faith to be faith in this or faith in that. But we say to you that, as far as we know, faith is the faith that all is well. It is not a belief; it is not a dogma; it is not complex; it does not have an object. Faith is an attitude of confidence that there is a plan, that the plan is working out perfectly, and that any difficulties that we are having with the plan are part of the plan. Therefore, no matter what the suffering, all is well and all will be well. The only responsibility of the faithful entity, then, is to maintain that faith and to deal with the suffering in a way that has as much as possible of humor, patience and perspective. For it is hoped that when it is seen that there is a plan, that this may release the spirit to dance within that plan, to look for ways to create style in responding to the nuances of the plan and finding ways to inject humor and a lightness of being into those reactions to the plan. And, above all, that ability to refrain from judging the self as stupid, unworthy or otherwise less than a perfect partner with the Creator and Spirit in experiencing and responding to the love and the light of the one infinite Creator.

There may well be the concept that there are things to do that are part of the plan of incarnation, and may we say that it is never part of an incarnational plan to do, but, rather, to be. Naturally, when entities achieve greatly within the illusion that is a cause for rejoicing, but that is part of the illusion. In terms of incarnational plans and incarnational lessons, what each seeker is working with are intentions, thoughts, hopes and dreams. In terms of metaphysical seeking it is not a matter of finding answers. It is a matter of coming to respect questions. It is never doing. It is always essence.

Faith is the willingness to abide in the essence of self, in the knowledge that the plan is good, and in the willingness to do the best that one can to interpret and respond to the situation as it unfolds. The actual decisions made are not that important. The intentions and the reasons involved for those decisions are important. Consequently, when the one known as Tom asked, "How do we get these crises, these problems that cause worry and the need for patience into the heart?" we would say that the answer involves allowing those things that are not of the heart to fall away, realizing that the issues are not in the physical world or the decisions made in the physical world, but, rather, the issue revolves around finding the most respect, the most honor, support, and encouragement for that heart of self that rests within the plan.

We may see the plan as outfigured in that Holy of Holies within the heart which holds the truth of being. In that Holy of Holies the Creator dwells in Its full original vibration. And the seeker, too, is there in its own heart, if it can remember to go there. With all of the buzzing noises of brain and intellect and thought, it is almost impossible to remember to go to the heart. It is only when there is a decision made to release the intellectual thought in the workings of the decision-making mind and to move into faith, trust and hope that the self can become silent, the mind can stop its chatter, and the self can use the key of silence to enter that tabernacle that is the heart. The beauty and the excellence of silence cannot be overrated in this regard. Often, we speak of meditation, but we find that you within third density attempt to make a project out of this meditation and create complexities and difficulties within this practice as well, which is completely normal for those who are within the heavy illusion of Earth. We encourage all movements into silence, whether they be called meditation or simply sitting and soaking in the now. In any case, there is a release involved, a release of control, a surrender to the will that is the Creator's and at the same time the heart of self's will.

And this brings us to speaking of will, for it is the faculty of will that supports faith. This will is an interesting phenomenon. It is created from the discipline of the dark side of self. To those who have not begun to work upon the discipline of the self and its personality these words mean little. To the one who has begun the attempt to look at and to work with the emotional and intellectual responses and to begin to learn more and more about the self in this way it will make more sense. For it will be seen that each and every seemingly negative characteristic of self has its own strength when it has been tamed and placed in a configuration in which it lies within the deep heart and self, acknowledged as part of the self, but disciplined as to its expression within the outer expression of a daily life. This is not the same as the repression of unfortunate thoughts, for it demands that each thought that is seen by the self to be angry, or in some way unacceptable as seen by the self, as that which can be worked upon, that which can yield fruit, that which can become that which it does not seem to be.

In this work the creative principle is used by the self, not to tear the self down or to judge the self, but, rather, to accept the self as it is, to balance the emotions that seem to be unbalanced by seeing their opposites, and then to integrate that whole range of being represented by that seeming negative emotion into the universal self that is the Creator. For you and the Creator are truly all that there is, and often much will be seen in the experience that is within that universal self along the lines of the dark side as perceived by the self. Thusly, will is honed by forgiveness as the self works on the self to come into self-acceptance, self-love, self-forgiveness, and self-worth.

The one known as J suggested that, in a situation where there was a decision to be made, that an entity simply choose what it really wishes to do. It may be seen that in incarnational lessons that crises may have nuances that are so puzzling that it is not immediately clear to an entity what it wishes to do. However, we suggest that in these situations the faculty of will be called upon to hone the desire to invoke faith and then that the faculty of faith be called upon in order that the being may rest from strife and may find a peace that dwells in midair, in total unknowing. For what is impatience but a refusal to realize that periods of unknowing occur and are acceptable?

We do not suggest that any of this is effortless. We only suggest that it is a most carefully thought out and a most blessing-filled procedure. We suggest that each of you has created a perfect environment for learning and for service. And each of you has created an excellent plan which is in effect, and that each of you will do well to create within the self more and more ability to invoke faith and will and to know that all is love and, even in the midst of suffering, all is well. Shall you die? Shall you live? Does it matter if you are moving along the lines of spiritual evolution? We ask each to trust. And we assure you that every force of nature and spirit wishes to help and is ready to express the hints and harbingers of synchronicity to speed the awareness of the truth.

This instrument informs us that we simply cannot speak further, and we will even, with your permission, forgo the usual further questions, for we are aware that we have spoken far beyond our normal time. May we have your permission to leave this instrument, or are there some questions that we would answer through the instrument known as Jim? We would ask the ones known as Jim, J, and T to indicate.

(No further queries.)

We felt sure that this was the case, but we thank you for confirming that which we felt was so. We want to thank you for raising this question, which was very interesting and for allowing us to speak through this instrument. We leave each, as we found you, in the most beautiful and ineffable love and creative light of the one infinite Creator. We are known to you as those of Q'uo, and humbly we say to you, adonai, Adonai vasu borragus. ☙

L/L Research

L/L Research is a subsidiary of Rock Creek Research & Development Laboratories, Inc.

P.O. Box 5195
Louisville, KY 40255-0195

www.llresearch.org

Rock Creek is a non-profit corporation dedicated to discovering and sharing information which may aid in the spiritual evolution of humankind.

ABOUT THE CONTENTS OF THIS TRANSCRIPT: This telepathic channeling has been taken from transcriptions of the weekly study and meditation meetings of the Rock Creek Research & Development Laboratories and L/L Research. It is offered in the hope that it may be useful to you. As the Confederation entities always make a point of saying, please use your discrimination and judgment in assessing this material. If something rings true to you, fine. If something does not resonate, please leave it behind, for neither we nor those of the Confederation would wish to be a stumbling block for any.

CAVEAT: This transcript is being published by L/L Research in a not yet final form. It has, however, been edited and any obvious errors have been corrected. When it is in a final form, this caveat will be removed.

© 2009 L/L Research

Sunday Meditation
December 17, 2000

Group question: Today we are going to take pot luck, and since it's close to Christmas and New Year's, perhaps Q'uo would have a Christmas message for us.

(Carla channeling)

We are those of the principle known to you as the Q'uo. Greetings in the love and in the light of the one infinite Creator, in whose service we are. We are most delighted to speak with your group this evening and we thank each of you for seeking the truth and for joining in this circle to do so. As always, we request that each listen to what we have to say with the awareness that we are merely offering opinions and are not authorities. And we would appreciate each of you discriminating as to those things which you find useful and those things which you leave behind.

The request for a Christmas message is a charming one and certainly offers us a beautiful array of directions which we might pursue. The time that you experience as the Christmas season is a part of a cycle that is remarkable to your planet, the situation being cleverly planned so that there are variations in the amount of light that you upon your planet enjoy in any one diurnal period. This Christmas season is that season of the least light and, indeed, some portions of your planetary surface are almost entirely in the dark for some portion of your winter. It is at this time of darkness that your story of Christ begins.

What is the message that this entity comes to offer? Indeed, the heart of that message is a kind of light. However, it is the kind of light that can be generated without your sun body or any other source of what you think of as light radiation. The light that gleams when no other light shines is the light of love, and it is that quality of light which the one you call Jesus the Christ embodies, for us as well as for you. For we feel that this entity expressed in a supernally perfect way the essence of pure love.

This instrument received a little story in her web mail this day which we would like to retell. In this story a wife who dearly loved her husband became aware that he was disenchanted with Christmas, not necessarily the sentiments and ideals of the season, but the commercialism and the hustle and bustle of it. And so she began thinking of what she might do to give her husband a better Christmas. One day they went to a sporting event and one of the two teams had no uniforms and also seemed to be made up of young people that had no advantages or money even to pay for their bus ride there. This woman found a way to purchase uniforms for that scruffy little team and when she had finished her act of charity she wrote a little note about it and placed it in an envelop and placed her husband's name on it and put it in a tree. This little, white envelope with its little message became the favorite present for the whole family that year, and it was so successful that the wife decided to do that every year.

And sometime during each year she would find a charity to do anonymously, quietly. A couple that had lost everything in a fire, a young child that needed an operation. Each year she found someone that needed something and found a way to be that person's Santa Claus, and each year everyone would look for that envelop. The year came when the husband died. The wife barely managed to get the tree up. There were many things that she was not able to do, but she did place a white envelop in the tree. When Christmas morning came, she and her four children gathered for a very difficult Christmas together, and they all discovered that every single person there had place a white envelop in the tree. Each child, being concerned that their mom would not be able to continue the tradition, had taken it upon themselves to find someone to give to because they wanted to give their dad his favorite present. The story ended with a hope that this would be a tradition that the family would continue, and each year the favorite presents would be those white envelopes. They talked about giving to someone nobody knew and nobody wanted to impress, but just someone who needed something and who had found a Santa Claus.

We could talk to you about Jesus the Christ, for we greatly admire this teacher. We could access the history of this entity's life, and, yet, we find that this entity would much prefer that we speak of the love itself to which he came to bear witness—the love that is beyond the love of possession, the love that is beyond human love, the love that created each of you and that will destroy the universe. For each of you is as Jesus the Christ, not in the literal way of being identical to this particular personality but, rather, each of you is as Jesus the Christ in that you enter the dark world, both in your incarnation and at that point within your incarnation when you awaken to the light within, when you become aware of the infinite passion and beauty and works of ideals and principles that have a truth that rings far beyond time and space, life and death.

Firstly, you come into a dark world physically, gaze at the illusion about you, listen to your nightly news. This instrument often calls it the bad news, for seldom do they give good news on the news. It is the nature of the Earth scene and of third-density scenes in general that the grime and the tatters of life will appear far more dark and serious than the light and the laughter and the delight that co-exist with the darkness of the illusion. In the outer manifestation of third density will always seem to be a fairly dark picture. It will always seem that there is a battle between good and evil and that the evil is winning. May we say that this is an illusion, that, in actual fact, the light is increasing as more and more of your people awaken to their spiritual identity. However, it is one of the great advantages of the illusion that it appears dark. This is a requirement of the third-density experience: setting the stage upon which each spirit entering the world walks into the center of that stage knowing that the audience has come, the play is going on, and the lines are not known. There is only one clue that each player has as to the nature of the drama that is taking place. And that clue comes from a place within the self rather than from the props and the other characters on the stage.

Each spirit enters the world to bring and to share, to bless and to transduce the love and the light of the one infinite Creator. In order for this to be a meaningful activity, there need be that backdrop of darkness. On the second level, the level of the purely metaphysical, the concept of each spirit's being as Jesus the Christ becomes more focused because here it may be seen that as each spirit awakens within incarnation to the basic nature of the experience and of the self each is awakening as an infant into a manger in a stable, not into a comfortable and secure place, but into a most humble and sparing abode. For each infant spirit is helpless and brand new, and it needs a great deal of help.

The spirit of love is the heart of each spirit that takes flesh. That perfect love expressed in Jesus the Christ dwells in each heart, but it is as though each spirit needed the help of the being that has become aware in order to thrive. So each of you is as the caretaker, the parent, teacher, and the comforter of his and her own spirit. Each of you can encourage the spirit of love within you. Each can clothe that infant spirit in the garments of care and self-awareness and time, time given to silence and the awareness of the love that rest within in that cradle that is the heart.

How shall you parent your own inner spirit? How shall you help this spirit to mature and to begin to try its wings? Remember that this spiritual child within is a creature that is moved and strengthened by the choices that you make. In so many of the dark aspects of the daily round of activities there is a decision to be made, and as this instrument was saying earlier, decisions can be made in fear or in freedom. When an ethical decision comes, when there is a crux, it is very well to pause and ask the self, as the one known as Ra has said, "Where is the love in this situation? Where is the light in this moment? Where is the service that can be rendered?" Often these questions create a clarity and the spirit within is able to flower and blossom a bit because the time has been taken to look at a situation that seemed dark within the illusion of the world and to find the light and love and service hidden within the darkness of that puzzle, that worldly situation. If you can draw back to the extent that you are able to ask yourself these questions you have succeeded in using the darkness of Earth to find ways to light the candle of the heart's great and often untapped resources of faith and hope. It is truly a dark time, your winter.

We bless that darkness. As we look back on our own third-density experience we see the gift of unknowing for what it is: a necessary prerequisite to the free choice of faith. We do not at all discourage the worship and love of the one known as Jesus the Christ. This entity is as the most excellent of models for love. We encourage each to gaze long into the stories of this entity and to see how this entity was able to love. But more, we ask that you look into your own hearts and see the spirit of love within that is the essence of each of you. And know that you have within you the love that you seek, the truth that you seek, and the beauty that you thirst for. We encourage each of you to value each hard choice and each time of apparent darkness.

The choices that you make during these incarnational times of unknowing have a weight, potentially, that can change the course of the development of your soul. We encourage each to know that you have the resources within you to be that candle that is lit within the darkness, that the darkness shall never overcome.

We would at this time transfer this contact to the one known as Jim. We thank this instrument and leave it in love and in light. We are those of Q'uo.

(Jim channeling)

I am Q'uo, and greet each of you once again in the love and in the light of the infinite Creator. At this time it is our privilege once again in the attempt to speak to any further query which those present may have for us. Is there another query at this time?

S: I had a question last time about some of those of your group who had come here as wanderers and who had gone slightly off track and gotten lost in this illusion. Can we help those of your group on this side of the veil?

I am Q'uo, and we are aware of your query, my brother, and we appreciate the concern that comes from the open heart in search of those who need this love, those who have found a great love, who have sacrificed much for it, and who in another form continue to seek it. We can assure you that each entity, whether previously that which you call a wanderer or an Earth native, as you may call one whose origins are this planetary sphere, will find the great love of the life to be that one Creator which resides within, as we have spoken of previously. For though each incarnation seems to be a great span of time, measured in your years, from the point of view of that which is infinite and eternal, each incarnation is merely the blinking of an eye. And those lessons that can be learned in such a relatively short span of time are intense, pure, passionate and do make their mark upon the soul identity. Thus, though one may seem to be lost from the many, the journey of being lost is that which, in itself, holds great potential. For the ability to move with faith and to power this faith with the will to seek the truth is that which aids any entity in its journey of seeking. Many there are who move in a fashion which seems to reflect this being lost, and yet we know there is a day in which all shall be found. There is within each heart that which may be seen as a beacon, a homing device which ever brings one nearer to the source of the self, to the source of love. And in each daily round of activities the opportunities are presented to the entity to avail itself of its desire to seek the One. Though the period of being lost may be what you would call extensive, always is the higher self offering to the incarnated self the opportunity to find the way home. There are many hints upon the trail, shall we say, and each entity shall eventually find each step on the journey to be complete.

Is there a further query, my friend?

S: One last one. We were talking earlier about a series of lessons in which our eldest daughter took one of our puppy dogs and it got lost. The idea of getting another dog and there seems to be a lot of issues and lessons and many things going on when you look at all of the ramifications of what is happening. Could you shed some light on some of those issues?

I am Q'uo, and am aware of your query, my brother. Whatever the catalyst may be in any incarnation in the third density, the ability to utilize the catalyst depends on large degree upon the ability to open the heart and to accept that which seems to be unacceptable, to give love where it would not seem to be welcome, indeed to be the fool in the desire to open the heart and freely share that which you call unconditional love. If one can remember that there is love in each moment, that each form of catalyst offers the opportunity to either express that love or to receive that love, or to utilize a combination of the two, then each season of catalyst may be seen to be complete and to be seen to offer these endless opportunities for the sharing of love. One may take each kind of catalyst seriously in that the catalyst is seen to be an end in itself, and this is in many cases to miss the point. Yes, it is important to a certain entity that one or another outcome result from a set of situational circumstances. And yet if each within the situation is aware that it is love to be learned from all of the catalyst then it is much easier to find that harvest within the catalyst.

Is there a further query, my brother?

S: I was requested to ask if the dog which is lost is OK?

I am Q'uo, and am aware of your query, my brother. We pause to scan and feel there is no infringement to report that the creature that you call the lost dog is well.

Is there any further query, my brother?

S: Not at this time. Thank you very much.

I am Q'uo, and we thank you as well, my brother. Is there another query at this time?

Carla: I am dealing with orange and yellow-ray blockage at this time. I am experiencing some illness and am trying to work with that and the issue of psychic greeting and of opening and clearing these energy centers. I would appreciate anything that you might have to say that would help me to work on this.

I am Q'uo, and am aware of your query, my sister. Without infringing we may suggest that in any situation with any other entity if one feels the lack of love then one may look to that shared catalyst as that which may profitably be explored.

Is there any further query, my sister?

Carla: No. Thank you.

I am Q'uo, and we thank you, my sister. Is there another query at this time?

R: Not a question, but as the year draws to a close I would like to thank the entities of the Confederation for speaking to this group, for their work and effort in communication.

I am Q'uo, and, my brother, we greatly appreciate your appreciation, and we return it as well. Is there a final query at this time?

(No further queries.)

I am Q'uo, and we greatly appreciate the warm reception and humorous vibrations that typify this group, especially at this time of year. We are always filled with joy to be called to your group and we cannot thank you enough for offering us this opportunity to be of service in our humble way. We hope that our words in some way may find a home within your heart. For those which do not, we bid you drop them and think not twice about them. At this time we shall take our leave of this instrument and of this group. We leave each, as always, in the love and in the light of the infinite Creator. Adonai. Adonai, my friends. ☙

Year 2001

January 6, 2001 to December 23, 2001

L/L Research

L/L Research is a subsidiary of Rock Creek Research & Development Laboratories, Inc.

P.O. Box 5195
Louisville, KY 40255-0195

www.llresearch.org

Rock Creek is a non-profit corporation dedicated to discovering and sharing information which may aid in the spiritual evolution of humankind.

ABOUT THE CONTENTS OF THIS TRANSCRIPT: This telepathic channeling has been taken from transcriptions of the weekly study and meditation meetings of the Rock Creek Research & Development Laboratories and L/L Research. It is offered in the hope that it may be useful to you. As the Confederation entities always make a point of saying, please use your discrimination and judgment in assessing this material. If something rings true to you, fine. If something does not resonate, please leave it behind, for neither we nor those of the Confederation would wish to be a stumbling block for any.

© 2009 L/L Research

Sunday Meditation
January 6, 2001

Group question: The question today has to do with the contrast between religion and spirituality, seeking from without and seeking from within. We are asking if Q'uo could give us some ideas as to the direction that is appropriate for each person, how each can be helpful, what the hindrances might be for each, and how a person can determine what is right for him or her. And is there really a precise answer or direction for each of us, or is there a certain amount of uncertainty that we need to be able to accept?

(Carla channeling)

We are known to you as those of the Q'uo, and we greet you in the love and in the light of the one infinite Creator, whom we serve. It is a great privilege to join this circle of seeking, and we greet each of you, thanking you for your great thirst for the truth, for all that has brought you to this meeting. It is a very special time for us when we are able to communicate with this group. We welcome each of you. Those in our principle known to you as those of Hatonn and those of Oxal wish especially to greet the one known as Kyra and to greet all of those who are new to this group. For each of you has your unique and beautiful music that you embody in your energy, and we greatly enjoy sharing this meditation with the beautiful harmony that you make together.

We ask one thing before we offer our opinions, which we are glad to share, and that is that each of you use your powers of discrimination, knowing that we are not authorities but, rather, we are as you: seekers after a mystery that recedes before us as we pursue it through density after density and experience after experience. The mystery remains and our thirst for that mystery continues to motivate and inspire us in our seeking and in our service. We want to thank each of you for helping us to perform that service which is simply to share our thoughts with you through this instrument. If any thoughts that we share do not seem right to you, we ask you to leave them behind and move on. For the nature of personal truth is resonant. When something is yours, some truth, some aspect of the truth, some inspiration or thought, it will ring true. It will have a resonance, and those thoughts that do not resonate are simply not a part of your own personal truth at this particular time.

Truth is a very slippery word, and we find that it evolves as we evolve. The principles and ideals remain the same but we ourselves, and you also, are in a constant and unremitting state of evolution. We cannot stop it. We can simply accelerate it or let it proceed at its own pace. Each of you has chosen to attempt to accelerate the pace of your spiritual evolution, and we commend you for that. It is effective. It is working. The problem with it, of course, is that increased rates of change are concomitant with increased rates of discomfort, spiritually and emotionally speaking. Consequently, the more successful that each of you is at seeking the truth, the more likely each of you will be to feel at times that you have lost everything; that you cannot possibly make heads or tails of what the truth might be, and that you might as well give up. We assure you that this is part of the pattern of spiritual evolution. And wherever you are, whatever the lightness or darkness of your own interior heart at this particular time, you are part of a pattern of spiritual lightening that, as you look back on it from hindsight, you will see to have been effectual and inspired.

Your question for beginning this evening is about the contrast between two words that, on the surface of it, mean very much the same thing in your language: religion and spirituality. Religion might also be called the outer path and spirituality might also be called the inner path in order to point up the basic point of tension between these two terms. Your question is most interesting, and we are very glad to spend some time on it. You asked concerning the advantages and disadvantages of each path, and we will talk a bit about each path in those two aspects. In order to orient the discussion, we would take a moment to step back and ask each to come with us. See yourself at this time resting upon your seats, your limbs relaxed and your minds quiet. See the beauty of the evening, the patchwork of snow and earth and tree. And see yourself lifting away from that chair and that close environment of home and friends, and drawing back in space until the Earth becomes smaller and smaller and disappears, and you are one with the stars and space and distance that is the outer appearance of the house of the Creator, the infinite creation of which you are a part. Rest in this larger identity and know that you are loved by the one infinite Creator, that you have been with that Creator since before there was time or space. Without duration. without dimension, you are a citizen of eternity, a being of infinity. In your heart of hearts, in your deepest self, you have no limitations, you have no location, and you have no set personality shell as you now experience these things. Your truth, beyond all telling, lies in this oneness with the one great original Thought that has created each long before there was a planet or dimensionality or sequence.

And if you are all these things, why did you choose to be in such a heavy and deep illusion at this particular moment in eternity? Why did you choose to come into the body of flesh that is heavy and illusory and limiting? Why did you choose to forget that you were a citizen of eternity and instead take flesh and join an incarnation? Each of you has desired greatly, before this incarnation, to partake in this experience at this particular time. Each of you felt that there were things that you wished to learn in this density, in this darkness, and at this time. And above all, each of you was moved to service. Each of you saw before incarnation an incredible opportunity, for truly this is the dawning of what this instrument would call the fourth density. Your planet itself is at this time and space traversing the boundary between what this instrument would call third density and fourth density. You are moving from a density in which the lesson is one of choice into a density where that choice has been made and you then are able to build upon that choice and to learn further lessons of love.

At the dawning of this density of love it is a dark-seeming hour. This instrument has the phrase, "It is always darkest before the dawn." And we would say that this is indeed the case as regards this particular planetary sphere and its inner planes as well. For there has been a great deal of building up of unbalanced karma, as this instrument would call it, in the interactions betwixt selves in individual lives, in betwixt groups of selves in societal lives, and in betwixt the selves that live upon this sphere, and this sphere itself. And all of these imbalances cry out with the voice of sorrow. There is a tremendous amount of suffering that rises from your planet. At the same time there is a tremendous amount of lightening of this darkness that has begun to occur because more and more entities are awakening to their spiritual identity. And it is for this awakening that you took the tremendous risk of incarnation. Certainly you hoped to enter that process of catalyst and experience that involve so much suffering, for you hoped to learn better and better how best to make the choice of this density for yourself. And it is this choice of polarity, this choice of how to serve and how to be, that riveted your attention before incarnation. For before incarnation, between incarnations, each of you saw the big picture, spiritually. You saw the plan. You saw the opportunities, and you saw, looking deeply within yourself at what you have learned and what you have chosen so far in this density, how to make an even more polarized choice for love. It is this context of how to love, how to open the heart, and how to be upon this Earth in order to increase the light that has riveted your attention and continues to offer you the challenge of the moment, and it offers us this same challenge. However, we are not upon your sphere. We are not in third-density bodies. We do not have the right to bring light into planet Earth. Only those who have paid the price of flesh, who have come into the darkness of the illusion of Earth, have the right to open their hearts and ask to become crystals for transducing light.

Each of you receives an infinite and continuing supply of love and light from the one great original Thought, which is the Creator. This infinite supply streams through the energy system of each of you continually. When a seeker becomes aware that she wishes to live so as to increase love and light upon planet Earth, she then begins to gaze at how to do that, how to be a more clear channel for the love and the light of the one infinite Creator.

The movements of culture upon your planetary sphere work because of the nature of the mind that all of you share. We would call this mind the archetypical or archetypal mind. In these deep roots of consciousness, certain key truths spring up as if from a fountain. And they flow through all of your lives in common. The high principles and spiritual truths that have inspired one have, at their proper season, inspired many. And they come up again and again in each seeker's life as if living were done in a spiral. Each time that one approaches the same concept again, whether it be an ethical choice or the structure of religious thought or spirituality, it comes into the field of a different person in that you are in unique place in your own time line. You have had perhaps had this lesson before, many, many times, but this time is different. It is always something new that you are looking at when you seem to be receiving an old problem.

In the outer path, the choice of what this instrument would call a mythology or religion has to do with how your particular archetypical mind and its connections to your conscious mind work, because moving into a mythological system is like making an electrical connection. It has to work, or it's no good. If you plug in an appliance and it is not the right kind of electricity, it will blow the circuit or it simply won't work. You cannot get power. And so if there is an attempt to follow an outer path and it doesn't work, this doesn't mean that the electrical system doesn't work for someone who is hooked up right. It just means that you are not of the sort of hookup that is going to plug into this particular structure of ways to think about the archetypes or the archetypical mind. Again, there is the concept of resonance. This instrument was talking earlier about the comfort that she receives from the old words that have been the same, for the most part, since this instrument was a child. This instrument carefully organized itself before incarnation to give itself every opportunity to reconnect with this particular mythological system called Christianity and with the entity known as Jesus the Christ. It was a choice made before incarnation. There were gifts placed in the personality shell of this instrument in order to make the hookup work. For many others this particular Christian myth or religion is an outer path that has a tremendous amount of power available. And we would suggest that this is the way that you look at the search for a religion, a mythology, or an outer system. Realize that it is a spiritual aid of tremendous power that is available in many, many different configurations, even within the Christian religion, and certainly within the family of religions, philosophies, and myths, enough differentiation and variety so that anyone seeking with enough patience can find resonant religions, resonant myths or philosophies from which at least to gather some gifts and resources and assets that can be used on the spiritual path.

The glory of any outer path is also its limitation. The glory of power is also the limitation of power. The glory of depending upon that which is outside of one is also the limitation of that which is outside of one. For many, many entities the great limitation of the path of outer religion is that it seems to demand a surrender. This instrument has not found that surrender to be necessary. However, it was born into one of the less radical or dogmatic sects of the particular religion called Christianity. We do not find any criticism of the desire to seek via the outer path. And may we point out that each of you to some extent in coming to this particular meeting at this particular time is accepting a certain degree of outerness to the path, for there must be some agreement in every group before there is a spiritual community. And as each of you came through the door this evening, including this instrument and the one known as Jim, there was a shift of universes, and it is powerful to shift universes. It is powerful to set time aside, to join a group of people of whom you wish nothing except to learn more about how to love each other and how to love the one infinite Creator.

May we say that whatever the spiritual group, it is blessed, and it has a tremendous company of angelic and inner planes entities which move to support each of you, to support the group, to support us, and to support the construct that is this particular channel that we use to speak through this instrument. All of these activities are part of the positive nature of that outer path that brings people together in devotion and in service. Many are the hard lessons learned beginning with any spiritual group, but also many are the blessings that come from the interaction that comes from those who seek and that chemistry that exists when the universe has shifted and you have moved into the acknowledged desire to seek.

The inner path is often seen as a rejection of the outer path. Spirituality can be seen, and has been seen by many, as what remains after religion is rejected. We would only suggest in this wise that it is helpful to look at the structures of outer paths as what they are: buildings for the seeking spirit, places to sit and look in a certain way at a certain pattern of concepts. Any myth that is so constructed that you begin to see a way to live a life in faith is a good match for you. And if you do not find such a match, then it is that you must turn within and leave the outer world behind, for at that level you are not finding resonance. The peace and the power of the devotional or spiritual path lies not in how happy it makes one, although it often makes one happy. Rather it lies in the satisfaction of another kind of surrender, this time an inner surrender, a surrender to the Creator within.

You have just passed through that season known to you as Christmas and we would suggest to you that each of you has moved through this Christmas season welcoming not only Jesus the Christ but also that Christ consciousness within yourself that yearns to be born and to be nurtured and to grow and mature. Each of you has within your heart a manger in which lies your own spiritual being, and it is a young being in need of protection, in need of encouragement, and in need of love. Any time that you can spend within your mind and within your heart acknowledging this child that is truly the heart of yourself is worthwhile. Time spent in the heart rocking this cradle is worthwhile. Coming into the heart and seeing the self as a spiritual being of which the fleshly being is a kind of parent we feel is worthwhile.

It would seem that the spirit could reach down and grab the soul from within you and bring it to a better place. And yet we say to you that many times that this is not the way that spirit works. For every time that there is a sudden and dramatic change in the outer picture, there are ten and twenty times when the lesson has to do with limitation, patience, and faith. This instrument said earlier that faith is not faith in anything. Faith is the trust, without any proof or supporting evidence, that all is well and that all will be well. And this is the surrender that is demanded on the inner path. It is faith stripped of dogma. It is faith not *in,* but simple faith. It is that faith that leads one to leap into mid-air as the Fool, not seeing the safety net, not seeing the next step, not knowing the answers, and yet being willing to act as if all were well by faith. It is a frightening concept when thought about without the activity of the self as a living being. And if thought about it will often bring that living self to a state of paralysis.

The great virtue of the inner path is that it is unshakably yours. There are no words from without that can dismay the one who is upon the inner path. There is no discouragement that is effective. For there is no point of dogma which another can use to bring to the mind confusion and despair. There is no cleverness to the inner path. There is no pretext and there is no knowledge. There may be many wisdoms that come to one and are useful at the moment they come, but the basic tenet of the inner path is simple faith. The great disadvantage of the inner path is that all connections with others shall be fortuitous and synchronistic and cannot be planned aforetimes. Instead of visualizing the spiritual journey as a physical journey to a physical place with a certain group of people who are fellow travelers with whom you shall find the truth you are operating at another level of being where each is alone. For some this is so inevitable that it feels comfortable. It feels like the right place to be. It feels like the only place to be. For others it is a tremendously arid and desert-like experience, that experience of being in the mid-air of simply faith.

We would not offer one path as superior to the other. In fact we imagined that for most entities over a lifetime of seeking there will be dipping into both aspects of spirituality: the outer and the inner. There will be a mixture of finding outer concepts and structures of thought with which to resonate, and of finding surrender to simple faith the only real answer in a specific situation. Realize, if you can, at each time that you find yourself getting into the tangle of intellectual thought, that all words and all structures of thought partake deeply of the illusion which you experience as your separateness. We communicate with this instrument in clusters of concept that this instrument is often heard despairing of being able to translate. There is, in such a cluster of concepts, a whole world of assumption and structured thought that precedes the necessity to translate it into the structures of words, sentences, and thought concepts. It is difficult to explain the stepped down nature of language and thought as opposed to the unified power of concept. We shall simply say is part of the illusion that you have embraced for a reason.

Be aware that no structure of thought will ever hold you completely. Only the emotions that you produce in your work with these structures of thought have a value in your own alchemical process of growth into the light and the love of the one infinite Creator. Trust those times when you do resonate. Trust those moments when your heart soars, and for a moment the limitations drop away and you are in the light, and you see the plan, and you know that all is well. Trust the bare memory of those times and always come back to the heart. Whether it be in spiritual groups or in working on your own, always we would suggest the great virtue of coming back to the heart. When we say this we are really describing in the heart a kind of structure like a church which we might call the holy of holies, for it is in this particular part of the energy system of your body that the connections are rooted that move into the infinite Creator, into guidance, into inspiration, into the ability to surrender.

The one known as Joyce asked if perhaps we were attempting to become too precise if we attempt to define the path for each person, and we would agree that indeed it is not a precise science to steer the boat on an ocean where there are no landmarks, no directions, and no sextant. The guidance in this three-dimensional ocean that is the spiritual search is an impelling from within. And at times it may feel that you are being kicked about the universe by a Creator who has a wry sense of humor. And yet we ask you to move back into the heart when you are discouraged, to sit in the silence of that holy of holies, and to become aware of the presence of the one infinite Creator. For when you enter your heart, the Creator is already there. It is you who have been away. You have forgotten to turn the key of silence and surrender. We always suggest, whatever your path, that silence is a powerful helper. As long as the intellect and the busy mind are engaged it will be correspondingly difficult to enter that portion of yourself that is sacred, not only because everything is sacred but also, relative to the outer life, there is that most inner self which is a spark, unadulterated and pure, of that one great Logos that is love.

We would at this time continue this transmission through the one known as Jim. We thank this instrument and would leave it at this time. We are known to you as Q'uo.

(Side one of tape ends. The second side did not record.)
♣

L/L Research

L/L Research is a subsidiary of Rock Creek Research & Development Laboratories, Inc.

P.O. Box 5195
Louisville, KY 40255-0195

www.llresearch.org

Rock Creek is a non-profit corporation dedicated to discovering and sharing information which may aid in the spiritual evolution of humankind.

ABOUT THE CONTENTS OF THIS TRANSCRIPT: This telepathic channeling has been taken from transcriptions of the weekly study and meditation meetings of the Rock Creek Research & Development Laboratories and L/L Research. It is offered in the hope that it may be useful to you. As the Confederation entities always make a point of saying, please use your discrimination and judgment in assessing this material. If something rings true to you, fine. If something does not resonate, please leave it behind, for neither we nor those of the Confederation would wish to be a stumbling block for any.

© 2009 L/L Research

Sunday Meditation
January 14, 2001

Group question: Our question today concerns the healing practices of the Christian Science Church versus the more orthodox use of medications and treatment by physicians, with the emphasis for the Christian Scientist being the relying upon the truth that we are all one, we are whole, and we are perfect. And we would like for Q'uo to give us any information possible that would pertain to the healing that can be achieved by the Christian Scientist's point of view versus the healing that can be obtained by the more traditional orthodox medicine. Would one be more likely to result in a cure? Any other comments that Q'uo could make about healing would be appreciated.

(Carla channeling)

We are those of the principle known to you as the Q'uo and we greet you in the love and in the light of the one infinite Creator, in whose service we come. It is a great privilege to be with this group, and we thank each for choosing to make the effort to be a part of this circle of meditation and seeking. We are very happy to share our thoughts with you on healing and request only that each of you listen with a discriminating ear to our opinion, realizing that we are not authorities but, rather, those like yourselves: fallible and error prone. We are glad to share our thoughts, but we do not wish them to become a stumbling block before any. Therefore, if an idea or thought is not helpful to you, we ask that you leave it behind. With this infringement on free will protected against, we feel free to share our opinion with you.

The healing of the mind and body and spirit of the human animal, as this instrument would call all of you who are living in third density at this time, is often a complex project because of the fact that there are some illnesses which have components which are physical, mental, emotional, and spiritual. Indeed, [for] each of you, with a complex of different kinds of energy and different levels of awareness and types of being and entrance into the mind/body/spirit unity that you call a human being, the essence of each of you is spiritual. Each of you is, basically, thought, not a single linear thought but a round, three-dimensional essence which expresses itself as a vibratory complex that creates a harmonic with at least three basic tones and sometimes more plus overtones and undertones of being.

This complex, harmonious chord of being that you are is beautiful. Whatever your situation, whatever the difficulties and challenges that each of you faces, this basic essential self that is you is unable not to make music no matter how dark the chords, for each of you is essentially a thought which is love, and love is that which is beauty and truth. And each of you expresses as a truth that is unique to you, and your being sings a song that is your identity and your name in the metaphysical universe, the universe of thought, which gave birth to the universe which you now experience.

In the mechanical process of coming into incarnation, each of you entered into the inner planes or the spirit world, shall we say, of your Earth world. For within your Earth world there is recapitulated all the densities of creation, and these inner planes worlds hold everything from the perfect idea of all structures upon your Earth world to, in their lower densities, the challenging monsters and fairies, elves, pixies, all of the childhood seemingly make-believe creatures which are a part of the lore and mythology of your planet up into the higher inner planes where reside entities between incarnations, those who have not chosen to take incarnational bodies but have chosen to remain with their guides and teachers. We, ourselves, are, shall we say, parked in one of your inner planes at the fifth level where we are welcomed and are able, from this vantage point, to have access into your Earth world.

In the highest of these inner planes lies one of the seven subtle bodies which each of you enjoys as part of your energetic life, that which this instrument refers to when she talks about chakra energies and balancing the chakras of the physical body. These various centers of energy within the physical body are connected to all of the finer bodies. But we refer to this form-maker body because it is that body which instructs the energetic body as to how the perfect body is conformed and created. When those whom you have referred to as Christian Scientists work upon healing a human being what they are doing is simply addressing their thoughts to what this instrument would call the form-maker or the Buddha body and asking that body to reassert its ascendancy over the physical body which has departed from that pattern.

Because each of you is basically, in essence, a thought, thought, itself, if refined sufficiently, has the power to heal. There are some entities which have the gift of awareness of this thought body. And such entities are natural healers. There are many healers who work with other of the subtle bodies and in each case there is a degree of effectiveness of such work with thought in healing. And again the reason that this is not miraculous but, rather, natural is that all of the seven subtle bodies are connected into the energy system of the physical body so that if there is a combination of a healer who is able to work upon that level of thought and of one to be healed who is willing to accept a new pattern of thought that can change the physical experience, then there is a good possibility that such mental or thought healings may be effective.

However, the subtleties of the practice of healing continue due to the fact that illness within the human being is not usually a simple thing but, rather, a multi-layered set of departures from various parts of the natural balance of energies in various of the subtle bodies as well as the physical body. So that in Earth terms, for instance, using this instrument as an example, there may be the physical stomach ache, the mental distraction, the emotional challenges, and the spiritual tension, this spiritual tension then having its home in various subtle layers or densities of the inner planes. Within certain entities' illnesses there are levels within the inner planes where pre-incarnational lessons have been put into place, meaning that a certain condition cannot be healed because it is protected. At other levels of the inner planes, there are points of opportunity for leaving the incarnation which are also protected, so that it is only the will of the one who is ill that can choose life or death at a certain crisis point, so that no healing can be effective at those points except it be the healing of the person by the person, by that person's will and choice.

No two situations are identical and this is the subtlety that is missed completely, for the most part, by those whom this instrument would call medical doctors. A medical physician in your culture is not trained to probe deeply into spiritual issues. There are doctors which are aware of emotional or mental issues, and there has been increasingly within your so-called modern times the effort made to begin to attempt to heal entities whose emotional and mental bodies contain illness, illness which only secondarily shows up within the physical body. But for the most part, when faced with physical illness, those of your medical professions will look for linear and mechanical answers. They will treat the body as a machine, and a machine it is. And certainly many conditions have been healed by the correct mechanical operation or the correct adjustment of chemical and biochemical properties of the physical body through the use of what this instrument calls medicine. It is no wonder that a physician does not always achieve the desired results, for mechanical, chemical, and biochemical agents do not address the issues of the finer or inner planes' bodies. And they cannot correct ill health in those bodies. The only way to address those issues is by moving into the arena of thought and vibration.

Within the very recent of your past there have been very creative and intuitive entities, which have begun to create so-called machinery which is actually a combination of physical machine and vibrational machine. These so-called black boxes of which this instrument is aware can in some cases affect some of the finer bodies by virtue of sending certain vibrational energies, which have a sort of shadow effect on these finer bodies. And this is a technology which is limited only by the creativity and intuition of those who become able to work with these technologies. However, the judgment of all may be withheld from choosing one technique or mode of healing as better than the others, for in truth it is rather the case that each person which is ill represents a picture which has a certain number of levels. And each level of the illness may take a different level of healing. Thusly it may be effective to offer the surgery, medication, the use of subtle energies sent through so-called black boxes, the healing of intercessory prayer, and the healing of one who knows the truth. It may be that health will not be achieved before all of these levels of healing are employed. And always it must be remembered that in some cases, no matter what healing modes are offered, certain illnesses are protected and are impervious to any form of healing because they are a portion of the pre-incarnational plan of the human being that is experiencing the illness.

The one known as D asked about the aspect of the healing of Christian Science in which parents choose for their children the healing mode which is preferred. There have been cases where this healing mode has not been effective and the child has entered larger life, not able to retain the physical vehicle and remain a human being. There are those who feel with justification that this kind of choice made for others constitutes murder[4]. And we agree that this is a very difficult ethical quandary. We would point out that frequently, when people choose to believe in a dogmatic approach, when they limit themselves to feeling that one avenue of healing or of belief is the only acceptable way, they may limit themselves to the point they have removed from themselves simple, common sense.

However, it is a part of the free will of each entity in choosing how to be and how to believe, to decide whether there is the need for the kind of structured belief that this instrument would call dogmatic. For many entities there are lessons that this soul has chosen to learn that can only be learned within incarnation by embracing a dogmatic approach to belief. From the standpoint of this instrument, for instance, it would look as though the one who holds to faith healing at the expense of all other techniques that indeed might be effective in saving the life, [are refusing healing], and yet for that person there is an intensity that is desired in the path of following the Creator that cannot be gained without the choice of utter, dogmatic belief. Certainly it can be argued that it is not acceptable to make these choices for others. And it seems most sad that such children as have died because medical help was refused are most sadly lost. Yet insofar as the metaphysical aspect of this agreement betwixt child and parent, it may be said that almost always, such a death is part of the agreement that was put into place before the incarnation of the child or the parent and that this is a plan acceptable to spirit and to the Creator.

Many aspects of that which you call the physical death have this quality of being other than the way it looks on the physical plane in terms of the actual metaphysical situation. In suicides, in abortions, in crib deaths, in accidents, in many times where there seems to be great and sudden tragedy, the metaphysical situation looks completely different. In terms of the metaphysical situation in many of these

---

[4] From a reader: "I am a Christian Scientist and found several comments in this meditation inaccurate and therefore misleading about Christian Science. No one wants to have a child die or suffer. It's a tragedy. And every loving parent would do everything in their power to save their child. Christian Scientists are no exceptions. They turn to prayer as a first resort because spiritual healing has proven so effective in their family's lives. Choosing Christian Science treatment rather than medical treatment shouldn't be characterized as 'denying' or 'refusing' reliable care. It is choosing a spiritual treatment with a long record of success.

"Because health care choices are so personal, there is no dogmatic church policy to dictate to members which course of action to take with ill children or themselves. It's entirely an individual's decision what form of treatment they choose. Over the last 125 years, countless cases of all kinds of illness, including those deemed incurable or hopeless by medicine, have been healed through this system of spiritual healing. For a complete explanation of Christian Science please see *Science and Health with Key to the Scriptures* by Mary Baker Eddy. The full text is available online at www.spirituality.com. If you have any further questions, please email me, Valerie Minard, at valminard@aol.com."

patterns, all of the actions involved have been planned as part of a pattern that has been considered helpful and useful by the soul before the incarnative pattern was begun. We say this realizing that in no wise can this keep entities who remain after such deaths from feeling the most deep sorrow and profound grief and loss. Yet as each life creates its final shape, it is a perfect and beautiful shape, and we offer this to comfort those who are dealing with those who are ill and who have resisted healing.

We would like to encourage each to think of healing in a slightly different way, not ignoring death, not ignoring illness or discomfort, but, rather, seeing that the pattern of illness and healing is a multi-layered thing and that prayer continues to be effective on many levels whether or not there is any visible sign of healing, whether or not the entity seems to thrive or improve. We again use this instrument to avoid infringing upon free will because this instrument already is aware that there have been many healings within the finer bodies of this instrument, healings of suicidal feelings and deep depression, healings of the spiritual, the emotional, and the mental bodies that have cemented this entity's energy and greatly improved this entity's quality of life without removing the physical discomfort or limitation which is a protected aspect of this entity's situation.

Each of you is able to heal. Each of you is able to work on the self. And each of you is well able to pray for others. For you are, above all things, creatures of thought, creatures of intention and emotion, and the great gift of the healer is the unifying of the human will and the compassion of the heart. Let us look first at the healing of the self by the self. May we say, as an over-generalization, that the great illness of the human spirit is a lack of forgiveness of the self. Often it does not seem to the self that it is the self that is not forgiving the self. It seems as though the lack of forgiveness were coming in from the outside. Members of the birth family, members of the marriage family, those in the work environment, the various environments of the life, always contain challenging relationships. And it may seem that it is those voices that hurt, harm, and make us ill. Yet metaphysically speaking, the great majority of pain is inflicted by the voice that one uses to talk to one's self. Often the challenging voices from birth family, marriage family, work environment, and so forth, seem to be others' voices but are actually internalized. Those entities may be gone from the life pattern. They may have passed into larger life. They may have moved into other relationships, but within the mind they have become adopted children of the self, and the voices then have the right to continue talking to the self in rude and unkind ways: criticizing, making fun, ridiculing, discouraging, doubting, and fearing. These voices are difficult to catch. It takes time and effort to begin to tune into the things that are said to the self that go down into the body, the mind, and the spirit to create ill health. But when you do catch yourself criticizing yourself, then it is that you have the opportunity to stop and say, "Wait, I would like to change that voice. I would like to encourage myself, and, most of all, I would like to forgive myself."

When this entity began working to forgive itself, it ran into a brick wall and we feel that this is true of most people who begin to attempt to create a spiritual practice of speaking to the self in a loving way. The problem is that part of being a human being on planet Earth is being imperfect, and not just slightly imperfect, but continuingly and maddeningly imperfect. It is, in fact, your responsibility to be imperfect on planet Earth, to be confused, to be foolish, to miss signs and signals and to remain somewhat confused at all times. This is the most beneficial atmosphere for growth and this is the atmosphere which each of you enjoys. How can one forgive oneself when one is constantly discovering that one has once again been mistaken? Been a bozo? Been a fool? But here is the key: it is when you see the imperfection of the self that you may realize that you are here, not to be perfect, but to love. You are not here to love perfection, but to love. You are not here to love this and not that, but to love. And the first object of your love needs to be yourself. There is a process of falling in love with yourself which is most salubrious and helpful, and we recommend it to each of you.

When you can look yourself in the face and see every imperfection and say, "I see a child of the one infinite Creator, and I love you," then you have begun to forgive yourself. We recommend the attempt to do this most profoundly, for it is only when you have come into a condition of love for yourself that you can truly begin to love each other. It says in your holy works that virtue lies in loving the Creator with all of your heart, with all of your soul, with all of your mind and all of your strength, and loving your neighbor as yourself. On these two commandments hang all of the law and the prophets. How can you love your neighbor as yourself if you do not love yourself? So the heart of healing the self is the continual and persistent attempt to speak to yourself with the voice of love, to see yourself with eyes of love, to hear yourself with ears of love. Not to condone that which is amiss, not to gloss over those things which are errors. Indeed, we recommend the attempt to satisfy every obligation, to correct every mistake that can be corrected and so forth.

However, beyond those attempts at restitution, it is essential to come into a state of forgiveness concerning that pattern which surrounded that particular mistake or error, to say to the self, not "You fool. You criminal. You have done something wrong." But to say to the self, "That was wrong, and I am sorry. I will attempt to correct that error, but I love the self that is trying to do the best that I can. And I love the self that is small and confused and feeling terrible." For it is that kind of imbalance in energy that comes through into the physical body to create more and more illness. So when you are working at self-forgiveness and self-acceptance, you are working on the mental body, the spiritual body, the emotional body, and as the shadow passes the sun, the physical body as well. Never doubt, when you are doing this work, that it is a good work.

We find that this instrument is instructing us that we have run out of time and, therefore, we will stop at this point on this interesting subject, aware that there is much more to say, but also aware that we have taken up too much of your time to move further in this basic first look at healing. We thank you very much for this question and would like to focus on any other questions that you might have at this time or follow-ups that you might wish to make of this first material. In order to do this we would transfer this contact to the one known as Jim, thanking this instrument and leaving it in love and in light. We are those known to you as Q'uo.

(Jim channeling)

I am Q'uo, and greet each once again in the love and the light of the One Creator through this instrument. At this time it is our privilege to ask if there might be any further queries to which we might speak in a briefer sense. Is there another query at this time?

S1: First, last week the second side of both tapes did not record, and I wondered if you could comment on the reasons behind that?

I am Q'uo, and am aware of your query, my brother. We find that there was a difficulty with the recording devices as they were operated in a dim light with some misapprehension of the correct buttons by this particular instrument. Hopefully, this has been corrected. We apologize for him. Is there another query at this time?

S1: Yes. My wife has broken her leg and we have thought a lot about what the lessons were in that and we have a pretty good idea. Could we have a few words or thoughts from you in that direction?

I am Q'uo, and am aware of your query, my brother. When one is engaged in a process which requires the slowing, and the deeper portions of the subconscious mind are in agreement with the conscious mind, and the conscious mind is unwilling to follow through with the agreement to slow the physical vehicle, then it is that the subconscious mind will move upon its own to do that which has been agreed upon. The nature of the slowing process is various for each entity and those opportunities that present themselves will be utilized in this process. In the case of the one known as C, this entity found the necessity of slowing its pace of the daily round of activities to be profoundly necessary. However the conscious mind was also dedicated to carrying those activities upon which importance had been placed. Thus this entity, as it is known well to each here, was able to apply the brakes, shall we say, to this process and the wintry conditions of the exterior walkway were used to literally break the pedal appendage that was necessary for continuing that which it wished to discontinue for a period of time. Thus the ability to reflect upon the life pattern was given in the form of the broken bones. These techniques of slowing the physical vehicle are, shall we say, stop-gap measures so that the conscious mind may once again become able to find a harmony with the true wishes of the entity to reassess that which it does on a daily basis. Is there a further query, my brother?

S1: Lastly, referring the initial question you were talking about, I have been in contact with some people who have created some subtle medical devices. One had to do with channeled information from one known as Hilarion. It is a combination of electromagnetic and inert gases. I am curious if you had any comments on that?

I am Q'uo, and am aware of your query, my brother. Such devices as these are indeed quite beneficial when the basic receptivity of the subconscious mind of the one to be healed has been awakened by the desire to be healed. The healing of any entity by any device, any intervention, any medication, any thought is aided when the entity itself, at a very deep level of the mind, desires this healing. Most entities are unaware that they have within themselves the ability to heal each affliction that may occur within the life pattern. However, within this and most cultures upon this planetary sphere the process of healing and the powers of healing have been given to those who you call medical doctors or healers of one kind or another so that the emphasis upon healing and the power of healing is given away by the self to another. However, even in these instances healing can occur when the one to be healed wishes it strongly enough and believes strongly enough that this or that entity, this or that device, this or that medication can be helpful in this regard. Is there a further query, my brother?

D: I have a query. Is it permissible to discuss the travails that L is going through and all the thoughts and prayers, her own included, to complete her sojourn on this planet? Is there any enlightenment that you can give us as to why the situation is as it is?

I am Q'uo, and am aware of your query, my brother. We find that we may speak in a certain degree without infringing upon free will, and this we do gladly. This entity, the one known as L, has successfully completed that which she has come to do. Though the purpose of each incarnation may be shrouded from any eye, including the entity living the incarnation, when this purpose has been completed and there is no further work to do for this entity within this incarnation then the entity takes its leave in a certain manner in order that those who are beloved of it, by it, and who love this entity as well may be allowed to say their farewells, shall we say, may be given the opportunity to express their love for this entity, and this entity for them. Though there may seem to be a great deal of suffering as the entity takes its leave of the incarnation the suffering is that which strengthens the soul, which strengthens the bonds between it and all who know it and love it. The one known as L has been able to express her love to each in her care, and each has had the opportunity to look upon the shared experiences and achieve a kind of review of not only her incarnation but their relationship throughout the incarnation with the one known as L. This entity hovers between this world and the next, moving more slowly into the next world so that there is a gentle transition, shall we say. When the incarnation is known to be ending it is often easier for a soul to finally make the transition after a period of awareness and lingering that brings a resolution for those it leaves behind. This entity shines brightly with the life-force that has been, for the most part, transferred to another world and remains here for but a brief time longer in order that this process might be as gentle for each involved as possible. Is there a further query, my brother?

D: Thank you for that explanation.

I am Q'uo, and we thank you, my brother. Is there another query at this time?

S1: Would you say that is L's gift to her parents?

I am Q'uo, and we would say that this is L's gift to all those who know and love her. Is there another query at this time?

Carla: On behalf of myself and D I would like to ask about the similar lessons that we are involved in at this time concerning physical discomfort and limitation and the continuing ability to do quite a bit of creative work and so forth at the same time. We have identified our lessons, among others, as faith and patience and are encouraging each other daily. I would be interested to ask if there are other key words or concepts that would be helpful for us to think about at this time for us?

I am Q'uo, and am aware of your query, my sister. To those concerns and those qualities we would add that quality known as a sense of proportion or that which you call humor, the light touch. For when one is able to gain a perspective on one's incarnation and the daily round of activities that occur within each incarnation one is able to partake more fully in the creative process. To become the Creator in each instance, to see the glory, the humor, the imperfections, the attempt, the perseverance, all of these which make each in third density human. And we would also suggest concentration upon the quality known as gratitude, for each portion of each incarnation is a gift to the entity within the incarnation. When one is born into this third density there are no contracts, guarantees, or promised that are made to any entity. All is a gift. All is an opportunity. All may be seen as the stairway to heaven, shall we say. These steps, humble though they be, faltering though they be, confused though they be, are each made by a portion of the Creator that moves in a certain fashion, mysterious to many, perhaps most mysterious to the entity taking these steps. However, each step is a step of the Creator, moving in closer harmony and rhythm to the music of the spheres, as you may call it. There is much within each incarnation that may be counted as blessing, much that may be seen as difficulty and burden. However, each offers the opportunity to move into a more full realization of the nature of one's being as the Creator. The entire process is one which may fill the Great Record of Creation with the most hilarious stories, the most tragic of dramas, the most incredible of experiences. It all depends upon the mind of the entity, the attitude of the seeker, the desire of the heart, and the openness of the being to move itself into places which are mysterious, which are difficult and confusing, and to open the heart there just to see what happens. Is there a further query, my sister?

Carla: No. I think I'll be pondering that one for some time. Thank you very much.

I am Q'uo, and we again thank you, my sister. Is there another query at this time?

S2: I would like to ask again how H is doing and if she is happy and well.

I am Q'uo, and am aware of your query, my sister and of the great concern that is within your heart for this small entity that has been separated from you. And we would assure you that this being is quite happy, for it not only carries your love with it but has found love with other entities as well, and it is most well cared for. Is there another query at this time?

S2: Yes. My question is did the people, or person, or family that has H, did they take her for a reason or a reason that they haven't tried to contact her owner? Are they trying to learn a lesson themselves? Or is it a lesson that I am trying to learn myself?

I am Q'uo, and am aware of your query, my sister. The motivation of the entities which have, shall we say, acquired the one known as H is not that which is consciously deleterious or meaning to be difficult or mean but more that which is ignorant of the actual situation of the one known as H, feeling this entity to be without a home and without an owner and feeling that they were fortunate to give the one known as H both. Is there a further query at this time?

S2: Thank you.

I am Q'uo, and again we thank you my sister. Is there another query at this time?

T: I have a question about awakening the life force every day. From just common exercise such as Tai Chi or others specifically designed to raise the energy throughout the body to just common everyday exercise like I do: swimming, tread mill, and stuff like that. Would you comment on how beneficial it is to engage in such to raising your energy to the point where you can utilize that energy in your spiritual life?

I am Q'uo, and am aware of your query, my brother. The primary quality here is, again, the attitude of the entity undertaking the exercise, whatever the technique used, is enhanced, enabled, and powered by the desire of the entity to do such. If the desire is born within the heart, reinforced within the mind, to raise the energy level of the mind, of the emotions, of the body, and of the spirit then the technique used to do this is at the entity's choice. Many techniques would work if the desire is present. Is there a further query, my brother?

T: No. Thank you very much.

I am Q'uo, and we thank you, my brother. Is there a final query at this time.

R: I would like to thank Q'uo for once again finding a way to communicate with our group and for laboring mightily to translate concepts into words that we can use.

T: Me, too. Thank you.

Carla: As a final question, to follow up T's question on movement I have long been a fan of dancing myself and feel that when you move you are creating a rhythm and not only the physical body but the finer bodies like a rhythm and are able to do a lot of harmonizing work not only with the physical body but the finer bodies too in the context of rhythmic movement, and I wondered if that was an accurate perception on my part. Could you comment on that?

I am Q'uo, and am aware of your query, my sister. Indeed the rhythmic physical activity energizes the physical body, the mental body, and the emotional bodies of an entity in that as the physical health is increased the muscle structure is enhanced and the pathways for various levels and kinds of energy is made more secure, shall we say, so that the entity is able to channel through its various vehicle higher and more intense levels of energy that, in themselves, are enablers to the expression of mental energy, physical energy, of emotional energy, and of spiritual energy. The rhythmic movement of the physical body is also that which tends to bring out the childlike nature of each entity that has perhaps been ignored as one ages in your culture. The physical body is too often seen as that which is as the mule, shall we say, to carry one about in a workaday world. When one is able to stop this normal round of activities and to engage in the rhythmic movements the entire complex of bodies is enhanced in its ability to express more intricate and advanced levels of energy. Is there a further query, my sister?

Carla: No. Thank you Q'uo.

I am Q'uo, and again we thank you, my sister, and at this time we would thank each present once again for inviting us to join your circle of seeking this day. It has been a great privilege and an honor to do so. Again, we apologize for causing each to sit for a greater portion of time than we had intended. We are not good measurers of your time and we would, if unrestricted, speak far too long and would probably cause each to enter those realms of theta and delta brain activity. We are known to you as those of Q'uo and would leave each at this time in the love and in the light of the one infinite Creator. Adonai, my friends. Adonai. ✸

L/L Research

L/L Research is a subsidiary of Rock Creek Research & Development Laboratories, Inc.

P.O. Box 5195
Louisville, KY 40255-0195

www.llresearch.org

Rock Creek is a non-profit corporation dedicated to discovering and sharing information which may aid in the spiritual evolution of humankind.

ABOUT THE CONTENTS OF THIS TRANSCRIPT: This telepathic channeling has been taken from transcriptions of the weekly study and meditation meetings of the Rock Creek Research & Development Laboratories and L/L Research. It is offered in the hope that it may be useful to you. As the Confederation entities always make a point of saying, please use your discrimination and judgment in assessing this material. If something rings true to you, fine. If something does not resonate, please leave it behind, for neither we nor those of the Confederation would wish to be a stumbling block for any.

© 2009 L/L Research

Sunday Meditation
January 21, 2001

Group question: The question today has to do with how a group can help us to develop our patience, whether it's patience in what we seek: truth, love, the purpose of our life, the purpose of a situation. Or how a group can help us to develop patience in accepting things that don't change or won't change: a rift in a friendship, a job situation, relationships with family, etc.

(Carla channeling)

We are those known to you as the principle of Q'uo. Greetings in the love and in the light of the one infinite Creator in whose service we come. We are most happy to find ourselves called to join your group and we are delighted to speak upon the group worship experience and its effect upon such spiritual qualities such as patience. As always, we would simply ask that in hearing what we have to say that each monitor our thoughts for that inner resonance which comes when a thought which has personal relevance to you. Respect those powers of discrimination that offer those resonances and leave any thoughts which do not have that resonance for you to one side and move on. This gives us the freedom to share our thoughts without any possible infringement upon your free will.

As members of social memory complexes, as this instrument would call them, we ourselves have the highest opinion of the help offered by the ambiance of a group. It is deep in what we perceive to be the Creator's plan of creation that entities not be alone. In a very important way, of course, each spark of spirit, each portion of the Creator that is experiencing self-awareness is indeed alone and we would not quibble with the inevitable and inexorable forces of individuality. Each of you chose, in coming into incarnation, to leave the stream of the soul, shall we call it, and choose certain relatively unbalanced portions of that soul stream, both in terms of limitations and in terms of gifts and resources to furnish the personality shell that each of you brought into incarnation. Each of you chose this veil of solitude that flesh represents, not just at the level of being unable to merge physically with another third-density entity but in terms of metaphysically finding many divisive factors in relating to other selves.

A legitimate and continuing portion of the experience of the illusion is and will continue to be that pressure of solitude that this instrument would express by the old spiritual song, "You have to walk that lonesome valley. You have to walk it by yourself. Ain't nobody else going to walk it for you. You have to walk it by yourself." There is a simplicity and a sorrow to that old spiritual phrase that is legitimate and is real. Only the release of physical death will assuredly and reliably remove from you the illusion of aloneness at the personal level. However, in all densities and between all densities, save this density, all portions of the creation is indeed aware that none is alone.

The entire fabric of increasing light contains warp and woof of connection between entities, between groups of entities, between groups of groups of entities until finally all truly is one being, all knowing what all parts of the Great Self have thought, done, and intended. There is a strength and power to this kind of unified knowledge that is part of the rightness of creation. And there is, naturally, a hunger and a thirst for this connection in each and every mind/body/spirit complex as this instrument calls people, spiritually speaking, that is most understandable considering the basic nature of creation.

We are aware that each of you has a good working knowledge of the reason for this veil of forgetting that places each entity upon your planet in a cocoon of solitude. Each of you is aware of the helpful nature of this cocoon and of the challenge that it represents, for the cocoon of a lifetime incarnation is as the stage of life of the butterfly that precedes the flight. Unlike the undeveloped butterfly, however, which is as it is and will develop along instinctual lines within the cocoon the third-density human cocoon is one ripe with possibilities. There are entrances into this cocoon, entrances which unify and strengthen the work that is done within the cocoon. It does not mean that there is an escape from the process of maturation. It does not mean that the pupae does not become a larva, and the larva does not have to do the work that is involved in becoming a butterfly. What it means is that the work is not only on the level of the development of the physical vehicle, although in many cases the cocoon of an incarnation does include a progression of more and more learning about how to take care of and cooperate with the evolution of the physical vehicle.

For the most part the work done within the cocoon of an incarnation is emotional, mental, and spiritual. The emotional and mental being far more obvious, but the spiritual being tremendously important as well. The feelings of isolation and independence from others create that opportunity that cannot be bought outside, of incarnation, to live by faith. Outside of the cocoon it is obvious that all are one. Inside of the cocoon it is isolated and protected. And the only thing that is obvious are the thoughts and the entity inside of the cocoon. What are those thoughts? Do they lead to an open heart? Do they lead to other thoughts along spiritual lines? Do they lead along threads of forgiveness, forgiveness of the self, forgiveness of others? Do they lead along lines of communication, more and more openness between the self and others within the environment? These are all good questions to ask when the self is feeling isolated within that cocoon. For as one moves through the day one may pass a dozen people. Each of those is also an immature being of light within a cocoon. Each of those also feels isolated and alone. In what way? By what smile or gesture or word could a connection be made? These are questions to ask the self within the cocoon.

Within relationships there is an enhanced opportunity, both to feel isolated and to search for connection. And certainly when there is the opportunity to work with a settle friend or mate or spouse this opportunity becomes most attractive, for each entity touched by the cocoon of self is an entire universe with connections through the energetic body in virtually every chakra and every finer body. Thusly there are, if not infinite ways to connect with others, certainly many, many ways at many levels to make genuine and helpful connections with those other selves that share that vibration that expresses your own nature and divinity. Company is a precious thing whether or not an entity has mated. There very few entities within your Earth plane which are able to grow in true solitude, and even when it is apparent solitude that surrounds an individual the threads of connection that exist in actuality are yours. For no entity can live without procuring the supplies needed to preserve life. And in order to do that there is the need to depend upon, to trust, and to interact with, either directly or indirectly, hundreds and even thousands of other entities who manufacture goods, who create goods, who distribute goods and deliver them to you. So in all these ways there are connections through the cocoon that empower and strengthen the self.

The spiritual community is the certain kind of connection, but it holds a special place. In one way this special place is created by the simple mechanics of multiplication. In this instrument's holy works it is written, "When two or more are gathered together in my name I will grant their requests." This message from the teacher known to you as Jesus was a hint about how groups of a spiritual nature work. We would, rather than hint, simply say that the vibratory energy of one entity, when joined in meditation with another entity, doubles the strength of that entity. When a third entity joins a group sitting in a circle of seeking, that energy doubles the energy of two, meaning that three people have become four. When a fourth entity joins the circle of seeking, again the energy of the group is doubled. Thus four entities vibrate with the power of eight. And when a fifth joins the group, the strength of the group doubles bringing the power of a sitting group of five to be equal to sixteen people who are sitting unconnected to each other. You may extrapolate from this to see how rapidly the power of a sitting group, of a unified nature, can grow. But there is an increase in not simply the vibratory power of a sitting group because of its being more than one person.

Secondly, there is a strength and a power that is drawn from being a portion of a group that is attempting to be a spiritual community that is of service one to the other. There is a feeling that there is someone to talk to, someone to share with, someone to laugh with and even cry with. There is a sense of comradeship and a sense of shared principles and beliefs. This is very strengthening.

The area of the third strengthening, however, is the most difficult to catch in words, and at the same time by far the most important of the three aspects of the helpfulness of groups. In joining a metaphysically oriented group there is what this instrument has often called the switching of universes. And when a group of entities does this together there is a strengthening of the thought structures which exist in the very deep mind, which this instrument would call the archetypal mind. Normally this material remains in the very deep and unconscious portion of the mind and only sparks through the threshold of consciousness in visions or dreams and then in a muddy or confused fashion. Within the influence of a group the shifting of universes means that the power of spiritual coincidences increases and the sheer number of things that are said and seen and heard, both in and out of the environment of the group, will greatly increase in the sense that more and more of those things that are seen and heard will have bearing on the spiritual journey that is undertaken by each of you. The universe is always trying to speak to the cocooned being. The creation of the Father is constantly trying to get its messages through. It does not know that it is trying to get the messages through. It is simply sending forth that message with every fiber of its being. To the flower, to the tree, to the plant a human being is a portion of the creation like any other and the vibrations of the plant pour out to it in glad fullness. Further, those second-density creatures are trying to drink in all of the vibrations which each of you might offer to them. There is no fear that that which is felt, intended, or said might not be attractive to the plant. There is only that all-accepting experience of welcoming and inviting all energies from the other. This is what the creation of the Father has to offer, not simply the welcoming of the human into the environment but the willingness to hear whatever that human has to say. What this means is that many things that cannot be said to other cocooned beings—that is, other humans—can in the context of the group soul nature not only be said but be heard.

Further, the creation of the Father has the power to heal that which is broken, especially in the realm of the mental, emotional, and spiritual. So there are many finer body adjustments that can be made when interacting with that group which is the second density. In the third-density group such as this one, or any other spiritually based group, there is that nature shared with second density and all higher densities of absolute love for the waking human consciousness within the cocoon and absolute willingness to absorb and accept all energies coming from the cocooned energies that the being within the cocoon is experiencing. This means that through the subtle connections made within the meditation within the group there lies the potential for vast amounts of healing that can come only from the surety of being loved and the realization that one is completely and totally acceptable. It is not that the other human beings within the group are giving each of you this although they may well be on the conscious level. It is that the connection of the circle of seeking opens to each, with a power of the group on an individual basis, the deeper self within.

You asked about how the group could offer to the individual an enhanced ability to have patience and we are sure that the question extends to other spiritual characteristics that are greatly desired and difficult to obtain within the illusion of experience within the illusion of separateness. For faith, a sense of humor, persistence, and compassion are certainly those qualities which are often sought but usually imperfectly found, and yet how blessed it is when the seeker can find a moment of utter patience, utter humor, utter acceptance, or utter love. And all of these streams of emotion flow through the channels of the deep mind in pure and undistorted vibrations, for they are part of what this instrument would call the default setting of the vibration of creation itself, the Logos of the one infinite Creator which is Love.

When one attempts to talk about love one ends up talking about qualities such as compassion, faith, hope, patience, and humor. But these are all as the rays of light which comes from the sun of Love, each a slightly different color, each a definable and recognizable quality but yet each a ray of light from the heart of the Creator. And what the spiritual group does is to bring that sun a little closer to make it more possible to find a conscious, honest faith in the existence of this sun or source of love and light. It is a permeable cocoon, this cocoon that your experience of incarnation in flesh. Through your energy body there are tremendous numbers of entrance into finer densities. Through the gateway of intelligent infinity which is part of the energy body there is access to inspiration and realms of teachers and guides.

And through the openings into the self which are through the heart, not just in the chakra or in the finer bodies but in the physical heart, there is entrance into the deep mind. And all of these sources of light are aided in the clarity with which they enter the energy web within the cocoon by the subtle enhancement of group energy. Each of you is much more than you know or can sense. Each of you brings to a group such as this one a variety of qualities over which you have little or no control and many of these qualities are greatly helpful to the group. Each of you brings, in essence, the universe and all the energy and power that fuels that universe that is yourself. And when you open that universe in meditation there is a golden connection and in any circle of seeking there is that connection that encompasses the group, that runs between each member of the group, and that exists within the finer bodies with a physical, if you will, truth. No connection is ever lost. And each connection increases the light. Indeed, it is by a series of connections with other awakened beings that each of you creates the net of love that is lightening your planet at this time. We are happy to say that this net has become more and more articulated as more of those upon your planet awaken.

There are many around your world, none of whom this instrument or any in this group knows, who have joined this group because they are aware that this group meets at this hour. And these unseen friends also add greatly to the power of the work done by each within the group. And, finally, of course, there are those many, many beings of spirit who are drawn to a group such as this and whose delight is in enhancing the experience of the group for all those who are attending.

We would at this time encourage each … We correct this instrument. We would at this time transfer this contact to the one known as Jim that this instrument may continue this contact. We leave this instrument in love and light and thank it. We are those of Q'uo.

(Jim channeling)

I am Q'uo, and greet each again in love and in light through this instrument. It is our honor at this time to ask if there might be any further queries to which we may respond.

S: I'll start off. My wife wishes to ask concerning our trying to sell our business. We are not real happy with the people that we are working with. She wanted to know if we are going in the right direction, with the right people, should something not be done, should we do something that we are not doing? Could you shed a little light on that?

I am Q'uo, and am aware of your query, my brother. We would speak to the point with a desire of avoiding the infringement upon free will, for it is matters such as this one that entity's are, for the most part, upon their own when it comes to receiving advice from those such as are we. For it is in the give and take of difficult decisions that the ability to exercise decision-making power is most enhanced. In this regard, and with this consideration, we would recommend that when you feel that there is a point upon which there is a disagreement, a point upon which there is confusion, whether it be the entities with which you work, the terms of the agreement, or any matter pertaining to this situation that you look together within the meditative state that you might seek your heart's direction. For the steps that you take within each incarnation are steps well taken when they are, shall we say, in the context of the incarnation, the direction, the attitude, the mode of seeking that which is most helpful to the learning and serving that each has come to do. Thus within the meditative state one may ask any question, then wait in patience, and receive a direction from that which we have called the heart. Or perhaps it would be more clear if we called it the higher self, angelic presence, guidance, unseen hands. Each entity has this assistance available. Knocking upon that inner door is the most, shall we say, salubrious method of achieving a direction and an answer.

Is there a further query, my brother?

S: Touching on something you said earlier about the group dynamics and learning and growth. With those such as yourself where you don't have the limitations and have a broader view of things, how do you spiritually advance or continue with your seeking?

I am Q'uo, and am aware of your query, my brother. Those such as ourselves. We assume that the removal of the veils that hide the truer self and the appropriate path are the qualities that you have referred to as advanced. We would, in our situation, be able to make a decision by simply following the path that we now move upon, for we move without the so-called veils that hinder perception, that remove confusion, and that allow us to do that which is appropriate but without the challenges which you face. For the illusion in which you move is one in which the veils are very much in force and which make more challenging, shall we say, the determination of direction. However, these veils also enhance one's ability to grow in the metaphysical sense in that with this degree of difficulty provided by the mystery of the veil one is able to move one's feet in an appropriate manner and one has achieved much. One then has achieved far more than we who move without these veils, who move without such encumbrances but who move without the degree of learning that is possible in each instance that is possible for you within this third-density illusion. Thus though we move in a more efficient manner we move in a more pallid sense in that there is not the challenge, not the intensity, not the difficulty that so enhances your experience in this third density as you make your choices as to the direction of seeking and the path to the heart.

Is there another query, my brother?

S: Not right now. Thank you.

I am Q'uo, and we thank you, my brother. Is there another query at this time?

Carla: I have two, but I would like to follow up S's and ask if you would describe the learning that you do now as refining or would you describe it as continuing to increase the light, or how would you describe it?

I am Q'uo, and we must pause briefly that this instrument be allowed to work the recording device. We are those of Q'uo.

(Pause)

I am Q'uo, and am again with this instrument. We would ask that you repeat the query, for this instrument was distracted and was not able to perceive the entire query.

Carla: I'd be glad to. Q'uo, I was wondering, to follow up on S's question, how you would describe your learning at this time. Would you describe it as refining or as increasing the light or as working with your groups to learn that way? How would you describe the spiritual evolution that you are now participating in?

I am Q'uo, and we thank you for the repetition of the query, my sister. This instrument's mind is often divided and it is not well trained in concentration. Our experience is one of the refining of those choices which we have made in a far more previous experience, that being both the third-density illusion in which we were able to achieve our polarity and in the fifth … We correct this instrument. And in the fourth density in which the compassion necessary to fuel our wisdom was gained. The choice which is made by any in third density as to the nature of the polarity is one of such a fundamental nature that there is constant refinement of the desire to serve as the compassion is gained that allows one to develop a method of propulsion, shall we say, where the desire to give love to the Creator is foremost upon the mind and within the heart. The gaining of wisdom in the third … We correct this instrument once again. The gaining of wisdom within the fifth density is an experience which is, again, a refining of the basic query to the self of how best to serve. The blending of the compassion and wisdom qualities of sixth-density experience again refines that which has been made as basic choices in previous densities' work. Thus we continue to refine that which has been chosen previously and seek continually the transformation of the self into the one Creator which we feel is our basic lesson in each experience.

Is there a further query, my sister?

Carla: Yes, there is. Thank you for that. Quickly, just with procedure. I like to be responsible with my channeling and right at the end there I was moving along and I got just the beginning of the phrase, "We would encourage each" I think it was, and it just stopped so completely. It is so unusual to have something like that happen. Usually you get the concept cluster that you have started with and you go through that and then there is another. But you stopped right in the middle and then started with a whole new cluster and said that you were going to transfer. That was unusual, but what I thought was that you realized that it was time to stop and not launch into the next portion, and I just wanted to know if you could confirm that is what happened?

I am Q'uo, and am aware of your query, my sister. We find that we must invoke the Law of Confusion in this situation. We apologize for being unable to speak further.

Carla: Could you give me some ideas as to what boundaries you are protecting?

I am Q'uo, and am aware of your query, my sister. This instrument is somewhat distracted in general and is unable to pick up our contact in a reliable fashion. We find that this difficulty was somewhat of a problem, shall we say, for your contact. Further than this we cannot go. Is there another query at this time?

Carla: Thank you, but I am wondering if it might be better to hold the query and let you and the instrument decide. My original query was somewhat divided. I was going to ask about patience since it was not covered overly much in the beginning query and I was going to invite you to say something about patience, but I would also be perfectly happy if it would be better for the instrument and you to end the contact at this time. I'll just leave it up to you. I want to thank you and also the instrument.

I am Q'uo, and we appreciate your concern. It would be well if we ended the contact at this time, for this instrument is not in a proper state for reception. We appreciate your concern. We are those of Q'uo. Adonai, my friends. Adonai.

L/L Research

L/L Research is a subsidiary of Rock Creek Research & Development Laboratories, Inc.

P.O. Box 5195
Louisville, KY 40255-0195

www.llresearch.org

Rock Creek is a non-profit corporation dedicated to discovering and sharing information which may aid in the spiritual evolution of humankind.

ABOUT THE CONTENTS OF THIS TRANSCRIPT: This telepathic channeling has been taken from transcriptions of the weekly study and meditation meetings of the Rock Creek Research & Development Laboratories and L/L Research. It is offered in the hope that it may be useful to you. As the Confederation entities always make a point of saying, please use your discrimination and judgment in assessing this material. If something rings true to you, fine. If something does not resonate, please leave it behind, for neither we nor those of the Confederation would wish to be a stumbling block for any.

CAVEAT: This transcript is being published by L/L Research in a not yet final form. It has, however, been edited and any obvious errors have been corrected. When it is in a final form, this caveat will be removed.

© 2009 L/L Research

Sunday Meditation
February 4, 2001

Group question: Our question this week concerns the ascension. A lot of different sources have described the ascension in different ways, speaking about its rapidity of occurrence, those to whom it occurs, how it occurs, when it occurs, what it means, and we would ask Q'uo to give us some information from Q'uo's perspective as to what the ascension, or the rapture, or the graduation, or harvest is like now for us on planet Earth and what it is likely to be like in the near future.

(Carla channeling)

We are those known to you as Q'uo. Those of our principle greet you in the love and in the light of the one infinite Creator. May we say what a blessing it is to be called to your meditation. May we thank you for calling us with your thirst for truth and your effort to join the circle of seeking at this time in each of your lives. We are honored and grateful and thank you for helping us to fulfill our chosen service at this time, which is to share information and what inspiration that we can with those who seek light in the third-density environment of your outer world.

We find that this day we experience not only those of Latwii and those of Ra, but also those of Hatonn and those of Oxal. The constitution of the principle varies somewhat from meeting to meeting, depending upon the vibrations and the needs of those who are attending the circle. As always, we ask that each use discrimination in listening to what we have to say, for we are as fallible and error-prone as any seeker on the spiritual path. We do not consider ourselves or put ourselves forward as authorities but simply as those who may have a slightly different point of view and one that might be helpful. For we are those who have taken a few steps more while upon the path that you are now engaged in navigating.

We are glad to speak with you about ascension, rapture, graduation and harvest. These terms are not precisely interchangeable, but certainly closely associated and it is an interesting field of inquiry. As often happens we feel the desire to step back into more basic material and look at the ground from which we would like to talk about these subjects. The song which the one known as Jim chose to aid in the tuning of the group at this session was speaking of love, and it said that, basically, the living was all about the appreciation and recognition of beauty, the beauty of nature, the beauty of thoughts, and so forth. It is the beauty of thoughts on which we would like to focus.

The creation is a thought. For lack of a better word, the creation is a Logos, a concept at one time simple and unified and infinitely complex. It is a metaphysical or non-physical thought. The physical world that you now enjoy is also a thought, but it is a much weaker thought, much stepped down from the energy of the Thought of the one infinite Creator, that Logos which, for lack of a better term, we can also call love. Each of you is a thought and that thought is of love because all things that are thoughts are distortions of the one great original Thought which is love. Before all manifestation, each of you is and exists as an energy, an essence, a concept, a complex of thought. Each of you, to put it another way, is a kind of crystal, an energy field that takes in energy, transduces energy, transmutes energy, and sends energy through the energetic system of the body, the mind, and the spirit.

The thoughts that you think, the emotions that you feel, the spiritual experiences that pass through your energetic system are all kinds of thought and they constitute your basic metaphysical identity. Every thought that you think, every thought that you pursue, every thought that you bring to a fruition, creates slight changes in the vibration that is your energy signature. To those of us, and others upon the spirit planes, looking at the metaphysical entities that you are, these vibratory nexi are very evident, and it is as clear to us as day who you are, how you are, whose you are.

To the entity within physical manifestation this is not at all clear. In the physical illusion, as each of you knows all too well, there is much confusion. And there will continue to be confusion generated by the very nature of third-density experience. All of the confusion may seem tremendously destructive. The suffering may seem to be erasing your identity when things become difficult. This too is an illusion, for beneath the surface confusion those energies of deeper thought, emotion and spiritual feeling continue to pulse rhythmically, continue to process energy, and continue to send out the fruit of the energy that has moved through your energetic bodies. Each of you, then, is sending out your own harvest of received, blessed, transduced and transmitted energies.

We might describe this energy output to light, that of a candle, let us say. Many times, it seems to each, that there is no way that one person can be of service, that one person's light can make a difference. However, this instrument is fond of saying that in a dark place the light of one candle can be seen for quite a distance. Metaphysically, this is far more true even than the physical truth of candles and sight. Each of you makes a significant difference to the lightening of the planet as well as to the lightening of your soul. For when each of you does one, each of you is doing the other. To work on the self is to work on the world. Indeed, to work on the self is the most direct and effective way to work on the outer world in a metaphysical sense.

And it is in a metaphysical sense that your Earth is experiencing that which this instrument calls harvest. The Earth itself has come to a crux in its own development. It is as though the Earth must needs give birth to itself. The third-density Earth is in the process of being transformed into a fourth-density, positive sphere. Your Earth is having difficulty with this birth. There are various reasons for this difficulty having to do largely with the negative concepts which have fed into entities choosing negatively polarized actions towards each other over a period of centuries and millennium. It is as though the Earth's energy system were clogged with a good deal of toxic material of a metaphysical nature. As entities such as yourselves awaken to their spiritual identity and become more and more conscious of the positive value of thinking along positive lines and pursuing positive orientations of polarity in thought, that toxic material is gradually given permission to be released. For as the light brightens, the new energies of instreaming fourth-density nature are able to find more welcome. And in that atmosphere it is gradually more and more possible for negative energy to be released and disbursed harmlessly.

We are not talking, in this wise, strictly about non-physical events, for certainly there are physical aspects to the metaphysical birth of fourth-density Earth. There are problems having to do with excessive heat within the mantle of your Earth, which, again, have to do with these negative thoughts, over a long period of time, being driven into the very Earth itself. And we find that there have been disasters and catastrophes aplenty within your Earth sphere, difficulties of weather that offer flood, earthquake and fire, causing much suffering and loss of life among your peoples. However, in actuality, were we to have spoken with this instrument a quarter century ago, we would have been less sanguine about the possibility that your physical Earth will be able to enter fourth density relatively unscathed and with the planetary population relatively unscathed.

As Earth entities awaken, the planetary energy lightens and global catastrophe has become instead a series of small and survivable catastrophes. Certainly they are not small catastrophes to those who lose the life or have loss of life in their families. Nevertheless, the great majority of Earth entities see the difference between local catastrophes and global catastrophes, and we feel that this is a very hopeful portion of this subject: that things are better, metaphysically speaking, for the Earth than they were in terms of the Earth's harvest.

The concept of ascension is a concept that we have found largely within your cultures' Christian belief systems. The beliefs vary, but the basic commonality of this idea centers upon the concept of some entities being physically removed from the surface of the Earth to safe places at a time when the remainder of the population of the Earth will be destroyed by the end of the world or some other version of the apocalypse, whether the cause of it be man or spirit. It is not our understanding that this concept is a helpful one spiritually. It is not our opinion that this is the way things work in any physical sense. In our opinion the processes of ascension or harvest are subsumed within the process of moving through the physical death and entrance into larger life, as this instrument would put it.

The concept of the harvest of Earth is, more than ascension, in line with our understanding with the way things work metaphysically. Each of you is a spark of the Creator, and each of you may think of yourself in a way as that which has been planted in the Earth, for you have been planted as a soul into flesh. And at the end of that work done within the school of life, the door of death opens, the Creator beckons, and through that door each goes. Upon the other side of that door, the decision for your harvest shall be made. However, it is not our understanding that this harvest is one of judgment placed upon one from the outside. Rather, it is a matter of that vibration that you and how that vibratory energy field works. Each crystal soul accepts light in a certain range and finds it difficult to accept life outside of that range. Consequently, the harvest of each of you consists, basically, of the careful and guarded process whereby the soul walks along a gradually increasing line of vibration of light. The light increases as the soul walks, and as the soul walks it senses whether or not it is most comfortable. It walks into that increasing light until it is at the spot of fullest light that it can enjoy and appreciate in a stable manner. And it stops at that point because it is uncomfortable to go further. Where that soul stops is either still in third density or has moved over into fourth density or higher. If that soul has stopped in third density, then it chooses, completely on its own and with no judgment involved, to repeat the third-density experience. In many cases this decision will not simply be for another incarnation, because this is the time of Earth harvest. It will mean there will be a 25,000 year period during which that spirit will enjoy third density upon another planet. However, it is not a punishment to repeat a grade. It is simply the right place for that soul that enjoys that range of light. If that spirit has stopped across that quantum divide between third and fourth density, that entity may then choose to begin a series of incarnations in fourth density and can be said to have graduated from Earth's third density. For each person that experience will be unique. To our knowledge, there is no general harvest but, rather, the individual harvest of each soul upon each soul's schedule.

We are aware that there is much confusion between metaphysical harvest and physical concerns having to do with the environment and other physical, scientific facts. May we say that is specifically not our province, and we feel that to discuss some of the concerns of those who seek scientifically is to infringe upon the free will of those who seek spiritually. This is, for us, a delicate area, for we too are both physical and metaphysical. However, in terms of our relation to this group or to any of those of Earth, we are at this time carefully non-physical. For we have found in the past when we have attempted to move physically among your people that there was no possibility of doing so without gross infringement upon the free will of planet Earth. Consequently, we have learned the hard way to allow some confusion in terms of scientific queries. And for this we offer our apology. It is an honest one. We do not withhold information for petty reasons but, rather, because we think that it is not only the right thing to do, but the clear and concise thing to do, for anything that we say about your physical situation upon planet Earth is not fact but a possibility vortex. By entering into discussion we become part of that possibility vortex. This is not acceptable. This would compromise our polarity and make it necessary for us to leave your people. Therefore, it is our judgment, fallible though it may be, to create these boundaries of that which we feel free to talk about and that which we do not.

It all comes back to the thoughts that each of you thinks. Only you know your hearts. Only you know the desire that you have to seek, to love, to serve. Only you know how you crave the love and the light that is so often missing from your Earth world. And so we ask you to be support for yourselves. Believe in yourselves. Feel that you are important and that the things that you think are important. And see that expression of what you think as valuable and a listening ear for supporting those things that someone else might think spiritually as being greatly valuable also. For as the ones known as Carla and S were saying earlier, for each person the self is blind to the self. Each can see into another's patterns far better than one can see into one's own patterns. Therefore, each may help each in that search for what one really thinks, what one truly feels, and for what one truly thirsts.

Know that your thirst is greatly important, and pursue your desires. Pursue those intuitions and inklings. Listen for those hints that come in the wind of everyday detail and coincidence. And know that whatever is occurring on the physical plane, what is important in terms of your harvestability is your response to what is occurring. Look at your responses and see what you can do to sit with them, to work with any fear that you find in them, to comfort yourself through any suffering that occurs from them, and to encourage yourself to move always to the higher plane, the loftier principle, the belief that all is well and that all will be well. It is said in your holy works that "in quietness and in confidence is your peace." Know that in terms of harvestability it is very helpful to have a high place within the self, a holy place within the heart, to which you may retreat and fall into the arms of the one infinite Creator who loves you dearly. When you are lost, when you are suffering, when you are alone, remember and move into the heart, into the sanctuary and peace of the one Creator's love and dwell there as long as you need to, in order to feel that balm of Gilead which is that energy of being loved, being valued, and being understood. These things the Creator does. In fact, the Creator greatly values each and every thought that you have, for it is this way that the Creator learns about Itself.

We encourage as much silence in the day as you may find, whether it may be a walk with the dog, a form of meditation, the time spent working in the garden, or simply time spent without the television or radio or other sounds of the creation of man in the ear. The key of silence is a powerful one.

We would at this time transfer this contact to the one known as Jim. We leave this instrument in love and in light and thank it for its service. We are known to you as those of Q'uo.

(Jim channeling)

I am Q'uo, and greet each again in the love and in the light through this instrument. At this time it is our privilege to attempt to speak to any further queries which those present may have for us. Is there another query at this time?

S: After reading last week's session one thing intrigued me and that was that you said that there were many unseen friends that join us at these meetings. I was wondering if you could elaborate at little more on this topic or can we welcome them or make any contributions to them? What can you tell us?

I am Q'uo, and am aware of your query, my brother. This group has, in one form or another, been sitting in these sessions of working for a number of your years and has, throughout this time, been able to receive communications of what is hopefully an inspirational nature from various members of the Confederation of Planets in the Service of the One Creator. When an entity has spoken to this group then there is formed a kind of bond with the group that is always honored by giving the attention to this group's proceedings when this group sits in a circle of seeking, as it now does. Thus though most such entities choose to remain silent during these sessions, each is keenly aware of the transfer of energy back and forth between the entity speaking and the group itself. This is a blessed event for many such as are we and those who seek to serve in a manner which is largely unseen by the great majority of your Earth population. It is a blessed event because it is so rare. So seldom are we, and others of our group, able to make direct contact with your peoples that when such is made there is attention given to it, a protection, shall we say, a wall of light that is formed of love and the attention of those who wish this group well. Thus there are many who have been known by name to this group who join silently but certainly as this group works. There are also, from time to time, other entities who have yet to speak from this same Confederation of Planets who nonetheless offer their vibrations of love and protection as this group works.

Each entity that joins this group from your illusion and sits in your circle of working, whether it asks questions or is silent, also may have certain guides, friends, and teachers that are not incarnate who are also desirous of blending their vibrations with this group and those of the Confederation as well. Thus when this group sits in a circle of working there is what you may call a heavenly host that joins with you and rejoices with you and feels sympathy and empathy and all those great emotions that third density is so richly populated with. For not only is there inspiration passed from each to the other, but there is also the opportunity for many of us of the Confederation of Planets in the Service of the One Creator who value being able to feel the emotions that those of your group bring to this circle of seeking and express not only in their queries but the very timbre of their being. It is a rich exchange of the experience of each shared with the other.

Is there a further query, my brother?

S: Interesting. Certainly welcome. It's nice to know that they are here and I request that they not be so bashful, I guess … Is there any … I'm puzzled what we do for them and the opportunity to help us in unseen ways. Is there truly that much that we can give or help in return?

I am Q'uo, and am aware of your query, my brother. Each entity such as yourself that joins this circle of seeking brings many riches in the nature of the variety of experience, the purity of emotion, the passion with which truth, love, etc. are sought so that those of our group may be able to appreciate the difficulties that each of you are able to labor under successfully even though you may think that your ability is far less than successful. When you are able to express a difficult emotion, the emotion, situation, relationship, or other Earthly adventure that is not offered to those of us who are now discarnate, to those of us who live, shall we say, on the other side of the veil of forgetting, then it is that our appreciation grows as you are pulled one way and the other in the struggle to remember love.

(Side one of tape ends.)

(Jim channeling)

I am Q'uo, and am again with this instrument. Just as you within this circle of seeking would enjoy reading a new novel that is in your area of interest, we of the Confederation of Planets are always interested to observe that which is freely shared within this circle of working. For it allows us to see how each entity may work with the catalyst which is presented in the daily round of activities, to see how the love and light of the one Creator may yet shine forth from the darkest of experiences, from the most confusing of experiences. This gives us a great deal of joy, to see that, indeed, that there is no place where love may be hidden so deeply that it will not shine forth in a brilliant and inspiring way. Thus you inspire us as much as we attempt to inspire you.

Is there a further query, my brother?

S: My last query is something that you mentioned earlier about your appearance in third density was not as successful as you had hoped. Could you give me an idea of what happened, what you did, how it was perceived?

I am Q'uo, and am aware of your query, my brother. As you are aware, we of Q'uo are what you might call a conglomerate or group principle formed of other groups such as those of Latwii, those of Hatonn, and those of Ra. And it is to this latter portion of our group, those of Ra, that the feeling of being less than successful in our contact with third-density entities a great portion of your years ago within that area which you call the Holy Land was undertaken and was, of necessity, abbreviated because of the difficulties in communication not only with words but in the appearance of our very being, our physical vehicles being much unlike those of the entities of Egypt with whom we sought to share the Law of One. There were enough misperceptions resulting from our words and our being that we found it necessary to take our leave of this group at that time and to retire to what you would call the inner planes of your planet to consider more carefully how to be of service in sharing the Law of One without giving to it those distortions of power which the entities of that land had attributed to the Law of One because of our work with them. The words which we chose were not always perceived in the manner which we had hoped and the message in general, we found, was reserved for those of royal and powerful position rather than being shared equally and freely with all. It is this particular experience that we seek to balance and have sought to balance since that time in days of old.

Is there a further query, my brother?

S: Not that I can think of right now. Thanks.

I am Q'uo, and we thank you once again, my brother. Is there another query at this time?

Carla: Yes. What S was asking kind of sparked me, and I wanted to ask about how it looks when we sit in meditation because when I tune upstairs to pray and sing a hymn after I work on my energies to channel and protect them and so forth, I call the archangels and I ask for all those who come in spirit and in the name of Jesus Christ to help us, as you said, the host of heaven. When I call them and ask them to protect the place and protect the channel and protect everybody in the circle I not only get a sense of their presence but I also see a kind of dome kind of structure where there are ribs going up in the dome, and it's kind of like a cathedral space, but it's made out of light. I wondered, since you were talking about this, if this was an accurate perception or if this was just something that my intellectual mind was stirring up to visualize what I was praying about?

I am Q'uo, and am aware of your query, my sister. Indeed, as we gaze upon this group, from our perspective, we see light, various shades and coloration of light, each entity offering a unique coloration and variety of colors as various energy centers are activated. Some are blocked. Some are spinning rapidly and brilliantly. And the group itself is producing yet further light so that there is, as you may see, a kind of dome or vortex of spinning light energy that has both the characteristics of each individual and the characteristics of the group itself blended with the light of the heavenly host, so that in sum there is a mass of light which reaches in an upward spiraling fashion as you may imagine or image the pyramid having a flame that reaches infinitely upwards yet inwards as well.

Is there a further query, my sister?

Carla: I just wanted to clarify what you are saying. The light is not only forming a vortex but at the peak of the vortex at this time there is a flame going forth, spreading out from that point like an upside-down pyramid. Right?

I am Q'uo, and am aware of your query, my sister. We followed your description until the last and would suggest that the pyramid is right-side up.

Carla: OK. Let me try again. The pyramid itself, of this group, has a point and what I thought that you said was that coming from this point and going outward into the creation was the sum of the light of the group, and it was coming out of the top of the space of the dome or the pyramid. Is that correct?

I am Q'uo, and this is correct, my sister.

Carla: Thank you. That is very inspiring. It looks like within the dome the energy is moving in a clockwise fashion. Is this true?

I am Q'uo, and this is correct for the inner portion of the dome or pyramid. The great majority of that which we see as light and that which forms the pyramid is simply in place, without movement. Is there another query, my sister?

Carla: No. I thank you.

I am Q'uo. Again, we thank you, my sister. Is there another query at this time?

Carla: One final query. Procedural only. There are a number of entities who have asked for Confederation entities such as Yadda and Nona. I perceive that I am removing the opportunity for these entities to speak because of the way I tune. I ask for the highest and best source that I can contact in a stable manner in a waking consciousness, and so I get you all. Is it permissible at the end of a session if someone wants to talk to Yadda or to listen to Nona that they would simply ask for that entity and then the contact be transferred back to me? Is that possible? I believe that both Yadda and Nona would vibrate harmoniously within your range.

I am Q'uo, and am aware of your query, my sister. This, indeed, would be possible if it was desired and requested. Is there a further query at this time?

Carla: No. Thank you.

I am Q'uo, and again we thank you, my sister. Is there another query at this time?

(No further queries. A couple of members express appreciation to Q'uo for speaking this day.)

I am Q'uo. We are also most grateful to each of you for inviting our presence for this particular session of working. We feel that there has been a great deal of love and light offered from you to us. We hope that we have given to you as well. At this time we shall take our leave of this instrument and this group, leaving each, as always, in the love and in the light of the one infinite Creator. Adonai, my friends. Adonai. ☥

L/L Research

L/L Research is a subsidiary of Rock Creek Research & Development Laboratories, Inc.

P.O. Box 5195
Louisville, KY 40255-0195

www.llresearch.org

Rock Creek is a non-profit corporation dedicated to discovering and sharing information which may aid in the spiritual evolution of humankind.

ABOUT THE CONTENTS OF THIS TRANSCRIPT: This telepathic channeling has been taken from transcriptions of the weekly study and meditation meetings of the Rock Creek Research & Development Laboratories and L/L Research. It is offered in the hope that it may be useful to you. As the Confederation entities always make a point of saying, please use your discrimination and judgment in assessing this material. If something rings true to you, fine. If something does not resonate, please leave it behind, for neither we nor those of the Confederation would wish to be a stumbling block for any.

© 2009 L/L Research

Sunday Meditation
February 11, 2001

Group question: The question today has to do with the concept of the new Buddhism. There seems to be a new interest in the practice of Buddhism around the world and we would like Q'uo to give us information that might shed light on why interest has increased for Buddhism, the effect it has upon people, the philosophy of how Buddhism connects to other world religions, and how it connects to the philosophy of the Law of One.

(Carla channeling)

We are those of the principle known to you as the Q'uo. Greetings in the love and in the light of the one infinite Creator, in whose service we are. It is a great privilege to be called to your circle of seeking, and we thank each of you for the thirst and hunger for truth that has lead you to this circle and this moment. It is a blessing for us to be able to pursue our chosen service at this time, which is to share thought and inspiration with those who may seek it upon your planet. For the most part our duty is carried out by simple presence in visions and dreams and moments of inspiration. Seldom it is that we have the opportunity to communicate using words such as we are able to do using this instrument and others that are similar to it. It is a real treat to be able to express our thought in these slippery things called words. We appreciate the efforts of this instrument and instruments in general who provide us with the opportunity to share our words in this fashion.

As always, we ask of each of you that each use her discrimination, for each of you has a very finely tuned, resonant awareness that springs into life when a personal truth is heard at a deep level. And we would ask of you that, as we share our thoughts, each listen for that resonance, that feeling of rightness and truth that comes from the heart and is far more of an authority than the so-called authority of teacher or seeming outer authority. We consider ourselves to be your equals and ones who, perhaps, have had a bit more experience. However, we still are aware of ourselves. We are still puzzled and seeking the mystery of deity. And we consider ourselves to be fellow pilgrims with each of you. It is a privilege to walk with you and to share the beauty of your vibrations during this meditation.

You ask this day concerning Buddhism, as it has in recent times been reenergized in terms of the number of people who seek within the path of Buddhism as an outer and settled religion. And we are glad to share our thoughts on this subject with you from our own point of view. As is often the case, we would begin by laying a ground upon which we would speak. And that is, as several within the group said in the discussion beforehand, that there is one Creator of which the so-called revealed religions are attempts to discern, illuminate and express. Any religion, so-called, has what this instrument would call baggage. And in the case of Buddhism, as well as the case of several of the major world religions, that baggage is not the baggage of a few years but, rather, the weight and onus of generations, centuries, and millenniums of those within the religion, who practice the religion, finding ways to re-identify and reassess the valuable points of the religion.

Thusly, a religion such as Buddhism, just as Christianity, Shintoism, Judaism, Yogic disciplines, and many other world religions, goes through a continuing series of changes and cycles of changes within itself, as its members attempt to practice the path that is offered by the mythical system involved. Each religion, including Buddhism, has valuable aspects that are peculiar to it, but each, shall we say, has two sides. There is to each religion the revealed or outer aspect and the inner, occult or mystical aspect, and we find that it is in the mystical aspect that the religions have the tendency to unify and to harmonize, so that a mystical Buddhist can speak to a mystical Christian, a mystical Jew, or a mystical Oriental worshipper and have very few communication problems, because mysticism focuses on essence and not on detail.

It is in the revealed or outer aspect of each religion that we find the bulk of the challenging material for those who seek to be inspired by religion. For in each religion you will find in the outer or settled church aspect of the religion the tendency to be dogmatic. The advantage of dogma is a simple and vital one, and we find that many among your peoples have the necessity for a dogmatic type of belief system. In such a system there is a certain list of things that are believed and are held to be true and a certain list of things that are specifically not believed and are held to be untrue. We find that the more that a mythical or religious system attempts to define in a dogmatic way the theology or belief system of the religion, the more pronounced the tendency is for there to arise disputes and disagreements between various factions within the religious system, so that in the outer church there is the positive aspect of a group which thinks alike or is attempting to think alike over against the disadvantages of this same group attempting to define itself by stating those things which it does not believe and finds to be false within various other sects of the same religion. Consequently, the efforts towards ecumenical or unified belief and unified worship on a global scale will be found to be far more successful when they are mounted by the mystical or occult portions of any of the world's religious faiths.

Perhaps the most striking difference between the various religions is the energy center or chakra which is the seat of most of the germinal or seminal energy of that system of belief. We would discuss three basic systems, the first being Christianity, the second being the amalgam of Oriental religions which honor family ancestors and tradition and the third, the Buddhist way of enlightenment.

In Christianity the basic chakra energy that tends to be activated for the worshipper is the green-ray or heart chakra. This is due to the fact that the entity known as Jesus was a teacher concerned with one thing only, and that was love. This entity offered a simple system of beliefs, stating, "Thou shalt love the Lord thy God with all thy heart, with all thy soul, with all thy mind, and with all thy strength, and thy neighbor as thyself. Upon these two commandments," said the teacher known as Jesus, "Depend all of the law and the prophets." In this statement the one known as Jesus specifically moved from the Old Testament, so-called by this instrument, which was the holy work of his people, and delivered and offered a new covenant having only to do with love, love of the infinite Creator and love of each other, beginning with the self and continuing with loving the neighbor as if it were the self.

When this simple commandment is the focus of the Christian path, we find that this truly is the path of the heart and there are those mystics such as this instrument who tend not to wish to deviate from the path of simple devotion because of the fact that moving into a more dogmatic approach to belief seems to pull the focus away from the heart. We suspect that each has those relatives or friends or acquaintances whose Christian belief system has a dogmatic aspect sufficient to create an atmosphere of judgment and, therefore, we suspect that each is fully aware of the difficulties involved in moving into the dogmatic beliefs and leaving the simple faith in love behind. However, when those who are working along the positive path using the Christian system find themselves to feel at home in the heart we feel it is likely that they have been able to move from the outer aspects of worship to the inner aspect.

In the disciplines or myths of the Orient, such as Shintoism, the energy which is most involved in the system is the yellow ray or solar plexus chakra. This is the chakra of the illusion. It is the chakra of relationships like marriage and family that have to do with the groups with which one associates one's self as a human being, as opposed to the individuals with which one associates oneself in a relationship. The great advantage of the religions that move from the yellow-ray energy is that there is no translation needed between the holy and the everyday. Each entity within a family, a clan, a village or a nation is specifically and frequently honored as a part of a valuable whole. Thus the family is seen as sacred. Age, itself, is seen as a sacred and holy thing. Events within the life take on the glow of the revealed Creator in bodily form. While it is not a system of seeking that specifically opens the heart, what it does in terms of the human experience is render it into a kind of liquid in which the elements of everyday life are specifically seen to be holy. And thus the life experience of everybody can be taken by one who has worked in this discipline as having a resonance of rightness that is profound, and there is a peace that this produces that is similar to that feeling of groups of entities at one of your games where instead of two sides there is only one side, and all portions of the game are winning. In this kind of experience there is a solidifying and strengthening of the bonds of simple humanity in the valuing of family, in the valuing of the wisdom of age, in the valuing of the death process as a part of life. There is a tremendous peace.

In the case of Buddhism, the energies involved tend to spring from two centers: the communication chakra or the blue-ray chakra of the throat, and the indigo-ray chakra of the forehead or the pineal gland. These energies of communication and work in consciousness have a tremendous advantage for people within third density at this time for two reasons. Firstly, there is the peace of working from the higher centers. The yellow-ray chakra is the chakra where the rubber hits the road in terms of everyday experience. It may render the everyday experience sublime, but it shall not render it completely peaceful, for peace is not the nature of the passing passion play that is life. Neither is it peaceful to dwell within the heart, for the heart is not only the shuttle for the spirit but also the seat of the emotions. And the tumult of the rising and falling away of emotions is constant. Consequently there may often be the transcendent experience of bliss and peace, yet it lies within the rising and falling of emotion. For in love's focus, in the heart's focus, there is the specific value of passion, desire and thirst. And this cannot be said to be completely peaceful.

Therefore, there is a tremendous appeal to the peaceful rounds of, shall we say, the wisdom aspect of Buddhism. Buddhism takes a far more distant view than either Christianity or the Oriental religions of suffering. In positing the reality of suffering within the world, Buddhism's only prayer is that it end. It gazes at that which a heart-centered religion would find full and sees it as empty. It gazes at the everyday round that the Oriental religions see as holy and finds that everyday round to be completely illusory. And, therefore, it is focused upon the reduction of suffering, the reduction of confusion, and the welcoming of nothingness, that nothingness being held as a holy thing and greatly to be prized. As this instrument said earlier, "First there is a mountain. Then there is no mountain." It is the hope of one who seeks along the path of Gautama Buddha to become able to gaze at all of the passing scene and see nothing, as opposed to the Christian hope of gazing at the passing scene and seeing the Christ or love, and the Oriental or Shinto hope of looking at the passing scene and seeing value and worth in the thing itself.

This peacefulness of working as an observer from the higher centers is very attractive because it promises a surcease from struggle and perceives struggle very much a part of third density at this time. There is a tremendous amount of pain at the emotional, mental and spiritual levels within the more comfortable and more economically advanced nations of your world, which has begun to be toxic in terms of perceived struggle. And in the light of this unceasing struggle, the opportunity to move into clear communication and work in consciousness is seductive and almost irresistible to many.

We do, however, see an implicit challenge in moving along the path of Buddhism. And that is in its remoteness. There is, shall we say, an intellectual cast of thought which is easily awakened within the Buddhist mentality. And an enormous literature of speculative theological works is evidence of the intellectual fruitfulness of this type of inquiry and discussion. Indeed, we may say that those who seek along the Buddhist path have done far more investigation into the specific discrete realms of the inner planes, identifying and describing various states of consciousness, various places where teachers dwell, and so forth, than any other system of religion. The difficulty with this tremendous panoply of assets and resources is that entities will remain within the higher centers without bringing the lower centers into balance with this work in consciousness. This weakens the integrated self and we suggest to those who wish to seek along the path to Buddhism that care be taken in a persistent and continuing way to reintegrate into the practice those lower energies of orange and yellow ray and of green ray so that there is not simply talk, discussion, thinking about the Creator, and the releasing of the illusion, but also the awakening of the heart and the valuing of the structures of the illusion. For the structures of the illusion, the relationships, the families, the friendships in groups are an elegant and eloquent design for learning. Into each relationship has been poured a tremendous amount of preincarnative thought. You may see each relationship as a carefully prepared lesson in the giving and receiving of love. And it is well to reconnect persistently with these lower chakra energies as one works within clear communication, the reading of material, and all of the work in consciousness that is so delightful to those who seek after wisdom as opposed to love.

The second advantage of Buddhism is an advantage of position and perception. The Christian and Judaic religions and the Moslem religion are all patterned with extreme similarity, to the extent that one may see that their holy works are shared. The stories are shared. The origins and springs of religion are shared. At the same time that this unity exists, there is also a tragic history, millennia of discord, and there is no religion that comes out any better than any other in terms of the folly of the wrong uses of power. In the name of religion it is well known throughout all peoples upon your globe that Christian, Jew and Muslim are a contentious and war-like people whose gods tend to be as aggressive as they are loving. And this is a difficult burden for the spiritual seeker to carry no matter how much the entity may adore Yahweh, Christ or Allah. No matter how much the seeker may feel the resonance and rightness of this path for him, yet too there is a perceived burden of shame and guilt than cannot be ignored.

It is not that the Buddhist religion as a system has not had its hassles and its fights, for indeed, if the scholar were to penetrate the outer details of this world system it would find the bellicose and aggressive actions and disputes of petty gods which indeed offer shame and guilt. Yet because of the fact that those who worship along Buddhist paths do not and have not for many centuries had ascendancy as race, people, nation, economy or society, there is little known of this history of shame and guilt. And instead it is possible for those who are seeking within the supermarket of world religions to come upon Buddhism in an innocent and fresh way. There is more of the feeling that this is a religion of peace and enlightenment, not a religion of war and dispute. And this perception is extremely valuable.

As we said, the great virtue of any outer religion is that it offers a place to be within the illusion. When one is within a path that is known, one may feel that one is not alone, that one belongs, that one is part of something that is beautiful and continuing and holy. When no sparks come to a seeker from looking at the various religions, then it is that the seeker must decide to create her own path. And this is a challenge. Certainly it is one that each is capable of rising to and meeting. But it does throw one upon one's own resources in a way that an outer path of religion does not. We sympathize with each who seeks, for we, like those within your circle, do not necessarily feel that one path has all the answers but, rather, that each path offers advantages. We would simply suggest to each that the seeking for the right path be done in the atmosphere of the trust of self and of the self's powers of discrimination and choice. For the seeker will know what is truly for him. And may we say that no matter what the path chosen, the creation speaks equally to all. The crocus that this instrument spoke of as growing where none was planted offers its own lesson in any religious system, speaking of faith, the generosity of spirit, and the endless possibilities of the present moment. Each day, each hour, and each moment offer sight to the eye and sound to the ear for one who is looking and to one who is listening for the truth.

We would encourage each, no matter what the path followed, to focus upon those aspects of the faith that unify and harmonize, that bring the self to a deeper feeling of the immediacy and the essence of the self. For beyond all perceived religion lies the self within that is each of you, and that self is the essence of holiness. That self is the spark of the infinite Creator, and those thoughts that you think are but distortions of the one great original thought that is

Love. No matter where you seek you dwell in precincts of love.

We would at this time leave this instrument and transfer this contact to the one known as Jim. We thank this instrument for its service. We are those of Q'uo.

(Jim channeling)

I am Q'uo, and greet each again in the love and the light of the one Creator through this instrument. It is our privilege at this time to offer ourselves in the capacity of attempting to speak to any further queries which those present may have for us. Is there another, shorter query at this time?

R: There have been actions in my life that I have taken that have left me with guilt and shame, and I wonder, in general, what we are to do with the realization of having hurt others and how to remedy such actions?

I am Q'uo, and am aware of your query, my sister. When one feels that there have been those experiences shared with others that have been hurtful to either party, then it is well, if it is possible, to utilize both the green and blue energy centers in the opening up of the heart and of the communication to any one may have injured in any way, to speak from the heart what is now felt and to offer it to the other, with the heartfelt apology. This not being possible for one reason or another, perhaps one entity no longer being incarnate, it is well, then, that this dialogue take place within one's own mind, within one's own meditation, so that that experience which was shared of a difficult nature may be brought again into consciousness, examined for the roots of the cause within the self, then be able to be forgiven both by the self and any other self involved, so that there is a healing and a harmony which comes from this reexamination.

As human beings within the third-density illusion, each of you moves as best as one can through this illusion, knowing that there will be those times when the misstep is made. However, with the faith that all is well and shall be well, one may also know that any misstep or injurious action can also be utilized for healing and harmony that will bring the entities closer together in the unity of thought and compassion that binds all beings within the One Creation. Thus one may utilize any previous disharmonious action or misstep as a method of working both upon the self and upon clearing communication between the self and any other self with which one has a relationship in the daily round of activities. It is well, however, that this communication and opening of the green and blue-ray chakras take place first within the meditative state so that one may begin the healing process there, as a seed within a garden is nurtured so that it grows to a certain degree of maturity before the sharing is sought with the other self.

Is there another query, my sister?

R: On a different topic, I wonder what the purpose of D's and my relationship and being together is?

I am Q'uo, and am aware of your query, my sister. If this purpose were not already known to some degree by each of you we would not be able to speak, for we do not wish to infringe on the free will of any who seeks the path of his or her own evolution. However, since each of you is, shall we say, strongly suspicious of the path shared by each, we may say that that which you share together is a mutual awakening process that allows each of you to open your heart to the other and to develop that quality that you may call compassion, unconditional love, mercy, understanding, forgiveness, surrender and acceptance. These are the qualities of the green-ray energy center, of the heart and are indeed the salvation of this illusion. For each entity comes here to work in some degree upon the heart. This is the energy center through which connection with all the creation is possible, and as each of you moves through your daily round of activities, making those small adjustments each to the other in compassion and understanding, you continue this process that has been ongoing through the entire length of your relationship and which shall be the strength and foundation as your relationship continues into what you call your future. There is much of understanding which each of you has developed for the other and for all other selves because of your relationship to each other.

The mated relationship is one which has been called by some an ordeal, for in this relationship one comes face to face with those qualities that are strengths, that are weaknesses, that are latent, that are possible. One is face to face, in short, with one's humanity, with that which enlivens your being and gives a vitality to your step, a purpose to your life and to the sharing that is possible also with others because of that which you have done with each other. Therefore, that which you undertake in this life is, in general and specific terms, the awakening of compassion and the forming of that kind of relationship which can be seen to be ideal; that is to say, where the heart of each is opened not only to each but to all others as a result of the work that is at times difficult, that is always undertaken between the two of you. Thus, work done between the two of you is work which can benefit the entire planet, for as you are able to find harmony, love, understanding and acceptance within the self so will you be able to find it within others as all others mirror to you that which is the heart of your self.

Is there another query, my sister?

R: No. Thank you.

I am Q'uo, and we thank you. Is there another query at this time?

S: I have a comment more than a query. I was going over last week's session in which what you had accomplished in the past hadn't turned out the way you had hoped and you are attempting now to make amends for that. Thinking on it this week, those days in Egypt have been pretty much forgotten by the population today. I guess I felt that you seemed too harsh on yourselves concerning your roles then and considering what you do now. We appreciate your being here and talking to us and we hope that you do it more out of enjoyment than a feeling of obligation. It's an opinion that you can take or leave from third density. I just want to let you know we appreciate the role you do play now. Have I misinterpreted what you said from last time? Would you comment on that, please?

I am Q'uo and am aware of your query and your generosity of heart, which we greatly appreciate. We do not mean to be harsh in our analysis of our previous interaction with the population of this planet, but wish instead to look at the ramifications of our interaction, which seemed from one perspective to have produced fruit that was not as we had wished. For when we share as we do now with any other entities we are hopeful that that which we share will be seen also as it is; that is, that we share our opinion freely from our hearts for all. Our experience with those of the Egyptian culture many thousands of your years ago was an experience in which our words were reserved for the few. That we were not able to see how our interaction would result in this reserving of that which was freely given only for those of power and position was, in our opinion, of a short-sighted nature, the eagerness on our part to be of service overshadowing the possibilities of being of less service than we were.

However, we are at this time greatly overjoyed to be able to speak to this group or to any group, whether it be through words as we do now in mind-to-mind communication, or whether it be in the dream state or in meditation or the inspiration that comes in the midst of waking activity. It is the greatest of honors to speak to those who call by their very essence, their very being, for our assistance. For it is a portion of ourselves that calls to us. Any call of any entity for assistance through the sorrow of the entity's being, the pain of existence, the confusion of the mind, the doubt of the heart, is a calling from one portion of the self to another portion of the self. Such a call cannot be refused. Thus we seek in joy to serve now as we sought in joy to serve then. And we appreciate greatly those who offer the call to us and present us the opportunity that we may be of such service.

Is there another query at this time?

S: One last one. Have you considered possibly dictating a book on the Law of One that we could share with all freely?

I am Q'uo, and am aware of your query, my brother. We are available for any queries which those within this circle of seeking find worthwhile in offering to us. We do not plan any, shall we say, curriculum. We wish to observe the free will of each present in the offering of our service. Thus we offer that which is ours to give in response to the queries which we receive.

Is there another query?

S: Not from me. Thanks.

I am Q'uo, and we thank you, my brother. Is there another query at this time?

(Pause)

I am Q'uo, and as it appears that we have exhausted the queries for the nonce, we shall express again our great appreciation to each present for offering us this opportunity to join you in your circle of seeking this day. We are aware that each has made great sacrifices in order to be here at this time, and each has been patient with us as we take a great portion of your time to speak those words which are ours. We are known to you as those of Q'uo, and we shall now take our leave of this instrument and this group, leaving each as always in the love and in the ineffable light of the one infinite Creator. Adonai, my friends. Adonai. ❧

L/L Research

Sunday Meditation
March 4, 2001

Group question: Our question today is how can a person who has a great deal of sexual energy available from the red ray but who has no sexual partner allow that energy to move through the various energy centers of the body in the most harmonious way possible?

(Carla channeling)

We are those known to you as the principle Q'uo. Greetings in the love and in the light of the one infinite Creator. We thank each of you who has called us to this group this day. We thank you for your searching, and we thank you for your question. We are glad to respond with our thoughts and opinions. For your part, you will use discrimination and realize that we are in no way authorities but those who are pilgrims upon the path and are glad to share what experiences we have had with you. We share as soul to soul and being to being and, in terms of learning and in terms of teaching, we feel you are our teachers to a greater extent than we are yours. We greatly appreciate this exchange of learning and of teaching. We thank each and bless each, for we are all desiring to be of service and all desiring to seek the truth. This is the bond that blesses us with its companionship, one to the other.

You ask this day concerning red-ray energy, and we are happy to talk about this interesting subject. As is often the case with us we would like to establish the ground upon which we will speak by moving back a step and looking at not just the red-ray energy center but at the energetic body and its location with regards to the physical body and its connections to the physical body.

Firstly, we would posit that each entity is an essence, a field of energy that has complex characteristics on many different levels. A soul essence vibrates through all densities and has chakra connections in all seven bodies on the inner planes, so when one is dealing with the energetic body one is dealing not simply with an adjunct to the physical body but rather a system of fields of energy that extend far past time, space and incarnational situations. Consequently, in dealing with the energetic body, the relationship of the energy body to the physical body is not as straightforward as it may seem to be when thinking in a linear fashion concerning issues connected with the various chakra energies.

The energy body is a system of bodies which occupy, in your terms, the same space and time in that they are all potentially available as sources of information within the incarnation so that as an entity becomes increasingly familiar with the feeling of the energy body in balance there becomes a kind of feedback system that is greatly helpful in working to balance the system. We will discuss this at more length later.

It is the tendency of this instrument, and certainly many who work with the concepts of the chakra centers, to tend to categorize energies as to chakra and to analyze them as to chakra source. This is in some cases of a limited amount of help. It is sometimes quite possible to analyze a situation in terms of chakra origination when it comes to blockage or over-activation. However, the limitations of this way of gazing at or analyzing chakra energies is that the chakras do not work separately, but rather work as a system and in addition have important and significant connections between finer bodies within higher densities as the process of learning by faith and receiving by faith now goes on.

We would begin then by suggestion that it is well, when faced with a perceived imbalance in the energy body, to realize that the situation is non-local, no matter how local it may seem. That is, it may seem that there is a red-ray over-activation or a red-ray blockage and that this is then removing energy from the red ray. In actuality, the energies of the system are seldom blocked in only one ray because of the interrelationships between the rays, especially between the primary rays and also because of the centrality of the heart to those who are working in service-to-others polarity.

In the case of perceived red-ray blockage, for instance, it is well to gaze carefully at the nature of red ray. It is that first gateway of the energetic body. It is that first gateway that allows in the infinite energy of the one infinite Creator. The easy way to gaze at energy systems is to look at the blockages and, one by one, to remove them. However, the subtleties of each chakra move beyond the stated venue or placement of that chakra. That is to say, certainly the red-ray blockage has to do with sexuality in a linear sense, but in a very significant non-linear sense it has far more to do with the processes of love and fear as regards survival. Survival is a vital and hidden issue for an entity that is well fed, decently clothed, warm and with a roof over the physical head. It does not occur to the waking consciousness that there is a survival issue with regards to sexuality, for sexuality is clearly not necessary for survival. However, in the gateway to the metaphysical body or energy body one also is gazing at the gateway to the physical body, and this connection between physical and metaphysical bodies creates the situation in which the instincts of the physical body have a sometimes striking and, again, hidden effect upon the perceived experience of blockage in red ray, so that that which is perceived as sexual frustration is actually the cry of the heart to survive.

This instrument was talking earlier about the simple, fundamental necessity of having one's need met. Obviously, in terms of your experience within incarnation, there is a constant and unremitting traffic of requests from the self concerning those things which it needs to survive. The stomach cries out for food. The physical body cries out to reproduce. The body demands to breathe, to work, to move and to function. When there are gateway challenges that are persistent, such as the denial of a perceived sexual need, the energy system is set up to become blocked along certain lines that create the perception, in the soul that is experiencing this, that there is a red-ray energy blockage, and on the level of the observation, this is correct. On the level of the solution of this observation, if there can be said to be a solution, this is not correct.

For, as we said, there is much more connection between the chakras and the effect of one chakra upon another than this instrument, and many perhaps, give the energy body credit for possessing. So in truth, a blockage in red ray, in the most linear sense, does block energy so that it cannot rise up into the heart chakra and, therefore, be available for work in consciousness. But more than that, it is a non-physical energy that is not a sexual energy, nor is it a survival energy, but it is, rather, energy. In truth, you see, the energy body does not respond to physical stimuli. In an energetic sense the body is completely a creature of the mind and the spirit and the emotions. So those feelings that are within, those desires and thirsts, as complex and interrelated as they usually are, are actually, at the heart, a blockage within the energy body. And because the needs of an incarnational being are complex, the blockages, over-activations and other distortions within the energy body, are significantly more complex than can be determined by analysis using the intellectual mind.

We would suggest that one way to work on blockages within the energetic body is to give to the self the resources of the energy body clearing or balancing, which we have talked about through this instrument before. Since we have talked about this before, we will recapitulate rather succinctly by saying that the point of energy balancing is simply to go through the day's experiences as one remembers them, sitting quietly at the end of the day, in a reflective mode and simply being with each distortion that can be remembered from the harvest of the day's emotions, whether that distortion was towards a positive emotion or towards a negative emotion, as perceived by the seeker. For all distortions from balance are equally useful for looking at and for allowing into the arena of the meditational mind in order that, in silence and in the release of control, there may be allowed to enter into the energy system that help which is available from those unseen beings which surround and guard and guide each seeker.

This instrument works with her own energy balancing in this way very seldom because the technique involves looking at each emotion, allowing it to intensify to the point of really heavy intensity, and then allowing that emotion's exact opposite to enter into the equation until both sides of, say, impatience and patience can be seen in a balanced fashion. However, this instrument does use a visualization technique in order to balance its energies. This is helpful for those whose visualization abilities are dull enough that there is not the danger of over-intensification or over-dramatization of emotion which would sweep away the possibility of balancing. In this visualization technique there is simply the request for help from guidance, and when that guidance has been secured, there is the request that this guidance help in seeing in an inner or intuitive sense the actual colors of the chakra centers to see if they are at the same color tone, the same color intensity, and the same degree of lightness of tone within each color. This way, it can be seen intuitively if an energy center seems muddy or dark or weak or attenuated.

It is possible to work with balancing techniques using the balancing meditation or using the visualization technique. Either one of these signals to the energy body that care is being given to the body, that concern from the heart is being offered to the body, and this is greatly reassuring to the body and helps, whether or not the balancing meditation or visualization seems to be successful from the conscious standpoint.

Another aspect which may well help with unclogging blockages is simply to act on the emotion which has been engendered. By this we mean that the basic emotion engendered is located, to the best degree of accuracy possible by the seeker, and then expressed. In the instance that the one known as R spoke of and related the one known as P's speaking of, the experience was that of waking up [from a night's sleep] and immediately feeling such a degree of frustration that the desire is to scream. We would encourage moving to a place of safety and screaming, when this feeling occurs. It is not wise to upset others, nor is it wise to upset the environment. However, it is very wise to acknowledge and express emotion when it can be done without infringing upon the free will of others or destroying something within the self. There is a real spiritual value in acknowledging primal distress and in expressing it, even in the most primitive emotional release such as the scream, for it is a scream from the heart that wants to survive, not simply the body that wishes to reproduce or to express its sexual nature. This is the surface of the energy distortion but not its essence. And the seeming catalyst for energy distortion is almost never a linear match with the catalyst that produced it. For within the energy body the system of unconscious memory connection and memory within other lifetimes which includes relationships with this issue or with the entity which is giving catalyst on this issue are numerous. And, consequently, the rational mind, in waking consciousness, shall not be able significantly to penetrate the nature of the actual energy distortion.

Perhaps we may say that beyond a certain point, it is well to rely on faith. We always come back to the simplicity of the situation and the unity of the situation, for all energy is one. There is not sexual energy, personal energy, family and group energy, heart energy and so forth. There are aspects to the energy, colors, shall we say, to the energy as it moves through those centers of energy and connection within the energy bodies. But the energy itself is limitless white light and although it may be distorted in its shadows within the energetic physical body connection, within the energetic body itself and at the source of the problem, it is all the same energy. And this is a key concept, we feel. For this lifts the seeker beyond the limitation of a concept of her problem and places the waiting heart and the energy body which is listening to that heart in a situation of being aware of the larger picture. And what one accepts into the waking mind becomes the door that opens the potential of the solution to be approached and released from its stricture.

First, there is the faith that all is well. This is a significant step for one who is suffering, for the physical body wants to react in a fear-based manner. The instincts of the physical body are to protect and control for the safety of the physical body. And so there is the feeling, when one is in discomfort, that one needs to control that situation. One needs to achieve a comfort zone. However, often within your density you have made choices as a seeker before incarnation that place you in a situation where you will continue to suffer, and that is what was intended. It was not seen before incarnation that this would be precisely suffering. It was seen that this would be learning. It was seen that this would be a great opportunity to make the breakthrough, the step forward as a spiritual being in evolution. Evolution is change. Change is difficult. Change is painful. Change engenders suffering. Consequently, some blockages that are looked at and are experienced are placed there by the self before incarnation, not in order to break through quickly, but in order to initiate a process of self-acceptance, self-understanding and self-forgiveness that is far deeper than the issue that begins this process of understanding, acceptance, healing and forgiveness.

Secondly, there is the faith that there is help available beyond what is available to the rational mind, and that this help is benign, kindly and intelligent. Once one has the basic attitude of faith, that regardless of appearances all is well, there is a door within the heart that opens, that has been closed by fear. It will continue to wish to close, again and again and again. And this is why daily meditation and the entering of the silence is so central, even if it is but for a few moments. That connection with the silence empowers the resources of the connections between physical and energetic bodies and between the connections in the energetic body to those bodies which are involved in the guidance of the higher self that is moving to help the self within third density. The faith that all is well, and that help is there, together, have a tremendously comforting and strengthening effect. However, as we said, in the face of apparent physical imbalance that continues over a period of time, this sense of well-being will again and again be compromised by the instinctive fear-based reactions of the physical vehicle which feels that it is being threatened in its ability to survive.

There is, as this instrument has said, no issue tougher than the red-ray issue because that natural function is so strong in the physical body, and the emotional need for connection and companionship, which sexuality is the door to within your peoples, is so very strong. There is, certainly, no way that any can control and, by doing or not doing some physical thing, solve the discomfort of the physical body when its natural sexual functions are denied. When this occurs, according to the nature of the individual and its energy system, there will be some degree of suffering. For some entities it is negligible, unnoticeable, or minor. For others it is an enormous and very substantial problem and certainly one that cannot be ignored. This instrument is aware that the one known as P has said that the mechanical satisfaction, on a solitary basis, of the physical desire for sexual completion had not been satisfactory, no matter how many times repeated, and we are not surprised at this because of the fact that the sexual energy blockage is actually not what it seems, but rather, a much deeper and more profound suffering that extends throughout the body system of the energetic body, if not the physical body.

In one very basic sense we must say that as far as we know there are times of suffering for all people. There are always needs that will not be met that seem important, and this is part of the way that the school of love that planet Earth is works. For again and again, it allows the senses of the physical body to inform the intellect that there is not enough, that there is no safety and that there is no healing. It is the challenge of the spiritually oriented entity to gaze at the limited and crying needs of the body, not with eyes to solve, but with eyes to love and understand, to enter into the experience, to enter into the suffering, to enter into all of the emotions that this brings up and to see the self in its needs, in its wants, in its character as defined by those cries of hunger. What one desires is extremely interesting to the developing soul, and it is very well to look at what one desires, not with the eye to judge, but with the hope of fully embracing the self, of being in love with that suffering self, of rocking that self within the heart and saying, "Yes, these needs are beautiful; these needs are worthy; these needs are fully acceptable and simply are not being met by the circumstances of my life."

This is, again and again, in one way and then another, the situation of the seeker within the physical plane. There is not enough. There is no healing. There is only suffering. This is a dark picture, and we would say to you that it is dark as the earth itself. The soil beneath the feet is dark. It is dark, mysterious and fertile. It is the seed of something that will grow through the soil, through the suffering, through the point of pain, to blooming at last in ways that cannot be comprehended at the moment that the suffering is being experienced. Perhaps you could look at the picture as a puzzle that one is so close to that one can only see thirty-five pieces out of the two thousand, and it looks, therefore, like the problem is about a dog and a man. But if one pulls back to gaze at the entire picture, the dog and the man are at the edge of a much larger conflict that involves many more characters and many more issues. When a cycle of suffering has been completed, it is far more easy in hindsight to look into the pattern and say, "Yes, I see the sense of this suffering. I see the point of this catalyst being offered to me. I see where it took me and what I learned, and I am grateful." We are suggesting that that attitude of gratefulness and thankfulness for the suffering be adopted by faith beforetimes, so that in the midst of suffering, control is released; needs are expressed to the self by the self and then let go. And it is acknowledged that beyond all need, beyond all distortions of energy, beyond all suffering, beyond all limitation, the essence of self is perfect and resting in the most divine love and in the most strong and healing light.

We would at this time transfer this contact to the one known as Jim. We thank this instrument for offering itself as channel and we thank the group for its very interesting question. We leave this instrument in love and in light and transfer at this time. We are those of Q'uo.

(Jim channeling)

I am Q'uo, and greet each again in love and in light through this instrument. We are privileged at this time to offer ourselves in the attempt to speak to any further queries which this group may have for us. Is there another query at this time?

S: I'll start. The thing I am curious about is when we gather each week we talk about what we have been doing during the previous week, and I thought I should give you the opportunity to tell us how your week was.

I am Q'uo, and am aware of your query, my brother. The experience which we have had since last joining with this group is one of the exploration of the interior of the self, shall we say. This is our means of becoming the one Creator. We continue to move along our evolutionary path in what might be seen to be small steps, investigating those portions of the self that is the Creator which have been, shall we say, less well appreciated in our previous experience. And, of course, we move in service to others where possible. In most instances this is accomplished by making an appearance, as you would say, within the dream state of those whom we seek to serve. Thus, we are modest in our work and in our service.

Is there another query at this time?

S: Are there any messages from any of our other unseen friends at this time?

I am Q'uo, and am aware of your query, my brother. Those of the host of heaven, as we have heard it called, merely send their love and light to all who are available to receive it.

Is there another query, my brother?

S: Not at this time. Thanks.

I am Q'uo, and we thank you, my brother. Is there another query at this time?

R: I don't ever remember being aware of Q'uo in my dream state. Do you do it more on an energetic level rather than as an identity?

I am Q'uo, and am aware of your query, my brother. When we are able to make such a visitation, it is most often in a situation in which the entity which we seek to serve has found itself in what you would call dire straits and is calling for aid by the amount of suffering and pain that the entity experiences in its life. In such a situation of extreme need, we are sometimes able to make our presence felt in an inspirational manner to such an entity. This is somewhat rare, as you would term it, but is a means of service which we have pursued from the days of old, in this planetary sphere's history.

Is there another query, my brother?

R: No. Not a question. But thank you for that answer. I derive some comfort from knowing that we all do have unseen help.

I am Q'uo, and we thank you, my brother. Is there another query at this time?

S: Recently a woman we work with had her mother pass away. Today my sister-in-law's father came very close to dying, and I was wondering if there were any words or thoughts or ideas that I could share with them to help them with the struggle that they are going through now?

I am Q'uo, and am aware of your query, my brother. When one wishes to serve in a situation in which there has been the loss of a loved one and there is much suffering and grief on the part of those who remain, it is often the best service simply to be available for whatever needs are felt by those who grieve. Thus the offering of one's efforts in providing the foodstuffs, as we are aware you have prepared to do, is one such means of service that is much appreciated by those who are at such a time thinking about little else than the loved one who has departed. It is also possible that if one feels there is an opening in the grieving entity, that they be approached by suggesting that there is the completion of a grand design or plan that has been accomplished by the one who has left, and that this plane continues beyond this earthly experience, where an ending is a beginning upon another level. Then there may be some comfort that can be given to the heart, to the mind and to the soul. For as those who grieve are reminded of that which they know—that all life continues, that all springs from one Creator, that we do that which is ours to do, and that there is truly no loss at any time—this reminding of the basic elements of the spiritual journey is often helpful and appreciated.

Is there a further query, my brother?

S: My wife still has much swelling and pain from her broken ankle and she requested to know if there was any other lesson, meaning or whatever that she should further examine at this time?

I am Q'uo, and am aware of your query, my brother. As we consider the situation of the one known as C, we would recommend that she has processed well that catalyst which has come before her. The healing that remains may be bothersome and lengthy, yet it is that which is necessary in order that the catalyst be utilized to its fullest. We see no further mental examination necessary for this entity. We add our blessing and healing vibrations to those many wishes of renewed health which have been offered to the one known as C.

Is there another query at this time?

S: No. Thank you.

I am Q'uo. Again, we thank you, my brother. Is there another query at this time?

Carla: I'd like to follow up on S's query. It seems like if you need to do one thing to solve catalyst that has come up for you, it doesn't necessarily solve the problem. Is there ever a situation in which the problem is what you think it is, and something that you do in the physical will take care of it nicely, or is it always, metaphysically speaking, that the roots of the situation are hidden?

I am Q'uo, and am aware of your query, my sister. Though we do not wish to discourage any from examining carefully each portion of catalyst that comes before the notice, when the conscious mind has finally noticed the catalyst that has come before it much has already been lost to the determination of the proper path to travel. This is merely the nature of the heavy, chemical illusion in which you find yourselves in third density. It is very difficult to perceive clearly those messages which are sent from the subconscious mind and the metaphysical realms, for it is as though a different language were being spoken and the ears that hear this language perceive only dimly that which is intended. Thus it is well to use not only the conscious analytical mind but also wise to employ the intuition, the hunches, those feelings that come through the veil of forgetting and leave the trace of meaning, the—we give this instrument the phrase—the niggle of direction that one may follow as one would follow the trail of bread crumbs in the deep forest, looking again for the path that one took into such an imposing and isolated area.

When one examines carefully the subconscious mind, as carefully as one can, shall we say, one will discover that there are trees of immense size, ferns of indescribable beauty, mosses unknown before, creatures strange and exotic, air barely able to be breathed and yet exhilarating in its intake. Thus when one examines catalyst for its origin and direction to utilize, one may rest assured that this is a process which itself can become a journey into exotic realms. The fruit that is found in such a place is well worth the effort, whether one is able to feast at the entire meal or only the hors d'ouvres.

Is there another query, my sister?

Carla: I had more questions but I feel the energy is getting low. If you wish to comment, you said that there was a language of the energy body, and I was thinking: was that the language of emotions? When I work with music or words, as in poetry, or with colors, all of those things seem to me to work well with the energy body and to clarify my own emotions and bring them out. I was thinking emotions would be the better language for the energetic body than would be intellectual analysis.

I am Q'uo, and am aware of your query, my sister. We also are aware that the energy of the circle is low. We shall comment briefly.

The emotions are an avenue of exploration that also deserve a great deal of effort. The attempt to interpret catalyst and its application to future action—this is the direction that we were intending when we suggested that intuitions be examined, for intuitions are a more purified kind of emotion from another source, these intuitions being that property of the subconscious mind, the first translation, shall we say, of the language that the conscious mind attempts to understand. Thus we suggest that the intuition and, as you have suggested, the emotions, be employed more as a fundamental means of examining catalyst, rather than allowing the intellectual mind the sole effort in this endeavor.

Is there a further query, my sister?

Carla: No. And I really thank you for that answer, Q'uo.

I am Q'uo, and we thank you, my sister. Is there a final query at this time?

(No further queries.)

I am Q'uo. We would take this opportunity to thank each once again for inviting us to join this circle of working. We are aware that the effort that each has made to become a member in this circle this day has been great, for there have been obstacles that made it difficult for each to partake. And we thank each for being a part of this circle, for inviting our presence, for seeking with a true and sincere heart that which is our opinion, and that which we joyfully give, though we recommend that each observe those words which ring of truth for each. Take those and leave all others behind. We are known to you as those of Q'uo, and we would take our leave of this instrument and this group at this time, leaving each, as always, in the love and in the light of the one infinite Creator. Adonai, my friends. Adonai. ❧

Sunday Meditation
March 18, 2001

Group question: We have just about got *A Wanderer's Handbook* ready to be printed, and we are going to be sending a flyer for it out to people on our mailing list. Many of them likely are wanderers or spiritual outsiders of one kind or another and we are wondering if Q'uo today would like to say something to these people about the concepts in the book or the quality of being a wanderer, of being alienated and isolated in the spiritual journey.

(Carla channeling)

We are those of the principle known to you as the Q'uo, and we greet you in the love and in the light of the one infinite Creator, in whose service we are. We thank you for calling us to your group this afternoon. It is, as always, a great privilege and pleasure to speak to you. We want to thank each who has come for the sacrifice of those other things that were not done this day in order that each of you might seek the truth and rest in the silence that binds us all in the love and in the light of the one Creator. It is wonderful to be able to share our humble thoughts with you. We do want to be clear that we are not authority figures, but seekers upon the same path with you. Perhaps we have walked a few steps more. Perhaps we remember a few more of the experiences that we have had, and, therefore, perhaps we can offer opinions that may be useful and may be interesting to each of you. But we do ask that each of you listen with a discriminating and careful ear, listening not for all of our words but for those words that seem to resonate within your heart. For truth is a very subjective thing, and when something is part of your personal truth it will have a certain ring to it, and you will recognize it. Trust that resonance of recognition and not the seeming authority of any source, for you have responsibility for your mental, emotional and spiritual evolution. You may choose the rate and the process of change. And we would not wish to become a stumbling block as each of you seeks the truth in his or her own way.

With that said, we are very happy to share our thoughts on the occasion of this special newsletter, which speaks to those who have enjoyed other material that we of the Confederation of Planets in the Service of the Infinite Creator may have offered in times previous to this. For many to whom we speak, we simply say, "Welcome home," for one thing that is very common among wanderers and all those who have begun the process of awakening from the sleep of Earth is a feeling of not being at home in the Earth world, of not recognizing the colors and shapes of your beautiful planet. As lovely as it is, yet still it does not feel like the shores and the fields of home. And this is because in many cases we speak to those who do not originate from the planetary environment that you call Earth but, rather, are those who have chosen very deliberately and specifically to come to Earth on a voyage of service and learning.

For many others to whom we speak, Earth is the native sphere, the beloved home, and yet the spirit has awakened from the dream of Earth. And more and more, in the awakening process, Earth has become an alien place, not because its shapes are unfamiliar but because the thinking of its peoples and its culture has begun to jar against the newly found shapes and resonances of an awakening awareness of the self as a citizen of eternity and infinity. Whether you listen as one who is an Earth native or as one who has come here from elsewhere, yet still we speak to you as absolute equals, for all of those who have awakened have become wanderers upon Earth. All begin to experience the dislocation of living in two worlds at once. There are certain characteristics to this experience of awakening and finding one's self, attempting to make sense out of that which seems more and more not to make sense about which we can speak.

One very common experience is the experience of isolation. It is as though a separation had occurred between those who think in physical terms and the self, who is thinking in metaphysical terms. The reasons and the considerations for making choices in the Earth world have to do with practicality, finances, schedules, what people think, what the mores of the culture are and so forth. To the spirit who has awakened, there has been a switch of universes, and the reasons for doing things in the Earth world do not seem to hold the fascination and the attractiveness, if ever they did hold attractiveness. Rather, there comes, more and more, to be a yearning of the heart, for truth, for essence and for service.

The self, once realized as a metaphysical entity, is also realized as an ethical principle. And you can see yourself more and more clearly as one who truly can be responsible for doing her absolute best to do the ethical thing, to hold the highest principle, to hew to the road that seems the most beautiful, the most moral and the most right for the self. Often that which the world considers right and that which the inner self considers right will coincide. However, not infrequently issues looked at from the standpoint of Earth are looked at with an eye to the protection of the self and the maintenance of the environment, whereas looked at as a metaphysical issue, often the solution is transformed, and roads may be chosen that do not seem as practical, as convenient or as down to earth. For in the switch of universes there is the release of the forms of the world and the realization of forms that are higher in the metaphysical universe. All things are energy and vibration and your thoughts and intentions are far more important than whether or not, in the eyes of the world, you have succeeded. It is a cliché among all cultures of Earth that many a fool cannot seem to be practical, and yet many times, from the standpoint of spirit, it is very important to be impractical and to hew to that which this instrument calls the highest and best. Again, such value judgments are very subjective, and another's opinion of what is the highest path or the finest or most beautiful principle by which to live may not agree with your opinion. And we say to you, one way to become more at home in this strange world of the awakened spirit on Earth is to be decisively impractical and to know, going into decisions, that you shall be making decisions with an eye to spiritual values. Often these decisions will not make sense to others. And we encourage each to have the courage and the faith to follow your principles, your guidance, your light. For what each of you has awakened to is a precious awareness of self as essence.

Each of you has become aware that you live in a very busy physical world. It is a world of never ending detail, a world which this instrument often characterizes as one offering too much good work to do. It is not that the world offers one bad choice after another, though this is often the case. There are many beauties and blessings to the world as it is, in all of its confusion. Yet there is a simple factor underlying all of the busyness and detail of physical life, and that is the essence that you are, that each of you is. We would look at this essence for a moment, for it is at the heart of what we have to say. Each of you is very, very real. Beyond the dream of Earth, beyond the dream of ether, beyond the dream which is at that level at which we are now speaking, beyond all dreams of which we know, each of you is very profoundly, ultimately, uniquely real. You are, in fact, the stuff of creatorship. Each of you is a spark of the divine, and without each of you the divine would not be complete. Each of you was, before time and space existed. And each of you will be, beyond all thought, beyond all telling, beyond any creation's end, for in infinity an end is always a beginning, and you shall forever be the only you that exists, precious, beloved of the Creator, an essence, a light, a love.

You are here as awakened beings to be, not to do. This is a terrifically difficult concept to receive within the context of incarnated life because life as you know it, as you experience it, as the culture teaches you to experience it, is about doing. You were taught to value yourself as a worker, as a producer, as an accomplisher of deeds. They may be many different kinds of deeds, but at the next gathering to which you go, you will be asked not, "Who are you?" but, "What do you do?" And you will be valued by many people according to how that answer goes. And yet we say to you that you are not here primarily as a doer, but as an essence. In the energetic or metaphysical sense, each of you is a field of energy. Now this energy is not simple. Each of you has, as a core vibration, the one great original Thought. Each of you, at the core, is the Creator. Indeed, the basic goal of evolution is to come once again into full vibratory congruency with the one original Thought that is the Logos. This Logos could be described as love, and yet that word has been so sullied by being used for different kinds of passion and emotion and devotion that it is inadequate at heart to express the fullness of that quality that is creative and divine love.

To this original Logoic energy you have created distortions or variations or complexities that add to that basic vibration and that make you that unique essence that you are. As we see your vibratory pattern, we see your name metaphysically. You are as a rainbow of color and a certain pattern of shape that is, in its own way, exquisite. And we would know each of you anywhere, not from what you are thinking, not from what you are feeling at any particular moment, but rather from the great accumulation of self, through many experiences and many densities. Each of you comes to the present moment vibrating in a very discernibly identifiable way, and this is the great gift of each awakened being to the self and to planet Earth and to the peoples of Earth. For once each has awakened, each becomes an agent of the love and the light of the one infinite Creator.

It is part of the nature of the ethical, biological entity that you are that you shall express in this way. Here is the plan that we believe each of you set before yourselves before incarnation. The plan was to choose a set of relationships and a set of lessons as the one known as T. was saying in the conversation before this meditation. "I know that this problem has come to me," he said, "because I set this up for myself, and I am looking to sit with this difficulty, to enjoy this challenge, and to move through this process with as much love as possible." Your plan as learning entities, interested in the evolution of spirit, was not to be here and be wise, but to be here and be confused. You are hoping, by coming into this very dense physical illusion, to become completely disoriented and to wake up in the midst of a true sea of confusion. And the reason that you hoped for this was that you had the feeling that you could come to a better balance of self, a more pure choice of polarity, and a more passionate desire to seek the truth.

Before incarnation it seemed not so hard, because before incarnation, gazing at the scope of the entire incarnation, it seemed fairly obvious what these lessons were and why these relationships were important to follow through. It seemed unlikely that we could possibly avoid awakening. Yet in most cases awakening is not an easy thing but a process that moves in jerks and fits and starts, going through many an epiphany and many a dark night of the soul. Your hope here was simply to become so aware of the confusion of planet Earth that you would finally stop attempting to control things from the mind, from the ego, from the head, and would abandon what would appear to be an inadequate resource for dealing with that sea of confusion that is Earth life. You hoped that you would begin to move into the heart, for it is the heart, its intuitions and emotions, which contain the true harvest of wisdom, love and truth that lie within you within the sea of confusion.

When the awakened seeker begins to move into the heart and allow the heart to open and remain open, even when it is the most vulnerable, then it is that somehow the issues begin to seem simpler. Then it is that unseen hands begin to lend their aid and messengers of bird and beast, word and sign, and relationship and association seem to begin to pop up here and there and everywhere, forming a synchronistic web of coincidence and connection that teach and offer help when it is least expected and least seen ahead of time.

Attempting to live by essence, attempting to be oneself, is the work of the heart. Often it does seem very impractical as a way of living, for the opened heart seems very unprotected and very vulnerable. And so it is vulnerable to confusion and challenge of all kinds. The strength of living in the heart is that slender strength called faith, that lifts one on angels' wings and takes one above a problem, so that even if the body is troubled and the mind is confused, there is a serenity that comes from the release into knowing that all is well, and that all *will* be well. This trick of living which is called faith is a great key in switching universes, for faith takes the place of control in the Earth world and doing becomes being. Details become essence, and a life moves from the inside out rather than being driven from the outside in.

Another aspect of being a wanderer, which is common to those from elsewhere and to those who are native to the Earth sphere, is the enormous yearning to serve. And we say to each that the main service of each of you is the service of being yourself. For when you are most truly and deeply yourself, when your heart is open and vibrating in its fullness, you become a crystal capable of receiving energy, transmuting energy and releasing energy into the Earth's sphere. Many of you from other planets have come here specifically to do this. It is a simple process. You breathe in. You breathe out. You allow the truth to flow through you. You allow the infinite supply of energy that is the love of the Creator to flow through your energetic system and out into the Earth planes, and as you bless this process, encourage it, you intensify and enhance those vibrations that move into the Earth plane. Each of you, by being the way you are, is at this time a servant of the light, and you need do nothing more than live and love to fulfill your mission upon Earth. Naturally, each of you gave yourself gifts to share, lessons to learn and outer services to perform. And we encourage each to move along those lines of talent and gifts as you perceive them, looking for ways to share those gifts. But realize that, more than those outer doings, the inner essence is the true and central gift of the life, which you have come to offer. It is a beautiful gift. It is a gift that will take you all your life to give, and our encouragement to you is to give this gift and do this service regardless of what else you seem to be doing in your life.

You can work on opening your heart within the process of the workaday world, within the process of any present moment, under the storm of any challenge. It is impossible for any thing or any one to keep you from pursuing this service of being, and we want you to know that you have many helpers to aid you in this service. For each of you has guidance, personal guidance, deeply impersonal sources of guidance, inner planes teachers that shall come to you if you have a desire for that which they have to share. Many are the unseen spiritual aids that are available to the persistent and asking seeker. The key here is simply to ask and to keep asking with all of your heart. For it is true, as this instrument's holy work says, "Seek and you shall find. Knock and it shall be opened to you." Your desire shapes a tremendous amount of that which you shall receive spiritually. So trust that self that desires. Do not scorn it, but rather seek to know yourself more and more, and to define and refine to yourself that which you truly do desire, that which you truly do seek. For that which you seek, you shall surely find.

Each of you is a tremendously powerful principle, spiritually speaking, and a wonderful haven of help and healing to others. You are a particular kind of spiritual being, and although it may seem that you are isolated, that you are different and that you cannot be effective, yet we say to you that this is far from true. You cannot know what importance a smile or a word from you may have to another. You cannot know who will oversee some action or thought that you take and become comforted and inspired. You do not know, when you reach out your hand, how it will be received, and yet the impulse to do that is gold, spiritually speaking. Know yourself to be one who is truly powerful to serve, one who is worthy, one who, by doing her best, shall have done all that is necessary. This instrument often says, "Is there ever enough?" having noticed in so many ways that she is seldom satisfied. Yet we say to you, "Yes, you are enough, just as you are at this moment. Know yourself to be of great value as you are, as you sit, as you rest, at this moment. And know that all of the confusion of Earth cannot remove that essential quality from your being."

We greatly sympathize with the confusion that each feels within the Earth plane. We admire your courage. We rest in the comparative sureness of knowing of our density, in which many, many things are known, in which all thoughts are clear. Our confusion and our seeking lie in the mystery beyond that knowing. But to you, even that, the knowledge of self and the knowledge of other self, is so often hidden. It is as though each of you were in a scene from the television program this instrument knows as "The X-Files," looking around with flashlights in one dark corner after another. Such is the spiritual world. Within the Earth plane it is a very dark plane. The inner planes are not clear, and often there is no observed light. And yet we say to you, trust the light that is not seen. Trust that candle that is your heart, and know that as long as you keep that candle lit, that is your only responsibility, not for other's thinking, not for other people, and not for outer issues, but only to open the heart, to offer the self to love and be loved, to know the self as part of the Creator.

I am Q'uo, and we are aware that we have taken a great portion of your time speaking to you this day. We would, at this time, take our leave of this instrument and this group, leaving each, as always, in the love and in the light of the one infinite Creator. We are known to you as those of Q'uo. Adonai, my friends. Adonai.

L/L Research

L/L Research is a subsidiary of Rock Creek Research & Development Laboratories, Inc.

P.O. Box 5195
Louisville, KY 40255-0195

www.llresearch.org

Rock Creek is a non-profit corporation dedicated to discovering and sharing information which may aid in the spiritual evolution of humankind.

ABOUT THE CONTENTS OF THIS TRANSCRIPT: This telepathic channeling has been taken from transcriptions of the weekly study and meditation meetings of the Rock Creek Research & Development Laboratories and L/L Research. It is offered in the hope that it may be useful to you. As the Confederation entities always make a point of saying, please use your discrimination and judgment in assessing this material. If something rings true to you, fine. If something does not resonate, please leave it behind, for neither we nor those of the Confederation would wish to be a stumbling block for any.

© 2009 L/L Research

Sunday Meditation
March 25, 2001

Group question: Today our question concerns the fact that we reincarnate from life to life with friends, time after time, in clans or groups, and learn to serve and seek the Creator with them. We are wondering how this process of reincarnation in groups affects the planetary consciousness. Does it aid the planet and how does that work? How does this process aid the individual harvest when that time comes?

(Carla channeling)

We are those of the principle known to you as Q'uo. Greetings, in the love and in the light of the one infinite Creator. We offer that name and that signature because we are in the service of this same Creator, this one great original Thought which has spun out of Itself the infinite patterns of the evolving universe and which draws all things inexorably to harmonize, beautify and come together once more in the fullness of that dimension or quality we call time.

We are very happy to speak with you about some aspects of reincarnation and harvest and ask only that each be responsible for listening with a discriminating ear to that which we have to say, for we are not authorities which wish to impose our opinions on you. Rather, we are happy to share our thoughts in the hopes that some of them might be of use. Please keep those thoughts that resonate to your inner sense of truth and discard the rest without a second thought.

It is in the light of time that reincarnation unfolds its patterns. It is more accurate, metaphysically speaking, to look at the systems of reincarnation involving the repeated joining of relationship with certain other entities as a part of a circle of being in which each incarnation is a spoke out from the center and in which all experiences harvested by the entity in each incarnation are fed back into that central pool of self, than to describe reincarnation as a series of successive lifetimes. However, within the constraints of time and space, time is seen to be linear and directional and, indeed, were this not to seem so, the entire pattern of reincarnation would become fruitless. It is essential, in terms of third-density experience, that those moving through incarnation be unable to see the great circle of lifetimes and the nuances of each issue with which the relationships that seem to be karmic bring forth and create the opportunities for the work in consciousness.

Without time, taking the infinite viewpoint, all is the Creator. When time has begun unrolling its scroll in a creation sequence, it offers each spark of the Creator the opportunity to learn, to investigate and discover that which it will. Through lifetime upon lifetime entities go through a gradual process of awakening to the self. This awakening is the product of a great deal of inner exploration. The exploration involves many meetings with those who become to us the bearers of good things. Each is aware already of the process by which the self prepares for incarnation. Each is aware of the careful process of choosing those with which one shall come into relationship within the incarnation.

Within the course of these relationships which we have given ourselves, certainly it may seem from time to time as if we have chosen for ourselves harsh lessons and confusion as an inevitable part of the relationships that we have chosen to investigate and help to blossom forth. It may well seem that instead of becoming more and more unified with those with whom we are in relationship, that we have not made progress, and we may wonder about the efficacy of our work within these relationships and within these lessons. And yet we say to you that it is well to trust the rhythms of relationship and to allow them to be of the shape and the texture that they will be rather than attempt to remold them according to a desired outcome or a preferred status. This instrument earlier was speaking of a relationship that she would like to mend, and yet is not the work of mending work done upon the self? Is not the process of forgiveness and healing that forgiveness of self that sees the other self as the reflection of the Creator?

Consequently, we have this pattern of repeated relationships and may we say that rather than having one fairly small group of people with whom there are repeated relationships over the course of a creation process—that is, over the course of many densities of that process—each may expect to become intimate, to go through the processes of catalyst, healing, harmonization and unity, with each other spark of the infinite Creator. Thusly, this process of each helping each to learn the lessons of each density is not in any way seen as a malignant or an undesirable process, no matter how confused or muddied the relationships seem to be. Rather, it is the outworking of the tremendous force of spiritual gravity calling each to become more and more aware of the true nature of the self and calling each to do that in ways that are native to each density and which work differently in each density.

You asked concerning the way the relationships which have karmic weight impact the planetary subconscious, and we would say that the actual events in the physical illusion concerning relationships are as shadows upon the surface of the pond compared to that tremendous amount of inner work that is going on within the entities who are working with the catalyst of each other in their inner work, or as this instrument has called it, the work in consciousness that each does, however each person frames that attention. Some choose to work upon this incoming catalyst by daily meditation, and as always we recommend that process of moving into the silence very highly. It is the single most effective resource the spiritual seeker has for opening the channels to the guidance which each has in abundance within the confines of the archetypal mind which resides within and which is accessed by that door of silence more effectively than by any other means of access.

There are various ways to meditate and a contemplative walk, the reading of inspirational material, the musing upon an inspirational seed thought, and many other approaches to the silence, move one through that door as well as the more traditional ways of prayer and formal meditation which some may feel are more desirable than other methods. In our way of thinking, the method that is the most workable in each seeker's life is that method which is right for him. Again, it is a matter of the individual seeking within herself as to what choice feels right or resonant. So often in the spiritual life the seeker will find that the great authority present is the self. For within the self lies all knowledge that is sought, not in the conscious mind, not even in the subconscious mind but in those realms which are able to be accessed through the subconscious mind, the roots of mind, as this instrument would call them.

And as each moves into this silence, as each does the work of the incarnation, getting to know the self, becoming able to be that self more and more, the patterns of that vibratory nexus that is the self grow ever so slowly and ever so inexorably clearer, more lucid, and more full of that great original Thought. Consequently, the effect of this process upon the archetypical mind of your planet is that simple effect of the mind feeling that its self is moving well through that process upon which it has come to work. All the storms of confusion that ruffle the archipelago of entities and issues and situations are as nothing to those roots of mind. For to those roots of mind these processes have a virtue, not by any outer standards that this instrument would share concerning courtesy or ways of progressing that are desirable rather than others which are undesirable. Rather, the attention of the roots of mind is upon the intensity of desire and the seeking of teaching of these agents of the Creator that is attempting to become every more Itself. That which appears to be a tremendous storm upon the surface, when gazed at from the level of the roots of mind, appears to be a series of small details. It is a matter of perspective.

We would at this time pause to ask if there is a further defining of the question that we may answer before we move into the portion where other questions are entertained besides the original question for the day. May we ask at this time if there is a pursuing question upon this point of reincarnation and the metaphysical roots of mind or the archetypal mind?

(No further queries.)

We are those of Q'uo. In that case, we would at this time transfer this contact to the one known as Jim that any other questions that are entertained at this time by those present may be asked. We would thank this instrument for her service and leave her in love and in light. We are those of Q'uo.

(Jim channeling)

I am Q'uo, and greet each once again in love and in light through this instrument. At this time it is our privilege to ask if there might be any further queries that those present may have for us. Is there another query at this time?

D: I was wondering about the confusion that I have concerning delusions of grandeur and why the pathway to the source isn't clearer for me to encompass understanding with.

I am Q'uo, and am aware of your query, my brother. The feelings of the self being that which is expansive and that which is, as you have said, grand, are feelings which in and of themselves [are correct], for each entity within incarnation is the one Creator, and each entity partakes of the glory, the joy, the power, and the peace of the one Creator. However, within the illusion which you now inhabit, there are accompanying these feelings of being the one Creator also the more specific, narrowed and focused feelings and experience of being a personality with distortions of the one Creator; that is to say, each entity within the third-density illusion has those portions of itself which are yet to be fully realized. There are lessons to be learned, areas to be enhanced and seeking to be undertaken in order to accomplish the learning and serving.

Thus an entity such as yourself may, with the aid of certain substances or experiences, be able to penetrate the shell, shall we say, of the personality and to move beyond this shell to the reality of the self as the one Creator. However, there is the necessity of living the daily life, of experiencing the daily round of activities that are normal and mundane and focused upon the aiding of each entity in the pursuance of the becoming of that which one wishes to be, of learning those lessons which have been set before the incarnation. So we would say to you, my brother, that it is not necessarily a delusion, but it is not a balanced view of the self to see the self as the one Creator. Such experiences of feeling the self as being the one Creator, of being all that there is, are glimpses of the reality of each entity that need to be balanced with the experience that is now at hand in the mundane, workaday world where each works toward realizing a more full expression of this personality which has been chosen to aid the self in such growth and service.

Is there a further query, my brother?

D: What is the connection to the White Brotherhood regarding this group?

I am Q'uo, and am aware of your query, my brother. We find that there is no direct connection between this group and that group which is known as the Great White Brotherhood; that is to say, within the third-density illusion, for all are a portion of the same Creator in truth. However, the Great White Brotherhood is composed of those entities who from ages past have achieved the graduation that each here seeks. These entities, in achieving this graduation, have chosen, rather than to pursue further personal growth, to remain within this planetary sphere in the attempt to serve those brothers and sisters who yet seek this graduation.

Is there a further query, my brother?

D: If you wouldn't mind speaking about the probability of altering our harvest dates so that more may become awakened.

I am Q'uo, and am aware of your query, my brother. We would suggest that the harvest is now, that many who go through the doors of what you call death are able to harvest themselves in the service-to-others polarity predominantly. Some few in the service-to-self polarity are also achieving harvest, and as the choices that each entity within this illusion makes are made towards sharing of the love and the light of the one Creator, so is the harvest of each and all made more possible. The dates, shall we say, are relatively unimportant at this time, for the future is mazed to all eyes, and the choices of the peoples of this planetary influence are the primary force, shall we say, that determines any potential dates for harvest. The future is flexible, so that it is possible in one great turning of the mass mind to the light that a harvest date could be at any particular point in time. Though this is not probable, it is ever possible that all may see the light within themselves and other selves as well and move the compass of the needle to the service-to-others polarity in one fine moment of inspiration.

Is there another query, my brother?

D: I could probably go on all day, but thank you.

I am Q'uo, and we thank you, my brother, for your desire to seek the truth and to share the love and the light of the one Creator with those about you.

Is there a final query at this time?

Carla: I'm thinking about what you said about time, that all incarnations are occurring at the same time, and it a model of creation as a moment in which everything happens at once. It boggles the mind, and I wanted to pursue that because I had been thinking earlier about how the structures that you give us, like the Council of Saturn, for instance, the way your principle is made up of different group entities, and so forth, it has in common with the structures of time that it makes it possible to think about what I called mystery specific language. I was wondering first, if non-linear time or instantaneous time has a center like a circle and if the geometry of the circle would help us to understand more about infinity and eternity? And I was wondering if all structures of thought are these approximations that seem to have less substance than they do in space/time?

I am Q'uo, and indeed we would look to the construction of the circle, or more particularly, the sphere, as an example of the simultaneity of time and experience within the one creation. One may look at a line of experience, a line of time, that moves from the center of the sphere in a particular direction and observe the entities affected by this line of experience. Within the third-density illusion you may see yourselves as experiencing various of these time/experience lines, moving from the center of your being to another location, also within your being, intersecting experiences of others, also located within the center of your being and their being so that the center of experience is shared for a portion of the experience as it is moving along this line. This line may also be seen to be able to describe constructions of entities, groups of entities, and experiences shared so that there are various ways of seeing the formation of relationships, of seeing the means by which one creation may be experienced by a number of entities moving along these lines of time simultaneously. Thus, within this sphere there is an infinite potential for experience. Each individual experience, seen from the third-density illusion, then seems to be complete unto itself, seems to be linear from point A to B to C and so forth, whereas if this experience is seen from without the third-density illusion, it is seen as a portion of a simultaneous experience of the one Creator, these experiences being infinite in number.

Is there a further query, my sister?

Carla: So when you have a breakthrough in a relationship, does it resonate through the other lifetimes in which this issue or this relationship comes up? Does it have a ripple effect through the circle of being?

I am Q'uo, and am aware of your query, my sister. And, indeed, this is so for those who have eyes to see. However, as you are well aware, the limit to the sight is the veil of forgetting.

Carla: Indeed. But sometimes I wonder why something comes to me so clearly and I wonder why I was so puzzled before, and I just wonder if it's because that in another lifetime that I am working on this question, I may have made a breakthrough that is registered in this lifetime as a clearer understanding. If that's so, then do you still believe that there is virtue in offering these structures of thought about the mystery, deity, and the way that we begin to experience ourselves as you talk about reincarnation or as you talk about anything. What's your level of feeling that the words that you are offering through instruments such as Jim and me are of avail?

I am Q'uo, and am aware of your query, my sister. Indeed, we find a great virtue in the words offered through any instrument and, indeed, in the words which any entity may use to form a means of understanding for the self. For it is the effort to understand that is important. The words form what you may see as a channel through which ideas and inspiration may be offered from deeper portions of one's own mind which connects to the universal mind, the one infinite mind of the one Creator. Thus such constructs bring from more fundamental levels of the self and the great Self the desire to seek certain information. This information, then, finds its way to you, through you, by becoming a kind of nourishment, a kind of—we give this instrument the picture of rain falling upon the ground causing seed to sprout, a crop to grow and food to be harvested therefrom. The desire to speak causes a form to be made that itself transmits that answer to the seeking.

Is there a further query, my sister?

Carla: No. Thank you. I appreciate your words.

I am Q'uo, and again we are grateful to you, my sister. We would take this opportunity to express our gratitude to each present this day for inviting our presence in your circle of seeking. We are always grateful to join you in your seeking, for there we find great inspiration from you as well as you move within this heavy, chemical illusion seeking the one Creator with each step. We would remind each that we do not speak as authorities but would encourage each to utilize personal discrimination in taking those words which we share, those ideas, and reserving only those which ring of truth, leaving behind those that do not.

We are known to you as those of Q'uo, and would take our leave at this time of this instrument and this group, leaving each as always in the love and in the light of the one Creator. Adonai, my friends. Adonai. ✦

L/L Research

L/L Research is a subsidiary of Rock Creek Research & Development Laboratories, Inc.

P.O. Box 5195
Louisville, KY 40255-0195

www.llresearch.org

Rock Creek is a non-profit corporation dedicated to discovering and sharing information which may aid in the spiritual evolution of humankind.

ABOUT THE CONTENTS OF THIS TRANSCRIPT: This telepathic channeling has been taken from transcriptions of the weekly study and meditation meetings of the Rock Creek Research & Development Laboratories and L/L Research. It is offered in the hope that it may be useful to you. As the Confederation entities always make a point of saying, please use your discrimination and judgment in assessing this material. If something rings true to you, fine. If something does not resonate, please leave it behind, for neither we nor those of the Confederation would wish to be a stumbling block for any.

© 2009 L/L Research

Special Meditation
March 29, 2001

Group question: What is the nature of the Matrix of the Mind and how is it related to the Potentiator of the Mind? How might we apply this information to our daily lives?

(Carla channeling)

We are of the principle known to you as the Q'uo. We greet you with joy in the love and in the light of the one infinite Creator. We are most happy to have this opportunity to speak with this unique group, and we thank the instrument and the group for its dedication in making the sacrifices needed to come together at this point. We greatly appreciate that thirst for truth, that hunger for words of beauty and sustenance, that create the energy of this working and that draw us to you. We will be glad to share some of our thoughts on the archetypes of the Matrix and the Potentiator, as always requesting that each listen with very discriminating ears, taking those thoughts which may have value and leaving the rest behind, for we would not wish our thoughts to be a stumbling block before any.

When the infinite Creator wished to know Itself, Its great heart beat out the next creation with all of its densities and sub-densities and all of the patterns of those densities and creations. Time and space were invoked and that which before was immeasurable and unknowable became a series of illusions that, paradoxically, were to some degree knowable, and these shadows of knowing were much desired by the Creator. And each of these sparks and shadows became agents of the one infinite Creator, thoughts in and of themselves, thoughts rounded and centered in the one great original Thought which is Love. And so each of you is a Logos, stepped down and stepped down until you are able to experience the very illusion you now experience. And each of you has come through many experiences and many densities to this particular time, at this particular place, each balanced exquisitely in the present moment.

And as each rests in this present moment, what is the nature of each? Each is Logos and yet not Logos, not fully realized. Each is human, earthly and limited, and yet not fully human, not fully earthly, and not fully limited, for there is the growing awareness of the creatorship within. And so each is as an entity with one foot in each world, the world of the Earth and the world of infinity; the world of things and the world of thoughts.

Coming into that world of thought, that world of intention and principle, that world of desire and ideal and love, moving into the heart, we ask each to let the world of flesh retreat. As each of you rests in this world of the spirit, you have an unique viewpoint, for you are still within the body, within the incarnation, within the confusion, and yet by resting in the metaphysical, in the spiritual awareness of the heart, you have a release into spiritual things, into those things that can be trusted and depended upon to exist today, tomorrow and forever. The concerns within which you rest are concerns that will matter just as much in a thousand years, in ten thousand years, in a million years.

How easy it is when attempting to understand the archetypal mind to attempt to see that mind in the context of a busy world. And yet it is in the spiritual realm, entirely, that the world of the archetypes moves, feeding, informing, fructifying the structures of the roots of mind that, as the spirit gazes at its evolutionary spiral, it may have tools and resources with which to guide the self in the choices related to its perception of itself as an ethical being. It is in this context that we look at the nature of the Matrix and the nature of the Potentiator and their relationship with each other.

This Matrix/Potentiator axis or dynamic may fruitfully be seen as the two portions of one energy, and yet because of the complexity of these relationships it is also very useful to see these two figures as completely separate. A foundation of your density is polarity. The hope with which each comes into third density is that this thoroughgoing environment of polarity shall create more and more ways to see into the making of the choice of how to serve. And so these figures within the deep, deep roots of mind, the Matrix and the Potentiator, dwell as sigils of ways of relationship, ways of mutual thirst, mutual help, mutual feeling.

Matrix is a word that seems not even to indicate a living being but, rather, a structure, a container, a grid, qualities and aspects of self. The basic figure of Matrix is figured forth as royal. And this is not by mistake. For as a spiritual being each seeker is indeed the highest royalty, is indeed prince and king and Creator. This figure of Matrix has tremendous potential, for it is empty and waiting. The hunger for evolution is stitched and knitted into every fiber of the carefully articulated web of being that the Matrix experiences as its nature. Possessed of crown and power and royalty, it is a figure with no lack of self-respect, with no concern for being unworthy, with no unhealed issues. And coming to the mind of the Matrix as a human is the work of some time. For much of human sorrow, shame, guilt, low self-esteem and unworthiness need to be, not denied, but taken off as shoes, as garments that are upon the body of the self, but are not the self.

To enter into the Matrix one must become naked, and it is a powerful thing to accept the self as one is, powerful enough indeed that it is difficult to do.

And this is the first gate that we would suggest that each unlock to come into the unfed mind of the deep self. You do not, when you put off the clothing of self-opinion, put off the essence of self. You are not able by any trick of mind, by any cleverness of intellect, to remove from the self the essence of the self. For you are yourself. You cannot escape that energy field that you are. The vibratory nexus that you are echoes from lifetime to lifetime, from density to density throughout the creation of the Father. You are who you are, and your signature is beautiful.

Seldom can the entity within incarnation have a direct experience of the reality of that essence, and so we say to you it is something that you may take on trust. You may become naked of your self-perceptions and you shall still exist. And you may place that self that the Creator adores, that is the true you, into the Matrix of the unfed mind. And that Matrix can accept all that you are as an essence. This fit is natural and ongoing, and it is helpful to go through the exercise of moving into the unfed mind of the Matrix of the deep mind and to experience at once the royalness of being who you are and the utter humility of being empty. For as the Matrix you know nothing but thirst and hunger. You are a creature yearning and seeking with an appetite that is keen, unending and driven by the wind of spirit from creation to creation. As the Matrix, once settled in that persona, all thought moves to the reaching, the seeking, the hoping for fulfillment.

The Potentiator is cast also as a royal being. And it is perhaps efficacious in terms of what we would give to this entity at this time to figure forth this Potentiator as the guardian angel, the guidance, the guru, the agent of divine change. This is an entity royal with that same creatorship, full of the essence of that great Self which is the one original Thought which is love. Although each may fruitfully at other times see this agent as the self, yet in this discussion we will allow the seeing of this agent as a gift-giver to one who opens the hands without knowing what it has. For as the Matrix reaches to the Potentiator, the need of the Matrix creates the gifts of the Potentiator. It is not that spiritual evolution consists in step A, step B, step C and so forth, a lesson plan and a linear set of things to learn, things to do, things to encompass with the mind, but, rather, it is as though the unfed mind, by its thirst, by the intensity of its thirst, and by the direction of its seeking, creates an unending grove of trees whose fruits drop into the hands of the seeker, who then eats that fruit and receives knowledge peculiar to the soil in which that fruit grew, the soil of that particular seeking, the soil of that particular response from spirit.

There is a constant organic and mutual back and forth of information between the Matrix who reaches and the Potentiator who awaits the reaching. And all that is hidden within the Potentiator changes every time the Potentiator releases fruit from behind that veil. That is the hidden nature of things unknown. One person on one day shall receive fruit from spirit. That same person on another day with just the tiniest change in seeking, in attitude, in state of mind, shall receive an entirely different fruit. So we cannot offer the comfortable assurance that all is in safe hands, that all is prepared, that all will go one way. The archetypal journey is far more creative and far more plastic.

What can be trusted beyond all telling is the protected nature of this work in consciousness. It is as though, as the seeker dedicates itself to the seriousness of its desire, it alerts a large body of discarnate protection which this instrument would probably call inner-planes or angelic. Whatever the description of this energy, it is devoted to being sure that, whatever the incarnational situation, whatever the physical situation doing this seeking, this work shall be protected. This thirst and its fulfillment shall be blessed.

We stand, in speaking of the Matrix and the Potentiator, at the beginning of a deep, deep road, a very fruitful road, a most promising road that shall be wended not just within your present lifetime or your present density, but through several densities to come. You are at the beginning of a journey of self-knowledge that shall bring surprise upon surprise, awareness upon awareness and yet we say to you that at each of the spirals of awareness, including that one at which you now are, you are already that being which you hope to become. And by the bare attempt to seek within the archetypes you bring resonances of that being to your waking personality which strengthen and have a tendency to heal the waking personality. We would thusly encourage each to do this work in consciousness. Not hastily. Not without respect. And certainly not without preparation.

For doing this work without preparation can be unbalancing to the energetic body. And so we would caution each before doing such work in consciousness, always to begin with the meditation, with the balancing of the energy system, with the clearing of the lower to the higher energy centers to a minimal degree so that the energy system that is doing this work is without significant imbalance. For when there are shadows that block energy into the heart, then it is that there is not energy coming through into the green, blue and indigo-ray energy centers where this work in consciousness is taking place. Consequently, we do encourage that work, before a session of meditating upon the archetypes, where there is the attempt to balance the energy system and to settle it so that not only the physical body but also the metaphysical body is rested and balanced and ready to receive those piercing energies which flow from the roots of mind and fructify the waking consciousness.

We would at this time transfer this contact to the one known as Jim. We thank this instrument and leave it in love and in light. We are those of the Q'uo.

(Jim channeling)

I am Q'uo, and greet each again in the love and the light of the one Creator through this instrument. It is our privilege at this time to ask if there might be any further queries from those gathered here to which we may respond.

S: Yes, I have a query. First I would like to thank those of Q'uo and both instruments for what I consider to be heroism above and beyond the call of duty. This has been very, very helpful to me, and I appreciate it. My question brings in the concept of the Significator as this relates to the coming together of the Matrix and Potentiator. I am particularly interested in the concept of sacrifice and whether it would be useful to see it in relation to the Significator and the coming together of the Matrix and Potentiator?

I am Q'uo, and we are aware of your query, my brother. We are also grateful for this opportunity to blend our vibrations with the vibrations of those present today.

We would respond to your query by suggesting that the concept of sacrifice, the giving of the self for the benefit of another or for the benefit of a principle, shall we say, is indeed a salient feature of the blending of the Matrix and Potentiator so that the fruits of this blending, the stuff of your third density, may become a portion of the quality known as the Significator or the significant self. For it is the Significator that is the actor upon the stage of creation that is able to become more than it is because of the efforts of those qualities known as Matrix and Potentiator. That there is the sacrifice of comfort, of convenience, of opportunity, of any quality that gives stability and assurance to the entity, is significant and is registered as a great desire that seeks fulfillment by the significant self. The self of each seeker desires union with the Creator, desires knowledge of the Creator, of the self and of the creation. This knowledge, passionately sought, willingly sacrificed for, may only be obtained when one is willing to give of the self in a degree which is reflective of this great desire. Thus the experiences that each so eagerly seeks within each incarnation are dearly bought. The greater sacrifice purchases, shall we say, the greater knowledge, experience, union and presence of the one Creator. Is there a further query, my brother?

S: Yes, thank you. That too is very good. One other, and this is one that I feel comes from my beloved M. It is very difficult to feel one's self to be one for whom sacrifices are made and to feel a sense of self-worth and to try to keep one's head high and to feel that one too is making a contribution. Can you give us some words of encouragement that speak to that issue?

I am Q'uo, and am aware of your query, my brother. We would respond by suggesting that in the relationship in which you are so completely engaged with the one known as M, that there are sacrifices upon both parts which are most courageous for we see that it is in your illusion so easy to mistake that which is of value. There is the worldly measure of accomplishment and potential for accomplishment that is in truth only of peripheral value, for it is the heart of desire in each entity as each entity seeks the Creator within which is of most importance. The one Creator has flung from Its being the infinite creation and all entities that populate it in the attempt that It might know Itself in ways unavailable to It before such creation came about. When one, especially within the third-density illusion, sets one's self the task of seeking this Creator within the self as purely and as passionately as the one known as M has done, this reverberates to the heart of the one Creator in a manner which is most significant. For by removing the ability to work in the worldly sense one has set the challenge before one's self that is as focused as is possible within this illusion. All of the mundane world, shall we say, has been set aside for the single purpose of opening the heart in love and service to others. This, done as the one known as M has accomplished it, will achieve the metaphysical polarity in a significant sense, in a most efficacious sense, and all who touch this entity's being are aware of the brilliance of the light within.

Is there a further query, my brother?

S: No. Thank you very much.

Is there a final query at this time?

(No further queries.)

I am Q'uo, and we would again thank each present who has joined this circle of seeking this day. We are most grateful to be with you and at this time we would take our leave of this instrument and this group. We leave each, as always, in the love and in the ineffable light of the one infinite Creator. Adonai, my friends. Adonai. ☥

L/L Research

Sunday Meditation
April 1, 2001

Group question: The question today has to do with what is the most harmonious way to achieve closure in a relationship when the person that you are trying to achieve closure with won't talk to you? And when you feel a strong emotion in desiring to close a relationship, is there anything that you can do internally for yourself that doesn't involve another person? How much of this is an internal process?

(Carla channeling)

We are those known to you as Hatonn, and we greet you in the love and in the light of the one infinite Creator. It is our privilege and our blessing to be called to your group this afternoon, and we thank you for this blessing. We send each of you our love and our blessing as well. We ask that each of you discriminate carefully in listening to what we have to say, taking what is good to you and leaving behind the rest. We travel with you as companions, not as authorities, and would not be a stumbling block in any way.

We almost hesitated to begin speaking because the meditation was quite beautiful to us, and we know that our words are not as full of meaning or beauty as the silence. But you have asked for some information about how to end a relationship when the ending must be done by one and not the other. And so we must use words to offer our opinion on that interesting subject. This instrument requests that we express why we are here instead of those of Q'uo. It is the nature of this particular question that has brought forth the energy of our social memory complex of Hatonn. We are of the love vibration, and truly there are some concerns that are addressed through the totally open heart rather than through wisdom or any mix of love and wisdom.

One of these concerns of the open heart is forgiveness, and although it may not seem that affecting closure of a relationship has particularly to do with forgiveness, in actuality it has a great deal to do with this somewhat difficult concept. The relationships that come into the life, any life in any density, are a gift of the self to the self. Incarnation is a special period within the timeless circle of being, when time and space take hold and the personality that you are sets off on an adventure. You give yourself resources and things to carry for this adventure. You give yourself targeted issues that you wish to explore for incarnational lessons, and you give yourself relationships by whose means these issues may be addressed most efficiently. Relationships are ideally experienced as the coming together of two entities who work with more and more harmony until all of the learning between them has been accomplished, and all of the possibilities of service between them have also been explored and generous gifts given. So it is that each relationship teaches and gives us the opportunity to share our gifts and to be of service. And in actuality this is what happens, but on the level of the physical illusion it often may seem that the expression of a relationship is sadly incomplete and must be left in what seems to be an inharmonious condition.

In some cases there is no recourse upon the level of the physical illusion from seeing relationships end before the self is ready for them to end, before the expression has been or is felt to be complete. The other entity in the relationship may well have passed from this physical illusion, thus ending the direct chance of communication. There may be such a separation between the two entities from the impact of circumstances and differences of opinion that there is no longer the opportunity to communicate. Certainly many emotions can come between two entities, making it impossible for them to be successful at speaking with each other, whether because of anger and guilt or simple misunderstanding.

The desire of the spirit within incarnation is mixed because the spirit within incarnation is a mixed being, and by that we mean that on the one hand there is the personality which wishes to be comfortable and to manipulate and control situations for comfort and safety. There is also that completely spiritual being which has very little to do with time and space but has a great deal to do with ideals and inspirations and mystery and, oddly enough, ethics, so that there is that part of a spiritually awakened entity that at all times wishes to do everything possible to create the most ethically pure situation where all respect has been given, all communication has been harmonized, and all differences have been healed as well as words can heal them.

In many cases for a spiritually awakened entity the situation is that the other entity has chosen not to follow the call of the highest and best and has, therefore, simply decided to end a relationship without communication. When you are faced with this situation we may suggest that the first work to be done is simply to release the situation from your conscious control. It is amazing that there is not more pain connected with relationships, for indeed in almost all cases two entities in relationship will have many areas of pain and soreness. We encourage again and again the communication between loving beings that is honest and clear, saying the hard thing as well and as kindly as possible, for it is in the saying of the hard things and in the bringing up of difficulties, in the exposing of the self in its vulnerabilities and its pain that entities begin to become closer and start to generate the kind of unconditional trust that is necessary for that experience of having true intimacy between two people.

Within your density it is virtually impossible to know when you have hurt someone, how you have hurt someone, where the sore spots are, where the sensitive areas lie. And if another entity will not share this information with you, then what intuition does not tell you remains unknown. And how painful this is, both for the self who is missing the mark unknowingly and for the other self who has not the strength of character to speak up and express in a gentle and loving way the needs that must be met, the limits of being that must be confessed, the self-perceived faults that must be shared.

The second thing that we would say is that this situation of unrequited communication is sometimes part of the lesson that is yours to learn in having this relationship. When one is dealing with a repeated issue, especially one they see repeatedly crop up, where it is not simply the releasing of another entity, it is also the releasing of an issue that lies behind the failure to communicate within the relationship. For those lessons which you came to learn and those gifts which you came to share may in some cases overpower the personalities involved in a relationship, so that it is helpful to probe what was brought up within that relationship that it may be seen that there were impersonal elements in the relationship that have no need to be discussed with the other but only with the self.

In this entity's experience, for example, this one known as Carla has had the experience of discovering after the fact that communication intended to help has indeed hurt to the extent that further harmonious relationship was impossible. Was this entity at fault? To any way of perceiving, no. Is another entity at fault because it cannot defend itself? To any perceived way of thinking, again, no. Sometimes for two entities the issues become larger than the relationship, and for the entities it is well to think, for the one known as Carla, what is the issue that sits squarely at the heart of the inability to communicate? For this entity the incarnational issue happens to be, "How do I serve another entity?" And it is in the light of service to others that this entity will then find closure to a relationship that seems to be hanging.

But at a level deeper than this, at a level deeper than lessons and personality shells, the lessons are all about love. And we would pause that each within the circle may re-center the self upon the realization in this moment of the utter love in which each abides. Each is the one infinite Thought of love, brought into flesh, given a voice and hands to do, to serve and to be. But each moves with the breath of love, with the energy of light, with the power of deity. And from the standpoint of that loving nature, each is as a vibration and that vibration is an expression of love. It is well to remember this deep and constant nature of self, for certainly upon the surface of the physical incarnation, in the everyday experience, there are many rough waters and puzzling events aplenty.

It is well to remember that all things come down to issues of love, forgiveness, acceptance and release. In this particular instance where there is a desire to find closure in a relationship without the advantage of communication from the other party, the largest issue is forgiveness. And it is not simply forgiveness of another self although this certainly is involved, but rather it is coming to see that that person is a part of the self which the self does not happen to be able to control. However, the self can control the emotions and the direction of thinking within the heart. It can determine for the self to release and forgive all shadows that appear to blot the beauty of another person at the soul level and to know that person again as that person has been known before, as perfect, without blot or blame or sin of any kind. For this is the true nature, not only of that person, but of the self and of all that is. Once that other entity has been released from its stricture within your heart, the remaining work of forgiveness lies within the self. For although the issue seems to have to do with another entity, in truth all things come back to the self, and the other self is not forgiven until the self has forgiven the self.

When there has been a great deal of trauma, emotionally and mentally, it may not seem to the self that there has been any blame attached to the self. It may seem that all has been done beautifully and with a perfectly intended positive outcome hoped for. And we do not say that these things are not true. We only say that they are true for each entity, so that if one were to speak to the other in the relationship in this situation where two cannot speak together it may be that an entirely different story would come forth, a story unrecognizable from the standpoint of the self, so changed are the events that actually took place between the two by the viewpoints of the two different people. However, spiritually speaking it is perfectly possible and very highly recommended by us to pursue the closure of such a relationship until the heart within the self is completely satisfied and the processes of healing then can progress. Once all blame, anger and so forth have been lifted from the other person and the focus has shifted to the heart within the self, then it is that the true work can be done with much more helpfulness and efficiency. There are no issues within the self of infringing on the free will for it is the own free will of the self that is involved, and you can decide that which you wish to do without fearing that you have trodden on sore feet.

For many a physical action is very helpful in attaining closure of such a heart-breaking and difficult situation. In order to invoke the forces of what this instrument would call Mother Nature we would suggest something direct such as writing down all of those things which you wish to say, one after the other, in exquisite detail, leaving out nothing, but saying everything that you hoped to say. Then we would suggest one of two ways of alerting nature and the forces of nature of your need for closure. One way would be ritually and carefully to burn such a letter, offering it up to the infinite Creator. Another way would be to take such a letter, to wrap it around something physical such as a piece of tree root or a rock or small pebble and burying it, again with some ritual words designed to express the willingness to release this situation from human control and judgment.

Underlying this act is a faith in the rightness of the relationship as it is in its seeming imperfection. If there is absolutely no desire for further relationship with the entity with whom closure is desired we would suggest burning. If there is the desire to invoke the forces of time so that in any future in which such relationship and such issues may again be worked upon that there is willingness to do the work, we would suggest burying. But in both cases we would suggest the most careful thought as to the expression you wish to make as you burn or as you bury, seeing this in true terms of closure, seeing the making of an end and asking the self, "How can I make the most loving and most harmonious end? How can I release this soul to move along its path with the most open heart?" Let this be a concern that brings forth the words that are the highest and the most loving that can be found while at the same time being completely honest and sincere.

Remember that you deal with fragile, fragile beings when you come into relationship. It may seem that you are fighting a tremendously powerful force, yet you are only fighting yourself. The shadow of self within this other self, just like you, is a delicate, sensitive, vulnerable spirit, often confused, and often out of control. Even when we think we are in control, many times there are emotions that are impure and issues that have not been fully realized that bias and distort perception. This is the nature of the physical illusion that you enjoy at this time. To some extent it is still the nature of our environment. We can be fooled by ourselves. We can be fooled in subtle ways in relationship. This work goes on past your density. Yet it is good to deal with. It is indeed the very stuff of spiritual evolution. To work on relationships is to purify the emotions and to center the self again and again in humility and a desire to be of service.

Realize in a very deep way that the job of the self is to give and receive love. The work of receiving love is done when it is perceived as being offered. The work of loving is endless, for it does not take the agreement of another person to love that person. All beings may be loved without infringement of free will. So we encourage each to work on loving without expectation of return, without attachment to the outcome of a letter or a telephone call or any other communication, but loving into the void, into the abyss, that is a life lived in faith.

We would at this time transfer this contact to the one known as Jim. We thank this instrument and leave it in love and in light. We are those known to you as Hatonn.

(Jim channeling)

I am Hatonn, and greet each again in love and in light. We would ask those present if there may be any further queries which we might address this day?

Carla: I would ask if you would like to comment on why we got you instead of Q'uo. You did say something about that. I would be glad to hear anything further.

I am Hatonn. We are always eager to lend our vibrations to this group, for we have been with this group for a great portion of your time. When there is a certain configuration of seeking within your circle of seeking, then it is our privilege to join you in word and with our vibrations. And so we do so today. May we ask if there is another question?

Carla: No. I am glad to talk to you. I just asked about it because it is unusual and hadn't happened in a long time. I'm very glad to talk to you. There have been requests to talk to Oxal and Yadda as well, but I haven't exactly known how to request certain entities because I just ask for the highest and best contact that I can carry in a stable manner and that almost always comes up Q'uo. Thank you very much.

I am Hatonn, and we thank you, my sister. May we ask if there is another question at this time?

S: My niece has very few things that she will eat, and even the things she does eat, she is removing some of those from her diet now. My brother and his wife are concerned, and I am curious as to the reason for what she is doing. Is there anything that we can do to help her?

I am Hatonn. We are not well aware of this entity and must speak in most general terms, for it is not our forte to look to individual vibrational complexes in order to diagnose the difficulties therein. We may suggest that when an entity finds that there is little of the foodstuffs that it is interested in, and this is most often especially the case with the young children of your peoples, that the need [is] for the intake of love from those that are the parents and the, shall we say, significant entities in the life pattern. For in its most basic sense, your food is love. It allows the life force to continue to move through the physical vehicle, and the young entity will equate the foodstuffs with this quality of love that is needed most basically by all entities, especially by the younger entity. If there is some manner in which attention may be given to this young child in a more understandable manner, perhaps then the reflection of being full of love will manifest in the eating habits as well. May we ask if there is another question, my brother?

S: Are there any words of wit or wisdom from our unseen friends that join us in our circle today?

I am Hatonn. We consider your query and may report that the verbal communication has been left to us this day, which we are happy to undertake.

However, we would remind each entity present that the means of communication that is most effective is not that which is mind to mind or mind to ear, but that which is heart to heart. Those entities which join us this day, who are not visible to your physical eyes, send this vibration of love to each present with greetings, with blessings and with benedictions that each may be well and may reflect this love to all about it. Is there another question, my brother?

S: Not from me right now. Thank you.

I am Hatonn, and we are grateful to you as well, my brother. Is there another question at this time?

R: I have no question but feel that I want to say that it is nice to hear Hatonn. It does not always happen, and thanks for speaking of love because it does come through.

I am Hatonn. We are also grateful for your presence and the love that we feel from you and indeed that we feel from each within this circle this day. We would ask if there may be a final query before we take our leave of this group?

(No further queries.)

I am Hatonn. We find that the thanks and the love and the sincere desire to seek that we have found within this circle are reflected also within our hearts to each here this day and to all those who hunger within the population of your planet. For there is to our ears a great call for love at this time from this planetary population. We are honored to be but a small number of the great heavenly host that answers this call at this time. If each will take the time in each day to meditate and to seek there the one Creator, there is where this love may be found in its most obvious quality and sense. For within the daily round of activities that is normal to most of your population, the noise and static, the hustle, the bustle, the hurrying is much too loud for most ears and heart to hear. But within the heart of your heart, there is the voice of love speaking directly to each. We are know to you as those of Hatonn, and we would take our leave of this instrument and this group at this time. Adonai, my friends. Adonai vasu borragus. ☥

L/L Research

L/L Research is a subsidiary of Rock Creek Research & Development Laboratories, Inc.

P.O. Box 5195
Louisville, KY 40255-0195

www.llresearch.org

Rock Creek is a non-profit corporation dedicated to discovering and sharing information which may aid in the spiritual evolution of humankind.

ABOUT THE CONTENTS OF THIS TRANSCRIPT: This telepathic channeling has been taken from transcriptions of the weekly study and meditation meetings of the Rock Creek Research & Development Laboratories and L/L Research. It is offered in the hope that it may be useful to you. As the Confederation entities always make a point of saying, please use your discrimination and judgment in assessing this material. If something rings true to you, fine. If something does not resonate, please leave it behind, for neither we nor those of the Confederation would wish to be a stumbling block for any.

© 2009 L/L Research

Sunday Meditation
May 6, 2001

Group question: The question today has to do with the eternal spiritual principles that each seeker of truth pursues. At some point in the spiritual journey a seeker will lose some of the original passion that propelled the seeking to begin with, and we would like Q'uo to give us information about how the seeker can find again that passion in the seeking. How can we as seekers of truth keep our passion high, or is it necessary to have periods of rest?

(Carla channeling)

We are those known to you as the principle of the Q'uo. We greet you in the love and in the light of the one infinite Creator. It is our privilege and our blessing to be called to your group this afternoon, and we thank each who is a part of this circle, those present and those who are joining this circle from a distant location. The dedication and desire for truth that each of you expresses creates the vibration that has called us to you. And we thank you very much, for it is our chosen service to offer our thoughts to those who would seek to hear a slightly different slant on that story which is always and ever the same. That story that is always the same is a story about love.

Your question to us this day is also, in an important way, about love. For when you are in a passionate stage of seeking your heart is on fire with that which is love. The story of love is a very simple story. The Creator loves each and every spark and atom of creation with a love that is beyond all that can be imagined. This love is as the energy which drives the infinite universe, and it is the spark within the heart of each of the Creator's children. The love of the Creator is as a unified, infinitely intelligent Thought that we have often called the Logos. Logos is the word which the one known as St. Paul the Apostle used and the one known as St. John when they wrote those books of your Bible in which the love of the Creator was discussed. The one known as John, who wrote the Gospel of John in your Bible, also used this word when this entity wrote, "In the beginning was the Word." In the beginning was the Logos. And each of you is made of that same Thought that is the Creator and the created. And each of you, having received this infinite gift of life and spirit and being, has created through the winding trail of experiences and thoughts many, many shadows and variations on that original Thought of Love so that each of you vibrates in love, and yet with many unique characteristics of your own which mark each of you with a signature which is unmistakable. We would know each of you in any density and in any form of body which you would take, for each of your souls is unique.

The question this day concerns the cycles of seeking that you experience, the ups and downs of being very excited about a certain body of material that seems to hold true and then being not so excited about that material and perhaps, then, being drawn to another body of material and becoming excited about that. As this instrument was saying earlier in the discussion that preceded the mediation, there is only one truth. There is nothing new under the sun. And we would be the first to agree with this instrument. We have often said to this group that our story is too simple to be told in an understandable fashion. We work through channels such as this one because each channel has a personality and an attitude which enrich our simple story with words and images that we are able to use to find a new way to share our hearts with you. And this is what the thousand thousand entities who are inspired with the love of the Creator offer. Some of these sources have been codified as holy works. Some of these sources have never written their words down at all. And many are somewhere in between.

Each entity that you may meet as a seeker, each book that has been offered, is one of the thousand thousand faces of the Creator, one of the million stories about the Creator, one of the myriad of structures in thought for happening upon the Creator. Within the incarnational cycle of living there are numerous cycles. The day revolves light and dark. The year in its seasons brings about the warmth and the chill of summer and winter. Each cell of the body is renewed every so many years of your physical vehicle, and each has experienced daily, monthly, yearly and multi-year cycles of growth within the emotional, mental and spiritual parts of yourself. It is natural indeed that even the most devoted student of the very best story would find after a certain period of time that there was enough of that source within the being, that the self is full and sated with that story, with that truth, with that face of the Creator. This does not necessarily mean that it is time to move on, as this instrument has experienced within her walk within the Christian faith. She has found that walking through the desert of unbelief, walking through the difficult and bleak times when there is no spontaneous inspiration has its own very powerful effect upon faith.

And those who choose a religious path or a philosophical path as a life path are very wise to remain upon that path in good times and in bad. But there are many entities, many sparks of the one infinite Creator who are not able, for one reason or another, to resonate and respond to the story, the truth and the face of the Creator that lie within that religion or philosophy that is offered. These are entities that will make their own paths, and these are entities that may well find themselves not simply moving in and out of a passionate love of one body of material but in and out of respect for and devotion to and learning from several or even many different sources of inspiration and guidance as the path moves through years of living and experience. We do not in any sense recommend one way of pursuing truth over another. For entities such as this instrument we find one path to be extremely helpful and the sticking to that one path extremely wise. For those who do not resonate to one path but who find their food from this and then another and then another source we simply commend to those seekers all that is old and all that is new in their experience.

Even if the seeker attempts to stick with one body of material she will be cycling each time she reads through the same holy words into another period of her own learning and, therefore, she will come to that material as a new person, so that spiritual words are never actually old, for each time that you come to them you are a new entity with a new and more informed mind and heart. Sometimes it may seem to you that you are actually moving backwards and regressing, and this is expressed well by the one known as T who was somewhat disappointed in himself because his passion for the particular material that he had previously loved so much was no longer running so hot. And yet we say to those who may feel this way that even were you to move back into that same material and be kindled anew for that material, it would not be coming back to the same material. Rather, it would be looking at it with new eyes and finding a new level of learning and inspiration within those pages.

That which the seeker seeks may seem to be within the words of holy works or inspirational works, but in fact the truth lies beyond the words of those books. For truth cannot be written down. Truth lies within the heart. Truth lies within essence. Within your illusion, within the poor words which we offer through this instrument, within all words, lie nothing more substantial than dreams. The world as you experience it is a very thick illusion made up of atoms and molecules and a great deal of space and energy fields. Those energy fields are thoughts. You as an entity are a kind of thought. And what you hope to do, what you seek to do, what you yearn to do when you are seeking for truth, is bring your thought, your energy field, your light, if you will, more and more into tune, into harmony and eventually into unison with the Thought that is the one great original Logos of love.

This desire is what calls you through all of your seeking and whatever reading or studying that it may call you to, you will find, as you move more into a particular study, that this study is not bringing you to truth, but, rather, is bringing you to a place from which you can begin to think about truth in a way that resonates to you. And this is why it is very important for those who are not inspired by a certain book or a certain source any more to move forward, to keep the eyes open and the heart open to receive a new story, a new image, a new way to think about the Divine. Whatever inspiration comes to you, the truth within it lies beyond it. The truth of all words, philosophy and religion lies in the silence that is invoked when the seeker comes to the end of the words, releases all from the mind, and allows the heart to open to the silence that is the true essence of the ether or fluid within which true learning takes place, within your spirit or soul.

Religious and philosophical seeking brings the student to the place where finally all the stories fall away. The heart is opened, and at last the soul can rest and tabernacle with the one infinite Creator in power, in peace and in love. The comfort, the joy, the bliss of that companionship of the one infinite Creator is not out there somewhere, but, rather, within the heart, that same heart that beats so strongly within the body. This heart has a metaphysical component that is just as powerful a pump as the physical heart. And the Creator waits for each of us within that heart energy.

We wish that our words were not so poor. And yet at the same time we are grateful that we are able to share them. We wish we could share truth instead of the story about truth. But as long as we use words we will be telling a story. We will be dreaming dreams. Yet know that within the dream of each of your lives, within the seeming illusion of everyday, the reality of truth and love abides. There is nothing unreal about your illusion. It is very real. It is just not what it seems. The Creator is everywhere. Your heaven is everywhere, within you, without you, in every speck of the creation of the Father. Teachers are everywhere: the frog upon the rock, the iris blooming in the garden, the raven out the window. All the familiar images of this particular day in this particular year within this particular life experience are divine as well as mundane, enspirited as well as illusion.

In many ways we have nothing to say. There is nothing to teach and nothing to learn. For that which is truly within each of you is already perfect. It is a matter, always, of finding those resonances, those special words, those special people, those special images that bring the Creator alive to you that you must value and be on the alert to look for. They are everywhere, and the Creator is extremely redundant about being sure that you have many messengers to keep you on the track that you hoped to be on within your incarnational experience.

You asked whether it was a good idea to attempt to be on fire for the Creator all of the time. And we would say to you that it is not a state of mind that on the surface is passionate, that we would encourage seeking as a steady state. In terms of the surface experience we would encourage experiencing as truly and really as possible what is being felt at each moment, for you are not attempting to direct the way you experience the Creator. Rather, you are simply attempting to know more of the Creator. And so we ask you to release from any judgment your view of yourself as being good when you have passion and being not so good when you are less passionate about a way of seeking. Rather, we would encourage in terms of the steady state the remembrance of the Divine, the remembrance of who you are and whose you are. It does not matter how you feel about that. What matters most is the persistent and heart-felt orientation of the self with the Creator. Simply to remember the Creator is what we would recommend as the request made by the self of the self for every day. Attempt, if you can, to remember every day that you are the Creator's child and that the Creator loves you more than you can ever imagine.

Try to remember every day to find a thankfulness for the opportunity of life and being. If you can but remain faithful to the remembrance of your true essence the flow and the stream of life will bring you every lesson you need, every inspiration, every truth, every opportunity for service. It may not seem at times as though this were true. It may seem at times as though there was nothing but confusion and chaos and not much comfort. And yet we say to you simply remember in good times and in woe that you are the child of Love and that you are here to love and to be loved.

If you can but enter the silence for five minutes within each day and tabernacle with that love that created you, that would be a tremendous achievement, and certainly all that you need to ask of yourself as a seeker. Of course, each of you will be inspired to many more than five minutes in the silence in many days. There will be times of excitement and they will cycle predictably. Realize that when you see yourself going through the cycles that it is a natural phenomenon, not born of your shallowness or your unworthiness but, rather, of the seasons of your soul, that come and go, that blow hot and cold with the warmth and the chill of a close or a distant Creator. These are the ways things will feel to you and this is part of the experience of life. It is acceptable to us, each shade of that cycle. For no matter where you are on that cycle, you still are vibrating with that unique signature of self. You still are a creature made of love and expressing love.

Every moment of your life will not be inspired. But every moment of your life will be filled with love. For that is all that there is, the Love that created you and the light from which the Creator made your body and all of the creation. We always greet you in love and in light because that is all that there is. All that there is, is the one infinite Logos.

We would at this time leave this instrument and transfer the contact to the one known as Jim. We leave this instrument in love and in light. We are known to you as Q'uo.

(Jim channeling)

I am Q'uo, and greet each again in love and in light through this instrument. It is our privilege at this time to ask if we might be of service to those present by attempting to answer further queries which may be upon the mind. Is there another query at this time?

Carla: I have a question *(from M)* that asks, "I am a follower of Rael and it was revealed to him in 1973 and 1975 that all life on Earth was created scientifically by extraterrestrial Elohim as it was described to him in religious texts. What is the role of Rael in the spiritual evolution of humanity?"

I am Q'uo, and we are aware of the query, my sister, but we find that there is a concern that you are well aware of, that we are not willing to infringe upon the free will of what this entity has to share. We are aware that there has been a great deal of, shall we say, assistance from sources of extraterrestrial, as you would call them, visitation from your days of old in which there was interaction between the population of your Earth at that time and many who came from elsewhere with the intention of assisting in the evolution of not only this planet's population but this planet itself as well. This we can confirm. However, we would not suggest that the entire population of this planetary sphere was so seeded by extraterrestrial sources. There have been much, shall we say, later additions by more normal means to this planet's population. The entity, Rael, is one who works in this area with a desire to be of service. However, we find that our ability to speak upon this entity any further must be bated by our concern for the first distortion. Is there a further query, my sister?

Carla: As a follow up I was wondering if you would identify this group Rael is talking about as the entities Sitchin is talking about in his books as the Anunnaki who came to the Sumerian and Egyptian regions allegedly about 11,000 years ago?

I am Q'uo, and am aware of your query, my sister. There is a connection that is related to this entity from those called Anak, the Anunnaki. However, there is much distortion as well within the writings of the one known as Sitchen so that there is more emphasis in these writings given to the influence from elsewhere. There is also the difficulty of the time frame. We do not choose to correct this difficulty, for there is some infringement possible there as well. Is there a further question?

Carla: No, Q'uo. I would just say that those are two more stories about the infinite Creator. Thank you very much.

I am Q'uo, and we thank you as well, my sister. Again we apologize for our lack of information in this area. As you have correctly noted, all such stories are stories of the one Creator and Its movement within the one creation. However, some of the entities of your peoples are enough swayed by this kind of information that we must take care that we do not influence such beliefs overly much. Is there another question at this time?

T: Yes. I have a grandson named D, and I have a very strong feeling that he and I are connected, more so than we all are part of the Creator. I feel that there is some connection to my former wife, E, and I don't know if you can comment, but I would appreciate some elucidation on your part.

I am Q'uo, and am aware of your query, my brother. As you have yourself realized there is indeed a connection that is karmic and is one which has connections [to] other entities as well as the one which you have mentioned. As is often the case in the reincarnative pattern of entities upon this third-density sphere there has been interaction between you and this entity, the one known as D, in many previous experiences. However, we are not able to give more specific information at this time because of our desire to maintain the free will of both the one known as D and yourself. Again, we must apologize for being shy of information. Is there another query, my brother?

T: No. Thank you. Thank you very much.

I am Q'uo, and we thank you for your sincerity, your compassion and your dedication to seeking the truth. Is there another query at this time?

S: I have a question. My wife has many times fallen back into the patterns that cause her a great deal of stress. Is there anything that I can do or provide to alleviate this stress that she feels?

I am Q'uo, and am aware of your query, my brother. When an entity such as your wife has repeated experiences of a similar nature, in this case the carrying of the load of stress, it is difficult to share such a load until this entity has been able to fathom the depths of the lesson to be learned. There is the matter of the feeling of responsibility which is felt by this entity that is connected to the feeling of the stress. The responsibility itself is also added unto by the entity's feelings regarding sustenance, abundance, plenty. This entity explores these areas of its own nature in order that it might more fully experience the presence of the one Creator in its daily round of activities. This exploration of the connection to unity, to power, to peace is one which this entity has long pursued and which this entity wishes to balance by its current experience of that which you call stress. There is much which can be done to support such efforts and lessons in that there is the need to value both upon your part and hers the amount of work that is truly necessary for this entity's learning of that which she has set before herself. The basic questions in this series of lessons concern the amount of effort necessary to secure the feelings of abundance, self-worth and the providing for those in this entity's care. There is a boundary now that we find beyond which we do not wish to go, for again there is only so much of the setting of the table that is possible before infringement occurs. Perhaps at a future time further queries may be appropriate and further response given. Is there another query, my brother?

S: It gives me plenty to share and think about myself. Thank you. I guess my last question is again, our unseen visitors seem to be bashful and I was wondering if you could tell us anything about our unseen friends here today?

I am Q'uo, and am aware of your query, my brother. Those of the goodly company, shall we say, are what you may call somewhat boring in that their constant aim is to assist each by offering the vibrations of love and light to all those within the circle of seeking to be used as each sees fit. This unspoken offering of assistance is one which is offered to many of the inhabitants of this planetary sphere, indeed to each by some entities, for this is their work, as you would call it, in regards to this planet's current position in the harvest of souls. For the population of this planet at this time is seeded according to those whose likelihood of attaining harvest is greatest. Oftentimes it is not possible to do any more than send this unseen love and light, for many entities are not open to any other kind of communication or assistance from those of the Confederation of Planets in the Service of the one Creator. Those within this circle of seeking, however, are more familiar with such entities and the concepts which are shared in these sessions of working. Thus, the assistance can frequently be altered into more perceptible offerings, that being the hunches or intuitions which each feels when considering certain options or actions, paths to pursue in future endeavors. Thus it is well for each seeker to not only seek with persistence and sincerity but to take careful note of those feelings or flashes of inspiration, of intuition, of purpose, of direction that come in the silent and sacred times of meditation, contemplation and prayer. Here, within the inner room, is the opportunity to meet more closely those who stand in the shadows behind the curtains of light, shall we say, to offer what is possible to offer. Is there a further query, my brother?

S: So, is it appropriate to not only appreciate the efforts that they have given, to also ask for that assistance from them to help others when the opportunity arises?

I am Q'uo, and this is most appropriate, my brother, for the request for intercession on behalf of other entities is one selfless means of service that is always appreciated by the goodly company, or the heavenly host. Is there another query, my brother?

S: I just want to say that it is greatly appreciated from this side, too. I have no other queries. Thank you.

I am Q'uo. And again we thank you. Is there a final query at this time?

(Pause)

I am Q'uo, and as we feel that there is no further query at this time we shall thank each present for inviting us to join your circle of seeking this day. As always it is a great privilege and honor for us to do so. We would remind each that we do not seek to be authorities and would ask that each use the personal discrimination to take those words which we have offered that ring of truth and to leave all others behind. At this time we shall take our leave of this instrument and this group, leaving each in the love and in the light of the one Creator. We are known to you as those of Q'uo. Adonai, my friends. Adonai.

L/L Research

L/L Research is a subsidiary of Rock Creek Research & Development Laboratories, Inc.

P.O. Box 5195
Louisville, KY 40255-0195

www.llresearch.org

Rock Creek is a non-profit corporation dedicated to discovering and sharing information which may aid in the spiritual evolution of humankind.

ABOUT THE CONTENTS OF THIS TRANSCRIPT: This telepathic channeling has been taken from transcriptions of the weekly study and meditation meetings of the Rock Creek Research & Development Laboratories and L/L Research. It is offered in the hope that it may be useful to you. As the Confederation entities always make a point of saying, please use your discrimination and judgment in assessing this material. If something rings true to you, fine. If something does not resonate, please leave it behind, for neither we nor those of the Confederation would wish to be a stumbling block for any.

© 2009 L/L Research

Sunday Meditation
May 20, 2001

Group question: The question today has to do with the process of growth that the spiritual seeker seems to go through. We would like for Q'uo to give us some idea about the nature of this process. Most of the time, when something happens internally, we may or may not feel the repercussions externally in our life. We are wondering if Q'uo could give us an idea of how this process of change occurs, the various types of change, the stages of change, the ways the seeker can use to survive the change. And could Q'uo give us an idea of how the process and practice of meditation enhance this change?

(Carla channeling)

We are known to you as the principle of Q'uo. Greetings in the love and in the light of the one infinite Creator. It is, as always, a great joy to be called to this group, and we are most blessed by being asked to speak with you this afternoon on the subject of spiritual growth and how to survive it with some degree of comfort. Certainly that is an endless topic. We are still learning how to enjoy the natural, inevitable processes of evolution. We are most happy to speak to you and are gratified by the opportunity, but as always we ask each of you to listen with a discriminating ear and retain only those ideas which seem helpful to you, leaving the rest behind.

As we consider how to speak about this process of evolution we rest within each of your vibrations and experience the beauty of each of you as if you were flowers, each of you with its own scent and shape, each blossom at a different stage of unfolding, some personalities with more thorns than others, some hardier plants than others, but all blooming beautifully according to each soul's nature. Perhaps this is the place of starting in considering the processes of growth, that realization that nothing can truly harm this process. Maturation and evolution are protected processes. They cannot, in fact, be halted, not for long, although certainly some entities attempt to escape change. The mills of destiny grind fine and that which has been rough has been refined. This is the nature of your experience. You are those who have chosen an environment which is a spiritual refinery, what your Holy Bible called the refining fire.

It may be said that experience is a refining fire and in the ways of the world this is so. There is a certain amount of maturation and evolution that occurs because of the outer events of a life. However, we believe that the question was directed from the standpoint of the inner landscape rather than the landscape of the world. There is a level at which the feeling associated with outer events percolates and distills during the refining process, and it is this inner portion of this process which has attracted the interest of the questioner. For no matter what the vagaries of the outer world are, generally in the emotional part of the self there is a different density or feeling to the material that is processed. The outer events may be large or small, but what they bring up for the seeking soul is as the attention-getter that pulls the feeling, the focus and the arena or work away from the literal and mundane details of a situation into those areas of sensitive feeling and fragile vulnerability that seem to limn the treasure box of the unconscious.

The irony of spiritual catalyst is that the more material, emotionally and spiritually speaking, that catalyst offers, the less articulate and simple will be the words that will satisfactorily encompass the feelings, the emotions and the processes of suffering that take place during the burning of that refining fire. When the seeker stays on the surface level it is very easy to explain to others what is happening. When there is a situation when there is an illness, a death, a change in employment or some other large and obvious catalyst, the entities about one are able without any effort to grasp and sympathize with the situation. When the difficulties arise because of tender feelings and the inner winces and shudders that accompany difficult experiences emotionally, new experiences, times of risk and times of fear, it is far more difficult to frame a simple conversation with a friend and describe what is going on. And, indeed, once one begins plumbing one's emotions, the opportunity to obtain a larger point of view is, for the moment, lost. Consequently, while it is seemingly helpful and, in a bittersweet way, even pleasant to probe and press and explore into those areas of difficult experience or feeling, in another sense it is more skillful simply to accept the feelings that are sweeping through the energetic being.

The great trick of the intellectual mind is to consider itself capable of understanding situations and, again, for outer situations the intellectual mind generally has the promise of being able to assess a situation adequately. When it comes to matters where there is fear and a desire to be comforted in the processes of growing spiritually it is more helpful to move into that portion of the being which has no words. For those feelings do not need words in order to move through the various filters of each chakra, working like the energetic brooms that they are, cleaning, purifying and moving through the system like weather. Begin to see yourself as a far sturdier being than you feel as though you are. See yourself as much a solid being as a planet or a star. Lift away from the thought of self as body and move into the concept of self as an energetic being and you may see a model of yourself as this fantastically complex flower that blooms in good weather and bad and that enjoys both the rain and the sun in their seasons.

When there is the experience to the flower of the rain, the flower simply accepts the rain. When the sun is shining the flower gratefully accepts the sunshine. Both of these states of weather are necessary for the health and the evolution of this bloom, and both perceived times of halcyon days and perceived times of terrible internal weather are times that are good for you as a growing being. We cannot say to you that suffering is not truly suffering because each of you is fully aware of the depths of suffering of which you are capable and which you have experienced. Each of you has undergone great difficulty. We would be fools to try to tell you that you have not suffered. What we are saying is that this suffering is a tremendously helpful force that is powerful to offer those refining energies that you came to experience, not because you wanted to suffer but because you wafted to investigate and see if you could remake with even more purity that choice to serve the light with which you came into this incarnation.

You had very carefully thought-out hopes for this incarnation before it began. What this instrument calls the Holy Spirit, what many call guidance, what those known as the Ra group have called the higher self, took counsel with you before this incarnation and considered just what goals you would hope to place for service and for learning within one lifetime. With great thought and care you chose those people that are in your life: mates, parents, children, friends and enemies, each carefully positioned to rub against you this way and that and knock off the sharp edges. Each is as the refining fire to others around you, and those around you are as the refining fire to you. And yet the fire is not of the person, but rather, it is of the spirit. This entire refining process is powered by spiritual energy. It is the energy of the Creator to know Itself, and you mirror this by your desire to know yourself.

What we encourage for each of you is a mixture of high ideals and utter down to earth practicality. It is a wonderful thing to be awake to the reality of spirit. Yet this awareness is seated in a life of flesh and blood and dust. You came into incarnation to experience the grit and the friction of a very real physical illusion. This is the chosen arena for this season of your bloom. We suggest that there is great survival value in trusting that the soil in which you were planted and the blooms that you see around you are the correct ones for your best growth and learning at this time. We suggest that the very nearest things to you can provide you a tremendous opportunity for service. We suggest that there is an enormous value in realizing the permanent in the ever changing world of your heart.

Where does the world's reality leave off and metaphysical reality begin? We suggest to you that they are both centered in your heart. If you dwell within your mind and think many thoughts and skitter across the surface of ideas you may make a great noise but you may not make a great deal of sense. If you move into the silence and reality of the heart you may say nothing, but you will be resting in the peace that lies within the precinct of that heart. We have described you as energy beings, and when we speak about moving into the heart we speak about moving into the very center of that energetic being where body and soul come together. Realize that while your brain and your personality shell are pumping out one idea after another, your heart is serenely beating, moving in rhythm with the creation of the Father. The instinctive wisdom that you as a living being possess is incredible, and the challenge is to tap into what you already have within you.

The one known as R asked about meditation and what enhancement it might offer to those in the process of growth and as this entity is well aware we very much agree that the one most powerful method of enhancing the processes of evolution is meditation. Moving into the silence in any way that one feels comfortable is always a powerful helper, for it is within the silence that love may abide most comfortably and may express most fully. We do not know what realms may open up to you in the silence, but within that room to which silence opens the door lie many mansions. We simply suggest that the habit of silence is helpful, profoundly and continuingly so. It is, to our knowledge, the single most attainable way of moving from the level of the outer world into the levels of that inner world where the feelings and the processes of being revolve.

To hear us speak you would think we never laughed. You would think that we never cried but that we were always calm and wise and dispensing of words. In fact, this is not so. We struggle to find ways to share our experiences with you and we do not feel that we are tremendously successful. But what we have to share, more than anything else, is an awareness of and a certainty in love itself and the power and rightness of that love—that is your very being and is our very being. We encourage each to be lifted up by whatever light comes into the heart to comfort it, that it reach hands willingly up to the angels that hope to help. We ask each to know that you are not alone and that there is comfort for the asking, for prayers are answered, and when help is requested presences are with you that love you and wish to safeguard you in every way. The Creator is not far off. The Creator is very, very near. This is good to remember.

We hope you find many moments of peace, but we assure each that the unrest and the disquiet have a purpose too. The more serenely that you can look at the troubles in your life the more trust you can develop that these are not simply difficulties that seem to challenge but are also helpers whose purpose will be seen much more easily from hindsight when the process is through. And we encourage each of you to use each other as lifelines. If there is a hard time find someone you trust and talk it over. It does not make the process of refinement any easier, but it makes it much more bearable because the sharing lightens the load.

We would at this time transfer this contact to the one known as Jim. We thank this instrument and leave it in love and in light. We are known to you as the Q'uo.

(Jim channeling)

We are those of Q'uo, and we greet each again in love and in light through this instrument. At this time we would offer ourselves in the attempt to speak to any further queries which those present may have for us. Is there another query at this time?

Carla: S phoned one in and he asked about light centers around the world such as Mt. Shasta, Sedona, Machu Picchu, etc., and what their significance might be.

I am Q'uo, and am aware of your query, my sister. These areas which have been described as centers of light have an influence upon those who are sensitive or psychically aware, shall we say, in that these centers or areas are both located at points of intelligent energy ingress and have the advantage of attracting seekers for many of your years. These centers then are steeped in those energies which are transformational in nature. For the intelligent energy that is sent by your sub-Logos, the sun, makes its way into the Earth sphere through various vortices that are distributors, shall we say, of this energy that the entire population of the planet shall eventually be able to partake of their transforming nature. These vortices are in a regularized grid—we search for the word within this instrument's mind and complex is the closest we can come. Where there is an intersection of these lines of force there is formed a vortex that is an opening for such energies to be easily assimilated into the Earth's mantle. Entities who are sensitive to such energies oftentimes gravitate to these areas in order to feel more of the pulse of life, shall we say. Is there a further query, my sister?

Carla: No. Not from me. S may want to follow it up when he returns. Thank you very much.

I am Q'uo, and we thank you and the one known as S. Is there another query at this time?

M: To follow up on Steve's question, what is the closest vortex of energy in our area, Indiana and Kentucky?

I am Q'uo, and am aware of your query, my sister. Within this particular geographical region there is a vortex of energy that is very close to this location, that is, the city of Louisville, and there are other vortices located within a radius of five to six of your miles, both east and west of the center location that is congruent with this population center. There is a map which this instrument may be able to locate that could be of help in the determination of these locations. Is there another query, my sister?

M: No. Thank you.

I am Q'uo, and we thank you, my sister. Is there another query at this time?

Carla: We had a visit from a Toltec magician this week, and listening to his descriptions of his inner landscape I wondered if he was working on one of the inner planes, the astral or devachanic and so forth, if I could frame his reality in terms of thinking of it that way. How would you suggest that I think of it? What level is he seeing what he sees on?

I am Q'uo, and am aware of your query, my sister. We must be general in our response in this instance and would suggest that this entity is one who is partaking in both the space/time illusion which each here inhabits and in the time/space illusion as well which is that which is more metaphysical or invisible to the third-density eye. That which is approached in meditation, in prayer, in contemplation reflects the milieu in which this entity has a richly populated interior landscape, shall we say. Is there a further query, my sister?

Carla: No. Thank you.

I am Quo, and again we thank you, my sister. Is there another query at this time?

R: You usually are not able to speak in much detail about things such as the location of the vortices in our area. Is it because we already knew about it that the Law of Confusion did not apply? I am curious about why you were able to be more specific than you usually are?

I am Quo, and am aware of your query, my brother. In the case of the query concerning the centers of energy influx we are able to give that which this instrument can transmit without any fear of infringing upon any entity's spiritual growth, for these centers of energy are available to all entities and do not affect one's future, shall we say. Is there another query, my brother?

R: No. Not from me. Thank you.

I am Q'uo, and we thank you, my brother. Is there another query at this time?

M: Will you be coming to watch over our group for the summer until next fall when we get together again?

I am Q'uo, and am aware of your query, my sister. The period of time between the gatherings of this group …

(Tape ends. The answer was basically in the affirmative, although no channeling would be attempted, only the aiding of the meditation.)

L/L Research

Special Meditation
August 29, 2001

Question from R: This first question concerns [a] pattern in my life that has to do with feelings about my work. My criticism of myself is that my work should be more service-to-others oriented. I then proceed to find a different type of work or employment that has energy in it that grabs me and that I start working with it but that passion or that energy dissipates quickly once that new work begins. I am looking for suggestions or different points of view that would help me get deeper into this pattern that I am seeing.

(Carla channeling)

We are those known to you as the principle of Q'uo. We are a slightly different voice than the Q'uo [that] normally speaks through this instrument because the vibrational characteristics of this particular question and group seem to be better met if the brothers and sisters of Hatonn take the position of speaking for the principle which includes those of Hatonn, those of Latwii, and those of Ra. Normally, we speak with this group through the brothers and sisters of Latwii. However, each session of working has its own dynamics and this particular group seems to call forth the strengths of the brothers and sisters of Hatonn. If there are any differences, they are probably due to this unique voice.

We greet each of you in the love and in the light of the infinite Creator. As always, it is a great joy to speak with this group, with whom we have not spoken for some of your time. Truly, it is a blessing and a privilege for us to be with you and to share in your meditation and your seeking. We thank each of you for this special occasion which we are heartily enjoying.

As always, we ask each of you to ponder our words with your hearts, keeping those thoughts which seem helpful and resonate within your being as true and leaving aside all other thoughts as not applicable to you at this time.

The challenge of right occupation is not a challenge that is entirely that which it seems on the surface, any more than an activity at which one spends a substantial portion of one's waking hours can be simply a job, simply that which it appears on the surface.

The concept of an occupation has been distorted by the needs of your peoples for money. In a world where there was no need to earn money in order to live a life that was comfortable to a minimal extent, it is likely that many, many of those that work at the jobs at which they now work would immediately cease to report for their hours spent at the job because they would no longer need the money that the job offers.

However, there would still be an incarnation with lessons to learn and gifts to share. And even those who come into incarnation with absolutely no need to earn money usually find themselves at least tempted to choose to occupy a substantial portion of their waking hours pursuing an activity which could be said to help the seeker learn its lessons and share its gifts.

It is easy to see the materialism of the world and its ways. It is less easy to see how the materialism in which the seeker lives may have penetrated into areas of the metaphysical and caused elements of the work ethic to become elements of spiritual materialism. This is a subtle area of contemplation but we recommend it to the one known as R.

For the rules and the ways of the world and the spirit are genuinely, from the core outward, different. And when evaluating the spiritual work of issues such as this—which have so many elements in the physical and so many elements in the metaphysical world—it is well to ponder how to frame that great and genuine desire of the heart to serve in a way that allows the seeker to see into, to penetrate into the deeper workings of desire, and to sift out those elements which have to do with the world and its ways, in order that the real form, the real skeleton, the real muscles and sinews that underlie the flesh of spiritual seeking may be viewed.

For there is a structure to right occupation in the spiritual sense. And that has to do with those things that are of worth in the spirit rather than in the world, in the heart rather than in the mind, and in the intuition and the resonances of feeling rather than in the logic and reason that characterize intellection and ratiocinated thought.

One thing we would suggest in pondering this issue is a review of the gifts which have been brought through into the personality shell available to the seeker in this incarnation and to ask the self how best these gifts might be shared. We are aware that the one known as R wishes, for instance, to investigate the possibilities of working with the younger entities among your people, feeling that perhaps working with these young entities may be of more service than working with the adult versions of the entities which are all the Creator.

We suggest to the one known as R that this may well be a reasonable concept. The one known as R may well have gifts that would feed into these relationships with younger entities. This can be investigated in several ways: by thought, by research, and to an extent by experience.

We would point out that the job, the career, is, in form, connected more with money than with the gifts that one shares, whereas activity that can be chosen of oneself offers a clear and far more elastic form of inquiry. In other words, it is possible to place oneself in certain organizations through what this instrument would call volunteering time and attention in certain ways, and to allow oneself to come into contact with and interact with entities of that younger age so that many questions upon the seeker's mind might be explored.

Is there indeed a special gift that seems to be called for by younger entities who may have greater needs than the simple need to learn? Is there a resonance when actual experience replaces theoretical thought?

We suggest this for the simple reason that interaction with another self or other selves, while often very confusing, contains within it a tremendous potential for learning. When one is confined within the privacy of one's thoughts, suppositions that may or may not be true cannot be at all examined with the same efficiency as when these suppositions are placed cheek by jowl with actual experience. In the process of following relationships begun with such younger entities among your peoples, much data may be taken in; much, certainly, of linear information but far more than that, much of the visceral, the gut reaction. In this way there may be more of a rounded and full shape to the thinking.

We would at this time transfer this contact to the one known as Jim. We are those of Q'uo. We leave this instrument in love and in light.

(Jim channeling)

I am Q'uo, and greet each again in love and in light through this instrument. In addition to that which we have spoken through the one known as Carla, we would add through this instrument the utilization of one's passion in determining that occupation into which one places one's desires and dreams as a means by which to serve others. As one looks at the skills which have been brought forth into this present incarnation and evaluates that level of expertise, shall we say, added to this, we would heartily recommend the investigation of any area in which one finds excitement, interest, passion—a desire to serve increased by the pleasure of serving.

In truth, there are truly no mistakes, for all entities are the Creator. One can only serve the Creator. All expenditures of energy are a service to the one

Creator. Therefore, in order to serve in a most fulfilling manner and to achieve that brilliance and vividness of the variety of colors of service, shall we say, it is well, whatever choices one makes, that there be a passion for the choice made to propel one, in a day by day manner, into the service and through the service to those whom you serve.

In this way the lessening of excitement which the one known as R has observed occurring in his patterns may be ameliorated and the most full expression of the heart of the desire to serve might be achieved wherever passion is found. For passion is a kind of a pre-incarnative gift. [It is] a continuance of that which has previously opened one's heart [which] again finds resonance in the present incarnation by the expression of a passionate desire to be of service in a certain manner.

At this time we would suggest the asking of the second query.

R: The second question I have concerns a pattern of looking for a mated relationship in my life, finding one, and then the relationship ending soon after. I wonder if there is a spiritual structure to such a relationship and if I am putting expectations in such a relationship from the beginning and therefore not allowing the passion or the true love to flow. If you can comment on it, I appreciate it. I am once again looking for suggestions on how to explore this pattern deeper.

I am Q'uo, and am aware of your query, my brother. The mated relationship is a specific kind of service, an experience of mutual desire for seeking the one Creator, for serving the one Creator, and for sharing the life pattern out of which seeking and service are born. Thusly, you may consider the words which we have spoken concerning the occupation and its service as being applicable to the mated relationship as well.

There is the need to love and to be loved which is as normal and natural a function of the human being as is the sleeping, the eating, the breathing, and the moving about within your illusion.

The experience of being of service with the mate is one which has a great deal of joy and direction in that each in the mated relationship feels a kind of wholeness which is not present outside the mated relationship when one is alone.

Although it is quite possible for each entity to be of great service and to seek with great purity in a solitary fashion, the yoke of such honor/duty/experience is more easily borne when shared.

In opening oneself to such a relationship there is the need to become truly open, to prepare the self for change and to be willing to accept the changing currents and depths of the river of life. For once there is an expectation to which one holds strictly or dearly, then that expectation can become an obstacle to this opening of the self to that which the potential mated relationship brings to the self.

Thusly, it is well, when considering the possibilities of the mated relationship, to truly examine the heart's desires. For when allowed to express truly, these desires may move far past the boundaries of mental contemplation. Thusly, the romantic involvement within your illusion has oftentimes been seen to originate in the stars, shall we say, so that forces outside of the self are given the opportunity to move the self as the wind and the weather move a sailboat upon your sea.

At this time we would transfer this contact to the one known as Carla. We are those of Q'uo.

(Carla channeling)

We are again with this instrument. We are those of Q'uo.

For you see, my brother, the entire self is here to love and to be loved; not simply the conscious self, the self with expectations, but the entire self, the whole, utter, real, complete, universal self.

And one can not approach that which is a consuming fire, that which changes the life, that to which one must surrender at one level, as if it were hiring someone to fill a position. One cannot choose a mate. That is, one can choose a mate, but one shall get what one has chosen. The product of rational thought may or may not be that emblem of love which so speaks to your own whole self.

There is that element in that other person that is the face of the Creator that allows you to see into the Creator through that person. There needs to be something within the choice that must be made, that cannot be denied, that is felt passionately to be sufficient cause of the discomfort, suffering and pain of surrender to a relationship.

For any relationship, while it will not change you, precisely, will change so much about your experience! It is as though you will have set into motion the wheels of transformation in such a way that they are never under your control in any substance of sense. Nor are they in the hands of the other involved in a mated relationship. For that entity, too, will be challenged to so love you as the face of the Creator that she can see more of the Creator in herself because she has you as her mirror.

Certainly, a relationship can be made; a home can be created with any chosen mate. But to move beyond pattern into spontaneous energy which creates its own patterns, there is the need to find that focus that is worth the sacrifice of the old self and that inspires the faith and the trust of the self to release the protective layers around the heart, that the self may offer itself its life and its service to another.

Each in a mated relationship does this and it is not an "I" or a "she" but a "we" and an "us" to which each surrenders; that oversoul or higher self that the two become in union when mated. So there is not simply the self and the other self but there is that divine union which contains the Creator to which both have surrendered.

This is the glory of the committed or mated relationship. This is the beginning for great potential for learning and for an expansion of service depending upon that creature that both have become as a "we" and an "us."

Again, to move from the head to the heart is to find reasons for what this instrument would call sacrifice. In any new choice there is, as the one known as R has said, the initial joy, the initial thrill of something new, and something perhaps better. But then, no matter how good that new choice is, there comes the moment when the new job or the new relationship is more fully seen and something akin to despair can crop up, for it is now seen, as the one known as R has said, that here lie feet of clay; here lie, in a job, tasks that ring hollow and do not resonate.

This instrument has been working at the occupation which she now enjoys for some stretch of time and from this instrument's experience there seems to be, even for the most fully fulfilled worker, still those times when the job seems sterile and without true appeal.

And we find that in this instrument's mind that this instrument has often said to herself at such times that this is not about the job, this is about the process. It is not the fault of those situations that define a job description. It is about what cycles and what patterns through which the entity, as a personality and as a deeper spiritual seeker, is going and which can be expected to continue throughout the incarnation that is full of its cycles and will always be so as long as third-density conditions exist which encourage cyclical patterns: waking and sleeping, eating and being hungry, being happy and being unhappy.

These cycles are very stubborn within the human personality and are built into that constant pulse of spirit in order that the illusion may be what the illusion is intended to be: a disquieted, confusing, distracting and ultimately successfully humbling experience that brings one out of oneself and down upon one's knees in many ways, and ready to open the self to that which is desired.

For all things that are desired will create the new patterns of change and change is always difficult. All new choices will seem wrong at a certain point, at many points in a cyclically repeating pattern.

What shores up the confidence of one who is moving from the heart is that feeling of being true to the self, right or wrong, and that feeling of being able, if one is wrong, to accept that and move forward, bolstered by the passion that moved the seeker in the first place to make a change so that the self may see into these cycles and yet may still, by following the heart and following desire, locate those precious elements that need to be within the life—be it the job or the people. Identifying not by sight but by the eyes of the heart, not by reason, but by confidence in those memories of desire that the heart speaks.

(Side one of tape ends.)

(Carla channeling)

For the Creator wishes each child to fulfill every desire, to ask every question, to knock at all the doors that call to him.

We are aware that the one known as R wished that we keep this session brief and we are aware too that the sound of the tape recorder means that we have not fulfilled his expectations. However, we can fulfill it at this time by relinquishing our hold upon this instrument and this group and thanking the one known as R for these very heartfelt and genuine questions.

It is a mark of spiritual maturity to see the patterns of one's life. It is a mark of even more maturity, spiritually speaking, to look not only for ways to solve the puzzle but for ways to love and to know the self ever more deeply, and knowing it more deeply, to find ways again to love.

Truly, every difficulty can be untangled by persistently turning to those gentle fingers of love that, through time, will untangle every knot and remove every obstacle.

We leave you glorying in the love and the light of the one infinite Creator. We leave each of you with our thanks and our true, true gratitude [for] our relationships with you and [your] invitation to share our thoughts with you. Adonai. Adonai vasu borragus. We are those known to you as Q'uo.

L/L Research

L/L Research is a subsidiary of Rock Creek Research & Development Laboratories, Inc.

P.O. Box 5195
Louisville, KY 40255-0195

www.llresearch.org

Rock Creek is a non-profit corporation dedicated to discovering and sharing information which may aid in the spiritual evolution of humankind.

ABOUT THE CONTENTS OF THIS TRANSCRIPT: This telepathic channeling has been taken from transcriptions of the weekly study and meditation meetings of the Rock Creek Research & Development Laboratories and L/L Research. It is offered in the hope that it may be useful to you. As the Confederation entities always make a point of saying, please use your discrimination and judgment in assessing this material. If something rings true to you, fine. If something does not resonate, please leave it behind, for neither we nor those of the Confederation would wish to be a stumbling block for any.

© 2009 L/L Research

Sunday Meditation
September 2, 2001

Group question: The question today has to do with the situation concerning our planet and all of us who inhabit it. We would like for Q'uo to give us some information concerning the quality of consciousness on our planet when you consider the various wars, diseases, famines and crises that occur on a daily basis as each of us as individuals go about our daily lives, dealing with the various levels of stress of family, work, community and so forth. We are wondering how we as individuals find a centering point, the joy in the moment? How can we really be of service to each other and to ourselves?

(Carla channeling)

We are those of the principle known to you as Q'uo. Greetings in the love and in the light of the one infinite Creator. We come to you as a voice of love. To this planet we speak the ways of One, the ways of unity. We have a very simple tale to tell, and we thank you for bringing us to you to be able to share this simple philosophy, a philosophy truly too simple to be easily understood. We are most grateful to you for your infinite genius that looks at that subject, which is always and ever the same, in ever-new ways, giving us new opportunities to work with the words of your language and the biases of this instrument in order to share our heart through the heart of this instrument and the one known as Jim.

We are extremely gratified to share our thoughts and would only ask in return that each of you is extremely careful about what you choose to listen to in what we have to say. For what we have to say is a truth to us, but it may not be so to you. That which resonates within your heart, by all means, consider. For we hope to offer interesting and helpful thoughts. But those things which do not resonate we ask that you leave behind without a second thought. Some thoughts are for you. Some thoughts are not. That power of discrimination which each of you has is golden, as this instrument would say. Treasure it and trust it. No one else can tell you what is right for you. You are the authority for yourself. You are the teacher for yourself. You are the guru in a very important way, for those things which you desire to know lie within you now. It is a matter of remembering and coming again into awarenesses [of] that you have had many times, not necessarily within incarnation.

One great goal of each of you within this incarnation is to become aware that you are dreaming and to become able to make the dream of incarnation a lucid and a conscious dream, one that is, in some ways and to some extent, a matter of your choices and your control. For these skills much is required of time and attention and discipline. And each of you is well aware of these things as are we, for we too seek, unendingly driven by the desire to be truly one with the Creator and yet still aware in many ways of our own biases and our group biases. Always, it seems, the spiritual path has another turn and another, and the road leads ever onward. We rejoice in this endless journey that truly is not endless but cyclical.

For in the fullness of the time and space that you now enjoy within this creation of yours and ours we all will come to the octave. We all will coalesce once again into the one infinite Creator and become an unpotentiated unity. And in that beating of the great heart of creation, one creation shall end and another begin. We share this walk with you, this walk from source to source, from light to light.

We greatly enjoyed your conversation and thank each of you for all that you laid aside in order to attend and place time and attention on things of the spirit. How precious that desire and thirst for truth is, my friends! We can never thank you enough for your desire, for it is your desire that calls us to you, your desire and your sorrow. For we do hear the sorrow of Earth. We hear the sorrow of its people, and we want to respond, hopefully, in ways that are of service. That is one of the questions that is on your minds today.

But we shall not start with that. We shall focus briefly on the state of the planet, for that is one thread of your questioning: is there a gain or a decrease in love upon planet Earth? Indeed, there are a number of ways to answer that question, but we shall choose two. Firstly, as the one known as R has said, the surface of life has a spurious and shallow reality that is nonetheless undeniable. It is a world of complete illusion, and in that world the dragon thrashes its tail. And angels in flesh quiver, defend, worry and hope to respond in ways that add love to the illusion. A little positive, a little negative, and the illusion wags on, doing the job it was meant to do, thoroughly confusing, baffling and frustrating. All efforts of the linear and conscious intellect to control it bring each inevitably, surely, if each is honest, to the realization that the self knows nothing. That the life of the surface has nothing. That all is "vanity and striving after wind," as this instrument would quote from her Bible.

Such is the surface of life. Such is the design that was intended for that illusion, and at the same time may we say that there is tremendous growth in the metaphysical sense among the peoples of your planet. It is abundantly, richly clear on the metaphysical planes of your planet that a tremendous outpouring of love and concern has streamed into the Earth plane. Many Earth native individuals, and by that we mean those who have been within the planetary influence as souls since pre-history, in your terms, have come through the many waters of many, many incarnations over thousands of years and have slowly but surely come to the point where the alarm clock has gone off. The awakening of the spirit within flesh has taken place, and there is now the realization within many, many individual Earth native souls that they are citizens of eternity, that they are infinite beings and that the surface of life, while due great honor and attention, is not all that there is but is only the gateway to the present moment, which is infinite. And these voices have become a great choir asking and seeking and knocking at the door of truth.

There is a call going out from your planet at this time that has been going out from your planet for a considerable number of years now, that has activated and doubled and redoubled the light energy upon your planet. Further, as many within this room are intimately aware, many entities have chosen to travel to the earth plane from other planetary influences for the purpose of entering into the experience of being an Earth native, plunging the self into the third-density atmosphere once again in hopes of serving the planet and its people but also in hopes of doing work upon the self: a reevaluating of that all-important choice of third density: the choice of whether to love by radiation and unconditional love or to love by control and magnetic attraction and the overriding sense that people need to be managed for their own good or for the greater good of the whole. This is work that is common to all at this time, all who are awakened, all who have begun that transforming opening of the heart and the spirit for which each took birth.

We hope that you feel very good about the work that you have done so far, and we hope that you will redouble your efforts, not to do, but to be. For the work of consciousness is the work of asking the self to be the self most truly and most deeply. What is the self? Upon the surface of the incarnation the self is a personality, a collection of biases, opinions, beliefs and suppositions, an amalgam of gifts and quirks and challenges. The interesting thing about personality is that each of you chose both your gifts and your limitations, your abundances and your lacks, for very good reasons. The challenge is to come into some fuller realization as time goes on as to what the pattern is behind those challenges and those gifts. What was hoped for by the higher self that is you when you and your higher self planned the big points, as this instrument would say, the plot points of this incarnation? Why did you put that blockage there? That remarkable gift there? That incredible stupidity over there? These things were placed there for a reason. Why did your choose relationships with this, this and this entity that delight you and aggravate you and make you angry? In each connection there is a fullness of goodness, if one can but see the plan. As the one known as C has said, that is the challenge, and one seldom sees the plan until the pattern is complete and one has the blessed advantage of hindsight.

How to be one's self? [This is] a question we still seek the answer to ourselves. We know that our direction lies along the trail that leads to the Creator, along that ever seemingly darkening trail that rounds curve after curve until, at last, that creature that eats its own tail that is the Creator has found its tail again and the self is swallowed up once again in absolute divinity. Light shines within that direction, yet in a way that is hidden from the outer eye and from the eye of circumstance. Most often the spiritual riches are found when life is at its darkest and most challenging. For it is then that the little hammers and chisels and acid water etch and smooth and craft and sculpt and find the gems within the ore that is the personality shell. So the learning to be the self is a *geste* of tremendous patience and persistence. And yet, at the same time, advances are often made in blinding steps forward that seem like the dawning of a sudden sunrise, the turning of a corner which opens into a new world, the epiphany of the senses and the soul.

Be prepared for sudden and stupendous moments of awareness because, you see, you are a being. You are not an activity or a process. And you surprise yourself being yourself sometimes. And in those moments when you have hit a resonance that strikes deep down into the self, suddenly the moment opens up and you become aware of all that you are, of the tremendous unity that you have with everything that is. This state of mind is an actual opening into one of the inner planes or perhaps more than one of the inner planes, depending upon the experience, so that you simply are seeing more into your self, more into the reaches of your true nature, which is inclusive, universal, timeless and divine. You have to remember that you are the product of the Creator's thirst for knowing Itself, and your seeking to know yourself is part of the Creator's seeking for Its own identity. And what fascinates the Creator endlessly is how that identity is the same, and yet it continues to grow because of the fecund and fertile nature of spirit.

You seem to stand upon the Earth, sticking out into space, upon this ball that is revolving, day/night, day/night, day/night around a minor sun at the edge of a rather small galaxy. And yet you are standing upon holy ground within the creation of the Father, and you are the womb of stars, the grave of dreams, all emotions, all feelings, all thoughts, all possible processes. Out of all these things you have chosen a certain eccentric pattern of personality and experiencing, a certain set of filters to further confuse the already illusory data of the incarnation. You have set yourself within a situation where you are at once universal and unique. You are living a life and at the same time you are living forever, never stationary and yet unified. This is the key to grasping the nature of the spiritual journey. It is truly a journey because the Creator is never still. The Creator's nature is extremely strong in freedom. This freedom of will creates a state of cyclical discovery, the desire to know more, the desire to seek. It is your nature because it is the Creator's nature.

And what the Creator actually is evaluating and, shall we say, feeding upon is the essence of those emotions which have been brought up in various muddied states again and again until there has begun to be more and more clarity within that particular emotion. In a way, you are a refiner of emotions and one way to look at the work of spiritual seeking is to use some discipline in evaluating your thoughts and your emotions on a daily basis, if possible, certainly as often as possible. For there is always the temptation to let the good and the bad slide by with the oil of time and to seek the doing, and to seek the rest, and keep busy or unconscious, thereby removing oneself from some of the less comfortable aspects of those thoughts and feelings which you have had during a day's time. Yet these responses you have had to catalyst are grist for the mill. These are the clues that you have, the harvest of the day at the end of each day that will help you to investigate your own nature.

We would suggest time spent perhaps just as you are drifting off to sleep wherein these emotions are looked at one by one as you remember your day. And there may be seen in each memory and in each cluster of emotions the opportunity to revisit those feelings, to see into the dynamic of those particular feelings. If it is a feeling of impatience, for instance, that you are investigating, you may accentuate the impatience and really give permission to the self to feel very impatient and then give permission to the self to allow the opposite of that emotion to come into and flood the senses so that you ask, "Show me patience. Let me feel what it is like to sense true patience." This flexing of the emotional muscle in a very meditative and contemplative ways is most helpful to the unconscious mind and will, to some extent, clarify those dreams that are also hints and inklings that help one upon the spiritual path.

One of the threads of inquiry this week was having to do with service to others and how to evaluate such service. Truly this is a question that moves to the very heart of spiritual work in third density and beyond. It is a question that we answer when we come and speak with you through this instrument rather than landing on the lawn, impressing you with our looks and our differentness and then attempting to persuade you to our point of view. We attempted service in such direct manner at one time, and we found that it was not acceptable in terms of [the] infringement of free will that we caused. We now are perfectly content in ways that can never be proven as real because we feel that the information will speak to those for whom it is helpful. There is a law of attraction in seeking so that we know that, one way or another, the thoughts that are needed will come to those who truly are asking. And so we add our voice to those voices that are available if someone seeks such a voice.

Much of service to others is wrapped up in the study of polarity. However …

(Side one of tape ends here; side two did not record.) ❧

Sunday Meditation
September 16, 2001

Group question: The question today, Q'uo, as I am sure that you already know, concerns the recent acts of terrorism that have come to the United States. Many people have died, and much property has been destroyed and there is a lot of talk about retribution, about war, and a lot of fear and anger, a lot of confusion. And we are wondering what this situation looks like from Q'uo's point of view. We are told that this world is an illusion. It is a place where we come to learn to love. From our point of view, right here, right now, it is a very difficult place to learn to love. We are wondering what Q'uo can add to our knowledge of just exactly what has occurred, what does it mean to us in the spiritual sense, and what can we as individuals do to help the situation?

(Carla channeling)

We are those known to you as the principle of Q'uo. Greetings, love and light to you each, the light and the love of the infinite Creator and the infinite unity of all that is. We thank each of you for joining our group this afternoon. We thank you for calling to us with your thirst for truth. We thank you for your sacrifice of time and your attention. We thank you for a great privilege, for it is a great privilege to be allowed to share our thoughts with you.

It has been asked of us this day that we tell you what our point of view is upon the events taking place within your earth world at this time. May we say, first of all, that we greatly appreciated the comments that were made in the sharing of thoughts and reflections that preceded this meditation. We are aware, to some extent, of the distress and the discomfort of the normal tenor of life your peoples have greatly suffered, and it is a particular kind of suffering which is not only the suffering of particular nation but a suffering which goes beyond your nation states and into the overriding ethos of your culture.

What it looks like to us is somewhat different because we see in a wider range of things that are visible. We are not limited by physical limitations in what we see, what we hear, shall we say, what we are aware of, but rather are limited only by our distortions which to us is limit enough. Because of being able to see into the finer planes of your planet's ongoing developing nature and essence we are able to report both that there is genuine suffering going on within your earth world in the finer planes and that there is at this time, as this instrument and as the one known as Steve has mentioned, a tremendous outpouring of love, light and energy.

To express our point of view is to ask all of you to come from a standpoint of looking within the parameters garnered by physical limitations to the realm of concepts. For in the metaphysical creation which is the counterpart of the physical creation, concepts are that which is, shall we say, real and form is a matter of choice. Consequently it is the color and structure of thoughts that creates meaning. It is a creation in which what this instrument would call ideals are geography, and these ideas, these concepts, these thoughts are of an order which your peoples have studied in various ways as mythology, as religion, as philosophy of a certain kind, always attempting to express truths that are too fine for the physical senses to comprehend.

One system, which this instrument is somewhat familiar with, of studying this creation of concepts is that system which predated the tarot deck as used for divination and consisted of the twenty-two archetypal images which this instrument and this group have previously questioned about. One of these images is called, in the system offered by those of Ra, the Tower or the Lightning Struck Tower, and it is at this level of meaning that we would look at your planetary situation from a metaphysical point of view. Your planet as an entity, as well as each of you as a part of the human family of Earth, is moving through a tremendously transformative period.

We speak now not in terms of physical transformation, although physical transformation is, to some extent, likely. We have no idea to what extent. That will be determined by people such as you and the thoughts that they think within your next fairly finite period of time.

We speak of the metaphysical aspect of intense transformation as this planet changes densities, changes the very nature of its core particles, changes the nature of its light, changes the way that light is able to come into the planetary aura or grid of energies. It has been transforming for approximately two thousand of your years to some extent. It has been beginning to accelerate for the last, say, two hundred years to a marked degree. And as each of you is aware, it is profoundly accelerating in exponentially shorter amounts of physical time/space as the cusp of transformation is reached. As far as we are aware that cusp will be reached within the next decade. At that point your planet will have awakened its fourth-density nature. That indicates magnetic change, electrical change; change of a profound nature that has already been showing up for some of your years in newly discovered, very quirky, sub-density particles. It will continue to be a situation where the finer energies keep showing up for brief periods of time within the physical universe as these transformative processes continue.

In this climate of change, the Earth is as vulnerable as a pregnant mother that is giving birth to a child. It is vulnerable in a way that it has not been vulnerable, as entities are always vulnerable in times of change. And from the standpoint of the entity Earth, which this instrument is fond of calling Gaia, it has been given an unending amount of negative emotional catalyst by those entities who are attempting to polarize towards service-to-self and by the careless actions of those who are not attempting to polarize in either direction and who occasionally create suffering almost casually. The thoughts entities have habitually thought over a long period of time have created difficulties in the health and the welfare of Gaia. And as the physical parameters of the Earth are nudged into change or catapulted into change—and this is your choice—there is the possibility for natural global catastrophe, not simply the catastrophe of mankind against mankind. It has happened frequently enough in other third-density graduations where the process of maturation of the species upon a planet was not able to endure through the lessons of love. We are grateful to the one known as Jim who witnessed to the lack of love upon your planet. Truly, no truer words, no truer thought has been spoken than this one. Your people and Gaia desperately need to be loved; to be seen, to be apprehended for the first time as part of the self.

Many times we have said in response to your questions about this transformative time that we prefer not to give specific information. For one thing, at best we would be approximating the largest probability/possibility vortexes. We would be telling you what is likely to occur, for the future is not fixed. It is liquid. It is a creature of thought, and it will be the fruit of the seeds that you are planting now. It is said in your holy works that others have planted and you have reaped, that which you have planted others shall reap, and this is deeply so. Many are the painful, angry, furious, negative emotions that have been sprayed across this planet by the self to the self. For my friends, that is what the situation truly is. All of you are sparks of one flame. All of you are one thing. You may choose at this time a direction of how to think, and we simply encourage you to focus the mind, the heart and the commitment upon love.

Let us go back to that Lightning Struck Tower and look at its significance again. Within your next decade or two this transformation will have taken place. This is the time to acknowledge fully the need to learn the ways of the self, to become more and more familiar with the thoughts of the heart with an eye to working with these thoughts, to accentuating the tendency towards positivity, towards compassion, towards tolerance, towards creativity, towards hope and faith. For that which has crashed your tower of the physical world and brought it down is a very literal symbol of an archetypal process. The Matrix of the Spirit in this tarot system is called the Devil. And the Lightning-Struck Tower is the Potentiator of the Spirit. The Matrix of the Spirit is called this because those who bring light have always had a bad reputation. Lucifer is one of the names that is most telling that is used for the Devil in your culture. The roots of this word mean "light-bringer."

The lie of your metaphysical dynamic is concerned with the value of wisdom in spiritual seeking within third density. Knowledge and wisdom, in the spiritual sense, can be seen to be highly negative when unlit, unillumined, by love. That is why love is learned before wisdom. That is why love must be learned before wisdom. For when wisdom is learned first it is fair to the taste and so smooth within the intellectual digestion, and so handy and useful in the intellectual display of personality and intelligence that it is often not clear, for lifetimes at a time, that without love, wisdom is utterly devoid of content. No matter how many fine thoughts roll around inside of an intellectual system, if it does not come into the heart and become grounded by what this instrument would call good works, good living, it will not abide in the sense of being spiritually useful for the evolution and the maturity of the soul.

The Lightning Struck Tower is a kind of signal at this time that great catalyst is now available for the spirit. In the tarot system, which this instrument is somewhat familiar with, the Catalyst of the Spirit is Hope. You could also call this entity Faith. We think you will find that honing the faculties of faith, hope and love will be an agenda that will keep you profitably busy for the rest of your incarnation doing what you came to do, serving as you came to serve. We hope you will realize that you have already begun, that you have already done much work. We appreciate the sentiments of the one known as Cindy who, like so many, feels that she may be the least among the assembled. Each is the least among the assembled, for each is one with all that are assembled. Each has done great work in this lifetime and in previous lifetimes. Each comes to this moment with some sense of awareness that this time is special, and we hope that each of you will believe yourselves and will take courage, and become ever more faithful simply in being creatures of light. This is your nature. We do see the inconveniences, the suffering that has occurred. We see the possibilities that continue to open, not simply from this vortex, but from others. And we say to you, in the words of the Holy Bible, "Let not your heart be moved. In quietness and in confidence shall be your strength."

You are now those who bear a kind of light to Earth. In a way, you are Lucifer now, but you are not evil, nor was Lucifer intending towards evil. Indeed, much in this story is mis-told, but archetypically speaking we see your situation as one that is much more blessed and much more hopeful, because of the change in the last ten years, the last twenty years, the last thirty years. We see an acceleration of the light on this planet as well as an acceleration of the dark. To us, it is very clear that the forces of light are gaining strength.

We would at this time transfer this contact to the one known as Jim. We leave this instrument in love and in light. We are those known to you as the Q'uo.

(Pause for a few moments.)

(Jim channeling)

I am Q'uo and greet each again in love and in light through this instrument. We are aware that there are many questions upon the minds yet remaining, and in hopes of speaking to some of these we would now open this session to those questions. Is there another query at this time?

T: I am sure it was probably covered but I did my usual thing and went away for a while and didn't hear the whole channeling. In everything that I read there is always a need for balance and while I don't use the word evil too often, this would make one think of that word for sure. But this is a thing that has happened that is on a very big scale. Is this something at this time that is a polarity balancing sort of thing? I mean, in order for us to see the good and finally start pulling together as a people everywhere, do we have to see something so terrible that it is called evil or is called bad but is the opposite of the good that we try to do if we would all try to pull together. I hope that that made sense.

I am Q'uo and am aware of your query, my brother. That this event would be seen and experienced as that which is catastrophic is as you have correctly surmised, a necessary culmination of those energies which have, for many of your millennia, been in motion upon your planet, and this present expression of anger and hatred is that which can be seen in one of two ways: as that which demands retribution and a continuation of those energies of which it was born, or it can be seen as the alarm which rings the alert to those observing that there is something tremendously dislocated, shall we say, in the relationship between the various members of the family of humanity upon your planet and which needs attention, which needs understanding, which needs love and compassion. So difficult is it to look beneath the surface of events to see the genesis of such that most of your peoples do not make this effort. It is far easier to rest upon the simple and quick assessment of things.

Thus this experience of the loss of life and love can be that which ignites many hearts to love, to light and to service. For each entity upon this planet can be of service in this event, for each has those with whom difficulties have arisen in the daily round of activities. Each experiences this same loss of love, and each has the power within the heart to open in love to those with whom one is in relationship. Each time that love is given instead of hate, instead of confusion, instead of reprimand, instead of ignoring, instead of walking away, then there is the magical transformation that is possible when faith and will work together in each life. Then it is possible that such an event such as this great tragedy can bring more of the peoples of this planet into an awareness of the heart of their heart, of that which wishes to be awakened, of that which each took incarnation to awaken.

There have been tragedies aplenty throughout the many millennia of human inhabitation of this planet. None before have brought this awareness of the need of love to the consciousness in a strong enough way that there was a general response of love. It may be that this event also does not draw this response. It may be that this event does indeed draw that response. As we have said, the future is liquid. It is determined moment by moment by each of the many billions of entities upon this planet. Each entity can love. Each entity can heal. Each entity can have an effect upon how this scenario plays its course.

Is there another query, my brother?

T: No. Thank you very much.

I am Q'uo, and we thank you, my brother. Is there another query at this time?

S: Could you tell us what role, if any, of the Orion, service-to-self group, and their agents of influence had on this issue?

I am Q'uo and am aware of your query, my brother. We can begin by stating that the influence of those of negative polarity, those of the so-called Orion group, has been great for many thousands of your years upon this planet. Their endeavor to create the concept of the elite has been seeded throughout the many cultures and religions of this planet so that there is seen by all of the various religions, in their narrower or, as it is called upon your planet, fundamental, sense that there is reason to act as they act. It is for those within all cultures and religions who have the deep desire to truly serve the one Creator in all that may see beyond and behind the illusion of the elite, the illusion of separation, to that which binds all entities into one. This is the great *geste*, my friend: to see love where there is little reason to see it, to find unity where separation seems the only logical path, to see a brother or a sister instead of an enemy. It is not easy, my friends. But you did not incarnate with an easy plan for learning and for service. For this is the culmination of your planet's great Master Cycle of third-density evolution. It is at this time that those great swings of power over people can be balanced by love for people.

Is there another query at this time?

S: Any particular suggestions as to how we may be of service in this situation, for others, not only current needs but as further events unfold, to help them balance things?

I am Q'uo. We are aware of your query, my brother. Our recommendation is to love. When each situation, whether large or small, whether global or familial, or simply pointed towards the self, arises, ask yourself, "How can I love? Who can I love? Where can I love?" To love is enough, for to love is the reason for which each took incarnation. Is there another query, my brother?

S: Not from me right now. Thank you.

I am Q'uo, and we thank you, my brother. Is there another query at this time?

Carla: I would like to follow up on S's question by noting that we started doing an additional meditation at 9 o'clock at night to balance the one at 9 o'clock in the morning, with the thought that maybe others would like to join in spirit from around our global family and wondered if you would comment on this method of expressing love and any other concrete suggestions for ways that we could come together as a group to make a difference?

I am Q'uo and am aware of your query, my sister. We heartily endorse the efforts of joining together in group meditation in order to heal the rupture in the garment, shall we say, of this country, this planet, this family of humans. For to focus upon the inner world of spirit is to take refuge in that which is real. This world, the one which you inhabit now, the one which suffers mightily, is but an illusion born of the truth of spirit. Here, you are offered the opportunity to serve under adverse conditions, and so you shall.

(Tape is turned.)

I am Q'uo and am once again with this instrument. We greet you again in love and in light. May we ask if there is another query at this time?

S: Carla had mentioned earlier that she had many people contacting her for assurance that everything is OK. Are there any briefer words of wit or wisdom for those looking for that type of assurances? What would our best response be?

I am Q'uo and am aware of your query, my brother, We, again, as we are wont to do in many situations, recommend that each utilize the tool of meditation upon a daily basis, utilizing the opportunity to commune with the one Creator and to find the strength of that unifying connection that leaves one with the conclusion that truly all are one, and that whatever occurs to a brother or sister, occurs to you. So that when one loves those who have not been loved previously that one is loving all beings, that when one can heal any misunderstanding or wound in a relationship that one aids the healing and the loving of this planet and its population.

We would recommend to each entity that within the meditative state one see the ruptures in this planet's beingness. Perhaps you can locate them geographically within your mind, seeing them as dark and hurting, in pain and confusion. And then, begin to bring the light and the love of the one Creator into the image. See that rupture of hurt and pain lightened by this love of the one Creator, shining forth through the eyes of all. Focus upon the injury, the hurt, and the pain until it is also as bright as the noonday sun.

Though one may feel that such an image is a small thing compared to the immensity of the agony in your world today, we can assure you that when your inner world of spirit is illumined by your free will choice with love and light these thoughts are things, and this is more and more truly so as your planet moves into fourth density at this time, and this light and love goes where it is needed. And there is healing. And there is hope. And there is a direction that leads each into that unity with each other self upon this planet. The process may not be short. It may not be easy, but it is ever possible to those who have the faith and the will to persevere. All things are possible when entered into with love, acceptance, compassion, humility, tolerance and the light touch. These are your allies, my friends, and each other heart in love [who is] joined with you in this great quest which you are upon ever more fully at this time in your planet's history.

Is there another query, my brother?

S: No. Thanks.

C: I'd like to ask if the same method can be applied to healing the Earth as you recommend for the healing of humanity?

I am Q'uo and am aware of your query, my sister, and this is indeed so. This technique of visualization may be used for any kind of healing, whether of the self, of another self, of a people, of a country, of a planet. Wherever there is that which is broken, that which is hurt, that which is injured, healing is possible for mind, for body, for spirit and for the ability to continue where there seems to be little reason. The imagining, the imaging is that which calls for from the deeper levels of the subconscious mind the connection with the one Creator, with the Logos of Love, that enables that love to move through your being to wherever it is needed. This is a means by which each may avail the self of that ability to open to love, to give love, to direct love, to feel love, to be love.

Is there another query, my sister?

C: In addition to meditation is there anything that we can do with crystals to aid in the healing process?

I am Q'uo and am aware of your query, my sister. There are various aids, shall we say, that one may employ in the persistent meditation. By persistent meditation we recommend that a time and a place for meditation be set aside on a daily basis so that when one retires to that place at that time that these become signals, prompts, if you will, to the subconscious mind that it is time for a working; it is time for a healing. If one wishes also to utilize crystals, incense, any type of sensory deprivation, such are means of refining this type of visualization in meditation which may be utilized as the meditator desires. Each entity will find a slightly different means by which to accomplish this healing meditation. And whatever rings of truth to the entity is that which we would heartily suggest and encourage. For each entity has come into this incarnation with the ability to do this kind of work. Indeed, each has come with many abilities which can be brought forth in times of heavy catalyst, shall we say. Each will feel a certain kind of awakening, a certain kind of enlivening of the spirit within as this kind of daily meditation and visualization is undertaken. For as you retire to the world of spirit you retire to that which is real, which powers you through this world of illusion. We cannot recommend meditation enough, my friends, for this is your link with the infinite. This is your link with truth. This is your link with love. This is your link with your true self and all other selves on your planet.

Is there another query, my sister?

C: No. Thank you very much.

I am Q'uo and again we thank you, my sister. Is there another query at this time?

M: I have one. Is there a particular time of day or of year that is most conducive to meditation?

I am Q'uo and am aware of your query, my brother. We find that indeed for some who have a great deal of time to meditate that there are times that are more opportune than others. For some the dawning hours are most helpful for they signify the beginning of a new day, a day fresh with opportunity, a day ready to be painted, shall we say, by the heart, by the creative and curious mind, by the passion for living and sharing, for learning and loving.

For others, the time nearest the sleep is helpful, for some feel more desire to heal that which has occurred, to experience again the difficulties of the day that then, as the day ends, there may be an effort to heal them.

For some there is much of strength and empowering that occurs with meditation at the noonday when the sun is at its zenith and the light of your day is its strongest and brightest. Thus you see there is a great variety of times which might be helpful to each entity. We recommend that each consider for itself the daily round of activities and their requirements and to look at those times when one would feel the most comfortable and ready to enter into the meditative state and to do work upon consciousness for the whole planet. Regularity of the time chosen is that which is most helpful, whether it be the beginning, the middle or the end of the day is really not as important as that the time be regular and be done each day at the same time.

Is there a further query, my brother?

M: Not from me. Thank you.

I am Q'uo and we thank you, my brother. Is there another query at this time?

(Pause for thirty seconds.)

I am Q'uo. As it appears that we have exhausted the queries for this session of working we would once again thank each for inviting our presence this day in your seeking in your circle of working. It is a great honor for us to be here. We may say that we feel the great desire for truth, the desire for healing, the desire for serving that is present in this circle this day. We can say to each present that you are not alone. There are many more circles of seeking upon this planet that are shining most brightly at this time, for it is apparent to many more entities upon this planet at this time that there is the need for such healing, for such seeking and for such serving. Know that you walk with a goodly company of lighted souls who see and seek beyond the illusion and who walk with you each step and who encourage of you through their own meditations, their own circles of working. For each of you is likened to the other. Moreover each of you is the other, and when this truth can be seen and known and felt and experienced and lived in the daily round of activities more and more fully upon your planet, then will the difficulties that you experience at this time and for so long in the history and culture of every country [be eased], then will you be more fully able to channel that love and that light in your everyday activities and to heal the wounds that have long festered in the population of all countries and all hearts. Then will it be more possible to know the love of the Creator and to see it expressed about one. Know that you are joined by those of the Confederation of Planets in the Service of the Infinite Creator upon a daily basis, and when you do meditate or think upon these things a simple request is all that is necessary for various entities from this Confederation of Planets to join you in your meditations, in your thoughts, in your love and in your healing.

We are known to you as those of Q'uo. We would take our leave at this time of this instrument and of this group, leaving each as always in the love and in the light of the one Creator. Adonai, my friends. Adonai. ✤

L/L Research

L/L Research is a subsidiary of Rock Creek Research & Development Laboratories, Inc.

P.O. Box 5195
Louisville, KY 40255-0195

www.llresearch.org

Rock Creek is a non-profit corporation dedicated to discovering and sharing information which may aid in the spiritual evolution of humankind.

ABOUT THE CONTENTS OF THIS TRANSCRIPT: This telepathic channeling has been taken from transcriptions of the weekly study and meditation meetings of the Rock Creek Research & Development Laboratories and L/L Research. It is offered in the hope that it may be useful to you. As the Confederation entities always make a point of saying, please use your discrimination and judgment in assessing this material. If something rings true to you, fine. If something does not resonate, please leave it behind, for neither we nor those of the Confederation would wish to be a stumbling block for any.

© 2009 L/L RESEARCH

HOMECOMING MEDITATION
SEPTEMBER 23, 2001

Group question: The question today has to do with the concept of the "light-bringer," the knowledge-bringer, whether this is Lucifer that was the knowledge-bringer or the light-bringer, or Eve who gave Adam the apple from the Tree of the Knowledge of Good and Evil, we are wondering if Q'uo could give us some information about the nature of these entities, or these qualities that bring knowledge. Are these entities themselves either good or evil? How does the concept that they deliver to us give us the ability to pursue that which is good or evil, service-to-self or service-to-others? Last week Q'uo gave us some information concerning the Lightning Struck Tower which is also a concept or an image that shows light in its sudden and fiery form causing what seems to be destruction. We are wondering if there is other fruit from this destruction? Can something positive come out of the Lightning Struck [Tower] and, literally, the towers in New York City that were destroyed?

(Carla channeling)

We are those known to you as the principle of Q'uo, and we greet you in the love and in the light of the one infinite Creator, in whose service we are. It is a great privilege to be called to your group this week, and we thank you for the privilege of sharing our thoughts with you and for sharing this time of meditation. Each of your vibrations are beautiful to us, and we thank you for the gift of yourselves, the gift of your time, and your seeking.

We are most grateful to be able to speak with you and ask of you only that you be very careful in listening to what we have to say, for we are error-prone, those of opinion rather than of authority, seekers upon the path just as are you. And we do not want to constitute in any way a stumbling block to your seeking. Take those thoughts that appeal to you and leave the rest behind. This is the way of truth. All truth is not for all entities. There is a resonance to that truth that speaks to your own seeking and to your own situation. We ask you to trust your own powers of discrimination. For truly you have a very keen radar for truth and for falsity.

You ask this day concerning the Matrix of the Spirit and the Potentiator of the Spirit. And may we say that this is a very interesting subject and certainly one that challenges our ability to use this instrument to create a structure of sense and truth. For this is a mazed subject. The construction of archetypal images in a certain system is a tool, a resource of learning about the architecture of the deeps roots of your mind. It describes things that are impossible to put into words in terms of imagery and combinations of images. These are subjective images that are intended to act as triggers as much as patent images. They are not necessarily to be literally interpreted but to be felt, to be sensed, and to be entered into.

In the system of the images which we of the Confederation have often spoken to your group concerning, the archetypal images are divided into three groups: those that pertain to the body, those that pertain to the mind, and those that pertain to the spirit. In each of the three systems there is a matrix which is a still and unmoving structure that is a receptor web that has only very limited ability to act. What it can do is desire. It can reach. This is the nature of the matrix. It is essentially a structure into which catalyst will come and through which catalyst will be processed into experience. In these three systems the potentiator is that which is able to fertilize or to make fruitful the matrix. There is a dynamic between matrix and potentiator then. The basic dynamic is that, in the mind, the reacher and the reached; in the body, the body in constant motion, and the controller of that body; and in the spirit, the unreaching, unhasting darkness of spirit waiting for, hoping for, yearning for, and desiring information about itself. And out of the dynamic of that dark yearning comes the Potentiator of the Spirit, which is light.

Let us take a moment to gaze at the power and the peace of this situation, of the empires of mind and body and spirit, of the supple and lithe connections between body and mind, mind and spirit, spirit and body. The spirit, the soul, the entity that each of you is, is a crystalline shape, a snowflake, shall we say, a beautiful crystal. Each of you is unique. Each of you has your own beauty. Each of you has your own symmetry. And within your crystal each of you is working with those perceived flaws, those clinging barnacles of matter that are not the gem. Each of you seeks the light of spirit to inform and advise. Each of you, then, has laid before you a tremendous range of resources upon which you can rely with your linear, intellectual mind, with all the powers of ratiocination that you have at your command, with the grace and rhythm of the pulsing body that in its instinct and in its essence is so completely aware as a second-density creature is of the love and the light, of the harmony and the unity of the creation and the infinite Creator. And of the tremendous strength of that creature which is the spirit.

The kingdom of the spirit is a dark one. And we say this not because darkness is evil, for darkness is not evil. We say this because it is the nature of spirit within third density to be largely impossible to see. It is dark because it must be dark, and the light that is the Lightning Struck Tower, though it may seem radiant to the physical eyes when seen as a symbol in your World Trade Center bombing, in terms of metaphysics it is a frail and flickering candle of a lightning bolt that is all too quickly extinguished and shows all too little of the hidden landscape of the spirit.

Each of you will spend the incarnational time that you have in this estate of peering into darkness using seemingly the dimmest of lights, occasionally receiving that lightning, that bolt of epiphany that speaks, that is as the star that guides, that brings that moment of clarity and spiritual truth that is so blessed. Thusly the Matrix of the Spirit is called, in the tarot system, the Devil simply because the spirit seems, in its form, to be antithetical to the body. It seems that there is a tremendous sacrifice involved in moving from things of the body to things of the spirit. It seems as if one must give up the life, in a way, when one chooses the life of the spirit because the life of the world no longer fits, no longer applies. When light has been brought to the spirit there is tremendous change and transformation that takes place. And there is a death process that goes on as the allegiance and the thinking of the seeker moves from one system or realm or kingdom to another.

Is this an evil matrix? Is there something evil about the spirit that has brought the energy of Lucifer and Satan into identification with it? We would say, no, absolutely without hesitation there is no evil whatever in the spirit, nor is there good. But, rather, there is simply essence. There is that which is. This is how you are made. This is the way your vibrations are structured within the energy pattern or the energy field of your being. This is the way the Creator is articulated at this point in the Creator's progress. And what you are looking at is, as this group has mentioned several times during the conversation, somewhat abstract and hard to get hold of because it is not the familiar. It is not the everyday. But, rather, it is what is moving below the surface of self in very deep portions of the self that help to shape the options that are available to each of you within the incarnation. The more that you can see into these relationships of Matrix and Potentiator of Spirit, the more hardy you may be in terms of being able to withstand and to be able to use the light which there is because it is so precious and so rare.

Those who bring light are, shall we say, a way or a symbol of the same thing as saying those who bring polarity. It is not precisely knowledge that the tree involved in the Garden of Eden story was bearing as its fruit. That is not it, precisely. It is not simply a body of knowledge that was forbidden. Rather, it is the essence of third density that is being talked about in this story. The creatures of Eden were basically second-density entities. They did not have free will. They did not have self-awareness. They were the created opportunities for spirit growth without the indwelling spirit. The story of the one known as Satan offering this fruit of good and evil to the one known as Eve is, as the one known as Eric points out, a delightful way of shifting the blame for the entire fall of human nature to women and that, shall we say, incorrect solution has entranced and delighted men in many different religious systems of those of your planet and has led many into sweeping generalizations concerning biases towards the feminine gender and their unworthiness which have been quite stubborn in balances within your peoples as a race.

Each of you, we find, within this circle is fully aware that this is not a correct solution. It is neither a masculine or a feminine quality, good and evil, but rather each of these genders is opportunities to learn certain lessons, and the souls that inhabit these bodies of gender are both sexes and neither sex; in other words, simply souls. But the reason, the logic behind the woman giving to the man this fruit of the tree of good and evil, this polarity, this third-density essence, is simply that in the system of archetypes the Matrix of the Mind is the unfed spirit, the unfed seeker and the Potentiator of the Mind is a deeply feminine character, the High Priestess, which represents, shall we say, the fructifying influence of the subconscious, so that the unfed mind is reaching into the subconscious for its knowledge, for its truth, for its beginning of experience. This is the only reason for this attribution of so-called evil to the feminine character. It is well, when looking at stories such as the Adam and Eve Story, to look at them in symbolic terms, in general terms, in terms that would suggest and would provoke contemplation of deeper issues.

The darkness of the spirit is like unto the darkness, the apparent darkness, of the starry heavens. As you gaze from the side of your planet out into your outer space, that thick velvet of infinite space is as are you in your spiritual aspect: an undiscovered country of hills and valleys unknown. And every place is sacred. And every place is full of information. And every place looks to be that which it is not. There is thick darkness and great depth of unknowingness to the spirit within third density. The veil of forgetting is very deep. And the life-giving light, when it falls, yet does it not always disclose truth. And so there is a great peering into what light there is to see beyond the falsity of the complex and intricate patterns of spirit.

Even when the veil of forgetting is lifted, even when you ascend into densities which are full of light, yet still that spirit is stubbornly unknown, and layers of misinformation and false patterning will fall away as the densities roll, and we find this still to be true with our selves. We find we still peel away another layer and another layer of that deception of spirit which is part and parcel of the situation which we all enjoy as part of the Creator. It is not that the Creator intends to deceive. It is not that the light means to be false. It is that there is so much of untold riches to the infinite Creator that It is not all articulated. There is much still for the Creator to know about Itself. And yet that seeking is a slow, slow process. For all that the Creator finds out about Itself, It finds out from you, each of you, each of us, each of all of those entities that live and move and have their being within the creation of the Father.

We find great beauty in this pattern. We do not understand it completely. As each of you works with your own spiritual journey we ask simply that you not fear the light-bringer who brings seeming destruction. For there must be that taken down as a preparation for that which is builded anew. There needs to be the removal of false concepts before the building of a fresh and vital concept.

We would, at this time, transfer this contact to the one known as Jim, pausing only to offer to the one known as M the comment that we see the wanderers among your peoples because of the overlay of the vibratory patterns of their home density. Those who are wanderers can only feel this, as you have said, rather indirectly and by inference. However, it is our feeling that all those who are awakened upon this planet are wanderers at this time and functioning as such. We would now leave this instrument in love and in light and transfer to the one known as Jim. We are those known to you as Q'uo.

(Jim channeling)

I am Q'uo, and greet each again in love and in light through this instrument. At this time it is our privilege to ask if there might be further queries on the minds of those present. Is there another query at this time?

M: I'd like to know how the patterns of the matrix of the souls looks to you. Does it look geometric? What is it made of? What is its purpose?

I am Q'uo, and am aware of your query, my sister. The pattern of the matrix of souls who have taken incarnation and who have moved into the physical third-density for their incarnation is a pattern which is formed of light, formed by love, in a fashion which is useable by the mind complex for the purpose of pursuing information-gathering and decision-making, shall we say. For the Matrix of the Mind, in the system of images which you call the tarot, is a quality which allows for a nurturing of experience and the utilization of this experience in a useful manner. We would ask the questioner to query further as to more specific information.

M: I'd like to know how we can make use of it, for example. Can we visualize its form or its flow to help us learn better or see more and make better informed choices, or heal ourselves? Things like that.

I am Q'uo, and am aware of your query, my sister. All of which you have mentioned are possible for any seeking entity by the fruits of the seeking process. The Matrix of the Mind is a concept complex which is a tool for the seeker of truth, as are all the images of the Major Arcana of your system of tarot. For each one forms a kind of library, shall we say, that allows access to various portions of the mind itself. If we look at the mind as a jewel, each concept complex of the tarot is as a facet of this jewel. The jewel, the mind itself, is brilliant in its appearance to us, for there is light in each entity which is emanating from this jewel in such and such a fashion according to the proclivity or tendency of each seeker to seek in its own way. Thus some facets of the jewel of the mind are brighter than other and the overall balance of brilliance is that which reflects or measures the seeking intensity and efficiency of each seeker. We would see the Matrix and the other facets of the mind as avenues which a seeker may pursue in any manner chosen by free will, including each of those which you listed. Is there another query, my sister?

M: That's all at this time.

I am Q'uo, and we thank you, my sister. Is there another query at this time?

Carla: I received a letter yesterday from Bruce Peret, and he said that the Earth had once again accepted us and wanderers in general as those whom it would accept love from and accept healing from. Can you comment on this situation with our planet and its feelings and experience right now?

I am Q'uo, and am aware of your query, my sister. The entity which you call Earth, or Gaia, is one which is in the process of its own evolution as is each entity upon it. The Earth entity at this time, realizing that it is preparing to move into a more intense portion of the birthing of a new Earth is, as we have mentioned previously, particularly vulnerable as is any woman who is about to give birth to new life. The experience of many thousands of years of difficulties between the populations of this planet has caused the entity of Earth to be, shall we say, infected with a great deal of anger and hostility, the vibrations of the bellicose actions of your peoples over a great portion of your time. This heat of anger has caused the entity of Earth to release the excess heat in various places in various manners. Those geophysical eruptions of your volcanoes, the earthquakes, and so forth have been able to release some of this buildup of heat so that the mantle of the Earth, in some places, is rearranged in a fashion which causes a great deal of physical destruction. Yet the alignment possible after such rearrangements is that which welcomes the newer vibrations of love and compassion which are now moving more fully into expression within some portions of, not only the Earth entity, but large portions of the Earth's populations. Thus the entity of Earth has begun to vibrate more fully in harmony with both the newer vibrations of love and compassion and those of the population of this planet which has also sought to harmonize with these vibrations as well. Thus there is, within the Earth entity, a feeling of excitement at this opportunity, of distress at the difficulty of the birth, of compassion for those who suffer, and a kind of maternal disapproval of those who yet linger in the ways of war. Is there a further query, my sister?

Carla: Yes, Q'uo. I would just like to ask then: is our daily meditation practice the best shot that we have at reassuring Mother Earth that we do love her and wish to help her through this birth?

I am Q'uo, and am aware of your query, my sister. We would respond by suggesting that the regular meditations, focused upon the healing of this planet and the possibility of peace for its populations, is most helpful at this time and at any time. For as one is able to see light entering into the darkened world awaiting war, there is a balancing that is given yet another avenue to enter into the Earth vibrations. There is a point of balance, a fulcrum, which you may see created by your efforts to visualize peace and healing. This fulcrum is within the mass mind, or the planetary mind, of the population of this planet. It is that new mind, shall we say, which is being born at this time as the fourth-density positive population which shall remain as the remnant in its path of evolution at some point in your future, in all probability. When groups such as this one, and many, many others around this planet, meet for the purpose of visualizing peace and healing it is as a level moving through this fulcrum, lightening the vibratory pattern that has been prevalent for a great portion of your time. We recommend that such meditative experiences be regular and include not only this country but all those who are engaged in the pursuit of war, or the destruction of fellow humans. For each entity is quite closely connected to each other entity. The concept of unity is that which eludes most peoples of your planet at this time. That concept of linkage of one to another is most important to enhance at this time so that the vibrations of healing, acceptance, compassion, forgiveness, mercy, understanding and so forth may be injected into the peoples of the various geographical vicinities of this planet, thus strengthening the bond that each is aware of at some level of the life experience. Thus the vibrations of light sent forth in meditation move where they are needed most, into those areas of the planet and the population which are engaged in the destructive effects of separation and the thinking which brings it about. Is there a further query, my sister?

Carla: No, thank you. That was plenty. Thanks.

I am Q'uo, and we thank you once again, my sister. Is there another query at this time?

C: Could you say something further about the remnant that will remain here for fourth-density work?

I am Q'uo, and am aware of your query, my sister. The so-called remnant, that portion of this planetary population which shall remain with this planet, is labeled as such by many for there is in all likelihood a far greater portion of the population which shall need to find further experience within the third density in order to balance the difficult vibrations which have not allowed the graduation into the density of compassion. Thus those who do remain and who seek in the positive sense are from various locations, shall we say, not just this third-density planet which you call Earth. For the population from this planet that will be able to welcome and enjoy the vibrations of love and compassion is small in comparison to what this planet could comfortably welcome and stably house.

There are many entities coming from other third-density planets who have made the graduation at this time, who are incarnating early within the fourth-density experience of this planet in order to help it in its birth process. This is considered a great honor, for there is much catalyst at this time which these entities seek to utilize in a positive or magical sense; that is, the transmutation of the vibrations of separation into that which enhances the unity between all the peoples and the creation itself. This population of the new Earth is that which is like unto the vanguard that moves first into the difficult areas of conflict and seeks to combat the difficulties with the vibrations of love. There is no direct conflict, as you are undoubtedly aware, for those who move under the banner of love are those which welcome the opportunity to transmute the dark and heavy vibrations into those which are light and full of love by the effort that they make in these latter days of your third density.

Is there another query?

C: Not at this time. Thank you.

I am Q'uo, and we thank you, my sister. Is there another query at this time?

M: How will we physically clean up the Earth? Will there be magical means? Will we be able to clean it up?

I am Q'uo, and am aware of your query, my sister. One of the primary qualities of the fourth-density experience is that which may be seen to be the ability to utilize the frontal lobes of the human brain in a manner which is able to participate as a co-Creator. The ability to create with the mind those tools and resources necessary for the revitalization of this planetary entity which you call Earth is the primary means whereby the healing of this planet may be achieved.

Is there a further query, my sister?

M: I am concerned about the loss of species of animals. I wonder if they can be restored?

I am Q'uo, and am aware of your query, my sister. And we can assure you that through both the processes which we have just mentioned and the natural regeneration of the Earth itself will make it possible for this planet to become inhabited by those species which have previously been present upon and within its being. This is correct.

Is there a further query?

M: No. Thank you.

I am Q'uo, and again we thank you, my sister. Is there another query at this time?

C: I would like to ask about working with frustration. I seem to have a great deal of it these days. A lot of people are dealing with it now and struggling against daily things as well as larger things. Do you have any recommendation other than meditation?

I am Q'uo, and am aware of your query, my sister. We would suggest the further use of meditation in a specific fashion in order to deal with the increased stress and frustration which the daily round of activities for each of your peoples has brought in this time of turmoil for most of your population.

When the end of the day has come, or at some portion just prior to retiring for the day, we would recommend the sitting in meditation and the reviewing of the portions of the day which were perceived as frustrating. Look again at each situation. Relive the experience of frustration and observe the components of this experience: each entity, each event, thought, response, each detail which you can remember, so that the experience is once again alive in the mind. Then when this frustration is felt in this particular type of meditation, allow the balancing emotions of peace, of understanding, of acceptance, of tolerance, of humor to begin to surface as well within the mind until there is an equality of power between the frustration and the peace. This is a kind of short course, shall we say, in experiencing the incarnation. If one is able to accept the self, both for having the frustration as an experience and for being able to find within the self the ability to balance that with the feelings of acceptance, compassion, mercy and so forth, then you are able to move in a more balanced fashion within your daily round of activities, having laid the foundation within both the subconscious and conscious portions of the mind for being able to deal with various other frustrating experiences in succeeding days and rounds of activities.

Is there a further query, my sister?

C: No. Thank you.

I am Q'uo, and we thank you once again, my sister. Is there a final query at this time?

E: I would like to know if it is possible for us to straighten out the situation on this planet without straightening out the situation between the sexes?

I am Q'uo, and am aware of your query, my brother. The situation, as you have described it, is one which has many, many facets, being rooted first in the concept of separation. What is the first separation? Self from self. As each individual entity views portions of itself as needing punishment, as being less than valuable, as being unworthy, then is born the concept of the separation of self from others as well. So that which you have described as the difficulty between male and female sexes upon your planet and the subjugation of the latter by the former, then, this kind of separation is also possible between groups of peoples, one state and another, one country and another, one religion and another, and so forth.

Thus it would be helpful to begin the healing, not only between the female and male portions of the populations, but between those portions of the self which have been rejected for one reason or another and have made the possibility of rejecting other entities a reality. The healing of this planet and its peoples is a healing which begins with each self and moves outward to include all other selves.

Is there a further query, my brother?

E: Then, if I have you right, then, it basically starts with the self? Straightening out my relationship with my self is where I need to begin rather than worrying about gender relations. Is that correct?

I am Q'uo, and am aware of your query, my brother. We would recommend that indeed the effort at healing begin with the self but at the same time include all other relationships of self with other self, the male and female relationship being primary among all relationships. Thus the healing process may be far reaching in its overall scope but indeed begins with the self.

Is there another query?

E: No. Thank you.

I am Q'uo, and we thank you once again, my brother. At this time we feel that we have spoken as fully as this particular instrument is able to, for there is some distraction and fatigue. We thank each once again for inviting our presence this day. It is a great honor to be invited to join your circle of seeking, and we can assure each that the Confederation of Planets in the Service of the One Infinite Creator has many emissaries present at this time observing the movement of your peoples from one concept of love and acceptance to another. As this concept begins to spread from one grouping of peoples to another we see a great deal of light being generated so that your planet at this time is a combination of the light and the dark in many different patchwork places so that the light very slowly but surely begins to burn brighter in those areas where there are hearts to open to the concept of love more and more fully as the catalyst becomes greater and greater. You are not alone, my friends. There is a great company of the heavenly host which moves at this time to send its light where it is most needed according to the difficulties that various portions of your planet now experience. As your meditation groups meet and send their light it is joined by the light of many, many others and moves into those areas at this time that are in difficulty.

We are those of Q'uo and we add our light to yours, and at this time we would take our leave of this instrument and this group. We leave each, as always, in the love and in the light of the one Creator. Adonai, my friends. Adonai.

L/L Research

L/L Research is a subsidiary of Rock Creek Research & Development Laboratories, Inc.

P.O. Box 5195
Louisville, KY 40255-0195

www.llresearch.org

Rock Creek is a non-profit corporation dedicated to discovering and sharing information which may aid in the spiritual evolution of humankind.

ABOUT THE CONTENTS OF THIS TRANSCRIPT: This telepathic channeling has been taken from transcriptions of the weekly study and meditation meetings of the Rock Creek Research & Development Laboratories and L/L Research. It is offered in the hope that it may be useful to you. As the Confederation entities always make a point of saying, please use your discrimination and judgment in assessing this material. If something rings true to you, fine. If something does not resonate, please leave it behind, for neither we nor those of the Confederation would wish to be a stumbling block for any.

© 2009 L/L Research

Sunday Meditation
October 7, 2001

Group question: The question today has to do with the healing meditations that you recommended a couple of weeks ago in response to the terrorist attacks of September 11 and various other places on the planet which are full of anger and war and hatred, famine, poverty, disease and so forth. We would like to know a couple of more ways that a person could use to send love and light to all the areas, the people, the places that need it.

(Carla channeling)

We are those known to you as the principle Q'uo. Greetings, love and light to you. The love and the light of the infinite Creator to you this beautiful autumn evening. What a pleasure it is to rest in meditation with each of you and to join your circle of seeking. We greatly thank you for the privilege of being called to your group, and, as always, we would simply ask that as we offer our ideas, that each be confident in her own powers of discrimination. If an idea or thought seems resonant to you, by all means, we offer it as our opinion and our best answer but not as authority. If it does not interest you, then by all means lay it aside and move on. We thank you for that discrimination because that allows us to express ourselves with the most accuracy that we can through this instrument without abridging the Law of Confusion.

It is a pleasure to speak with you concerning the question of how to be instruments for the love and the light of the one infinite Creator. It is a most central and key question for us as well as for you. We have long hoped to offer our part in positively affecting the process of the birth of fourth density positive upon your planet and among its peoples, so we, too, are focused in our own ways on the questions of how to offer love and light to the planet and to its peoples. Obviously, our current solution is communication within the rather narrow confines of a meditation which has a trained channel of the type such as this instrument and the one known as Jim are. This enables us to offer impressions and to tell stories as the one known as S suggested, to weave tapestries and structures of words that may constitute resources for you, as you think about these questions that are infinite in their possibilities for fruitful contemplation and further realization and understanding, if we may use that term.

This communication of ours is bound in silence. It is silence that fuels the channel, silence that fuels the desire of those present, and silence that enables that desire to be honed. It is silence that enables the self to be known to itself. It is in silence that trust and faith abound. It is in the shared silence of prayer that miracles happen.

Prayer is a word that has emotional overtones for many, and yet we use prayer not only for formal orison and for words beseeching the Almighty in the traditional sense of prayer, but also prayer as entering the silence, prayer as practicing the presence of the one infinite Creator. It is easy to open to the self an empty room by silence. It is more fruitful to visualize or to realize that room within that is the room of prayer, shall we say, or the room of silence as a room that has atmosphere and person, in that it has location within that person that you are most deeply are. It is like the sanctuary that is in the very heart of the temple that the priest may enter for private moments, those moments which fuel that ministry that serves others. For each of you is a temple and a priest within the temple. The temple is that body and that personality and those gifts. The priest is the consciousness within that directs that building and its stewardship, the disposition of the talents and treasures of the temple and the use and aid of those faculties of being that fuel the ministry.

Each priest needs to spend time in that sanctuary that has to do with no one but the self and that connection that is sacred between the self and the infinite Creator, between the loved and the lover, between the spark and the source of that spark, that great fire, that great light, that great love, that great Thought that is the one infinite Creator. It is helpful to picture entering, not that empty room of impersonal prayer, but a very personal room that is the heart of self and in which there waits the figure of the Creator as the Creator would appear to you. Many see the Creator as Father. Many see the Creator as Mother. Some see the Creator as the Christ, as does this instrument. Whatever that image is, realize that the Creator is waiting for you there and that you go to be with your true self when you enter the sanctuary of silence.

This enables the basic lining up of the energy body so that the silence may be offered and may be used to the Creator and for the use of the Creator. For meditation itself is something that feeds upon itself. There is the intention to meditate which becomes the meditation, which becomes the intention to meditate, which becomes the meditation. The one known as T was quite correct in stating that it matters not the perceived degree of efficacy achieved by the meditator or the one who prays. What matters is that the entity remember that the entity come into remembrance of that sanctuary, that infinite Creator, that presence that touches the life and in so touching the life creates the life for it.

We will speak to some extent about various techniques, but first we would like to say that beyond any technique of meditating, visualizing and sending light to a certain concern, there is the simple truth that as this instrument's Psalm says, *"Send forth your spirit, and I shall be created, and you shall renew the face of the Earth."* As each of you comes to that sanctuary, comes to that door of spirit, enters through it and practices the presence of the infinite Creator each of you is coming into his own higher self and is filling out and fleshing out a nature that is already there, that has been there before the world was. Each of you is a spark of the Creator. Each of you has within you that spirit which has the genius to know what is needed in a particular moment. The greatest and most courageous feat of faith is a surrender to that spirit and to that spirit's will for you. And that in itself is a prayer. "Send me forth. Create me. Play on me as you play on the face of the deep and create that which is a new world, that which is a new me. Let me be, for the first time, fully my true self. And let that true self become full enough of the higher aspect of self that it irresistibly begins to radiate."

As the one known as T noted, even a tiny bit of doing this, of allowing the heart to become open and golden and flowing, creates a joy and a blessing that is often startling. It is not that you are going in search of joy. It is not that you are attempting to create bliss. It is simply that you are attempting to line up the energy body, balance it, open it and ask it to work. Ask, shall we say, the Holy Spirit, the one infinite Creator, your guidance, however you frame your processes of communication with the divine, to make you an instrument of His peace. Each of you is a crystal instrument and truly it is not necessary to know precisely how you are creating the melody of love, how you are shaping that instrument which is your crystal being so that it is able to transmute, intensify and anchor into the planetary vibration the infinite light and love of the one Creator. It is only necessary that you surrender to that intention. The remaining details are useful, but they are more useful for the linear mind than they are in terms of the metaphysical.

In terms of the metaphysical, the clumsy and awkward attempts of sincere people are far more persuasive than the sophisticated, easily spoken and roundly shaped phrases of faith that do not come from the heart. It is not necessary to be clever, articulate or even to have words. What is necessary is that there be a process that is passionately being pursued whereby the seeker is seeking along the path of spiritual evolution. The desire to serve creates the opportunity to serve. The opportunity to serve creates the means to serve. The means to serve flow through the instrument and out into the world. Thusly, the main focus of the crystal is to be a good crystal, to open the self as a crystal, to give the intention of service, to give the intention of placing time in the silence for this service and to be persistent about offering this service in a way that speaks more and more to the question of how high an amperage is this light? How high in amperage are you as a crystal? [How committed are you to] this process of patient, dogged persistence, no matter what your self-concept is: to that which is most effective metaphysically. Those intentions are powerful. They are your strength, not any self-perceived skill or lack of it with entering the silence, maintaining the silence, holding a visualization and so forth. These are linear details that some are quite effective at dealing with and some not so effective. This instrument, for instance, is not a skillful visualizer and, in fact, is often blocked from visualizing.

The secret to visualization is finding an image that brings forth the passion and the desire to serve and opens the heart in a certain way. We speak now not of visualizations in the white magical sense but visualizations in the sense of taking an image and sending energy into that image, attempting to build an image of light and healing. Perhaps the simplest image is the globe itself. The book cover of this instrument's book [*A Wanderer's Handbook*], which shows the globe with the sun rising behind it in that dawn of the new age that is breaking over the Earth, is perhaps a good object to take visualization from, for in that visualization there is both light shining from the dawning of the new age upon the entire planet and the colored lights streaming into the planet which are all of the souls entering the Earth plane that wish to help the Earth at this time.

Realize that much light is being sent to this planet at this time, and when the visualization of this globe is done it is not a visualization that you have alone. For many, many entities visualize the basic globe and send light to that globe until it is bright all over. There are ways to embroider this basic image of the globe in space and the light coming to it and dawning over it that, perhaps, are more personal. One may picture oneself as one of many beings which are weaving a net of love and light just like a fisherman's seine or a butterfly net, something that moves across the entire stream, that wraps around the planet like a great, full skirt from an angel so that all of the planet is wrapped in this shining mesh that is made of individuals' love and light, woven energy upon energy, sent from so many instruments of love and light, from so many light workers, shall we call them, into this web or net of love.

One great problem is simply convincing your planet that you truly care. There has been a substantial amount of uncaring, neglectful and even destructive action of entities upon the Earth in ways that the one known as Jim was commenting upon earlier, creating ever-increasing lacks of good environment in which various species may thrive. The sheer passion and persistence of this effort is that which the Earth will hear. If visualization is a problem, it is possible simply to speak with, to give words to, the Earth, to explain to the Earth how much it is loved by you, how much you appreciate the Earth, how much you feel in unity with the Earth, and how much you want to help it come through this tremendously exhausting and difficult period of birth.

We find that we need to move on to speak through the instrument known as Jim. We are watching this instrument's energy level this day, and we feel that this is sufficient through this instrument. We thank this instrument and would transfer this contact to the one known as Jim. We are those of Q'uo.

(Jim channeling)

I am Q'uo, and we greet each once again in love and in light through this instrument. We would ask if we may speak to any other portion of this query if those present would examine that which we have given and put forth any refining queries at this time. Is there such a query at this time?

Carla: Would you like to discuss any other methods of meditation and sending the light that would be options for people to use?

I am Q'uo, and we are aware of your query, my sister. We are grateful that you have asked this portion of the query again, for there is indeed a variety of ways that those who wish to aid the healing of this planet and its peoples may do so. We have often mentioned the technique of visualization, as we did previously today, so we shall at this time discuss a technique which may be more helpful to those who are less skilled at the inner visualization.

When in the meditative state look at the feeling that one connects to the anguish of the world, of various locations, peoples, experiences and so forth. This ability to perceive the difficulties which others upon this planet are experiencing is yet another means by which those who meditate with the desire to heal may connect their experience with those who need light. Indeed, all are a portion of the one Creator, and the connections that bind each together with each other entity are those which are, shall we say, submerged within the subconscious experience. It is helpful to imagine one's own being within a certain set of circumstances, perhaps of having no home, being hungry, cold, alone or with a great mass of other entities in similar circumstances such as is now the case in the area of the world which you call Afghanistan. Imagine what your experience would be like to be without a home, hungry, to be fearful, to be uncertain of what the next day would bring. Allow your feelings to move into those areas of your being which can appreciate this experience. These are the subconscious levels of the mind.

Experience for as long as you are able the feelings of anguish, of pain, of loss, of confusion. See with new eyes how an entity such as yourself would respond to these severe circumstances. Allow that feeling to grow within yourself until it is truly palpable. Then, from within the center of your heart, allow that quality of love/light to emanate until the previous feelings of the stress have been, shall we say, engulfed, surrounded by the love and light emanations from within not only your heart but from within the hearts of all others who meditate with you as well. Experience the outpouring of these small streams of love and light until there is a great river of love and light that completely engulfs the feeling of distress. See these feelings of the distress begin to lighten as there is sent to them those streams of hope, of faith, of support, of unity. See these threads of light weaving together, feel them joining, experience this blending of the concerns of many such as yourself for those who are experiencing extreme difficulties. Allow this feeling to remain with you for an equally long period of your meditation. Then give praise and thanksgiving to the one Creator who made all that there is the opportunity to serve the One in this manner.

Is there another query, my sister?

Carla: That was very interesting. It seems like it is similar to the personal balancing technique but for the planet. I guess another question that comes to my mind is one that I was talking to C about because she and S have a great number of crystals. I had imagined them sorted into colors and used like a mosaic to create a glyph, some kind of shape that would help to intensify the self as a crystal and become a larger crystal and do better light work. I had thought of the Star of David with a cross inside of it or some such symbol that had a lot of energy to it that would be helpful. What do you think of this idea to use crystals or water as a kind of accelerator to help?

I am Q'uo, and am aware of your query, my sister. The use of the crystals for enhancing the meditative practice of sending love and light where it is needed is a practice which, indeed, can be most efficacious. However, there is some skill in the use of such accoutrement for the purpose of healing. It would be our recommendation that one or more crystals be chosen for their specific feeling or vibratory nature. There are many kinds of crystals which are each unique in their qualities of being able to enhance the imaging of light. For, indeed, the crystals themselves are often referred to as frozen light. To use a great number of crystals for such an endeavor would be, in our opinion, counterproductive, for this quality of uniqueness that each possesses would work against the unified acceleration or intensification of the light which is being sent as a healing device.

We would recommend that the crystals be examined for the appropriate feeling-tones, shall we say, and those possibilities for utilization be used one after the other separately in order that the most efficacious crystal be finally chosen and used in a manner which may be likened to a resonance chamber. The crystal may be held in the hand while the meditation is undertaken. The inner visualization would need to see the crystal and the heart and the third eye working in harmony in a synchronized fashion, the thought of the need for healing being held foremost in the mind. Then the crystal may be imaged as being the medium through which the thought would be sent. And the visualization of the recipient of this light, whether it be a planet, a country, or a person, would then be seen to be bathed in this light. Thus the thought or the image would be sent forth and enhanced by the use of the crystal in this fashion. Is there a further query, my sister?

Carla: I would like to ask a couple of questions from Dr. E Are there cultures of sentient third- and fourth-density, service-to-self nature of reptilian and gray beings located in subterranean facilities or cities located in the southwest of the USA that are busy herding humans as slaves, guinea pigs and labor?

I am Q'uo, and am aware of your query, my sister. As you are aware, we are hesitant to speak in specific terms concerning such a query for indeed there has been a good deal of interaction between various extraterrestrial races and those of your governmental structures, both within this country and many others. The activities of such interactions and the entities involved are those which we feel are, shall we say, subsidiary to the primary effort of those entities who seek to serve the Creator in the positive sense by the opening of the heart chakra and the shining of the light of love to all who are encountered and seen as the same as self, the same as the one Creator. Thus it would be our recommendation in this instance that the focus be removed from the fringe areas of concern and placed once again in the heart of the incarnation. Is there another query at this time?

Carla: His next question is, if so, if there are beings here which are service-to-self, what is the best way to thwart or greet their efforts?

I am Q'uo, and am aware of your query, my sister. We, again, would recommend the meditative state for any such effort to be of service to those who may be seen to be of a service-to-self nature. Those who are seen as such may also be seen as the same as those who were seen in distress; that is, there may be engendered this quality of love/light which may then be seen to be sent to these entities who are of the negative polarity so that they also are engulfed in the radiance of the noonday sun. Then this quality of love and light may also be seen to be surrounding and protecting those areas or persons that are felt to be endangered by such entities. Thus the quality of love and light may be utilized both as a healing and as protection. Is there a further query, my sister?

Carla: I think I will hold it to two questions from Dr. E. I know he will appreciate what you have said. Thank you.

I am Q'uo, and we thank you, my sister. Is there another query at this time?

S: A minor question. Carla just sent me the [transcription of the] first session of this fall's meetings, and side two didn't record. Do you ever change your mind and have the tape recorder not record, or is it just mechanical? Is there something else operating here that keeps the tape recorder from recording?

I am Q'uo, and am aware of your query, my brother. We give information and our opinions with a free and open heart. We do not change our hearts or our minds. Your recording devices are usually accurate in their functioning. However, there is occasionally the misdirection, shall we say, in the operation of such machinery. We find that this instrument is often unable to handle all the buttons and dials. However, he is diligent in his perseverance. Is there a further query, my brother?

S: We hate to lose any of your words. If there is any way that you could let us know if there is a problem with the recording devices we would appreciate that.

I am Q'uo and we are aware of your query. We are able to utilize an instrument such as this one and the one known as Carla with some difficulty, but we find that we are out of our league, shall we say, with the mechanical devices that are utilized in these sessions. We must apologize for our lack of ability to communicate with such entities. Is there another query at this time?

S: No, I guess I won't ask you to program a VCR then. Thank you.

I am Q'uo. We thank you once again, my brother. Is there another query at this time?

C: I would like to ask about a dream that V had, that she has had repeatedly at various times in her life. She has a dream of seeing a shore and darkness upon the water, infinite sea, and then above the sea there becomes one moon, and then a second, then a third, then a fourth, all full. And then she looks and sees the moon that is creating these four moons and these four moons are reflections of it. Then the fifth moon smiles and she realizes that it is the Creator and that the Creator loves her and that everything is perfect. Then that Creator's moon splinters into a million pieces of all different colors. She wonders if you could comment on this dream?

I am Q'uo, and am aware of your query, my sister. In this instance we find that we may speak in a limited sense, pointing the way rather than leading.

The concept of the moon is one which is, of course, central in this dream. The moon for this entity is a quality which is partaking of the feminine nature, that which is somewhat hidden and mysterious, illuminated by another source. The one known as V may look within her own experience for the recollection of the primary quality of the moon. The shattering of the Creator in the form of the moon into many colors may be seen as the many peoples and experiences which the one known as V has met or shall meet in her life pattern. The number of four also is significant. Moving from the lower to the higher in energy centers one finds that the heart is the fourth center which may be seen as a means by which the Creator may be apprehended or known by the one known as V. Each previous center or moon having distinct vibratory signatures that this entity would profit from examining. We would recommend that she be given basic information concerning these centers so that she may further contemplate the message of this dream experience.

We find that this is the extent of the information which we are able to give at this time without infringement. Is there a further query, my sister?

C: No. Thank you from V.

I am Q'uo, and again we thank you my sister. May we ask if there is a final query at this time?

(No further queries.)

I am Q'uo, and as we have apparently exhausted the queries for this session of working we would again thank each for inviting us to your meeting this day. It is a privilege for us to be able to join you, and we commend each for the great desire of each to be of service in the healing of this planet which has brought each to this circle of seeking this day. We would encourage each to continue in these efforts for indeed your thoughts of healing are things which are seen and felt and which have their effect upon the levels of the spirit which, indeed, is that place within each of us that enlivens our very vehicles of experience, our hearts, our minds, and our desires to learn and to serve grow from the seed of spirit that is firmly placed within each entity's heart. As you send love and light to any, you send it to all, and there is a kind of reverberation that feeds this process and moves it in the metaphysical sense.

We are known to you as those of Q'uo, and we would take our leave of this instrument and this group at this time. We leave each, as always, in the love and in the ineffable light of the one infinite Creator. Adonai, my friends. Adonai.

L/L Research

Sunday Meditation
October 21, 2001

Group question: Our question today has to do with fear. Before September 11th, everybody had the normal fears of having enough money, food, friendships, harmonious work relationships, and so forth. Now there seems to be a general tenor for many people of a foreboding, a fear, that there might be more attacks, that we are not safe, that we are losing our freedoms, that something is going to get us. We are wondering if Q'uo could give us some information concerning how we can handle our fears? How can fear best be handled by the sincere spiritual seeker? Is there a way of changing our attitudes, our behavior, our thinking? We would appreciate whatever Q'uo has to say.

(Carla channeling)

We are those of the principle known to you as the Q'uo, and we greet you in the love and in the light of the one infinite Creator, in whose service we are. We want to thank you for gathering this afternoon and for calling us to your circle. We want to thank [you for] your seeking hearts and your thirst for truth and for creating the atmosphere for such thoughtful comments as we are able to make about the interesting subject of fear. We are very happy to share these thoughts with you with the one request, as always, that each use her own discrimination and select those thoughts which may have value for you, leaving aside the rest.

Fear is a four-letter word, as this instrument would term it. The conversation before this meditation brought up the question of how fear could possibly be love, and perhaps that is where we shall start. Often it is helpful to move back to material that seems very simple and very obvious, yet within it lies the end of a string that can get very tangled. Yet if you tug at it from the end of its origin it unravels far more easily than if the attempt is made to tug on the string of fear past the tangle-point in the present moment, where the fear is living. So let us move back to the beginning of this particular string of reason and concept and gaze at love itself and what we think about love.

Love is another four-letter word. It is a very difficult word to deny knowledge of by anyone in any density, yet certainly within your density the word has so many overtones and undertones because of constant usage to mean several quite different kinds of affection that it is a difficult word to use precisely. When we speak of love we are speaking of that which is the essence of the Creator. The love of which we speak is far more powerful, far more coherent, shall we say, far more crystallized than the love of family or mates or even the overriding love of brotherhood and humankind. Love, as we speak of it, is not simply an emotion but, rather, an utterly coherent Thought. It is a Thought that is so powerful that it has created all that there is. This Logos which we call Love, this living entity that is the Creator and includes the created, is an infinite concept. Indeed, one word for Love is intelligent infinity. The essence of love lies in this infinity and in its intelligence which is the intelligence of the Creator.

This creative Thought, by the action of free will, by the indwelling of possibility, has chosen to create light. Using this building block, which is the very fabric of space and time, the Creator has builded a universe. All that therein is, is made of light. All that is light was created by love. Consequently, all that is experienced in the creation is one thing, and that is love. No matter how distorted that energy, its substance is the same energy, the same ancestry as the lightest and brightest of energies. All positive- and negative-seeming appearances, no matter how far from love and light they seem to be, are still made up of love. Just as that which is new can become old quickly, just as that which is whole can become broken in a heartbeat, the creations of the Father within your experience all have a great deal of plasticity. Each of you is an agent of this Creator with a certain degree of latitude in creating the sub-universe which is your personal reality. Each of you, then, is a creature compounded of love, moving and having your being within an energy field that is made of love and shaped by your distortions of that love. Each of you comes into contact with a varying number of other energy fields, whether people, groups of people [or] societies. All of these energy fields have their being within the larger energy field which is the Creator. And this is true whether gazed at from the perspective of third density or from a perspective of higher densities. Because of our experiences within higher densities, certainly we experience a different universe in terms of what we sense and see. And yet we too see the interplay of fields of energy and know that all truly is one.

To move a little further into the question of fear, if you will think for a moment of your energy body, you may see that each center of energy within your body is vulnerable to distortion in a particular way, and we use that term, distortion, to indicate fear. For fear is a very common distortion of love. Within the red-ray the energy tends to be blocked if there is a fear of survival. Within the orange ray in the lower belly the natural distortion of that energy comes with the experience of attempting to relate to other energy fields, to other people. When there is a difficulty and there seems to be a threat from the personal relationship, this lower belly energy can be blocked or otherwise uncomfortably distorted. In the upper part of the belly, in the solar plexus, the yellow-ray energy center can easily be blocked by fears having to do with the family, the society, one's place within that family or society; in short, one's dealings with the larger groups that go beyond personal relationships and move into the roots of being, the family, the mated relationship, and so forth. And a great deal of that which many are experiencing during this particular autumn season among your peoples has to do with the energies that became manifest on the 11th of September of this year. These are basically yellow-ray fears, and the solar plexus of many, many entities within your culture has been punched, shall we say, hard and given the opportunity to choose fear, not just once but many times.

When fear closes or even partially blocks the energy that is flowing through the energetic body, energy moving into the heart becomes less and less, depending upon how bad the blockage is. Consequently, the natural effect of allowing fear into the energy body in any settled way is to close the heart. When the heart center is not receiving very much energy, then it is that there is not sufficient energy to do work in consciousness. It may be said that one cannot hear when one is screaming, and in a way that is what fear does: it deafens the ears of the heart.

Yet this fear is a creature of love. And the patient seeker does have resources to bring to bear when a blockage is perceived in the energy body due to fear. These resources are generally not expressible in linear terms. When one sees fire, one has a perfect right to fear the fire. It is hot. It will burn. And it threatens the survival of the physical body. There is no linear way to suggest to someone that he not fear fire or that he [not] at least be cautious and careful when using fire. The feeling of being invaded, being encroached upon, being terrorized is a powerful kind of fear that moves both in red ray and in yellow ray, two primary rays that are most powerful. And we have no right to suggest to anyone that she not fear a terrorist attack. Yet in a non-linear sense if one can move back in thought, bringing the energy of the mind beyond the present moment and the present catalyst and into the realm of personal essence and consciousness, the resources are powerful and ready to help.

"For He shall give His angels charge over you to guide you in all your ways, lest you hurt your foot upon the stone." [*Holy Bible*, Psalm 91:1.] This is a quotation from the holy works of this instrument, and it is true. Each entity has angelic beings attempting at all times to help and serve, to save and protect, to bless and to nurture. "Behold, I bring you good tidings." [*Holy Bible*, Luke 2:10.] That is part of the Christmas story of this instrument's Bible. An angelic being speaks to those who are afraid and says, "This is the unknown, yet it is the birth of spirit, and this spirit is coming into the world. And this is the spirit of light. So have great joy."

In the beginning, dealing with fears, it may be necessary to move slowly to allow the fear to be with you, uncomfortably so. Sitting with that, feeling that discomfort, creates within the seeker a growing awareness of the nature of this fear. As the one known as R said, sitting at the campfire with this fear, sharing a story, enjoying the night together, allowing this situation within to be what it is, is a helpful beginning. It may seem like nothing, but simply becoming quiet and still and accepting of the feelings that are in the heart is very helpful. One thing fear greatly needs is a lack of ridicule and an honest respect. That which is fear is that which is contracting within the energy body, that which is battening down the hatches, armoring and defending. Becoming able to sit quietly and with acceptance with this fear creates within the seeker the eventual feeling that it may be acceptable to somewhat allow this contracted state to melt away. The angelic help that moves towards the seeker at a time of fear is looking for ways to help the seeker expand and disperse and diffuse that concentration or tangle of energy that has been created by the fear. It is attempting to send you the energies of radiated love, that which, according to your holy works and according to us, does cast out fear.

One may look at various elements of fear in order gradually to emerge from that contracted feeling. Certainly one energy that is prevalent in fear is the desire to control that which cannot be controlled. The issue of control is very difficult. Almost never does one have control over that which is the object of fear. That which can be controlled is generally not feared. It is precisely the inability to affect changes in something that seems desirable or undesirable that has created the fear. It is in this situation that archetypal images may help more than words, for images are not linear. Thus when we speak of the leap of faith we speak specifically of leaping into a void, putting oneself in a situation where there is no control. But, indeed, the straightest road from fear to love is faith, the ability to move beyond the tangle in the stream of energy, back to the source, and it is done not by moving to anything but only from the position of fear. The classic paralyzing Buddhist description of fear is a seeker hanging onto a rapidly decaying branch of a tree, on the side of a cliff, with a tiger above and a tiger below, and a chasm beneath. And the answer to that image is to let go of the branch, wave bye-bye to the tigers and welcome the abyss. There is, in faith, that realization that in no way, shape, or form can we know in a linear sense that all is well or that all will be well. And yet that is what we claim. That is what we believe, and on that we base our security and our confidence.

This energy of faith seems to come to those in the darkest of hours and in the most pressing of circumstances. And it is in this sense that the tragedies of your September 11th attack may be seen to be beacons of light as well as fires of disaster. For in unsettling the smugness of perceived safety these attacks at once made it very shiningly clear to all of those who speak the word, freedom, within your cultures that a free and unfearing way of life was indeed a precious and wonderful thing, something dear and valuable and worth preserving. And this opened the energy systems of many as compassion for those who were victimized poured through half of your planetary population at once.

Times of trial and trouble such as the one you experience now are those times when fear can be most crippling and when that leap of faith can be most powerfully effective. What thoughts are you thinking at this moment? What thoughts have crossed your mind this day? What are your patterns of thought? Where do you put the value in your thinking time? And how would you choose to change those patterns of thought? Work in consciousness can be dazzlingly fast and brilliant. Instantaneous changes and transformations can occur, but in an incarnational experience the great majority of time is spent not in the flashes of illumination but in those times between, in those valleys between the mountaintop experiences. And yet those valleys can be your heaven or your hell or anything in between. Each thought that you think is at once an accident and a creation.

The challenge for the seeker is to become more and more conscious of the patterns of recurring thoughts, looking at those patterns of thought, asking the self, "Are these radiant or contracting thoughts that I am repeating? And if I would rather radiate than contract, how shall I affect the processes of this recurring thought?" It is patient and slow work to gaze at the self and yet allow the self to function naturally and fully. But there is an interplay constantly going on between the accidents of creation and that which you bring to creation that transforms those accidents. You are part of what happens to you. The thoughts which you habitually think create an atmosphere [in which] you may see something completely differently than someone else may see the same thing. To another person that sight may be frightening. To you, that sight may be quite tolerable. The difference is in the attitude, and work can be done on that attitude, not in a weekend, not because of one book, not because of one teacher, not because of one idea, but over a period of time in which the seeker has been thoughtful persistently.

At the heart of fear is a situation which at once defines your experience and is irrelevant to your experience, and that is your physical life. The root fear, the fear that closes red ray, is the fear of survival. Within your physical incarnation you shall never be free of the fear of death, for death is inevitable. From dust was the body created, and to dust shall the body return. Once it is seen clearly and at a basic level that this physical death is an illusion, then there is much less distortion and contraction possible. But it is seldom given to the seeker to come into full knowledge of her true nature. Seldom is it that he can see the inevitability of this revival of consciousness through the death of the body. Insofar as it is possible we recommend daily immersion in silence because it is in that region of the self alone that the truths of the metaphysical reality can flower in such a way as to fortify the vagrant imagination and strengthen the ability to have patience with the self and with circumstances that are other than you would wish them to be. To see all of these elements of your personal story as simply what they are is a powerful resource. To know that faith can change that story is a powerful resource also.

We would at this time transfer this contact to the one known as Jim. We are those of Q'uo, and we thank this instrument as we transfer. We are those of Q'uo.

(Jim channeling)

I am Q'uo, and we greet each again in love and in light through this instrument. At this time we would ask if there might be any further queries to which we might speak.

T: I believe I have asked this before, but it has got a little more intense. Basically, how do you go about helping someone when there are other people involved and possibly you will hurt them by helping the other person? I would appreciate whatever comments you might be able to make.

I am Q'uo and am aware of your query, my brother. We would suggest that it is often helpful, in a situation in which there are many considerations affecting the service that one wishes to offer, to spend as much time as possible in meditation, not just to find the center of self and to make that kind of renewing connection which is always helpful, but, while in meditation, to explore the avenues available. Imagine one course of action that is perhaps to help as you are hoping to be able to help, to carry this out in your mind as far as you may, and to attempt to examine the repercussions of one's assistance. For a few periods of meditations, perhaps for as long as a week, each day, consider this possible avenue to be that course which you shall follow. In each meditation perform the service as you imagine it. Imagine how it will be received, and continue in this fashion until you feel that you are aware of this course of action and its ramifications. Then perhaps for another week, each day, take the opposite course of action, which perhaps shall be inaction. Imagine the repercussions. Be as thorough as you can. Experience this course as fully as the first. Then, after you have completed both courses of action and inaction, look within your heart to that to which you feel most committed. Is there a further query, my brother?

T: No. Thank you very much.

I am Q'uo, and we thank you, my brother. Is there another query at this time?

Carla: I'd like to ask two questions from Dr. C. E. One is, "Is there a sizeable asteroid called the Death Rock or Mynra on its way to Earth on a collision course?"

I am Q'uo and am aware of your query, my sister. At some point in the future of this sphere perhaps there shall be such an event. We are currently unaware of such. Is there a further query, my sister?

Carla: Yes. What effort, method or means could be employed by humans or others that would result in the U.S. government bringing to light all their secret agreements with all non-human sentient beings, including channeled sources, groups or agencies which the government has listened to?

I am Q'uo and am aware of your query, my sister. We find that the probabilities of both queries are almost identical. Is there another query?

Carla: No. I think that is enough of that kind of question. I don't want to detune the contact. Thank you very much.

I am Q'uo, and we are grateful for your efforts on this entity's behalf. We apologize for our lack of information in these areas. We do not necessarily dismiss such inquiries as those of small value but can see little possibility for either occurring. Is there another query at this time?

Carla: I would just follow up by asking if you would like to comment on this kind of specific question and how it affects a channeling group and a channel such as this one, with Jim and me as instruments and you on the other end? I would welcome any thoughts that you would have on that since all of Dr. E's questions are specific.

I am Q'uo and we appreciate your query, my sister, for it gives us the opportunity to comment on the nature of queries which are offered to us. We are, as you are aware, happy to give our opinions in those areas of our expertise which are primarily those of the metaphysical nature, the process and proceedings of the rate of spiritual evolution, the ability to open the heart in love, for this is the primary reason and activity for which each took incarnation. While in the physical vehicle operating within third density it is often easy to become interested in areas which are of momentary interest. And we say momentary realizing that for many of your peoples there are years spent pursuing such specific information. It is our hope that entities that are engaged in such activity will at some point realize the futility of seeking this kind of information. For even if one had each answer there would be little value to the personal or general evolution. The information which we seek for ourselves and which we seek to share with others is information of a lasting value:

that which is important to one's spiritual journey now and ever. There is a great deal of information which seems important for the moment, for it is full of the drama of your third-density illusion. Who did what to whom and why? And how? Yet how much more important is how can one love in this situation or that situation? We are always appreciative of those entities who seek beyond the illusion, beyond the seeming importance of trivial events that so congest your days and minds. For it is those who can penetrate beyond the veil and the illusion that shall eventually find the heart of their journey.

Is there a further query, my sister?

Carla: No. Thank you, Q'uo:

I am Q'uo, and again we thank you, my sister. Is there another query at this time?

(No further queries.)

I am Q'uo and we would like to take this opportunity to thank each for inviting us to join your circle of seeking this day. It is always a great privilege to be able to do so. We would again remind each that we do not wish to present any stumbling block for any seeker's spiritual journey. Any word we have spoken that does not ring of truth to you, please disregard it immediately, saving only those which do have that special ring of truth. We are known to you as those of Q'uo. We shall take our leave at this time of this instrument and this group. We leave you in the love and the light, the peace and the power of the one infinite Creator. Adonai, my friends. Adonai. ✣

L/L Research

Sunday Meditation
November 4, 2001

Group question: The question today, once again, is focused around the events of September 11th. We are wondering if you could give us some information about [whether] the people who were directly involved and who gave their lives in this event might have been the catalyst for all of us to become what you might call a "nation of priests," people who are desirous of being of service to others and following the way of the peaceful warrior, of discovering love in the life, in the heart and sharing it with others. Could you elaborate on how this kind of catalyst can work in all of our lives and how we can become a "nation of priests"?

(Carla channeling)

We are those known to you as the principle of Q'uo, and we greet you in the love and in the light of the one infinite Creator, in whose service we are. May we say what a privilege and a blessing it is to be called to this meeting. We greet entities we have not enjoyed in this group for some time. We greet those who are new. We greet those who have some small experience with this group. We greet each of you and thank each of you, for each of you brings beauty and grace to the circle. Each is a gem through which the light of the Creator shines in a unique and beautiful way. And we greatly appreciate the flavor of each of you and the coloration of your vibrations. We would ask of you that you employ your powers of discrimination in listening to what we have to say, for we are not without error, but are as you: pilgrims seeking along a path that sometimes is broad and pleasant and at other times seems to be a path in the desert that is difficult and dark.

We greet you at a time within your year when the celebration is made for those who have departed the physical incarnation in faith and are considered among the faithful departed. The time of all saints is celebrated in this instrument's church at this time, the time when all of those who have experienced incarnation in this world and have moved on are remembered. You ask this day about some few of those who have departed from the incarnation recently because of the events of the eleventh of September, and it is an interesting [question] that you ask and certainly one that moves into deeper material.

Your question has to do with how a death can be more than a death, how a tragedy can be more than a tragedy. And we say to you not only that this is so but that it is so again and again in large occasions that acquire global notice and in the very small tragedies that occur within the purview of one small life. And yet within that life is all of creation. The nature of mortality is such that the incarnational experience as a whole can be seen as that which is sacrificed. The breath moves in and the breath moves out of the body just so many times, and then that body again becomes dust. The heart beats so many heartbeats, and then that heart is stilled. The physical body of each entity has written within it its future history, and one finds in those who have gained a great deal of peace that there is no concern left when the question of dying is looked at. It is simply that which is known as part of the future history of that body. It is no longer, therefore, catalyst for distress or discomfort.

The nature of destiny is such that we cannot say to you that your future is fixed. What we can say to you is that you have made arrangements with a specific group of entities to be in the position of companion and minister to them, just as they are companion and minister to you. And you have agreements set in place to look at certain incarnational questions. For most entities those questions have to do with the giving and receiving of love. For many entities these lessons revolve around how to serve, how to give freely without expectation of return, how to be a healing presence without being an aura infringer, how to express the self without becoming a perceived negative in the lives of others. These and many other issues come up within the life repeatedly, and it is not to be amazed at that this would occur because there are careful arrangements in place so that no matter which way that you move, no matter which choices that you make in a given situation, the path somehow winds around to meet again those issues and to work with those people that you have made agreements with.

This is by way of saying that all of those souls whose lives ended on the eleventh of September in the World Trade Center or elsewhere did in a way have dates with destiny and in another way they were completely free up until the moment until that possibility/probability vortex turned into an actuality. The future is very much a creature of each of you and what you think and what you do. It is not fixed. We cannot look at the future and tell you what you shall experience because each of you is a co-Creator, capable potentially of generating tremendous light and tremendous love, not from within yourself but through the crystal of your being. Many there were who met their death that day in such a way as to embrace the light. Many there were that day who were as the unsung heroes whose stories shall never be known, who in helping others lost their own lives.

No death is ever a loss without a gain. There was for some of your time an issue which we were concerned with having to do with those souls who were not yet able to leave the inner-planes version of that locale in the New York City area. However, we are happy to say that over the two or two and a half weeks after that event there were those of what you would call your native American population—not those within this density, but those within the inner planes—which were able to work with those entities who were confused at that time so that at this time all of those souls which were involved in that tragedy have moved on into the realms of healing and are receiving the balm of Gilead.

Each of you, however, in living through this experience has, as several within this circle have said in the conversation preceding this talk, experienced emotional catalyst having to do with a change in the way the surrounding world is perceived because of that which occurred. Most of the surface events which come before your view are those pieces of information almost scientifically designed to reduce hope and faith and increase doubt and fear. As the one known as H has noted, the object of so-called terrorism is simply to instill terror, to instill fear and discomfort in the minds of those who were formerly smug and uncaring of the rest of the world. This has indeed occurred. There is a profound feeling of having been awakened from a sleep, a pleasant sleep that now is at an end.

The creation is made in such a way that balance is the strongest single force operating in situations that are unbalanced. And in the darkness of aggression lies the call to the light, and we do see that this call has, to an increasing extent, been heard by many among your peoples. The concept of unity is very simple. And, indeed, the name of the country in which each of you abides is called the United States, and yet may we observe that your states are more united at this point than before the events of the eleventh of September. The shock of such a general attack created the catalyst for many who had formerly thought of themselves as Americans with distinctions as to race or creed or color, [and who] now have found themselves as Americans without regard to anything but citizenship, feeling perhaps for the first time a fellow-feeling and a complete sympathy and solidarity with the man on the street of your towns and your cities and your countryside of America. Not because another looks like you or sounds like you but because that entity is part of that experiment that those known as the fathers of your country started so long ago.

You asked about the quote, "and ye shall be a nation of priests" and how one might focus on that quotation from your holy scriptures which this instrument's guidance which she calls the Holy Spirit offered to her when she was troubled and asking for guidance in this matter. If each of you will take a moment to think of the thoughts that you have thought today, the concerns that have been upon your mind, and then think of yourself as a priest and ask yourself, "Were I a priest would I have been content with these thoughts, these actions? Would I have been content with my day, with my service, with my walk? Would I have felt that I had touched into the presence of the one infinite Creator?" The sense of this particular quote at this particular time is that each of you is as a flower that is opening, and the awakening process is very much like a rose opening its petals to the sun. As the entity awakens and seeks and thirsts for the truth, that entity learns, and each of you in this circle is a veteran campaigner and has learned a great deal. There is much more to learn. There is always more to learn, yet there is a point at which the pilgrim soul can see itself not only as a student but also as a teacher, not only as a member of the congregation, but as a minister, not only as one who comes to the table asking to be fed, but as one who moves into the kitchen and makes sure that the feast is prepared.

This instrument has been saying lately that if ever there was a time to be steadfast it is now, and this thought, that you are a nation of priests, that you are a holy people, is along those lines. When you seek, when you learn, you develop a responsibility to share what you know, to live what you know, to express what you know in your daily life. Perhaps it is nothing more than a smile, a positive reaction to a negative situation, a word dropped at the right time, a thought that helps. At a time when it is easy to give negative thought, finding that one positive thought is to work magic.

When people realize their power they become much more effective. And so we would ask each of you to realize the tremendous potential within you. Realize that you are already exerting a great deal of power, so the question becomes, "What is the right use of power?" Where is the love in the situation in front of your eyes? That is the question that brings the most resonance and affords the most magic in terms of being able to effect change. More and more, allow yourself to come into the priesthood that you have so long studied for. Accept the mantle and vow to do your best to run the straight race, to be steadfast with what you believe, to find ways to share those things that only you can share, for they lie within the folds of your personality and they are your gifts to give.

Love one another. That is the heart of priesthood: to love, to bless, to witness to the light.

We would at this time transfer this contact to the one known as Jim. We leave this instrument in love and in light and in thanks. We are those of Q'uo.

(Jim channeling)

I am Q'uo, and am with this instrument. We greet each again in love and in light through this instrument. It is our privilege at this time to ask if there might be any further queries upon the minds of those present to which we may give our response. Is there another query at this time?

S: I'll start off. Recently I got a book from Carla called *The Emerald Tablets of Thoth the Atlantean*. It was interesting reading. The fellow seemed to ascend during his lifetime and I was wondering if you could tell me what he is doing now and what kind of service he is performing?

I am Q'uo, and am aware of your query, my brother. We find that this entity is one who has become that which you would call a source of channeled information. However, the contact which this entity has made is with a group of entities who seek in what may be called a solitary fashion, shall we say; that is, they seek specifically the kind of information which is contained within this volume and are a portion of this entity's larger family of seekers. Thus the work of this entity continues in another form, always seeking to give information which is of service to those who are interested in the kinds of mysteries and riddles that the secret or occult endeavors produce. Is there a further query, my brother?

S: There is another book which I got from Carla, *The Hathor Material*. I guess these were fourth-density beings who came either before or after Ra, in Egyptian times. Maybe you could tell me something of the service of this group?

I am Q'uo, and am aware of your query, my brother. Again the information that you seek in this area is as broad ranging as a race of entities can produce through their experience, their seeking and their service. We could only give a brief description without moving into many areas of interest which would consume a great portion of your time. The entities of the Hathor race were those who, as did those of Ra, make contact with various cultures of this planet's history, most notably those of the Egyptian culture, and this contact was not just one period or point in your past but has been that of a continual nature. Some aspects of this contact became more noteworthy or widespread than others. These entities were most helpful in planting the seeds of the concept of unity and infinity within the Egyptian culture which allowed those of this culture to be readied for consideration of the Law of One. Thus the entities of the Hathor race worked in conjunction with those of Ra in order to allow an expansion of the concepts in the philosophical or spiritual realms of the Egyptian culture so that there was seen to be not just many gods or powerful forces at work in the universe about these entities but that there was truly one Creator from which all else sprang. This was a revolutionary concept, shall we say, for those of the Egyptian culture. Is there a further query, my brother?

S: The last question would be do you have any suggestions on different meditation groups that have reached out to each other? How can they share information and service?

I am Q'uo, and am aware of your query, my brother. Truly, that which you do is that which is helpful: to communicate with each other, to share the information which you find of value with others who have such to share with you as well. The ability of each entity that is desirous of serving others actually to do so is dependent only upon the passion that each has within the heart, within the mind, within the will to be of such service. For as the will is set upon a course, so is a way made that the will may manifest as it is formed within the heart, mind and soul, the very essence of the entity. Is there a further query, my brother?

S: Not from me. Thank you.

T: I have a question. A couple of weeks ago N noticed white light coming from my knee when I twisted it in bed. J had a dream about that a few nights later and got the message that this was piezo-electric energy that was coming from the crystallized arthritis in my knee. It has to do with crystals having pressure exerted on them. Could you tell me anything else about this? How can I use this energy, if indeed I am supposed to use it?

I am Q'uo, and am aware of your query, my brother. As you are aware, the crystalline formation is that which is composed of light in a certain field or form. As one applies energy, or force, to a crystal this light energy expresses itself, or, quite literally, moves from the crystalline form in a fashion that may be perceived by those who are sensitive to the movement of subtle energies. That this occurred when you applied pressure to your knee is the result of the various secondary and tertiary energy center formations contained within the knee, the wrist, the elbow and the ankle that correspond to the primary energy centers or chakras that are located within the finer formation of the physical body, from the base chakra to the crown chakra. The energy which expressed from your knee location was that which has a relationship to the health of that portion of your physical vehicle, there being some imbalance in that area at this time in the form of what you may call the arthritis or bursitis. These are not absolutely correct terms but will suffice for the nonce.

The use of such energies is, to our knowledge, not specific to the physical vehicle itself but to the regaining of the health or balance of energies within this portion of your physical vehicle. Thus to utilize this energy most effectively one would need to engage in a program of meditative visualization that would allow you to see with your inner eye the overall experience of catalyst that has led to this particular imbalance in your knee. This is a product of the process of ageing and is a primary source of the catalyst with which you now deal. Is there a further query, my brother?

T: No. Thank you very much.

I am Q'uo. We thank you, my brother. Is there another query at this time?

C: I have one from B. He asks "What do wanderers expect of the Earth?" And the second question is "What is the society and cultures of the wanderers like?"

I am Q'uo, and am aware of your query, my sister. Those who have entered the Earth environments from those realms of higher densities are those who have left experiences which are far more harmonious and in touch with the unity of all creation than the Earth environment is found to be at this time. Therefore, the entities whom you may describe as wanderers are oftentimes, upon the discovery of their own nature, quite discouraged when viewing the environment which they now find themselves incarnated within in order to serve and to learn, for your third-density experience at this time, near harvest, is that which is quite confused in its overall orientation. There is found within most cultures of this planetary sphere a great deal of disharmony and even the bellicose nature being expressed upon a daily basis, not only between those entities you call the nation states but also within each entity in its relationship to other individuals within its daily round of activities. Thus the experience many wanderers find, when they have discovered that which they have come to do, is one of bewilderment, of confusion …

(Tape is changed.)

I am Q'uo, and am once again with this instrument. Is there another query at this time?

N: Could I personally thank them for the inspiration and devotion that they have given us?

I am Q'uo, and we are grateful to be able to do so, my sister. Is there another query, my sister?

Carla: Thinking about the question of joining with other groups and sharing, and thinking about the work I do each week writing people with these kinds of concerns, I feel that since this is an illusion we are connecting on the inner planes and we are together on the inner planes and we don't have to worry about that. I have this sense when I am writing the people that I work with through the mail that it is like I am doing two things. I am doing the individual sharing and listening and communion and communication. I feel an energy exchange being co-created with the other person and me, whatever we have to teach each other and whatever we have to learn from each other. At the same time that it is helping me or the other person it seems like it is creating the channels of communication for fourth-density positive. We are doing work at this time on the soul level and we don't even know that we are doing it on a conscious level. Could you speak to that?

I am Q'uo, and am aware of your query, my sister. Indeed, as each entity engages in such communication it is as though a muscle that has not been used previously is now being exercised. As one gains in the strength of sharing what is in one's heart then there is brought forth from that heart more and more information, inspiration and direction, not only for the entities with whom you communicate but a great deal more in the sense of the numbers of entities who share these concerns. As you are able to open yourself in communication with others you allow these others to share that energy and to move the energy in a spiral fashion, much as the light of the one Creator seeks to return to its source in the upward spiraling line of light. So as you are able to share the inspiration that is drawn from you by the questions of others this is as a seed. It is planted not only within the heart of those with whom you communicate but within the inner sense of self of humanity. As one learns, so do all have the potential to learn that which one has learned. Indeed, all are portions of the one Creator, cells within the body of the one Creator. And as one is enriched, so are all. Is there another query, my sister?

Carla: What is the Merkaba? M wants to know more about the Matrix of the Spirit, the Potentiator of the Spirit and how to use the Potentiator of the Spirit to work with these energies that have been archetypally jump-started with 9-11. I can refer her to the works of Drunvalo Melchizadek if you want to focus on the latter portion of the question.

I am Q'uo, and am aware of your query, my sister. It would indeed be our recommendation that the reference to the one known as Drunvalo Melchizadek be made for the one known as M in this area, for it is indeed a large area of study and we would not be able to do it justice with the energy that begins to dwindle within this instrument's vehicle.

As far as the second and third queries, we also feel that this is a large area of study in which there needs to be a further refining of the query, for there is a great deal of information that could be given here as well. We shall satisfy ourselves and hopefully begin to satisfy the one known as M by suggesting that the nature of the spirit itself is that which is immobile in that it does not move in the same fashion as does the physical vehicle or the mental vehicle but is that which is. The spirit of each entity which moves within the third-density illusion is that which is drawn from infinity. There is the body of the one Creator which may be seen as the creation itself. There is that from which the body is made, that which we find the ones known as Ra referred to as the unpotentiated intelligent infinity. This is the infinite source which each of your entities is able to make contact with, when the higher self is realized at any time within the third-density experience.

We realize that this does not speak specifically to various portions of the spirit [archetypes] that are described in the system of study called the tarot which the one known as M has queried concerning. However, we feel it is well to begin this study with a basic foundation of information that is able to include the nature of infinity as being that which is the basic source for each finite expression of the one Creator known as a mind/body/spirit complex. We apologize for being short of information in this regard, but we find that the energies and the concentration of this instrument are less than adequate at this time for giving further specific information. Thus we would recommend that there be one final query before the ending of this session of working.

Carla: In truth, Q'uo, I would suggest that we end the session now because we have gained so much, and I wasn't able actually to read M's question as she wrote it. I think the energy of that question and the thirst that she had for that question really wasn't there, so I will refocus for next time. A flashlight would help I believe. Thank you very much.

I am Q'uo, and we are most grateful to you as well, my sister. At this time we would take this opportunity to express our gratitude to each present for inviting our presence this day in your circle of seeking. It is a great privilege for us to be able to join you here, in your hearts, in your minds, and in your seeking for that which is known as the truth. We truly enjoy these gatherings and are unable to express adequately our gratitude to you, but we are most thrilled to be able to join you at any time. At this time we would take our leave of this instrument and this group, leaving each, as always, in the love and in the light of the one infinite Creator. Adonai, my friends. Adonai. ✿

L/L Research

L/L Research is a subsidiary of Rock Creek Research & Development Laboratories, Inc.

P.O. Box 5195
Louisville, KY 40255-0195

www.llresearch.org

Rock Creek is a non-profit corporation dedicated to discovering and sharing information which may aid in the spiritual evolution of humankind.

ABOUT THE CONTENTS OF THIS TRANSCRIPT: This telepathic channeling has been taken from transcriptions of the weekly study and meditation meetings of the Rock Creek Research & Development Laboratories and L/L Research. It is offered in the hope that it may be useful to you. As the Confederation entities always make a point of saying, please use your discrimination and judgment in assessing this material. If something rings true to you, fine. If something does not resonate, please leave it behind, for neither we nor those of the Confederation would wish to be a stumbling block for any.

© 2009 L/L Research

Sunday Meditation
November 18, 2001

Group question: The question today has to do with why human beings in the third density, especially here on Earth, seem to be so war-like. In this particular system we have had the experience of Mars, which was apparently so war-like that they destroyed their atmosphere. Maldek exploded its planet. Earth has had thousands of years of war. We are wondering what it is about the third density that seems to lend itself to entities in it moving in the direction of war-like actions. Is it the nature of our consciousness interacting in social groups? Is it our free will choice? Is it our opposable thumb? Our ability to make and use tools and, therefore, weapons? We would appreciate anything Q'uo could tell us about what it is that gives us this propensity for war and what it is we need to do as individuals, groups and nations to move in the direction of cooperation and working together instead of against each other?

(Carla channeling)

We are those known to you as the principle of the Q'uo, and we greet you in the love and in the light of the one infinite Creator, in whose service we come to you. We thank you for coming together to seek the truth and for joining in this circle of seeking. We thank you for calling for us, for we greatly appreciate the opportunity to share our thoughts with you. We ask only that you use your discrimination in listening to our words and set aside any words that trouble you, for we would not be a stumbling block but, rather, a resource for your seeking. We ask you to trust your discrimination and no outside authority. For you know what is comfortable and what is good within for you, and you may trust that instinct within you.

The question that you ask this day is an interesting one, one in which there is indeed a great deal to say but not as concise and crystalline a pattern as in some matters. The causes of war within third density in one way are unified into one cause, and in another way there are threads of cause. It simply depends upon the level at which you wish to attack the question. We will start with the threads, we think, because perhaps that is more where each of your minds are at this time.

One thread, having to do with third density and war, is the nature of the physical vehicle which you as a species enjoy and which others upon other planets have somewhat closely approximated in the sense of the basic structure of the two arms, two legs, one head, one torso makeup of the body. When you gaze at the instincts of the stock from which your species developed you may see that your instincts, those deep seated predilections for response in certain situations, are those of a territorial animal. Your great apes occupy a certain area in which they are upon their home territory for hunting food and protecting their source of water. The nature of this species is such that for the most part entities remain within various small groupings, each with its own territory, and with each territory being allowed its own way in what this instrument would call a *laissez faire* structure, each group being independent from each other group, no attempt being made to work together in larger groups.

This is the instinct basis which feeds into the mind's working, for a portion of the mind is involved with prioritizing messages from the body which have a tag which says, "Urgent." Therefore, even though these instincts are unthinking they represent a substantial bias that prejudices third-density entities in the direction of what is perceived as their territory or their possession. If you will gaze upon the tangle of reasons surrounding your bellicose actions you will find that territorial considerations almost always play a significant role. This is the energy of red ray, of survival, being expressed. When the territory is threatened the territory [must] be defended. When other territory is seen as necessary and it must be gotten, then aggression is considered reasonable. This remains a substantial portion of the reason for war in third density.

Another thread of this tapestry of third-density situations and areas of conflict is the nature of the third-density mind. This third-density mind, without the benefit of the consciousness that is you as an eternal being, is a choice-maker mind. It is designed to make one choice after another. It assumes, as a way of working, that there is always a right choice and, therefore, sees the process of living as a sequence of choices. Faced with a situation, the third-density mind will attempt to solve the situation—not necessarily to appreciate it, to understand it, to analyze it, or to plumb its subtleties. The first mental reflex is to solve it, to make it go away. The tendency to see black and white, yes and no, feeds into that ability to be belligerent which is indeed a hallmark of your density. The very nature of the mind is such that it tends to suggest to the most rational thinker that decisions must be made, that plans must be made, that all must be chosen and then whipped into order along the lines of choice.

Another thread that moves into the war-making ability of humankind and of third-density in general is as the one known as Jim suggested: the challenge of working with groups. The great question in any group is "What is the character of that group?" A group shows its character as it chooses its leaders. Those who attempt to be leaders within large groups tend to have personality structures in which the use of aggression seems fair; the use of influence, just; the use of all advantages, necessary. The tendency therefore is for leadership not to be as idealistic as the spoken ideal philosophy that is given respect in polite company, while at the same time, as the one known as Jim pointed out, ignores those same ideals when it seems to be of some advantage.

All of these threads feed into the situation where entities, feeling threatened, respond to their insecurity by aggression. You may see the fight for territory; you may see the greed for advantage, influence and power. You may see the tendency to do something as opposed to resting and gathering for extended periods of time, that impatience of leadership, that impulsivity. And a final thread that we would mention is that tendency of the stronger to bully the weaker. And by this we mean to indicate not nations against nations but rather, as the one known as C pointed out, male against female, one kind of energy over against its dynamic opposite, instead of coming into cooperation with that dynamic opposite. We have found that in populations of third-density entities who have chosen to seek the face of the Creator in a feminine face, the values of the culture include far less impulsivity and far more kindness than in cultures dominated by a Creator who is seen as a powerful male figure. The tendency to find positions of power held by male entities, the tendency of the very workings of the law and certainly the traditional underpinnings of your cultures upon your Earth at this time favor the values of strength, power, and force—the virtues of a strong male figure.

The very roots of your thinking, shall we say, from childhood have been saturated with testosterone-rich heroic deeds. This entity has a fondness for reading, and we find in this entity's mind many, many a story which involves the waving of the sword, the brandishing of the firearm, the assumption that weaponry and armament are natural concomitants of policy. And indeed we do not disparage war in and of itself. It is part of the almost inevitable confusion of third density. We do not suggest strict ways of thinking about conflict, for a case can be made for war as a game, as an excellent game, rich in glory and honor. Like many other things which from a wider point of view seem insane, going to war is a part of the expression of third density as most third-density planets experience the density.

Beyond all these reasons, the heart of war and the heart of the reason for war in third density is the nature of love. All things that you experience come to you as distortions of love. There is no other substance but love from which to draw life. So all of life, including murder, pillage, and rape is act after act of love: love distorted, love blocked, love asked to go where it would not go. Nevertheless, no matter how many times the stock seems to be hybridized and ruined, the basic root stock of all experience is love. Third density is a very focused, very intense density, the density of choice. The choice is not between love and hate. The choice is between two ways of seeking love: loving others as a way of choosing to love, or loving the self as a way of choosing to love.

Needless to say, the service-to-others path is not a war-like path. It is allegedly service-to-self entities that would move themselves into fighting against their own kind. And yet the struggle to see clearly the roots of love within the self is a tremendous one. As the one known as Jim has said, it is not that anyone knows not how to love. There are many examples of unconditional love. There are very simple words to indicate the qualities of forgiveness, compassion and love. However, all of these words are only within the mind until an energetic attempt begins to be made to translate these ideals into that which can be manifested in physical life. So the question becomes, "What is each seeker's response to the call of love?" And this is not a simple thing.

It is easy for us to ask each to go into meditation each day and seek the silence. The answers are there within the silence, not within our words. However, when it comes to attempting to step into your shoes as third-density entities we find that we are simply glad that each of you has the energy and the will for this great task of seeing the truth amidst the confusion. Love calls powerfully and pulls each entity forward. Third density is carefully designed to pull entities forward according to their desires and their thirst. The challenge of selfhood is to find out what you truly desire. What shall you desire? Truth? Love? Peace? Where is the substance to those words? Where is the reality beneath your feet? What is your understanding of your journey? If you understand that you are here to pursue spiritual evolution, that you are here to answer the call of love, then you will want to shape your questions to the infinite Creator in such a way that you are seeking your own essence and the essence of Love itself.

It is thought by some that if people would stop shooting at each other that we would have peace. And yet we say to you that it is not as simple as that. For as the one known as C said, if one stops doing that, then what does one do instead? At least aggression against a certain and very specific nation-state or group of entities is a limited and achievable battle and at the end of it one can say such and such has been achieved, and now there is peace. And yet we say to you, like love itself, peace is beyond all condition. Peace does not originate within conditions. Peace is a quality that is waiting for each third-density entity to take it and claim it as his own, his very own, a wonderful, blessed possession. Yet how many entities truly seek the peace within their own hearts which comes from stopping the striving and encouraging the resting in what is? How many entities truly embrace peace if peace involves releasing many other things which are dear?

The one known as Jesus answered the man who said, "I follow all of the commandments. What else shall I do to enter the kingdom of heaven?" by suggesting that he sell all that he had and give the money that he received to the poor. And the young man went away very unhappy because he did not wish to do this, even if it meant entering the kingdom of heaven. Pride, vanity, the need to be better than someone else: all of these are energies within the human heart that are natural to the instinctual, second-density body and third-density brain. Yet you as a consciousness, as an eternal being, are resting within these biases for an incarnational experience in which you are attempting to follow the inexorable pressure of seeking for the truth, and your question each day to yourself is always the same. "Where in this moment is the love? Where in this moment is the Creator?"

So we do not suggest that it is an evil thing to go to war in and of itself. We do suggest that it is not a productive way to seek spiritually compared to the ways of peace. Yet in many ways your third density will express conflict because that is the basic nature of people who see themselves as separate from and over against others. This is a part of the catalyst of third density. It is a part of the hard lessons of love. And indeed it does move through not just third density but also to some extent, fourth density. For there are those within fourth density who choose to continue as children of light or as children of darkness and continue the clash of polarities. As fourth density wears on, this great love of being a warrior begins to evaporate, as love is better learned.

Each has had crystalline, shining moments in his life, when love has become real, not just a word, not just a concept, but amazingly, vividly, powerfully real. Think about those times and the gift that those times have given you. Allow the consciousness that filled you at those moments to come back to you, just to remember how it feels.

We encourage each to ponder deeply her own essence and the nature of her own heart. The heart of one entity and the heart of the world upon which you live are the microcosm and the macrocosm of the same thing. And actually each of you is of an higher order than the world itself. As you choose to seek, to think and to act, so shall the reflections manifest in the macrocosm that is your globe. Work with the essence of self to find ways to choose not to promote conflict, ways to express the truths that do not do damage to those who think differently. But above all, seek that Presence within that is as the ray of light that is a fuller light, a light that blesses the darkness, a light that is not afraid. Open the self to that gentle, lambent flame that is the presence of the infinite Creator. Let that light take up and enlarge its home within your heart. As you seek the ways of peace within yourself, as you find ways to solve conflict within yourself, you are learning a little bit more for the planetary mind.

There is a fairly quickly growing group of those who are attempting to speak peace upon your planet, not in ways of public policy, but in ways of working within to become beings of peace. We see this body of energy enlarging upon your planet, and we feel very hopeful that, against all of the apparent news to the contrary in your Earth world, the lessons of love are more and more being seen, sometimes for the first time. Entities are awakening and doing some of this inner choosing of essence that we suggest. As more individual lives are transformed, so, we believe, shall your planet be transformed.

We would encourage each not to take to heart the appearance of things. It is said in your holy works that there will be wars and rumors of wars. There will be this, and there will be that, but the time is not yet. And we say to you that we believe this to be true. The true war for each of you is the struggle that the one known as Jim called the *jihad*, the internal struggle of the pilgrim to discipline the earthly self in order to make of the earthly self a vessel for the spirit within. In this *jihad*, in this holy conflict, your choices are not clear, and yet there is always a light that shines from within. And so we ask you simply to seek that light, to seek the face of love, and when you see that sun shine radiantly that is love, to learn from it and to offer yourself to it. For you, too, can be an agent of love within the confusion. You, too, can be a part of the eventual peace upon planet Earth. It begins with each individual seeker seeking the ideals within herself that she hopes to see in the world.

We would at this time transfer this contact to the one known as Jim, leaving this instrument with thanks, and love and light. We are those known to you as Q'uo. We transfer now.

Jim channeling

I am Q'uo, and we greet each once again in the love and in the light of the one Creator. It is our privilege at this time to speak to any further queries. Is there another query at this time?

S: From our e-mail group one topic that came up: a fellow named B anchored frequencies like love to the Earth. I asked if there was anything that I could do to be of such help, and it was agreed that it was a matter of intention, but many seemed to have certain abilities, abilities that I am not aware that I have. Is there anything that you can enlighten me on as far as that type of service and how to be of service?

I am Q'uo, and am aware of your query, my brother. We can speak to those areas which any seeker has access to. It is not our function to discover for another that which is latently possible, for this learning is that which is most important to each seeker. However, any seeker may simply share the quality of being which each has as a basic vibration, as distinct as one's fingerprint or voiceprint. For each of you resonates and vibrates in a certain fashion according to the nature of how you seek, of what you seek. And as you are able to communicate that very basic quality of your efforts to another, you share from heart to heart that which is of most importance. Each of you vibrates in a certain fashion the harmonics of love, for from love was each made. If one is able, through the process of seeking, to discover this basic vibration of love, then there is no greater gift that one may share with another.

Clearly communicating that which is your intention and that which is your desire is another method of sharing that is available to all seekers. Clear communication is a phrase which sounds simple, yet it is difficult for each to achieve within third density, for there is much confusion, not only among entities, but within entities. To take the time to seek the heart of self is a process which also enables one to reveal or to share clearly that heart of self with others.

To offer a service which is requested and which one feels able to offer is a third way in which any seeker may offer itself in service to others. This requires the seeker to look carefully into what the needs are from others with whom one is in contact. This looking also requires the seeker to listen, to listen to that which is requested, perhaps clearly requested, perhaps hinted at. Perhaps there is a means by which the seeker may elicit the needs of others through questions.

These are but a few ways in which any seeker may serve and yet though they are common to all, they are basic methods of being of service which are most valuable to any seeker. Is there another query, my brother?

S: Yes. We also discussed connecting the various meditation groups and circles of light and I suggested attempting to contact such groups in the Middle East or China or Africa and places other than just the western world to start seeds of a global consciousness. Could you share your thoughts on that topic?

I am Q'uo, and am aware of your query, my brother. To open the avenues of communication with those who are distant geographically and perhaps culturally as well is an effort which we encourage whole-heartedly, for there is far too little true sharing between such entities upon your planetary surface at this time. When people that are divergent in points of view, in backgrounds, in culture, religion, in socio-economic status are able to communicate with others, there is what we might call a commonality discovered between such entities which opens doors, shall we say, opens minds and opens hearts in a way which is not possible through any other means. To read about a culture, to hear about a culture is most informative to those who have little experience outside their own cultures. Thus this effort is one which could be most helpful at this time. And we encourage your efforts in this endeavor. Is there a further query, my brother?

S: Just one. When Atlantis disappeared under the waves what happened to the Maxim Stone, the spiritual center?

I am Q'uo, and am aware of your query, my brother. This is information which moves into the area of the infringing upon the free will of others which we do not wish to do. We apologize for our lack of information. Is there another query, my brother?

S: That's interesting. No more queries from me. Thanks.

And we thank you, my brother. Is there another query at this time?

(No further queries.)

I am Q'uo, and as it appears that we have exhausted the queries for this session of working we would take this opportunity to thank each once again for inviting us to join you this day. Please take those words which we have spoken and use them as you will, discarding any that do not ring of truth. It is our great honor to join you in these sessions, and we do not wish to be a stumbling block for any.

At this time we shall take our leave of this instrument and this group. We leave each, as always, in the love and in the ineffable light of the one infinite Creator. Adonai, my friends. Adonai. ☥

L/L Research

Sunday Meditation
December 9, 2001

Group question: (Our question today is from B.) It is my understanding that the formation of a social memory complex is crucial to fourth-density existence, and that the human race, due to factors already cited in *The Ra Material*, has been unable to even begin to form a social memory complex. My question is: What would be the areas of study, and the mental and spiritual disciplines required, of a dedicated group of people who wish to form a social memory complex in preparation for harvest?

I assume detailed communication between complex members is a necessity, with direct person-to-person communication being the most efficient, allowing communication to take place at multiple levels, but is physical proximity necessary to initiate the formation of a new social memory complex? Can a social memory complex be formed through a tool such as our Internet or electronic mail?

And how much a portion of this preparation for a social memory complex might be accomplished by seekers of truth simply seeking the truth and living a life? Is there something specific that we need to do?

(Carla channeling)

We are those known to you as the principle of Q'uo, and we greet you in the love and in the light of the one infinite Creator. We thank you for calling us to your circle of seeking. We thank you for your quest for truth and for your preservation of this special time of silence in meditation, for it is a beautiful and most helpful discipline to come together in silence and to invite the truth with all of the ardor of a courtier. For truly you do court that which is to you unknown, that which to you is a gift of your own spirit within. We thank you too because it allows us to perform a service that we feel is worthwhile. The one known as R was saying how remarkable it was that we continue to be happy to speak to you on subjects which seem to cycle around and perhaps cover the same material more than once and certainly in a generalized sort of sense this is true, yet we find that at each asking the direction from which the question comes and the seeking and vector of that seeking are different not only in a horizontal manner but different in a vertical manner. It is a matter of the cycles of questioning being spirals and perhaps not even that organized or logical because oftentimes the learning of a spiritual principle is completely nonlinear and some of the seemingly advanced bits will come very easily to a certain personality shell whereas some of the most simple things will be very difficult. Consequently, it does no good to take one's own spiritual temperature but simply to continue to live each day as though it were the central concern of your soul to live it well.

We ask one thing and that is that always each of you use the discrimination that has been created as part of your consciousness. Listen with an ear for resonance and when resonance is occurring, retain those thoughts and invite them to develop themselves more and to blend within your musing.

If the thoughts do not interest you, do not attempt to follow them, for they are not yours at this time.

The question today concerns how to form a social memory complex of fourth-density level while in third density. And we do find this an apt question and an interesting one. To begin with, let us look at third density as opposed to fourth density. There is a quantum break in between third density and fourth density. Consequently, the question cannot be answered as asked precisely because of the fact that third density is not fourth density; fourth density is not third density. The two have different locations within time/space or the metaphysical universe. It is easy to mix up in one's mind the question of how to be a fourth-density social memory complex in third density and the equally valid question of how to express fourth-density values within third density, thus foreshadowing or pre-echoing the fourth-density reality of which your foreshadowing is a gift of hope. It is far more simple to talk about fourth density as fourth density, and we will do this first. But we do not believe that it completely answers the question.

When a third-density entity allows or surrenders to that ineffable energy of unconditional love, which has often been called Christ consciousness, then the experiencer of this love vibration is dwelling, unknown to herself oftentimes, in fourth density. That quality of love, when the veil is removed, simply places one in a fourth-density environment. In this fourth-density environment the social memory complex is alive and well because the nature of consciousness in fourth density allows that pattern and that pattern is a model that is higher than or that will replace the lower density when there is the awareness to see the higher density. In other words, when the spirit is not embodied in incarnation and the soul involved is vibrating at this level, the disciplines and studies involved in creating a social memory complex begin to be available, certainly, but even before such study and discipline the roadway is there upon which the seeker finds it convenient and easy to walk. The difficulty in fourth density would be finding a motivation for shutting off any part of the self from the blessed company of all other selves that were part of your being.

So any time there is between two entities an energy exchange that is genuinely and authentically mutually loving, without reservation or purpose of control or manipulation, any time that there is the achieving of a state of trust that is pure between two entities, any time there is that insight and awareness of the oneness of the self and another, within that moment, within that communion, however long it lasts, you are walking the bright and golden path of social memory formation, weaving connections and experiences that redound to the personal process of evolution and also to the planetary process of birth into fourth density. Third-density entities finding themselves to be running fourth-density energy greatly aid in the formation of the fourth-density social memory complex simply by opening the heart to the extent that those moments are possible.

It is not, however, to our mind, a physical goal of physically incarnate beings to achieve the complete fourth-density social memory complex. The concern that we share with you here is simply that there not be the desire for outer achievement or for some kind of clique or society of elite. It is well to realize that the social memory complex is not that which is made up of certain selected entities whose personality shells seem to indicate a certain level of awareness. Rather, in the complete democracy of spirit the social memory complex is made connection by connection, energy exchange by energy exchange between all peoples who connect in all ways, on all levels, and in many, many cases without there being a noticeable catalyst. Consequently, it is well to work with those with whom there are special connections. It is also well to level the gaze to include all entities whatsoever who come within the purview of any being who is working on this very worthwhile line of direction in seeking to serve the one Creator.

Do not expect to be completely successful in third density except momentarily or briefly and always be aware that in seeking such goals there is the greed for moving quickly, perhaps more quickly than the wise old woman inside the heart would have you move. And you must listen to that grandmother within that says, "This is the day in which you shall be content to be silent and to surrender and to wait. This is not the day to go forth and achieve." Be aware of the energy that you have from day to day and work with the energy that is there that day, not towards an arbitrary goal of running Christ energy at all times. But simply live the goal of moving towards the self again and again. This instrument was saying earlier that where she has weaknesses in her thinking she finds herself moving back again and again, iterating the messages of faith and confidence and peace that she feels most deeply to be true, but that her emotions and her mental quirks of character do not find so appealing and, of course, in each situation where an entity has to repeat that particular lesson, whatever it is, again and again, the message is clear. This is something that we need to pay great respect and attention to and to sit with and to welcome as a friend. For this friend has something to teach us. Perhaps it may sit at our campfire with us for a long time. Perhaps it shall be the entire incarnation. Perhaps it shall be a month or a year. Whatever that time is, be hospitable and welcome that time. We simply encourage each not to go faster than the wheels will turn. The need here is not for any rate of speed but rather for the self in the daily moment to be paying attention and attempting to do those things that are felt by that entity to be important at this particular time.

However, it is more difficult to speak of the foreshadowing effect but much easier to find a sense of reality which we may share with you, which you might be able to see in a conscious manner. This flashing of fourth density is a magical thing. It is a matter of the state of mind of the person, and it is extraordinarily difficult to talk about that state of mind, but belief and faith are a state of mind, perhaps we would even say that *knowing*[5] is a state of mind. If one *knows* that something is true, that person becomes able to demonstrate that truth. It is the depth of the knowing that creates the state of mind which opens the gateway to intelligent infinity and allows that Christ-consciousness energy its freedom of passage, and when that energy is flowing freely, even if that entity has no idea of what is occurring, the planet itself and the people around that entity will feel the light shine, will feel the warmth that is radiated and will be drawn towards that light and that gentleness of energy that moves with those who are full of love.

All of you have seen this in your daily lives. You have seen the illuminated moments when those around you or even you yourself experienced something that made your everyday experience seem like a black and white movie in comparison because the colors are richer; the feelings are more intense and more pure; that which seems two-dimensional in third density is three-dimensional in fourth-density. And you flash on this awareness, not because you have changed, but because you have opened the door that is closed within yourself. Or the door has been opened for you because of your surrender to the silence and your discipline with persistence in keeping that silence daily.

One of the questions that was asked was "What studies or disciplines might be helpful for those perceived to be at the fourth-density level and to create a social memory complex?" Certainly the most important tool is silence, for truly until you have come to a certain degree of silence within yourself the energy exchanges of the quality of fourth-density would be difficult. For there will be fear. Times spent in silence over a period of time, a little at a time but daily, are extremely helpful for opening those higher densities to the self within so that the self is beginning to pre-echo and foreshadow fourth density without even thinking about it.

We believe that we have given enough for this sitting and would appreciate the one known as B refocusing and requestioning for further information, if this entity desires. We would at this time thank this instrument and transfer the contact to the one known as Jim. We are those known as Q'uo. We leave this instrument in love and in light.

(Jim channeling)

I am Q'uo, and greet each once again in love and in light through this instrument. We would ask at this time if there might be any further queries remaining upon the minds of those present to which we might attempt response? Is there another query at this time?

Carla: OK. I have been receiving some interesting communications, and I have developed the theory that I am receiving a psychic greeting at this time from an entity which has to do with me and which I met during the course of the Ra contact. This is the fifth-density entity. Some information that I got recently suggests that this entity is working to dismantle the Law of One and has been doing so for a long, long time. My feeling is just to love this entity as myself and to let the chips fall where they may. If you would like to comment in any way about this situation I would greatly appreciate it.

I am Q'uo, and am aware of your query, my sister. As you are aware it is with great care that we attempt

---

[5] Carla: I used italics here because when the Q'uo said this word, "knowing," I could feel a substance and depth.

any response to such a query. However, we feel that it may be stated that your relationship with the entity of the fifth density negative polarity was, shall we say, begun at a time previous to this incarnation but became more specific and personal, shall we say, with the beginning of the contact with those of the Ra social memory complex. This was of necessity for this entity has as its primary purpose in regards to this third-density planet the increase of the harvest of those who share its polarity and the reduction of the harvest of the positive polarity. This entity has been engaged in this activity for a great portion of what you would call time in your third-density illusion. The mandate, shall we say, that such an entity gives itself is that there shall be control over those in this entity's field of experience. It is the nature of the negative polarity to arrange itself in such a fashion so that there is a definite order in the movement of energies, thus allowing those controlling this ordered movement to benefit most in the harvest of energies and power. This entity has many areas in which it has invested its own energies in this manner and with these goals. It found the necessity of focusing upon your role in the contact with those of Ra, for it was with this contact that this entity felt the most opportunity for gaining power resided. That this entity would focus upon such a contact was logical from its point of view, but we would also suggest that this entity has busied itself with other endeavors as well.

We would speak briefly to the concept of dismantling the Law of One. This entity observes the Law of One with the attitude of using this law for its own gain. Thus it does not seek to dismantle this law as much as it seeks to bend it and form it in a manner which suits its purposes best. The Law is One. It is indestructible. However, there are means by which certain of its applications may be distorted by those who would seek to use it for their own gain. Is there a further query, my sister?

Carla: No. Thank you.

I am Q'uo, and we thank you for your query, my sister. Is there another query at this time?

Carla: I guess I would ask one more question, but feel free to tell me that you cannot answer it if it infringes on free will. My question has to do with a fellow who wants to create a simpler version of the Law of One. I have mixed feelings about this project. I'd love to see the Law of One available in more ways to more people at more levels. I am hoping that it could be accomplished without changing the material substantially. This is an entity who wants to serve very deeply and is willing to put a lot of energy behind the project. We may have the opportunity to be of more service here and want to do our best. Can you comment?

I am Q'uo and am aware of your query, my sister. In this particular question we find that there is so much of your free will available for infringement that we must not give any kind of response at this time.

Carla: That is fine. Thank you so much, Q'uo. I have no more questions today.

I am Q'uo, and we thank you for your queries and apologize for our lack of response to the second query. We would take this opportunity to thank each once again for inviting us to join you this day. It has been a privilege, as always, to do so. We would take our leave of this instrument and this group at this time, leaving each in the love and in the light of the one infinite Creator. We are known to you as those of Q'uo. Adonai, my friends. Adonai. ✼

L/L Research

Sunday Meditation
December 23, 2001

Group question: The question today comes from B and S. B was wondering if a social memory complex possesses a kind of consciousness that can engage in the exchange of energy with its members, either consciously or unconsciously, or if it is simply the sum of its members? We were assuming (in our conversation previous to this meditation) that a social memory complex could indeed engage in conversation of a very intimate and continuous nature with all of its members. If that is true, could you expand upon that, and could you let us know? And as S asks: As we are beginning to form a social memory complex, is there anything that we can do to prime the pump towards positivity in service-to-others acts, attitudes of mind, meditations, rituals, anything at all?

(Carla channeling)

We are those known to you as the principle of the Q'uo. Greetings in the love and in the light of the one infinite Creator, in whose service we are. It is a great privilege, as always, to speak to this group, and we thank you for forming a circle of seeking once again. It is a great blessing to us to share with your circle's vibrations, and it is a great blessing to us to be able to serve by speaking our thoughts. We ask, as always, that your discrimination choose which of these thoughts you will retain and which are not for you. We do not claim to be purveyors of truth. We claim only to share what we have concluded in our journey so far. But we are very happy to do so, and we do believe that it is a valid path of service.

The question this day is very apt for the time of year that this meeting is being held, for it is near Christmas and all over your world, in every nation, many millions of hearts turn now at this season to thoughts of peace, love and giving. The catalyst for this enormous peak in energy among the peoples of your planet is an outgrowth of the natural cycles of light and dark, fear and love. And, indeed, as was spoken of earlier, the Christian Christmas is a very old overlay to even older rituals from a previous time and a previous religion. It is a response of the heart of a society to the maximum amount of darkness and the minimum amount of light. It is a response to that which moves into the consciousness at such a deep level that there is no true defense against it. The lack of light creates a mood, and the tendency of that mood is towards poignancy and intensity and what this instrument would call negative thought patterns for the simple reason that life within third density is often, among other things, an accumulation of moments of pain that certain occasions seem to bring closer to the surface of memory.

However, this energy of Christmas has never been expressed in precisely the way that the one known as Jesus the Christ expressed it. And the way this entity expressed it has to do with this question about the formation of a social memory complex. Now, this entity who in his native tongue is called Jehoshua but whom we will call Jesus, because of this instrument's distortions and the distortions of the culture in which all of you live, was, in his own way, a politician. But he was a politician who was running for office in another world. As he said, "My kingdom is not of this world." This entity identified his kingdom as the kingdom of heaven. We feel that there has been a tremendous amount of distortion of this entity's message. However, there is enough in what is left of what he actually said to begin to form an idea of what it takes to form a social memory complex.

When one gazes, for instance, at what this instrument calls the Beatitudes, it is interesting to note who is blessed. Blessed are the poor. Blessed are the meek. Blessed are the hungry. Blessed are those who suffer for righteousness sake. Blessed is adversity. Blessed is the enemy. Blessed is he who despitefully uses you. In other words, no matter what you do you will be blessed. When this entity was on the cross dying painfully a thief asked him if he would remember him when he came into his kingdom. And the one known as Jesus said to him, "This day you will be with me in paradise."

Jesus was not a foolish man. He did not feel that all things were good. He felt that some things were sinful. However, he took it to a higher level in each and every case and said, "The past is past. Make a new beginning and you are completely and utterly forgiven." Would that the voices that surrounded this entity had the same message. Much has been lost of the message because others immediately misunderstood it and felt, during the time that this entity was alive, that this entity should become a political figure and rule a country, a physical country, the country of the twelve tribes. This the one known as Jesus rejected out of hand. So if the one known as Jesus was offering information about the vibration of a social memory complex then the direction that the entities who wish to help form a social memory complex need to go is the direction of forgiveness and love. Forgiveness of enemies. Forgiveness of the self. And the willingness to make a new beginning. These seem finite qualities, but in the metaphysical world they are infinite. The freedom to expand and strengthen light is complete once the soul has pierced the veil of forgetting.

Now a very tiny example of a social memory complex would be the couple or the family which is extremely close, so that the entities have begun to tune into each other and eerily have begun to know what the other was going to say, what the other was sensing, how the mood of the other was going without having to speak. There is a growing awareness from the soul level when there is complete trust between two people. This is difficult to achieve. It takes time and it takes persistence on the part of two human beings who will systematically fail at everything that they try to do at one point or another, metaphysically speaking. Consequently there is forgiveness built into trust so that when entities within a fellowship of complete trust misbehave they are allowed the room to do that. They are allowed the support to come out of that. They are allowed the chance to start anew.

These qualities of forgiveness and forgetting and moving on are sweet indeed, metaphysically speaking, because they free up the energy system, the energy body. The one known as T was asking about fear and whether that is an improvement upon anger which is an overlay of fear. And we would say that all overlays being taken away are improvements. The fear now is exposed because of the practice of the one known as T. He now is able to see and be aware of what that underlying emotion truly is, and indeed, no matter what the negatively oriented emotion, we assure you that it is a type of fear. Whether it is anger, grief or any other negatively perceived emotion, the dynamic is always between love and fear.

Now, how do entities in third density achieve such a heady and ambitious intention as forming a social memory complex beforehand, before its time? Almost anything that seekers can think of as ways to express their own individual desire and thirst for being part of the good and the love of planet Earth will help. So much of spiritual evolution is involved in sheer desire and persistence of intention in following that desire. Desire is the fire that drives. It can be a fire that is red-ray, orange-ray, yellow, blue, indigo, or violet-ray. Each of those types of desires, each of those combinations of types of desires, has its own characteristics. And an entity, in order to progress, needs not to follow someone else's idea of a curriculum or a study but, rather, each entity needs to follow his own heart, his own intuition, his own hunch of this or that book at the bookstore, this idea or that idea to think about.

Each of you already is part of a nascent social memory complex, but it is at a very low level at this time because it is not yet time. Priming the pump is a matter of desiring to prime the pump and desiring it just as much tomorrow and the next day and taking each moment of desire as it comes and asking, "Show me Thy ways. Teach me how to serve." And surrendering that cleverness of wit in order to open to deeper guidance and to purer fire. For there is help for those who wish to rise. There is an enormous company, as this instrument has often said, of angels, beings that wish only to help entities to evolve and to cherish them while they do, to keep them in a metaphysical sense safe and comfortable. There are angels around each of you. They truly desire to be of service. When you sit in the silence, lean into that help and ask that invisible company to give you signs, give you ideas, help with the guidance, help with the clues, so that you can choose what feels the most resonant as your own path of service.

The one known as Jesus tried to apply fourth-density ideas to third-density society. We grasp the fact that this has not been popular since, and we believe we grasp why, realizing as we do that the one known as Jesus was able to open his heart and trust in the infinity of supply. The closest that your peoples have come to the idea of Jesus, which was to hold everything in common, has been various socialistic and communistic societies in their theoretical form, where each entity is looked at as completely equal and equally deserving of the right to live and to have a place to be and food to eat. The ability of your culture at this time to tolerate the situation where many, many entities do not have enough to eat is, among many other things, acting as a, shall we say, drag on the planetary evolution. For it reflects a carelessness among its members and a lack of appreciation for the qualities that humanity offers long before it justifies itself by being useful.

We ask you to consider who you are. Your physical vehicle was created, according to the writer known as Sitchin and others, to be gold miners for extraterrestrials. Consequently, there are many among those who believe in extraterrestrials and believe in their interactions with those of Earth who believe that there is no resurrection possible because the physical vehicles are simply dust and were created only to be slaves. But we say to you that a physical vehicle is a physical vehicle. Yours, like most life forms in this universe, has been interfered with several times. But that has little or nothing to do with the consciousness that accepts the contract with the physical vehicle to have an incarnation together.

Each of you is truly a citizen of eternity. It does not matter what the makeup of your body is, whether it was created by the God of the Bible in six days or whether it was created by extraterrestrials. The fact is that, within the illusion that you now experience, you are here. There is a little sign with an arrow that says, "You are here." Whatever your age. Whatever your station. Whatever your challenges. That is the playground in which you are enjoying yourself at this time.

While you are enjoying yourself on this playground it is very seductive to come to the belief that you are on a playground enjoying the games. It is, however, an helpful thought always to move beyond the playground, to move beyond the lights, the glitter, and the drama of people doing righteous and unrighteous things to each other. It is possible to move back into the heart of being that was before this world was and which will be when this world has finally become energy again. It is an uneasy union, body and consciousness, but it is precisely that union of flesh and spirit that is needed for third density. The vehicles you have are sound for the work that you wish to do.

We encourage both an intensity of dedication and a very light touch with the seeking to accelerate the pace of evolution and to come into some expression of fourth density. Now, you may find as you continue seeking peace that ideas will come to you. We encourage you to respond to those ideas because each of you is a Creator. Perhaps you have a gift for becoming closer to another entity or to a new idea that no one else has. We assure you that each of you sings a different melody of vibration, so each of you has unique gifts to give. And those gifts are already held in common by the people of Earth. There is at this time a nascent fourth-density social memory complex of positive nature forming on planet Earth. It is occurring now.

The one known as B is attempting to do this by starting a community. The one known as Carla, this instrument, in her own way has dedicated her life to bringing more light; to running fourth-density energy within a third-density system. This entity, unfortunately, has not done this entirely efficiently within her personal life. But in terms of metaphysical efficiency, both the one known as B and the one known as Carla have made good efforts. And it is the continuation of those efforts; that is, the continuation of faith, that will avail the most.

For love has a way of teaching you without being obvious about it, without the two-by-four having to hit the forehead. There is no wakeup, often, with the lessons of love but, rather, you discover that your ideas have migrated a bit, that there is a different light from which you are seeing the same thing. It may be slight, but it may well be more fourth-density if that is what you are affirming and seeking.

When you are expressing this nascent fourth-density energy you, if you are very aware, will feel it as an energy exchange even if the entity with whom you are communicating is half a globe away. There is an energy exchange between those who are vibrating together in love with each other on the fourth-density level which is very heartening and very healing for both entities, and we encourage each to attempt in all relationships to move from a point of fourth-density love, acceptance, forgiveness and willingness to move on. That is the pattern of learning, not to linger too long in negative emotions but, rather, to honor that negative emotion whenever it arises, to sit with it as long as it needs to be sat with in order to be accepted, in order to feel that it has been honored. And then, when it has been honored and there has come a peace and a balance and some small understanding, it is time to say, "Amen. I am sorry. I begin again." And let mistakes be mistakes, but stay in the light and the love of the one infinite Creator while you make the mistake, and, after you make the mistake, allow yourself your own love rather than your judgment. For judge and grasp the lesson you certainly will, but then it is time to release that.

The great obstacle to peace among your peoples is the same obstacle that is in a family when they will not agree and they insist on leaving problems unadressed and unsolved. The one known as Jim has said very truly many times that this world needs a great deal of love. That is true at the individual level. It is also true at the societal level, at the racial level, and at the planetary level.

Does a social memory complex have its own ability to communicate? Certainly. Even within a marriage there is a social memory complex. Within this group, which today represents only four human beings (physically present), there is a strong and healthy social memory complex that is helping each. It is not that each has become wonderfully able in the human sense to comfort and support each other but that the wish to do so is pure within these four hearts sitting within this room. And within this atmosphere, since all things truly are one, naturally over a period of time there is formed not just these four souls into a union but these four souls and the Creator so that the Creator and the self multiplies with the Creator and the next self and the Creator in the third self and the Creator in the fourth self and the result is powerful, far beyond the sum of its parts. There is a feedback system that begins to work when entities meet spiritually and attempt to love each other, even when they misbehave, even when they have difficult times.

Many, many opportunities will come to each of you in small ways and in large. Opportunities to see an entity as the self or the other self. We do not say to ignore the needs of the physical life. We do not say that it is wrong to set limits when there are difficulties, to protect the self from damage. You are third-density entities and you need to respond to the pain and the suffering that you feel. If you do not respond to it, if you insist on being all love and light at all times and not dealing with your feelings, not dealing with your dark side, you shall never make a social memory complex.

So the first entity that you must fall in love with in order to form a social memory complex is yourself. If you can fall in love with the shadow self of your own 360 degree being you have become far, far more vulnerable to the light that is the new light of fourth density. So much of the light that you call to yourself is created by the nexus of desire and emotion within which you are seeking the light. So all aspects of light feed into making third density into fourth density because all aspects of light can be illuminated by love. Love makes food taste better. Love makes gardens bloom better. Love makes children grow healthier. Love makes businesses thrive. Love will also make positive fourth density occur because the love energy within many of your people is now approaching that energy which is the graduated third density, the Christ energy.

The one known as Jesus would laugh long and hard at someone who said that he was a saint or that he was holy or that he was better than the next sinner. This entity did not feel those things. This entity was seeking to become more meek, more poor, more hungry, and to achieve more suffering. Why was this entity doing this? This is the mystery of moving from third density to fourth density. Why did this entity find such joy in turning the other cheek? And in embracing death when he thought that by that sacrifice he would be able to save others from that suffering? Why was this very imperfect human act of choosing to die something that has riveted your culture for 2,000 years? That is the question that we feel may be most beneficial at this time [for you to ponder]. For the Entity comes into the Earth at this time. The one known as Jesus each year comes into the darkness, and the darkness knows Jesus not. And to that darkness Jesus is simply a mistake, a fool, a troublesome entity that must be stopped. For this entity simply wants to love. He wants nothing in return but simply wishes to speak the words of his Father, to do the will of his Father.

May you follow your heart. May you follow that which this instrument calls the cross. For fourth density is cruciform; that is, early fourth density especially. There is a cross involved. There is a sigil of sacrifice that needs to be grasped in a way that words almost cannot achieve. Silence itself, the tabernacle of the heart, and those infinitely blessed words that have no sound, that still, small voice, will bring to you that which you need. We encourage each to seek that silence each day and to affirm that all is well, that all will be well, that the life may be lived in faith. This rest that faith gives, again, frees one to love. It enables fearlessness. No one within your sphere is truly fearless in all ways, but it is well gently but determinedly to work on that fear, work on those separating emotions and realize that all actions expressed lovingly are metaphysically correct. It is not possible often within the Earth planes to make a pure choice because the physical vehicle won't stand it or the budget won't stand it, or the family won't stand it, or something will fall apart that you wish to keep together if you pursue a totally pure path of light. As we said, there are times when one must make decisions that do not seem particularly loving. But if they are made carefully, thoughtfully, and because of love then we say that is excellent work. It might not be right, but it is not important to be right. It is important to be loving. So attempt to be right. Attempt to run that ship that you have. But attempt more to open the heart to love.

We would at this time transfer this contact to the one known as Jim. We thank this group for asking such a good question, and we at this time would leave this instrument in love and light. We are those of Q'uo.

(Jim channeling)

I am Q'uo, and we greet each once again in love and in light through this instrument. At this time we would seek to offer ourselves to any further queries which may remain on the minds of those present. Are there any shorter queries to which we might speak at this time?

S: It is recently on my mind that, since yesterday we had a rear end collision and a couple of days ago we had another accident, I was wondering if there was some lesson that I had missed?

I am Q'uo, and am aware of your query, my brother. We apologize for the delay that was necessary for this instrument to work the recording devices. To your query, we can not see any particular lesson here other than there is always the unexpected, which occurs sometimes without any seeming rhyme or reason, yet which one can interpret by whatever means or attitude is prevalent within the personality structure. This attitude of mind then is set to work upon whatever catalyst approaches and will make the necessary adjustments to include the new catalyst within the established ways of thinking. The seeker of truth, then, may utilize any catalyst to achieve the desired perspective, shall we say. When one has one's spiritual feet firmly under one, there is no catalyst which can shake one's ground of being. All catalyst then becomes available as grist for the mill, shall we say, the catalyst being the means by which one seeks the heart of the being, if that is one's predilection, or seeks the more easily accessible surface interpretation, if one wishes to skirt the issue, shall we say, or move around the experience of one's being. Is there another query to which we may respond, my brother?

S: My wife has been feeling kind of low and down and I suggested it might be a psychic greeting, or it may be the doldrums but she couldn't seem to find a reason why she feels the way she is feeling. Do you have any perspective on that?

I am Q'uo, and am aware of your query, my brother. We show this instrument the picture of the ice and the broken ankle. We suggest that this entity, the one known as C, may be, in the memory of the body complex, remembering that which occurred nearly one year ago at this time. The memory of the body is much stronger than most entities in third density are aware of or give credit to the body for possessing. We assure you, however, that the body does remember those traumatic experiences and this memory bleeds through from the subconscious mind and becomes that which is seemingly non-directional, without source, a feeling of apprehension or anxiety. Is there another query, my brother.

S: That is most helpful and I am sure C will appreciate it too. I am curious from the last session, concerning Carla's fifth-density friend of negative polarity that occasionally attacks her. Does this entity have a name?

I am Q'uo, and am aware of your query, my brother. And this is correct. Is there another query, my brother?

S: And what is this entity's name?

I am Q'uo, and am aware of your query, my brother. We suggest that it be carefully considered whether or not this knowledge is desired. For it is polarized significantly in the negative direction to know the name of one's seeming adversary. To know such is to begin the trail in the attempt to have power over that entity. Is there another query, my brother?

S: I'll take the hint and leave it at that. The last question is: do those of Q'uo and the heavenly host have any message or thing that they would like to contribute to our group at this time?

I am Q'uo, and we cannot resist. Ho! Ho! Ho! Is there another query at this time?

S: Not from me. Thanks.

I am Q'uo, and we thank you, my brother. Is there another query at this time?

Carla: I've noticed that Christmas is a very difficult time for many people to the point that they have to work at surviving Christmas, to go and get some deli and some videos and shut out the horror until it passes. It's a terribly negative view of Christmas, perhaps because there is no one to share it with or because of a bad memory. I wonder why this is and what can be done to make people feel better about Christmas?

I am Q'uo, and am aware of your query, my sister. There is an infinity of possible reactions or responses to the season which you call Christmas as there are for any season, day, or event. Who can say why one entity feels such great joy and another such sorrow at the same experience. Each of you and each of us in all of creation is an individual, a spark from the same flame of the one Creator, yet a reflection in infinite variety according to choices made, experiences had, directions taken and not taken. There is no way to estimate the response of one entity over that of another entity to the same catalyst. For all lives are written by one soul in many experiences, some of which mark deeply upon the pages of the life pattern, while others seem to go unnoticed with the same seeming surrounding cast of characters. Life, for most, is a great mystery. To begin, and we stress begin, to unravel the various twists and turns of plot and character is the work of one entity for a lifetime. In short, my sister, we cannot give you a cure for the Christmas blues. Is there another query at this time?

Carla: No. Thank you, Q'uo.

I am Q'uo, and we thank you, my sister. Is there another query at this time?

T: When Carla asked the question a thought came into my mind. Sometimes it seems to me that some people at Christmas time get a glimpse of good cheer and people having a good time and what happiness could be towards this light. And some people take this and say that it's not this way all the time, and they get depressed. Could you comment on that, please?

I am Q'uo, and am aware of your query, my brother. Indeed, for many this is so. To see that which is desired but not realized and removed from one's experience seems to be focusing on that which is ephemeral, seems to be a trick, to be false. Others perhaps see the commercial nature of the season and are disillusioned. Others respond more to the lack of light, the days being shorter. Others perhaps respond to the loss of loved ones from earlier times who are not now available for sharing the joy. Others perhaps respond to events within the world stage which seem to be more evident at this time in your yearly cycle. As we mentioned previously there are many reasons for entities to respond in the negative sense, of joy or sadness, at this particular time of your year. Is there another query, my brother?

T: No. Thank you very much.

I am Q'uo and we thank you, my brother. We would take this opportunity to thank each present for the heartfelt queries. The concern that underlies each is most evident to us, and we are always grateful to be able to speak to those who have the great desire to know the truth, to share the truth, and to become the truth. We walk with you on that journey, as do many others who are not visible at this time but whose hearts sing with you in the joy of your own seeking and your own serving.

At this time we shall take our leave of this instrument and of this group. As always, we leave you in the love and in the ineffable light of the one infinite Creator. We are known to you as those of Q'uo. Adonai, my friends. Adonai. ✧

Year 2002

January 6, 2002 to May 19, 2002

L/L Research

Sunday Meditation
January 6, 2002

Group question: For the group question today we are going to take pot luck and see what Q'uo might have to say to us.

(Carla channeling)

We are those known to you as the principle of the Q'uo, and we greet you in the love and in the light of the one infinite Creator in whose service we are. We thank you for forming a circle on this day of winter. The snow and the difficult roads have kept many of your friends from their activities. We celebrate your faithfulness to these precious times together, and we are most grateful to you for seeking the truth as a group this afternoon.

It is the first time in a long while-we do not immediately remember the last time that we had a pot luck-and that is a novel thing for us. For we then need to use our own discrimination to the extent which you usually take off our hands. What would we wish to tell you? What would we wish to offer you? Left to ourselves we speak one tune. We tell one story. We tell of love. And yet we find that even within this small a group of three we would be able to rest within each of your minds to discover the genius that lies in the connections between those minds and to find a completely unique subject at any time that you would ask for pot luck. For the energy between even any two people, much less any three people, is a complex and multi-layered thing. The connections are there in so many ways that are difficult to understand in any linear fashion. Each of you is connected to each other by those things which you are working on in common, by those services which you share in common, by the outer gifts which you enjoy in common, and by the desires that resonate between each of you in common.

So that even among those whose path is fairly calm and whose seeking has become silent and only occasionally moving into the new book, the new tape, the new buzz, the new news. Each of you creates constantly the future forks in the road for yourself, those future choices of pathway. It is not only that you are choosing the road that you are on when you come to the moment and gaze at it, for indeed you choose not only the road that you are on in the present but turnings from that road that are implied in the depths of your seeking, in the quality of your attention, and in the sincerity of your humility at asking and knowing that you know not and that you truly wish to know. This desire is not a permanent or a fixed thing in anyone. Rather, it is that commitment that is revisited [perhaps] each day but certainly from time to time.

So rather than your life being a clarion call that once begun simply continues speaking we suggest that each of you has a voice, has an energy, has the potential to sing a certain beautiful and complex melody, but each of you, indeed, in the present moment is a sonata under construction, a musical piece that has not yet been finished. And so there is the rehearsal and the playing over of the tunes of self, those leitmotifs of being.

The one known as T said earlier that there was that in him that greatly missed the opportunity last week to come together in seeking in silence and in truth. And we would address this line of thought because there is a very valuable point to be made here, not simply for this group, but in terms of all groups that are seeking to increase the light upon planet Earth. It is very well to establish a group. It is very well to begin a practice of spiritual seeking. It is excellent to form a plan for seeking the truth, for finding the self, or for discovering one's service. All of these avenues are worthy. They all lie before each of you. When you come together as a group in a regular and persistent fashion these threads begin to weave themselves without your conscious awareness into a far more coherent and lambent pattern, banked and steeped in light because of the energy of those companions of the path that have entered the silence together over a period of time.

Opening to the silence in a group over a twenty year period that these particular three entities have enjoyed together is opening a very small social memory complex between the three seated within this circle plus the social memory complex existing betwixt each of the two in this group which have a close bonding, plus the social memory complex that exists within fourth density, that one which exists within fifth, and that one which exists within sixth density and which forms the principle which is our voice. Consequently, rather than bringing one entity into the silence, by meeting in a group over a period of time you are beginning to weave for yourself a solid and reliable resource which contains your energy spoken truly and reflected in the mirror of those who love you and those who would wish to help you.

Meeting in trust, coming together in humility and seeking, are motives and energies which ennoble and strengthen that within you which seeks so that you may have the grace to continue to seek. For, indeed, we do not advertise that there are easy answers. Indeed we do not advertise answers. We urge the questioning. We encourage the hunger and here we do not speak of intellectual hunger, although certainly that has its place and books and ideas and all sorts of outer influences are intended to come in and to speak to you and to move you, but beyond all of these things it is the silence, it is the seeking beyond the question where the whole self becomes the question and the only answer desired is wrapped in silence and lifted on the wings of angels so that you, yourself, are wrapped in angels' wings, those wings which bear one up when one knows nothing, those wings which hide one when the sunlight of pain is too bright, those wings that lift one up above the pettiness and the greed, the sloth and the laziness of other human beings that come before your eyes, that lift one up beyond the secrets of the heart, that are not worthy, that are error-prone, that mark one as a human that are the hardest of all to lift beyond, to fly beyond, to release from the judgment of one's self.

We are so pleased that you have sensed the power of simple, error-prone, third-density human beings in a group, dedicated to light and love and service. Is there within any of you some bright idea that will instantly change the planet? We do not know. We do not know where your outer gifts lie, where the footsteps of your heart will take you, not tomorrow, not even next year, not in the next decade. We don't know the final shape of your life but [only] that there is this moment together in time and in space where these three have come together and sought in silence and in the spiritually lived voice which this instrument has asked for. That which you know not is a great treasure, a great resource within your practice, and we are very, very pleased that you feel its value whether or not it is possible to see into this depth or quality of value in a conscious manner. It is there, and on the incarnational level contracts are being fulfilled. Collaborations continue, and the work that is common to all moves on to a fuller life because each has persisted in good weather and in bad, in good feelings and in difficult times, through all of the thicks and thins of living.

This is a time when your planet roots deep and sleeps. This is a time when many little snows visit the Earth and sink into it very slowly, watering in a much more beneficial way than the dazzling flooding rains of spring. The ground is preparing for its growing season, feeding the deep springs. Slowly, so slowly the energies of the light begin to strengthen as the day becomes minutes longer each day. Each within this group deals at this time with those difficulties which seem to smack of the cold and the ice of inconvenience, discomfort and pain. Yet we say to you that within the warm nest of hearth and home and heart the balm of Gilead lies sleeping, waiting to be taken up and used, and all of the energies of healing, peace and new life are upon the wind, harbingers of the spring and the blooming time to come. Know that all is well. Know that all seasons have their beauty, and rest in that faith and hope which inform your heart when it opens to the shining face of the one original Creator.

We would, if the instrument known as Jim is willing, like to exercise this instrument briefly as this is a good opportunity, since there is no message, to work with this instrument in a more general and creative way. If this instrument prefers, it is perfectly all right not to speak. We would at this time offer to transfer this contact to the one known as Jim. We are those of Q'uo and leave this instrument in love and light.

(Jim channeling)

I am Q'uo, and we greet each once again in love and in light through this instrument. We have at this time spoken about the process of evolution that each entity undergoes, both as an individual and as members of a group of individuals. The process of seeking the direction of one's path is a process which is chosen not only upon the conscious level of each individual seeker but is a process which is, you might say, encoded into the very cells of your bodies. For all of life which has been created is made of the same Creator and this Creator of us all seeks to know of Itself what can be known, and seeks as well to return to a state of being in which there is a complete stasis for but a short while in which the knowledge of being is fully assimilated. As this is a dynamic energy there is in fact no true stasis, for that which is garnered from knowledge is almost immediately put to use as a kind of fuel for the engine of beingness. There is always a use or burning of the fuel of knowledge which can be focused in an individualized sense so that there are infinite possibilities for those portions of the Creator which are able to individualize to do so. Thus are each of you, and all of the sentient beings who are children of the one Creator, fitted with a kind of homing device. For the portions of the one Creator who wander far, it would seem, from unity are in fact voyaging into those areas of unity which are yet unknown or unexplored until some portion of the seeking Creator moves into these areas, much as the-we search this instrument's mind-various expressions of biological life flourish in a pattern dance, growing ever more intricate patterns of life forms to once again express another facet of the one Creator being explored through free will.

We are those of Q'uo. We feel that we have taken this instrument far a field in this particular expression and would at this time ask if there might be any queries that we may attempt? Is there a query at this time?

Carla: I don't have a question but I would just like to ask that you be with Jim and me as we go through these two procedures in January and February. I would appreciate your help.

I am Q'uo, and we feel your desire for assistance, and this is of course an area in which we are most happy to join you in the healing efforts. For the energies which we have to offer are of a very basic level of vibration in accordance with the third-density requirements for expression. We are with you, my sister, and would be glad to join you in any meditative endeavors which would assist in the relaxation and healing process.

Is there any query at this time?

Carla: No. Thank you very much.

T: No. Not from me. Thanks.

I am Q'uo and we thank each once again for inviting our presence this day. Again, we would express our great joy at each opportunity to join this group in its seeking. At this time we would take our leave of this instrument and of this group. We are known to you as those of Q'uo. Adonai, my friends. Adonai. ✜

L/L Research

L/L Research is a subsidiary of Rock Creek Research & Development Laboratories, Inc.

P.O. Box 5195
Louisville, KY 40255-0195

www.llresearch.org

Rock Creek is a non-profit corporation dedicated to discovering and sharing information which may aid in the spiritual evolution of humankind.

ABOUT THE CONTENTS OF THIS TRANSCRIPT: This telepathic channeling has been taken from transcriptions of the weekly study and meditation meetings of the Rock Creek Research & Development Laboratories and L/L Research. It is offered in the hope that it may be useful to you. As the Confederation entities always make a point of saying, please use your discrimination and judgment in assessing this material. If something rings true to you, fine. If something does not resonate, please leave it behind, for neither we nor those of the Confederation would wish to be a stumbling block for any.

© 2009 L/L Research

Sunday Meditation
January 20, 2002

Group question: The question today has to do with the concept of how we create our experience, our reality, by the way we think, by the way we believe. We would like for Q'uo to give us any indication as to whether that might be correct and if it is, how does that work? We would like to have more information on how we can create a more harmonious reality.

(Carla channeling)

We are those known to you as the principle of Q'uo, and we greet you in the love and in the light of the one infinite Creator, whose service we share with you. We thank you for forming a circle of seeking on this snowy day. It is a blessing to us to respond to your request for thoughts on the notion that beliefs can change your future. We are aware that in the sense that the world sees things this may be very difficult to grasp. However, we believe it is correct and we would be glad to share some thoughts about it.

First of all, we must remember the creation that you experience and the creation that, shall we say, is the reality of which the creation is the illusion are very, very close together but are not the same thing. The illusion is as close as a heartbeat to reality but is invested with physicality so that you are actually a traveler in two worlds at the same time: the world of your outer experience and the world of your inner experience. To suggest that the inner experience influences the outer experience would not be to suggest something very unusual. For it is clear to all of those in the circle how much difference a person's attitude can make with regard to most situations faced. Certainly it is easy to see that the glad smile or the way of making light of some perceived difficulty will always create an atmosphere of the people around one, if not the self, to feel better about an existing situation.

Wherever the self or other people are concerned the words said create not just an atmosphere but a feeling. And that feeling predisposes the inner self in ways that are difficult to see, looking from the eyes of the world. In actuality even that reality that you sense that is a heartbeat away from the illusion is not the end of the seeking for reality, for each of you is part of a group oversoul, shall we say, or a larger self that contains many seeming individuals that are not the self but in actuality are part of the self. And these larger entities are part of even larger entities until you get to the level of planets and sun bodies and the kind of entities that have many orders of magnitude beyond the one that you now experience.

All of these orders of reality are alike reality and illusion. However, the level at which one is working is very difficult to pin down in words because in no case will it be that which is congruent with the outer reality which is an illusion. Consequently a great deal of the path of seeking the truth is, as the one known as R said, discovering the depth of the truth that one cannot control all things in order for the self to feel comfortable, for the self will never feel comfortable. For all things cannot be controlled, and most things are not even supposed to be controlled. That is, we suggest to you that the apparent chances and changes of an everyday life have elements of excellence in all of the offerings spread before your experience each day, not simply the seemingly fortunate happenstances but also those accidents and misfortunes which seem to be quite the opposite of fortunate and seem to be ill-starred and unlucky or even tragic.

The way the illusion is set up is almost guaranteed to make it impossible for you to be able to control the inner universe. It is a situation where the outer personality shell attempts to order things so that the self will be comfortable. This is the usual choice for entities. They attempt to control the environment for comfort and for perceived goals that have to do with security and protection.

The film that this entity was talking about earlier is an offering by a scientist who suggests that the role of the physical things that make up the body, the genetic structure of the body, is not as controlling and elective as it appears from the outside in, that what one has in the genetic structure of the self as inherited appearance is not necessarily that which must be experienced. This entity explained that these genetic structures have a garment and that garment is kept over the genetic structure in such a way that it does not appear or become activated in the life experience as long as this covering is allowed to remain over the genetic structure. This covering is made of proteins. These proteins are excited by incoming signals which cause these proteins to express themselves, first by electrical pulse, then by the exciting of the precise proteins that the electricity encourages. And then another electrical pulse to complete the errand started by the protein which come to either uncovering the genetic structure and causing it to be triggered or leaving it as it is.

This entity was simply saying that the belief of the person has the actual physical power to change the input signal that electrifies the proteins and that this change in belief will change the reaction of the physical body so that if there is a tendency towards cancer in the family, by figuring out what positive things keep that sleeve on the cancer gene and figuring out what things to avoid to keep from taking that sleeve off that gene that cancer gene never needs to be excited, never needs to be uncovered and never needs to be experienced. This is the basic idea behind this approach to attempting to bring the outer world and the inner world into one and create the reality that we would prefer, rather than the reality that we see in our genetic structures and our heritage from our parents.

This is the sense of this video tape that the instrument was talking about earlier. This is sound in terms of your own world's science. It is also sound in terms of what we believe to be so. It is very difficult for us to get into the real nitty-gritty of how you can talk to yourself as opposed to how someone else will talk to himself or herself. Each person has habits of mind which are not, shall we say, of the most hopeful or positive point of view. And with each person there are different areas. These areas are very quirky, as this instrument would say. It is very much a matter of the day, the hour, the mood, and the catalyst within the life in any one day as to what areas of the thinking that you do in talking to yourself you get into, what mistakes that you make in that particular day. And are they mistakes, indeed? For if you are telling yourself something that is disempowering, like "I don't think that I can do this job," perhaps you are telling yourself that so that you can stop and take a good look at the job and really ask yourself, "Is this the job I want to do?" Or with a relationship to ask yourself, "Is this the footing on which I want to be, or is there another footing that would not only be more skillful but actually make me a happier camper, a happier person, a more efficacious human being," one that is more capable of learning, loving, serving and all of those things that you hope to do?" So I suppose that what we are saying is that it is true beyond our ability to prove it that what you think to yourself, what you say to those about you, has, to the extent that you believe what you are saying, or that you do not believe to the contrary, a power over your future.

The question of time is most confusing, but is very relevant to this discussion because it is the nature of how time flows that is critical to the grasping of how it is possible for something as invisible as thought to affect physicality. So our first statement is simply that you may take it on faith, if you have faith, that this is so and work with a will to discovering how to talk to yourself and how to talk to those about you in order to express what you most truly think is true, what you most deeply feel to be the case. Consequently, we are not suggesting that it is possible to look at a situation where a house is on fire and say that this is perfect. This will not stop the house from burning down. We will agree completely that thought concerning a seemingly unfortunate situation will not change the structure of that situation, at least not in the physical.

However, think about the last time that you heard of someone who came through a fire. What were they saying? They were probably saying, "Thank God that my wife and children are safe. All we lost was the house." Somehow it is the function of bad fortune not to create tragedy in people's lives but to open possibilities for thankfulness and for positive change. It might be a terrible opportunity for positive change to see one's house burn up or to see other disasters strike. Yet at the same time, with the gift of hindsight one is able to look back on such passages through difficulty and one is able to pinpoint the real quality and appreciated nuances of that experience that seemed in the present moment to be a dreadful thing but seen from the future looking backwards becoming almost the opposite: almost a boon, almost a point of fortune because of the learnings and the maturity that were gained during the experience.

So when faced with something that you perceive to be a difficulty we are not suggesting that you put on rose-colored glasses and say that the difficulty is not a difficulty. Rather, what we encourage is that thoughtful approach that is willing to accept the two-natured quality of all apparent experience. There is an outer quality to the experience, and that is what you are seeing, feeling, tasting, touching, sensing in that way. There is also an inner quality to this experience. This inner quality is a very subtle thing and not a simple one. It is made up of the way you are at the moment on the surface, on the surface personality level, plus those deeper levels of the self where you have let some sunlight into deeper parts of the self where you are aware of some of your geographies of mood and emotion that have created themselves into structures in your inner life. You might be in that inner structure where you are comfortable and you are in a role that you might enjoy. You may be in a structure where you do not have everything explored yet. You are still the seeker, the discoverer of the self. You may be at that level where much is unknown and where you may feel relatively uncomfortable. Yet you feel that you are in a very true part of the self. It is just one which you have not become fully acquainted with yet.

And these structures of familiar roles and unfamiliar roles, old things and new things, create a kind of three-dimensionality to the inner life that is almost impossible to put into words, but we feel that you grasp what we are trying to say, that there is in the self that comes to the moment a great deal more than what meets the eye, not just the personality meeting the day, but the personality at a certain point in a very long journey, with a lot of energy behind that journey and a lot of energy in front of that journey. And you're just picking a point in the illusion to come into awareness and have this lifetime and have these experiences. And so you are just sort of sticking up into the outer reality with this physical vehicle, and this personality shell and this enormous weight of many, many lifetimes, many, many experiences and many desires fulfilled and yet unfulfilled. This is each seeker's situation as the awakening occurs. Again and again there is the awareness that the situation is far more than a simple present moment and that the full reaction to that present moment is coming from places near and far within the self so that the self that meets the moment is always a unique individual, unique to that day, that time, that mood, that catalyst.

We do not see time as you see time. We see time in more of a circle. We see your experiences as circles within that circle, and we see all of it with much more capacity to allow for the complexity of the true situation without needing to define it. Consequently we find it much easier to have, shall we say, a pleasant existence. We are not in that dense physicality that blocks much of the vision that you have in an inner sense. It blocks it specifically because you are supposed to be thrown off balance and disturbed by the illusion. You are supposed to become involved and lose your objectivity and make mistakes and when you do that you feel that you have failed and at the same time you are fulfilling each desire of your heart, just not in the order and with the comfort that you had perhaps intended. Yet all of these things that seem to crop up in the present are a mixture of those things that happen in the outer world without any rhyme or reason: the weather, the car breaking, and so forth and those things that happen for a great many inner reasons that create situations where it will be a totally different experience if there is poor weather or if the car breaks because of the richness of your inner experience and the way that it has delivered you to the present moment.

Now, in this present moment you are sowing the seeds of a future and this is where it gets interesting from our point of view because of the fact that this is what so many of those who have awakened have come here specifically to do at this time and that is to make a difference in the future of your planet in the short run. And the difference has to do with how each individual seeker sees the present and sees the future. And here is where self-fulfilling prophecy comes into play. It is easy enough to see that if this entity named Carla can smile when she is in pain she affects the lives of those around her to the point where, as they did before this meditation they asked this instrument, "How is it that you can feel pain and not react?" To this instrument it was not a question easily answered because as far as this instrument knew she was reacting to pain. She simply was apparently better than she thought at keeping it to herself.

This is true of each of you. Each of you has these areas that other people think "Oh, that person is doing very well." But to you, yourself, you are aware of the gap between that which was hoped for and that which was achieved in terms of the quality of the personal response of that moment, the quality of the response of the heart, to consciousness itself. But we say to you that each of you is a tremendously powerful fulcrum and the present is the pivot, and what you do in this present moment with regards to your belief about the future of humankind will redound either to the safe birthing of planet Earth into fourth density positive with all of the inhabitants of the planet more or less kept safe, or it will redound to a global catastrophe where all of the magnetic fluxes which are presently unstable will become stabilized. Either future is at this time, as far as we can see, entirely possible. The future is in the hands of you and you and you, each of you. And it is within the belief system of each of you.

Think how one person who chooses to bring faith into the present moment, to bring the love of the heart into the present moment, affects that present moment and affects the mood of those about that person that is expressing love and light. Think about those moments in your own life when you have found that moment of grace and won through to a good attitude and how empowered you did feel and how it did change the outward reality simply because you had risen to the occasion with a happy heart. Think of how you have blighted your own life in times when you have taken the negative view and talked yourself deeper and deeper into sadness and sorrow and despair.

It is not always possible to create the future in big, bold strokes. It is not always possible to express in a day, in a week, in a month, or in a year the beauty that you are capable of appreciating in even one moment. It seems on a thousand different levels that the treasure of life and its beauty were falling away far quicker than life's difficulties and travails. And we suggest that for the faithful one the path lies in continuing to play the hand that you were dealt, to enjoy the weather that the day holds, to deal with those chores that seem to need to be dealt with as best you can. And retain, insofar as you can, beyond all of those things a remembrance that has nothing to do with what has happened, a remembrance that is stubborn against seeming reality, a remembrance of an internal reality that, to you, overmatches the pale colors of the physical world. And that is that inner world of your own heart, your own soul, your own spirit.

When you are quiet in those moments that come to be so treasured when they do come you feel the truth of the self, the beauty of your sweetheart, the strength of your soul, and the power that is within you. Rest insofar as you can in the memory of those moments when you did feel connected to the Creator, when you did feel that you were part of the love that is all that there is, when you had the connections that made you unified, positive and hopeful.

A life in faith is not a life in which the faith is always expressed. Rather, it is a life that is full of mistakes that, when self-perceived, are addressed with the best that the self has to address those perceived mistakes. If you have the willingness to retain that sense of self when everything else goes wrong and to win through after all the difficulties and emotions have been expressed to the remembrance of that self, then you will be living a good spiritual life. For it is not living smoothly and wisely and all things being even that is the hallmark of the rich spiritual life but, rather, it is that often challenged self, that self that is held accountable after being comforted and comforted after being held accountable. That is where the skill lies: in not giving up upon the self, and not giving up because of perceived failure, but rather in seeing that one cannot see at all times into the pattern that lies beneath the seeming chaos of the day. That remembrance is enough to keep you faithful or faith-filled with regards to the future. It is as though that remembrance of the self beyond all of the mental and emotional patterns, the remembrance of that spiritual self, the remembrance of those times of connection with the Creator, enables the self to pick itself up, brush itself off, and try again. And there is that skill with which the future will become a positive and ever more shining thing, that bare remembrance of who you are and what the process is all about. It is not about creating beautiful moments, although it is wonderful to create beautiful moments. It is about being real, as real as the self can be, and that will often lead one astray, that will often lead one to errors in judgment, self-perceived by the self, to wrong decisions, self-perceived by the self.

The more the thought is taken, the more the mentality is invoked to rationalize and to analyze the less the self will be able to connect with those deeper strata of internal structures which actually are slowing up the deeper patterns of life in your incarnation in terms of the large strokes of life: the relationships, the jobs, the situations that are seen to continue from year to year and constitute continuing lessons for the self.

You are not a solid. You are a vibration. You are an energy field that has connections to absolutely all other energy fields in the universe. You are connected to them through a series of orders of magnitude and, shall we say, reality, that are understandable only from the larger viewpoint. Many times within the life experience you will not be able to see how a certain situation could possibly be one in which love abides. But this is always the question to turn to, that one offered by the ones of Ra, "Where is the love in this moment?" This is a question that is always productive, that one may ask the self in a crux in the present. And by finding where the love lies for you in this moment and placing yourself there, there is how you affect the future. You are choosing what you desire because you desire it. That is understood, but in terms of responding to that which is given you have the skill and you have the chance at each offering to ask the self, "Where is the metaphysical structure of this moment? What speaks to me from a larger point of view that really informs the situation for me?"

The one known as R suggested the fear contracting around the vehicle breaking down and needing to be fixed even though the financial situation was no longer so tight that this constituted an actual emergency, yet still even though money could now be spent on the car and it simply needed to be fixed there is the contraction around the event simply because of old impulses, old emotions have set a pattern of belief. Now, you may continue having that pattern and fearing and being glad when a repair is accomplished, or one can take the opportunity as the one known as R has done to ask the self, "Is this actually the best pattern for me to go through this experience holding, or should I perhaps hold a different pattern since my illusion has actually changed?" Naturally, we agree. We would suggest that the one known as R create a new pattern, one that makes this entity comfortable with having to deal with the necessary maintenance of all that is physical, for those things which are within your illusion have as their heart mortality, though it is known beforehand that all machines and engines will not work and they will have to be repaired. This is the inevitable price of being in the illusion at all. Your time is limited, and the time for you to think about what you truly desire for the future is limited. This is indeed the hour when all entities who wish to serve the light can feel assured that their service will count. Each of you is here upon Earth, as are we, within the influence of your Earth's inner planes, because of the exciting and interesting times in which you live. Each is aware of the powerful wind of change. Each is aware of the potential of the future for good or for ill. How shall you react to this present moment? How shall your beliefs create your future?

We assure you that you each have a great deal of power. And it is a power that is precious. For many, many upon planet Earth at this time this is a crowning incarnation. This is the end of a pattern or the potential end of a pattern and the beginning of new patterns. It is a very exciting time. It is a difficult time. Each of you has, shall we say, sacrificed a great deal to be upon Earth at this time to do what you could to serve the light. So we just encourage you to take heart. You are on course. Those efforts that you sense will be helpful are those efforts that you should focus on, opening the mind always for new ways, but trusting in your own inner feelings and hunches, those intuitions that tell you that, "Yes, this is where I should be, and this is what I should be doing. All is well."

You truly do hold a world in your mind. May you birth within your own mind that sense of self that is at peace with what is and that seeks only the presence of the one infinite Creator and the witness to that infinite Creator— to yourself, and to the world about you, as you are given the light [so to act]. Each of you has much to give. Each of you has inspiration to share, some in one way, some in another. Some by pounding nails. Some by walking streets. Some by what they say. Some by what they do to serve. Everyone is a part of a incredibly rich pattern in which you are involved in all of humankind, and all of the life within your density and within all the densities of this creation and of all creations beyond. Allow yourself to rest in the oneness of all that is. Allow yourself respite and comfort and yet at the same time ask of yourself always to be responsible when you have the light to see that responsibility. And notice simply the responsibility to be who you are and to be true.

We would exercise the one known as Jim and would leave this instrument in love and in light, with thanks to this instrument. We are those of Q'uo. We transfer at this time.

(Jim channeling)

I am Q'uo and greet each again in love and in light through this instrument. It is our privilege at this time to offer ourselves in the attempt to speak to any further queries which may yet remain upon the minds of those present. Is there another query at this time?

S: I am just kind of curious as to where Q'uo spent its third-density experience. What can you tell us about it?

I am Q'uo, and am aware of your query, my brother. As you may be aware we of the principle of Q'uo are a principle because we are of more than one source or origin. Those of Latwii, who are of the density of light, have joined with those of Hatonn, of the density of love, and also have joined with those of Ra, of the density of unity. Those of Ra, as you are aware, experienced their third density upon the planet which you call Venus and were honored to have a most efficient experience within the third density of Venus. The many entities which formed the eventual social memory complex of Venus had a most harmonious third density upon that planetary sphere and moved quickly, shall we say, through that experience with a significant portion achieving graduation within the first cycle of 25,000 years, a larger portion achieving graduation during the second cycle, and the third cycle saw the joining of the social memory complex by all of the population of that sphere. Those of Hatonn and those of Latwii had somewhat similar third-density experiences upon planets which are distant from this solar system and which are as yet undiscovered by your astronomers. Thus the name or place of such is meaningless, yet each social memory complex has found the third-density experience to be that which has produced the tempering of seeking, and the fire of the testing was intense and true. And we have been privileged to become that which you call Q'uo for the purpose of these transmissions at this time. Is there another question, my brother?

S: With all of these different originating points how did you meet or come together to become a principle?

I am Q'uo, and am aware of your query, my brother. As a planetary population moves from the third density, the density of choice, into the density of compassion, love and understanding there is at that time the obvious blending of each individual within the social memory complex. And this blending is assisted by those, what you would call, angelic presences or teachers and guides which represent the Confederation of Planets in the Service of the one infinite Creator. This confederation, then, when there is the opportunity to offer membership, shall we say, to a new social memory complex does so by sending emissaries of light to acquaint the potential members with the opportunity to expand their service to others and to the one Creator by becoming a part of this confederation of planets. And in this confederation there is the opportunity to blend energies, efforts and services with many other social memory complexes. The formation of the principle which you call Q'uo has been an effort to maintain contact with this group by those who have previously served this group in a particular fashion. Those of Hatonn have offered introductory messages for many years through this group and through many others as well upon this planetary sphere. This is true also for those of Latwii although to a lesser degree for those of Latwii are more, shall we say, silent in that they serve as what you would call Comforter for many individual seekers upon this planetary sphere and others as well. Those of Ra have had contact with this group in previous times and were desirous of maintaining a contact, however stepped down it was necessary to be so that there could be the continuing of the service which was begun more than two of your decades ago.

Is there another query, my brother?

S: When do you perceive that conditions would be right for making a more direct contact? Any time soon?

I am Q'uo, and am aware of your query, my brother. And we do not see any more direct contact with the population of this planet or any portion of it than that contact which we are now honored to pursue. Is there another query, my brother?

S: Not right now. Not from me. Thanks.

Is there another query at this time?

S: Maybe I lied. Maybe I have one more. My understanding is that Venus is not indigenous to this solar system. My understanding is that it is from 19 light years away. Was Ra's experience before or after Venus became a wandering planet?

I am Q'uo and am aware of your query, my brother. We are aware that there are many theories as to the origin of each of the planetary spheres in this solar system. There are many who seek to be of service by giving information of one kind or another. The transmission in many cases has been tenuous and occasionally misinterpreted. We are not aware of the planetary sphere which you call Venus having been of any other origin than the solar system in which it now moves and has its being. Is there another query, my brother?

S: No. Just curious. Information from another channel that I was curious about. Thanks.

I am Q'uo, and we thank you again, my brother. We do appreciate each query which this group offers to us at these circles of seeking, for we are aware that each entity does have within it the great desire to pursue those areas of mystery and the unknown, for both within and without each seeker there is an abundance of mystery. It is the purpose and the focus of the mind to seek those answers to queries which the heart asks. However, there are often more opportunities when both mind and heart are opened in harmony.

We are known to you as those of Q'uo. At this time we would take our leave of this instrument and this group. We leave each in the love and in the ineffable light of the one infinite Creator. Adonai, my friends. Adonai. ✣

Sunday Meditation
February 4, 2002

Group question: The question today, Q'uo, deals with the concept of self-doubt in relation to change and to the increased vibrations that everybody seems to feel: more stress, more choices, more anxiety in the life pattern. We would like for you to give us an idea of how we can deal with self-doubt when stability in the way things are seems so much more comfortable, how we can deal with change in making choices on the spiritual path.

(Carla channeling)

We are those known to you as Q'uo, and we greet you in the love and in the light of the one infinite Creator, in whose service we come to you this day. We wish to thank you for forming a circle of seeking and for your desire to serve and for your desire to know ever better and ever [more] purely. We can feel the gravity of the concerns which you bear this day. The experience of third density is ever poignant and pointed, full of emotion and challenge for the seeker. For truly the awakened seeker is caught between two worlds. Not necessarily stranded or snared but certainly aware of and needing to relate to worlds that seem very separate. Responding to the demands of physical incarnation, the need for supply, warmth, shelter, food, clothing, and all the considered necessities of the life is, in itself, not an easy or simple task.

The question of worth is always present. What is worth more, free time or more money? What is worth more, intensity of effort or material success from effort? Questions like this are not easily answered and in the context of an everyday life it seems that these demands of supply and finding ways of meeting [the] challenge of each day create more than enough opportunity for new things, new experiments, new ways, and new directions. At the same time as this world of the horizontal takes up the three dimensions of your days there is at the same time within you a vertical life that seeks always to reach higher and to go deeper, to find the springs of inspiration within the roots of consciousness and to find the guidance from up above. And it comes through earnest desire and persistent asking.

The one known as R spoke of sitting on the fence over decisions, and we find that this is often the skilful thing to do. There is, as far as we know, no indication, spiritually speaking, that it is better to move quickly than to move slowly.

Perhaps the direction that we would like to take this day is to talk about something that this instrument has been pondering at this time and that is the building of the road between the two worlds. The particular energies of this particular time and space for each of you have an unusually strong and generous energy at this time for the simple reasons that your entire globe is in that area of time/space in which your Earth's fourth density is coming into birth. We cannot say how long this labor shall last but while it is occurring there are great needs within your people and your planet, great pressures for change that are the product of this particular phase of planetary labor. And these things are affecting not only each of you in subtle ways but also the nature of time and space and the nature of light. In other words, your world is changing around you. So, is it any wonder that each of you senses that this is a time of change, that there is some urgency to expressing the truth of the self and that in order to better express this truth, this and the succeeding time, shall we say, in this next decade, is and shall be prime time for finding new ways more fully to express the self in its heart and in its soul. Not necessarily in grand or impressive ways but in those ways that create within the self the sense of completing patterns, serving more fully in expressing the self in an ever deeper level.

There are many things that fall away when change occurs. This instrument was attempting to fit her old desk's *accoutrements* into a new desk and was finding that many, many things do not fit. What shall she do with these bits and pieces of a workaday life, these small boxes and piles of physical items that no longer have a niche? So it is within the inner self when there is a change in the geographical location. The new home for the one known as S, the possibilities of new jobs for the ones known as Jim and R, and certainly all the possibilities that lie before this instrument at this time. They are heady things, things that can become larger than the underlying principles that created them and gave them their substance. We would encourage each of you not to be distracted into thinking that the outer details and the shifts and changes necessary in the physical world are the most difficult part of a change. For within the self there is the equivalent of many an old desk with many a niche that is filled with many a detail that is considered an important part, a significant part, of the personality. What shall be packed up and taken with the self, and what shall be left behind? What still fits in the drawers of self, and what must be abandoned?

These are far more challenging questions than how to make arrangements for a new situation in the physical. And there is far less support within the network of relationships in the matrix of the culture for these inner changes than there is support for the outer changes that all people understand and have in common. Many, many sympathize and grasp the nature of change when it is the new job, the new house, the new vocation, the new relationship, the new tragedy or illness. All of these changes, good and bad in the outer sense, can be seen by most people to be challenging. Yet it is more difficult to find support when the changes are within. There is no true social pattern for inner change. The entities that are fortunate enough to find spiritually oriented communities in which they can express their concern for others' needs are perhaps in the most favored position to express support and encouragement to those with whom they come into contact.

In the normal run of a life, sharing in the workplace and speaking on the surface of things how very little true support and encouragement there is for the chewing over of details, the turning about of the situation, looking to find those elements of the puzzle that are the keys to fitting all the other pieces, all the colors and the newness into a new pattern. And how mazed and difficult it is sometimes to see a new pattern. Indeed, sometimes it is impossible for the best of humans in third density, and we would not encourage you to be harsh with yourself when you stumble. For the outer portions of change are difficult enough and then those unexplored corners of self that are being left behind in the new change are at a level of difficulty that is almost impossible to express and, yet, each of those who hears can think back into his life and see again and again those times of loneliness and solitude when the outer life was tranquil and yet the inner life was full of tumult.

It is not that there is no balm for those heart-sore people who are moving through change, for there is. There is endless balm, endless compassion, endless assistance. The challenge is in becoming still enough to receive. For the self is used to the struggle, to breathe, to pump blood, to prepare the food, to keep things in order and move ahead. The third-density training is to do, to act, to meet and solve all incoming problems. So fear not those times of change but know that then is the time to turn to the silence with an especial understanding of the importance of this rest for your soul.

There is the need to make a full stop from time to time in the day. A disengaging from the details, the morasses and tangles of effort, relationship and profit. How precious it is simply to be able to stop, to rest, and to knock at the door of your own heart hoping, waiting for the moment when the key turns because the mind is finally silent and that door springs open into that holy place wherein the Creator awaits. There is a timeless temple made of silence, arched with beauty, steepled with hope, founded on simple faith that all is well. It is a spacious, spacious room, this holy of holies within. It is a wonderful slice of heaven, a small place of Eden where there is nothing rude, nothing imperfect, where there is never any change because all is truly one.

Perhaps one key that we would share with you in thinking about change is to refrain from thinking of it as a dialectic, for that simply perpetuates duality. Although yours is the density of choice, yet also is there a level wherein all is one. And each choice that is made is far better served by preparatory time spent in the unitary and unified silence of your own heart, practicing the presence of the infinite Creator and allowing the questions in your heart simply to be so that you and the Creator and the questions with which you come rest all together, loved and loving, Creator known to created, created known to Creator. Each time that you come into this space, move into it with empty hands, for you know not what gifts the silence will bring you. You do not know what beasts, birds, winds and weathers may respond and come to bring you messages, giving eloquence to the silence and hints to the wise.

When you do not have the chance to practice silence in a formal manner we encourage you to seek the ways of nature and enter the creation of natural things whenever possible, for there in that world you are a harmonious and beloved part of all. There, in that universe, the light is trusted. Life and death are equally embraced and all blooms and blossoms bow to the wind, to the weather, and to the seasons. Such seasons there are also in several layers within the personality shell, within the life experienced by that personality shell within incarnation.

It is a helpful thing, indeed, to glance back and see the shape of former spirals of learning, for the past can inform you about yourself. Memory can tell you where your strengths and weaknesses have been in the past. Certainly, that memory does not serve to create new solutions to the problems of the past or creative directions for those patterns of the past which are felt to be incorrect. It is difficult to separate the glamour of the way things seem from the simplicity that lies beneath detail, the pattern that lies beneath the chaos. The one known as Jim was saying that out of a couple of instances of complete chaos and dropping things and seemingly loosing the pattern, some items that had been sought for some time had been found. The pattern was restored in spite of itself, almost. And often this strange and arbitrary sequence of events will produce new gifts, new patterns, new beginnings, seemingly, almost by accident or in spite of oneself.

We wish that we could reach from our position into your world and arrange the details of your incarnation so that the worries that are upon your mind would not be there. For we sympathizes greatly with the sometimes formidable amount of difficulty which surrounds key decisions within the life pattern. Yet we have no way to enter into your pattern to smooth out the spirals of your learning and your growth. We can only say to you that the more you rest in trust and faith, the more room that you give coincidence to work for you. The stronger your belief that all is well the more quickly patterns will smooth out and reveal that, indeed, all *is* well. And, conversely, the more a fear is focused upon the more that fear becomes real, to the point where, as each of you has seen in the past, this self-fulfilling prophecy does occur and that which is most feared comes to be because it has been the focus for energy within the self, and it has created its own vortex and started to lay out its talons into your life.

When you feel those contractions of fear that surround a proposed change we ask you to honor those feelings, not to avoid them or replace them with affirmations, but to embrace them, to rest with them, to allow the process of balance to work itself out within you so that its strains run sweet and true and all of that which is catalyst for you is allowed to pass through the membranes, shall we say, of your desires and emotions and processes. Do not duck them or push them down below the level of consciousness but find time for them. Find time to sit with them as though they were your own children that were worried and concerned. Perhaps talking out loud to them may even be helpful. The one thing that is sure is that fears do not go away because of repression or because of consciously shoving a fear aside and shoving in a faith that is not felt from the inside out but is grasped from the outside in. There is faith within you. It is not something that you have to pretend but that faith begins with honoring and respecting [one's own feelings of] doubt and unbelief.

The healing of doubt is in balancing, and that balance is sometimes slow in coming, so we ask you to be patient with yourself. Allow time to pass. Allow destiny to roll. Allow the cry of the wolf, the honking of the geese, the keening of the wind and the storming of the rain to bring those elements to you that only time can bring, to allow those energies to move through you with only time to accomplish in the movement.

It is true that a new age has been born and your planet at this time is in labor with this new world. And so you, too, are in labor within yourself, birthing a new and hopefully more spiritually oriented entity, finding ways as you make choices to become more real. How do you forge a road between the everyday of earning a living and the fourth density of love unconditionally given and received? Each of you has part of the answer to that, for each of you is at work paving that road now with your thoughts, with your faith, and with your doubts.

As always, we are with you; we and many others are glad to join you in your meditations to strengthen them. It is our privilege and pleasure to find ways to bring you dreams and stray thoughts and coincidences, and this is not only our practice but many of those within the inner planes of your planet who wish to help you will find ways to communicate concerning those things that you are worried about. Keep open the ears and the eyes and behold those small beauties and blessings that each day brings.

We would at this time ask if there are any questions that any present would like to ask, a follow-up on this question, or any other questions. Is there a question at this time?

(No queries.)

We find that when the one known as Jim stopped answering the questions for us the questions dried up[6]. We shall, therefore, wind up our speech through this instrument, our "cosmic sermonette,"[7] as this instrument would say, by saying what a privilege and what a blessing it is to speak with each of you, and, as always, to ask that each of you listen to what we have to say with a jaundiced eye, or ear, taking those things that seem good to you and leaving the rest behind.

How we wish that we could express to you the gemlike nature of the processes of suffering and change that you go through, how we can see the tempering and annealing work that is being done within through the excellent processes of catalyst and experience within your density. Truly, all is well and each of you is on course. May you fare well. May you be bold. And may you be merry.

We leave you in the love and in the light of the one infinite Creator. Thank you for the privilege at this time of speaking. We are those known to you as the principle of the Q'uo. Adonai. Adonai vasu borragus[8]. ⚜

---

[6] Carla: Jim, a humble man, was concerned that his channeling was unworthy, and refrained from channeling Q and A on this day. After this comment from the Q'uo group, he decided that perhaps his channel, too, was needed! Thanks be to the Creator!

[7] A phrase from Brad Steiger's book, *The Divine Fire*.

[8] This salutation often draws questions from readers. I believe it is both a salutation and a farewell, and means, roughly, "Greetings in the Creator, dear brothers/sisters." George Hunt Williamson was of the opinion that the language from which it comes was that of Maldek, called Solex Mal.

L/L Research

Sunday Meditation
February 10, 2002

Group question: The question today has to do with the concept of the shadow self, the darker side of ourselves that we occasionally explore but which is mostly a mystery to us. We would like for you to help us discover what it is that we can do to get to know our shadow selves, to accept our darker side, and become 360 degree people, with light and dark. What is the most salient thing that we as seekers of truth could do to get to know and accept our shadow selves?

(Carla channeling)

We are those known to you as the principle of the Q'uo. Greetings in the love and in the light of the one infinite Creator in whose service we are. We honor you and thank you for all that you have done in order to have come to this circle of seeking at this time. For each there have been sacrifices and we thank each for the desire to seek the truth and for the honor of being called to your group by the tuning of this instrument and this group and the question that you asked. We are greatly in your debt, for you allow us to be of service in that way that we hope best fulfills our present capacities. Therefore, it is most precious to us to speak these words to you and we would ask of you only that as you listen you discard those things that do not seem to be useful and retain those things that seem to be worth a further look. For we would not be a stumbling block before any, and we encourage each not to allow the self to be a stumbling block in the sense of the received wisdom of authority. For truly the discrimination within that resonates, whether disturbed or elated by material, will tell you what material is for you. If there is no resonance, either of dismay or of love, then this material definitely can be looked at another time. It is helpful not to dismiss things with which one disagrees, but, rather, to examine it in order to see what others' perceived distortions might be. Information is often helpful, although not always in the manner expected.

Trust the discrimination that lies within in the emotional resonance that is retained when material is put down, that nags at the mind and causes the mind to iterate that process of thought, that little shift of dimension that somehow those words held. Notice those. Follow those. Those are the ripples that come to you so that you can follow well by your interests, trusting that that which you are seeking will be attracted to you by the natural energy exchanges that are part of all the densities of this universe where, as you would say, energies are not blocked in order to prevent these connections from being made and these roundnesses of occurrences to plump out the seemingly flat and linear horizon from time to time.

The shadow self is a most interesting query and to begin we would bring to your mind a symbol in this instrument's mind labeled "pop culture." It is the ying yang symbol with the S-shaped curve across the circle with one graceful arch being black and the other white, the black having a white dot and the white having a black dot. Certainly one can see the white from the black. One can also see that they create a spherical being and this is the 360 degree being that we have been talking about. In this instrument's communion service, which we present to the one known as C as an example of our sense of humor, the wording of the general confession is to be that of claiming the self to be a wretch, and within this instrument's mind there is often the ironic thought that she regrets that this was ever taken out of the service because it is helpful from time to time to connect with the wretched portion of self-perceived humanity. For it is the glory and the pain of humanity to express and experience two paths for the price of one. This is a density that is rather unusual even for later densities in the strength of the apparent wide chasm or abyss between the forces of light and the forces of darkness. And indeed there has been a very concerted effort on the part of many to conceive of this as a war and the light workers of the world as warriors that are fighting dark forces.

We do not find this to be the most helpful model from which to view the energies of your planet, as harvest is in the midst of its birthing and processing of so many energies and so very many entities. The temptation is to remain within the spiritual materialisms of fourth-density war. This density has never solved the question of war. Indeed, it is incapable of solving the question of the war between good and evil for it has, by its very definition, especially in the beginning of it, no balance. It is purely loving. Within third density there is the opportunity to come to balance, and this is the query that you ask, in effect, when you ask about the shadow self.

When one is in balance one sees and allows the enjoyment of and the preference for the radiation of beauty, the truth, and the very obvious unity of the positive that is around one, of the beauties and the blessings that are thick in the air in daily life, in all sorts of nooks and crannies that seldom are even seen because the creation is so rich in its gifts. And yet the creation is rich also in challenges and for each of you within this room the challenge is in seeing the dark side without its masks or rather, shall we say, with a more selective, with a more understanding choice of masks for the dark side. For is not the she-wolf a terrible hunter, greatly feared by its prey? And do you not desire to have the she-wolf run with you? She is a murderer. You can think about each and every aspect of the dark side of the self, the self that feels self-pity, the self that feels jealousy, greed, murder, adultery, all of your ten sins and, we assure you, many more which are more subtle and lie within the heart.

And yet within this same matrix of humanity lies also the tree of the new world, for as you are all things within this density so are you also things that are not of this density. Therefore, balance becomes a matter of retaining and refining a sense of proportion so that you are able to become a better observer of the self in its behavior. It is difficult to become aware of the self, the thoughts of the self, and what the self is doing. Usually for such intensive work as this it is helpful to have that entity who is able to see the self from the outside, and so groups such as this one are helpful. Friendships are helpful when there is sharing back and forth as this instrument and the one known as C have often done, encouraging each other in those truths that they both have an intellectual awareness of but of which they both do not yet grasp with absolute comfort the cloak, the crown, the scepter.

For you see, to come into an acceptance of the she-wolf that runs with you, to come into an acceptance of the liar whose dazzling footsteps dance one out of trouble, to love that self that is able to aim, group at three inches, and polish off a target at twenty yards that happens to be a human that is attempting to cause damage to a loved one … This instrument has certainly experienced the feelings of a murderer when a loved one was apparently struck and perhaps killed. There is no length of time between the sight of someone that needs defense in the mind of the perceiver and the feelings of murder. And it is a pure, clean, crisp and powerful emotion, not unlike anger but with deadly intent. Would any say that this instrument had an unintegrated murderer within her? No. And yet it is in this instrument's inner thoughts that she does indeed have a murderer alive and well and living in the hospitality of the temple of the body, the mind, and her spirit. And so each contains all that there is, and within your density the very fabric of your illusion is very much the ying and the yang, the give and the take, and it is a great achievement indeed when that dark side of self is seen as an asset by the self and as that she-wolf bares its fangs and seems to come at one as a werewolf, as a predator, as one that wants to tear out the heart, that is when you embrace that she-wolf and know that that is your powerful, brave heart that is capable of anything but that chooses to be your she-wolf, to be your totem, to be your seeker of truth that prowls in dreams and comes back with news of elsewhere.

All of those aspects of dark side that seem so grimed are actually no grimier than the excrement that passes from the bowels of your body. Is food fair and excrement foul? It may seem so, yet both are necessary and the intake and the outgo are equally necessary and the bowel is just as necessary an organ as the tongue. Both are valued equally by the body and whether dark or seemingly light, both are affected not by the literal nature of their seeming function but rather of the emotion that powers them. For cell by cell each of you is powered by an emotion or a mixture of emotions. We urge people over and over again to refine their desires. We urge them to seek the silence and to ask within the silence for the further refining of truth, for the further honing of the desire to know. This is because this is the path that yields to the seeker those abilities to move from the world of black and white into the world of moving energy, energy that passes through all the chakras, moving up and through and out, catalyst moving down and through and out in a majestic mixture of inner planes' and outer planes' function in which the human physical vehicle is an inextricable and valuable part of spiritual growth and the great sender of signals of that which is your mind, your body, and your spirit. And the person in charge of sending each signal to the mind, which sends to the body, and which shares with the spirit is that perception that is believed to have occurred.

What is that faith which each of your holds, to which each of you can cling? Where are there simple and easy ground rules for improving one's perception of these things? This instrument has found helpful and uses to this day the following prayer: "Lord, make us instruments of Thy peace. Where there is hatred, let us sow love. Where there is injury, pardon. Where there is discord, union. Where there is doubt, faith. Where there is despair, hope. Where there is darkness, light. Where there is sadness, joy. O divine Master, teach us to seek not so much to be loved as to love, to be understood as to understand, to be consoled as to console. For it is in pardoning that we are pardoned. It is in giving that we receive. And it is in dying that we rise to eternal life."

This is a prayer of light and dark and of the choices that we make in the way we feel. Entities surrounding one shall predictably offer one negative catalyst, catalyst that is perceived to be negative because it is dealing with other peoples' projections of one's own dark side, which is another way of saying that you are projections of their dark side and that all entities are busy demonstrating the humanity of the self to the other self. Each of you is valuable in that regard if in no other, for all of you are a bad example from time to time. And blessed are the bad examples as well as the good examples. Blessed are those moments when you despair and think that "I will never get this problem," because at that point that you realize that there is a bad attitude that is involved here, blessed is each moment when you are able to pinpoint anything about the thinking process with which you might quarrel. For there are things which can be improved by watching the thoughts one has and the comments that one makes to oneself about these thoughts. There truly are voices within the mind that need to be put into deep memory, into deep storage, into files that are closed, that do need to remain in the voices that speak in dreams, and in the voices that speak within the musing of inner thoughts. The voices that are needed are the voices of silence; not our words, not the words of your parents, not the words of any perceived guardian or authority can give you that which is beyond words, the presence of the one infinite Creator whose nature is absolute love.

The Creator has come through other generations of being and has found ways closer and closer to understand what love is and yet it remains a mystery. And the Creator is ever curious. Your experiment in positivity and negativity of such sharp characterization is very interesting. The Creator is most curious. We are aware that the challenges of coming into a balanced view of the self in which the self is forgiven are great. The many enculturated energies that tend, society by society, to keep people in their places within the scheme of things, as this instrument would say, are deadening, distorting, numbing, confusing teachings that either consciously must be removed or be removed by trauma.

In the face of this the challenges of coming into balance with the self may seem insurmountable and yet we say to you that there is a moment which is what this instrument was attempting to speak of when she said falling in love with yourself is needed. There is a moment when the horizon opens and one is able to accept responsibility for one's joy and one comes into a bliss that does not cease entirely. When there is even a bobble in the harmony it is painful enough that it is necessary to stop and correct the error. In each place where the entity perceives the self to be out of balance and stuck the things that are holding the pattern have to do with perception rather than truth, with, as the one known as C stated, inner balances of self in lessons that are being learned rather than the characteristics of the outside world as it impinges accidentally and in a random manner. It is not random. It is kindly producing the general catalyst for the kind of lesson that this instrument desired to learn within this incarnation. And this particular line of thought is one which, more than most spiritual questions, is not harmed by intellectual and analytical thought.

Perhaps if we were to narrow things down to one piece of advice it would simply be this, check it off and forget it. Whatever it is, if it is something that you genuinely feel that you do not want to do, check it off and forget it. The effect that this has will be the change in catalyst that will inform you as to the preferences which genuinely come into play in various situations. For many times things are other than they seem not by just a small degree but as if a house was constructed upon another house and that first house was buried and the archeologist must go down and dig up an entire structure and find out what keeps the energy in this pattern that is not productive.

When one is talking about balance one must talk without making generalities, for no two people have the same balance. Each entity will have a different kind of chakra system, a different way of using it, a different way of expressing it, letting it go, and moving it through the body. No two entities are at all alike. They may harmonize and then they are perceived as aura enhancers or they may tend not to harmonize. Upon the level that balance is achieved without dealing with the light and the dark, what is best is simply to come into loving relationship with the pattern as a whole so that you celebrate the dirt, the muck, the seeming darkness with honest and sincere appreciation, just as you have appreciation for fertilizers in fields and for the cleanliness of a cleaned out system that would be toxic if one were not able to process food and remove it through the bowel. The perceived darkness of things is negative and those who honestly believe that the heart is a false creator will attempt again and again to use only the light in order to achieve truth. The problem is that there is no balance in light that does not have love within it. Without love the light shall always bend itself into service to self. For without the heart there is no clearing house to take what this instrument would call the 90 degree shift from one type of energy to another. And this is what each is attempting to see: that shift in consciousness that is beyond doing well at a perceived task or finding better ways to do tasks.

What is actually the benefit and the service of the entity is far below that level, far below what an entity is aware that she is offering. It is in the being of the entity, the way the entity responds in a spontaneous and free manner to the present moment with those with whom she comes into contact, with those of whom she thinks, with those prayers with which she occupies her mind, and with those hopes and dreams that she holds dear and moves to in thought to create places of light in the spirit world.

That is the self that entities actually respond to, that they take fire from, and that without knowing why they feel as the light upon the hill that shines forth and radiates in a way that is beyond them and expresses spirit. It is not the entity that is skilful at directing the life. It is the entity who loves in and out of season that is truly serving. So where a balance is an excellent thing to seek it is not necessarily a goal because it is yet another thing about which to have a preference. It is yet another trap to lay for oneself to say that "If I have balance, if I have equanimity, then I am wise." True balance involves the knowledge that no one knows anything and that includes the self. Even the one known as St. Paul the Apostle said that "I am the least of all Christians." Even arrogance must at last, when speaking upon the level of the soul, own its humility and accept the imperfection of this entire experience.

Yet, within you also are all the inner planes and all of the entities who make up this octave. For many there are actual memories of other densities. For others there is the feeling of being native to Earth but being ready indeed for greener pastures as far as lessons to learn. And the path of service and learning at this time is, to a great extent, being able to have those moments when you have come into your bliss and you are running with the wolf. And that wolf is your will and your strength and has nothing to do any more with unbridled or negative darkness but only with that fecund and energetic power that brings into being the flowers that grant their beauty to a waiting world.

We would at this time transfer this contact to the one known as Jim whom we welcome back to our extensive stable of adequate channels. We are greatly appreciative of the adequacy of this channel and would like to encourage this entity to feel competent. This entity may be aware that we are teasing it. In reality we are jumping with joy and we want you to know that too. We are very glad to have you as an entity with whom we may share conversation, for greatly do we enjoy being with you and being able to express in your particular style. Consequently, we thank you and we would at this time transfer to the one known as Jim. We are those known to you as the Q'uo and we leave this instrument in love and in light.

(Jim channeling)

I am Q'uo, and we greet each once again in love and in light through this instrument. We find that its layoff period has been brief enough that we have little rust with which to deal. For this we are grateful. May we ask if there might be another query of a shorter kind at this time to which we may give our attention?

S: I'll start I guess. We were talking about the troubles and tribulations that Carla and Jim were having with their Law of One publisher in getting rights to their books back at this time. Could you tell us what issues and influences are blocking at this time?

I am Q'uo, and though we are aware of your query, my brother, we must apologize for invoking the Law of Confusion, for this is information which is that which could abridge free will. We are sorry to be short of information. Is there another query to which we may speak more freely?

S: Not from me right now. I think that Carla is very eager to ask you a question.

Carla: Yes, because I can't get the flashlight off with one hand. OK. We had a question from S from Metaphom Foundation Inc. He writes, "I have been studying the basis for spontaneous healing for 14 years. We know that there is virtually always a shift in consciousness, usually accompanied by great joy, in a spontaneous healing. However, we have been unable to discover what triggers this response. Is it possible for you to consult your source and see if they could come up with a simple definitive answer?"

I am Q'uo, and am aware of your query, my sister. The experience of the one to be healed in which there is an inpouring of great peace and comfort during the healing and the experience of the joy-filled mental and emotional complexes is that experience which one would have if one could but shed in an instant that which caused great pain, that which caused great ignorance, that which blocked one from the next step upon the path. This is, indeed, what occurs with what you have called the spontaneous healing, for the one to be healed has, in an instant, dropped that which was of difficulty, of limitation, of concern. This is responded to by the emotional body of the one to be healed as a kind of joyful noise, shall we say, a rejoicing of the spirit and a rejoicing of the soul. To be healed is to be brought into a closer balance with all that is. When one reaches home, shall we say, after a long journey there is the immediate feeling of relief, of joy, of completion, that one is once again within that place of peace that nurtures one and gives one the feeling of wholeness. To be healed is much like coming home and the joy that comes from the one to be healed is an expression of this instantaneous realization.

Is there another query, my sister?

Carla: No. I thank you very much, and I will send this on to them.

I am Q'uo, and we thank you once again. Is there another query at this time?

R: Yes. I have a question. There has been a lot communicated in the last decade or so about humanity polarizing itself into two groups. Basically a light group and a dark group and that the dark group in its own way will go away and pass over. Could you please comment on that?

I am Q'uo, and am aware of the query, my brother. There is indeed at this time, the time of the harvest of souls and of the planet itself, a great opportunity to seek further either towards serving the light and the other selves which one sees as the Creator and same as the self, or to serve that which one may call the self, the darkness, the left-hand path as it has been called. For it is within these two paths the ability to continue the journey of seeking the one Creator may continue from the third density forward into the density of understanding, the density which beckons each at this time.

We may say that there are far, far fewer of those entities which pursue the negative path than there are of those who seek the light and to serve others, for the negative path is one which is most difficult to pursue. This path requires the conscious functioning of an adept who is able to control not only the self but other selves to a degree of at least 95% so that there is very little which this entity does not seek mastery over. These entities who seek the negative polarization will have their day, in fact, are having their day at this time so that they may accomplish that which they have set for themselves with their only regard for others being that which affects themselves. This is what you may see as a very brightly burning flame that will consume much about it for a short period of your time. There will be, following the exit of this influence from this planet, the continued experience of service to others by those who have chosen this path, for there will be a continuing need for a great deal of each serving each other. There will be the obvious requirements of living the daily life under conditions which may be less than conducive to accomplishing this task with comfort.

We find that we must pause briefly that this instrument might be allowed to work the recording devices. We shall leave this instrument briefly. We are those of Q'uo.

(Pause)

I am Q'uo, and am again with this instrument. We thank each for your patience. The ability of entities to express their choice of seeking to serve other selves and to seek what you might call within the positivity will be enhanced by the difficulties which have begun and which shall continue apace. That which might be seen as turmoil, as lack of necessities and so forth in the days and years to come will be heavy laden with opportunity to others. Thus each will become aware more and more fully of the unity of all creation and all entities within the creation as it becomes more and more necessary for each to aid each other in the ability to accomplish the daily round of activities under circumstances which may be seen to be of a difficult, even severe, nature. Yet these entities shall prevail, for as one seeks to serve other selves and sees other selves as the one Creator, each is pursuing the path of that which is. For, indeed, each is a portion of the one Creator. Each is inextricably linked with each other self and these ties will bind each into what you have called a nation of priests. Each will feel the power of the one Creator moving through the vehicle in order that the one Creator might be glorified in each thought, each activity, each experience.

These will be times which few will have desired before going through them but which each and every one will be most grateful to have experienced when they are going through them and as they are completing these services.

Is there a further query, my brother?

R: Yes. I have a follow-up. Is it possible to have an approximate date by which all this will transpire?

I am Q'uo, and am aware of your query, my brother. The question of dates is one which is most heavily upon the minds of many of those of your population, for the frame of time seems short, and, indeed, this may be the case. Many of your peoples throughout your recorded history have spoken of times that were within a decade of the new millennium which has now arrived. We see this possiblity/probablity vortex as well and though it is most heavily weighted, shall we say, there are others that are potentially energizeable in that the free will choices of the population of this planet is of paramount importance in this regard. As those of Ra have said, it is possible that in one fine, strong moment of inspiration the population of this planet could turn the needle of the compass to seeking to serve other selves. Though this is not probable, it is ever possible. And the choices which are made by more and more people to seek to serve in the positive polarity makes the likelihood of the timeframe grow shorter. As people are less able to choose one service path or the other the time frame lengthens. We apologize for not being able to be more precise, but this is a fluid possibility. Your future is mazed from all eyes that look upon it. Seek then to serve each other as if this were your last opportunity to do so.

Is there another query, my brother?

R: No. Thank you.

I am Q'uo, and we thank you once again.

(No further queries.)

I am Q'uo, and as it appears that we have exhausted the queries for this session of seeking we shall once again thank each present for making those sacrifices in order to join this circle this day and for calling us to join you as well. We are most appreciative of this opportunity to be of service in the way in which we feel most helpful. At this time we shall take our leave of this instrument and this group. We are known to you as those of Q'uo. We leave each in the love and in the ineffable light of the one infinite Creator. Adonai, my friends. Adonai.

L/L Research

L/L Research is a subsidiary of Rock Creek Research & Development Laboratories, Inc.

P.O. Box 5195
Louisville, KY 40255-0195

www.llresearch.org

Rock Creek is a non-profit corporation dedicated to discovering and sharing information which may aid in the spiritual evolution of humankind.

ABOUT THE CONTENTS OF THIS TRANSCRIPT: This telepathic channeling has been taken from transcriptions of the weekly study and meditation meetings of the Rock Creek Research & Development Laboratories and L/L Research. It is offered in the hope that it may be useful to you. As the Confederation entities always make a point of saying, please use your discrimination and judgment in assessing this material. If something rings true to you, fine. If something does not resonate, please leave it behind, for neither we nor those of the Confederation would wish to be a stumbling block for any.

© 2009 L/L Research

Sunday Meditation
February 24, 2002

Group question: Our question this week has to do with communication, real communication. It's hard enough to be honest and to speak clearly to another person about what you are thinking and feeling. We are wondering how a person can also engage the heart so that the intellectual communication that you share isn't just a means of attacking or defending but that you are also able to engage how you really feel and maybe the higher principles that you believe in, the concept of love and forgiveness and compassion. How would you recommend that people having difficulty communicating—not so much being honest—how would you recommend people be able to get to their hearts, be vulnerable, share what's really of foremost importance in their lives?

(Carla channeling)

We are those of the principle known to you as the Q'uo, and we greet you in the love and in the light of the one infinite Creator. It is a great blessing to us, as always, to be called to your group, and we thank each for setting aside this time to seek in the silence for truth, that truth that often has no words but is shaped in the silence and molded in infinity.

We thank you for the thoughtfulness of this question. Truly, communication is a principle avenue through which learning and service may take place among your peoples. And we find it a provocative subject, one with many subtleties. We are glad to tackle it with you this day. We ask that, as always, each maintain a degree of discrimination concerning anything that we or any other seeming authority may have to say. Do not buy anyone's ideas because of the excellence of their character, but rather subject all incoming thoughts to your own indwelling powers of discrimination, for you will recognize those truths, pleasant or uncomfortable, that are yours. They will resonate for you and not leave you. Focus on those few thoughts that really ring a bell for you. And we would ask that you leave all others aside, for ideas that are not resonant to one can only confuse, and we do not wish to confuse but to aid. So, please, we ask each of you to use that discrimination that is yours.

To speak of communication is to speak of many levels of conveyance. Much more goes on within a communication between one entity in third density and another than is seen upon the surface. Upon the surface there is a two-dimensional quality to the shape of words and the structure of sentences, and if communication were a matter of the words then our discussion would be very simplified. Yet, in truth, communication is a far more multi-dimensional process than the words alone would suggest. When we speak words through this instrument, in actuality we usually are offering to this instrument concepts which do not come in the shape of words but, rather, have that quality of infinity which rounds the two-dimensional into the third, the fourth, the fifth, and the sixth dimensions, all of those dimensions being the layers of meaning and reference that each entity has created within its own internal structure, far below the level of words, into which incoming information shall be placed so that the same words coming into the field of twelve different entities will mean twelve different very complex sets of things. And when communication becomes more complex than asking for something to be passed or requesting that something be taken from one, when communication becomes a matter of expressing shades of opinion and discriminations of feeling, then the subtlety of possible techniques of communication becomes more and more obvious.

It is helpful, we think, to step back and look at who is communicating. As you sit in your chair within this circle each of you would seem to be a fairly well-defined physical object. You weigh so many pounds; you have so much mass; you have certain color hair; you have a certain color eyes; you present a fairly simplified picture of a finite entity. Yet in truth, within your finite bounds, each of you contains the heavens and the earth and all that in them is. Each of you is all that there is, and all that there is resides within you. How is this possible? It is not possible in a linear world. Of course, we do not believe that any of us lives in a linear world. We see that as a simple illusion, an illusion within a larger set of illusions, and all of these illusions are acceptable and proper and as they should be, not in order to keep people in the dark or confused but in order to express the endlessness of being. For each of you is, within the tiny structure of bone and muscle and heartbeat, the Creator, the created and all that between them is.

So you are infinitely valuable and of infinite proportions and size, and as you approach each other you are as stars that rotate in their orbits so that they come into contact with each other, two incredibly radiant, powerful beings whose effulgence and splendor is beyond description.

And how shall that star which is you shine in such a way as to communicate to that star which is shining back at you? If you hold this image you may see that within this image lies the question of energy fields and how they attract or repulse each other. It may be seen that some entities will be helped and pulled together by the forces that will naturally drive other entities apart because each entity has a certain quality of vibration which carries a certain charge. And we would not call this a positive/negative dynamic because that would suggest that in communication one entity may be positive and the other, therefore, must be negative. This is not so. It is more subtle than that. It is simply a matter of each energy field, each person, that is, having a very discernable, clear signature of being that expresses far below the level of self-awareness. You put out a very clear signal, each of you. We can recognize you as you and pick you out from all of the billions of entities that dwell now upon your planet. There is only one of you. There is only one of each of you, and each of you is precious and unique and quite necessary. If, in human communication it can be remembered that each entity is worthy of respect, is necessary for the survival of the group as a whole, and is that which is acceptable, then we feel that communication would perhaps become somewhat less difficult. In truth, we are fully aware that in the hurry and scurry of ordinary life it is extremely difficult to remember that entities that are upon the surface displeasing to the self, nevertheless are beautiful, necessary and perfect in their own way, just as you are beautiful, necessary and perfect in your own way.

The goal of communication often seems to be to come to a resolution, to effect a change, to get things done. And again we would suggest that it is helpful when working upon communication to realize that there are times when the goal of communication is not so much to obtain the desired goal but, rather, there are times when communication has the goal simply of expressing the dynamic that is occurring, not with a drive to find a solution but in the spirit of clarification, so that between two entities who differ there comes into being, as a result of the communication, the sense of each entity having a growing understanding or grasp of that fuller nature of that other self that lies behind the seemingly flat surface of a disagreement or a point of discussion.

Within your world, processes take on the qualities of chemical interactions where there is always a vector, there is always a direction, there is always an arrow pointing from one to two to three to four processes. This is what entities tend to expect from communication, that information will be received and processed, work will be done, decisions shall be made, and all entities shall be fully informed and able to go forward. And certainly there are many times when two entities may accomplish these things with very little effort, and those are blessed times. However, you asked concerning those communications which seem to have gone awry.

And as you ask these questions we could sense within you that assumption that the goal of a conversation would be to come to a conclusion, and we would suggest that this is not always the model that is most helpful for communication. We would suggest, rather, that there are times when it is important that each who attempts to communicate simply be able to express the emotions, mental structures, and spiritual considerations that have injected themselves into the matter about which communication is taking place.

For all of the things that are in your life are placeholders for things of the spirit. All things are alive. All things are ready to tell you their story, so you have a much more complex interesting, intricate, vibrant universe than the intellect perhaps can perceive. There are upwelling energies from the archetypal level that are simply waiting for the opportunity to work their magic within the fragile structure of human incarnation. There are wonderful, powerful spiritual energies that are just waiting for channels through which they may run, be blessed and come into the power and ownership of the Earth in general.

Communication sounds simple, but in the processes of communication lie the salvation or redemption of the entire group. And it is very much as a group that those of planet Earth shall move forward and not as an individual and then as another individual. But each of you is as an ineluctably intertwined portion of the group that is the humankind of planet Earth. And there is a tremendous amount of energy that wishes to cooperate with that group's working together to move forward as a group. Consequently there is a tremendous spiritual bias towards attempts at communication no matter how clumsy, awkward or seemingly unsuccessful.

In the face of this great bias on the part of the Creator towards communication we may say that it is tempting, even seductive, to enter the list[9] of communication as if it were a medieval jousting match with the communicators loading up their armor and getting on their destriers and heading towards each other with a shield in one hand and a lance in the other to communicate this idea and that idea and get across to the other person and in the process, of course, knock that person off of his steed and win at the list of communication. This is not a model that we would encourage. We would encourage rather the model that realizes that right and wrong have only a limited amount of energy whereas truth and love are equal in their energies so that there is not a one-time linear truthfulness to any opinion or feeling that is being communicated but, rather, that which is being communicated is the tip of an iceberg, and that when the skillful person hears that which is communicated that person is willing to open his awareness to take in, not simply the point of the iceberg that is showing above water, not simply the words, but is willing to open to the unseen presence of all that is below the waterline, all that is unsaid, all that fills out the substance of an opinion or a feeling that is being communicated so that each can see the other as a positive source of information and support, even when there seems to be huge discrepancies in opinion and ample evidence suggesting the impossibility of a happy conclusion to the communication.

It is not necessary to have a happy ending in order to have good communication. Nor is it necessary to have the opposite to have a seeming tangle and disagreement and one entity prevail over another. These dynamics are dynamics of illusion. That which is valuable is the spirit within each of the parties who communicate so that if left to choose between someone who says all of the right words and someone who is able in any way to enter into the respect of the infinite qualities of the self and other self, we would choose every time that fool who was not communicating with particular skill but who was receiving communication and offering communication in the humble awareness of the infinite qualities of self and of other self.

A growing awareness of this nature of hidden things in the most simple communication is very helpful to the developing spirit. And in any way that you can, we encourage you to support these growing awarenesses within the self that begin to see into that other self in a way that lifts judgment and takes it away from the field of vision so that the self may see the other self in a sweetness of reception based upon

---

[9] Carla: Even the Oxford English Dictionary said this word was obsolete, but it is in there, as a race track for horses or other paced off and fenced or otherwise demarcated place for contests or races. One joins a list in the sense of enlisting for the match. But the way it was used in the novels in which I became familiar with the term was that one entered the list as one signed up for the jousting and got one's armor on. It was always a "game," never a real battle, but the testosterone flowed.

the awareness of that entity's deeper nature and value.

How is this possible? How can the ordinary person give up the linear processes that seem so clear and obvious and, instead, embrace those values that lie beyond sense? We can only say that it begins within yourself. For the first entity with whom each of us, on whatever level of learning, must communicate is the self. How do you communicate with yourself? What conversations have you had with your self this day? Have they been clear communications? Have they been kind? Charitable? Have you respected yourself, even when those thoughts that you had in your heart were not what you would have chosen? Do you scold yourself? Are you honest with yourself? How do you treat your own self? We would suggest that many of you, if not all of you, have habits of abuse with yourself.

This may sound as if it were not so, but look into your treatment of yourself, and we think that you will find that you are as impatient, upset and rude with yourself as you are with others. Before others can hurt you, many times, by the way that you treat yourself, you have already caused yourself pain. We would suggest to you that there is great value in listening and in silence, in opening and letting go, in being empty and being comfortable with being empty. We would suggest that it is not the first goal of communication to make sense or achieve objects, but, rather, the first goal of communication is to open the heart to another entity and allow that entity to see your heart. In terms of energy, communication is far beyond that which is thought of as communication among your peoples. What passes for communicating among your peoples is that which never achieves any energy level beyond red, orange and yellow-ray concerns. Much communication among your peoples does not involve the heart, and we would suggest that skill in communicating involves becoming a spiritually viable entity that moves into the heart, anchors the self within the heart, and only then turns outward with a willingness to share ideas. Were entities to invoke their own open hearts before each communication, we feel that much that is contentious among your peoples would naturally fall away.

Again and again it is necessary to move into the silence of one's own heart. Call to yourself this day with that inner tolling bell of love unknown. Let that bell within toll for you. Let it ring out and resound in the shoals and the deep waters of your being. Open yourself to the wonder of that which is within you and allow a larger picture of self to emerge, a picture of a self that sees the creation as made and says that it is good. For you are co-creator in a far more specific way than perhaps you realized. You, by the seeds of love that you sow this day, create the love of tomorrow. Thusly, we simply ask of each of you to lift the linear judgment away from the limitations of eyesight. Lift away from the limitations of that which is seemingly being communicated in any situation so that as you come to the communication in its seeming outward form, which is words, inflections, and body language, you have as much realization as you can bring into your heart of the beauty, the sacredness and the worth of each and every entity that is within your world.

The processes of linear thought shall continue to work as they have for third-density entities for millennia. But the value of communication never remains at the level of problems solved and information shared. The value of communication lies in the reception of each by each in such a way that each is a helper to each. Each is a supporter and encourager to each. When communication finds ways to embrace this realization of the preciousness of each other then that which is communicated enters into the mutual systems of the two in a far more enhanced way which is very powerful in deep, subconscious levels of connection. For you see, what you are actually doing in communicating betwixt each other is creating connections of a certain kind. The hoped-for result of communication for those who are service-to-others oriented is an energy exchange which is helpful to both parties. It is this particular instrument's opinion that when she responds to a request for help from someone who assumes that she is a teacher, what she is actually doing is not sharing information so much as sharing love. And it is in the acceptance of that other self, the honoring and respecting of that other self, that the communication begins to have real worth, not simply in what is said, but in the energy that runs beneath the words.

Thusly, we ask each of you, what energy runs beneath the words that you say? Are you powering your communication from the heart? Are you powering and empowering yourself by the respect and honor that you give yourself, regardless of the mistakes that you may seem to make? What judgments have you made against yourself this day, and what merit do those judgments have?

We pray that each of you may ponder these things. Truly you ask a very advanced question when you ask concerning communication. Communication, when it is truly working, is a spiritual event, a mutually strengthening, mutually validating experience. When you can come to communication with yourself and feel that you have honored and respected yourself, only then can you be said to be ready to communicate fully with another.

It is extremely helpful to realize that the nature of communication is that of speaking to a mirror. The other self with whom you are communicating is a very faithful mirror of you. And those things that you see in that mirror are those things within yourself with which you either greatly agree or greatly disagree. Usually, amongst third-density entities the preponderance of reactions that one has concerning other selves remains loaded with bias and judgment and a lack of love. And this is as it should be in an environment in which each of you is attempting to fathom what love is and to begin to make choices that are loving choices. Realize each time that you begin to communicate that you are communicating with the Creator and that that Creator is communicating back to you, offering you a mirror in which you may see your nature.

We hope that these poor thoughts may not confuse but help each to open the heart to the profundity and limitlessness of the spirit. You are ethereal beings caught into a matrix of birth and death, living and dying, light and dark. You walk this road at this time for infinite reasons, but with finite steps. Thusly you are a creature of two worlds at once, one with measure and one which is immeasurable. And both of these parts of self are equally so. Yet dealing from the standpoint of infinity the life experience opens before one in a very different way from that life that is approached from the level of linear sense and activity.

Thusly, we point you always to the value of silence and the opening of the self within that silence to the infinite unknown and to the goodness and beauty of that which is not yet known. Allow the mysterious to empower your imagination. Allow those infinite qualities that do not seem to be a part of communication to enter into your willingness and that shall open up your ability to move through difficult material in such a way as to empower each, yourself and other self, in ways that move beyond linear truth. For the greater truth is always unity, harmony and consolidation of disparate things into beautiful and useful patterns. There is a beautiful and useful pattern in between each and every soul with whom you shall come in contact in this life. There is always a full possibility of resolution, peace and moving forward, no matter how infinitely impossible the two points of disagreement may seem to be.

We thank you for allowing us to speak with you this day and realize that we have spoken too long as we sometimes do, so we will take our leave of this instrument at this time and continue this communication through the one known as Jim. We thank this instrument and leave it in love and in light. We are known as those of the Q'uo.

(Jim channeling)

I am Q'uo, and greet each again in love and in light through this instrument. At this time it is our privilege to ask if we may speak to any shorter queries that may yet remain upon the minds of those present. Is there a shorter query at this time?

Carla: I have a question. Earlier the group was talking about our ongoing discussion with P and our strong feelings that it is better to accept P even though we don't agree with him than to attempt to control the situation and have our will over his and wrest our material back from him. We realize that it is a very unworldly way of thinking. I wonder, do you have any comments to make on our continuing feelings that this is the way we should act?

I am Q'uo, and am aware of your query, my sister. We feel that in this matter it is in the general area of "walking the walk as one talks the talk." This is a phrase that we have heard used many times in your metaphysical discussions where the principles by which entities such as yourselves live are tested. When such a test presents itself to the seeker it is well that the seeker set those priorities by which it lives its life and then remain steadfast in those priorities' observance though there may be a price in worldly terms to pay. For that which you seek to do, though it is in this world, is not of it. You seek to be more than you are. You seek to be beacons of light. If, therefore, you shall be a beacon of light worry not about the splinter that is in another's eye. Worry about how clearly you see yourselves. Is there another query, my sister?

Carla: If you will pardon me, I do have another one on a different subject entirely. I've had three different people say to me in the last two weeks that humankind needs more DNA than it has and something must be done to improve the DNA structure or humankind won't make it out of third density into the fourth and will be, as a group, stuck here repeating and repeating. The model that all three of these people have used is that we don't have it and we need to go out and get it. They are referring to extra strands of DNA that would enable us to do this and that. My model of it and the one that I feel at this point is more correct by far is that we have everything that we need and it's been turned off. We just have to find the place to allow it to be turned on again. Of those two models would you have an opinion as to which one is more accurate, or would you feel that this is even a valid concern at all?

I am Q'uo, and am aware of your query, my sister. As third-density beings your mind/body/spirit complex has been equipped with all the necessary prerequisites for utilizing the catalyst of this choice-making density. It is not that you need more equipment but to refer to your owner's manual. The answers are in your heart, not in your DNA. Is there another query, my sister?

Carla: No. Thank you.

L: I have a query, and it may be rather simple but I've taken to collecting quotes from readings in church, Bible reading, that kind of thing. And just from one I remember the last phrase, "Obey me," and that can mean "Obey me," taken from Bible text, or "Obey me," as like with what you hear from the Holy Spirit. What do you take that to mean? It's so hard to know if I am doing it.

I am Q'uo, and am aware of your query, my sister. To this query we would respond by suggesting that to obey is to give over one's personal decision-making in favor of another's who perhaps one feels is more wise, more powerful, more loving, and so forth. This is a free will choice which any can make. Each entity, as it matures within your culture, comes under the influence of many authorities that must needs be obeyed for a certain period of time: the parents in the upbringing, the teachers in the schooling, the bosses, the entities that are placed above one in the work environment, that this work may be accomplished in such and such a manner. However, at some point each entity must exercise its own ability to choose that which it shall do, that which it shall say, that which it shall believe, that star that it shall follow that it might reach the higher goals of the spiritual life. At some point the obeying of another is not enough to take one to the highest levels of being, of serving, of loving. It must be instead the inner-directed spiritual seeker that fashions its journey from all that it has learned, from all it believes, and from all that it seeks to gain.

Is there a further query, my sister?

L: No. That's a great help. Thank you.

I am Q'uo, and we thank you, my sister. Is there another query at this time?

(No further queries.)

Carla: Thank you so much, Q'uo. We are just grateful to have you to ask.

I am Q'uo, and we also are most grateful for each query that has been presented to us this day, for it allows us to serve in the way that we feel is the most helpful. Thus together we aid each other on the journey of seeking the one Creator in each experience, in each other, and in ourselves. For, indeed, the Creator resides in all things and in all people.

At this time we shall take our leave of this instrument and this group. We leave each, as always, in the love and in the ineffable light of the one Creator. Adonai, my friends. Adonai. ✣

Special Meditation
March 7, 2002

Group question: Our question today concerns the meeting that we have had this afternoon, the many ideas that have been exchanged about how to make the Law of One information available to more people, and we would like Q'uo's response, consideration, estimation as to the value of this particular effort and the likelihood of having an effect upon planet Earth in the positive sense and any effect that we might have in this endeavor. Could you give us your ideas and comments concerning this question?

(Carla channeling)

We are those known to you as the principle of Q'uo. We greet you in the love and in the light of the one Creator, in whose service we are. We feel very blessed to be able to be called to your group. We want to thank each of you for making the sacrifices necessary to join this circle of seeking. It is a great privilege to be able to function as we had hoped to be able to function when we made our promise to your people to be here in case there were questions in areas we felt that we could help to fulfill. For we truly feel the cries and the sorrow of our brothers and sisters on Earth now.

We thank you for this energy of your conversation that you have so deeply and so lovingly entered into. And we are most happy to speak to you on the subject of how to move forward to serve and to learn. We ask only that as you listen to that which we have to say you continue to discriminate carefully and to be the guardian of your thoughts, for truly you will know that which is to come to you for it will resonate. That which does not resonate to you need not be a stumbling block but simply that which is walked around and forgotten. And we truly ask that if our thoughts do not fit well with you, you drop them and leave them at once, for we would not function as a stumbling block.

We pause while this instrument refreshes herself.

We are those of Q'uo and are again with this instrument. We were unable to work this instrument's mouth because she had not drunk. And we thank you for your patience.

That which we think about your situation, for the most part, is simple joy that entities who so dearly wished before incarnation to come together in the grand collaboration have come to the moment of realizing just a bit of that wonderful, peaceful awareness of the lightness and worth of the ideals and principles about which you have been speaking. We confirm that this is a good plan for such efforts, for within your density at this time there is indeed an increasing transparency and fourth density is as close as your breathing. It is truly said that heaven is near at hand. It is necessary only to claim that awareness in order to begin, as the one known as K has said, to participate in an alternate reality, a reality of concept, intent and desire. An element of your universe would not be able to express within the metaphysical universe, yet those within the metaphysical universes are able to express through the density you live in.

Consequently, we ask each to remember, as endeavors are made, the truth of the energy flow concerning metaphysical law: it is not that which is of this world. Rather it is as if one planted a tree with the roots in heaven and the branches touching the Earth through people, through works of art, through every channel of living energy that has been created by thought, whether it be the original Thought of unconditional love which is the infinite Creator or whether it be that which is produced by the co-Creator that each of you is.

In the metaphysical world, chariots are your thoughts. That which you create which goes forth, in the metaphysical world, is created because of your desire, your will, your faith. Thusly we suggest that when each comes to the details and the planning of that linear nature, that it be remembered that the energy of the spiritual world is coming very reliably down the trunk of the Tree of Life and into its branches which are each of you. As above, so below is one of this entity's favorite sayings. And that we would suggest would be helpful to remember: that there is a shape hoped for by the very plastic and progressing thought processes of each of those who are collaborating within a given project, that each is a channel and receiving guidance concerning the collaboration. Consequently we ask that you trust and consult guidance as plans are made in addition to using the very sound linear and intellectual processes of analysis in the creative conception.

We would ask that each realize the sacredness of the life surrounding such a effort. For the life must support the work. If the attempt is made to merge the world of thought and that world which this instrument would call the world of commercial ventures or business, remember that the energy that is within the reach of each who offers needs to be respected and its path allowed to remain clear.

We would suggest to you that there is a great deal of unseen, hidden work [possible during communication] which creates far better collaboration. Conscious acceptance of the [ideal] of a spiritual community where each is nurtured by each, [is helpful for communicators,] for each of you has the ability to comfort and feed [others] by the attitude with which you greet your compatriots, and all of those about you have that same ability to function as support, encouragement and humor for you. Beyond all considerations, the chief lessons of the enterprise have always to do with accepting love from others and giving love to others without pride, vanity or feelings of unworthiness. The work that each of you does in truly entering into the energies of each of you will create creative pathways that will link in a more, shall we say, telepathic or whole-concept level so that the synergy of energy fields becomes consciously validated by belief in the opinion of those present, thus freeing those energy exchanges between each to take place at an enhanced rate.

We find that this is the sum of that which is without the possibility of infringing upon free will in general, and so we shall turn to questions that you may have following this initial cosmic sermonette.

Is there a question at this time?

B: I would like to state for clarity and see if I have this right. Clearly the spiritual teaching portion of this effort is much more important than its commercial outcome. And that must remain a goal in the background if this work is to succeed for the maximum good. Is this correct?

We are those of Q'uo, and we are not skilled at estimating commercial enterprises, but we feel in general that you are correct in saying that the heart of any enterprise is sacred in nature and the abilities of all concerned to cleave to the perceived ideals and purposes with which such an enterprise was engendered are far more important than considerations having to do with creating more of a splash or even a place of survival within the physical world. May we speak further, my brother?

D: We keep asking questions about what brought us together here. I have to think that there is a deep spiritual something, love, something, that brought us together. It is quite coincidental that we all got together.

We are those of Q'uo, and we thank you, my sister, for this query. We did not know, nor will we ever know in events of human occurrence, precisely when or even if connections will be made. The situation is that creation as you know it is a matter of strobe flashes of awareness within your mind so that you are recreating the world at this moment. Further, before the beginning of the incarnative period upon planet Earth each of you created for yourselves a curriculum of study for your school of hard knocks that is your planet. In this plan certain entities were involved, many more entities than sit within these walls. Agreements were made during the time when memory had not yet failed, to work together at this time on many levels, personal and service-to-others oriented. Each of you has already moved past many opportunities to attempt to serve in this thematic or general kind of way, and were each of you not to connect with the people within this particular group of collaborators within your near future you would make other connections that would inevitably offer you the same lessons and same opportunities for service. That being said, we celebrate the fact that each of you chose this probability/possibility vortex to make into your present moment. We salute each of you for moving, not to dictate arbitrarily or with authority, but to move with the promptings of intuition and the whisper of the dove's wing.

Can we answer you further, my sister?

(Inaudible)

Is there another question at this time?

K: We are a very loving group. I particularly find this life a very happy place for me, not always, but pretty close. Through work with D and B can we change the world to one of higher consciousness? Can we teach people love? Can we be involved in a higher consciousness?

We are those of Q'uo, and are aware of your question. Resoundingly, profoundly, the answer is yes. This instrument has been saying that each is the heart of a grand conspiracy for the light and that it is close to critical mass. The efforts of a very few in statistical percentages of population of planet Earth may well, in this very transparent time period where metaphysical energies are ever stronger, bring many to a successful harvest very quickly. Finally, as this instrument would say, it is that gift of the past saints, sinners and fellow travelers that has created both the challenges and the glory of this moment in your history. That which you receive has been produced by others, and that which you sow shall be reaped by your children. That ability of each to sow seeds grants to the seeker who asks to become a channel the ability to bring that hope into manifestation.

This is the time where, more than ever within history, each individual action, our own and yours as well, and each connection made in loving service, is tremendously blessed. The reason is—we are urged to pick this instrument's brain for a story, a joke actually—these considerations are often helpfully illustrated by laughter. The acolyte peeks out at the congregation in order to tell the priest how many are there for mass. In answer to the priest's query the altar boy replies, "Well, sir, out there in that church there are angels, cherubim, seraphim and all the company of heaven, and Mrs. Brown." The unseen help, the unseen presence is tremendous at this time for those who seek to be healed. Purify your intentions; discipline those forces of personality that block your heart. Open to inspiration and trust intuition. And know that each has tremendous power to make a difference and to achieve effective and transformational improvement of the harvest of planet Earth.

May we answer further, my sister?

A: How can one go about finding truth personally?

We are those of Q'uo, and, my sister, that is difficult to speak of in a short answer. However, we will say that the beginning of such work is a respect for the self and an honoring of the self to the extent that one sets about the mission of getting to know the self. May we answer you further, my sister?

A: Can you tell us if T is to be part of this group?

We are those of Q'uo, and are aware of your query. My sister, we cannot within the bounds of the Law of Confusion, for there is much value and virtue in the energy people bring to spiritual work. It is very important in the creation of a collaborative effort or any effort by anyone alone or in a group when attempting to be of service to come to a grasp of the true reasons for the desire and the purest heart of expression in terms of methods and how to do things. May we answer further, my sister?

B: I have a question regarding that. M met with us but had to excuse himself and at the same time he seems to be interested in helping us with the internet consumer project. Is it OK for us to use M's assistance even though he is not here at this time?

We are those of Q'uo, and are aware of your question, my brother. In general let it be said that the virtue of an entity depends not upon his conscious beliefs but upon his signature or vibration. Thusly, it matters not whether the one known as M would go through certain specified behaviors which could be considered the impression of one belief system upon another who does not share that belief. That would be that which would enable us only to be silent. We would always encourage those who do not wish to experience contact of this kind not to, for we have no desire to make anyone uncomfortable. The ethical question remains concerning the use of entities who may not enter into the ideals and the spiritual hopes of this group. It is up to each of you within the group to evaluate the heart and the intentions of potential group members, not according to the outward dictates of any sort of ritual, including this one. We are sorry that we cannot answer more specifically, but this is the general principle upon which spiritual collaboration may take place, not an agreement from the letter of every law, but a total and complete consensus on the vibratory level of the efforts made.

May we answer further, my brother?

B: That was very helpful. Thank you.

We thank you, my brother. Is there a further question at this time?

K: How can one open and sharpen the throat chakra?

We are those of Q'uo, and are aware of your query, my sister. When working upon the energy system the method that we would recommend is that of beginning at the beginning whenever working on the higher chakras and being very sure that all energies up into the heart are flowing easily and effortlessly. It is often the experience of your peoples that the energy system becomes partially blocked in various energy centers because of the affairs of the day. And the problem of working upon higher centers than the heart without working upon the lower centers is simply that the higher work emphasizes and further distorts the chinks in the armor of light, shall we say, that the lower difficulties present.

Consequently, people who yearn to do higher density work often find themselves with very sickened and failing bodies because the physical complex has not been strengthened to receive higher energy. Consequently, the prelude to working upon the blue ray or the throat chakra is the same as any other energy work. It begins with red ray and clears blockages sequentially, red, orange, yellow, green. Once the energy into the heart has been secured as a good supply then it is that entities may work further and begin that which is truly a blessed and healing thing, work in consciousness. Work within blue ray is helpfully preceded by time spent in silence within the heart chakra, for there is the need to become undefended and it is only in the heart chakra that you are able to reprogram fear into love.

Once as a seeker you are convinced that your heart is fully open and flowing then work upon the specific difficulty may begin. Communication is often much more a matter of that which is between the words than that which is text. Consequently, once the heart is opened there can be the conscious request to include that green energy of the open heart.

Meet the entities that you meet within the, shall we say, role-playing mask that you wear so that you are aware that you are an actor upon the stage and are creating your lines in accord with the truth of your being. Your hope then is to remove those blockages from speech which have visited you as fear and replace them with motives and energies that have to do with vulnerability, humility, compassion, forgiveness and absolute honesty. When you have been able to create a safe atmosphere with another entity then communication becomes far easier.

May we answer you further, my sister?

K: No. Thank you.

Is there a final query at this time?

D: Can we assume that everyone in this group is a wanderer?

We are those of Q'uo, and can indeed confirm that. It is a great privilege and pleasure to speak with you. Your beauty warms our heart. Your courage and your desire are wonderful to behold. We thank you for wishing to be harvesters, for truly the fields are white with harvest. We also are here as helpers. And if we would be helpful in each person's practice we encourage you to call upon us, for although we do not speak through channels usually in such encounters we are able to strengthen what this instrument would call the carrier wave so that your meditations may be useful and the connections to your guidance more effortless. May we answer you further?

D: No. Thank you.

We are those of the Q'uo, and we leave you in power and in peace, in the arms of each other, and in the spirit of love. Go forth in the knowledge that all is well and that all will be well. Follow and cooperate with those forces of destiny that roll in ever quicker breakers into the tidal basin of your consciousness. Trust the promptings of the guidance within. We are those of the Q'uo, and we leave you in the love and in the light of the one infinite Creator. Adonai, my friends. ✺

Sunday Meditation
March 17, 2002

Group question: The question today has to do with what we in the group have perceived as a lot of personal energy getting moved around, a lot of chances for change. People seem to be dealing with issues that they have let go for a while. There seem to be a lot of new issues popping up. There seems to be a lot of energy to be used now for catalyst for spiritual growth. And we would like Q'uo's comment on whether this might be a correct perception, and if so, what are the opportunities that are being offered when we have so much energy available to us?

(Carla channeling)

We are those of the principle known to you as the Q'uo, and we greet you in the love and in the light of the one infinite Creator. We serve that Creator as best we know, and at this stage of our own maturity that service is oriented in offering thoughts to those who seek them among your peoples, through instruments such as this one. It is, in our estimation, the best way that we have of sharing information without infringing upon your free will. And we greatly appreciate and thank each of you who has come to make a circle this day, for your seeking is what calls us to your group. As always, we ask that you use your discrimination in valuing our thoughts. For all things that we say are truthful as far as we know, yet truth is ever a subjective and limited item which appears in one guise and then in another as the rounds of experience become cycles and the cycles become octaves. We cannot say what will resonate to you from the words that this instrument chooses from our concepts. Were we able to speak with each entity telepathically we would be more sure that our thoughts were helpful because we can link in with the dynamics with any one entity. However, this instrument asks for universal information. And it is at that level that we wish to speak. Consequently, we speak always to a group and each entity within the group has a unique way of processing the information that comes to it. Each of you has a slightly different truth, a slightly different universe, a somewhat eccentric take on the construct which this instrument calls consensus reality. You seem to share one world between each of you, and in truth each of you does. Yet each of you creates that universe, and, therefore, each of you creates a different universe. So be careful as to what truth you accept as your own. Be sure that it rings loud and clear, and if it does not, leave it behind. For we would not be a stumbling block before you.

You ask this day about the impression that each in the group has had that there is an enhanced amount of energy available for work in consciousness and we would confirm that this is indeed so. And we are glad to speak about it although it is easy to oversimplify this very interesting line of thinking. The experiences that this instrument has had have been somewhat alarming to it, indeed, because recently the personal guidance of this entity, which she has always called the Holy Spirit, has begun to express through her instrument while she and the one known as Jim are in meditation, whereas formerly this entity spoke to this instrument in silence. This entity, indeed, inquired about this recently within the personal meditation and we would confirm that which this instrument received and that is simply that because of decisions which this instrument has made, because of choices which this instrument has made to support those decisions, having to do with the concept of being a responsible minister or priest, this entity has allowed its channel to open to a far greater extent than was previously possible.

Each entity's guidance system is quirky, and is quirky along the lines of love and loyalty and friendship and devotion, all of those positive emotions that feed into a sense of safety and well being. Thusly, this instrument has found faces for that guidance which she calls the Holy Spirit, and these faces have changed as this instrument's needs have changed. Currently this instrument's faces are friendly, familiar, loved, even adored and much appreciated. Thusly, when the connection is purified of all dross of fear and fear-based emotion, that connection with one who has passed on or with one who is physically present upon the planet takes on the possibility of being used as the face of guidance. Many entities wish for a name. This entity's mind works with pictures. Consequently this entity receives many pictures and guidance will always have a face for this instrument.

The situation in general, at this time, is that the people of your planet have entered planetary fourth density. The labor is ongoing of the planet itself. However, the vibrations have changed. The energy has changed. And you are experiencing the dawn of that which some call fourth density and some call fifth density. It is the density of love or understanding. In this environment guidance is ever closer and ever more powerful to help. In this environment emotions and desires call forth the appropriate vibration of guidance. That is to say, entities at this particular time have a maximum ability to polarize, positively or negatively. All guidance is not positive. The guidance comes because of the vibration of calling that is sent out. This is as if one were a radio listener who was tuning that radio that was the self, looking for the best station, the most pleasant and desired station within that band of vibration which carries the radio waves.

Whatever signal is put out has the potential of a tremendously enhanced and enlarged response. May we say that your planet at this time is fascinating to many, many entities within your inner planes who have come here to observe and some, hopefully, to help. There are many positive and negative entities very interested in the harvest at this time upon your planet. It is not that the present and this next decade, as this instrument has been receiving lately, is the beginning of the end. Rather it is the end of the end, and what we are saying at this time is that approximately for the next decade what you will see within the Earth plane is an increasing transparency of desire to guidance so that efficacy to guidance becomes ever more efficient and, further, we are saying that once it is realized that there is extra help available and it may be asked for, then the effect can even be squared and squared again and increased exponentially.

So there is a tremendous amount of positive energy available, what this instrument would call angelic energy available for those who seek to purify their emotions and to see into their desires to the heart of desire. Those who are doing that, focusing and learning of self, shall indeed find miracles occurring, peace becoming possible within the heart. All of the fourth-density environment is available within the mind's eye, within the chambers of that sacred heart, which is the metaphysical heart, the seat of the one infinite Creator within each of you. As you are able more and more to come into a state of trust and faith, as you are able more and more to find the heart of self, the heart of desire, the heart of service, that which means love and positivity to you personally, the more you shall receive angelic or positive guidance, the more you shall see helpful coincidences occurring, the more you shall see evidence of unseen hands at work.

On the other hand, [the more that] those who choose to identify this energy as that which has to do with fear, or power that cannot be controlled which results in fear, the more such entities will become confused and misguided. And the more situations will increase exponentially to give more opportunities for negative catalyst. So it is not the catalyst that is the work of this additional energy that is in the Earth planes at this time. The energy is there and is available to the spirit within, to the soul that you are, as you work on whatever catalyst that you receive. But guidance does not have to do with the catalyst. Your guidance has to do with you. Catalyst is an interesting subject in itself. For there is the impression that there are some things that are excellent, and there are some things that are terrible, and then there are many things in between. And each within this room knows pretty much what those things might be. Pain is bad. Pleasure is good. Yet we say to you that this can be easily subverted, not because entities wish to become confused and misguided but because your surface cultural environment has a somewhat negative bias at this time. Entities function according to fear. Consequently, almost all of incoming catalyst, left to itself, will have somewhat of a negative spin.

Thusly, it is not catalyst that is positive or negative. This instrument has gone though much in the way of surgery within the last season of your year. Was this a negative experience? Emphatically not. For this instrument it was a blessed and inspiring time of studying and healing. It is just as easy to have great difficulty and to find great negative emotion when experiencing what the outer world would think of as positive catalyst as it is to experience the same difficult negative emotions because of seemingly negative catalyst. Any catalyst gives one an entry into a full range of response. Guidance has to do with the mechanism of the entity attempting to discover how to look at its own thoughts and its own responses. Guidance helps an entity take a longer point of view and see into interior patterns that are not necessarily obvious upon the surface. Often guidance will come second-hand and indirectly through those very flesh and blood angels that are about each of you every day, the friends and the family that seem to be either good or evil, yet are all equally perfect souls in perfect expression in terms of their own universes.

The one known as S has a good grasp on this aspect of that which we are saying because of having a nature which is more inclined to be philosophical than reactive, and this is a gift which many entities have brought into incarnation with them to help them deal with the discomfort of living upon a planet that is somewhat more negative than their native vibrations. However, those who seem to be very negative are very often expressing pain and negative emotion when they deal with each other because of being in the interior of self, extremely sensitive and very much in pain because of the same sensitivity to vibration as those who are expressing positively. The mood of an entity does not indicate an entity's basic polarity. It is more subtle than that by far and much more a matter of that which goes on well below the surface of thinking. However, when an entity realizes that there is help available, then it is that there is the possibility of linking the conscious mind and the subconscious or unconscious mind so that the guidance may come from the deeper part of self and appear above the surface of that threshold of awareness. It usually comes in a still, small voice of silence. That this instrument has opened a larger channel to a conscious word-based form of guidance is simply a function of its long years of work in this area.

The guidance said to this entity, and to the one known as Jim, "You are now able to listen to our words because you are tough and have become tough enough to listen and yet make your own conclusion." Thusly we are free to speak. Each of you needs to be tough, to hew to your own sense of things, to seek your own guidance and to see all of those who come within your own purview as equally valid and valuable regardless of how they are expressing. This is your gift to each: the level of awareness with which you see them, hear them, and understand them. What can you do for another? You can see another. You can empathize with another. You can love another. You can forgive and accept another. These things are ineffable. They are not quantitative. Often they cannot be spoken. But we assure you that they can be felt and that they can help. And when the desire is to help and intercession goes up and the prayer is offered for those entities that you see in pain, that they may resolve their issues and may come to a balanced awareness that does not give them so much pain, these prayers are very effective. These very invisible and very silent voices that speak in the house of prayer have a real effect within the entities for whom prayer is offered.

Trust then, when there is concern, to turn it from anger, grief or whatever other emotion does not feel as if it were the emotion of the true heart, to prayer. For turning to prayer, turning to hope that another individual's suffering may be alleviated, is a turning to that love within the self and the worth within the other self that is not expressing at the moment but remains the truth of that entity. It is not always necessary that all entities know the truth. This instrument heard just yesterday that the subconscious works, psychologically speaking, without the necessity for words; that is, if one person knows something and is able to make a subconscious contact with another person, what one person knows will become what another person knows also. Trust this level of metaphysical reality because it forms that reality which you speak of as the physical illusion or maya.

We would at this time transfer this contact to the one known as Jim, as energy begins to wane for this instrument and for this group, in order that we might address any questions that remain upon the minds of those present. We greatly thank you again, and leave this instrument thanking it also, in the love and in the light of the Creator. We transfer to the one known as Jim. We are those of Q'uo.

(Jim channeling)

I am Q'uo, and greet each once again in the love and in the light of the one Creator. Is there a shorter query that we may attempt to speak to at this time?

S: I have a question related to the initial discussion on our seemingly dysfunctional family affairs. My wife has a desire to help her family as best she can in working with us. It seems that with her brother this desire has really blown up in her face. When the desire to help another does kind of fall flat on its face, do you have any suggestions on how to help, what to do, where to go, what to say?

I am Q'uo, and am aware of your query, my brother. We do not specialize in the attempt to unravel the personal tangle of perceptions as a normal part of our service to those of this planet. However, we may speak in some general terms in this particular case. It is not often easy to determine when one has been of service when one looks at any particular situation, for all experience is in motion. This is to say that as one step is taken in a particular direction in the uncovering of personal blockages of energy that the step shall be recognized as that which is helpful. For oftentimes the momentary experience and expression of growth may seem difficult and be beneficial, may seem beneficial and yet prove difficult at a later date.

In this instance, where there has been the emotional tear in a relationship, it would seem that the effort to assist has failed. And yet, is this true? If an entity, in this case the brother of the one known as C, moves himself to a point of distress and expresses this distress in a public fashion, as was done, perhaps there is in this expression a movement of energy which was necessary, yet difficult, aided by those around this entity so that this entity might experience what you would call a traumatic experience and share this trauma with the one known as C, and with others as well, then can one say that there has been no movement in this entity's growth and in the growth of those about it? For indeed, there has been movement. There has been experience and the sharing of intense emotions. That there has not been a resolution in your terms at this time may be interpreted as failure. Yet is this true? It cannot be said with certainty, not even by those of Q'uo, for the future is mazed by free will. We see possibilities. We see possibilities for great growth for all concerned, depending upon current and future choices. The stage has been set. Parts have been assigned. Roles are being played. Ancient energies are being expressed. There is the opportunity for further efforts in this endeavor. Do not ever feel that failure is all that is possible to determine from a situation in which anger has played a large part. Growth comes in many packages, my brother. Keep the heart open, the mind clear, the effort ever strengthened by the will to serve wherever possible.

Is there a further query, my brother?

S: No. Not right now. I would like to wish you a happy St. Patrick's day. I hope that you're wearing your green.

I am Q'uo, and we are indeed green with envy at the opportunity that each of you has within your illusion to celebrate such occasions and to move in the mysterious ways that are ever possible within the third density where the veils are so, so present within each experience. We thank you, my brother.

Is there another query at this time?

S: Not from me.

Carla: I am going to ask a kind of open-ended question because the catalyst for the question is the private guidance that I have got that seems to me to be somewhat ego centered, having to do with being a prophet of Mary, a prophet of the New Testament, a prophet of Sophia, these things that I have heard recently. I have seen many groups go down a bad road starting with some identified part of buying into some existing mythology and then painting oneself into a corner out of which one cannot go. I very much do not want to participate in anything of this vibration, and I simply would appreciate your response to my concern.

I am Q'uo, and am aware of your query, my sister. As we said to the one known as S, it is not our speciality to speak in specific terms to personal questions that are of pivotal importance in one's growth. However, to this query we may speak briefly, for there is great possibility for infringement in this area of your concern. You have been, as you are aware, opening yourself to more possibilities for the energies of change, of growth, and of sharing yourself with others. As you have done this, so there has been a response from the time/space portion of yourself in the form of many tendencies, many urgings, many energies that are open-ended in that you may work with the effort to grow in a number of ways with the energies that you have experienced [in response] to your invitation. You know well how to challenge such energies and entities and have done this without fail. Look then to your own inner guidance, to that hand in whose grasp you place your being. Find there the comfort and security that you seek. We only ask that you return to that which you have chosen as your own North Star, shall we say.

Is there a further query, my sister?

Carla: Let me just follow up on that (and thank you for that answer, Q'uo) by saying that were I a practicing Buddhist I would probably be getting that I was a prophet of whatever energies of that particular myth would bring one into the heart more, and because I am a woman and because I am a Christian, I am receiving the rays of that energy which is Jesus Christ, which are especially intimate and fit in with my gender and personality. Could you confirm that?

I am Q'uo, and am aware of your query, my sister, and we can indeed confirm that which you have spoken well.

Carla: So that I do not need to take it literally. I can continue to invite the mystery and not lean on this as some kind of other mission. It is part of the same thing. Right?

I am Q'uo, and this is so. Is there a further query?

Carla: No. I don't have any further questions.

I am Q'uo, and we thank you once again, my sister, for your query, for your concern, and for your fastidiousness. Is there a final query at this time?

(No further queries.)

I am Q'uo, and we are most grateful to have been invited to your circle of seeking this day. As always, it was a privilege and an honor for us to join you. At this time we shall take our leave of this instrument and this group, leaving each in the love and in the light of the one infinite Creator. We are known to you as those of the Q'uo. Adonai, my friends. Adonai.

L/L Research

L/L Research is a subsidiary of Rock Creek Research & Development Laboratories, Inc.

P.O. Box 5195
Louisville, KY 40255-0195

www.llresearch.org

Rock Creek is a non-profit corporation dedicated to discovering and sharing information which may aid in the spiritual evolution of humankind.

ABOUT THE CONTENTS OF THIS TRANSCRIPT: This telepathic channeling has been taken from transcriptions of the weekly study and meditation meetings of the Rock Creek Research & Development Laboratories and L/L Research. It is offered in the hope that it may be useful to you. As the Confederation entities always make a point of saying, please use your discrimination and judgment in assessing this material. If something rings true to you, fine. If something does not resonate, please leave it behind, for neither we nor those of the Confederation would wish to be a stumbling block for any.

© 2009 L/L Research

Sunday Meditation
April 7, 2002

Group question: The question today has to do with some of the finer aspects of service. If we wish to be of service and offer ourselves in that way, is there any danger that we could distort the service or make it less than it could be by being proud of our service, by making it public, by doing it in a way that is not hidden, not pure. We would like for Q'uo to talk to us about the optimum way of really being of service to others in a way that does serve other people and doesn't activate our egos.

(Carla channeling)

We are those known to you as Q'uo. Greetings in the love and in the light of the one infinite Creator, in whose service we come to you this day. We offer you many thanks for gathering in a circle of seeking and for calling us to your group with your question concerning service to others and how to optimize it. We are very glad to share thoughts upon this subject and would ask only that each of you listen to those things which we would say with an ear for that which is yours, being very quick to lay aside any thoughts that we offer that do not seem to you to be helpful. We would suggest that your powers of discrimination are very keen and are true for you, far in excess of what our opinions might be.

We give this instrument the vision of a blank, black night sky without even the twinkling of stars, but simply the black, full night that expresses itself as the foundation of your consciousness as it gathers itself into an energy web and forms itself into that which you know of as yourself. That gathering of energy, that swirling into pattern, is a gathering from fullness into fullness. And we use the color black because it is that which cannot be seen, yet we might as well say a fullness upon fullness of light. However, the purity of this image is in that which forms itself as an energy field without any visual cue, without any proof of its existence or its identity.

Such is the foundation stone of each of your incarnational selves. The self within incarnation is a collection that you have put together for this particular life experience. You have chosen, very carefully, the attributes, limitations and gifts that you have within this incarnation. From a rather vast array of distortions which appear as gifts, and distortions which appear as limitations, which lie within the confines of a soul self, you might call it, that has been formed through many, many experiences, each adding its torque and twist to the swirling, spiraling energy of the self which has been formed without sight, without vision, but of energy itself, that energy which is love, that energy into manifestation which then becomes light, you have chosen that which becomes form, becomes being, becomes body, becomes personality, becomes ego, becomes "you." And that "you" then enters the blinding light of incarnational consciousness.

And yet what are you? It is well to reckon with the infinity of your own being. At the beginning of the discussion of service to others and of optimizing it is the foundation stone of knowing who and what you are. You are not a new being, and yet you are brand new to this moment. But by saying that you are not new, we mean to indicate that those quirks and quiddities which make you just the personality that you are have a value that is not obvious to the conscious, human eye of reason. Your value to the Creator is precisely in those irregularities, eccentricities and inconsistencies that form you as you are, that distort and bias you as you come to the questions of your life and the pondering of those questions throughout your life.

Realize always that there is beneath your feet a profoundly concrete unmanifested security. You cannot fall from being who you are. You cannot fail to be who you are. Anything that you do, anything that you may consider a gross error, a silly mistake, or a foolishness remains part of the glory and goodness of who you are. It is useless and beyond useless to attempt to measure the quality of your self or the quality of the giving of the self. Not perhaps useless in the sense of being food for thought or "grist for the mill" (after Ram Dass) but useless in the sense of achieving a sensible and meaningful answer to the question of self-worth. You cannot estimate your worth. You cannot criticize your biases. Beyond a certain point, they are those things about you which are most powerful and strong to serve because only you can express within the infinite universe precisely as you express. Each of you is as the cub reporter who works to tell the story and write it down for the paper. Each of you sees the same world scene, and yet each of you writes a different story. What the Creator is fascinated with is the differences in the stories.

Therefore, in terms of pleasing the infinite Creator and in terms of fulfilling your hopes of serving, you cannot fail. For all that you do will inform that one great original Thought which is Creatorship as It cannot be informed by any other spark in the infinite universe. Each of you is precious and beloved by the Creator. So we ask each, beyond all discussion of this question, to move immediately to a place of resting when such concerns occur within the mind, bringing up the doubts of self and the worth of the self. Move to that place of safety and resting that this instrument would call Gilead and allow yourself to feel the balm of the Creator's love. For truly, in the Creator's eyes you can do no wrong.

The rhythms of your work days and your leisure days create within you the suggestion that the passage of time is real, that there is a coherence of truth and meaning based upon the sequence of events, the past, the present, and the future. Certainly within your incarnational experience this is the literal truth of experience. The days flow into nights, flow into days, the months flow into years, flow into decades. All the rhythms of your world of nature cycle round once again: spring, summer, fall, winter and spring again. As this instrument has been so exalting the past few days to see, the new green shoots forth from the withered branch, the blossoms come forth from the hopeful leaves. Daffodils and tulips, fruit trees in blossom, all scenting the air with their sweet odors and resting the eye with a delight of color and life.

And beneath these transient events lives an energy as slow and as firm as the heartbeat of the Creator Itself. It is a matter of gradually becoming able to cease the noise of worry, to cease gradually, little by little, the fretting of fear. It is this kind of allowing a slowing of the rhythms of conscious thought that will bring to the seeker the optimal frame of mind or point of view for being of service to the self, to other selves, and to the Creator. There is a surface to what this instrument would call consensus reality, much like the surface of a glass ceiling or a floor that cannot be seen, yet it seems to hold up the bodies and the experiences. Many are the entities that move through the incarnation that they experience upon your planet without once falling through the glass ceiling into the great reaches of deeper consciousness. It is possible to move from infanthood, to childhood, to teenagehood, to adulthood, through to the grave, without ever leaving the surface of life. It is not particularly easy to maintain this comfortable shallowness of existence which allows almost complete control over the environment. Yet many attempt nothing more than simply to remain comfortable and, as this instrument would say, keep body and soul together. For those within this circle that has never been a distinct possibility. Each within this group seeks not just the surface of the truth but those blessed regions that lie beneath the surface, those areas which are more like a water world than an air world, a world of smooth, rhythmic gliding, the characteristics, shall we say, of water rather than of air.

The way that energy moves through water is pertinent here, for as water is pushed by a force from behind, it expresses itself in a way which is not from here to there. For water simply pushes on its force to the next drop of water to the next so that something that occurred off the coast of Japan can eventually express itself upon the shores of your beach of California. The same energy, the same reason, is infinitely expressed across the ever interconnected drops of water. Study the way that water works to see a little bit more into how entities come together in their patterns and how they may express in ways that do not show but yet have their effect on a distant shore. Many times there is the hope of seeing a result and there is a demand put on service that it be quantifiable. This is an easily understood desire, to be able to measure the service that one is, that one can offer. And yet it is not always at all obvious how the service is going to express. For it may express not simply within a small pond of being, not in the immediate ripples but rather at a distant shore when that wave that you began washes up and expresses itself finally in just such and such a way.

So, we would suggest that there be a releasing of tension when that tension of worry is felt concerning the worth of an effort. Ask the self to release judgment. Releasing the judgment of how one is doing is very helpful in simplifying and regularizing the energies surrounding those gifts which you hope to offer.

Let us shift to another gear here and look at the question of being and doing, an old theme for us and for you, too. Some of service-to-others does have to do with doing, indeed, and we praise each for those kindnesses and services that each has agreed to offer freely from the heart of self. It is a wonderful thing to behold the helpful desire of each entity to do good, to serve truly, to run the straight race, to be a child of the Creator in all things. And each of you has these outer gifts that have been expressed by you in service to others in many different ways throughout your life, and yet always the truer and deeper elements of service have to do with your being. It does not matter in terms of the worth of service what that service is. Some services may seem more noble than others, some entities more able to serve than others, and yet all service is equal.

What ennobles service is the love with which it is offered. And that love can be held within the heart, can be withheld, or can be released. It is tempting to attempt to hold the picture of service within the mind and to adjudge the self then from that position within the mind, and yet this is what this instrument would call the mind game.

We are finding, as we discuss this topic, that the energy within the circle is quite low, and consequently we would choose at this time to open the meeting to further questions. We would attempt at this time to transfer the contact to the one known as Jim. We are those of Q'uo, and would transfer this contact at this time.

(Jim channeling)

I am Q'uo, and we greet each once again in love and in light through this instrument. We appreciate your patience, as we have worked with this instrument, and would ask at this time if there might be a query to which we might respond.

T: Yes. I have a comment and I would appreciate your elaboration. I believe from what I just heard you say that our working on ourselves in any way is a slow chipping-away process. I had spoken earlier about having one very good day one day last week, and even that evening when I watched the boys usually I would be a little upset because I would like to read or watch some TV and they would be making noise. But it didn't seem to bother me that evening. Do you have any suggestions about how, once having attained that feeling or mindset, to continue, or to get that feeling back?

I am Q'uo, and am aware of your query, my brother. How to bottle the magic! It is our recommendation that to be and to accept yourself as you are is the quickest road to attaining those goals which you desire in terms of being as harmonious as you can be, learning what you can learn, and yet being aware that you have a distance yet to go. It is the fate of humans in this third-density to be in some degree seemingly deficient, for this is the lot of those who dwell within this illusion. This is not to be mourned or bewailed, for this is a process that is long in terms of your time and energy, yet which need not bring discomfort or concern to the hearty seeker. This is, rather, to be worked with as a given, shall we say, for each of you has those qualities which are what you would call strengths as well as those which you would call weaknesses. You will do well when you are able to exercise discrimination to the degree where you are able to accept one as well as the other. For your journey is one which is best accomplished when you are evenhanded, shall we say, when you are able to work with yourself, with these strengths and these weaknesses, and bless the Creator, the creation, and yourself for being as you are. For in truth, all is well, all is one, all is as it should be. Yet this great dance, which all do as they progress through the creation and the evolution of the self, is accomplished in a movement that is truly fluid, that is ever present, and which can lead one on into the greater realms of understanding.

When you have achieved what you would call a success and have been able, to your own discrimination, to be able to do that which you wish to do, again do not feel overly glad, for to become attached to one form or another, one expression or another is, to some degree, to place small stumbling blocks within one's way. It is a balancing act, my friends, for you on the one hand realize that you have a journey to make and on the other hand are wise to realize that you are the Creator, that all is truly well, and that there is no need for any thing. This is the paradox in which each of you moves.

We hope that we have not overly confused you, my brother. Is there another query at this time?

T: No. Not from me. Thank you very much. It didn't confuse me at all.

I am Q'uo, and we thank you, my brother. Is there another query at this time?

Carla: I have a couple. First of all, I wanted to ask concerning a dream theme that I have experienced lately. I've had several dreams about a baby, and in this last dream I was able to get to the baby and pick the child up. My thinking about this is suggesting to me that I am going back to my own childhood and comforting the child that was not comforted when I was a child. In general, could you confirm that this is the direction that my dreams are attempting to speak with me on?

I am Q'uo, and am aware of your query, my sister. And we confirm that which you have supposed. Is there another query?

Carla: The other question simply has to do with my experience of the channel today. It was coming from a very deep place and I can still feel the energy. It was very powerful but there were fewer words than usual. It was very hard to bring up any content, but it seems like a very rich place and seems like a new area of conscious channeling, and I would be glad to hear anything that you have to say about it because it is very new to me.

I am Q'uo, and am aware of your query, my sister. The practice of the vocal channel is that practice which one may become more, shall we say, capable of producing as the experience continues. There are along the path of this service various steps or stages of growth which are apparent in some cases and in others not so apparent. You have begun to experience the beginning of a newer phase, shall we say, of serving as a vocal instrument. There are levels of consciousness that are available to each entity and to those who serve as vocal instruments that open doors, that offer great access to pure information or inspiration. Through another door you are beginning to pass. Is there another query, my sister?

Carla: Yes. One more. It's pretty silly, but I do want to ask it. I have had the inspiration lately to wear clothes for the channeling and only for the channeling and have them just be for that. I wonder if it is acceptable as a service to put the clothes on as part of being tuned, or is it simple vanity? I almost put on my brand new channeling outfit today and then I thought it was just too vain to be changing my clothes. I don't know where the judgment is and where the truth lies. If you can make a comment, fine. It it's too specific, that's fine too.

I am Q'uo, and am aware of your query, my sister. The use of special garments for the providing of the service of a vocal channel is completely at your discretion. If you feel that this would enhance your ability to serve, then by all means do so. If you feel that it would, on the other hand, set you apart and make you feel better than, then by all means do not. This is your decision, my sister.

Carla: Thank you.

Thank you, my sister. Is there another question at this time?

T: Yes, it also concerns vocal channeling. In this last newsletter from Jim and Carla a graded group was mentioned and Carla explained it to me. I've never been much of a channel at all and never have had much of a desire, although I would like to do it if I felt it would be helpful. She also mentioned that in groups like this there were people who functioned as a battery or a conductor and I would like some guidance as to whether I should pursue active participation as a vocal channel.

I am Q'uo, and am aware of your query, my brother. Again, we come to that point which is more appropriate for your own decision-making according to that which you feel drawn to do. You may be either, according to your desires, for you have abilities in both areas. However, the choice must come, not from any source outside yourself, but from that voice within yourself.

Is there a final query at this time?

R: I have one. Speaking of dreams, I want to encourage the dreaming activity because I look at it as a way of speaking to your self. Is that all that is necessary, the desire?

I am Q'uo, and am aware of your query, my brother. Desire and perseverance. Continue in the effort until you have been able to produce the fruits which you desire. Practice. Practice. Practice.

We are those of Q'uo, and we again thank those present for taking the time to join this circle of seeking and to blend your desires as one as you speak with your own hearts and with those of all of the creation. We appreciate your efforts and your sincerity. At this time we would take our leave of this instrument and this group. We leave each, as always, in the love and in the ineffable light of the one infinite Creator. Adonai, my friends. Adonai. ✣

L/L Research

L/L Research is a subsidiary of Rock Creek Research & Development Laboratories, Inc.

P.O. Box 5195
Louisville, KY 40255-0195

www.llresearch.org

Rock Creek is a non-profit corporation dedicated to discovering and sharing information which may aid in the spiritual evolution of humankind.

ABOUT THE CONTENTS OF THIS TRANSCRIPT: This telepathic channeling has been taken from transcriptions of the weekly study and meditation meetings of the Rock Creek Research & Development Laboratories and L/L Research. It is offered in the hope that it may be useful to you. As the Confederation entities always make a point of saying, please use your discrimination and judgment in assessing this material. If something rings true to you, fine. If something does not resonate, please leave it behind, for neither we nor those of the Confederation would wish to be a stumbling block for any.

© 2009 L/L Research

Sunday Meditation
April 21, 2002

Group question: The question today has to do with opening the heart and the center of love in our daily round of activities. Each of us from time to time has found ways of accessing this energy of compassion. We have insights and prolonged experiences of one kind or another that have let us know that there is an energy there. We would like for Q'uo to let us know how this process of opening the heart is really accomplished by those of us who live here in the third density but still behind the veil of forgetting, still trying to discover the unity with all things. How do we go about opening our heart centers and carrying that love with us into our daily round of activities?

(Carla channeling)

We are those known to you as Q'uo. We greet you in the love and in the light of the one infinite Creator, in whose service we are. It is our privilege and pleasure to be called to your circle of seeking, and we thank each of you for the room that you have made in your life to ask for and to welcome these questions, this seeking, and the possibilities of new life. It is a great blessing for us to be called to your group by this energy, for it is our form of service at this time. And because of your dedication it is possible for us to do what we came to the inner planes of your planet to offer, and this is our greatest blessing. For we too are those who seek to be of service and to share our hearts. We are happy to share our opinions and ask only that each of you monitor that which we say, asking that you keep only those things which resonate to you on a personal level and do not view us as authorities. For you are that one unique person who knows what the truth is for you, and we would not wish to put a stumbling block in your way.

You ask how to find the way back to the open heart when you have gone away. We would step back from this question and ask you to come with us in an envisioning of the beginnings of your creation, that which the Creator expressed when this intelligent infinity burst forth in the infinite number of sparks, each of which contained the stuff of the Creator in a holographic form and each of which was sent out to collect information. You are beings of light, beings of love, beings of infinity. You are citizens of an eternal universe that expresses itself at this time in illusion upon illusion upon illusion. Each of these illusions set in place in exquisite regularity and discrimination a fastidious arrangement offering experience after experience designed to create environments in which these sparks of creatorship would become progressively more and more articulated, expressive and unique.

What does the Creator hope for from you but that you be yourself and that you explore what the self is in an ever more profound sense; that you come to experiences with your whole self and allow them to affect you. The Creator's interest is in learning more about Itself and each of you is as the detective on that same path of discovery and transformation into ever more authentic versions of you. For in cameo, in small, you are the microcosm of which the Creator is the macrocosm. Each of you contains that jewel that is perfect, but each of you has gone through incarnation upon incarnation in which you have been colored by experience. It is as though each of you has come through the refining fire that has progressively clarified and refined your nature so that you are ever a little more able to see that which is truly you. Your responsibility to the Creator, then, begins with being who you are. Not striving, not making efforts, but, indeed, letting go and releasing that which is not you.

This instrument experiences constantly the journey from the center of self as perceived by the self outward towards the expressions of outer experience, becoming entranced by various things of the illusion and finding the self dissatisfied with that position, that state of awareness, that experience of self, and cycling back into the heart of self by choice by the techniques of momentary prayer, remembering who she is, why she is here, what she hopes to express through her presence. There is no one within the energies of your third-density world that remains at all times in a perfect state of self-awareness. Truly, this is not the reason for which you took form within the Earth world. Indeed, each of you came specifically to be thrown off balance, to be confused, to be puzzled, even to be in distress and to suffer. For you knew before incarnation that the great opportunity that one has only within the illusion is that it cannot be seen or proven that spirit exists, much less that it is a transcendent state which, in fact, doubles the illusion. You are not here to be masters of the illusion but rather to be confused, puzzled, foolish and wrong. And in the process of this scramble and this struggle that aura which you bring into manifestation with the embedded gems of creatorship hidden within it is offered the refining process of your Earth, and in that friction and suffering you are processing this confusion and this suffering in ways that create great beauty as your emotions stabilize, deepen and purify themselves through the hard-won experience of all of the confusion and suffering.

Certainly, it is to be hoped that more and more of your experience within the illusion is able to take on that centered feeling which graces and blesses all environments with a beauty that comes from within. But the concept of remaining centered at all times sets up for entities such as this instrument the incorrect idea of coming up to a standard or being considered inadequate, and we would not suggest in any way by what we are saying that any state of mind is inadequate or wrong. Precisely what you feel is that which is right for you, yet you are creators. You are those who have all of the infinite resources of that spiritual part of self that has nothing to do with the illusion. You are people of magic and power, and you can, as this instrument was saying earlier, dream a new present for yourself and envision a new future. You can use techniques that allow you to release old pain and embrace the present and the future with confidence.

Perhaps we would say that there is a secret to coming into the open heart once again. The secret is buried in each religion and we encourage each to play with and sense into the various religious and mythical systems to find those images and icons of the Creator that pierce your heart. For this particular instrument that image is of Jesus Christ. Whatever your image of unconditional and sacrificial love, the secret is to know in the deepest part of your soul that who you really are is the Creator, so that moving into the open heart is a matter of coming home. There is a home within your heart that this instrument would call the sanctuary or the *sanctum sanctorum*, the holy of holies, the inner temple of self. You might consider it a room that is locked against casual visitors, even yourself. The key that unlocks this door is silence. There is the momentary stopping of the voice within, the coming into the silence of sacredness and, once there within the heart, you are in a tabernacle with the Creator. And you may sit and rest and even, as this instrument often does, picture the self crawling into the lap of the Creator and resting against that comfortable, strong breast. For the Creator has a very deep and infinite love for you and is waiting for you in every moment of every day, hoping and rejoicing when you do come home.

One of this instrument's catch phrases is, "Christ is the I of me." In the cosmic sense, whatever your belief system, unconditional love is not something for which you need to strive because at the very center of your self, the truth of your self is this same shining, unconditional love. When all other things of the self are released, this is your truth. This is your nature. This is your being and your essence, and your outer personality becomes as a pane of glass, clear and transparent and able to let the light shine through.

The day has many moments, many common and ordinary chores, and we would suggest of you that you investigate each of these moments as if all were new and re-experience those common things of life, for they are full of light. They are open energies which include always that energy, bliss and peace. Again and again this instrument has asked these last months, "What is peace?" for each day there is a peace meditation and this instrument and the one known as Jim sit in silence visualizing Earth being healed and being brought to a state of peace. And so each night since that day in September of last year there has been this exercise in asking once again to "Show us the ways of peace." And as the energies begin to consolidate about this daily peace meditation, what this instrument is discovering is that peace is already established within the heart of self. We each know the ways of peace. Each of you knows what it is to love with every fiber of your being, to be open, flowing channels for the love and the light that is the essence of the Creator.

Wisdom is not "out there." Wisdom is not that which needs to be grasped for. Wisdom is that which comes in a moment when there is at last a willingness and a humility that allows the self to release all the preconceptions and all of what the one known as J was speaking of as the old way. Is there anything wrong with old ways? We would say, certainly not. What there are, are unending variations in a pattern. Each time that you do a day you are creating one set of ripples in the ocean of common being, and that which you think and that which you do and that which you envision for that day is your expression of beauty, of essence, that you give as a gift to the common race of humankind and to the energies of planet Earth of which you are her stewards. You cannot see the effects of that day, just as ripples move into the ocean and finally fetch up on a distant shore. You do not know what you have done. The joy of it is in the doing, not in the results. The gift was the day and the life is a gift to the future and others will reap those seeds that you now sow with your being this day. Each day is a brand new gift, a brand new life, a new opportunity to be you and to find the most creative ways to love.

Before we leave this instrument we would like to say something about this love. When you talk about coming back to the open heart, each of you is perhaps thinking mostly about how you can serve other entities, for that is your energy and your hope: service to others. And yet how essential it is that you retain the energies to give to the self that love that you hope to give to others, and to do that before you attempt to give to others. It is as though each of you wishes to beautify the lives of others while leaving at home that self within that is as the neglected child. In this instrument's holy works the directions are to love others as you love the self. It is important to love the self. This is not selfish, nor is work done to untangle the threads that keep you from loving yourself selfish. It is important work. It is work that will probably need to be kept up day after day, ministering to yourself with the same joy that you minister to others.

Each of you has seen how easy it is to minister to others, and we ask you to forgive yourself in just that way for all perceived faults, not attempting simply to ignore those faults. You have a mind and a power of analysis. You have techniques and resources that you can use to work with yourself. And we are happy to speak to you about this. Each of you needs somewhat different ways in order to work upon various distortions which you have picked up, places where you are holding energy within yourself so that your energy is not flowing into the heart and through the heart in full measure. As the one known as R said, in the great urge to get into the heart and to do work in consciousness often that self that is expressing in the lower energy centers is simply left behind. What are your issues? Are they diet? Are they exercise? Are they emotional healings? Are they moving back into an abandoned and lonely childhood and bringing that child into the heart and giving it the love that was not perceived in the young days of that soul? Whatever your issues are, honor them, respect them, and minister to yourself. It is not selfish. It's needed work in order to free you up to be that essentially joyful self that you already are when you are not burdened with concerns.

We cannot take the concerns of the day and suggest to you that they not be attended to. We can only suggest that there is a rhythm and a harmony and a dance surrounding the energies of all things, no matter how seemingly mundane. When the image of the self is as the dancer instead of as the bumbler, then even falling down is part of the dance. Even dropping everything. Even the cat's exploration of gravity in the other room as occurred during this meditation, making great noise and clatter, becomes a perfection of its own and a dance into the kitchen after the meditation to retrieve the tray and retrieve the broken cutlery and the broken glass. It's simply part of the dance of being for this day. It too shall be put to rest and a new day shall dawn. Cherish and protect your sweet, sweet essence of self, for each of you truly is a child of the Creator.

We thank you for this energy and this question, and at this time we would transfer this contact to the one known as Jim for further questions. We leave this instrument in love and light. We are those known to you as those of Q'uo.

(Jim channeling)

I am Q'uo, and greet each once again in love and in light through this instrument. It is our privilege at this time to ask if there might be any queries of a shorter nature to which we may speak. Is there another query at this time?

S: We're here to be of service to others. What are the others here for?

I am Q'uo, and am aware of your query, my brother. Each seeks to serve the Creator in each other entity that it meets in the daily round of activities and this is true of those who seek on the positively oriented path, that path of radiance, that path of that which is. As you are aware, there are some who seek to serve the self and who seek to manipulate others to serve the self as well. However, since all beings are portions of the one Creator, even these who seek upon the negative path serve the One, for there is no other.

Is there another query, my brother?

S: Not right now. Thanks.

I am Q'uo, and we thank you, my brother. Is there another query at this time?

Carla: I'd like to ask about this idea of envisioning a road to fourth density. From your point of view is this a good way to think about serving in the next decade, or is the concept of building a road into the next density an inadequate vision?

I am Q'uo, and am aware of your query, my sister. We feel that your image of constructing a road, a path by which those who seek love and seek to serve the Creator in all may move ahead, is indeed a most adequate image to envision at this time in your spiritual evolution. We give this instrument the picture from your tarot images of the Fool who seems to walk off the cliff and who is momentarily suspended in mid-air. As the seeker of truth moves along the path of spiritual seeking, many times this is the image which functions well to describe this journey. For when one seeks beyond what the world about you recognizes as real then there is that magic of the thinking, and the acting to follow the thinking, which creates the sure fundament under the foot as it is placed foolishly upon the path, and we say foolishly for many will feel that it is foolish to seek to love all beings. For is there not evil in this world? It is foolish to move intuitively in a world where reason wrests its reward from all. It is foolish to seek to give the self full of love to those whom you do not know. And yet, my friends, is it not foolish to love the Creator that you have not yet met? Is it foolish to seek the heart of love when love is that force which has created all that is? Is it foolish to walk upon the dusty trail of the seeker of truth when that trail so often seems isolated and alone, yet when explored fully is filled with fellow seekers and pilgrims who walk that same trail and who seek in that same vein to love without end, to give without stint, and to be in harmony with all that there is? Yes, you build a road. It is a road that is made of things not of this world but those principles and qualities that are the center of the heart of a Creator of love.

Is there a further query, my sister?

Carla: No. Thank you. That was wonderful.

I am Q'uo, and we thank you, my sister. Is there another query at this time?

S: What kind of changes and trends do you see as we go from third to fourth density on Earth?

I am Q'uo, and am aware of your query, my brother. As we look upon your Earth world at this time it is our privilege to witness to the growing of light within the hearts of those who have previously felt no urge to seek in this manner. For the events of your days, these latter days of third density upon planet Earth, have served and will serve as catalyst to bring forth that which is the highest and the best from the hearts of those who are beginning to sense that there is more to this life that meets their everyday eye. There is within many people at this time the beginning of questioning of those values which have long been held and which have held entities long within a certain restricted way of thinking and of being. When it seems that there is less security within a world filled with a desire for security, then it is that there is the seeking of that which is true, firm, sure and dependable. This brings the hardy seeker back to the heart of the self, the heart of the journey, the heart of the illusion in which each finds itself at this time. Each seeker, as a portion of the one Creator, has within it that, shall we say, homing device that is awakened at the proper time for each seeker, that reminds each it was planned aforetimes that this is the time to begin that conscious journey of seeking for truth, and so each takes the first step of a journey which in truth has never ended, shall not end in the foreseeable future, and which shall grow more fruitful and abundant as time and experience accumulate.

(Tape change.)

I am Q'uo and am once again with this instrument. Is there another query at this time?

Carla: In thinking about materials for building a metaphysical road, am I on the right track by thinking about qualities like faith, hope, will, the creation, the world, the lightening-struck tower?

I am Q'uo, and am aware of your query, my sister. Indeed, we feel that you have mentioned those qualities which are central to any seeker's journey and to the road into the fourth density, as it has been called this day. For, in truth, the faith which each seeker expresses as further steps are taken upon the journey of seeking is matched by the will which each seeker also expresses as the perseverance is called upon to continue the journey of faith. Indeed, these two are the rod and the staff which bring great comfort to the seeker as it moves through what your holy works has called the Valley of the Shadow of Death. For upon this journey there are many tests, the ordeals by which the seeker's desire to continue is burnished, is tempered, is made stronger by the testing. And as one exercises the faith that there is a journey to make, and a goal to reach, and a grail from which to drink, then it must be matched by the will to continue and to pass these tests that the daily round of activates will bring to each. For it is by such testing that one is able to measure the mettle. It is by this testing, that which seems to be negative at first glance, that you are able to build the metaphysical muscles, shall we say. It is such exercise of faith and will that makes you stronger as

metaphysical beings. It is your intentions, your desires, that have strength, that have power, in the spiritual world, for there, thoughts are things, and it is by the way you think, the attitude that is your fingerprint in the metaphysical sense that you are able to do work in consciousness, that you are able to change consciousness in the magical sense, that you are able to access deeper portions of the subconscious mind and to bring them forth into consciousness that they there might find a room and a reach into which they might have effect in your daily life. And that, indeed, you begin to change yourself as you continue this journey, a continual movement from one image of yourself to another so that you are a new and risen being moving into the fourth density of love and compassion.

Is there a further query, my sister?

Carla: No. Thank you.

I am Q'uo. Is there a final query at this time?

J: I would like to ask if the electromagnetic field energy work that I have been doing is, in your opinion, a good way to serve others? Or if there is another way that I could be of more service to others?

I am Q'uo, and am aware of your query, my sister. We do not as a regular practice care to judge another entity's efforts, for we see each entity making the greatest possible effort in its personal life each moment that that life is lived. However, in this instance we may comment in a general sense and suggest that that which you do in the way of magnetic healing has great benefit for those with whom you share this work. And we encourage that which you do, in that you will be able in your future to expand upon this work as each entity will expand upon all efforts that are made. This is the nature of growth: to begin at a point, to assess the situation, to gather information, to make choices as how to proceed, to proceed with or without fear, to learn how to drop fear, to enhance that which was begun, to add unto it, to alter it. This is your path. This is the path of each seeker of truth and we support each effort that is made at this time by those who intend to serve others. For it is your intention that is your strength, and your power, and your direction.

At this time we feel that we have spoken a relatively reasonable length of time. We are aware that the one known as Carla is concerned that we speak overly long. We do not mean to make each sit in uncomfortable positions for too long a period of your time. We thank each for inviting our presence this day. We bless each. We tell you now that there are many within the realms of what you call your heaven worlds that rejoice at the gatherings of entities such as this that occur all over your planet for the purpose of seeking and sharing the love and the light of the one Creator and to go forth then into the daily round of activities to take that with you and share there with those who perhaps share not so consciously but who appreciate your sharing of your love and your understanding.

We are known to you as those of Q'uo. We leave each now in the love and in the light of the one infinite Creator. Adonai, my friends. Adonai. ✣

L/L Research

L/L Research is a subsidiary of Rock Creek Research & Development Laboratories, Inc.

P.O. Box 5195
Louisville, KY 40255-0195

www.llresearch.org

Rock Creek is a non-profit corporation dedicated to discovering and sharing information which may aid in the spiritual evolution of humankind.

ABOUT THE CONTENTS OF THIS TRANSCRIPT: This telepathic channeling has been taken from transcriptions of the weekly study and meditation meetings of the Rock Creek Research & Development Laboratories and L/L Research. It is offered in the hope that it may be useful to you. As the Confederation entities always make a point of saying, please use your discrimination and judgment in assessing this material. If something rings true to you, fine. If something does not resonate, please leave it behind, for neither we nor those of the Confederation would wish to be a stumbling block for any.

© 2009 L/L Research

Sunday Meditation
May 5, 2002

Group question: The question today has to do with putting the puzzle pieces together, remembering our being, our knowledge, our ancestry, our connection with each other and with the planet. We are hoping that Q'uo can give us some information on how this spiritual journey works for us. No matter how long we've been on the journey, no matter how newly we feel revitalized, we need to know how it is that we remember our mission. Are there stages to our remembering? Is there a process that we could accelerate or harmonize with in our daily round of activities? How do we keep that excitement that we all felt at the workshop last weekend alive in our daily round of activities?

(Carla channeling)

We are those of the principle known to you as Q'uo. We greet you in the love and the light of the one infinite Creator, in whose service we come to you today. We thank you for putting so many things aside in order to make the time to form this circle of seeking. It is a great blessing to us to be called to your group, and we thank you for the dedication that it takes to form such a circle as this. It is an especial blessing to us because this is the service that we have entered your planet's energies in order to offer and it enables us to serve in speaking through instruments such as this one. So we are most grateful to you for giving us this opportunity to share our thoughts. As always, we would ask of you that you use your discrimination in listening to our opinions, for we are not authorities and we would not be a stumbling block before any. We would ask you to take those thoughts which seem helpful to you and leave the rest behind. This will enable us to speak freely within the limits of our own ethical feelings for the preservation of free will.

We thank you for the question concerning how to continue to remember more and more of the truths that create within the heart the peace that passes understanding and the joy of realizing who you are and why you are here. It is certainly a challenging thing to retain the freshness of the vigorous enthusiasm that accompanies initiations and transformation. There is that feeling of being lifted to a place that is infinitely more desirable than the seeming contents of consensual reality. The challenge always is to become able to express these feelings of bliss and joy throughout the moments and days and months and years. The expression of joy is a natural state. It has to do not with any portion of the physical body but rather the movement of the energetic body into a position of balanced openness so that the energies that are moving through are able to do so without what this instrument would call distortion. The set energy of the universe, that OM of which you were speaking earlier, is a vibration that is utterly joyful and blissful, much as those physical feelings that explode when there is the sexual orgasm. In the sense of higher consciousness this state exists as the steady state and when an entity reaches a certain balance within the energetic body and is able to open within that balance in utter trust, the result is that one comes into a state of consciousness which the one known as R was so eloquently describing.

We are aware that in the course of a lifetime there are many times when the intersection of circumstance and personality grants a window of opportunity for the opening of the gateway to intelligent infinity. It is a direct experience of the Creator. It is never to be predicted as to how this shall occur, under what circumstances it shall occur. There is no one combination of efforts or words or positions or rituals that can bring about this particular state of consciousness. It is almost as if one emerges into it from a fog, a fog that you did not see, a fog that you did not know you were in the midst of until suddenly the mist clears and the sun shines, and all is made perfectly, and quite perfect. This state is a true state. It is not the same as happiness which, as it comes, guarantees its own departure. This is a state that can be and has been by many allowed to remain through tragedy and times of personal difficulty. This is a state that cannot be destroyed. This is the temple within that no power of life or death can destroy. Yet the experience that many have is of coming into this temple and going out, coming out and going in, being in that state and then abruptly being abandoned on the shores of consensus reality.

The techniques of hard work and dedication have a certain justice and a right place within the efforts to find and to retain that state of consciousness which sees all beings as one. There is a certain degree of simple persistence which equals very hard work for most entities in keeping a practice that is daily. This instrument has oft spoken of a rule of life, for she has found it helpful in her own process of coming into her bliss and certainly we would recommend this simple, hard work and the perhaps rigid ethic of a daily practice that places before the eye in every day that lit candle at the altar within where time is spent in silence and in opening the heart to the tabernacling with the one infinite Creator that always awaits within the tabernacle. This tabernacle is your own heart and it is a blessing indeed that so many entities upon your planetary sphere have at this time that practice of daily seeking through silence. More and more entities among your peoples are awakening and are feeling that need to move within to a place of worship, of ideals, of adoration, of dreaming that within your Western culture has become increasingly unavailable from the standpoint of those religious institutions that attempt to offer the feelings of the spiritual community.

Perhaps it is well to say at this time that the freshness of love is that which spiritual communities are most excellent at maintaining within the members of that community. We do not wish to criticize or to judge your churches and temples and holy places except to say that, more and more, those entities which are awakening have not found their home within the established buildings that hope to be spiritual communities by virtue of their name. What we find is that, as it has always been, the liveness and freshness of spiritual seeking is a matter of people and not institutions. The hope of creating an institution that will carry on the practice and make it available to people is in essence an anthropomorphism where the spiritual entity seeks to re-create the family as a permanent thing when in fact each family is always renewing itself as entities leave this plane and other entities are born into this plane within their family. Consequently, those who are moved to be pastors and ministers and priests may well have that open heart which creates a loving atmosphere and authors a place of safety for those who wish to seek together. It is possible to find this within the church, within any religious practice, but it is a matter of moving from group to group until one has found not only the way of worship that appeals but also the energy within the leader and also within those within that particular group that is comfortable and supportive and encouraging to you personally.

We find that in groups such as this one which gather in homes and are unofficial and spontaneous, the likelihood of fresh energy is higher because there is no reason to come to a group such as this one to express a social or a political or an economic kind of feeling or beingness, but rather, the only reason to come is that sense of a spiritual family that together may more efficiently and effectively seek than each by himself alone. We would say that this is extremely true and is a great help to remembering who one is, for there is within the earth plane at this time a tremendous number of people who have incarnated in large groups of people to serve together and much of the joys of spiritual community are involved in re-linking with those entities with whom you have spent lifetimes in the past serving together and learning together. Each time that you reconnect and re-link with these beloved strangers that are very much a part of your energy of being, there is laid another golden strand of connection within the net of love which surrounds the Earth and is glowing brighter with every day. We are rejoicing at this point to see the outburst of newly awakening people. There is a tremendous, shall we say, population explosion of those who are awakening at this time. It makes us feel most blessed to see entities taking hold of their being and knowing themselves and their power for the first time.

As each of you moves into this awareness of the open heart and desires more and more to live there and to express that love within the light, each effort to do so makes it easier to do so once again. And each persistent effort to remain open to that which this instrument would call the Holy Spirit creates an atmosphere in which others find it easier as well, so that each of you becomes that light that is set upon the hill, that is not hidden any more beneath a bushel basket, that is not tucked away but that is glowing and burning for all to see, glowing not with the energy from the self but with the energy that moves through the self, so that this is not a tiring or effortful thing but, rather, an expression of the utmost peace.

This instrument has for some time had the feeling that she dwells within a very critical and interesting time, and we also have that bias towards that feeling that these are very precious and very powerful times within your planet's cycle. The new heaven and the new earth of fourth density has been nearly completed now. Your Earth entity which may be called Terra or Gaia has come through most of her labor. She still labors and each of you may be very strong in helping her through these labor pains. The practice of moving into the creation of nature, the kingdom of the Father, as this instrument is wont to call it, is very helpful in stabilizing and deepening the energies of the balanced and open heart, for each flower, tree and breeze that blows, each element that exists, exists within a complete awareness of the one infinite Creator. Rocks, fire, wind, grasses and blooms do not have words and they do not move in the way of being self-aware in choosing in each movement whether it is in or out of harmony. The creation of the Father has no knowledge of how to be disharmonious. All things, rather, are working towards the help of the entirety of the Earth.

This natural energy has been distorted and compromised by those feelings of aggression, greed and other heated emotional states which tend not towards peace but towards the unwise use of power, whether by money, by influence, or by various means which your civilizations have developed through the millennia of your history to collect the resources that seem to be fair and to attempt to create a safety that is forever specious because the vehicles which you have chosen for this incarnation are in no case free from the limitations of birth and death. Consequently, there is a great energy within your Earth sphere at this time which tends towards the breaking down of coherent energy and the invitation to chaos which is the result of the unwise use of power.

Each of you has a tremendous ability to alter this picture, not because you can change it physically but because belief is the truth of perception. What you choose to accept as true has a very powerful effect upon that story that you tell yourself, and the story that you tell yourself is that which creates within you a safe place from which to love, to accept, and to embrace those that seem like you and those that seem distinctly unlike you, those that seem positive and those that seem drawn to a darker shadow world. Every difference that can be distinguished is helpful to that self that must conduct a life within third density. However, that ability to distinguish and discriminate betwixt souls does not serve the spiritual life. Certainly it is well to use the intellect and the powers of analysis that were given as a portion of those resources with which you meet the world. And yet beyond the intellect and its limited ability to assess true situations or the truth of the self, there is that within you which does have a far more informed point of view. You may call it your higher self. You may call it guidance. In this instrument's case she calls it the Holy Spirit, but however you personally find it useful and fruitful to characterize to yourself that guidance that comes from deep within you and which was yours before this incarnation and will be yours after this incarnation, this is that which you may depend upon. This is the foundation upon which the feet truly rest.

As each of you becomes more spiritually mature you will go through cycles of losing the balance and regaining it. This is a natural occurrence. There are very few entities who move through a life without going through these cycles or spiritual seasons of light and dark. Certainly this instrument has had experience with the Dark Night of the Soul. We believe that each in this group has had significant suffering to bear. This is as it should be, for although it is a hard truth to understand, it is a simple truth that each of you chose a plan for incarnation, some have said a contract, and in this contract certain lessons were chosen to learn and to share in the learning of with those beloved entities with which you made agreements before this incarnation. As well, there were services that you hoped to offer.

Each of you has one central service in common and that is the ministry of essence. The task of each that is primary is simply to be yourself. It always seems as though one must do something in order to be of service and yet as we have said many times through this instrument, it is in how you are within yourself that you serve in the greatest capacity since each of you is as the crystal that transmutes and sends forth the light that is received from the infinite Creator. Each of you is an unique crystal, then, which can allow the light to flow into the Earth plane in just such and such a way that is unique to you. And when your heart is open and the light is flowing through you and you feel transparent to that energy, then it is that the most beautiful light of all colors, depending upon the personalities involved, is able to move into that grid that this instrument has sometimes called the Christ grid and which others have called the grid of unconditional love or the Buddha. This grid is that web of light, that pattern of love, that is beginning to stabilize fourth density upon your planetary sphere. Each of you is doing tremendous work for those who shall come after you, sowing seeds of light and seeds of love whose blossoms you shall not see, for you shall move on. Yet those who come after you will be able to do as they do because of reaping the harvest that you now sow with each loving thought and each contact made in love and in light.

We may say that it is well to be aware that there are many who are uncomfortable with unconditional love, as the one known as T has said. Do not be discouraged if it seems that your light is not accepted by those about you. That which is upon the surface is an illusion. The energetic work that you do is as it is, and it is not necessary for any to be aware that you are doing this work. It is not necessary for people around you to respond or seem to accept you as you would hope to be responded to and accepted. It is only necessary that you do the work, that you keep your body, your mind, and your spirit in enough balance that energy may flow through and not be stuck in this or that place, or overstimulated so that there is a distortion because of that hectic energy of overstimulation. Realize that the spiritual path is one which extends throughout the incarnation, moment by moment, and unexciting chore by unexciting chore. There is no life which is nothing but the glitter and the sheen of holiday times and mountaintop moments. Realize too that by connecting with those around you who are of a like mind you are helping them and you are allowing them to offer their love offerings to you also.

But be steadfast in those situations which do not seem to be so full of love. Allow yourself to be the love that is brought to that meeting, to that moment, to that situation. And if, for some reason, you are flagging and your emotions are tumbled and you are weary, reach out and allow someone to give to you that which you have so often given to others. For there will be times of weariness for each soul within illusion. There will be times when circumstances come upon one which seem most difficult. And there are those stubborn traits which each of you carefully brought into this illusory incarnational experience for the express purpose of butting your head up against, of being confused by, of seeming to be flattened by, in order that you may stand in the refining fire of the spiritual distillery that Earth is and work upon these traits that you have chosen to balance within this lifetime.

It is easy to feel discouraged when the process takes you into your shadow side and you find yourself dealing with blockages or over-activations or some other kind of imbalance that seems to vitiate and attenuate your ability to be a crystal that is steady in its opening to the light and the love of the one infinite Creator. Do not be discouraged when these times come upon you. Do not chide yourself because you are not in a state of bliss. Know that your memories of that time are perfect, that they are valid, that they are the truth of you, and know that in honoring that memory and in remembering those mountaintop times you allow yourself to rise once again to that mountaintop where all is well and all people are one.

We would speak a little bit more along this subject before we open to questions simply in iterating the efficacy of meditation. The joy that lurks within the center of your being is invited by silence. It is a playful energy. It is full of light and full of dance and each of you was intended to be a dancer through this illusion. Each of you, upon the brink of incarnation, gazed at that which was to come and thought, "This will be so much fun. This will be so simple. How could I possibly forget any of the truths that I know simply by being born into this illusion? I will remember. I will remember." And yet birth comes and the air of Earth hits the face and there is the necessity to breathe in order to live, and all of a sudden the environment has completely changed and you are a helpless infant, dependent upon others for absolutely every need.

This creates a situation where the tiny child that is newborn has its first experience of vulnerability and a lack of emotional safety. Within your experiences as a child there are almost guaranteed to be repeated times where this feeling of panic and distress becomes almost overwhelming, as the environment seems not to be a safe one, not to be a secure one emotionally and spiritually. And the understanding of others about you seems to be lacking. The pressures and distortions of the birth family, the parents and so forth, almost always create these biases within one which are carried upon the back like a burden until they are once again named and greeted and faced and embraced and loved and forgiven and placed within the heart to be healed and to be forever then part of the strength of the entity that has come through many waters and is as fresh and young and strong as in the days of greatest youth.

This is the permanent state of each entity which has no age and has no falling away from strength. And it is from this perspective that it is most helpful to gaze upon the world of ten thousand things. It is far more accessible, this world, in meditation, in silence, in contemplation, in walks within the natural world, in all ways in which you can remove yourself from the various, shall we say, pernicious thought structures of your civilization. Your song that you began this meditation with was about living on the outskirts of civilization. And we recommend that you think of yourself in this way, not physically. Physically it is helpful for entities to be everywhere, especially in the urban areas that are so crying out for positive energy, but rather in terms of being in this world but not of this world.

Thinking of oneself as an outsider is a way of preparing yourself to be a dweller upon the road to fourth density and not simply one who is stuck in third density. For the one known as R is correct in saying that heaven is here. Heaven is now. It is so each time one becomes aware of the self as a lit candle and encourages that light, that vulnerable, living light that depends upon the oxygen of the open heart. Breathe that love and light in. Breathe that love and light forth through your being, for truly it comes in and it moves out, and the blessing that you give it creates infinite brightness within it.

This instrument is instructing us that we have overstayed our time, and so we thank you for your question, and we transfer this contact to the one known as Jim so that more specific questions may be asked at this time. We thank this instrument and we leave it in love and light. We are those of Q'uo.

(Jim channeling)

I am Q'uo, and greet each once again in love and in light through this instrument. At this time it is our privilege to ask if there might be any shorter queries to which we might speak. Is there another query at this time?

J: My question today is about a blockage in the red ray and I would appreciate a suggestion about how to clear this with grace and ease. Thank you very much.

I am Q'uo, and am aware of your query, my sister. We would recommend in the meditative state, at the end of your day or during a portion of your day where you have time to relax and reflect, that you look at the blockage as it has been experienced in your daily round of activates. Within the meditative state then look at the experience which represents to you the blockage of the red-ray energy center. Re-live that experience, allowing it to fill your being, and then in a natural fashion allow that image to dissipate and allow its opposite to emerge into your consciousness so that you see it with the same intensity that you saw the blockage to begin with. Allow this image to continue for as long as feels comfortable. Then see both the blockage and its balance as means by which the Creator may know Itself through you, and accept yourself for having both as means for the Creator to know Itself in your being. Repeat this exercise upon a daily basis for as long as is necessary for the blockage to be resolved.

Is there a further query, my sister?

J: No. Thank you very much.

I am Q'uo, and we thank you, my sister. Is there another query at this time?

S: Sometimes I wonder if my dog is in more pain than I am aware of, or if you could comment to me on the right course with him?

I am Q'uo, and am aware of your query, my sister. We examine this entity. And we can suggest that the pain which this entity feels is ameliorated to a great extent by the love which you give this entity and that any pain which this entity feels is worth the continued existence within the shower of your love. For this entity learns most by being loved and by being able to give love. In this manner then, this entity then is able to become, shall we say, inspirited, vested in a fashion which increases its consciousness and its ability to perceive the love and the light of the one Creator.

Is there a further query, my sister?

S: I understand. Thank you.

I am Q'uo, and we thank you, my sister. Is there another query at this time?

Carla: I was contemplating using a technique in counseling where I help the person focus by moving that person down into a fairly deep state of concentration which is the essence of hypnotism, and I was wondering whether it is recommended, as an ethical person, to help a person in this manner? And also I was wondering if by my tuning I am able to assure the person's safety throughout the experience?

I am Q'uo, and am aware of your query, my sister. We are also aware of the potential for the infringement upon your free will as we attempt to comment upon a choice which you have not yet made of your own free will. We can suggest that the tool of that which you call hypnotism is indeed a powerful tool for some entities who are susceptible to entering the trance state in an easy fashion. Whether your tuning is able to provide a safe place is uncertain, for the susceptibility of each individual varies greatly. We suggest your continued meditation upon this topic and the consideration of other means of allowing a focus to be achieved.

Is there a further query, my sister?

Carla: No. Thank you. I will do just that.

I am Q'uo, and we again thank you, my sister. Is there another query at this time?

T: To follow up Carla's question, if Carla engages in counseling someone but if this person also comes to her with an intention of receiving counseling is this not the choice of each person, and should we not allow each person to decide whether to enter into something like this that may have an effect in one way or another?

I am Q'uo, and we are aware of your query, my brother. Indeed, each entity which enters into the counseling relationship is doing so of its own free will. However, many entities are unaware of their susceptibility to such techniques as the use of hypnosis and would not be able to give a free will choice from this inability to assess its own susceptibility. Thus care must be taken. Is there another query, my brother?

T: No. I understand. Thank you.

I am Q'uo, and we thank you, my brother. Is there another query at this time?

R: I have some medical problems and I think it's related to emotional blockages that I have. I have chosen to treat it with an alternative healing method. Is this a good method for me?

I am Q'uo, and am aware of your query, my sister. Again, we wish to be of service by responding to the query which has been offered to us, yet we fear that there may be some potential for our infringement upon your free will if we speak too clearly or if we advocate one means over another, for the seeking of healing from whatever means of healing, whether it is orthodox, alternative or any other kind of healing is a choice which is fundamental to the spiritual path of the seeker. For any medical problem, as you call it, is a reflection of catalyst for growth which has been offered the seeker and which the seeker has in some degree appreciated but in another degree been unable to penetrate, so that the lack of understanding of the catalyst then transfers itself to the physical or the spiritual realms in order that the attention might be gained upon another level of experience where it has been, shall we say, unappreciated upon the mental level where all catalyst begins its journey and transmutation with a seeker.

We may suggest that the course of action which you have chosen, being that which was chosen by your free will, is helpful in that regard, for you in your conscious and subconscious abilities have assessed your situation in such and such a fashion which then has resulted in your choice of alternative means of healing. We suggest that you continue in choosing that which feels most appropriate to you. There are many means of seeking healing. That which speaks to your inner voice, to your heart, then, is that which will, in most cases, be the most efficacious in bringing about a resolution of the medical situation, shall we say. We apologize for seeming to be unable to speak to this query more directly, but we hope that you will appreciate our desire to maintain your free will. Is there another query, my sister?

R: Can you give me any advice on my spiritual development?

I am Q'uo, and again we find ourselves up against the full stop of the infringement upon free will, for to give advice in such a general fashion would be to seem to judge, and we do not wish to be a judge of any entity or the path that any entity follows. We affirm each entity's choices and can suggest again that the path which you follow in your spiritual seeking must needs be that which speaks to your heart rather than that which another suggests, whether that other be revered and honored and seeming to be possessed of greater knowledge or to be an ordinary entity upon your street. For there are as many paths to the one Creator as there are entities who seek that One within all and within the self. Follow, then, that which is in your heart. Follow that which speaks to your heart and be always willing to increase the intensity of your seeking, the intensity of your desire, and the meditation that we always recommend for every path, for every seeker, for meditation is the surest means that we know for any seeker in third density to approach the infinite Creator.

Is there another query, my sister?

R: No. Thank you.

I am Q'uo, and we would ask if there might be a final query at this time?

Carla: A question came to me as I was looking in the mirror. Sometimes I just look into my eyes in the mirror and I am always struck by a quality that is more than me and really I can see the citizen of eternity that is living within me. Is there something about the eyes that has this capacity to reveal the soul? And is there some way to encourage that?

I am Q'uo, and I am aware of your query, my sister. The optical apparatus which you have described as the eye is the primary means by which stimuli are appreciated by entities within your illusion, for most do not see with their hearts the great panorama of experience that is available to each within every moment of the incarnation. Yet this way of seeing is possible for those who have opened their inner eye. Thus, the ability to see is that which has been relegated to the physical optical apparatus and the inner ability to see then must needs be translated, shall we say, so that when an entity begins to see with more than just the outer eye then there is the ability to apprehend more qualities of the self and of the life experience than are normally to be had with the physical eye. Thus, when one who seeks in a conscious fashion upon the spiritual journey takes the opportunity to look within a mirror, as have you, the perception begins to expand beyond the image first seen. There is the possibility of viewing other qualities, other resonances, shall we say, within the current incarnation, so that the experience of seeing within this fashion and with this feeling/tone becomes enlarged and there is perceived more than the image in the mirror. This ability to enlarge the range and depth of vision then can be extrapolated so that previous incarnational characteristics may begin to flash before the outer and inner eye. Thus, one may begin to see other aspects of the self, not just from this incarnation but from those previous to this one which have significance to the current incarnation. Thus, the experience of looking within the mirror and concentrating upon the eyes may indeed begin to show more of the soul aspect of the entity. And this may also begin to trigger memories that are from other incarnational experiences but which play a role in the current incarnation.

Is there a further query, my sister?

Carla: No. Thank you.

I am Q'uo, and we thank you, my sister. And as we are aware that we have spoken overly long this particular session of seeking, we would close this session by thanking each once again for making those sacrifices which were necessary for each to join in this circle of seeking this day. We are always most honored to be invited to join you in your meditations. We cannot thank you enough for the heartfelt queries which each has offered to enhance the understanding of the spiritual journey. We assure each that you do not walk any portion of this spiritual journey alone, for each has those teachers and guides that are unseen to the physical eye but surely walk with you each step of your way. There are no mistakes upon your journey, my friends. There are many coincidences and to the seeker which keeps the open eye, there is much that each journey's experience can offer. And we thank you for your diligence, for your intensity of desire, and for the love in each heart that springs forth at these times and at many other times during your daily round of activities.

We are known to you as those of Q'uo. At this time we shall take our leave of this instrument and this group. We leave each in the love and in the ineffable light of the one infinite Creator. Adonai, my friends. Adonai.

L/L Research

L/L Research is a subsidiary of Rock Creek Research & Development Laboratories, Inc.

P.O. Box 5195
Louisville, KY 40255-0195

www.llresearch.org

Rock Creek is a non-profit corporation dedicated to discovering and sharing information which may aid in the spiritual evolution of humankind.

ABOUT THE CONTENTS OF THIS TRANSCRIPT: This telepathic channeling has been taken from transcriptions of the weekly study and meditation meetings of the Rock Creek Research & Development Laboratories and L/L Research. It is offered in the hope that it may be useful to you. As the Confederation entities always make a point of saying, please use your discrimination and judgment in assessing this material. If something rings true to you, fine. If something does not resonate, please leave it behind, for neither we nor those of the Confederation would wish to be a stumbling block for any.

CAVEAT: This transcript is being published by L/L Research in a not yet final form. It has, however, been edited and any obvious errors have been corrected. When it is in a final form, this caveat will be removed.

© 2009 L/L RESEARCH

SPECIAL MEDITATION
MAY 16, 2002

Question: Q'uo, this is a question for T1. The question will be sort of broad and possibly double-based: "I'm interested in the best way to deal with the catalyst in my marriage and how I can be of service and love in that area as opposed to adding to the catalyst and direction for life in general. I feel there is a beating in me that I can touch and feel, and I seem to be doing something with the soul purpose sort of like what I was reading about in *The Law of One*, Book V, what you had mentioned about 'silver flecks'; how everyone has their own knowing that they are on the right track. Well, sometimes mine, I guess, may be just a quickening pulse, shivering, you can call flecks at some times. The burning in my lower and upper chest, sometimes, throat. I'm of the mind that this is a 'use it or lose it' type of phenomenon, and I don't want to lose it because I'm not focusing or listening in the right direction to what's happening. Synchronicities happen all the time in my life, but I don't know what they mean. I dream and record my dreams many times a week, but I have no idea how to interpret them even though I attempt to. Even trying just sort of confuses me, or they're more complicated. I know this is a way for God to guide and direct me, anyway. I know there are two big, huge issues or maybe one in the same, basically, about my marriage and the catalyst there; how to learn from it; how to take advantage and learn from the synchronicities in dreams and moments in my life that are filled with soul and direct them into what I should be doing with my life or even spare a love time that I could have to be creative, write, sculpt, etc."

And, Q'uo, we'd also like to know how you feel about doing personal sessions like this. We'd be interested in your comment, maybe, this time.

(Carla channeling)

We are known to you as those of the principle of the Q'uo, and we greet you in the love and the light of the one infinite Creator. It is a great privilege to be called to your group this evening, and we thank you very much for this opportunity to serve. We are glad to share our opinions with you upon the interesting subject of how to be a part of the good in someone's life and not part of the difficulty and of how to use those bits of pieces of guidance that drift from the infinite world of the metaphysical and the unconscious up into and across the threshold of the conscious mind. As always, we ask only that you use discrimination in listening to and judging those things which we say. For we are not authorities but, rather, your brothers and sisters of sorrow. If something seems good to you, then by all means use it as a resource, but those things that do not seem good we ask that you lay aside and think no more about them. For, truly, each knows the resonance of truth within her own mind.

The one known as T1 has said that the two prongs of this double question are perhaps intertwined and perhaps more unified than double, and we would agree that in a way they are two sides of a mirror or two faces of a coin. For the same information is, perhaps, helpful in many ways in answering those questions. Let us start with that question concerning how to be a servant of the light within a personal relationship such as a marriage. Our model or paradigm for responding to this query is a simple assumption but a sweeping one, and that is that all is one, that that entity which is a mate is the projection of the self into the face of another self; both entities being the Creator. The efficiency of this method of mirroring and projecting images upon the screens of each other's field of energy is precisely the purpose for which many entities chose to make commitments and form relationships. The catalyst, indeed, is the prize, not the problem, of the relationship. For it is in working with the catalyst of the self as projected onto the other self that the entity comes face-to-face with the refining fire of realization that this, too, is a part of me. This is what enables people to look at, to accept, and to come to love what this instrument has sometimes called the shadow side, the darker side of self, that side which knows the good but enjoys that which is of the darkness. It is not possible to remove the shadow from the self, for each contains the seeds of all things; each is truly the holder of the universe within the self. And if the self is all things, then it also is in part a shadow self; a darker, richer-hued, and more difficult to comprehend part of the self.

It is easy for this vision and view of the self to generate fear, and, as the one known as T2 was saying earlier, in whatever guise this fear is, it is there that the catalyst will be rich upon the ground and ripe for the plucking. So we would suggest that in a relationship it is, perhaps, not a skillful goal to wish not to perform the function of acting as catalyst for another, for this would suggest that catalyst is an unfortunate thing. And, indeed, we would suggest that that which is truly unfortunate is that which never changes, for it is not a part of the experience of rock or air or wind or water or plant or animal to remain the same. There is a flow to the destiny of each entity that is as close as breathing, too close to reach for, for it is already part of the environment, the ambient atmosphere of the self. It can be sensed, although usually within the conscious, daily round of activities it cannot be seen or heard or touched. There is, as the one known as T1 has said, that quickening of the self that gives the intuitive, conscious mind a small affirmation that energy is moving, that magic is near, and that there is guidance and power in the very atmosphere about one. And, truly, these are what the one known as T1 called soul moments, and yet we would suggest that each moment is, to the one whose senses are fully unguarded and undefended, a soul moment. Each instant is a now that is infinite, and the possibilities of each present moment of now are stupendous.

We would suggest that in the outworking of dynamics between two entities there is a fine and movable line betwixt viewing catalyst as difficult and viewing catalyst as a rich and welcomed opportunity. That fine line has to do with safety and trust, and the question then becomes within relationships: "How does one become a place of emotional safety for another entity so that even within a disagreement, even within the tangles of personality and circumstance, there is a feeling of trust that enables each to feel comfortable in misbehaving and apologizing and discussing with utter honesty those things which lack between the two?"

The grit of life can easily be seen to be a thing that is unfortunate, and we would offer the image of the pearl, which is the result of the irritation of the sand within the shell of the shellfish known as the oyster. Without the refining fire, without that distillation of spiritual maturity that such seeming difficulties offer, that pearl, which is each of you, should never properly be polished into its complete and perfect beauty. We do not suggest that there is an easy way to do spiritual work, either by the self or within relationships. It is not even easy to deal with the self or with relationships following the rules of the physical world and what this instrument would call consensus reality. The advantage of dealing with such issues as a spiritual entity is that advantage which sees a wider and more fundamentally powerful point of view, a point of view which offers a more sturdy resource than the shifting values of your third-density world.

The values of the density which calls each are very simple. If one looks within your holy works and reads those words which this instrument calls the Beatitudes, much can be learned of the way of love. For those who are humble and poor in spirit, those who mourn and those who are peacemakers, are those who are blessed; are those who have gifts in their hands and good work to do. This is what this instrument calls process: the moving into the tangled part of a relationship buoyed and lifted not by rules and regulations and agreements and those things of the linear world that keep the lawyers among you so busy. But, rather, we speak of a spiritual world that calls one to look for ways to offer the self, as a radiant sun offers sunshine upon the whole earth; not judging betwixt one person and another, one species of plant and another, one place and another but, rather, shining impartially and lovingly upon all.

When one allows the wings of faith to lift one, there is much love that begins to circulate around in that spaciousness that is made by living in faith. There is something about the leap into midair that strengthens that which was being sought: faith itself. There are times when it is very helpful by faith alone to realize the most fundamental truth of all relationships, which is love, unconditional, absolute love from one soul in its perfection to another in its perfection. All those things that seem imperfect are part of the illusion of personality and what this instrument would call ego. Beneath each difficulty that tangles two upon the soul level lies a unity, a oneness, a union, that is profoundly more the truth of the relationship than any structure of description that contains itself in words rather than in the open heart which knows that it loves, though it knows not, perhaps, how to respond to a certain situation or to a certain moment.

It is an interesting thing to look at what the self tells the self, for there are many times when the self that is not fully aware of the possibilities may find many faults within the self and within another. And it is well to be able to speak of these things, yet, beneath this level, there is the level in which the truth is love. Consequently, when the moment comes to have a response to catalyst, let that response be the response that answers the question, "Where is the love in this moment?" The goal between any part of the Creator and another self that is also part of the Creator, is to serve, to love, and to accept the love offerings of others. Often, these love offerings are clumsy, mis-expressed, even meaningless in a linear sense but only containing the non-logical meaning of emotion itself; emotion that is carried, perhaps, even from lifetime to lifetime, looking for a way to balance those energies that are unbalanced.

So, we suggest that each see a relationship as an opportunity to be in love with the Creator, to tend to an angel that is in your care, and to refrain from the judgment of behavior but rather find ways to express those positive aspects of love which come from the open, accepting and forgiving heart. We do not offer that which is easy to do as a suggestion, but we do offer that which is, shall we say, the higher path, the path that will tend to bring the relationship into its own balance, whatever that may be. For beneath the questions of this kind of love or that kind of love flows the current of friendship, companionship and that wonderful ease that comes to those who truly and unguardedly love.

We would gaze now at the question concerning the use of synchronicities and dreams and the concern that there might be a bus that the one known as T1 is missing, because there is not very often at all that feeling of linear understanding and the feeling of controlling or being able to grasp that which is occurring within that flow of the unconscious into the conscious mind. And we would say to the one known as T1 that she is in her young years for working with this question and that this is, indeed, a very profound and central question within this particular incarnational experience and certainly looms large in that experience that is the life of any awakened soul.

The nature of the subconscious or unconscious mind, as it is known among your people, is that which is of a different order of magnitude than the conscious mind. Rather than having a tremendously complex machine, which is that which your brain is as a human being, your consciousness is one atom of an inorganic organism which is the infinite Creator, so that you are the sun within your own constellation of being and are the center of your world, and yet, at the same time, every other soul is also a sun. And so, those near to you are as the galaxy, and you dance as stars dance, rotating about each other and swimming in a sea of infinite possibilities. In the subconscious mind an infinite number of things may be happening at any moment that are coming into the unified soul-stream of the entity from various places within the circle of incarnations that is all of the incarnations that you have experienced and will experience within the entire octave of densities that makes up this particular creation. Consequently, that which makes it through the threshold from the infinite metaphysical unconscious into the relatively limited, structured, almost cartoon-like shapes of the conscious mind and its logical thought constructions, is, indeed, only the hint and the whisper and the nudge that suggests and creates feelings and emotions. Thusly, it is not well to bear down too hard upon attempting to understand how each message works.

The magic lies within the feelings that synchronicities, dreams, visions, coincidences, magical experiences, in general, create and rouse within the self. These emotions are precious, precious things and throughout the incarnation each is working to purify, beautify and make more truthful those expressions of pure being that emotions are. So, in looking at synchronicity, in looking at the parts of dream, ask the self, "How do I feel? What color is this emotion? What part of myself does this seem to figure for?" If the synchronicity has to do with an animal, what does that animal make you feel like? What emotion has it roused? If it is a dream, the purpose of such as dreams is to speak to the self concerning the self. Consequently, each figure, each detail, each process within the dream is the self. There is no need to seek far for who these characters are, for they are all the self. It is as though each entered a world, within dreaming, where everything was a symbol that is used because it is the closest construction to create a precise shade of feeling that can be found by the ever-creative subconscious mind in its great desire to communicate its essence to the conscious self.

The sharing of gifts is a portion of the question that can be responded to best taking the fruit of the statements that we have made concerning the expression of radiant love that flows through one, rather than from one, and the allowing of symbols to enter the life and to move the heart and the emotions and then simply to realize that one is on a voyage of service and discovery. Sometimes one is about one's lessons, sometimes one is concerned only to serve in a certain situation, and sometimes the opportunity comes to share that most precious thing of all, the essence of the self.

And that is what we would share with you concerning the question of what one "should" do in order to express the joy of spirit and the pleasure of service to others. We would ask each, then, "What do you desire if you close your eyes and envision the peak of peace and contentment? What do you start to imagine?" In times of change, in times of awakening and transformation, often it is that the most meaningful ways of sharing gifts are not seen, because they are too common and too ordinary. However, the ministry of essence, as this instrument has called it, the priesthood of being who you are and allowing your truth to shine, is a most precious gift to give, and it is truly the deepest and the most central gift that each life does give to the world. For each came into the world to be the light of the world; each has the capacity to be the hands, the arms, the loving hearts, the loving mouths of the Creator that speak, that reach to hug, that curve to smile and stop to recognize and honor the divinity of each other self. This principle that is you is unique, and yet you carry crystal within you through which the light may shine.

This energy does not need to come from you. All you need to be concerned with is allowing yourself to be ever more truly and deeply yourself and in that comfort of self to bless and welcome and open to the infinite energy of the one Creator as it flows through from the limitless white light of the great original Logos. Once that energy has been begun, the energy itself, as it circulates, rotates and spins, begins to bring naturally to the self those opportunities for outer service that one has planned aforetimes for the time when spirit within was mature enough to take it up.

We may suggest that there are many opportunities to heal, to be a healer, to be an agent of healing energy and that this healing has as many avenues as there are personalities. It is as though each of you were as the stained glass of a rich and beautiful design. All those colors within the window that is you are your very own; no one else has selected the way that you move energy through your energy body. And this means that you are creating a constant tapestry of color and music that is the personal signature of yourself, and this energy vortex, as it moves through the cosmic energy vortexes that are figured forth in the outer world by your planets and your stars, moves you along with the flow that you and your guidance created at the beginning of that web of energy that is called a given incarnation.

We would suggest that the silence and the intent are those two things which shall be most helpful as practice that creates habit that creates a predisposition to an increase in the level of awakening. There are many ways to be silent, meditation being one, contemplation being one. Any form of silence within is to be welcomed and to be applauded, for that is an atmosphere which opens the self to the self; that is that attitude which allows the intent within to come clear, to speak lucidly within the self so that the self ceases asking and begins to know. The asking comes first and then repetition and persistence carry one forward. It is not known when such a process will ripen and come into the conscious mind as a pattern that is seen and [understood]. But we ask that there be the continuing attempt to trust this process and to trust the self and its discriminatory powers. It may seem that much is not understood, and yet we have often said through this instrument that understanding is not something that any within third density may expect to achieve. Rather, what one may achieve [in] third density is an increasing purity of choice, and, once that choice is made to the full satisfaction of the self, that choice of radiance, of service to others, of unconditional love. Once the path of the open heart has been taken, then we would suggest trusting and embracing the light that you feel and moving as a dancer even when you stumble and fall. Let there be the light touch as well as light, and let the self be merry and have its laughter and its happy times.

We would at this time speak a bit more through this instrument and then we would transfer to the one known as Jim. The one known as Jim asked concerning our feelings about working with this instrument on the behalf of the questioner who has made a donation to this instrument's bank account. And we would say to you that our issue is always with the preparation and the tuning of the channel. It is not relevant to us whether or not your money, which is a kind of energy, has been given a spin. What is our concern is always the honesty, the integrity, the purity of effort made by a sincere and willing servant of the light to speak those things which we offer. The only difficulty that we see is in the instrument's own reservations concerning the appropriateness of such actions as the one known as N and she were laughing about earlier within this situation.

It is entirely appropriate to seek the truth, and when it is done with the sincere effort that this instrument and that this group offer, we are grateful and overjoyed to be of service by offering those humble thoughts we have to share. We would ask this group to realize that there is energy in all actions. There is as much energy in refusing to take money as there is in the energy of taking money. It is a different energy. Both energies could be positive or negative. Allow the energy to spin always clockwise, to move always towards the light. Follow those magical principles which the one known as Jesus the Christ offered so simply. Each is here within the Earth plane as a messenger from the Creator. May your light shine forth; may you serve, and, truly, you cannot help but serve.

We would at this time transfer the contact to the one known as Jim in case there are any remaining queries within this group. We thank this instrument and leave her in love and in light. We are those known to you as Q'uo.

(Jim channeling)

I am Q'uo, and greet each once again in love and in light through this instrument. We would offer ourselves briefly for any shorter queries which may be upon the minds of those present. Is there a query at this time?

Questioner: Yes, I have a question that concerns a great and grand friend of mine, my son, M. He at this moment is experiencing catalyst with his employment and also with his status of being about to become a new father, and he's caught up in a thing, a situation, job-related, that is sorely testing his self-esteem, and I've tried to advise him as I can, but I guess I'd just like any comment that you may have. Now, I either myself can go about helping him, or he can help himself which, ultimately, is the same thing. Anything that you could comment with, I would appreciate it.

I am Q'uo, and we are aware of your query, my brother. When one wishes to reassure another who is worrying and fretting concerning an outcome that rests within the future, it is well to do as you have done and that is to give your patient counsel that all will be well, for, indeed, there is a plan which each entity follows, whether it is known or not consciously. This plan has been created by each of you with assistance previous to the incarnation from those teachers and guides who are your fellow travelers, who themselves move in other realms yet walk closely with you here in this illusion as well. Though it may seem that there is difficulty, doubt, confusion and a myriad of other emotions and possibilities, each foot is set upon firm ground to teach just that lesson the moment has to offer, and this lesson is appropriate to each entity. Though those times of difficulty may not be sought consciously by any seeker, yet they teach as well as any and, perhaps, better than most, especially if one is able to look consciously at each situation for the fruit that may be gained by partaking fully within that situation. You do not live lives that are truly chaotic, out of balance or off the beam, shall we say. It may feel that way to you for a while, yet, this too teaches. Learn everywhere, everything, at all times! This is a possibility; this is actually what occurs for each. Most of what is learned remains between the worlds of the subconscious and the conscious mind. The conscious seeker seeks to make this a more conscious activity. Many blessings on this journey and for this effort. It is a valiant one and the outcome is well. Be assured the outcome is well.

Is there a further query, my brother?

Questioner: No, thank you very much.

I am Q'uo, and we thank you, brother. Is there a final query for the evening?

Carla: Yes, I have a question concerning my vital energy and the frequency with which I can accept such channeling opportunities. My guess would be no oftener than once a week. Would that be something that you can confirm?

I am Q'uo, and am aware of your query, my sister. As we assess your vitality as an instrument expressing the vocal channeling, we would suggest that there be no more than the one session that you have determined yourself in addition to any regular channeling that you partake in on your first and third Sundays of each month. Thus, most weeks would have but one; two each month would have two as possibilities. Do you understand, my sister?

Carla: Q'uo, I think I do. You're saying that I can have one a week for private people and once every two weeks for the public channeling, and that will be adequate, and there's no lower limit; it's okay if I don't do any and just do two a month. I should not do more than six a month. Is that correct?

I am Q'uo …

Carla: Or seven …

This is correct, my sister. We would agree with your former number, that being six.

Carla: Ah, but, Q'uo, four times a year, there are five Sundays in a month, so that was why I added seven, because four times a year I would have seven opportunities instead of six. *(Laughing)* Moving right along … Thank you very much. Thank you so much. I appreciate that.

I am Q'uo, and we thank you once again, my sister. We find that this session of working has exceeded the comfortable period of your time, thus, we shall take our leave of this instrument and this group, thanking each for asking for our presence and thanking also the one known as T1 for her heartfelt query. We hope that we have been of service.

We are those of Q'uo. We leave each now in the love and in the light of the one infinite Creator. Adonai, my friends. Adonai. ✷

L/L Research

L/L Research is a subsidiary of Rock Creek Research & Development Laboratories, Inc.

P.O. Box 5195
Louisville, KY 40255-0195

www.llresearch.org

Rock Creek is a non-profit corporation dedicated to discovering and sharing information which may aid in the spiritual evolution of humankind.

ABOUT THE CONTENTS OF THIS TRANSCRIPT: This telepathic channeling has been taken from transcriptions of the weekly study and meditation meetings of the Rock Creek Research & Development Laboratories and L/L Research. It is offered in the hope that it may be useful to you. As the Confederation entities always make a point of saying, please use your discrimination and judgment in assessing this material. If something rings true to you, fine. If something does not resonate, please leave it behind, for neither we nor those of the Confederation would wish to be a stumbling block for any.

© 2009 L/L Research

Sunday Meditation
May 19, 2002

Group question: Our question today is sort of two-pronged. The first part has to do with the energies, the spiritual vibrations, of the evolution of the planet, its population, and each of us individually as well. Some people spoke of being able to feel these vibrations more intensively now, and we are wondering if you could describe these vibrations to us, their nature, and how we could work more harmoniously with them so that they are not so overwhelming. The second part of the question was: when you speak to groups like ours, could you give an indication of how it is you feel when you have been successful? What are the usual needs of the group and what are the services that you provide to meet those needs?

(Carla channeling)

We are those of the principle known to you as Q'uo, and we greet you in the love and in the light of the one infinite Creator, in whose service we are. We thank each of you for being part of this circle of seeking. It is a true blessing to us to be able to be called to your group and to share in your meditation and the beauty of your energies. It is a unique pleasure, different each time, as each of you has come to a different place in your seeking and in your process, and each shows us new colors and tones of colors each time that we meet. We also greet those who have not been to our group before. Each is most appreciated. The time that you have found for the seeking creates the opportunity for us to serve, and we are most thankful. We ask only that you listen to our words with discrimination, taking only that which seems good to you and leaving the rest behind. This enables us to share without being concerned that we will infringe upon your free will.

Your query this day is most interesting, covering as it does two seemingly disparate subjects: that of the energies that are transforming your planet and that of the way that we serve and the kind of results that we hope for.

Let us begin by becoming more aware of the energy that each of you sits with, as if you were the center of an energy nexus, which, indeed, you are. Feel that feeling of being the self, the energies of essence, those energies that are so familiar and so near and at the same time perhaps often unthought-of, as though because they do not show, because they do not have substance within the physical world, they are left somewhat neglected. Relax all of those tensions that are confining or narrowing your energy stream and come into the full feeling of yourself. For each of you is a spark of the Creator. Through each of you the universe has its being. That consciousness which you carry is the heart of yourself and is infinitely precious.

Now we would ask you to become aware of the energy of others within this circle of seeking. Feel that entity upon your right and that entity upon your left. Begin to sense the link between each, the overriding unity of identity between you and those within the circle with you. Allow that sensation of shared aura to begin to rotate in a clockwise manner about the circle. What color is that light? It will be somewhat different for each as each views from a unique point of view. To some it may be white. To some it may be golden. To some it may be violet. Whatever your perception, for you it is an accurate and helpful one. It is your subconscious way of describing to yourself, for yourself, this sensed energy.

Now we would ask you to become aware, if you will, of our energy, as a kind of engirding support to your meditation. It is as if we are a carrier wave that enables your meditation to be somewhat more sturdy and more stable.

Now we would ask you to open up your senses and become aware of the energies of the earth under your feet, the sky, the air, the wind above this roof, the warmth of the sun, the motion of the planet, and the energies of the planet and stone, sea and river, plants and animals. As your heart beats, so the rhythm of the earth itself is affected. As the tides turn, so the beating of your heart is affected. Each of you has ripples of effect upon each other. Each whom you meet ripples out and affects you by the wake of energy that each brings and shares.

This is the world of your energetic body. This is the world of an incredible variety of beings that live within the inner planes of your planet, many teachers and many healers, many wise entities and certainly many beings of mischief and fun as well as those darker entities that would delight in feeding upon the darker emotions that you may offer: pain and fear, the suffering. It is a rich and challenging atmosphere, the atmosphere of this energetic being that you are. It makes the world of physical reality very simplistic and almost like a comic book. For the strokes are broad and not as subtle as the gentle and infinitely moving and flowing waves of the energy that you are.

At this time among your people and, as the one known as D says, for some time before this, the energy upon your planet has been transformed as the Earth mother of your planet itself moves inexorably to and through the process of giving birth to fourth density. The change within your planetary energy grid is remarkable. Indeed, there is a new grid which this particular instrument tends to call the Christ grid but which may be seen in general to be a pattern of energy nexi which surround the planet like a net, we would say a net of love, a net that is made of fourth-density light. It is woven with golden strands offered by each of you and offered by many, many entities within the inner planes of your planet as well. There are many beings who have dedicated themselves at this time within the inner planes to the ceaseless task of offering thanks and praise as they move along these lines of energy and connect one point to another with strand after strand of coherent light which is that stream which is created when each of you prays, meditates, or opens the heart in any way.

This transformational light is profoundly different from that light which you have been processing through your physical body and the finer bodies of your energy system in previous years. Its energy is of an entirely transformed nature and may we say that this energy is oftentimes that which creates some discomfort for those who have become aware of it and who have begun to respond to it. In any change there is discomfort, even in the happiest of changes such as in the occasion of marriage or upon the occasion of birth, and in a way there is both a birth and a marriage taking place at this time.

The birth is that of the planet beneath your feet, and the marriage is that between the self and the fourth-density portion of yourself which you have brought within you into this incarnation to be activated by this light at this time. It is a marriage of self with a higher aspect of self. And yet this new aspect of self is a stranger, a new portion of the self that has yet to be fully recognized. Under the influence of this light, at the cellular level, your genetic structure is being offered the opportunity to become more organized. This instrument's scientific knowledge is slim but we find within her mind the concept of DNA and we say that at this time, each of you is capable of creating new strands of DNA which allow a far more open door between the contents of the conscious mind and the treasures of the subconscious mind.

Many of you, perhaps, are experiencing various aspects of your subconscious at this time flowing far more freely into physical awareness. This can have very discomfiting effects at different times. It depends entirely upon the amount of attention that you are paying and the growing ability that each has to see through the circumstances of your daily life into its essence. Some of you have been speaking of experiencing various symptoms, and this is to be expected. This is a typical response to new vibrational levels and, indeed, it does create a sense of great intensity from time to time in most awakening entities.

Is this a blessing? We feel certainly that it is. We feel that it is a very helpful and powerful time for each of you. It is as though you are rediscovering an aspect of yourself that we would call mastership or priesthood. For within this new vibration, it is possible to sense yourself as a spiritual being entirely, a creature of spirit, a minister of love and light. Within this very exciting time among your people, our hope is to assist in opening the awareness of those who seek to do so. The one known as S was asking what sort of service we provide and what the results are. The service that we provide through this instrument is linear and yet we find that when we speak these poor words of language through instruments such as this one, we are able to use the coloration and timbre of that instrument's emotions and personality to enhance and to stain our very simple message of love and light with the colors of individual personality, incarnation, and point of view. We must blend with the energies of instruments such as this one. We find it a most interesting and creative way to work with those concepts that fit so poorly into the shape of human language and yet explode with meaning when allowed to rest in the space between the words.

In the next density you will be able to open that telepathic sense that eludes you most of the time within this density and you will grasp the poverty of language compared to the richness of concept communication, for words are a filter to the wholeness of truth, straining out many things in order to say one. Perhaps our most fundamental service, as we perceive it, is in bringing to people, in groups such as this and as they ask individually, an experience of unconditional love. We do come to you in love. We come to you in radiant light. We float upon the wings of utmost purity and meaning that we know. We hope to blend with each of you in such a way as to enhance your own sense of joy and peace and balance. We open our arms and embrace you. We love so much. Each of you is a master who has not yet become fully aware of that. This instrument was speaking earlier about how foolish she felt. We find that this is the human experience in cameo, that feeling of being inadequate to the moment, of being imperfect and one step behind. Of not being the one who has a clever word, but the one who stands in silence thinking seriously of something clever to say.

How true it is that each of you suffers within this illusion of life on Earth, each in a very unique and personal way. Not all entities experience the same thing, but each has its patterns of light and dark. Each has its travails and sorrows and its joys. Each has those shining moments and those moments of bleak despair. Our hope in this work is to enter into relationship with those who ask for communion and companionship in such a way that there is an enhanced sense of the reality and sturdiness of love within your being, within your life experience, and in the very air around you. We would like to create for each a more substantial bubble of fourth density that you may walk within as you go about your business upon planet Earth.

Oftentimes we work on the individual level to join a meditation. When entities do not meditate or ask for us on the conscious level, but are calling for comfort upon the unconscious level, then it is that we work with dreams in order to create within the dream state that comfort and safety that oftentimes is missing in the life of those who wish to serve the light. It is a peculiarity of the spiritual path that it at once brings all entities together and isolates each within its own process. We hope to be a healing influence for those who sense themselves as being isolated and stuck in lack of communication and lack of companionship.

For those who, like this instrument was saying earlier, are attempting to pray on the run we simply attempt to act as a carrier wave beneath the chores of everyday. Our advantage is that we are very used to working with the energy bodies. It is our version of a physical body. As beings of energy, in a far more conscious manner than each of you, we are somewhat more able to facilitate the blending of energies.

It is as though we come to encourage and support each of you and then call you forth, as the spirit and spiritual energies always do, to minister to each other. For in truth there is nothing that we do that you cannot do as well. It is a matter of experience on a conscious level versus inexperience on a conscious level. However, beneath the threshold of consciousness we are completely and utterly equal and that which you know within yourself is precisely as full and whole a knowledge as that which we hold and know.

Our results are, in the sense of feeling that we have been effective, enormously uneven, and we are quite content with this apparent variation in success. It is not a matter of filling a specific quota or creating a specific result. For us it is a matter of finding ways to communicate within your density that do enhance, but do not infringe upon, the identity, the wholeness, or the integrity of each of you. If we could give you a feeling of how we see you, it is as entities of enormous courage, sacrifice and beauty. Each of you, in choosing to come into incarnation, did, indeed, take a chance in terms of the sacrifice of comfort. For within the spirit world, there is that lack of a veil between the self and the glory of all that is. Wordsworth once wrote in a poem that infants come into this world trailing clouds of glory. Glory is a much underused word in that there truly is a glory to the present moment, there truly is a glory to the universe and there truly is a glory to thank the Creator for. One has only to gaze into the creations of the Father to become aware in a deep and an intimate way what glory is there, the blooms of the iris and the coral bell, the shoots of the tree that are fully green. This burgeoning and swelling time of spring among your people is truly bursting with glory from every hedgerow and every roadside.

Yet, there is always that glory within, there is always that urge to seek for the Shangri-la, the place of perfect meditation, the place of great power that somehow will assist in bringing those powers to a place where they can be used. And we say to you that it is your divine self that contains the power that you seek. Certainly one can feel the strength of places of power, and yet we suggest to you that as the planet itself evolves, those places of power move around. Also as the fourth-density energy takes hold and becomes stronger, each of you will become more and more aware of yourselves as places of power, people of power.

How much you did give when you gave up the knowledge of who you are, of the tremendous experience that has been your palette upon which you have drawn to create this particular lifetime! There is within each a watchtower. In this watchtower, there is a light. When you turn on this light you are as a lighthouse that beckons the weary sailor home from the sea, that warns of rocks and shoals so that the boats may come in and land safely.

We call you masters and then, perhaps, your question is, "What shall we do with this mastership?" And we say to you that you came here to be healers of one kind or another, but not in the old sense of the healing arts, such as doctors and nurses, for each has the capacity to heal in his own way, some of you by the things that you say, some of you by those whom you attend and take care of, some of you by the sharing of the energies, some in the more specific ways of healing nature, in the laying on of hands and body work.

The difficult thing to express to you is the healing nature of many things that do not appear, within your culture or your experience, to be those things that have a profoundly healing influence. Yet those that clean their house with a certain kind of love and blessing are creating a healing space and claiming that space as sacred. When one is scrubbing a toilet, one does not particularly think that one is healing and yet you are creating an atmosphere for yourself of cleanliness and beauty, taking care of, loving, and nurturing your environment. This too is a healing, the cooking of food, the paying of bills, all of these very mundane things that this entity was speaking of earlier as her "Quick Books week." All the ledgers and columns and figures are not abandoned to ugliness, but yet contain beauty also, contain sacredness also, when they are approached with love, when they are approached as honored and respected activities within the life, they too become lessons and create blessings. Most of all they come to invite you to a fuller life, to an expanding and enhanced life. And we hope to help in your stability as you open like a flower.

We would at this time transfer this contact to the one known as Jim. Ask any questions that remain within the group before we adjourn. We thank this instrument and leave it in love and light. We are those of Q'uo.

(Jim channeling)

I am Q'uo, and greet each in love and light through this instrument. It is our privilege at this time to ask if there are any further queries to which we may speak. Is there another query at this time?

S: Well, I'll start out. I have one of major universal import. War Emblem won the Preakness and the Derby. Is he going to win the Belmont?

I am Q'uo, and am aware of your query, my brother. We have but a small idea as to the outcome of such events, for we do not move along those lines of investigation that would require that we invest a great deal of our energies in such endeavors. The kind of contacts that we are able to enjoy, given our origin outside of your planetary system, is that which we enjoy at the present moment, the mind-to-mind contact that has as its focus the nature of the spiritual journey and how it is accomplished through the daily round of activities. We are sure that there are sources more formidable than ours that may offer an opinion upon this topic.

Is there another query at this time?

S: No, not from me, I was just yanking your chain.

I am Q'uo, and we thank you my brother. Is there another query at this time?

T: Yes, I have a question. My son is going through quite an emotional ordeal with his job and he is going to be a new father. I am trying to advise and help him, but there is only so much that each person can do. Each person has to push their own load. It all boils down to trying to advise someone about their spirituality, whether they name it as such or not. Do you have any suggestions as to how I can aid a person who is going through a pretty hard time?

I am Q'uo, and we must pause briefly so that this [instrument] be allowed to work the recording devices. We are Q'uo.

(Tape change.)

I am Q'uo, and am once again with this instrument. We apologize for the delay and appreciate your patience. It is the desire of many seekers such as yourself, my brother, to be of service to those who are in a kind of distress, as you might call it, needing that which they do not know, seeking in a general fashion that which specifically speaks to the spirit. As you seek to be of service to such entities, our only recommendation is to speak those words from your heart which are appropriate for the moment. Each moment is different, each entity is different. Thus, there is great room for individual expression in the sharing of that which you have to offer. As you are the same as they, your opinions may be weighed in an evenhanded manner, shall we say, there being no great reason why any entity should listen to or follow your advice. You are free to speak as you will. We have oftentimes recommended that it is well to put oneself in another's place mentally before attempting to serve that entity, in order that you may achieve a certain amount of appreciation of what the entity whom you wish to aid experiences in its personal life. We would recommend this once more, as you seek to apprehend the qualities, the energies, and the opportunities that are making themselves available to such an entity in order that this entity may take the next step upon its own personal journey.

Is there a further query, my brother?

T: Yes, just a little follow up. There are lots of times that I feel that I know what to say to a person like that, my son or whoever. Sometimes I want to leap ahead and say this is something that he or she would want to hear. What I hear you saying is, speak from your heart, speak the truth, and if that person doesn't like it, then that is probably catalyst for them to move ahead. Anyway, is that correct, just to speak the truth and whatever happens will happen?

I am Q'uo, and we agree with your estimation of the message that we were attempting to deliver. We find that you have spoken with eloquence and have spoken to the point.

Is there a further query, my brother?

T: No, not from me, thank you.

I am Q'uo, and again we thank you, my brother. Is there another query at this time?

Carla: I just want to thank you, the vibrations were beautiful.

I am Q'uo, and we are most grateful to you as well, my sister, for each in this group has provided us with the vibrations of love and compassion which make it possible for us to blend our energies with those of your group. We are most appreciative of the effort that each entity has made in order to be here this day and to share those vibrations that are from the heart.

Is there another query at this time?

(No further queries.)

I am Q'uo, and it appears that we have exhausted the queries for the nonce. We shall again thank each for inviting our presence on this day in your circle of seeking and we shall at this time take our leave of this instrument and this group. We are known to you as those of Q'uo. We leave each in the love and the ineffable light of the one infinite Creator. Adonai, my friends. ✦

www.ingramcontent.com/pod-product-compliance
Lightning Source LLC
Chambersburg PA
CBHW080420230426
43662CB00015B/2159